Advanced Microeconomics for Contract, Institutional, and Organizational Economics

Advanced Microeconomics for Contract, Institutional, and Organizational Economics

W. Bentley MacLeod

The MIT Press
Cambridge, Massachusetts
London, England

The MIT Press would like to thank the anonymous peer reviewers who provided comments on drafts of this book. The generous work of academic experts is essential for establishing the authority and quality of our publications. We acknowledge with gratitude the contributions of these otherwise uncredited readers.

This book was set in Times New Roman by Westchester Publishing Services. Printed and bound in the United States of America.

Library of Congress Cataloging-in-Publication Data

Names: MacLeod, W. Bentley (William Bentley), 1954– author.
Title: Advanced microeconomics for contract, institutional, and organizational economics /
   W. Bentley MacLeod.
Description: Cambridge, Massachusetts : The MIT Press, 2022. | Includes bibliographical
   references and index.
Identifiers: LCCN 2021023060 | ISBN 9780262046879 (hardcover)
Subjects: LCSH: Microeconomics.
Classification: LCC HB172 .M273 2022 | DDC 338.5—dc23
LC record available at https://lccn.loc.gov/2021023060

10   9   8   7   6   5   4   3   2   1

For Ben, River, Gabriela, Raisa, and Janet.

Contents

Preface

This book is intended for use in a graduate economics course, either as a text or for supplementary material. It reviews, "from the ground up," the microeconomic theory of exchange, which includes decision theory, game theory, and the foundations of contract theory. A distinguishing feature of this book, relative to the many fine books on contract theory, is the references to related empirical work. Ultimately, good theory should provide insights into observable phenomena. A course in optimization theory and general equilibrium theory is a recommended prerequisite. The appendix provides a brief introduction to optimization theory and the welfare theorem of general equilibrium theory.

Such a book would not be possible without the support and insights from many people. I am very grateful to my teachers from graduate school, particularly Charles Blackorby, Curtis Eaton, Tracy Lewis, Keizo Nagatani, Hugh Neary, and John Weymark. After graduate school I was very fortunate to spend time at CORE in Belgium, where I learned a great deal about game theory and mechanism design from Claude d'Aspremont, Jean Gabszewicz, Jean-François Mertens, and Jacques Thisse. I also learned a great deal from the other visitors, including Jean-Charles Rochet and Jan Svenjar. I am particularly grateful to Jim Malcomson, with whom I started to collaborate at CORE. Our work on relational contracts began by combining the insights from Jan Svenjar's work on self-management with Jim's ideas on incomplete labor contracts.

I also learned a great deal from a wonderful set of coauthors, including Jennifer Arlen, Elliott Ash, Jim Bergin, Jordi Brandts, Lorne Carmichael, Surajeet Chakravarty, Daniel Carvell, Janet Currie, Herbert Dawid, Armin Falk, Mehdi Farsi, Paul Gomme, Jon Hamilton, David Huffman, Yoshi Kanemoto, Lewis Kornhauser, Thomas Lemieux, George Norman, Daniel Parent, Mark Pingle, Evan Riehl, Juan Savedrea, Jessica van Parys, and Miguel Urquiola.

Finally, I greatly appreciate the feedback on the book from colleagues and graduate students. These include Iain Bamford, Thomas Braun, Danny Bressler, Daniel Deibler, Matthias Fahn, Ricard Gil, Jared Grogan, Florian Grosset, Tianshu Guo, Sakshi Gupta, Utkarsh Kumar, Lorenzo Lagos, Rui Duarte Mascarenhas, Suneil Parimoo, Roman Rivera, Yifan Shi, Carol Shou, Meredith Startz, Katherine Strair, Haoran Wang, Ding Yuan, and Georgio Zanarone. I also appreciated the input from the many graduate students who attended lectures based on this material at USC, Princeton, Caltech, and Columbia. Finally, I would like to thank both the Institute for Advanced Studies in Princeton and the Russell Sage Foundation in New York who hosted one-year visits while I was working on this book.

1 Introduction

And as for principles of law, he should know those which are necessary in the case of buildings having party walls, with regard to water dripping from the eaves, and also the laws about drains, windows, and water supply. And other things of this sort should be known to architects, so that, before they begin upon buildings, they may be careful not to leave disputed points for the householders to settle after the works are finished, and so that in drawing up contracts the interests of both employer and contractor may be wisely safe-guarded. For if a contract is skillfully drawn, each may obtain a release from the other without disadvantage.
—Vitruvius (1914, bk. 1, chap. 1, sec. 10), ca. 15 BCE

The purpose of this book is to present a review of the theory of exchange that can be used to produce a set of models and hypotheses amenable to empirical exploration, with particular focus on models that are useful for the study of contracts, institutions, and organizations. This introduction provides an overview of the terrain. The next subsection discusses price theory and why it is the dominant tool in economics. That discussion is followed by a summary of some work that extends price theory. The introduction concludes with a review of the agenda for the book.

This book is appropriate for the second part of the graduate sequence in microeconomics. As such, it is assumed that the student has taken general equilibrium theory and basic constrained optimization theory. Debreu's 1959 book *A Theory of Value* remains a good source for general equilibrium theory. This book views the microeconomics for contract, institution and organizational economics as building upon the ideas outlined in Debreu's brilliant work. The appendix of this book includes a brief outline of general equilibrium theory for reference purposes. There are many excellent sources for optimization theory, though the work of Luenberger and Ye (2008) for finite dimension problems and Luenberger (1969) for infinite dimension problems, such as control theory, remain among my favorite sources.

A feature of this book, which distinguishes it from the many excellent texts on microeconomics, is a discussion of evidence and how one might link theory and evidence. The discussion on this point is necessarily incomplete but it is included to highlight the fact that all models are imperfect representations of observed phenomena. Advancing knowledge entails exploring the empirical implications of the many models described here and documenting how they may be used to explain features of observed economic institutions that are difficult to describe from the perspective of price theory alone.

1.1   Price Theory

The fundamental theoretical building block of modern economics is general equilibrium theory, developed by John Hicks, Kenneth Arrow, and Gerard Debreu. The theory, laid out beautifully in Debreu's (1959)'s *Theory of Value*, provides a clear definition of an efficient allocation of resources, along with the conditions under which such an allocation can be achieved via the price system. The theory is the cornerstone of a modern graduate education not because it is "true," but because it provides a precise general framework within which it is possible to define what one means by an efficient allocation of resources.[1] The theory provides few normative presumptions beyond requiring that commodities are well defined and that each person has a way to evaluate and then rank commodities according to their preferences.

1.1.1   Commodities

A necessary condition for determining an efficient allocation is the requirement that commodities are well defined (Debreu 1959, chap. 2). A commodity can be either a good or a service. A good is a tangible object, such as food. In contrast, a service, such as the stream of images one experiences while watching a movie or attending a concert, cannot be physically owned. In this setup, an *asset* is some physical or intellectual property that provides a stream of services. For example, a pair of shoes is an asset that provides services to one's feet as one walks around. The distinction is meaningful because at some future point the service might be used by one's children (my son sometimes borrows my shoes). The services provided by an asset can be contracted upon and delivered to different individuals over time as a function of future events. Examples would include renting an apartment or car for use over a limited period of time.

The description of a commodity requires specifying the quality of the commodity, as well as the place and time of consumption. In addition, uncertainty can be introduced by allowing the commodity to be state-contingent (Debreu 1959, chap. 7). For example, one might buy a particular type of wheat on the Chicago futures exchange to be delivered next year. In addition to carefully specifying the characteristics of the wheat to be delivered, the futures contract would also specify what will happen if delivery cannot occur. All these features can be viewed as characteristics of the commodity, with the implication that the same wheat that is delivered under different contingencies, such as with different penalties in the event of nondelivery, will be traded at different prices.

Thus, part of economic development is the definition and creation of new commodities, a process that has long been recognized as a key feature of economic growth. Karl Marx (1981), like Adam Smith (1776), was well aware of the fact that economic development is concurrent with increasing commodification of exchange. Marx identifies commodification with the "alienation of labor." By this he means that the worker loses control over their day-to-day work. This is the essence of modern contract theory—agents voluntarily agree to provide services to a principal in exchange for income. Marx was worried about the differences in bargaining power between the employers and employees. As we shall see, the allocation of bargaining power plays an important role in the design of efficient contracts.

More recently, Lisa Bernstein's work provides a number of interesting studies illustrating the process of commodification in practice. Bernstein (2001) discusses trading norms within the US cotton industry that helped standardize the notion of a "cotton bale," which in turn led to a more competitive market for cotton because parties could enter into arm's-length agreements to trade a specific number of well-defined cotton bales. Bernstein (2014) has a wonderful discussion of a "2 × 4," the piece of lumber that is not in fact 2 inches by 4 inches but whose exact size becomes standardized over time.[2]

The approach taken in this book is that commodification—the precise definition of the good or service to be exchanged—is the first step of a three-step exchange process. The next step is assigning value to different commodities. The final step is to agree upon and enforce trade. Let us now turn to the determination of value.

1.1.2 Value

The next ingredient of price theory is determining the value of a commodity. Models of competitive markets assume that value is determined by consumer demand based upon rational choice between alternatives. The rational choice model is a common target for criticism; however, its power lies in the fact that it is a very simple and elegant model of decision making (and certainly not because it is the "true" model of human choice). It is built upon two assumptions. The first is that individuals have well-defined preferences for ranking commodities. Without loss of generality, one can begin with a finite set of choices, $\{A, B, C, D, \ldots\}$. The second assumption is that if an individual prefers A over B, then she will choose A. A person is considered *irrational* when she knowingly chooses B if she really prefers A.

Debreu (1959) shows that under these assumptions, the choices of a rational person can be represented by assigning a value to each choice, say V_{choice}. By construction, choice A is chosen over some other choice B if and only if the value of A is greater than the value of B ($V_A > V_B$). The rational choice model is the starting point for what Bandura (2001) calls the *agentic* approach to social cognition—the notion that individuals have goals and make decisions based on whether the consequences of their decisions advance their goals.[3]

Once preferences have been defined, then an *efficient allocation* is a feasible allocation (one that satisfies the resource constraints) with the feature that there is no other allocation that makes a single individual better off without harming any other individual. This notion of efficiency is typically considered to be ethically neutral from the perspective of individual preferences. Most economists would take the normative view that, if possible, one should choose an efficient allocation. Under the standard assumptions of general equilibrium theory, efficient allocations can always be found, though there can be an infinite number of such allocations.

The purpose of the rational choice model is to provide a simple and coherent representation of how millions of individuals in an economy will respond to changes in their environment. It should also be noted that the model allows for interpersonal judgments. There is nothing in the theory that bars a person from choosing an outcome that is more equitable, even though it may lower her personal income. The theory also allows individuals to change their mind based on new information regarding the characteristics of a commodity. The empirical power of the rational choice model does not come from the rationality hypothesis per se (individuals have complete and transitive preferences over outcomes), but from the assumption that preferences are *time invariant*. That is, if we can observe preferences today, this will tell us what a person's preferences will be tomorrow. Not only is this assumption difficult to test, it is certainly false—the advertising business is built upon the hypothesis that consumer preferences can be modified over time.

Less well appreciated is the role of the rational choice model in modern behavioral economics. Before the work of Kahneman and Tversky (1979), there had been a great deal of work attempting to model human decisions from the ground up based on models of human cognition. A good example is the treatise by Newell and Simon (1972). This work had little impact in economics, even though it is widely recognized that Newell and Simon are correct to suppose that individuals are not perfectly rational. The genius of Kahneman and Tversky (1979) was to use a standard rational choice model as a benchmark against which to measure *deviations* from rational choice. This approach has been enormously influential because the rational choice model provides a good first-order representation of behavior, and hence it helps organize features of human behavior in terms of deviations from rational choice. (See Camerer, Loewenstein, and Rabin [2004] for a collection of seminal articles.)

Thus, in order to understand modern behavioral economics, a first step is to understand the rational choice model. What is possibly less well appreciated is that once uncertainty is introduced, and choice occurs over time, then preferences depend upon both the characteristics of the commodities to be consumed and beliefs regarding their future characteristics. This in turn is consistent with a wide variety of possible behaviors. Hence, with the introduction of uncertainty about the future, it is quite difficult to reject the rational choice model. Thus, throughout the book it is assumed that individuals are rational in the sense that they make choices consistent with maximizing their expected payoffs. As we shall see, once we relax the assumption that commodities are well defined, then efficient exchange depends upon a number of features of human decision making that are often associated with other social sciences, such as social norms, the potential for conflict, and personal beliefs.

1.1.3 The Welfare Theorems of General Equilibrium Theory

General equilibrium theory provides a model of resource allocation assuming that the set of commodities in the economy can be observed and contracted upon. In this case, one can characterize all efficient allocations by giving each commodity in the economy a value per unit called the price.[4] This price is a purely technical construct that follows from the requirement of (Pareto) efficiency.

It turns out that there is a beautiful connection between these prices and the prices in a competitive market. By a competitive market, I mean a situation for which every commodity can be traded at a price and that prices are set so that demand is equal to supply. The first welfare theorem states that every competitive equilibrium is efficient. An obvious concern is that competitive equilibria may be extremely unjust. For example, Sen (1977) points out that one of reasons for the Bengal famine was not the lack of food but the fact that many households did not have the resources to purchase food at the going prices.

These concerns are addressed with the second welfare theorem. Under the appropriate conditions, every efficient allocation can be achieved via a two-step procedure. In step one there is a redistribution of initial endowments and in step two parties trade in a competitive market. This is a very powerful idea that can be viewed as consistent with many of

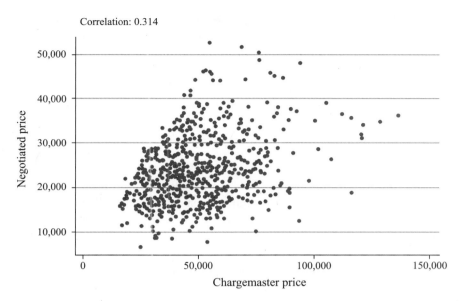

Figure 1.1
The trade price of knee surgery versus the contract (list) price in the United States.
Source: Appendix figure III, Cooper et al. (2019).

the ideas in Friedman (1962). Friedman makes the normative claim that a society with free markets is preferable to the alternatives because distributional concerns can be addressed with an appropriate redistribution of initial endowments (such as vouchers for the provision of school services and a negative income tax system), with the final allocation determined by free markets.

However, as Gary Becker (1976) observes, the notion of price used in general equilibrium theory does not correspond to its everyday use, and it certainly does not correspond to "price" as used in a legally binding contract. Price as used in general equilibrium theory represents the value of any constraint upon the set of feasible allocations, and does not necessarily correspond to the price paid by consumers.

A good example of this is the price of surgical services. Cooper et al. (2019) provide evidence on the price of a wide variety of services in the health care market. They find that there is a great deal of variation in the price of services across the United States that cannot easily be explained as resulting from variation in either costs or quality. Figure 1.1 illustrates the price that insurance companies pay for knee surgery as a function of the list price. There is a positive correlation, but it is relatively weak (the correlation is 0.314). For example there are several cases in which the list price is over $100,000 while the insured price is less than $40,000.

Thus, for exactly the same service—knee surgery at a particular hospital—the price paid varies with one's insurance status. It is theoretically possible that providing services for the uninsured individual may be two to three times higher than for an insured individual, though most health economists would find this very unlikely. This example illustrates the point that "price" in practice can mean different things. When using the theorems of general equilibrium theory, price is precisely defined as the resource cost of a commodity. The power of price theory is that in principle, such a price is always well defined and should be used when deciding on how to allocate resources. The danger, as Nobel Prize–winning economist Paul Krugman (2014) observes, is that economists are often temped to use a "bait and switch" strategy—namely to go from the true theoretical result that efficient allocations can be supported by some set of "economic prices" to the false claim that free markets are always efficient. To spot this strategy, let us explore a more nuanced notion of "price."

1.2   Beyond Price Theory

1.2.1   The Trade Price

The notion of an economic price for a well-defined commodity is quite different from the *trade price*. This corresponds to the everyday concept of a price given by the observed terms of trade at the time of sale. When we speak of the price of milk or housing, it refers to the price we pay at the store—the trade price. The trade price is a *legal* rather than economic concept: it defines your obligation to the store should you wish to leave with the milk. The *economic* price of the milk, in contrast, reflects the *full* cost of leaving home to buy milk and then returning home.

This is important because although the economic price *always* refers to the actual resource cost of delivering a commodity to a specific location at a specific time, the trade price refers to the single market price for a *basket* of different commodities. For example, in his famous "The Market for Lemons" paper, Akerlof (1970) considers the market for cars that are characterized by their age, make, and quality. He also supposes that the mechanical quality of the car for sale cannot be observed by buyers, which in turn implies that high-quality cars and low-quality cars ("lemons") fetch the same trade price in the market, even though they are distinct commodities. In this case, the word "price" in Akerlof corresponds to the trade price—the amount one would pay in this market for a car whose quality is uncertain. Akerlof shows that the trade price is equal to the average value of low- and high-quality cars. This in turn creates an incentive for owners of low-quality cars to enter the market since their cars are overvalued, while owners of high-quality cars exit the market because the trade price is less than the value of the car in their possession. This result is a complete breakdown of the market, with all high-quality sellers leaving, a phenomenon Akerlof calls "adverse selection."

Akerlof's paper is extremely influential in economics because it illustrates the role that asymmetric information plays in determining the volume of trade. Akerlof observes that the presence of adverse selection can explain a number of market institutions, such as a reputation for quality, and why jurisdictions with light regulation of quality experience lower economic growth.

Another good example that illustrates the different notions of price is the labor market. The competitive labor market model supposes that wages are equal to the economic price. In such a market the employment contract is very simple—the employer hires the employee for a certain number of hours, q, and pays $w \times q$, where w is the hourly wage rate. It is assumed that both employers and employees accept the wage signal as given, which in turn determines the number of hours, $L^D\left(w, \theta^D\right)$, demanded by the firms, and the hours, $L^S\left(w, \theta^S\right)$, supplied by workers, where θ^D and θ^S are exogenous parameters that change over time.

In the Hicks-Samuelson model, it is assumed that wages adjust to remove the imbalance between supply and demand so that the wage, w, as a function of the exogenous shocks, θ^D, θ^S, is given by the formula:

$$L^D\left(w, \theta^D\right) = L^S\left(w, \theta^S\right). \tag{1.1}$$

The power of the competitive model lies in its ability to make predictions on wage changes as a function of shocks to supply (θ^S) and demand (θ^D).[5]

Of course, it is well appreciated that the Hicks-Samuelson model is a highly stylized model of employment. Yet, it remains one of the most useful approaches to think about and organize evidence regarding secular trends in inequality and the returns to education.[6] However, the model has proven to be much less helpful in trying to understand many aspects of the labor market, such as persistent unemployment. By unemployment, we mean that at the current market wage rate workers are willing to work but firms are not willing to hire them. Such an outcome is not possible within a complete market framework because if wages are above market clearing, then wages are predicted to fall until supply is equal to demand.

Some unemployment is due to search costs and is part of the normal functioning of the labor market.[7] The puzzle is that job loss typically leads to a permanent loss of earnings rather than a new job with earnings similar to the previous job.[8] Thus, one would expect that many workers would accept a wage cut rather than job loss. Although such wage cuts do occur in practice, they are relatively rare.[9] Moreover, one would expect that workers would only care about real wages, though it seems that nominal wages exhibit some rigidity (Card and Hyslop 1997). Recent work shows that such "irrational" behavior also occurs in contexts in which individuals are very poor and hence have strong incentives to avoid inefficient behavior (Kaur 2019).

To account for these observations, the traditional approach has been to maintain the conceptual approach of price theory and try to "patch" the model. Beginning with Keynes, it has been common to suppose that wages are downward rigid, and firms set labor demand given the market wage. The problem, then, is to explain why unemployed workers refuse to accept lower wages in order to exit unemployment?

A number of patches to price theory have been suggested. One of the most popular patches is the class of "efficiency wage" models.[10] The basic idea builds on Leibenstein's (1958) observation that in a development context, workers have such low incomes that their productivity can be enhanced if wages are increased above the market-clearing rate. With higher income a worker can eat more, and therefore they are physically stronger, which in turn leads to more output. By increasing workers' income, worker productivity increases at a faster rate than the cost of the wage increase to the firm, and hence the term "efficiency wage."

There are a number of papers that use the idea that increases in workers' wages increase the quality of labor. Salop (1979), Calvo (1979), and Weiss (1980) build on this idea to provide equilibrium market models of unemployment based on information costs. Subsequent work by Malcomson (1981) and Shapiro and Stiglitz (1984) provides an efficiency wage model based upon the hypothesis that worker performance cannot be formally contracted upon. In these models, the employer uses the threat of dismissal to provide performance incentives, and thus, wages have to be above the market-clearing wage, which in turn leads to unemployment.

Each of these models takes the basic framework of price theory and then shows that a particular form of market incompleteness can generate observed downward rigid wages. In these models the "problem" is that wages are too high, which in turn focuses attention upon wage setting and finding ways to make the trade price of labor closer to the economic price. For example, the OECD (1994, pt. 1d) jobs study explicitly makes the point that wages are an economic price that is used as the primary mechanism to connect jobs to workers. Yet, twenty years after this report there is, if anything, more rather than less regulation of employment (see MacLeod 2011). Such regulation can restrict contract terms that parties are permitted to use. This can be addressed with the notion of a *contract price*.

1.2.2 The Contract Price

A typical sales contract entails a seller agreeing to supply a commodity at a future date for a well-defined trade price. Contract breach occurs when one or both parties fail to perform as promised. When a breach occurs, the harmed party has the right to take the dispute to a court of law. As Justice Oliver Wendell Holmes (1897, 462) observes: "The duty to keep a contract at common law means a prediction that you must pay damages if you do not keep it—and nothing else."

Thus, if the seller chooses a quantity or quality different from the agreement, then the payment she receives will be reduced.[11] Notice that a key feature of such a contract is that the payment to the buyer is state-contingent—it varies with the level of performance. The use of such contingent pricing, such as warranties for cars, is one of the solutions that Akerlof (1970) argues markets use to solve the adverse selection problem. Another example of such state-contingent behavior is documented in Banerjee and Duflo (2000), who observe that suppliers of software services mitigate low quality by providing after-sale services and support for product defects; this is the remedy of "cure" that is allowed under UCC §2-508.[12]

By *contract price*, I mean price terms that vary after delivery as a function of events in the relationship. In addition, these terms are associated with the notion of *contract breach*, actions that contravene the terms of the agreement. The notion of a contract price is best discussed in the context of some simple examples.

I consider a number of cases for which the relationship between seller effort and payoffs remain unchanged, but the information available to parties varies. From the perspective of price theory the relative costs and benefits do not change and therefore the economic price does not change by case. However, the variation in the information and legal instruments available results in variation in the contract price.

The payoffs

Consider the case of a one-off exchange between two agents, "A" and "B." We keep the payoffs fixed, but vary the context and information structure to illustrate the impact that this has upon the predicted contract price. "A" might be a seller in some cases, and a buyer in others. The stages are as follows:

1. A and B meet and agree on a contract. If no agreement is reached, then both parties get zero.

2. Individual A chooses effort $\pi \in \{\pi_L, \pi_H\}$, where $1 > \pi_H > \pi_L > 0$ represents the probability that there is a good outcome, g. In general this effort is not observable, though it might be with sufficient cost. The currency is normalized so that the monetary cost of effort π is π.

3. The state $s \in \{g, b\}$ is realized. If g occurs, the value of trade is $v_g = \beta > 1$; if b occurs, then trade has no value, with $v_b = 0$. The value of trade is assumed to be easily observable by both agents.

4. Parties choose to trade or not as function of the state $s \in \{g, b\}$, their choice is denoted by $q_s \in \{0, 1\}$, and transfers occur under the terms of the contract. The cost of production is c, and it is assumed to satisfy $\beta - 1 > c > 0$.

In this model, the substantive decisions are the level of effort, π, and the trade decision as a function of the state, $\{q_g, q_b\}$. Working backward, we can determine the efficient allocation for this model. If there is a bad outcome, since the cost of production is $c > 0$, then no trade is optimal and hence $q_b^* = 0$. If the outcome is g, then since $\beta > c$, trade is optimal and hence $q_g^* = 1$. Consequently, the expected total surplus (dollar value of A + B payoffs) from choosing effort π is:

$$W(\pi) = \pi(\beta - c) - \pi = \pi(\beta - (1 + c)) > 0.$$

The total return from effort is positive and therefore greater than the sum of the outside options for the two parties. Thus, the gains from trade are maximized when effort is high (π_H), and trade occurs if and only if the state is high (g).

Moral hazard: Seller effort is not observed

Consider a stylized version of Bernstein's (2001) cotton industry. Suppose the seller is a cotton farmer whose unobserved effort, π, determines whether the cotton is of high quality, with benefit $\beta > 1 + c$, where c is the cost of delivery. If the quality is low, then the cotton has no value. Suppose the farmer agrees to sell a certain quality of cotton to a firm in the future at a price p. If the contract simply states that the farmer must deliver cotton, then she will be paid a price p. In that case her payoff is:

$$U_{seller} = p - c - \pi.$$

Therefore, under this contract there is *moral hazard*: in the absence of a contract enforcing quality, the farmer will always choose low effort π_L.[13]

Bernstein (2001) observes that one of the roles of a trade association is to provide *observable* quality standards. If upon receiving the cotton, the buyer finds that the cotton does not meet industry standards for quality, then the buyer can sue for expectation damages, and the court would order the farmer to pay β to the buyer. The probability of breach (low quality) is given by $(1 - \pi)$, where π is the farmer's effort. Thus, the farmer's payoff is:

$$U_{seller} = p - c - \pi - \text{ProbBreach} \times \text{damages}$$

$$= p - c - \pi - (1 - \pi)\beta = p - c - \beta + \pi(\beta - 1).$$

Since $\beta > 1$, such a contract incentivizes the farmer to choose high effort π_H.

This solution is *not* efficient. If the good is substandard then it is efficient for the farmer not to deliver the good to avoid paying the transportation costs c. Thus, a standard contract enforced with specific performance (the farmer must deliver the goods) and expectation damages (the farmer must pay the value that the buyer expected to get) does not necessarily imply efficient trade.

Rogerson (1984) observes that a feature of US contract law is that parties are free to renegotiate contract terms in the face of new information. In this case, the farmer can let the buyer know that the crop failed and hence she cannot deliver. The farmer is still liable for damages β, but he can save transportation costs. Assuming that parties have equal bargaining power, then they can split the savings $c/2$ evenly. With renegotiation, the farmer's payoff is:

$$U_{seller} = p - c - (1 - \pi)(\beta - c/2) - \pi,$$

$$= p - \beta - c/2 + \pi(\beta - c/2 - 1).$$

Since $(\beta - c/2 - 1) > 0$, under this contract the farmer will choose efficient effort and there is efficient trade.

In this simple example, to achieve efficient trade the contract must simultaneously ensure that the farmer's income varies with her effort and that the level of trade varies with the value of trade. Contract law can achieve an efficient allocation with *contractual instruments* that give parties the right to voluntarily change the terms of the agreement, and give to the buyer the right to sue for expectation damages. This might lead one to the view that the trade price should always reflect the seller's effort. It turns out that this is not always the case.

An informed, but liquidity-constrained buyer

Consider a stylized version of Bernstein's (1992) diamond market example. Suppose A is a buyer of diamonds, and B is a seller. A feature of this market is that the buyer is often liquidity-constrained and therefore prefers to pay the seller after he has had an opportunity to cut and sell the diamonds. In that case, the contract would stipulate that the buyer inspect the diamonds (with effort $\pi \in \{\pi_L, \pi_H\}$) before taking delivery. He would be required to pay after a reasonable period, say sixty days. Given that the buyer inspects the goods, the contract assigns all liability regarding the quality of the good to the buyer.

Here one can suppose the buyer buys only diamonds of high quality β, and that c is the cost of cutting the diamond. With probability $1 - \pi$ the buyer makes an error in judgment, and learns that the diamonds have no value. Under these assumptions the diamonds are sold to the buyer with no warranty at price p, and the buyer has sixty days to pay.

In the absence of a warranty, the payoff for the buyer is:

$$U_{buyer}(\pi) = \pi(\beta - c - 1) - p.$$

In this case contract *breach* would simply be nonpayment of p. Under the standard expectation damages rule for contracts, damages would be p. Since $(\beta - c - 1) > 0$ then it immediately follows that it is optimal for the buyer to choose high effort (π_H).

Thus, when the buyer is in the best position to evaluate the quality of the good, it is optimal to have a fixed-price contract under which the buyer accepts all liability for defects. In this case, the role of the law (or diamond merchants association) is to ensure that the buyer pays the seller.

Relationship-specific investments

Consider now the case of *relationship-specific investments*, or what legal scholars have called the *reliance interest* (Fuller and Perdue 1936).[14] These are ex ante investments that increase the gains from trade but have no value outside the relationship. For example, suppose the seller is agent "A" and can make an investment into a cost reduction that allows her to offer a specialized good to the buyer at a lower price. In this case, the effort $\pi \in \{\pi_L, \pi_H\}$ is the probability that production costs are low. Let $c_b > c_g > 0$ be high and low production costs, respectively, and suppose $c_b > c_g + 1$. In this example, the value of trade to the buyer (agent "B") does not vary with the state, so let $V = v_g = v_b$ be the value of the good to the buyer and zero to anybody else.

Consider first the case in which it is always efficient to trade, and suppose the seller is offered a fixed price p that ensures her participation, then her payoff is:

$$U_{seller} = p - \pi c_g - (1 - \pi) c_b - \pi.$$

In this case, since $c_b - c_g > 1$, then under the fixed-price contract the seller would choose high effort. The point is that a fixed-price contract does not imply an absence of incentives. Rather, it provides incentives to the seller to find ways to lower costs.

However, suppose that trade is not always efficient because $c_b > V > c_g$. For example, costs might be high because the seller's factory burned down. Thus, the seller would like to renegotiate the agreement, which in turn results in the sharing of the ex post rents between the seller and the buyer, leading to what Victor Goldberg (1976) calls "holdup." In some cases, this may make efficient trade impossible (Hart and Moore 1988; Che and Hausch 1999).

In other cases, efficiency can be achieved with an *option contract* (Nöldeke and Schmidt 1998; Edlin and Hermalin 2000). The structure of the contract is as follows. The buyer offers the seller the *option* to sell at price p, with no penalty if the seller decides not to sell. Suppose the price is set to satisfy:

$$c_b > V > p > c_g + 1,$$

then the buyer will always be happy to buy at price p. On the seller's side, she will supply the good if and only if she has low costs, and thus her payoff is given by:

$$U_{seller} = \pi (p - c_b - 1).$$

Since the term in brackets is positive, the seller will set $\pi = \pi_H$, and the result is efficient investment combined with efficient trade.

These examples illustrate the point that contract terms can vary a great deal depending upon the characteristics of the commodity being exchanged. In the case of moral hazard, the seller's effort determines the quality of the good, hence a fixed-price contract with damages for contract breach results in efficient effort and trade. In the case of buyer liability, enforcement is purely financial; it is up to the buyer to inspect the good and determine quality. Finally, in the case of specific investments, the seller's effort determines the cost of production. In that situation, efficiency is achieved with a fixed-price contract that gives the seller the right, at a price, to terminate trade.

These examples illustrate that exchange of a commodity can entail a complex combination of compensation mechanisms. One might wonder whether we observe any of these mechanisms in practice. As it turns out, construction contracts use a variety of contractual instruments for different stages of the construction process (see Chakravarty and MacLeod 2009). Moreover, employment contracts, particularly formal union contracts, can be very complex and have a number of moving parts.

However, if contracts are too complex, then parties may not abide by their terms. This point was nicely made by Macaulay (2000), who provides a number of examples of contracts that parties have signed but ignored. In such cases, Macaulay observes that in such cases, the parties rely on long-term relationships to regulate exchange.

Relational contracts

Even if employment occurs in a spot market, most employment relationships last more than a few periods. For example, day laborers in Los Angeles can be found at the same location each day, where prospective employers can hire them on a day-to-day basis. In such a market, each side of the market learns about the other so that employment conditions and the trade price can vary with the characteristics of the match and the expectation of future employment.

A relational contract model begins with the situation in which contracting parties will meet again in the future and explores how the expectation of future trade affects current compensation and quality of work. In particular, in situations in which an efficient spot transaction is not possible due to, for example, incomplete information, the expectation of future trade may enhance performance. Greenspan (1998) explicitly made this point when he advised against the regulation of the over-the-counter market for securities:

> Professional counter-parties to privately negotiated contracts also have demonstrated their ability to protect themselves from losses from fraud and counter-party insolvencies.... A far more powerful incentive, however, is the fear of loss of the dealer's good reputation, without which it cannot compete effectively, regardless of its financial strength or financial engineering capabilities.

The importance of reputation has also been illustrated in a number of other contexts. Greif (1989) shows that social groups in medieval times played a crucial role in contract enforcement, while Greif, Milgrom, and Weingast's (1994) work on the law merchant provides historical examples of exchange that were enforced in the absence of formal law. More recent work includes McMillan and Woodruff (1999), who point out the importance of informal contracts in Vietnam, while Johnson, McMillan, and Woodruff (2002) highlight the complementarities between informal enforcement and courts.

The theory of relational contracts builds upon the research that applies the prisoner's dilemma game to social interactions. Axelrod (1981) started a body of literature that supposes life can be viewed as a repeated game between two individuals who, in each period, choose between trusting each other or cheating. The basic idea is that trust is sustainable if parties are in a social environment in which others can observe their behavior. This simple idea has been very fruitful and has been applied to a variety of questions, such as Kranton's (1996) work on sustaining reciprocal trade relationships, and more recently Dixit's (2003) work on explaining the rise of private governance relationships.

The prisoner's dilemma problem was extended by Telser (1980) to include contracts, and then fully characterized by MacLeod and Malcomson (1989). Formally, a relational contract is *self-enforcing* if both parties find it in their self-interest to perform as promised. Using Abreu (1988), one can characterize all the payoffs possible with such a contract. The key ingredient is the assumption that in every period there is a future surplus V^* that is larger than the parties would get if one were to breach the agreement.

More precisely, a relational contract is an agreement between the worker and the firm for which there is a legally enforceable payment w to the worker. The worker agrees to select effort π_H. In exchange, the firm agrees to pay a bonus b if the worker chooses π_H. If the worker does not choose the high effort, then the firm believes that the worker has breached their agreement, and therefore the firm terminates the relationship.

Similarly, if the firm does not pay the bonus, then the worker believes the firm has breached their agreement, and the worker terminates the relationship. What makes the contract relational is that rather than asking the court for relief, the parties threaten to leave the relationship; this may be their only option if effort is not observable outside the relationship. If termination occurs, then the surplus, S^*, from future trade is destroyed:

$$S^* = V^* - \left(U_F^0 + U_W^0\right) > 0.$$

If neither party breaches the agreement, then they continue to trade. As part of their agreement, the worker gets a share $\alpha \in [0, 1]$ of the surplus. In practice, the allocation of the future share can be achieved via a set of trade prices. However, I adopt this formulation in order to focus on the important role that the allocation of future rents plays in relational contract theory.

Consider first the firm. If no party breaches the agreement, the firm has payoff

$$U_F^* = \pi_H \beta - w - b + (1 - \alpha) V^* = \text{Current Profit} + \text{Future Profit}. \tag{1.2}$$

After the worker has chosen effort, the firm might be tempted to cheat on the agreement and not pay the bonus. Thus, a necessary condition for this contract to be self-enforcing is

$$U_F^* \geq \pi_H \beta - w + U_F^0 = \text{Defect Profit} + \text{Outside Option Profit}. \tag{1.3}$$

Notice Defect Profit − CurrentProfit = b = Bonus, hence (1.2) and (1.3) imply:

$$\text{Future Profit} - \text{Outside Option Profit} \geq \text{Bonus}. \tag{1.4}$$

This is the firm's *incentive constraint* under a relational contract. When the firm breaches its obligation to pay the bonus, the cost is the termination of the relationship and the loss of any rent it earned in the relationship. The firm performs as long as the gain is less than the cost of termination.

A similar situation holds for the worker:

$$U_W^* = w + b - \pi_H + \alpha V^*.$$

If the worker shirks, then the firm will not pay the bonus and will dismiss the worker. Thus, for the relational contract to be self-enforcing we have:

$$U_W^* = p + b - \pi_H + \alpha V^* \geq p - \pi_L + U_W^0.$$

This implies the following incentive constraint:

$$\text{Future Utility} - \text{Outside Option Worker} \geq \text{Incentive to Cheat} - \text{Bonus}. \tag{1.5}$$

These expressions illustrate that there is a connection between the division of the rents and contract form. If the firm has a greater share of the surplus, then it can credibly commit to a larger bonus, which in turn reduces the rent that it must leave to the worker to provide incentives.

Consider two polar cases. Suppose that the market for the firm is perfectly competitive, that is, the future rent for the firm is equal to its outside option. Thus, equation (1.4) implies that $0 \geq bonus$; that is, bonus pay must be zero. This implies that in equation (1.5) we have:

$$\text{Future Utility} - \text{Outside Option Worker} \geq \text{Incentive to Cheat} > 0.$$

In other words, the worker must receive a rent or she will shirk. This case corresponds to the well-known efficiency wage model of Shapiro and Stiglitz (1984), in which workers are paid a high wage but fired if they are caught shirking. The rent needed to enforce the contract is generated by equilibrium unemployment. Klein and Leffler (1981) have a similar model, though they argue that firms with good reputations dissipate rents with wasteful advertising.

A robust prediction of the theory is that the efficiency of the relationship is related to the size of the rent and does *not* depend upon the contract form. If we add constraints to (1.4) and (1.5), we get that the future value of a relationship must be greater than the sum of the outside options by at least the size of the temptation to cheat:

$$\text{Gains from Trade} - \text{Outside Options} \geq \text{Incentive to Cheat } (\pi_H - \pi_L) \,.$$

MacLeod and Malcomson (1989) show that this condition is not only necessary but sufficient for the existence of self-enforcing relational contracts. If it is satisfied, then relational contracts that implement the efficient allocation exist. The form of the contract (the size of the bonus) is a function of how the surplus from the relationship is divided between the two parties.

These observations illustrate that the move from economic price to a relational contract provides an economic model of many phenomena that appear to be "noneconomic." For example, Akerlof (1980) introduces a theory of social norms to explain why wages are downward rigid. It turns out that when relational contracts are modeled as a repeated game, then the existence of a social norm with these features is a *necessary* condition for the existence of a relational contract. This provides a way to integrate the theory of norms with efficiency wage theory that assumes, without justification, that it is an equilibrium for firms to offer above market-clearing wages.

A second—possibly more important—issue is to understand the limits of the theory and why things can go wrong. The prior quotation from Greenspan (1998) claims that reputation effects (as used in relational contracts) are sufficient to ensure good behavior in financial markets. Yet, ten years later, after the 2008 financial crisis, Greenspan (2008) states:

As I wrote last March: those of us who have looked to the self-interest of lending institutions to protect shareholder's equity (myself especially) are in a state of shocked disbelief. Such counter-party surveillance is a central pillar of our financial markets' state of balance.

1.3 The Agenda

To address the issues that are raised in the two Greenspan quotations, one needs a framework that relates reputation to observed economic outcomes. In particular, the 2007–2008 financial crisis teaches us that price signals alone are not sufficient to ensure a well-functioning economy. The purpose of this book is to review research that extends price theory to the exchange of commodities when markets are incomplete. Like the law itself, the theory I outline in this book is complex and builds upon a number of interlocking elements. In particular, a complete economic theory of exchange relies upon ingredients that are often viewed as "noneconomic," including individual beliefs about the future, norms of behavior, and the potential to engage in conflict with others. Depending on the context, each of these ingredients is shown to affect the quality and quantity of trade.

Chapter 2 is on the relationship between theory and evidence. It highlights two distinct goals for economic theory. The first is to provide a way to measure and synthesize evidence. The second is to view models as decision aids. Savage ([1954] 1972) explicitly introduces the idea that rational choice requires the creation of a "small model" of the world. Such a model can be used to organize evidence and systematically evaluate the consequences of different choices. The unprovable assumption here is that the use of an imperfect model improves decision making. As Robert Solow (1956) comments at the beginning of his classic paper on economic growth:

All theory depends on assumptions which are not quite true. That is what makes it theory. The art of successful theorizing is to make the inevitable simplifying assumptions in such a way that the final results are not very sensitive. A "crucial" assumption is one on which the conclusions do depend sensitively, and it is important that crucial assumptions be reasonably realistic. When the results of a theory seem to flow specifically from a special crucial assumption, then if the assumption is dubious, the results are suspect.

Since Solow wrote those words, we have gained a much better understanding of how to do credible empirical work. We do not yet have a firm understanding of the empirical relevance of many, if not most, of the work discussed in this book. The purpose of chapter 2 is to provide a brief introduction to the potential outcome framework of Rubin and Holland (Holland 1986) that forms the foundation for much of modern empirical research in economics. It is introduced at this point to highlight the importance of counterfactual thinking when evaluating models. A better model is not merely a way to summarize observed phenomena. As Solow observes, no model is "true," so the goal is to produce models that do a better job than the alternatives. In this regard, price theory is an important starting point as it can often serve as a useful counterfactual against which to evaluate a new model.

Chapters 3–5 review models of individual and group decision making. Chapter 3 provides a brief review of decision theory as it is used in contract theory and institution design. This is material that is traditionally part of a first-year graduate course in economics. These models build upon the influential work of Savage ([Savage (1954)] 1972) who introduces the idea of a "personal probability." Savage emphasizes the point that it is impossible to build a truly objective model of the world. Rather, all that is possible is to be objective relative to some imperfect worldview, a viewpoint that turns out to be consistent with the way contract law works.[15]

A core ingredient for the Savage model is the subjective beliefs that individuals have regarding the future. Savage realized that in many, if not most, real-world decision-making problems it is impossible to accurately assess future events, yet one must nevertheless make a choice. This observation is particularly evident in law, where in order to finish a case, the judge or jury must make a decision; neither party has the luxury of waiting a century or so for the science to be worked out. Savage's approach is appropriate for such situations because it allows individuals to build a model of the future, and then decide whether to use that model. When the science is uncertain, one builds the best imperfect model one can.

Many important decisions remain that require a discussion of possible future events and of how today's actions will affect them. In social situations, one of the essential ingredients is a model of how others will behave. Chapter 4 provides a brief review of game theory. The goal of this theory is to extend decision theory to model belief formation and then make predictions regarding how individuals will select actions when they realize they are interacting with other strategic individuals.[16]

As the example of knee surgery discussed above illustrates, there can be large variation in the gains from trade and how they are divided between parties in the market. Chapter 5 reviews both axiomatic and strategic bargaining theory. Axiomatic bargaining theory is concerned with the question of how one *should* divide the gains from trade based on some explicit normative principles. An alternative view is that the division of the gains from trade depends on how well parties are able to play the "bargaining game." The second part of the chapter introduces a set of models in which parties explicitly make offers and counter-offers until an agreement is reached.

Chapters 6–8 introduce agency theory and what is now considered in economics to constitute "contract theory." This is a class of models that builds upon three ingredients. The first is that there is a temporal separation between actions and payments. Second, parties are assumed to understand the relationship between their actions and outcomes and to correctly anticipate how their counterparty will respond to contract terms and conditions. Finally, parties are assumed to have imperfect information. They use events during trade to appropriately update beliefs. The theory uses the tools of decision and game theory to design efficient, one-period performance contracts.

Chapters 9–10 review the theory of relational contracts, a class of models in which contract enforcement relies upon informal rewards and punishments that occur during the course of the trading relationship. Chapter 9 explores the theory of relational contracts when parties have common knowledge regarding their payoffs. Chapter 10 extends the theory to situations in which evaluations are subjective. In that case, one has a trade-off between the provision of performance incentives and conflict, a feature of many exchange relationships. Thus, chapter 10 extends the models developed in the earlier chapters to include subjective evaluation, which in turn has the potential to provide new insights into organizational conflict. The final chapter is a nontechnical review that highlights the distinctive features of each class of models to provide a guide to which model is the most appropriate for a particular application.

2 Evidence, Models, and Decision Making

Make your theories elaborate.
—R. A. Fisher (1945)[1]

2.1 Introduction

A ubiquitous feature of modern training in economics is the division of duties between theory and evidence, particularly in graduate programs where microeconomic theory and econometrics are taught as separate subjects, often with little overlap. A common view among theorists, as nicely articulated by Ariel Rubinstein (1991), is that economic theory (more specifically, game theory) is a form of storytelling about the world since it does not present a realistic representation of the world. In many ways this is an update on the views of Friedman (1953, 7) who states:

> The ultimate goal of a positive science is the development of a "theory" or "hypothesis" that yields valid and meaningful (i.e., not truistic) predictions about phenomena not yet observed. Such a theory is, in general, a complex intermixture of two elements. In part, it is a "language" designed to promote "systematic and organized methods of reasoning." In part, it is a body of substantive hypotheses designed to abstract essential features of complex reality.

The standard first-year graduate textbook in microeconomics, Mas-Colell, Whinston, and Green (1995), does not have a single citation to empirical evidence. Since that text was written there has been a large increase in empirical research in economics. Angrist, Caldwell, and Hall (2017) document the trends in economics publishing and show that from 1980 until 2015 there has been a 20 percent increase in the number of empirical articles published in economics journals (going from 50 to 60 percent of papers published in top journals). This does not mean that theory is less important, but it does imply that with better data, theory can face more discipline from evidence. By including references to empirical work, this book aims to highlight areas where there can be fruitful interaction between theory and evidence.

The purpose of this chapter is to provide some basic language and concepts for the empirical study of socioeconomic phenomena. This will allow discussion of how one can move from the theory to evidence at various points in the book. One of the reasons this issue is often sidestepped in graduate training is because it is very hard. Economics, like physics, has a wide variety of models, and for a particular problem the most appropriate model may be found among many options. In the case of physics this is beautifully illustrated in the classic text by Feynman, Leighton, and Sands (1963), in which every page is full of both theory and evidence. There, the theory is chosen as a function of the phenomena to be studied.

In chapter 2 of volume 3, Feynman explicitly discusses the problem of the wave and particle views of matter and the impossibility of ever having a completely deterministic model of the universe. The point is that even in physics there is not, nor is there likely to be, a single model or worldview that is useful in all contexts. Thus, modern physics consist not of a single model but of a collection of models, whose choice depends upon the phenomena at hand, as well as the time and space scales. One uses different models for the study of stars from the ones used for studying subatomic particles.

This is even more true for complex socioeconomic phenomena and naturally leads to some controversy regarding the best way forward. For example, the June 2010 issue of the *Journal of Economic Literature* is devoted to the question of how best to perform applied research in development economics.[2] Deaton (2010) suggests the recent emphasis on the use of experiments has resulted in less integration of the theory with the evidence. More generally, theory is sometimes viewed with suspicion by applied economists, as we can see from Angrist and Pischke's (2009) conclusion to their entertaining and insightful book:

If applied econometrics were easy, theorists would do it. But it's not as hard as the dense pages of *Econometrica* might lead you to believe. Carefully applied to coherent causal questions, regression and 2SLS almost always make sense. Your standard errors won't be quite right, but they rarely are. Avoid embarrassment by being your own best skeptic, and especially, DON'T PANIC!

The advice "DON'T PANIC!" is good advice that Douglas Adams also embraces, as it appears inscribed in large friendly letters on *The Hitchhiker's Guide to the Galaxy*.[3]

A serious lesson one can learn from Adams's brilliant book is the impossibility of predicting the future. The author begins his book with the imagined destruction of the earth by the Vogons' completing an intergalactic construction project. This example illustrates a number of points.

First, this might be fiction, but there are many real-life examples of the difficulty in predicting events that lead to monumental upheavals in individual lives, such as the 2011 tsunami in Japan, the 2008 crash in financial markets, or maybe Donald Trump's becoming president of the United States in 2017. These events were difficult to predict and resulted in thousands of individuals and firms having to make unexpected, life-changing decisions. We can certainly expect similar events in the future, although maybe not in the form of an interstellar superhighway, but maybe in some other unexpected form.[4]

For example, there might be the discovery of cheap energy from nuclear fusion. What would happen to all the long-term supply contracts between fuel suppliers (coal, oil, natural gas) and utilities that have explicit incentive terms that make it costly for one or the other party to leave the relationships?[5] At the time the parties entered into these contracts, they had a model of how the future would unfold and designed their relationship in the context of this model. A dramatic fall in energy prices would necessarily lead to both contract renegotiation and contract breach, which in turn would require courts to decide how contracts should be enforced to deal with these unforeseen contingencies.[6]

In this chapter, I briefly outline the role of models in the assessment of empirical evidence and how this evidence can be used to modify our beliefs and expectations regarding an uncertain future. For our purposes a model has three roles. The first is to provide a *representation* of observed phenomena. This means that a model provides a parsimonious way to encode and represent information numerically. The second is to provide information about a *population* of units: individuals, firms, or countries. The goal of such a model is to capture statistical relationships between observed characteristics that are common to the population. This allows us to make inferences about the characteristics of any member of the population. Finally, models can provide a representation of causal mechanisms that explicitly address the question of how changing a choice affects observed or experienced outcomes.

Thus, I explicitly assume that building better models of the world helps us make better decisions. This is an unprovable assumption that is controversial. For example, in his book *The Poverty of Historicism*, Popper ([1957] 2002) explicitly argues that one cannot hope to have a scientific theory of human affairs. However, there is evidence that model building is a fundamental ingredient for decision making for any successful individual. This point was nicely illustrated by B. F. Skinner in the case of pigeons.

2.1.1   "Superstition" in the Pigeon

The ability to see patterns in data, even when such patterns do not really exist, is a skill that is not restricted to humans. Skinner (1948) reports an ingenious experiment in which he provides food pellets to a number of pigeons. Before I describe the experiment, consider first the observed outcomes. After one treatment, the birds exhibit a variety of behaviors. One repeatedly turns counterclockwise in the cage, another repeatedly thrusts its head into one of the corners of the cage, while a third develops "a 'tossing' response, as if placing its head beneath an invisible bar and lifting it repeatedly" (168).

If presented with these data, one can imagine building an area of research for understanding why different birds have different behaviors. These observed rituals might be due to the way they were raised, the types of parents they had, or maybe their genes. Skinner convincingly shows that it is none of these. Rather, food was randomly supplied to the birds, and each bird learned to repeat the behavior it was doing at the time the food arrived.

For example, if a bird was turning at the time food arrived, then it was natural for the bird to believe that further turning would lead to more food. If food supply was sufficiently frequent, then further turning would be rewarded with more food, and the bird would believe that its turning in its cage *caused* food to arrive! Skinner carefully modified the arrival rates of food and showed that in this way he could extinguish the behavior or increase its frequency.

This experiment has a number of useful lessons. First, it illustrates that animals, humans included, are designed to build models of the world, including false models. The difference between humans and birds is that we have developed a statistics toolbox that can help distinguish between good and bad models, and particularly the difference between causal relationships and spurious correlations.

Second, and more importantly, it is very easy to build a false model. For example, the pigeons might have underlying characteristics that lead them to turn or toss their head. In the absence of an experiment, one might easily collect data that are correlated with many of the observed behaviors without actually understanding that the root cause is a spurious correlation between behavior and food supply.

In human affairs there are many examples of such behaviors and "superstitions," including astrology, palm reading, lucky tokens, and so on. A particularly important example is predicting future prices in financial markets. Low and Hasanhodzic (2010) provide an interesting history of "technical analysis" in financial markets. Technical analysis involves identifying patterns in past financial data to predict future trends and thereby identifying profitable trades. The potential gain from such predictions encourages a large industry in financial advising in which some individuals claim to be able to do this better than others.[7] It is a sad fact that even though we have some excellent statistical tools, individuals continue to be attracted to "experts" who claim to be able to beat the market.[8] There are also the "experts" who are engaged in criminal activities, such as Bernard Madoff, who was convicted of a Ponzi scheme using funds from many respectable investors.[9]

A goal of economics is to help improve the rules that regulate economies given the actual behavior of individuals. This begins by building good, evidence-based models, which in turn provide a guide to decision making. These models will not be perfect. One reason unscientific models and worldviews survive is in a large complex economy there is a strictly positive probability that some trader using unscientific technical analysis beats the market several periods in a row, even though he or she has no special skill. The challenge is to build models of the world that can distinguish the lucky trader from one who has true insights into how markets work. The next three sections outline three distinct reasons for building useful models and how we can disentangle luck from causation.

2.2 Models for Representation

One of the most ubiquitous applications of a formal model is as a *parsimonious representation* of physical phenomena. For example, modern photography is heavily reliant on representing visual data in computer memory. Most casual photographers use the JPEG standard. When a photograph is taken, the image is divided into a grid of pixels that record the intensity of each of the three primary colors. This information, called a raster image, is a large vector $\alpha = \{\alpha_i\}_{i=1}^{10^7}$ where each pixel i, $\alpha_i = (R_i, G_i, B_i)$ provides the intensity of each of the three primary colors.[10] The intensity is recorded as a binary number, usually with 16 or 24 bits (and hence 2^{16} or 2^{24} intensity levels). The original file typically contains millions of bits of information, which require large amounts of storage space. The JPEG format is a *mathematical model* that is used to reduce the image to a smaller set of parameters while retaining quality as measured by the perception of a human viewer of the image. Essentially, the JPEG algorithm projects this information into a lower-dimensional vector space, in the same way one does a linear regression.[11]

Formally, the JPEG standard produces two functions. The first takes the data and produces a lower-dimensional representation: $\beta = f^{jpeg}(\alpha, r) \in I^{n_{raw}/r}$, where r denotes the degree of compression, I is the set of possible intensity levels, $2^{24} - 1$, and n_{raw} is the size of the original file. The JPEG standard relies on how the brain interprets visual data to interpolate between pixels. The function f^{jpeg} is programmed into most cameras, so that only the data β is recorded and sent to the computer. Given these data, a second function recreates the raster image that is displayed on the screen that is the "inverse" of the function f^{jpeg}:

$$\alpha' = g^{jpeg}(\beta) \in I^{n_{raw}}.$$

In general, since β is in a lower-dimensional space than α, it is normally the case that $\alpha \neq \alpha'$. In other words, the rendered image is of lower quality than the original image recorded by the camera.

This example illustrates the point that even though we could in principle store the high-quality raster file, the JPEG model provides a more parsimonious representation of the data. This is a good model, even though, as Pauli observes, all models are wrong in the sense that they do not perfectly represent the original data.[12] Rather, the best way to evaluate the JPEG algorithm is subjective—does the *perceived* image accurately represent the original?

The representation problem is complex because it can be hierarchical, with models building upon models. Figure 2.1 is based on a JPEG image of New York City (NYC) from circa 1964.[13] This image can be viewed as a very useful model. First, it is not "true" in the sense that it provides a perfect representation of NYC. Rather, it provides information about the streets in the city at the time. Moreover, it can be used for a "what if" analysis. For example, starting from a particular location, the map can be used to determine the route that will get one to the sea coast as quickly as possible.

Second, the map provides a natural way to think about the "external validity" of models. That is, to what extent can I use a model for new questions? We would expect that in 1965 the map would still be accurate and useful to determine how to go to a particular location or to discover the name of a street in a particular location. Today, more than fifty years later, the map is still useful, but we would expect changes—some street names have changed and there may be new construction that changes the optimal route we might use. In other words, this map is a "false" model in that it is not perfectly accurate and is less accurate today than at the time it was produced. But in a pinch, in the absence of a better model/map, it remains useful even today.

We can push the map analogy further and observe that one may choose different maps/models for different questions. The map in figure 2.2 is a 2010 subway map of New York City.[14] This is a model of the same thing, New York City, but at a different time and with a different goal—providing information on the subway system. In particular, the subway map is intended to answer a different set of questions than the street map. Street maps can contain subway information, but it can be hard to see the subway markers, and adding line overlays would cover some streets. Thus, subway maps can be viewed as models with a different goal from a street map—they allow individuals to make decisions on how to use the subway quickly and efficiently.

As with a street map, the external validity decreases with time. Moreover, notice that the external validity of this model is *nonlinear*. For example, when a new subway line is opened, large and discrete changes in transportation options occur that are not reflected in the map. Hence, individuals living close to the new line would make very suboptimal transportation decisions if they relied upon an old map.

In summary, the map perspective captures the main features of a good model. The most important feature is that a map/model is a decision aid; the model's representation allows one to make better choices more quickly than in the absence of the map/model. Second,

Figure 2.1
Map of New York City.

Figure 2.2
Subway map for New York City.

maps/models of the same phenomena are not unique. The map one uses to represent a city depends upon the question one is going to ask, such as where is the closest park? or which subway should one take? Maps/models have external validity when the world they are describing changes slowly and smoothly enough that the representation from a period is useful for many periods into the future. However, the failure of a map/model can be very rapid and can occur in nonlinear, unpredictable ways. For example, if New York were hit by an asteroid the map would quickly become historical evidence rather than a representation of the city after the incident.

All these observations are true for economic models as well. For example, we can study the US economy from the perspective of microeconomists, who might be concerned about the level of inequality and appropriate policy responses. In contrast, macroeconomists are more concerned with issues such as inflation and monetary policy. These questions are clearly linked, yet in practice one does not use a single model to study them, but rather one custom-builds models for specific problems. Hence, the models in this book should not be viewed as end points but as a set of potential starting points for building models to address specific issues and problems.

2.3   Population Models

The map example illustrates why models are useful for decision making. The example also illustrates a feature that is common to all models: they are not "true," but rather useful, though imperfect, decision aids. A second feature of a map, say the map of New York City, is that we do not expect it to be useful for other cities. However, there are features of New York City that we might expect to apply to other places (e.g., the relationship between population density and rents). The purpose of a population model is to be able to make statements about situations we have not seen before based on information from similar situations.

More precisely, a population model begins with many units, denoted by $i \in I$. These units might be cities, but more often in economics they are individuals (workers or consumers), firms, or countries. Suppose that at date t there are potentially three sources of information. The first is a vector providing individual specific characteristics or properties, denoted by $x_{it} \in X \subset \Re^n$. This might be the gender of a person or the number of employees in a firm.

The purpose of a model is to understand and evaluate choices. Hence, the second ingredient is the set of possible choices that the unit might make, given by a finite set A, where the action is $a_{it} \in A$. The combination of choices and characteristics can be associated with a set of *potential outcomes*, Y, where $y_{it} \in Y$, is the realized outcome at date t for unit i. For the current discussion we remain agnostic regarding the relationship between these variables. Specifically, we discuss the statistical properties of the population that in turn allow us to describe the expected properties of a unit randomly selected from the population.

Table 2.1 provides some examples of population models. Notice that the same information can appear in several columns. For example, the current health of an individual can be an X variable because it affects labor supply. However, it can also be an outcome variable because choices, such as the level of education, can affect health.[15]

As an example, consider the 1979 National Longitudinal Survey of Youth, better known as the NLSY79. This is a nationally (United States) representative survey of 12,686 men and women born in the years 1957–1964. These individuals were interviewed annually from 1979 to 1994, and biennially since 1994.[16] The data include information on a variety of characteristics, including gender, age, education, wage, and hours worked in a year.

Table 2.1
Population features

Unit $i \in N$	Characteristics: $x_{it} \in X$	Actions: $a_{it} \in A$	Outcomes: $y_{it} \in Y$
Person	age, sex, race, wealth, health	education, labor supply	income, health
Firm	age, size, location	location, investment	growth, profits, size
Country	health, climate, geography	taxes, services	health, climate, wealth

Suppose we let education, $a_i \in \{0, 1, 2, \ldots, 20\}$, be a choice or action variable, and let the outcome $y_{i,2000} \in \Re$ denote the log wage for a male worker i in year 2000. Let N be the set of male workers in the United States in the year 2000, and let $z_{i,2000} = \{a_i, y_{i,2000}\}$, $i \in N$ be a potential observation. The population information is denoted by:

$$Population = \{z_{i,2000} | i \in N\}.$$

A number of population models are possible. For example, this set could include several million observations if one had data from every individual in the economy. This is not practical; hence the actual data are from a small survey that is used to make general statements regarding the whole population. The survey results can be denoted by a set $N^s = I^s \times T^s$, where $I^s \subset I$ are the individuals observed and $T^s \subset T$ is the set of dates at which observations are taken, where T is the set of possible dates. Let $N = I \times T$ be the index set for the whole population, and let $n = \#N$ and $n^s = \#N^s$ be the size of each index set.

In this case, letting $z_{it} = \{a_{it}, y_{it}\}$ denote the observations, the data set is given by:

$$Data = \{z_{it} | it \in N^s\}.$$

The *population* of units is given by:

$$Pop = \{z_{it} | it \in N\}.$$

A central concern of statistics is to ask what we can learn about the population *Pop* using the observations in *Data*. For example, we may wish to know the basic features of the population as given by *descriptive statistics*, such as the mean and variance:

$$mean\ (Pop) = \sum_{it \in N} z_{it}/n,$$

$$var\ (z_{it}, N) = \sum_{it \in N} (z_{it} - mean\ (z_{it}))^2 / (n-1).$$

Notice that z_{it} is *not* being viewed as a random variable. The mean and variance are in principle well-defined numbers that we could measure if we had data on all individuals. In general, obtaining access to such data is very difficult. One can estimate these numbers by drawing a random sample from N of size $n^s < n$. Let $N^s\ (n^s)$ represent this sample and then create the statistic:

$$mean\ (Data) = \sum_{it \in N^s} z_{it}/n^s.$$

If the sample is randomly selected it follows that

$$E\ \{mean\ (Data)\} = mean\ (Pop).\tag{2.1}$$

(See exercise 3.) This statement makes no assumptions regarding the distribution of the underlying observations. Rather, (2.1) is the consequence of supposing that the sample with N^s individuals is randomly selected from the whole population.

In practice, it can be difficult to obtain a random selection. For example, suppose that the data are collected by a phone interview and that lower-wage individuals are less likely to have a phone. In that case, *Data* would have a higher fraction of high-wage individuals than are in *Pop*, leading to a sample for which the mean wage is higher than the mean wage in the population. When one uses the statement that the sample is "representative," one supposes that equation (2.1) holds. There are many applications for such models. For example, Gallup polls try to work out how a population of individuals will vote based upon a sample for a small subset of the population.

To move beyond simple means, the statistician must add some additional structure, such as supposing that the z_{it} are realizations of a random variable with specific properties. For example, if it were the case that $z_{it} = z_{it'}$ for all $it, it' \in N$, then a single draw from the population would reveal all the other values. The more common case is to suppose that $\{z_{it}\}_{it \in N}$ come from a set of independent and identically distributed random variables, whose distribution is from a parametric class of distribution functions:

$$Z_{it} \sim f(z|\theta), \tag{2.2}$$

where $\theta \in \Re^k$ is an unknown parameter. For example, one might suppose that Z_{it} is normally distributed with unknown mean m and variance σ^2, in which case $\theta = (m, \sigma^2)$.

This assumption provides one with another way to *represent* the data, as discussed above. Given the data, one can estimate the value of these parameters using maximum likelihood estimation (MLE):

$$max_\theta \sum_{it \in N^S} \log(f(z_{it}|\theta)). \tag{2.3}$$

In the case of normally distributed data, if $\theta_0 = (m_0, \sigma_0^2)$ is the MLE solving (2.3), then the best guess of any value of z_{it} would be m_0, with standard deviation of σ_0. A good example is the Mincer wage equation.

2.3.1   The Mincer Wage Equation

The work of Jacob Mincer (1958), Theodore Schultz (1961), and Gary Becker (1962) introduced the idea that education is an investment activity that increases a person's future earnings. By education, they mean the number of years of formal schooling. These ideas are influential because they provide a way to explicitly measure the value of education via what has become known as the Mincer wage equation. The basic form supposes that:

$$w_i = \log(wage_i) = \beta \times e_i + \alpha + \epsilon_i,$$

where $wage_i$ and e_i are, respectively, the wage and education level of worker i. If ϵ_i is normally distributed with mean 0 and variance σ^2, then we can compute the maximum likelihood estimates of the parameters $\theta = \{\beta, \alpha, \sigma^2\}$ using ordinary least squares (OLS). The year 2000 sample of the NSLY used in Lemieux, MacLeod, and Parent (2009) has about 2200 men, with OLS estimates given by:

$$w_i = .087 \times Education_i - 0.43 + noise_i. \tag{2.4}$$

The coefficient 0.087 is the correlation between a person's log wage and education, while -0.43 is a constant term. These coefficients are chosen to minimize the mean squared error:

$$MSE = \sum_{i \in I} noise_i^2 / 2200 = 0.43,$$

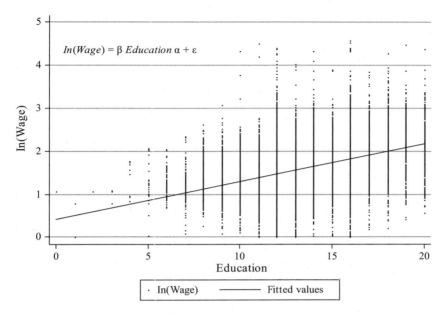

$In(Wage) = \beta\ Education\ \alpha + \varepsilon$

Figure 2.3
Wages versus education.

where I is the set of individuals in the sample. The relationship between wages and education is illustrated in figure 2.3. Wages clearly rise on average with education, but there is also a great deal of variation. This equation has several interpretations. One interpretation is as a parsimonious representation of the data, where the vector $\{.087, -0.43, 0.43\}$ provides estimates of the return to education, the intercept and the variance of the error term. Thus, one reduces a data set with 4400 parameters (wage and education for each person), to one with $2200 + 2$ parameters. For each person there is an education level, with the wage given by (2.4).

This is of practical importance for an employer who is trying to decide on what wage to offer a worker. If the only information the employer has is the years of education, then a reasonable offer might be the expected population wage conditional on years of education:

$$\hat{w}_i = E\{w_i|e_i\} = \frac{\int_w wf\ (w|e_i)\ dw}{\int_w f\ (w|e_i)\ dw} = .087 \times e_i - 0.43\ .$$

It is worth emphasizing that the kinds of predictions one makes using population models are relatively "atheoretical" in the sense that they do not depend upon a specific mechanism linking education to wages. The key ingredients in a population model are the characteristics of the individual unit i, e_i, which in turn allow one to make an inference regarding their log wage, w_i.

Like the JPEG algorithm, this regression can be viewed as creating a lower-dimensional representation of the data. However, there is still a great deal of unexplained variation. In this case the R^2 is .18, and hence *noise* accounts for about 82 percent of variation in log wages, with the rest "explained" by a person's education.[17]

One can dramatically improve the quality of the fit by conditioning on more variables, such as the age of the worker, occupation, and so on. This would result in a fit with a larger R^2, though it would not explain why workers in different occupations earn different amounts. Rather, the model describes a pattern in the data that can be used to provide a good prediction regarding the expected wage of a randomly chosen member of the population with particular characteristics.

2.4   Causality

The Mincer wage equation and its extensions are very useful for employers who would like to know how much they should pay an individual worker who is randomly chosen from the population. However, without additional assumptions, it cannot be used to reliably guide individuals as they decide how much education they should accumulate. For an individual worker, the decision they face is choosing between an additional year of education and the *counterfactual*—the wage she would get if they enter the labor market immediately. To make a rational choice they need to begin with the *potential outcomes* for student i:

$$\vec{u}_i = \left\{ u_i^0, u_i^1 \right\},$$

where u_i^0 is the lifetime utility from going to the labor market immediately, while u_i^1 is the lifetime utility from an additional year of education.

One can always frame the choice as if one is performing an experimental trial. In this case, an additional year of education can be viewed as the treatment, while going to the labor market immediately is the control. The *treatment effect* is defined by

$$\tau_i = u_i^1 - u_i^0.$$

The difficulty is that one makes this choice only once, so there is no way for the individual herself to experiment with both choices (there is no way to undo the treatment of an additional year of schooling). Holland (1986) calls this the *fundamental problem of causal inference*. The only reliable way to do this is via time travel. For example, in the film, *Groundhog Day*, the hapless hero, Phil Connors, played by Bill Murray, keeps reliving Groundhog Day in Punxsutawney, Pennsylvania, until he works out how to deal with his personality and connect with the heroine of the movie, Rita, played by Andie Mac-Dowell. In that case, each day is exactly the same, so Phil can experiment with different strategies, until finally he is able to win Rita's heart.

Given that time travel is not possible, then, as Holland (1986) points out, to make progress one necessarily has to make some untestable assumptions. In labor economics the most common approach is to suppose that one can group individuals with similar characteristics, some of whom get the additional year of education, and some of whom do not.[18] The difficulty with using population-level data to measure τ_i is because in many, if not most, cases individuals choose whether to be treated or not. For example, one reason educated individuals earn more is because they are more able and consequently they would earn more than noncollege educated individuals even in the absence of a college education (e.g., Bill Gates, the founder of Microsoft, is a college dropout).

It is easy to see such an effect in the NLSY data. It contains the results from the Armed Forces Qualifying Test (AFQT) that can be used as a measure of skill (see Altonji, Bharadwaj, and Lange [2012] for a detailed discussion, including caveats on the use of the AFQT). If we run the Mincer regression with the addition of the AFQT score we get:

$$w_i = 0.067 \times Education + 0.006 \times AFQT - 0.552 + \epsilon_i. \tag{2.5}$$

The addition of this single variable reduces the coefficient on education by almost a fourth. Moreover, the standard error on AFQT is small, so that the statistical significance of AFQT is the same as education. In this case the R^2 is now 0.36, twice the size of the R^2 in the case without the AFQT score. This result is consistent with the hypothesis that more-able individuals get more education and that wages are determined in part by ability. This leaves open the question of how to measure the return to education; that is, for a given person, how will their future outcome vary with the education they receive?

The solution outlined in Holland (1986) proceeds as follows.[19] We begin with a universe of individuals whose characteristics are described by a compact set $X \subset \Re^n$. For example, this might be all persons in a country who had a fever last year. Individuals may also be firms or countries, though for the current discussion we can think of them as a collection of persons denoted by:

$$U = \{i \in P | x_i \in X\},$$

where P denotes the universe of all possible individuals whose characteristics are taken from the set X. The reason for being explicit regarding set membership is to highlight the fact that the external validity of an experiment depends on who is in the experiment. For example, if X consists of only males, then the estimated casual effect may not apply to a set of females. Notice that this formulation includes the special case in which each person is a unique point in X.

For each person i, we would like to know for each choice $d_i \in \{1, 0\}$, the set of *potential outcomes*:

$$\left\{ \left(x_i, u_i^1, u_i^0 \right) | i \in U \right\},$$

where u_i^1, u_i^0 are the outcomes for choices 1 and 0 respectively. These are potential outcomes because the choice is made at a given date, with payoffs realized in the future, and hence for each unit we can at best observe u_i^1 or u_i^0, but not both. We maintain throughout the *stable unit treatment value assumption* (SUTVA)—the decision for unit $j \neq i$ does not affect the potential outcomes for unit i. The *average treatment effect* (ATE) of choice 1 is given by:

$$\tau^{ATE} = E \left\{ u_i^1 - u_i^0 | i \in U \right\}$$

$$= E \{\tau_i | i \in U\}.$$

This is the parameter estimated with a randomized control trial (RCT). One procedure to measure ATE is as follows. Randomly select $2n$ individuals from U, the set of individuals who match the criteria in set X. Then randomly assign n to group 1, U_1, and n to group 0, U_0. This generates data, $Data(n) = \left\{ x_i, u_i^{d_i} | i \in U_0 \cup U_1 \right\}$, where $d_i = 1$ if $i \in U_1$ and $d_i = 0$ if $i \in U_0$. The point here is that $Data(n)$ cannot contain both potential outcomes for the same unit, but it can be used to compute an estimate of ATE:

$$\hat{\tau}^{ATE}\left(Data(n)\right) = \frac{1}{n}\left\{\sum_{i \in U_1} u_i^1 - \sum_{i \in U_0} u_i^0\right\}.$$

When the assignment is random ($x_i \perp\!\!\!\perp d_i$), then we have the well-known result:

Proposition 2.1 *If units are randomly assigned to choices 1 and 0, and the stable unit treatment value assumption is satisfied, then the average treatment effect satisfies:*

$$\tau^{ATE} = E\left\{\hat{\tau}^{ATE}\left(Data(n)\right)\right\} = lim_{n \to \infty} \hat{\tau}^{ATE}\left(Data\left(n\right)\right).$$

Proof. We follow Deaton (2010). First:

$$E\left\{\hat{\tau}^{ATE}\left(Data(n)\right)\right\} = \frac{1}{n}\left\{\sum_{i \in U_1} E\{u_i^1 | d_i = 1\} - \sum_{i \in U_0} E\{u_i^0 | d_i = 0\}\right\}$$

$$= E\left\{u_i^1 | d_i = 1\right\} - E\left\{u_i^0 | d_i = 0\right\}$$

$$= lim_{n \to \infty} \hat{\tau}^{ATE}\left(Data\left(n\right)\right).$$

Next observe that:

$$E\left\{\hat{\tau}^{ATE}\left(Data(n)\right)\right\} = E\left\{u_i^1 | d_i = 1\right\} - E\left\{u_i^0 | d_i = 0\right\}$$

$$= E\left\{u_i^1 | d_i = 1\right\} - E\left\{u_i^0 | d_i = 1\right\}$$

$$+ E\left\{u_i^0 | d_i = 1\right\} - E\left\{u_i^0 | d_i = 0\right\}.$$

Observe that by SUTVA and random assignment, the final line is zero. Random assignment also implies that the expected value of a potential outcome (observed or not) is not affected by the assignment. Hence we have:

$$lim_{n \to \infty} \hat{\tau}^{ATE}\left(Data\left(n\right)\right) = E\left\{u_i^1 | d_i = 1\right\} - E\left\{u_i^0 | d_i = 1\right\},$$

$$= E\left\{u_i^1 - u_i^0 | d_i = 1\right\},$$

$$= E\left\{u_i^1 - u_i^0 | i \in U\right\},$$

$$= \tau^{ATE}. \qquad \qquad \square$$

Though quite simple, this result nicely illustrates the power of RCTs: under the appropriate assumptions, they allow for the measurement of the average treatment effect for a *population*. There is a large body of literature on constructing bounds to τ^{ATE} given finite data from an RCT. Our concern here is not with the implementation details for an RCT, but with the problem of making *decisions* using observational data.

The first condition, $\tau^{ATE} = E\left\{\hat{\tau}^{ATE}\left(Data(n)\right)\right\}$, is called the *ignorability condition*. It means that regardless of the sample size, the mean is an unbiased estimate of the treatment effect. This result has helped stimulate a literature in experimental economics (see Roth [1995b]; Duflo, Glennerster, and Kremer [2008]; and Charness and Kuhn [2011] for reviews). A typical laboratory experiment in economics draws from a pool of students and randomly allocates them to different treatments. The results of these experiments provide information on the average effect of the treatment for the population. Experiments are often viewed as the gold standard for the estimation of a causal effect.

These ideas have also influenced empirical work using observational data. A famous example is Angrist and Krueger (1991), who measure the effect of compulsory school laws on education and wages. The idea is that all compulsory schooling laws are based on requirements for students to be in school up to a certain age, such as sixteen. They observe that the law binds differently depending on the quarter of the year in which an individual is born. Individuals born in the first quarter of the year are relatively older compared to their peers in the same class. This means that they can drop out earlier and hence on average would have less education than individuals born in other quarters. The idea is that the change in years of schooling depends only on the quarter of birth and the law. As long as the quarter of birth is not related to labor market earnings in some unobservable way, then we have a *natural experiment*.[20] This is a feature of the environment that leads to a random assignment of individuals that, when combined with the unit homogeneity assumption (defined below), allows one to estimate the casual effect of a treatment.

The external validity of these studies—the extent to which the treatment effects are the same in other situations—explicitly depends upon some version of *unit homogeneity*.[21] This means that the effect is the same for all units (individuals, firms, or countries) with similar characteristics. More precisely, let $\Xi = \{X_1, X_2, \ldots, X_n\}$ be a partition of the characteristics space X.[22]

Definition 2.2 *The effect $\tau_i, i \in U$ satisfies unit homogeneity with respect to partition Ξ if for all $X_k \in \Xi$:*

$$\tau_i = \tau_j, \forall i, j \in X_k.$$

In other words, one can control for the effect of heterogeneity by having experiments that condition upon X_k. In particular, the following result is an immediate corollary of proposition 2.1:

Corollary 2.3 *Suppose for population U the effect of treatment satisfies the stable unit treatment value assumption and unit homogeneity with respect to partition Ξ. Further, suppose for all $X_k \in \Xi$ the units in $U_k = \{i | x_i \in X_k\}$ are randomly assigned to choices 1 and 0. Then for all $i \in U_k$ the average treatment effect satisfies:*

$$\tau_k^{ATE} = E\left\{\hat{\tau}^{ATE}\left(Data(n, X_k)\right)\right\} = lim_{n \to \infty} \hat{\tau}^{ATE}\left(Data\,(n, X_k)\right)$$

$$= \tau_i.$$

where $Data(n, U_k)$ are n observations randomly drawn from the population U_k.

This is the implicit assumption in any experimental design that conditions upon observables X. The expression requires the use of an expectation because the outcomes may themselves be random. However, as long as the SUTVA assumption holds, the unit homogeneity allows one to estimate the treatment effect.

It should be emphasized that unit homogeneity is a strong assumption that typically does not hold in practice for a variety of reasons. For example, suppose that we wish to know the effect of treatment of an infection with a new antibiotic. For some people who have natural immunity, an antibiotic may have no effect; for others it may save their lives, and still for others who are allergic it may cause death! Let $U = U_R \cup U_{NR}$ be the possible individuals, where U_R have natural resistance while U_{NR} have no resistance. For $i \in U_R$ the treatment effect is $\tau_i = 0$, while for $i \in U_{NR}$ we can suppose $\tau_i = 1$, where 0 means not cured and 1 means cured.

In general, we cannot observe the characteristics of individuals, and hence if we run an RCT we will estimate:

$$\tau^{ATE} = p,$$

where $p = Pr[i \in U_{NR}]$ is the probability that a person is not resistant. Since the treatment effect is either 0 or 1, this is an example where an RCT will not be able to estimate the individual treatment effect. However, such a trial is useful because it provides information on whether a treatment will be helpful for a whole population, even if the treatment effect for a particular individual is not known ex ante.

2.5   Discussion

This chapter discusses the role that formal models play in organizing and summarizing large amounts of information. In the case of economic models, the first step in building a useful model is to identify the units to which the model will apply. This could be an individual, a family, a firm, or even a country. The extent to which the model has empirical content depends on the extent to which observations of a number of units provide information regarding the characteristics or behavior of similar units in the future. These predictions take two possible forms.

The first are population models. These are models in which it is assumed that a group or population of units has similar properties. For example, observing the wage for a randomly selected group of workers provides information on the expected wage for the population at large. These models can be used to address a number of useful questions; however, they are not causal in the sense of providing substantial information on how a decision can affect an outcome.

This is the domain of the second class of empirical models that rely upon counterfactual analysis. Specifically, when choosing between different courses of action, one would like to know how the outcome varies with choice. As Holland (1986) has observed, the *fundamental problem of causal analysis* is the impossibility of simultaneously observing the outcome for each choice. Hence, every empirical study has an explicit or implicit identification strategy that allows one to infer the consequences of different treatments. Typical solutions include supposing that one has *time homogeneity*—the same unit can be used to compare the outcomes of decisions at two points in time—or alternatively, *unit homogeneity*—the effect of the decision is the same for different units with similar observable characteristics.

This book aims to promote an understanding of exchange between entities, whether those entities are individuals or firms. The analysis very much depends upon the hypothesis that parties can anticipate the consequence of terms of trade for future behavior, which in turn depends upon some form of unit invariance that we need to make precise. Given that the environment within which entities act varies with time, even an experiment with a credible identification strategy may not necessarily apply to a new environment. The purpose of a good theory is to allow us to extend our ability to make decisions using past experiences to new situations.

2.6 Exercises

1. Consider the market for financial advice and the problem of picking stocks that will go up in the next month. Suppose that there are N stocks and that one goes up and the rest go down. They have equal chance of going up. Now suppose that there are M advisers who pick one stock at random and get a reward R if their pick goes up and $-R$ if it goes down. What is the probability that at least one adviser is correct in a month? Given a particular advisor, what is the probability that they choose correctly? How do these probabilities change as M gets large and N is fixed?

2. Now suppose that adviser A picks a winning stock with probability $p_A > 1/N$ (she is better than all the other advisers). What is the probability that this adviser is among the best-performing advisers as M becomes large? Is there a lesson here?

3. Prove equation (2.1) when there is sampling with no replacement and sampling with replacement. In the latter case, after a worker is randomly chosen, that same worker is eligible for being chosen again. In each case, compute the variance of the statistic $m\left(Z_i, N^S\right)$ and compute the variance as the sample size n^S approaches n. When sampling with replacement, the variance of the estimate does not go to zero as $n^s \to n$. What is the difference in the implicit models that underlie each estimate? Another way to think about this is to find conditions under which the variance does go to zero as $n^s \to n$.

3 Decision Theory

Though the "Look before you leap" principle is preposterous if carried to extremes, I would none the less argue that it is the proper subject of our further discussion, because to cross one's bridges when one comes to them means to attack relatively simple problems of decision by artificially confining attention to so small a world that the "Look before you leap" principle can be applied there.
—Leonard J. Savage ([1954], 1972, 16).

3.1 Decision Making and the Economics Paradigm

For the purposes of this book, we are interested in decision theory to the extent that it can *represent* behavior (see section 2.2), as opposed to explaining behavior (see section 2.4), as one does for example in the field of psychology. Arrow (1958) explicitly makes this point when he observes that psychologists distinguish between behavior and preferences. The former is what individuals actually do in some situations, while the latter is what one *would* do with sufficient time and conscious reflection.

Psychology is the science concerned with understanding observed behavior under time constraints and how that behavior gets modified over time. In contrast, the norm in economics is to suppose that behavior reveals a person's time-stationary preferences. Thus, there is no distinction between preferences and behavior. This is the approach used in modern behavioral economics, beginning with Kahneman and Tversky's (1979) prospect theory that suggests modifications to the structure of preferences to model observed behavior.[1]

This book follows the economics approach and assumes that individual behavior is governed by preferences among alternatives. The next section outlines this model and makes the point that the rational choice model is a highly simplified representation of human behavior. Like the subway map of New York discussed in chapter 2, it is not intended to be an accurate model of single person's decision making. Rather, it is a robust model of choice for a population of individuals that has proven to be very useful for understanding how economic institutions work.

Section 3.3 extends the basic model to address the issue of decision making in the face of risk, where risks are events with well-defined probabilities of occurring. When individuals are risk averse, this generates a demand for insurance. Incorporating risk into the model of decision making is essential for understanding the role of insurance contracts.

However, "risk" can be a slippery concept. Frank Knight (1921) argued that one should distinguish between events for which past experiences would allow us to have a reliable estimate of the probability of the event occurring in the future and events for which there is insufficient experience to accurately assess the likelihood of the event actually happening. He called the former "risk," for which insurance markets can be expected to work well, while the latter correspond to "uncertain" events.

When an event is uncertain there is no objective way to quantify the likelihood of the event occurring (for example a business person launching a new product). This problem gave rise to a great deal of controversy in statistics regarding what one means by "probability."[2] Section 3.4 outlines Savage's ([1954], 1972) solution to the problem based on the concept of a "personal probability."

From the perspective of statistics, the probability of an event is the number of times it is likely to occur divided by the number of times it could occur. This requires repeated experimentation. In daily life many decisions involve uncertain events that are not likely to be repeated. Savage realized that when one makes a choice, one can derive one's personal or subjective probability from the decisions one makes.

This leaves open the question of how to connect subjective probabilities with objective probabilities that are used in science. A solution to this problem is provided by Anscombe and Aumann (1963). They realized that one can ask individuals to compare an uncertain choice with a truly random outcome, such as a lottery whose payoffs depend on the outcome from a roulette wheel. For example, if a person is indifferent between an investment that returns either nothing or 10 dollars and a lottery ticket that pays 10 dollars with a probability of 0.1, then the person's subjective probability of the investment paying out is 0.1. Conversely, this allows one to calibrate subjective beliefs. Such an idea is not only conceptually important, but it is of practical use because one can use lotteries to measure individual beliefs over uncertain outcomes in experiments involving humans.

In short, Savage's model supposes that rational choice is a two-step procedure. In step one, the individual builds or invents a model of the world that details how her possible choices map uncertain events to outcomes or consequences. Next, the individual ranks these choices. From this information, Savage shows that when choice satisfies a number of conditions, then one can derive a person's assessment of the probability of an event. Given this probability, a person's preferences can be represented by expected utility.

For much of the analysis in this book it is sufficient to suppose that preferences are represented by von Neuman–Morgenstern utility functions. Because probabilities are preference based, the Savage model has the benefit of allowing us to model "nonrational" behavior. For example, Yildiz (2004) shows the time it takes for parties to reach an agreement varies with their optimism regarding their bargaining power.

3.2   Behavior and the Rational Choice Model

The rational choice model is based on the idea that the pursuit of well-defined goals provides a way to describe behavior in a wide variety of situations. To see why, let us begin with an abstract but general model of individual behavior. As a matter of convention the word *individual* is used to denote a person, firm, or any other decision-making entity that may be pursuing well-defined goals. For the moment, preferences are assumed to be stable over time, and only the resources available to the decision maker change with time.

Formally, let A denote the set of potential actions available (eating an apple or taking a trip). The existence of information and resource constraints implies that in period t only a subset of these actions is feasible, denoted by $A_t \subset A$. The decision taken in period t is denoted by $d_t \in A_t$. If we observe d_t then the individual has, in the sense of Samuelson (1938), revealed a preference for d_t over the other actions in the set A_t.

An immediate difficulty is that the individuals may be indifferent over several of the options in A_t, and in this case the individual is in fact choosing randomly from a set of acceptable decisions that can be denoted by D_t. The possibility of indifference is an essential ingredient for some models described later in this book because in some situations, one may ask an individual to reveal information. One way to ensure truthful revelation is to make the individual indifferent over which report to provide, thus removing any incentive to bias her report.

An individual's behavior is formally described by a function $D_t = B(A_t, t)$ that defines the set of acceptable decisions at date t given the set of feasible choices A_t. In order for the model to have some empirical content, we need to add some additional restrictions. The first of these is that an individual makes a decision at each date, and hence $B(A_t, t) \neq \emptyset$. This may seem straightforward, but it is not an innocuous assumption. It implies that an individual acts even if she does not have all the information or knowledge necessary to make a decision.

Second, we need some hypotheses to connect data collected at one point in time with actions at another point in time. To achieve this, two most common assumptions are *unit homogeneity* and *time invariance*.[3] In the context of choice, unit homogeneity can be captured by supposing that individuals with similar characteristics have similar preferences. At this stage we have no basis for such a hypothesis. For much of the analysis in this book, *time invariance* is also assumed—namely, a person's behavior as defined by B does not change over time. It is given by the function[4]

$$B : 2^A \setminus \{\emptyset\} \to 2^A \setminus \{\emptyset\}. \tag{3.1}$$

This is a function from the set of feasible choices at date t to a set of choices over which the individual is indifferent. Such a model predicts that at date t the observed decision is given by some $d_t \in D_t = B(A_t) \subset A_t$. In such a model, variation in individual choice arises via variation in the set of feasible choices given by A_t.

In the context of the potential outcomes framework, the unit of analysis is the individual decision maker. The treatments are the different sets $A \in 2^A \setminus \{\emptyset\}$. These sets also define the potential outcomes. Notice that, as written, the model already has significant empirical content, namely that the choice set A defines the outcomes that we should observe. This may seem obvious, but in the context of a budget constraint, it implies that changes in prices may make some options unaffordable, and therefore we get some predictions on how prices may affect demand.

In terms of the rational choice model, new predictions can arise when some choice x is available in both sets A and A'. Now suppose the individual chooses x when offered A, but chooses an alternative, y, when offered the set A'. If choice y was not available in set A, then the individual has revealed a preference for y over x. The theory of rational choice builds upon this idea and *assumes* that one can learn about an individual's behavior from the way an individual makes *binary* choices. Namely, for any pair $\{x,y\} \in A \times A$, the individual is said to prefer x over y, written $x \succsim y$, if and only if $x \in B(\{x,y\})$.

A person is said to be *rational* if their preferences satisfy the following conditions:

Axiom A preference relation $\succsim$ defined on $A \times A$ is *rational* if:

1. It is complete, for every $x, y \in A$, $x \succsim y$ or $y \succsim x$.
2. It is transitive, for every $x, y, z \in A$, $x \succsim y$ and $y \succsim z$ implies $x \succsim z$.

Completeness ensures that it is always possible to rank two alternatives, and consequently the individual is always capable of making a decision. This is equivalent to supposing $B(\{x,y\}) \neq \emptyset$. The condition of transitivity is at the core of the theory of rational choice and is the condition that allows one to deduce how individuals are likely to behave when faced with any number of alternatives. Thus, if we are given three alternatives, x, y, and z, and $x \succsim y$ and $y \succsim z$, then we conclude that $x \succsim z$. This means that given the set $\{x, y, z\}$, the individual would choose x over both y and z.

When $\{x,y\} = B(\{x,y\})$, then $x \succsim y$ and $y \succsim x$ and the individual is *indifferent* between x and y, written as $x \sim y$. Alternatively, x is *strictly preferred* to y, denoted by $x \succ y$, if $x \succsim y$, but not $y \succsim x$. Preferences can be used to define behavior for any set A' by supposing individuals choose the most preferred outcome available to them. More formally, an individual's behavior given preferences $\succsim$ is defined by:

$$B(A', \succsim) = \{x | x \succsim y \text{ for every } y \in A'\}. \tag{3.2}$$

The agent chooses actions that are preferred to all other actions in the feasible set.

The axiom of transitivity ensures that this set is always well defined. For example, suppose the choices are s, v, and c, corresponding to strawberry, vanilla, and chocolate ice cream, respectively. If $v \succ c \succ s \succ v$, then an agent faced with the set $\{s, v, c\}$ would never be able to make up her mind because no matter which choice she makes, there is always a superior alternative, and hence $B(\{v, c, s\}, \succsim) = \emptyset$. Thus, the requirement of transitivity is intimately linked to the requirement that individuals are able to make a decision when the number of alternatives is greater than two. When preferences are transitive, not only does this ensure that $B(A', \succsim)$ is never empty, it also implies that observed behavior is consistent with the individual's maximizing some *utility function*.

Proposition 3.1 *Suppose A is a finite set, if preferences, $\succsim$, are rational then:*

1. $B(A', \succsim) \neq \emptyset$ for all $A' \subseteq A$.
2. There exists a function $U : A \to \Re$, called a *utility function* such that $x \succsim y$ if and only if $U(x) \geq U(y)$ and $B(A', \succsim) = \arg\max_{x \in A'} U(x)$.

Proof. See exercise 3. $\square$

This result shows that when behavior is described by rational preferences, then the individual behaves as if she maximizes utility. In this theory, the values that a utility function provides are used only to make comparisons among alternatives and do not have any independent normative value in and of themselves. In this case, with a finite number of n alternatives, a completely equivalent way to represent preferences is with a partition of

A: $\{P_1, P_2, \ldots, P_{n'}\}$, $n' \leq n$ where $P_i \subseteq A$, $P_i \cap P_j = \emptyset$ for $i \neq j$.[5] Then for all $x \in P_i$, $y \in P_j$ they satisfy $x \succsim y$ if and only if $i \geq j$. The indexes $i = 1, \ldots, n'$ also define a utility function for the preferences $\succsim$.

In social choice theory, it is quite common to suppose that preferences do not allow for any indifference, in which case preferences are simply represented by a list $\{x_1, x_2, \ldots, x_n\}$, rather than with a utility function. In particular, utility does not correspond to any notion of happiness; it is simply a way to rank alternatives. The prisoner may be miserable, but she will likely choose drinking water over no water, even if the impact on her overall wellbeing may be small.

3.2.1 Is the Rational Choice Model Restrictive?

We begin with a general model of behavior rather than the more traditional approach of defining preferences immediately to highlight the fact that the purpose of rational choice theory is to provide a compact *representation* of behavior. It is not intended to explain all behavior but it is intended to provide a model that is simple and yet sufficiently accurate that it can provide better predictions than one would make in the absence of the model. This section makes more precise the extent to which rational choice constrains behavior and hence can be falsified with data.

Suppose that there are n alternatives in A. For simplicity, restrict attention to behavior with the property that for any set $A_t \subset A$, the individual makes a unique choice given by $B(A_t) \in A_t$. In particular, this implies that the individual is never indifferent between two choices, and thus only strict orders on A need to be considered (for any $\succsim$ and $x, y \in A$, $x \neq y$ then $x \succ y$ or $y \succ x$). The number of such rankings can be computed by observing that there can be n top-ranked alternatives, $n - 1$ second-ranked alternatives, and so on. Therefore, the total number of possible rankings is $n!$. With n alternatives, there are at most $n!$ different behaviors that are consistent with the rational choice hypothesis.

Now consider the different types of behavior that are possible that do not necessarily conform to the rational choice hypothesis. Here we are explicitly allowing *framing effects*. There is a great deal of evidence from behavioral economics that choices can depend upon the other options in the choice set. For example, given a set $\{a, b\}$ a person might always choose a, but when offered the set $\{a, b, c\}$ always chooses b. Such behavior is clearly inconsistent with rational choice (why?), but certainly in the range of possibility. For example, the choice might be a customer choosing between suits. Upon viewing suit c, it causes the person to reevaluate her preferences over a and b.

Consider now how the potential for framing increases the number of possible different behaviors. Observe that there are $\binom{n}{k} = \frac{n!}{k!(n-k)!}$ different sets A_t of size k. For each of these sets the function representing behavior, $B(A_t)$, can take on k values; hence the total number of different possible functions is given by:

$$\prod_{k=1}^{n} k^{\left(\frac{n!}{k!(n-k)!}\right)}.$$

Table 3.1 summarizes the results of these computations for $n = 3, 4$, and 5.

As the number of possible alternatives increases, the rational choice model is extremely restrictive. When there are five alternatives, only 0.00000004 percent of possible behaviors

Table 3.1
The restrictions imposed by the rational choice hypothesis

Number of choices in A (n)	Number of subsets of A $(2^n - 1)$	Number of possible behaviors	Number of behaviors consistent with rational choice
3	7	24	5
4	15	20,736	24
5	31	3.0959×10^{11}	120

are consistent with the rational choice hypothesis. Thus, rational choice is a very restrictive hypothesis. However, as discussed in chapter 2, an important role of a model is to provide a parsimonious representation of data. The rational choice model is a representation of individual behavior that has proven to be a very useful way to think about a wide variety of economic institutions. At the moment, there is simply no alternative model of behavior that is as concise and is systematically superior.

3.2.2   Continuity of Preferences

In practice, individuals make mistakes, forget how they acted in the past, and so on, implying that rational choice theory is rarely, if ever, a perfect representation of individual behavior. Thus, it is useful to have a way to discuss behavior that "approximates" rational choice, which in turn requires a notion of "close." This section extends the model to allow for a continuum of choices to allow for a meaningful discussion of "approximately" rational choice. The theory for choice over a finite set of elements extends naturally to a continuum by supposing that small variations in quantities have correspondingly small effects upon one's preference for a good. This is captured formally by requiring preferences to be continuous:

Definition 3.2   *Suppose that A is a closed subset of $\Re^n$. A rational preference relation, $\succsim$, defined on A is continuous if for any two convergent sequence of decisions, $\{x'_n\}$ and $\{x''_n\}$ in A such that $x'_n \succsim x''_n$ for every n, then*[6]

$$\lim_{n \to \infty} x'_n = x' \succsim x'' = \lim_{n \to \infty} x''_n. \tag{3.3}$$

Gerard Debreu (1954), Theorem I, proves that this condition combined with rationality is sufficient to ensure the existence of a continuous utility function. The reader is referred to Debreu (1954) for the proof. The statement of the theorem is as follows:

Theorem 3.3   *Suppose that preferences $\succsim$ are continuous and rational on a closed and connected subset A of $\Re^n$; then there exists a (continuous) utility function $U : A \to \Re$, such that for every $x', x'' \in A$, $x' \succsim x''$ if and only if $U(x') \geq U(x'')$.*

This book maintains the hypothesis that individual behavior can be well approximated by the rational choice model with continuous preferences.

When individuals do not make optimal choices, then (hopefully) they learn from these mistakes. This can be easily incorporated into an economic model by viewing the quality of choice as a *skill*. For example, when playing, tennis, one might be observed "choosing" to hit the ball out of the court. However, what actually happened was that the choice was made so quickly that a mistake occurred. Any situation entailing choice in real time is subject to error. These errors can be reduced with training and practice. Such improvements in decision making can be viewed as *human capital*—decisions whose quality improves over time due to practice and training. See MacLeod (2016) for a discussion of how to view human capital theory as an extension of rational choice that allows for boundedly rational decision making.

3.3 Risk

One reason parties enter into a binding contract is the insurance motive.[7] For example, there is a small chance that one's house will burn down in the future, causing great harm to the affected family. However, the total number of houses that burn from year to year is relatively stable, and the reasons for these accidents are normally random. Therefore, it is possible for an insurance company to *diversify* the risk and sell policies to individuals that will reimburse them in the event that their house catches fire. In this case, an individual is choosing between facing the risk of a complete loss of the house and a consumption bundle that in effect shares the losses from each individual with a group of homeowners, so that his net consumption does not depend upon whether his house burns down. The theory of decision making in the face of risk begins with a rational choice model that represents individual aversion toward risk. From this representation we can compute how much an individual would be willing to pay for insurance.

As with the basic rational choice model, the analysis is greatly simplified if attention is restricted to a finite number of consumption bundles defined by the set $C = \{c_1, \ldots, c_n\}$. For most cases, these outcomes represent money payoffs and effort levels by individuals, though they may also represent an allocation of goods, the distribution of income between individuals, or even one's work environment. For example, c_i might be one's salary or a bundle of groceries. It may also represent working sixty hours in a week and receiving a paycheck of \$1000 at the end of the week.

Risk is introduced by supposing that the probability of receiving bundle c_i is a potential choice variable. For example, an insurance company can ensure that an insured never loses income due to a car accident or accidental burning down of his house. Similarly, lottery companies regularly sell tickets that pay off in millions of dollars with a low probability. Formally, the set of *lotteries* over C is denoted by $\Delta(C)$ and defined as the set of probability distributions over C:

$$\Delta(C) = \left\{ p = \{p_1, \ldots, p_n\} \in \Re^n \mid \sum_{i=1}^{n} p_i = 1, \ p_i \geq 0 \right\}. \tag{3.4}$$

Suppose that in each period the feasible choice set is a *closed* subset $L_t \subset \Delta(C)$, from which the agent chooses an allocation $B(L_t)$. Suppose that this behavior is represented by a preference relation, $\succsim$, that is continuous and satisfies the axioms of rational choice. From proposition 3.3 there exists a continuous utility function, $U : \Delta(C) \to \Re$, representing these preferences. Without additional structure, general preferences over lotteries do not provide much in the way of testable implications. Our concern here is to find a way to describe risk aversion and to differentiate between the preferences over goods and preferences over risks.

Von Neumann and Morgenstern (1944) solve this problem with their celebrated *expected utility theory*.

Before formally outlining this theory, it is useful to consider an early attempt to model behavior when lottery outcomes represent money payoffs. Suppose that $c_i \in \Re$ represents a monetary return. Then an individual is an *expected monetary value* (EMV) *maximizer* if preferences are represented by a utility function defined to be the expected monetary value of a trade:

$$l' \succsim l'' \text{ iff } \sum_{i=1}^{n} p'_i c_i \geq \sum_{i=1}^{n} p''_i c_i, \tag{3.5}$$

where p' and p'' correspond to the probabilities for the lotteries l' and l'' respectively. For example, suppose that an individual can buy a lottery ticket that pays off $1 million with a probability of 0.00005. The EMV of this ticket is $0.00005 \times \$1\text{million} = \$50$. In other words, the individual buys such a ticket if and only if its price is less than $50. Though this is in many respects an appealing criterion, it does not do a good job of representing observed individual choice in many situations. Bernoulli (1738) pointed this out with the following example: a coin is tossed repeatedly until a head appears, and if there are n tosses before the head appears, then the individual is paid 2^n ducats. The EMV of this lottery is:

$$\frac{1}{2} \cdot 2 + \left(\frac{1}{2}\right)^2 \cdot 2^2 + \left(\frac{1}{2}\right)^3 \cdot 2^3 + \ldots = \infty. \tag{3.6}$$

Bernoulli argues individuals are unlikely to offer more than 20 ducats for such a lottery, even though the expected value is infinite. He solves this problem by positing a declining marginal utility for money and supposing that individuals maximize *expected utility*

$$U(l) = \sum_{i=1}^{n} p_i u(c_i), \tag{3.7}$$

where $u(x)$ is called a *Bernoulli utility function*. In this example, if one supposes $u(x) = \log(x)$, then the utility of this lottery is:

$$\sum_{n=1}^{\infty} \left(\frac{1}{2}\right)^n \log(2^n) = \log(2) \left(\sum_{n=1}^{\infty} \frac{n}{2^n}\right) = \log(4). \tag{3.8}$$

Thus, in this case, the individual would be willing to pay at most 4 ducats for this lottery, much less than its expected monetary value. Von Neumann and Morgenstern (1944) provide an *axiomatization* for Bernoulli's idea.

Axiomatization means finding a set of principles of behavior represented by axioms that imply a particular utility function. For example, if $a \succ b$ and $b \succ c$, then we would consider a person irrational or erratic if he chooses c when offered a choice set $\{a, b, c\}$. In this case, the axiom of transitivity is violated.

In the context of risky decisions, the first normative principle is that probabilities are correctly interpreted. This idea is formalized by requiring individuals to correctly evaluate compound lotteries. A compound lottery is denoted by $\{\alpha_1, l^1; \alpha_2, l^2; \ldots; \alpha_n, l^n\}$,

$\alpha_i \geq 0$, $\sum \alpha_i = 1$, and corresponds to running a two-stage lottery for which a number $m \in \{1, \ldots, n\}$ is drawn with probability α_m, after which the lottery l^m is played. If these two lotteries are independent, then the probability that the individual receives consequence $c_i \in C$ is $\sum_m \alpha_m p_i^m$. A rational person should be indifferent between the compound lottery and the simple lottery paying c_i with probability $\sum_m \alpha_m p_i^m$, for each $i = 1, \ldots, n$. Formally we have:

Definition 3.4 *An individual with preferences over simple lotteries $\Delta(C)$ satisfies* reduction of compound lotteries *if she is indifferent between the compound lottery*

$$\left\{ \alpha_1, l^1; \alpha_2, l^2; \ldots; \alpha_n, l^n \right\}$$

and the simple lottery

$$\left\{ \sum_m \alpha_m p_1^m, \sum_m \alpha_m p_2^m, \ldots, \sum_m \alpha_m p_n^m \right\} \in \Delta(C).$$

The implicit assumption is that the compound lottery is carried out in a sufficiently short time span so that time preferences do not matter. The substantive content of this axiom is that individuals are able to use the rules of probability to judge outcomes, an issue that is discussed in more detail later in this chapter. The next axiom states a substantive restriction upon preferences that does not follow from any principle of rationality:

Definition 3.5 *The preference relationship, $\succsim$, on $\Delta(C)$ satisfies* independence *if for all lotteries $l, l', l'' \in \Delta(C)$ and for every $\alpha \in (0, 1)$*

$$l \succsim l' \text{ if and only if } \left\{ \alpha, l; (1 - \alpha), l'' \right\} \succsim \left\{ \alpha, l'; (1 - \alpha), l'' \right\}. \tag{3.9}$$

This axiom requires that when one prefers lottery l over l', then combining each of these with another lottery, l'', does not change the ranking. Suppose that $L_1 \sim L_2$; then notice that for all $\alpha \in (0, 1)$

$$L_1 \sim \{\alpha, L_1; (1 - \alpha), L_1\} \sim \{\alpha, L_1; (1 - \alpha), L_2\} \sim \{\alpha, L_2; (1 - \alpha), L_2\} \sim L_2.$$

Figure 3.1 illustrates this axiom when there are three consequences satisfying $c_1 \succ c_2 \succ c_3$ and provides a pictorial representation of the simplex $\Delta\{c_1, c_2, c_3\}$. The length of each side of the equilateral triangle is $\frac{2}{\sqrt{3}}$, and hence for any point in the triangle the sum of the perpendicular distances to each side is equal to 1. Therefore each point in the triangle represents a lottery in which the probability of choosing c_i is the distance to the line between the other two consequences. For example, the point of the triangle indexed by c_i corresponds to choosing c_i with probability 1. Given that $L_1 \sim L_2$, the reduction of compound lotteries and the independence axioms imply that an individual would be indifferent between any points on the straight line between L_1 and L_2.

If preferences are required to satisfy these axioms in addition to the standard axioms of rational choice, one has a generalization of Bernoulli's idea, namely that preferences can be represented by expected utility.

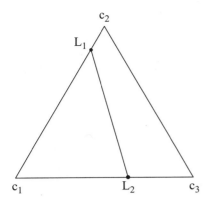

Figure 3.1
Lottery simplex.

Proposition 3.6 *Suppose that preferences $\succsim$ over $\Delta(C)$ are rational, continuous, and satisfy the axioms of reduction of compound lotteries and independence; then there is a function $u : C \to \Re$ (called a Bernoulli utility function) such that for all $l = (p_1, \ldots, p_n) \in \Delta(C)$ the function U defined by:*

$$U(l) = \sum_{c_i \in C} u(c_i) p_i \tag{3.10}$$

is a utility function representing the preferences $\succsim$.

Proof. (sketch) Given that preferences are continuous, there exists a continuous utility function representing $\succsim$. The continuity of utility and the compactness of $\Delta(C)$ imply that there exist lotteries, $l_{\min}$ and $l_{\max}$, the least and most preferred lotteries, respectively.

If $l_{\min} \sim l_{\max}$ then the individuals are indifferent over all lotteries, and we can set $u(c_i) = \bar{u}$, where $\bar{u}$ is some constant, which concludes the proof.

Suppose now that $l_{\max} \succ l_{\min}$, and observe that the independence hypothesis implies that for all $\alpha \in (0, 1)$ that $l_{\max} \succ \{\alpha, l_{\max}; (1 - \alpha), l_{\min}\} \succ l_{\min}$. From this result and the independence axiom, again it follows that:

$$\{\alpha, l_{\max}; (1 - \alpha), l_{\min}\} \succ \{\beta, l_{\max}; (1 - \beta), l_{\min}\} \tag{3.11}$$

for all $\alpha, \beta \in [0, 1]$, $\alpha > \beta$. To see this, suppose $\beta > 0$, and let $l = \{\alpha, l_{\max}; (1 - \alpha), l_{\min}\}$, and let $\gamma = \beta/\alpha \in (0, 1)$, then

$$l \sim \{\gamma, l; (1 - \gamma), l\} \succ \{\gamma, l; (1 - \gamma), l_{\min}\} \sim \{\beta, l_{\max}; (1 - \beta), l_{\min}\}.$$

By continuity, this implies that for every $l \in \Delta(C)$ there is a number, denoted $U(l) \in [0, 1]$, such that $l \sim \{U(l), l_{\max}; (1 - U(l)), l_{\min}\}$. It readily follows from the above that $U(l)$ is a utility function representing $\succsim$.

In the final step, observe that (3.11) and reduction of compound lotteries imply that for any $\alpha \in [0, 1]$ and $l', l'' \in \Delta(C)$, $U(\{\alpha, l'; (1 - \alpha), l''\}) = \alpha U(l') + (1 - \alpha) U(l'')$. In particular this implies that we can let $u(c_i) = U(c_i)$ and rewrite utility in the expected utility form: $U(l) = \sum_{c_i \in C} u(c_i) p_i$. $\qquad\square$

Table 3.2
Example of the independence axiom

		Ticket number		
		1	2–11	12–100
Situation 1:	L_1	$0.5 million	$0.5 million	$0.5 million
	L_2	$0	$2.5 million	$0.5 million
Situation 2:	L_3	$0.5 million	$0.5 million	$0
	L_4	$0	$2.5 million	$0

Axiomatization has the major benefit of making expected utility theory readily testable. One can present subjects with a finite set of choices for which the axioms make clear predictions. A famous example is the *Allais paradox*.[8] Allais asked a number of individuals to consider the following choice problem. Suppose there are three outcomes: c_1 corresponds to a payoff of 0, c_2 is a payoff of 0.5 million dollars, and c_3 is a payoff of 2.5 million dollars.

A lottery is then given by triples of the form $\{p_1, p_2, p_3\}$, where p_i is the probability of receiving c_i. One way of generating lotteries is to suppose that there are 100 lottery tickets, upon which c_1, c_2, or c_3 is written. An individual has an equal probability of receiving one of these tickets. Let us now consider the choice between different lotteries that allocate the payoffs among the tickets as shown in table 3.2.

Situation 1 corresponds to the choice between lottery $L_1 = \{0, 1, 0\}$ and $L_2 = \{0.01, 0.89, 0.1\}$, where $c_i = \{$0, 0.5 million, 2.5 million$\}$. Situation 2 differs from situation 1 only in that the payment of $0.5 million for tickets 12–100 is replaced by no payment. As the only difference between the two situations is the payoffs for tickets 12–100, then the independence axiom implies that any person choosing L_1 over L_2 must also choose L_3 over L_4. It is often observed in experiments that individuals rank L_1 above L_2 while ranking L_4 above L_3.

These observations imply that this theory does not in general correctly describe choices of many individuals in the face of risk, and thus in the spirit of Popper (1963), the theory has been refuted. Despite this, expected utility theory is the workhorse model of modern microeconomics because the model is a useful *representation* of behavior. As we observed in chapter 2, a useful model is one that provides a parsimonious representation of behavior, not necessarily a perfect representation.

Harless and Camerer (1994) and Hey and Orme (1994) reviewed a great deal of experimental evidence and found that although expected utility theory is not strictly correct, it does a better job of explaining observed behavior than the EMV model, just as the EMV model is better than one that assumes individuals do not care about expected income.

Active research in the theory of choice explores ways to relax the axioms of expected utility while maintaining the basic axioms of transitivity, completeness, and continuity (see the review by Epstein [1992]). Many of these can be viewed as allowing the indifference lines in figure 3.1 to be curved. As with the case of behavioral economics, a great deal can be learned by exploring the implications of the theory, given expected utility theory, while remaining open to the possibility that some failures of the theory may be due to the way preferences are represented.

3.3.1   Risk Aversion

This section discusses the problem of evaluating or measuring a person's willingness to bear risk. This discussion is typically carried out within the context of monetary rewards, and therefore we let the agent's choice set be given by monetary income from the set $C = (-\infty, \infty) = \Re$. The expected utility model extends naturally to incorporate preferences over random variables, X, with payoffs in $\Re$. Under the Von Neumann–Morgenstern axioms, the individual's utility function has the form:

$$U(X) = E\{u(X)\} = \int_{-\infty}^{\infty} u(x)\, dF(x), \tag{3.12}$$

where $u : \Re \to \Re$, is a Bernoulli utility function, $F(\cdot) \in \Delta(\Re)$ is the cumulative probability density function for income X, and $E\{\cdot\}$ the expectations operator. Demand for insurance is modeled by assuming individuals prefer sure outcomes to risky outcomes, a characteristic called risk aversion.

Definition 3.7   *An individual with preference ordering $\succsim$ over random monetary payoffs is* risk averse *if for every $X \in \Delta(\Re)$:*

$$E\{X\} \succsim X. \tag{3.13}$$

An individual is strictly risk averse if this preference is strict whenever var$\{X\} > 0$. The individual is risk neutral *(an expected monetary value maximizer) if:*

$$E\{X\} \sim X. \tag{3.14}$$

When preferences over monetary outcomes satisfy the Von Neumann–Morgenstern axioms, then it is possible to obtain a complete characterization of risk aversion in terms of the individual's Bernoulli utility function.

Proposition 3.8   *An individual whose preferences are represented by expected utility is (strictly) risk averse if and only if her Bernoulli utility function is (strictly) concave.*

Proof.   Suppose the Bernoulli utility function is concave. Then by Jensen's inequality one has:

$$U(X) = E\{u(X)\} \le u(E\{X\}), \tag{3.15}$$

from which we conclude that the agent is risk averse. Conversely, suppose the preference order satisfies risk aversion, but u is not concave. Then there exists an x and y such that:

$$\alpha u(x) + (1 - \alpha) u(y) > u(\alpha x + (1 - \alpha) y). \tag{3.16}$$

Let X denote the lottery that pays x with probability α and y with probability $(1 - \alpha)$. Then it follows that $X \succ E\{X\}$, a contradiction. The case for strict preferences is similar. $\square$

Example 3.9   *Consider an individual who wishes to buy home earthquake insurance and whose preferences are described by a strictly concave and increasing Bernoulli utility function $u(\cdot)$. Let $I > 0$ denote the individual's income, ρ the probability of an earthquake, and d the damage sustained to the house in the event of an earthquake. Let the price of earthquake insurance be q per dollar of coverage x. The amount of insurance, x, that the* *individual will buy is a solution to the following problem:*

$$\max_{x \geq 0} (1 - \rho) u (c_1) + \rho u (c_2),$$

subject to:

$$c_1 = I - qx, \tag{3.17}$$

$$c_2 = I - d + x - qx. \tag{3.18}$$

The amount that the agent consumes when there is an earthquake is c_2, while c_1 is consumption when there is no earthquake. Notice that the first-order condition for this problem is:

$$\frac{u'(c_1)}{u'(c_2)} = \frac{\rho}{1 - \rho} \frac{1 - q}{q}. \tag{3.19}$$

Thus the individual buys full insurance if and only if $\rho = q$, that is the price per unit of insurance is equal to the probability of an earthquake. Notice that at this price the expected profit of the insurance company is:

$$profit = income - outlay \tag{3.20}$$

$$= qx - \rho x = 0. \tag{3.21}$$

This price is called actuarially fair *because it ensures that a risk-neutral insurance company earns zero profits. When the price q is higher than ρ, then the individual underinsures ($c_1 > c_2$), while conversely, the individual overinsures when the price is lower than the actuarially fair price.*

When a person is risk averse, she is willing to accept an amount for a lottery X that is less than its EMV. This amount, called the *certainty equivalent*, it is denoted by $CE(X)$ and defined by:

$$u(CE\{X\}) = E\{u(X)\}. \tag{3.22}$$

Under the hypothesis that the Bernoulli utility function is increasing, the certainty equivalent also defines a utility function for preferences: $X \succsim Y$ if and only if $CE(X) \geq CE(Y)$. It has the attractive property that if $X = \bar{x}$ is a constant amount, then $CE(X) = \bar{x}$, and thus the certainty equivalent provides a way to measure utility in dollar terms. When $u(\cdot)$ is twice differentiable, one can obtain an approximate measure of the certainty equivalent as follows. Let $\bar{x} = E\{X\}$, and consider the Taylor expansion for u:

$$u(x) \approx u(\bar{x}) + u'(\bar{x})(x - \bar{x}) + u''(\bar{x})(x - \bar{x})^2 /2. \tag{3.23}$$

Substituting X for x and taking expectations, then when the variance of X, σ^2, is small we have:

$$E\{u(X)\} \approx u(\bar{x}) + u''(\bar{x}) \sigma^2 /2. \tag{3.24}$$

Using only the first two terms of the Taylor expansion we also have:

$$u(CE\{X\}) \approx u(\bar{x}) + u'(\bar{x})(CE\{X\} - \bar{x}), \tag{3.25}$$

from which we can conclude that:

$$CE(X) \approx \bar{x} - \frac{\sigma^2}{2} r(\bar{x}),$$ (3.26)

where $r(\bar{x}) \equiv -\frac{u''(\bar{x})}{u'(\bar{x})}$ is called the *coefficient of absolute risk aversion* and $\frac{\sigma^2}{2} r(\bar{x})$ is the risk premium, which is the amount that an individual is willing to give up to avoid the risk in the lottery X. Under the hypothesis that the individual strictly prefers more money to less ($u' > 0$), the coefficient of absolute risk aversion is greater than or equal to zero if and only if the individual is risk averse. The amount that an individual is willing to give up to remove all risk increases with the degree of risk aversion, $r(\bar{x})$, and the variance, σ^2, of the income stream.

An important class of utility functions are those with *constant absolute risk aversion* (CARA), where $r(x) = r$ for every x. In this case, the Bernoulli utility must solve the differential equation:

$$u''(x) = -ru'(x),$$ (3.27)

from which it follows that $u(x) = -ae^{-rx} + b$ if $r \neq 0$, or $u(x) = ax + b$ when $r = 0$, where a and b are indeterminate parameters. Exercise 9 shows that Von Neumann–Morgenstern preferences are invariant to any affine transformation. Given that $u' > 0$, then without loss of generality it may be assumed that $b = 0$ and $a = 1$ if $r > 0$ or $a = -1$ if $r < 0$. When $r = 0$, then Bernoulli utility can take the form $u(x) = x$. With CARA preferences and a normally distributed income stream X, it is possible to obtain a closed-form solution for the certainty equivalent $CE(X)$.

Proposition 3.10 *Suppose that an individual has CARA preferences with risk aversion parameter r. Then the certainty equivalent of a normally distributed random variable X, with mean m and variance σ^2 is:*

$$CE(X) = m - \frac{r}{2}\sigma^2.$$ (3.28)

Proof. By definition we get:

$$-\exp(-rCE(X)) = E\{-\exp(-rX)\}$$

$$= -\frac{1}{\sigma\sqrt{2\pi}} \int_{-\infty}^{\infty} \exp(-rx) \exp\left(\frac{-(x-m)^2}{2\sigma^2}\right) dx$$

$$= -\frac{1}{\sigma\sqrt{2\pi}} \int_{-\infty}^{\infty} \exp\left(-\frac{x^2 - 2(m-\sigma^2 r)x + m^2}{2\sigma^2}\right) dx$$

$$= -\frac{1}{\sigma\sqrt{2\pi}} \int_{-\infty}^{\infty} \exp\left[-\left(\frac{(x-(m-\sigma^2 r))^2}{2\sigma^2} + \frac{2mr - \sigma^2 r^2}{2}\right)\right] dx$$

$$= -\exp\left[-r\left(m - \frac{\sigma^2 r}{2}\right)\right].$$

□

Notice that this implies that when returns are restricted to be normally distributed, then individuals with *CARA* preferences can be represented by preferences that are linear in m and σ^2.

Example 3.11 *Consider an individual with CARA preferences with a coefficient of absolute risk aversion given by r and income I. Suppose that the individual is able to buy a number of stocks in a company whose future return for each stock, X, is normally distributed with mean and variance: (m, σ^2). Let the price of each stock be q. If the individual buys n stocks then her future income is $I - nq + nX$. To compute the individual's demand as a function of the price of the stock, $n(q)$, one can use her certainty equivalent:*

$$CE\,(I - nq + nX) = I - nq + nm - rn^2\sigma^2/2. \tag{3.29}$$

One concludes that the demand for the stock is:

$$n\,(q) = \begin{cases} 0 & \text{if } q > m, \\ \frac{m-q}{r\sigma^2} & \text{if } q < m. \end{cases} \tag{3.30}$$

Notice that demand decreases with the price of the stock and its riskiness. Also, the more risk averse the individual, the less stock she buys. When $m > q$, as risk aversion decreases, $r \to 0$, demand becomes unbounded ($n(q) \to \infty$).

3.4 Uncertainty and Beliefs

Expected utility theory explicitly assumes that probabilities of the lotteries represent the objective likelihood of receiving a particular consequence. For example, a lottery that pays $0 and $100 with equal probability has the explicit interpretation that if one were to accept this lottery repeatedly then one would expect to receive $100 about half the time. For a risk-averse individual, the certainty equivalent of this lottery played only once is likely to be much less than $50.

On the other hand, insurance companies rely on the law of large numbers to offer insurance policies that can be priced close to the EMV of a risk. More precisely, let $X \in \Delta(C)$ be a lottery, and suppose the lottery is run each period t, and the outcome is the random variable X_t. Then by the law of large numbers, one has almost surely:[9]

$$\lim_{N \to \infty} \frac{1}{N} \sum_{t=1}^{N} X_t = EMV\,(X). \tag{3.31}$$

Examples of such risks might include life expectancy, the probability of a traffic accident in Los Angeles on a particular day, or the probability of conceiving a boy or girl. In these cases, the notion of probability is well defined and can be interpreted as the frequency of occurrence if the risky event is repeated.

Frank Knight (1921) observed that many, if not most, important economic decisions are *idiosyncratic*. For example, if one is trying to decide whether to open a new restaurant, given that tastes are constantly changing, then it is simply not possible to use previous success rates to determine the likelihood of success for that particular business. Knight uses the term "uncertainty," as opposed to "risk," to describe business decisions such as these. Given that it is impossible to repeat this business experiment, then one cannot interpret the "probability of success" as the number of times such a restaurant would be successful.

Yet, in common language, it is normal to speak of the likelihood of success. For example, the local bank may believe that the restaurant fills a need in the neighborhood and therefore it has a "good chance" of success. Based upon these beliefs, the bank may decide to lend money to the prospective owner of the business. The difficulty is that these probability assessments cannot be based upon replicable experiments. Other examples are mutual fund investment choices, deciding to go to the beach based upon one's estimate of the weather, or making a career choice. All involve uncertain events whose true probabilities are unknowable, yet the individual must nevertheless make a choice. What does one mean by rational choice in these circumstances?

Savage ([1954] 1972) provides a brilliant solution to the problem that is now widely accepted in economics. His insight is to recognize that even though individuals face uncertainty, the fact that they must make *some* choice can be used to derive a *subjective* assessment of a probability. For example, suppose that an individual has to choose between buying a lottery ticket from one of two different organizations, A or B, each of which offers a $50 prize. If the individual chooses the ticket from organization A, then one may conclude that the individual believes that the probability of a win with a ticket from A is higher than with a ticket from B.

Savage shows that under the appropriate conditions, one can suppose that individuals act *as if* they are expected utility maximizers, where the probability used to compute the expected utility is derived from revealed preferences rather than from a series of experiments. Once an individual has constructed her subjective probability assessments, she can then incorporate new information using the standard rules of probability. A shortcoming of Savage's theory is that it does not explicitly allow for risky events—events for which there is some agreement regarding the probability of the event (for example, fair dice or the flip of a coin).[10] The existence of such events allows one to *calibrate* one's beliefs with an objective probability. It turns out that allowing a calibrating device not only allows one to make individual beliefs comparable but also dramatically simplifies the development of the theory, as shown by Anscombe and Aumann (1963). In this section, we begin with Savage's notion of a small world and then use Anscombe and Aumann's method to construct an individual's subjective probability distribution.

A second reason for using this approach is that it allows us to naturally model the role of information in decision making. Technically, information changes the probability assessments one assigns to events. Once it is recognized that these assessments do not have to be linked to objective probabilities, one can apply the full apparatus of probability theory to subjective beliefs and choice. This point is explicitly made by Kreps and Wilson (1982), who integrate Savage's model into game theory.

3.4.1   The Small World Model

The first step in making a choice is to identify the possible outcomes. Savage ([1954] 1972) observes that making a decision is akin to mentally constructing a small world in which one explores the results of different decisions. In constructing a small world model one acts as if the model captures all the relevant features of the decision at hand. One begins with the set of possible *states*, Ω, where each state $\omega \in \Omega$ provides a complete description of the world (for simplicity, suppose that there are N states, though everything can be generalized to sets of infinite size). In principle the state describes all aspects of the world, though in practice one models only those aspects that are relevant to the current decision.

For example, when deciding whether to bring an umbrella to work, the set of relevant states is given by $\Omega = \{R, NR\}$, where R = rain and NR = no rain. This idea can be extended to deal with events over time as well. Consider writing a contract for painting the inside and outside of a house that deals with contingencies for rainy days. Suppose all the work can be done in a week if there are at least two clear days to complete the outside work, and further suppose that one is certain to have two clear days during a ten-day period. In that case the state describes the days that it rains, and is a sequence, such as $\{R, NR, R, \ldots, R\}$, taken from the set $\Omega = \{R, NR\}$.[10]

Notice in this example the state describes the outcome for each day. We would like to model behavior as a function of the state, yet one must capture the restriction that it is impossible for individuals to condition their behavior upon *future* rain patterns. The *event* that it rains on day one is defined as *all* the states that have rain on the first day:

$$Rain\ Day\ One = E_{R1} = \{\omega = \{\omega_1, \omega_2, \ldots, \omega_{10}\} \in \Omega | \omega_1 = \{rain\}\}. \qquad (3.32)$$

The event that it does not rain on day one, denoted E_{NR1}, is defined similarly. Notice that $E_{NR1} \cup E_{R1} = \Omega$; that is, the events rain or no rain *partition* the state space into two, mutually exclusive, events. As time proceeds, and we learn more about what has occurred, this corresponds to a finer and finer partition of the state space. Once the weather has been observed for each of the ten days, then the exact state of the world is known (relative to the small world model constructed just for this decision).

In this model, the everyday notion of an event, whether it rains, whether the price of a stock goes up or down, whether there is an earthquake, and so on, corresponds formally to subsets of the state space. Learning corresponds to narrowing the true state of the world to smaller and smaller sets of possible states. The formalism provides a way to model both information and learning as events evolving over time. The information available in any period is represented by a set of events called a *partition*:

Definition 3.12   *Let $\mathcal{A}$ be a collection of subsets of Ω. Then $\mathcal{A} = \{E_1, E_2, \ldots, E_n\}$ is a partition if*

1. $\bigcup_{i=1}^{n} E_i = \Omega$.

2. If $i \neq j$ then $E_i \cap E_j = \emptyset$.

In our example the set $\{E_{R1}, E_{NR1}\}$ is a partition, where E_{R1} denotes rain on day 1 and E_{NR1} denotes no rain on day 1. If one learns whether it rains on day 2, then this results in a refinement of the partition into four sets: $\{E_{R1,NR2}, E_{R1,R2}, E_{NR1,R2}, E_{NR1,NR2}\}$. At the end of ten days the partition will be the state space itself. Partitions measure how fine or accurate one's information is regarding the true state of the world.

Another example is the measurement of some variable, such as one's height. If a person is six feet tall, then depending upon the precision of the measurement and time of day, this really means that the person's height is in some range, say, between $5'11.5''$ and $6'0.5''$. A person's height provides information upon the *set* of possible heights. A finer partition corresponds to a more accurate measurement of an individual's height and corresponds to having more information. More formally, a partition Π'' is a *refinement* of Π' if for each $E'' \in \Pi''$ and $E' \in \Pi'$ either $E'' \subset E'$ or $E'' \cap E' = \emptyset$.

Within Savage's model, a state conceptually represents a complete description of the world. In practice, it represents a partition corresponding to a description of those events relevant to the question at hand. It is worth highlighting this point because the conclusions of this model depend upon the way the world is modeled, and therefore any errors in model formation can result in decision-making errors. In particular, if contracting parties are using *different* representations of the world, involving possibly different partitions, then there is always some chance that contract terms and conditions will be interpreted differently.

For example, the homeowner might think in terms of rain or no rain, while the contractor might distinguish between rain, mist, and drizzle. Suppose the original contract states that work does not have to proceed if it rains. The contractor might believe that a drizzle is rain, while the homeowner might believe that drizzle corresponds to no rain. Thus, this apparently simple and clear contract can lead to a dispute because parties are using different models of the world.

We return to this question in more detail when we come to complex exchange. The issue is raised now to highlight the fact that this model is very rich and can be used to think about a wide variety of practical issues, including misunderstandings regarding what has occurred in the relationship. For the remainder of this and the next few chapters, we will proceed under the hypothesis that all individuals use the same model of the world; namely, they agree on the possible states $\omega \in \Omega$, though they might not have the same information.

The next step in the construction of a small world model is to associate *consequences* with different realized states. For example, we care about whether it rains because we might become wet if we do not have an umbrella. Being wet is a consequence. Bringing an umbrella to work to ensure that we do not become wet is a choice that in Savage's model is called an *act*.

As in the theory of decision under risk, suppose that there are a finite number of consequences c taken from the set C. In addition, it is also assumed that there are risky events, such as real lotteries, for which individuals know and agree upon the true probability distributions. This is the point at which the Aumann and Anscombe theory deviates from Savage's. It is assumed that individuals can, if they wish, implement an objective randomization system that allows them to experience consequences in C with specified probabilities. Hence, we assume that the set of consequences is the set of lotteries $\Delta(C)$, as in the theory of decision making under risk.

We now model the choice of a person deciding whether to bring an umbrella to work. The consequences are being wet or dry when coming home. Suppose the person considers three possible choices: bring an umbrella (U), flip a coin to randomly decide whether to bring the umbrella (RU), or don't bring it (NU). Using this definition of an event, table (3.3) illustrates the choices the individual faces.

In this example, each choice corresponds to an act that is given by a mapping from events (states) to consequences. For example, the act RU can be written as a function:

$$f_{RU} : \Omega \to \begin{cases} \{0.5, Dry; 0.5, Wet\}, & \text{if } \omega \in E_R \\ Dry, & \text{if } \omega \in E_{NR} \end{cases}.$$

Table 3.3
Consequences of umbrella choices

	Event	
Act	E_R	E_{NR}
U	Dry	Dry
RU	50% chance of dry	Dry
NU	Wet	Dry

Table 3.4
Entrepreneur's payoffs with debt versus partnership financing

	State	
Act	v_H	v_L
Debt financing	$v_H - I - R$	$v_L - I - R$
Partnership	$v_H/2$	$v_L/2$

More generally, any choice made by the individual can be viewed as an *act*, which formally is a function from the set of states of the world to consequences:

$$f : \Omega \to \Delta(C). \tag{3.33}$$

Let the set of acts be denoted by F. Observe that the definition of an act does not require the specification of the likelihood of states in Ω. Each act provides a complete description of how different states of the world affect the consequences to be experienced by the individuals. The primitive of the model is an individual's preferences over acts. From these preferences one is able to *derive* the *subjective probability* that is assigned to each event.

An example from finance illustrates this point. Suppose that an entrepreneur wishes to open a new restaurant at a new location and needs to obtain financing. Suppose that all the relevant decisions, such as the choice of decor, chef, and so on, have been made. Given these decisions, one still does not know whether the project will be successful. This is modeled by supposing that the restaurant will either be very successful or simply profitable. Let the total income associated with these two outcomes be given by the values: $v_H > v_L > 0$.

Though the entrepreneur has completed a business plan, she still needs to raise I dollars to finance the project, which can be done either with debt financing or in a partnership with a friend. With debt financing, she must repay the bank $I + R$ dollars, while in the partnership she agrees to split revenues equally. The payoff that the entrepreneur receives in each state is given in table 3.4.

Suppose that $v_H - I - R > v_H/2$ and $v_L/2 > v_L - I - R$. Then if v_H were to occur, debt financing is preferred, while a partnership is preferred in the state v_L. This is a classic decision in the face of uncertainty. It is very difficult to assign an objective probability to the states v_H and v_L. After building the small world model, the next step is for the entrepreneur to assign probability p to v_H and $(1 - p)$ to v_L and then choose the method of financing that yields the highest payoffs. Suppose that we observe the entrepreneur choosing debt financing; presumably this yields a higher return than a partnership, and hence:

$$p(v_H - I - R) + (1 - p)(v_L - I - R) \geq p(v_H/2) + (1 - p)(v_L/2),$$

or

$$p \geq \frac{2(I + R) - v_L}{(v_H - v_L)}.$$

In other words, by observing how the entrepreneur chooses, we can infer the range of probabilities that she assigns to uncertain events. Thus, we can *derive* constraints on the entrepreneur's belief in the likelihood of success. This calculation does not require assuming that the probability is an objective risk but rather that it is a subjective assessment made by the decision maker. Let us make these ideas a bit more precise.

3.4.2 Preferences in the Face of Uncertainty

Anscombe and Aumann's (1963) theory of decision making under uncertainty begins with the assumption that the decision maker has preferences over lotteries, $\Delta(C)$, satisfying the axioms of expected utility theory, given by a preference relation $\succsim$. This allows one to construct a person's Bernoulli utility function over consequences in C. The insight of Anscombe and Aumann is to use these preferences to *calibrate* subjective probability assessments.

If one can construct a lottery over consequences, then one can also define a lottery over acts. An example is the decision to randomize between bringing an umbrella to work and not. Let $\Delta(F)$ denote the set of lotteries over acts. Anscombe and Aumann call these *horse lotteries* to evoke the image of an individual randomly choosing which of several horses to bet on in a horse race. The choice of a horse can be viewed as an act because one is never sure of the objective probability that a horse will win. Preferences over the horse lotteries, $\Delta(F)$, are denoted by $\succsim^*$. It is assumed that $\succsim^*$ also satisfies the axioms of expected utility theory, where each act $f \in F$ is viewed as a consequence. Thus, preferences on horse lotteries have the expected utility form, where each act $f \in F$ is assigned a Bernoulli utility $u(f)$.

Thus, the axioms of rational choice theory alone ensure one has utility functions over lotteries and horse lotteries. The final step in the Anscombe and Aumann construction is to find a way to formally link the two sets of preferences. The first axiom requires that $\succsim^*$ rank constant acts in the same way as $\succsim$.

Definition 3.13 *Preferences satisfy the property of* constant acts *if for every $l, l' \in \Delta(C)$, $l \succsim l'$ if and only if $f \succsim^* f'$, where $f(\omega) = l$ and $f'(\omega) = l'$ for all $\omega \in \Omega$.*

As a minor abuse of notation, let the act l refer to an act with the outcome l in each state $\omega \in \Omega$. The next axiom requires that the agent always prefers to improve the outcome for a single state.

Definition 3.14 *The preference relation $\succsim^*$ is monotonic if for every act $f \in F$, lottery $l' \in \Delta(C)$ such that for some state $\omega' \in \Omega$, $l' \succsim f(\omega')$ then $g \succsim^* f$, where $g(\omega') = l'$, and for $\omega \neq \omega'$, $g(\omega) = f(\omega)$.*

Thus, an individual always prefers (under $\succsim^*$) an act that has an improved outcome in a particular state (under $\succsim$). Notice that this ranking cannot be strict because it may be that state ω is believed to be impossible, in which case the payoff in state ω is irrelevant. As Anscombe and Aumann observe, this axiom corresponds to Savage's *sure thing principle* (see Savage [1954] 1972, sec. 2.7).

The next axiom requires that the timing of uncertainty and risk does not affect preferences. Consider the horse lottery $\{\alpha_1,f_1; \alpha_2,f_2; \ldots; \alpha_n,f_n\} \in \Delta\,(F)$ with the interpretation that the act f_i is chosen with probability α_i. This lottery has two possible interpretations. The first is that act i is chosen with probability α_i and then state ω is realized, resulting in the consequence $f_i\,(\omega)$. The second is that the state ω is realized first, resulting in the *lottery* $\{\alpha_1,f_1\,(\omega)\,; \alpha_2,f_2\,(\omega)\,; \ldots; \alpha_n,f_n\,(\omega)\} \in \Delta(C)$, at which point consequence $f_i\,(\omega)$ is chosen with probability α_i. The next axiom requires individuals to be indifferent to the order in which uncertainty is realized.

Definition 3.15 *Preferences satisfy the* reversal of order in compound lotteries *property if for any set of acts,* $\{f_i \in F\,|\,i=1,\ldots,n\}$, *and any horse lottery* $f' = \{\alpha_1,f_1; \alpha_2,f_2; \ldots; \alpha_n,f_n\} \in \Delta\,(F)$, *then* $f' \sim^* f''$, *where* $f''\,(\omega) = \{\alpha_1,f_1\,(\omega)\,; \alpha_2,f_2\,(\omega)\,; \ldots; \alpha_n, f_n\,(\omega)\}$, $\omega \in \Omega$.

These axioms allow us to bootstrap from expected utility over lotteries to utility over acts. Suppose there is a least and a most preferred consequence, $c_{\min}$ and $c_{\max}$, such that $c_{\max} \succ c_{\min}$ (and hence $c_{\max} \succ^* c_{\min}$). Then without loss of generality we may choose the Bernoulli utility representing $\succsim$ such that $u\,(c_{\max}) = 1$ and $u\,(c_{\min}) = 0$, and let $U\,(l) = \sum_{c \in C} p_c u\,(c)$ be the corresponding expected utility function. Let $u^*\,(\cdot)$ be the Bernoulli utility function representing $\succsim^*$, normalized so that $u^*\,(c_{\max}) = 1$ and $u^*\,(c_{\min}) = 0$, where c_i represents the constant act $f(\omega) = c_i$ for all $\omega \in \Omega$. We may now state the main result of this section.

Theorem 3.16 *(Anscombe and Aumann 1963) Given that* $\succsim$ *and* $\succsim^*$ *over lotteries and horse lotteries respectively satisfy the Von Neumann–Morgenstern axioms for expected utility, and that* $\succsim^*$ *also satisfies constant acts, monotonicity, and reversal of order in compound lotteries, then there is a unique set of nonnegative numbers* p_s *summing to* 1 *such that for all acts* $f \in F$ *the Bernoulli utility for* $\succsim^*$ *satisfies:*

$$u^*\,(f) = \sum_{\omega \in \Omega} p_s U\,(f\,(\omega)) \qquad (3.34)$$

$$= \sum_{\omega \in \Omega} \sum_{c \in C} p_s \alpha\,(f\,(\omega)\,,c)\,u\,(c)\,, \qquad (3.35)$$

where $U\,(\cdot)$ *is the utility function representing* $\succsim$, $u\,(\cdot)$ *the corresponding Bernoulli utility, and* $\alpha\,(f\,(\omega)\,,c)$ *is the probability that* c *is chosen for the lottery* $f\,(\omega) \in \Delta(C)$.

Proof. Let f be an act and set $l_{\omega_i} = f\,(\omega_i)$. Given that for any pair of lotteries, $l \succsim l'$ if and only if $U\,(l) \geq U\,(l')$, then from the axiom of constant acts and monotonicity we can replace l with $U\,(l)$ and, with a slight abuse of notation, represent $\succsim^*$ by $u^*\,(U\,(l_{\omega_1}), U\,(l_{\omega_2}), \ldots, U\,(l_{\omega_N}))$. In particular $u^*\,(1, 1, \ldots, 1) = u^*\,(c_{\max}) = 1$ and $u^*\,(0, 0, \ldots, 0) = u^*\,(c_{\min}) = 0$. For each $\omega_i \in \Omega$, let f_{ω_i} denote the act such that $f_{\omega_i}\,(\omega) = c_{\max}$ if $\omega = \omega_i$ and $f_{\omega_i}\,(\omega) = c_{\min}$ otherwise, and define $p_{\omega_i} = u^*\,(f_{\omega_i})$.

Next we make the following observation.

Lemma 3.17 *Take any* $(r_{\omega_1}, r_{\omega_2}, \ldots, r_{\omega_N})$ *such that* $r_{\omega_i} \in [0, 1]$ *for all* $\omega_i \in \Omega$. *If for some* $k > 0$, *we have* $kr_{\omega_i} \in [0, 1]$ *for all* $\omega_i \in \Omega$, *then* $u^*(kr_{\omega_1}, \ldots, kr_{\omega_N}) = ku^*(r_{\omega_1}, \ldots, r_{\omega_N})$.

To show this, first suppose that $k \leq 1$ and notice by continuity there are lotteries l_{ω_i}, such that $u(l_{\omega_i}) = r_{\omega_i}$. Then $(kr_{\omega_1}, \ldots, kr_{\omega_N})$ represents the act, f', where for each ω_i the outcome is the compound lottery $\{k, l_{\omega_i}; (1-k), c_{\min}\}$. Let $f''(\omega_i) = l_{\omega_i}$ for all ω_i. Then from the reduction of compound lotteries we have:

$$f' \sim^* \{k, f''; (1-k), c_{\min}\}, \tag{3.36}$$

from which, using the expected utility properties of $\succsim^*$, we can conclude $u^*(kr_{\omega_1}, \ldots, kr_{\omega_N})$ $= ku^*(r_{\omega_1}, \ldots, r_{\omega_N}) + (1-k)u^*(c_{\min}) = ku^*(r_{\omega_1}, \ldots, r_{\omega_N})$.

Next, if $k > 1$, then:

$$u^*(r_{\omega_1}, \ldots, r_{\omega_N}) = u^*(kr_{\omega_1}/k, \ldots, kr_{\omega_N}/k) = (1/k)u^*(kr_{\omega_1}, \ldots, kr_{\omega_N}), \tag{3.37}$$

and multiplying through by k completes the observation.

Now we fix $(r_{\omega_1}, r_{\omega_2}, \ldots, r_{\omega_N})$ such that $u(l_{\omega_i}) = r_{\omega_i}$, where $l_{\omega_i} = f(\omega_i)$.

Let $c = r_{\omega_1} + \ldots + r_{\omega_N}$. If $c = 0$, then $r_{\omega_i} = 0$, and that is the end of the exercise. If $c > 0$, then r_{ω_i}/c are nonnegative and sum to 1. Let g denote an act such that $u(g(\omega_i)) = r_{\omega_i}/c$. But this implies $g(\omega_i) \sim \{r_{\omega_i}/c, c_{\max}; 1 - r_{\omega_i}/c, c_{\min}\} = l_i$, and hence the decision maker is indifferent between g and the act that in state ω_i plays the lottery l_i. Then from the reversal of order of compound lotteries property it follows:

$$g \sim^* \{r_{\omega_1}/c, f_{\omega_1}; \ldots; r_{\omega_N}/c, f_{\omega_N}\}. \tag{3.38}$$

Therefore, by the linearity of the Bernoulli utility and the expected utility property:

$$u^*(f) = u^*(r_{\omega_1}, \ldots, r_{\omega_N}) \tag{3.39}$$

$$= cu^*(g) \tag{3.40}$$

$$= c\left(\sum_{\omega_i \in \Omega} \frac{r_{\omega_i}}{c} u^*(f_{\omega_i})\right) \tag{3.41}$$

$$= \left(\sum_{\omega_i \in \Omega} r_{\omega_i} p_{\omega_i}\right) \tag{3.42}$$

$$= \left(\sum_{\omega_i \in \Omega} U(f(\omega_i)) p_{\omega_i}\right). \tag{3.43}$$

The final equality follows from the fact that $U(\cdot)$ is a Von Neumann–Morgenstern utility function. $\square$

Notice that the numbers p_ω are *derived* from the preference relation $\succsim^*$ and represent the *subjective probability* that the individual attaches to state ω. When the conditions of this theorem hold, preferences are said to satisfy the conditions for *subjective expected utility theory* (SEU). Preferences satisfying SEU can be used to derive the subjective probability,

p_E, of any event $E \subset \Omega$ by calibrating with a lottery. Begin with the act:

$$f_A(\omega) = \begin{cases} c_{\max}, & \text{if } \omega \in E \\ c_{\min}, & \text{if } \omega \in E^c \end{cases}. \tag{3.44}$$

Given that preferences are continuous, there is an α and lottery $\{\alpha, c_{\max}; (1-\alpha), c_{\min}\}$ such that $f_A \sim^* \{\alpha, c_{\max}; (1-\alpha), c_{\min}\}$ from which we conclude:

$$p_E u(c_{\max}) + (1 - p_E) u(c_{\min}) = \alpha u(c_{\max}) + (1 - \alpha) u(c_{\min}). \tag{3.45}$$

Thus $p_E = \alpha$ and since α is the objective probability of receiving $c_{\max}$, then $p_E = \alpha$ is the subjective probability of event E. In particular, subjective probabilities can be manipulated using the standard rules of probability theory. The next section on the value of information illustrates this.

3.4.3   The Value of Information

In many situations an individual may delay decision making to gather more information. This is particularly important for contract formation when individuals may not wish to enter an agreement until they receive more information or, as in the case of principal-agent models, the contract terms themselves are a function of information received. This section illustrates how to model information and to measure its value.

Consider the financing example above, and observe that there may be a number of distinct events or states that determine whether the restaurant has a high or low value. For example, one may be sure of a high profit if another restaurant opens on the same street, thereby attracting more potential clients to the area. Alternatively, the street on which the restaurant is located may be made pedestrian-only, again ensuring high profits. These are two different possible events representing two potential pieces of information.

For simplicity, suppose that there are two underlying states for each event corresponding to high or low profits: the states ω_{1H} and ω_{2H} result in high profits, while the states ω_{1L} and ω_{2L} result in low profits. In that case, the acts available to the decision maker are given in table 3.5.

Our risk-neutral decision maker is assumed to satisfy the axioms of decision making under uncertainty, with Bernoulli utility $u(x) = x$. Therefore the payoffs from the acts f_{DF} and f_P are:

$$U(f_{DF}) = E(u(f_{DF}(\cdot))) \tag{3.46}$$

$$= (p_{1L} + p_{2L}) v_L + (p_{1H} + p_{2H}) v_H - I - R, \tag{3.47}$$

Table 3.5
Entrepreneur's payoffs with debt versus partnership financing

Act	State	
	ω_{1L} or ω_{2L}	ω_{1H} or ω_{2H}
Debt financing: f_{DF}	$v_L - I - R$	$v_H - I - R$
Partnership: f_P	$v_L/2$	$v_H/2$

$$U\left(f_P\right) = E\left(u\left(f_P\left(\cdot\right)\right)\right) \tag{3.48}$$

$$= \left(p_{1L} + p_{2L}\right) v_L/2 + \left(p_{1H} + p_{2H}\right) v_H/2, \tag{3.49}$$

where p_{nk} is the subjective probability for state ω_{nk}. For purposes of discussion, suppose that $U\left(f_P\right) > U\left(f_{DF}\right)$ (and maintain the assumption made in the previous section that in the good state, debt financing is preferred, and vice versa in the bad state).

The reason for expressing the high and low outcomes as the result of more primitive states is that it provides a way to formally model what we mean by information. For example, one may be told whether the true state is in $E_1 = \{s_{1L}, s_{1H}\}$ or $E_2 = \{s_{2L}, s_{2H}\}$. Given that an event E has occurred, then the conditional probability of an event A is:

$$P\left(A|E\right) = P\left(A \cap E\right)/P\left(E\right). \tag{3.50}$$

Hence the probability of high (respectively low) profits conditional upon E_i is $p_{iH}/\left(p_{iH} + p_{iL}\right)$ (respectively $p_{iL}/\left(p_{iH} + p_{iL}\right)$).

In this case the information is represented by a partition of the state space, $\Pi = \{E_1, E_2\}$. The conditional expectation of an act f given by the information set Π is denoted by $E\left(u\left(f\left(\cdot\right)\right)|\Pi\right)$. Formally this represents a *function* from Ω to $\Re$ with the property that it is sensitive to the information contained in Π:

$$E\left(u\left(f\right)|\Pi\right)\left(s\right) = \begin{cases} U\left(f|E_1\right) & \text{if } s \in E_1, \\ U\left(f|E_2\right) & \text{if } s \in E_2, \end{cases} \tag{3.51}$$

resulting in payoffs:

$$U\left(f_{DF}|E_i\right) = \left(p_{iL}v_L + p_{iH}v_H\right)/\left(p_{iH} + p_{iL}\right) - I - R, \tag{3.52}$$

$$U\left(f_P|E_i\right) = \left(p_{iL}v_L + p_{iH}v_H\right)/\left(2\left(p_{iH} + p_{iL}\right)\right). \tag{3.53}$$

Formally, the function $E\left(u\left(f\left(\cdot\right)\right)|\Pi\right)$ is *measurable* with respect to the information set Π. This simply means that one's decision can vary as a function of event E_1 or E_2, but for any two states $\omega_a, \omega_b \in E_i$ then $E\left(u\left(f\left(\cdot\right)\right)|\Pi\right)\left(\omega_a\right) = E\left(u\left(f\left(\cdot\right)\right)|\Pi\right)\left(\omega_b\right)$. Essentially, one cannot vary one's actions with information one does not have.[11] More precisely:

Definition 3.18 *Given a finite set Ω and a partition Π of Ω, then a function $f : \Omega \to Y \subset \Re^n$ is* measurable *with respect to Π if for every $E \in \Pi$ we have:*

$$f\left(\omega_a\right) = f\left(\omega_b\right), \forall \omega_a, \omega_b \in E.$$

When applied to a choice function, measurability ensures that one's decision cannot vary with information one does not have. If $U\left(f_{DF}|E_1\right) > U\left(f_P|E_1\right)$ and event E_1 is observed, then the entrepreneur would choose debt financing. Notice that the assumption $U\left(f_P\right) > U\left(f_{DF}\right)$ implies that $U\left(f_{DF}|E_2\right) < U\left(f_P|E_2\right)$, and therefore the entrepreneur chooses a partnership if event E_2 occurs. In the absence of any information, the entrepreneur chooses the partnership, but if the information partition $\{E_1, E_2\}$ is available, then she would choose debt financing if E_1 occurs, and a partnership otherwise.

New information *refines* the set of states and allows us to update the probabilities of events that might occur in the future. In this example, learning about event E_1 is valuable because it would cause us to change our financing plan to debt from a partnership.

Let $U^*(\Pi)$ be the maximum utility when the partition $\Pi = \{E_1, E_2\}$ is available. Then if $P(E_i) > 0$, for $i = 1, 2$ we have:

$$U^*(\Pi) = U(f_{DF}|E_1) P(E_1) + U(f_P|E_2) P(E_2) \tag{3.54}$$

$$> U(f_P|E_1) P(E_1) + U(f_P|E_2) P(E_2) \tag{3.55}$$

$$= U(f_p). \tag{3.56}$$

More generally, we can define the value of information from having access to a partition Π. For any event $E_i \in \Pi$, payoffs conditional upon E_i are defined by:

$$U(f|E_i) = \sum_{\omega \in \Omega} u(f(\omega)) P(\omega|E_i), \tag{3.57}$$

where $P(\omega|E_i)$ is the conditional probability of ω occurring given E_i and our subjective probability assessments. Suppose that the space of consequences is lotteries over money payoffs, and the Bernoulli utility is continuous with no lower bound. Then we denote the *value of information* by $V(\Pi)$, and it is defined as the solution to the following equality:

$$\sum_{E \in \Pi} \max_{f \in F} U(f - V(\Pi)|E) P(E) = \max_{f \in F} U(f) \tag{3.58}$$

This is the maximum amount of money one is willing to pay to receive information Π. More generally, if Π represents one's current information partition, then new information Π' corresponds to a partition of Π (see section 3.4.1). Information has value because it permits the decision maker to tailor her decisions to finer sets of states, a result that is summarized in the next proposition.

Proposition 3.19 *Suppose that preferences over money satisfy the Anscombe and Aumann axioms of decision making under uncertainty, and that the Bernoulli utility is continuous with no lower bound. If Π'' is a refinement of Π' then $V(\Pi'') \geq V(\Pi')$. Moreover, $V(\Pi'') > V(\Pi')$ if and only if there exists an $E'' \in \Pi''$ such that $P(E'') > 0$, and $\max_{f \in F} U(f|E'') > U(f'|E'')$, where*

$$f' \in \arg\max_{f \in F} U(f|E'), E'' \subset E' \in \Pi'.$$

Proof. The fact that the Bernoulli utility is continuous with no lower bound ensures the existence of the value of information. Given that Π'' is a refinement of Π', then Π'' defines a refinement for each $E \in \Pi'$, denoted Π_E.

$$\sum_{E' \in \Pi'} \max_{f \in F} U(f - V(\Pi')|E') P(E') = \max_{f \in F} U(f)$$

$$= \sum_{E \in \Pi''} \max_{f \in F} U(f - V(\Pi'')|E) P(E)$$

$$= \sum_{E' \in \Pi'} \sum_{E'' \in \Pi_E} \max_{f \in F} U(f - V(\Pi'')|E'') P(E'')$$

$$\geq \sum_{E' \in \Pi'} \max_{f \in F} \sum_{E'' \in \Pi_E} U\left(f - V\left(\Pi''\right) | E''\right) P\left(E''\right)$$

$$= \sum_{E' \in \Pi'} \max_{f \in F} U\left(f - V\left(\Pi''\right) | E'\right) P\left(E'\right).$$

Given the continuity of U, it follows that $V\left(\Pi''\right) \geq V\left(\Pi'\right)$. The second result is a straightforward consequence of the fact that utility is a positive linear combination of $U\left(f|E\right)$, for E in the relevant partition.   □

It is also assumed that once subjective probabilities have been determined, then the decision maker is able to apply the standard tools of probability theory. In particular, it is assumed that beliefs are updated using Bayes's theorem. Notice that information is strictly valuable if and only if it allows us to make a strictly better decision for some event E that occurs with positive probability.

The fact that information is valuable only for events that have a positive *prior* probability of occurring creates a number of serious problems not only for decision making but also for contract formation and game theory. One of the reasons contract disputes arise is because an event occurs that neither party to the contract anticipated. In other words, an event with a subjective probability of zero has occurred. Unfortunately, when such an event occurs, Bayesian theory cannot be used to update beliefs. For example, suppose that $P\left(E\right) = 0$ and one wishes to contemplate the possibility that event A occurs after observing event E; however:

$$P\left(A|E\right) = \frac{P\left(A \cap E\right)}{P\left(E\right)} = \frac{0}{0} = \text{undefined.} \tag{3.59}$$

Thus, in cases in which the subjective decision maker has made a mistake and overlooked an event that actually transpired, the rules of probability theory can no longer be used to derive an individual's *posterior* beliefs. There is no satisfactory resolution of this problem in the literature, though several authors have explored the meaning of probability in these contexts. The interested reader is referred to Jeffrey (1965) and de Finetti (1974) for an extended philosophical discussion. Diaconis and Zabell (1982) review a number of alternatives to Bayes's rule for the updating of subjective probabilities.

The standard approach to this problem, advocated by Jeffrey (1965), is to use a diffuse prior and suppose that all events have strictly positive probability. This idea forms the basis for the concept of a perfect equilibrium in game theory, which is discussed in further detail in the next chapter (see also Myerson's [1991, 21] discussion of conditional probability systems). However, incomplete contracts often arise because the contracting parties are simply unaware that an event might occur; hence they cannot plan for it. Savage was well aware of this problem, which is precisely why he used the term "small world."

3.5   Discussion

When used as a positive model, the goal of rational choice theory is to provide a representation of behavior that is rich enough to capture the main qualitative features of human behavior. It is not a perfect representation of human behavior, but over the years it has proven to be the most successful model of human behavior for studying social phenomena. The recent advances in the psychology of economics have come from studying deviations from rational choice rather than from attempting to replace rational choice theory with a completely new model.

Even so, the model has a great deal of indeterminacy. The fact that individuals must make choices in the face of uncertainty implies that the individuals must choose even when their knowledge regarding the consequences of their choices is limited. Savage's theory of rational choice in that setting implies that individuals build a model of the world and then construct subjective evaluations of the likelihood of future events. The power of incentives is intimately linked to how individuals connect current actions to future rewards, which implies that the theory of incentive contracts must address the formation of these subjective beliefs.

The models in this book are concerned with how variation in information and the timing of choices affect observed outcomes. To focus upon these effects it is assumed that individuals, prefer more rather than fewer resources, and they are in many cases risk averse. Assuming that these preferences are fixed over time allows one to focus on the causal effect of changes in the environment on observed outcomes.

It is worth emphasizing that the rational choice model is merely a *representation* of a person's preferences or goals that is assumed to be stable over time. In particular, the rational choice model does not assume that a person is selfish or cares only about money. The theory outlined here can be extended to allow for social preferences and other features of human decision making. Sapolsky (2018) provides an excellent introduction to human behavior that brings together research from psychology, neuroscience, and behavioral economics. What is clear from the evidence is that human behavior is very complex and can vary in surprising ways from person to person. As economics is concerned with the effect of institutions upon millions of individuals, one necessarily has to use a simple model that characterizes features of behavior common to all individuals. The desire to have more resources is one such feature.

These simple positive theories can spill over to normative decision making. For example, there is some evidence that researchers in economics have a bias toward some models of choice over others. See in particular Fourcade, Ollion, and Algan (2015) for an excellent discussion of the sociology of economics. This is certainly a question that deserves further research.

However, for the rest of this book it is assumed that individuals are characterized by simple, stable preferences over outcomes. It turns out that when such individuals interact with each other, rational choice theory alone cannot always predict the outcome. The next chapter provides an overview of game theory, whose goal is to provide a model of the formation of expectations in such social situations. It is the foundation on which economics builds a rational choice model of complex exchange.

3.6 Exercises

1. Let n be the number of possible choices in set A. Suppose that an individual could face any subset of set A. How many distinct behaviors are possible as a function of n?

2. Suppose we allow indifference, and further suppose that the individual selects each outcome in her indifferent set with equal probability. How many observations within a choice set $C \subset A$ of size m does one need to be able to identify $D = B(C)$ with probability greater than $1 - \epsilon$? Now suppose that one can perform an experiment and observe how the individual will choose for different $C \subset A$. How many experiments does one need to identify the behavior $B(.)$ with probability $(1 - \epsilon)$?

3. Prove theorem 3.1. Hint: first show that transitivity allows one to completely order the set A, such that $x_1 \succsim x_2 \succsim \ldots \succsim x_N$, where $x_1, \ldots, x_N$ are the elements of A. Then use this ordering to assign a utility to each element of A.

4. Show that a group decision by majority rule may not satisfy the conditions for rational choice.

5. Let $A = \Re^2$, and suppose that $\{x_1, x_2\} \succsim \{y_1, y_2\}$ if $x_1 \geq y_1$, or $x_1 = y_1$ and $x_2 \geq y_2$. These are called *lexicographical preferences*. Prove that they satisfy the axioms of rationality but are not continuous.

6. Show that in the lottery simplex of figure 3.1, indifference curves must be a family of parallel straight lines.

7. Explicitly derive the demand for insurance in example 3.9 when there are two events and $u(x) = \log(x)$.

8. Given continuity and the independence axioms, prove the existence of a continuous utility function. Hint: begin by showing that we can set $U(l) = \alpha$ for all lotteries of the form $l = \alpha \bar{l} + (1 - \alpha) \underline{l}$, where $\bar{l}$ and $\underline{l}$ are the most preferred and least preferred lotteries, respectively, and $\bar{l} \succ \underline{l}$. These exist due to the continuity of preferences. Then show how continuity can be used to extend this utility function to arbitrary lotteries. Observe that the problem is trivial when $\bar{l}$ is indifferent to $\underline{l}$.

9. Suppose that an individual has preferences represented by expected utility with Bernoulli utility. Show that these preferences can be represented by another Bernoulli utility function $u'(\cdot)$ if and only if there is a $\beta > 0$ and α such that:

$$u'(c) = \beta u(c) + \alpha, \text{ for all } c \in C. \tag{3.60}$$

10. Fill in the details for the proof of proposition 3.6.

11. A risk-averse individual with initial wealth w can invest his wealth into two assets. One is risk-free, with a gross return of R; the other is risky, and its gross return is some normal random variable $\tilde{\theta}$ with mean t and variance σ^2. Let $\alpha \in [0, 1]$ denote the fraction of initial wealth invested in the risky asset.

   (a) Show that if $t \leq R, \alpha = 0$.

   (b) Show that if $t \geq R, \alpha > 0$.

   (c) Suppose individual has CARA preferences (see (3.27)). How does α vary with the coefficient of absolute risk aversion?

   (d) Assume that an agent has constant *relative* risk aversion. How does he modify his portfolio when he gets richer? In particular, how does the share of his wealth invested in the risky asset change?

   (e) Same question for decreasing relative risk aversion.

12. In this exercise we explore a way to model boundedly rational decision making. Suppose that you are in a company that is choosing to bring to market a software package to evaluate the value of securities. Let S be the set of all possible software packages. Suppose that at a cost c you can sample a package $s \in S$ and determine its value v_s. Your profits are simply the value of the package you choose less the costs spent in choosing a package. How would a rational entrepreneur model her decision problem, and what are the characteristics of the optimal solution? (See MacLeod 2002.)

4 Game Theory

And the king said, "Divide the living child in two, and give half to the one and half to the other." Then the woman whose son was alive said to the king, because her heart yearned for her son, "Oh, my lord, give her the living child, and by no means put him to death." But the other said, "He shall be neither mine nor yours; divide him." Then the king answered and said, "Give the living child to the first woman, and by no means put him to death; she is his mother."[1]
—1 Kings 3:25–27 (English Standard Version).

4.1 Introduction

Savage's theory introduced in the previous chapter allows one to use the full apparatus of statistical decision theory in situations for which probabilities have not been estimated by an experiment. This perspective views Nature as providing a fixed, well-defined environment that is considered *independent* of the statistical methods that one uses to uncover her secrets.

In contrast, institution and contract design must explicitly address the question of how each party expects other interested parties to act in the future. Game theory addresses the question of how to extend the rational choice model to situations in which there are interacting rational decision makers. Interactions with children are a good example of the problem, in part because they are often quite rational in their behavior (even though it may not seem so to adults).[2] They often enter into explicit agreements with their parents on how they should behave.

Consider going to a store with a child, who decides that she would like a candy bar, something that the parent would not normally wish to buy. The child might already know that asking for candy would elicit the typical response, "No!" However, once in the store, some children anticipate that their parents will become very uncomfortable if they start to scream and roll on the floor. They use the threat of a temper tantrum to extract candy from the helpless parent.

Notice that this is entirely rational behavior for a child who knows that her parents will be embarrassed by such a display and will succumb. This game can be formally modeled as seen in table 4.1.

This matrix is a game in *normal form*. When represented in a table form like this, it always has the same interpretation—the different rows correspond to the strategies by player 1,

Table 4.1
The candy game

	Buy candy (BC)	No candy (NC)
Tantrum if no candy (TNC)	$(2, -2)$	$(-1, -10)$
No tantrum (NT)	$(2, -2)$	$(0, 2)$

while the different columns correspond to different strategies by player 2. The table entries are for a strategy pair, and they are in the form (u_1, u_2) to represent the Bernoulli utilities for the strategies chosen by players 1 and 2 respectively. Unless otherwise stated, it is assumed that the players satisfy the axioms of subjective expected utility theory.

This simple game illustrates a number of features of strategic decision making that are important for understanding social interactions. Notice that if the child chooses TNC (tantrum if no candy), the parent is better off choosing BC (buy candy) to avoid the negative consequences of a tantrum, represented by the -10. If the threat is not actually carried out, then the child is indifferent between tantrum and no tantrum. Thus, the pair $\{TNC, BC\}$ forms a *Nash equilibrium*. Each person's strategy is optimal given his or her expectations regarding the other person's strategy. Notice that this is not the only Nash equilibrium. Because having a tantrum is costly for the child, then the outcome $\{NT, NC\}$ is also a Nash equilibrium.

The point is that if the child knows that she will not receive candy in any case, then she is better off not having a tantrum; but the child also understands that if she backs down too easily, then the threat will never work. Thus, children will often have tantrums to prove to their parents that their threat is *credible*. If the threat is to carry out a costly action when individuals do not behave as one wishes (in this case, the parent does not provide the candy), then enforcement of behavior may require the development of a reputation for having tantrums. Parents can of course fight back with their own strategies. One common strategy is to enter into a *contract* with the child. For example, if there is no temper tantrum while shopping, then the parent may offer ice cream at the end of the outing, under the assumption that the combination of ice cream and peace while shopping is preferred to the alternative.

In this case, there is also an enforcement problem. Once the child has behaved well and is in the car out of the public eye, the threat of a tantrum is much less costly for the parent. At that point the parent may attempt to renege on the original agreement. The extent to which a child would agree to such a contract depends upon the extent to which the child *believes* the parent will honor the agreement.

The example illustrates not only the potentially complex intertemporal behavior that is possible but also the extent to which behavior is determined by one's expectations regarding future behavior. This depends upon the extent to which one believes that the other person is rational. There is evidence that children do behave in a rational fashion, though the extent to which they can understand and respond to intertemporal incentives can depend on age.[3]

Behavior in this example is consistent with both parties making optimal choices and also expecting their counterparty to make an optimal choice. It turns out that what we mean by "optimal" is sensitive to the structure of the environment, and there is no universal theory of behavior is such environments. This can be very confusing when reading the technical literature because, depending upon the context, authors use different definitions of equilibrium behavior. Modern game theory can seem like a catalog of solutions concepts, with little guidance on which is the correct or "true" model of strategic choice.[4]

In keeping with the empirical perspective of this book, the term "self-enforcing" means the outcome of interactions between individuals with the feature that we observe people carrying out this behavior. Moreover, with further reflection, parties would not wish to change their actions. Different notions of an equilibrium can then be viewed as different formal ways to model self-enforcing behavior. The extent to which one notion or the other is preferred cannot be judged based on logical reasoning.

Rather, the appropriate model is the one that does the best job of representing average behavior for the problem or question at hand. In this chapter we review four solution concepts that are widely used in the literature: perfect (Nash) equilibria, sequential equilibria, perfect Bayesian (Nash) equilibria, and subgame perfect (Nash) equilibria. There are many books on game theory that readers can consult for in-depth study.[5] There is also a growing literature on behavioral game theory that extends these models to allow for behaviors that are not well modeled within the utility maximization framework.[6]

4.2   The Concept of a Strategy

Formally, Savage's concept of an act is sufficiently rich to provide a complete model of a strategy. However, his approach proves difficult because when one's payoff depends on the other person's decision, then those decisions are modeled as different states of Nature. One can view Nature as a player as well, in which case the model simply entails mapping all possible strategies by the other players into states, and then the decision maker forms beliefs over this state space before making a choice.[7]

Game theory begins with the hypothesis that all the individuals have goals and make choices consistent with these goals. The purpose of the model is to predict how parties will make choices, given that they are interacting with others who are faced with the same problem and there is common knowledge regarding each player's goals.

The notion of an extensive form game is introduced that allows an unambiguous definition of a strategy in a game. The definition is complex, and it might be argued too complex. We begin with an example that illustrates that the extensive form is not only a useful tool, but it also provides a framework for answering questions that even skilled mathematicians may get wrong.

The example is called the "Monty Hall Problem," based on the television game show *Let's Make A Deal*, which Monty Hall hosted. The problem, as posed by Selvin (1975), is:

Suppose you're on a game show, and you're given a choice of three boxes: In one box is a set of keys to a Lincoln Continental; the other boxes are empty. You pick a box, say A, and the host, who knows what's in the other boxes, opens another box, say C, which is empty. He then says to you, "Do you want to pick box B?" Is it to your advantage to take the switch?

This problem has produced a great deal of controversy concerning what is the "correct" solution. Selvin provides one of the first solutions to this problem, yet his solution was criticized. Selvin had to publish a response a few months after his paper was published. The controversy was renewed when Marilyn vos Savant published the problem in her *Parade* column in 1990, along with Selvin's solution. About 10,000 readers, many with doctorates, wrote claiming her solution was wrong.[8]

What happened was that many individuals approached the issue as a "problem in probability." However, the solution depends upon the strategies that Monty is following when he opens a box. Given that this information is not provided, the player's expected payoffs for her different choices are simply not well defined.

To solve this problem, we begin by specifying the formal definition of an extensive form game and then apply it to the Monty Hall problem. This provides a solution that is a simple matter of calculation and not open to multiple interpretations.

The first step is to enumerate the set of players, given by $N = \{0, 1, 2, \ldots, \bar{N}\}$. Uncertainty is introduced by modeling an uncertain event as a choice by Nature, who, as a matter of convention, is always player 0. Second, one constructs a timeline that orders the time at which players make their moves. This does not have to be real time but the sequence is important to allow us to properly model information flows.

At this point we could proceed by defining a game in *extensive form* (see, for example, Luce and Raiffa [1957] 1989), which provides a precise definition of a strategy and equilibrium play. However, it is also an extremely complex object. We solve this by providing an *algorithm* for the construction of the extensive form given the "rules of the game."

This is a natural approach because all games are typically described by their rule box, and not the extensive form. For example, in the case of chess, players take turns choosing "legal" moves that are given by the rules of the game. The winner is also determined by a given rule (checkmate or stalemate).

Technically the extensive form is a directed graph, in which each node represents the state of the game in progress. These nodes can be defined recursively from the rule book and the choices available to players. The start of a game is identified by the root of the graph that will represent the game. The construction proceeds as follows:

Definition 4.1   *Given players $N = \{0, 1, \ldots, \bar{N}\}$, a rule book R, and play starting at date $t = 0$ at the root r, an* extensive form game Ξ *is defined recursively as follows:*

1. *The game begins with the root node r and set $\Sigma(0) = \{r\}$. The set $\Sigma(t), t \geq 1$ represents the nodes created at date t as a result of legal moves made at date $t - 1$, for which there will be further moves. Let Z represent the terminal nodes of the game. Suppose that $r \notin Z$ and that the rule book R has clear criteria that determine whether a node n is in Z.[9]*

2. *The set $\Sigma(t)$ is partitioned into information sets, $E_{tk} \in \Phi_t, k \in \{1, \ldots, k_t\}$, where k_t is the number of information sets at time t, and Φ_t is a partition of $\Sigma(t)$. Each information set is associated with a player $i_{tk} \in N$, with the interpretation that the player has a chance to make a choice at this information set. However, the player cannot distinguish between nodes in E_{tk}. The action chosen by player i_{tk} at this information set is given by action $a_{ik} \in A_{tk}$. Player i's strategy at information set E_{tk} is given by the function $\gamma^i(E_{tk}) = a_{tk} \in A_{tk}$. Player i's behavioral strategy at information set E_{tk} is defined by the function $\hat{\gamma}^i(E_{tk}) = \hat{a}_{tk} \in \Delta(A_{tk})$, that is, the player randomly selects an action from A_{tk} as given by the probability vector $\hat{a}_{tk}$. If $i_{tk} = 0$, then this is a play by Nature. It is assumed that Nature always plays a behavioral strategy $\hat{a}_{tk} \in \Delta(A_{tk})$ that is known by all players and corresponds to the probability that*

Nature chooses an action in A_{tk} (it is not assumed that players can necessarily observe the choice by Nature).

3. New nodes in $\Sigma(t+1)$ for the next date are created as follows: For each $n \in \Sigma(t)$, and for each $a_{tk} \in A_{tk}$, where E_{tk} is the information set containing n, a new node $n' = a_{tk}$ is created, with the following additional properties. If a_{tk} leads to a final move of the game, then n' is added to the list Z, otherwise it is added to the list $\Sigma(t+1)$. Define the predecessor function by $n = p(n')$ and the successor correspondence by $s(n) = p^{-1}(n) = \{n' | p(n') = n\}$. Let $S(E_{tk}) = \{n' | p^m(n') \in E_{tk}, \text{ for some } m \geq 1\}$ be the set of all successor nodes, namely all the nodes that follow the information set E_{tk}, where $p^m(n')$ is the predecessor function for the choice made m periods ago.

4. Repeat steps 2 and 3 until $\Sigma(t) = \emptyset$ is empty, or equivalently, $s(n) \subset Z$ for all $n \in \Sigma(t-1)$.

5. Let $\Phi^i = \{E_{tk} | i_{tk} = i\}$ be the information sets for player i. Let Φ denote the set of all information sets.

6. For each $z \in Z$, the Bernoulli utility for player i of arriving at that node is specified by $u^i(z)$.

Whenever we use the symbol Ξ we mean a game in extensive form as defined above. The extensive form allows one to precisely define any finite game. In the game of chess, white moves at even dates, $t = 0, 2, 4 \ldots$, while black moves at odd dates. In chess there is complete information and hence each information set contains a single node. At time $t = 1$ the nodes are simply all the board positions consistent with legal moves by white at time $t = 0$, and so on.

In card games, such as poker or bridge, the first move is by Nature, which determines how cards are distributed. When a player acts, she does not know how the cards are distributed among the other players.

There is some indeterminacy in the definition of the extensive form when players are required to choose at the same time. In that case the ordering of moves does not matter. All that is required is that the players moving later cannot observe the choice of the players from the previous time period. Examples below discuss this.

Notice that the nodes $z \in Z$ correspond to a *unique* description of the actions that lead to that node, and hence the elements in Z correspond precisely to the notion of a *state* in Savage's model—a complete description of the outcome of the game. From this one can also see that defining games using an extensive form game that is defined in terms of a set of nodes $\Sigma(t)$ and endpoints Z is not very practical.[10] For many games, such as chess or Go, the set of terminal nodes is astronomically large. However, the extensive form is convenient to address purely theoretical issues, such as the existence of an equilibrium. Moreover, this approach suggests that the notion of a state or node in a game seems to be something that is exogenous and well defined.

The definition here highlights the idea that states in a model are *constructed* and that in practice, when playing a game, individuals are typically aware of only a small subset of the full state space. For example, in the game of chess one never thinks in terms of all possible endpoints but rather in terms of a few board positions that can be reached from the current position in the game. This perspective will become relevant when we turn to the issue of contractual incompleteness.[11]

Let Γ^i and $\hat{\Gamma}^i$ denote respectively the set of strategies and behavioral strategies by player i defined in step 2. A *strategy profile* for the game is given by:

$$\hat{\gamma}^0 \times \gamma = \hat{\gamma}^0 \times \left\{\gamma^1, \ldots, \gamma^{\bar{N}}\right\} \in \hat{\Gamma}^0 \times \Gamma^1 \times \ldots \times \Gamma^{\bar{N}} = \hat{\Gamma}^0 \times \Gamma,$$

where Γ is the set of strategies for the players. This generates a probability distribution over terminal nodes denoted by $\mu(\gamma) \in \Delta(Z)$. Given that Nature's strategy, $\hat{\gamma}^0$, is usually specified as part of the description of the game, it is not an explicit argument of μ. Hence the payoff of the individuals as a function of the *strategy profile* γ is defined by:

$$U^i(\gamma) = \sum_{z \in Z} u^i(z) \mu(z|\gamma), \tag{4.1}$$

where $\mu(z|\gamma)$ is the probability of $z \in Z$ given the strategy profile γ. Notice that all the information necessary to describe the game is given by the finite strategy sets, Γ^i, and the payoffs, $U^i(\cdot)$. When the strategies and payoffs are given in this manner without reference to the underlying information structure, this is called a game in *strategic* or *normal* form. In this case we can write $G(\Xi) = \{U^i, \Gamma^i\}_{i \in N}$. One can also use the notation $U^i(\gamma^i, \gamma^{-i})$ to indicate the expected utility of player i, given her strategy, $\gamma^i \in \Gamma^i$, and the strategies of the other players, $\gamma^{-i} \in \Gamma^{-i}$.

It is assumed that the game ends in a finite number of rounds, and thus the set of strategy profiles for player i, Γ^i, is a finite set.[12] A *mixed strategy* for player i is one for which the player randomizes over the elements of Γ^i, and thus corresponds to the set $\Delta(\Gamma^i)$. Given mixed strategies $\hat{\gamma}^i \in \Delta(\Gamma^i)$, the utility of agent i is:

$$U^i(\hat{\gamma}) = \sum_{\gamma \in \Gamma} U^i(\gamma)\hat{\gamma}^1(\gamma^1) \times \ldots \times \hat{\gamma}^{\bar{N}}(\gamma^{\bar{N}}), \tag{4.2}$$

where $\hat{\gamma}^i(\gamma^i)$ is the probability that pure strategy γ^i is chosen under mixed strategy $\hat{\gamma}$.

The notion of a mixed strategy is an essential element in many games. For example, in the game of soccer, when a penalty kick is awarded, the defending goalkeeper does not have much time to respond to the shot made by the attacking player. Hence, the goalkeeper typically "guesses" which side the shot will go and lunges in that direction as the attacker kicks. The attacking player would be at a tremendous disadvantage if he or she always shot to the same side, so the player will randomly choose one side or the other (see Palacios-Huerta [2003] for supporting evidence from professional soccer).

The problem is that mixed strategies are defined as randomly choosing from the very large set of possible pure strategies, something that is clearly impractical in many cases. The notion of a behavioral strategy is introduced in the definition of the extensive form because it has the natural interpretation of the player randomizing her choices at the time she acts. Clearly, each behavioral strategy corresponds to some mixed strategy. The converse is also true when players have perfect recall.

A player has perfect recall if she can recall all the strategies she has played previously.

Definition 4.2 *Formally, player i has* perfect recall *if for every information set $E_{tk} \in \Phi^i$, and for any choice a_{tk} at information set E_{tk}, then we have that for any other information set $E_{t'k'} \in \Phi^i$ either:*

1. $E_{t'k'} \cap S(a_{tk}) = \emptyset$; *that is, the player at information set $E_{t'k'}$ knows that a_{tk} did not lead to the current information set, or*

2. $E_{t'k'} \subset S(a_{tk})$: *player i knows for sure that a_{tk} has occurred before she arrives at information set $E_{t'k'}$.*

Given this assumption we have the following result.

Proposition 4.3 *Suppose that player i has perfect recall. Then for any mixed strategy, there exists a behavioral strategy that results in the same payoff for player i.*

The proof of this proposition is left as an exercise for the interested reader. Unless stated otherwise, it is assumed that players have perfect recall, so without loss of generality, players can be assumed to use behavioral strategies.

If attention is restricted to pure strategies, then the existence of an equilibrium cannot be assured. Thus, for the rest of our discussion it is assumed that the strategies $\gamma^i \in \Gamma^i$ refer to behavioral strategies, unless it is clear from the context that they are pure strategies. Consequently, we allow for a continuum of strategies. The game is still considered to be a finite game because there are a finite number of terminal nodes, $z \in Z$.

This implies that a mixed strategy can be represented by a vector in $\Delta(\Re^n)$, where n is the number of pure strategies. In the case of a continuum strategy space, as one would have for, say, a Cournot oligopoly model, then the mixed strategy would be given by a measure over the real numbers, greatly increasing the complexity of the analysis.

4.2.1 The Monty Hall Problem

Let us now illustrate the construction of an extensive form game using the Monty Hall problem. This is illustrated in figure 4.1. At time $t = 1$ Nature moves and places the key in one of the boxes, A, B, or C. When the player, denoted by P, chooses her strategy, Nature's choice is not observed. Hence, there is only one information set, denoted E_{21}, containing all the nodes generated by Nature. Given E_{21}, the player then selects A, B, or C. Notice that this implies that the same action must be applied to each node in the same information set.

For the purposes of the example, the player has chosen B. At that point Monty Hall (MH) plays. In this case he knows not only the location of the key but also the choice made by the player. Thus given P's choice, Monty Hall has three information sets, E_{31}, E_{32}, and E_{33}, corresponding to the three choices made by Nature (in total at $t = 3$, there are $3 \times 3 = 9$ information sets, three for each choice made by P).

In order to make her choice, P has to work out what she believes is Monty's strategy at this point, which is not always clear. Monty could, for example, show the location of the car key, but that would not be very interesting! What happens on the show is Monty opens a box with the following two properties: it was not chosen by P (and hence he opens A or C) and the car key is not in the box. Many analyses of the problem miss the fact that we are not really told the probability that Monty chooses box C or A. The Savage model implies that if P is a rational individual, then she assigns subjective probabilities to Monty's choice, say

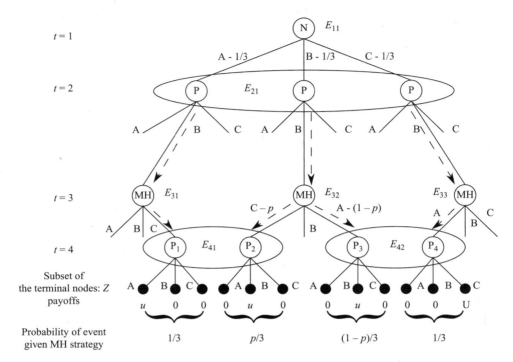

Figure 4.1
Extensive form for Monty Hall problem.

p and $1 - p$, respectively. That these probabilities are required to solve the problem but are not given in the statement of the problem implies that the problem *cannot* be just a problem in probability, as is sometimes claimed.[13] These probabilities are given by the preferences of the individuals and not by the information provided in the statement of the problem.

Consider information set E_{41}, corresponding to the event that P has chosen B and Monty has chosen C (with probability p when the key is box B). Given this information, the individual must choose box A, B, or C. Notice that a quick calculation shows that the probability of arriving at node P_1 is $1/3$, while the probability of arriving at node P_2 is $p/3$. We can conclude using the definition of conditional probability that $\Pr(P_1|E_{41}) = \frac{1/3}{1/3+p/3} = \frac{1}{1+p}$. Letting u be the utility from winning and 0 the utility for not winning, then conditional upon E_{41}, the utility of the player for each of the three choices is given by:

$$E(U|E_{41}, A) = \frac{1}{1+p}u,$$

$$E(U|E_{41}, B) = \frac{p}{1+p}u,$$

$$E(U|E_{41}, C) = 0.$$

Since $p \in [0, 1]$, then playing A is always an optimal strategy, namely changing her choice from the original box B is always optimal. This is the standard solution proposed: changing one's choice from the original choice to the box not chosen by Monty is always optimal. However, there do exist beliefs for the player under which it is optimal *not* to switch.

Observe that the player is indifferent between A and B if $p = 1$. If one makes a similar calculation with these beliefs, one will find that choosing C when event E_{42} occurs is optimal and yields a payoff $E(U|E_{42}, C) = \frac{1}{2-p}u$. When $p = 1$ then in information set E_{42} one believes that the key is behind box C with probability 1.

Put another way, suppose Monty follows the strategy of choosing the box to the right of the player's choice, unless that box has the key. If the player chooses A then the default is for Monty to choose C and so on. Notice that if Monty does not choose the box to the right, then the key must be there and the player would optimally choose that box. If Monty does choose the box to the right, then that implies that the probability that the key is in the other two boxes is equal, and therefore there is no need to change one's choice.

As is evident, this example illustrates the point that this is not a simple mathematics problem. In order to make a decision, the player needs to build a model of Monty's behavior. Conditional upon this model, the player can then choose.

In particular, if we observe that the player does not switch, we cannot logically conclude that the player is being irrational. Whether the player is irrational depends on the player's beliefs. Under some beliefs, it is rational not to switch. For any reasonably complex situation one cannot assess the rationality of choice without also making statements regarding the beliefs of the party making the choice. More generally, game theory extends decision theory with the addition of an explicit model of player beliefs (Kreps and Wilson 1982).

4.3 Rational Choice in a Game

We solved the Monty Hall problem by viewing Monty's strategies as a play by Nature that required the assignment of subjective probabilities to unobserved events. Game theory is concerned with modeling choice when it is common knowledge that all agents are rational (or, more precisely, decision makers satisfy the Aumann-Anscombe axioms of choice). Consider now the problem faced by rational decision makers in a game defined in normal form by $G = \{U^i, \Gamma^i\}_{i \in N}$. In game theory the standard hypothesis is that the rules of the game are common knowledge and that all players are rational in the sense that they satisfy the axioms of subjective expected utility theory. It is well known that these assumptions by themselves are not sufficient to uniquely determine the outcome of the game in all cases.[14] For example, consider the famous *battle of the sexes* game.[15]

In this game, the two parties, say George and Lucy, discuss the possibility of going out the next evening. George has a co-worker who will sell him hockey tickets, while Lucy has the chance to get opera tickets. Unfortunately, they were not able to finish their discussion on where to go, and then, while at work, each must independently decide whether to buy the tickets.

The problem is that George prefers the opera, while Lucy prefers hockey, and both hate to waste money. Thus, the question is should they buy the tickets? If they both buy, then they will both be upset, while if neither buys, they won't go out. The interesting point here is that even though both parties are rational, if they cannot communicate with each other, the hypothesis that they are rational does not provide a unique solution to this problem.

We will come back to this game in the next section. For the moment, let us consider another situation in which rational choice theory *can* guide us. Consider now the prisoner's dilemma.[16]

In this game, two white-collar criminals from the same firm have been arrested, and agree not to confess to the authorities. They are in separate cells where they must decide whether to keep quiet (cooperate with each other) or confess (cheat on the other). If neither confesses, they are free to keep their ill-gotten gains of 2 each. If one confesses and the other does not, then the cheater gains 3, while the cooperator loses 1. Finally, if they both confess, the payoffs are normalized at 0 each.

In this case, rational choice theory can make a unique prediction. Notice that regardless of the other player's decision, the strategy of cheating is *always* a better choice than the strategy of cooperation. The strategy of cheating is called a *dominant strategy* and would always be used by a rational player. When a dominant strategy exists, decision making by the player is easy because their optimal choice does not vary with the actions of the other player. Given that easy-to-compute optimal strategies are a desirable feature of any economic mechanism, a great deal of research considers the question of how to design institutions with the feature that players can restrict their attention to dominant strategies (see exercise 7).

Building on these examples, a solution is provided based upon the assumption that it is common knowledge that players in a game are rational. The battle of the sexes game shows that such a solution can be nonunique. Hence, the solution is at best a subset of the possible strategies. Because it eliminates some strategy pairs as inconsistent with rational choice, the theory has some empirical bite and can be rejected with evidence of such irrational choices.

Suppose each player knows that other players make decisions consistent with their preferences, and they all share this belief.[17] The most straightforward way to think about this problem is to suppose that each player i chooses an optimal action given her beliefs over possible choices by the other players. This implies that if there is a strategy $\gamma^i \in \Gamma^i$ that a rational player i would never choose, then other players must assign zero probability to this strategy in their own beliefs. Bernheim (1984) and Pearce (1984) provide a formal model of this idea that proceeds as follows.

In the context of Savage's model, players' beliefs are given by some probability distribution over the actions of the other players. Suppose that player i believes that the other players will select strategies from the set $\bar{\Gamma}^{-i} \subset \Gamma^{-i}$. Then a rational player's strategies will come from the set $H^i(\bar{\Gamma}^{-i})$, where:

$$H^i(\bar{\Gamma}^{-i}) = \bigcup_{\hat{\gamma}^{-i} \in \Delta(\bar{\Gamma}^{-i})} \left\{ \arg \max_{\gamma^i \in \Gamma^i} U^i\left(\gamma^i, \hat{\gamma}^{-i}\right) \right\}.$$

With a slight abuse of notation, the belief of player i is given by a probability distribution over the finite set of strategies in $\bar{\Gamma}^{-i}$, and denoted by $\hat{\gamma}^{-i}$. The payoff of player i extends naturally to this case. This is the set of strategies for player i that maximize her payoff when she believes that the other players choose their strategies from the set $\bar{\Gamma}^{-i}$. No restrictions are placed upon beliefs other than the support lie in the set $\bar{\Gamma}^{-i}$. Thus, this formulation is allowing for the use of mixed strategies. As we have no way to restrict these beliefs other

Table 4.2
The battle of the sexes

George	Lucy	
	Don't buy opera tickets (DB)	Buy opera tickets (B)
Buy hockey tickets (B)	(1,2)	(−1,−1)
Don't buy (DB)	(−1,−1)	(2,1)

than by saying that they lie in $\bar{\Gamma}^{-i}$, then we take the union over all possible beliefs. Because the set of strategies is finite, this mapping is always well-defined.

We now define the set of strategies that are *rationalizable*—these are the strategies consistent with the assumption that rational choice is common knowledge. Begin with the full set of strategies, $\Gamma_0^i = \Gamma^i$, then set $\Gamma_1^i = H^i(\Gamma_0^{-i})$. Given that rational individuals would only choose strategies from the set $\Gamma_1 = \{\Gamma_1^i\}_{i \in N}$, it also follows that the rational person i would only select strategies from $\Gamma_2^i = H^i(\Gamma_1^{-i})$. More generally, if one lets

$$\Gamma_t^i = H^i(\Gamma_{t-1}^{-i}),$$

then $\Gamma_t^i \subset \Gamma_{t-1}^i$. When combined with the fact that the number of strategies is finite, this allows one to conclude that these sets converge to limit sets $\Gamma_*^i, i \in N$, with the feature that $\Gamma_*^i \subset H^i(\Gamma_*^{-i})$. These strategies are called *rationalizable* because player i's strategy has the feature that it is a best reply to some beliefs that place positive weights only on the other players' *rationalizable* strategies.

As an example, consider the battle of the sexes game (table 4.2), in which George and Lucy are considering going to the opera or to a hockey game. Consider first the problem from George's perspective. Because George cannot communicate with Lucy, he may view her decision as a *state of the world*. In that case, the choice to buy or not are two acts, the consequence of which is determined by Lucy's choice. If George is rational in the sense of satisfying our theory of subjective expected utility, then we may suppose he assigns a subjective probability, p_L^e, to Lucy's choosing to buy the opera tickets. In this case George's payoffs from "don't buy" (DB) and "buy" (B) as a function of his belief regarding Lucy's choice are:

$$U^G(DB, p_L^e) = 3p_L^e - 1, \tag{4.3}$$

$$U^G(B, p_L^e) = 1 - 2p_L^e. \tag{4.4}$$

These payoffs are illustrated in figure 4.2. Notice that for belief $p_L^e < p^*$ the optimal strategy is to choose B, while for $p_L^e > p^*$ DB (don't buy) is an optimal strategy. When $p_L^e = p^* = 0.4$ either strategy is optimal, and hence any lottery $\{(1 - \rho_G), DB; \rho_G, B\}$ is optimal for George.

Let $\rho_G = 0$ denote DB, and $\rho_G = 1$ denote B. Then George's behavior as a function of his beliefs can be described by the *best response correspondence*:

$$r^G(p_L^e) = \arg\max_{\rho \in [0,1]} U^G(\rho, p_L^e) = \begin{cases} 0, & \text{if } p_L^e > p^* \\ [0,1], & \text{if } p_L^e = p^* \\ 1, & \text{if } p_L^e < p^* \end{cases}. \tag{4.5}$$

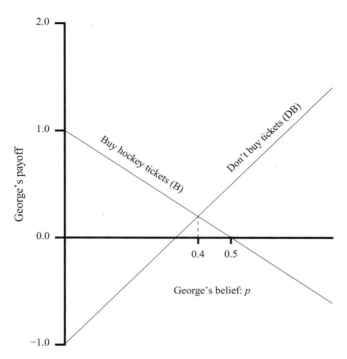

Figure 4.2
George's payoffs as a function of his beliefs.

Rational choice theory, as modeled by subjective expected utility theory, simply predicts that George chooses a strategy to maximize his utility *given* his beliefs. The central question of game theory is how to model the formation of these beliefs. Lucy carries out the same calculus and forms a belief p_G^e regarding the probability that George chooses B. In that case, her best response correspondence, where ρ_L is the probability that Lucy chooses B, is given by:

$$r^L\left(p_G^e\right) = \arg \max_{\rho \in [0,1]} U^L\left(\rho, p_G^e\right) = \begin{cases} 0, & \text{if } p_G^e > p^{**} \\ [0,1], & \text{if } p_G^e = p^{**} \\ 1, & \text{if } p_G^e < p^{**} \end{cases} , \qquad (4.6)$$

where $p^{**} = 0.4$ is the strategy by George that makes Lucy indifferent between buying and not buying the opera tickets.[18]

In this case all strategies are rationalizable; even though preferences are well defined and it is common knowledge that both parties are rational, there is no way to make a prediction if the only assumption one makes is that it is common knowledge that parties are rational. This illustrates the important point that rational choice theory alone is not sufficient for making a unique prediction regarding individual behavior in strategic situations. At one level this may seem unsatisfactory, but then again it does appear to be consistent with the casual observation that making predictions about economic events seems to be a difficult, if not impossible, task!

This book is concerned with incentive contracts—the kinds of agreements that individuals would make in the shadow of rational choice by parties. As a matter of law, a necessary condition for a contract to be enforceable is that parties have achieved a "meeting of the minds." This requirement can be modeled by supposing that individuals know or agree on how each person should or will act. This assumption combined with rationalizability implies the concept of a Nash equilibrium (Nash 1950).

4.4 Nash Equilibrium

The Nash equilibrium concept was first introduced by Cournot ([1838] 1974) in his famous formulation of the duopoly problem. He envisioned two firms adjusting their output in each period to maximize their profits given the other firm's output during the last period. He showed this process leads to an outcome in which each firm's output is optimal given the other firm's strategy. John Nash (1950) extended this idea to allow for an arbitrary number of players and provided a general existence proof. In the context of our model of rational choice, the Nash equilibrium concept adds to the criteria of rationalizability the requirement that each player correctly anticipates how the others will play.

Formally, consider a game (in normal form) given by $G = \left\{ \Gamma^i, U^i \right\}_{i \in N}$, where $N = \left\{ 1, \ldots, \bar{N} \right\}$ is the set of players, Γ^i is the set of strategies available to player i, and $U^i(\gamma)$, $\gamma \in \Gamma = \Gamma^1 \times \ldots \times \Gamma^n$ is the utility for player i. These can refer to either the pure or mixed strategies. As there is only one information set for each player, the behavioral and mixed strategies are identical.

Definition 4.4 *A strategy vector $\gamma^* \in \Gamma$ is a* Nash equilibrium *for the game $G = \left\{ \Gamma^i, U^i \right\}_{i \in N}$ if for every $i \in N$:*

$$U^i\left(\gamma^*\right) \geq U^i\left(\gamma^i, \gamma^{-i*}\right), \text{ for every } \gamma^i \in \Gamma^i. \qquad (4.7)$$

The vector $\left(\gamma^i, \gamma^{-i*}\right)$ represents γ^*, with the i'th coordinate replaced by γ^i. This definition does not depend upon the nature of the strategy space Γ and applies equally to the case where Γ is an infinite set, as in the case of mixed strategies. If the mixed strategies are defined over a finite set of pure strategies, then Nash (1950) proved the existence of an equilibrium. See exercise 8 for the proof.

Consider again the case of Lucy and George. Suppose they can agree beforehand that George will buy the hockey tickets when he goes to work. Notice that at the time George buys the tickets Lucy cannot observe this action, nor will she know the outcome until arriving home in the evening. Consequently, George buys the tickets because he *believes* Lucy will not buy the opera tickets and knows that he is better off with this action. This agreement is *self-enforcing*: both individuals have the same beliefs and have an incentive to follow through on the agreement.

For this game there also exists a mixed strategy Nash equilibrium. We can find this equilibrium by observing that Nash equilibria are best responses to the other player's strategy, and thus a mixed strategy pair (ρ_G, ρ_L) forms a Nash equilibrium if:

$$\rho_G \in r^L\left(\rho_L\right), \qquad (4.8)$$

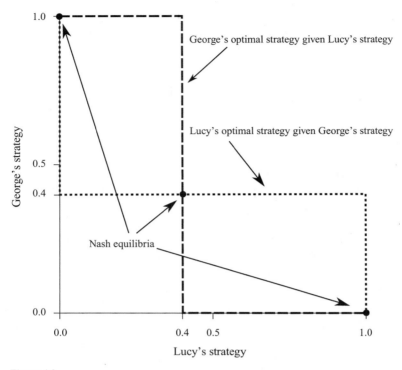

Figure 4.3
Response functions for the battle of the sexes game.

$$\rho_L \in r^G\left(\rho_G\right), \tag{4.9}$$

where these best response functions are defined in (4.5) and (4.6). The response functions for this game are illustrated in figure 4.3. In the case of George, it is optimal to buy the hockey tickets when the probability of Lucy buying the opera tickets is between 0 and 0.4. If Lucy chooses buy (B) with a probability of 0.4, then George is indifferent between buying and not buying. The situation is similar for Lucy. Thus, in this game there are three Nash equilibria: $(1, 0)$, $(0, 1)$, and $(0.4, 0.4)$. The first two equilibria are called pure strategy equilibria, while $(0.4, 0.4)$ is called a mixed strategy equilibrium because it entails randomization by at least one of the players.

The concept of a Nash equilibrium has proven to be quite durable in economics. It is almost universally accepted as a necessary condition for rational play. Strictly speaking, it is a purely static concept that is much more restrictive than the hypothesis of rational choice alone. One possible reason for its durability is that it is the plausible outcome of a number of different strategic situations. The first of these, as discussed above, is Cournot's dynamic duopoly model in which players are assumed to choose the optimal strategy with beliefs determined by the previous period's play. There is now vast literature exploring various behavioral foundations for the concept of a Nash equilibrium.[19]

For the purposes of contract and incentive theory, the Nash equilibrium concept is a natural *necessary* condition.[20] If it is common knowledge that two parties are rational then each would expect the other party to take actions consistent with their self-interest (as represented by their preferences).[21] A key feature of a legally binding contract is that parties have a *meeting of the minds*, a condition that is formally captured by the requirement that one's beliefs regarding the other person's play are correct. The rest of this book heavily relies upon this interpretation of a Nash equilibrium. However, a Nash equilibrium is not always a *sufficient* condition to capture the *meeting of the minds* interpretation of the concept.

4.5 The Problem of Commitment

This section shows that in many situations, the Nash equilibrium concept is not a *sufficient* condition for rational choice in many situations. A modified battle of the sexes game can illustrate this point. Suppose that George (the one who prefers opera) has the first chance to buy the hockey tickets and then leaves a message for Lucy saying whether he was able to buy the tickets. Lucy then decides whether to buy opera tickets *after* George has made his move. The strategies and payoffs can be illustrated using the extensive form, as shown in figure 4.4.

In this figure I1, I2, and I3 denote the information sets (nodes) for this game. In this case, George has no information when deciding what to do, but Lucy knows George's choice at the time she decides, and therefore is able to make a different decision depending upon whether she has information I2 or I3. Here the strategy is a pair that specifies how she will play in each information set. For example $\{B, DB\}$ represents B if I2 occurs (George buys the hockey tickets) and DB if I3 occurs (George does not buy the tickets). Lucy has four possible strategies. Given the payoffs at the terminal nodes T1–T4, the normal form for this game is given in table 4.3.

This game has three pure strategy Nash equilibria: $\{DB, \{B, B\}\}$, and $\{DB, \{DB, B\}\}$, resulting in an outcome of $(2, 1)$, while $\{B, \{DB, DB\}\}$ results in outcome $(1, 2)$. An interesting feature of the third equilibrium is that it requires Lucy not to buy opera tickets if George does not buy hockey tickets. This equilibrium has a familiar interpretation; it corresponds to Lucy saying to George:

"You better buy the hockey tickets, because under no condition will I buy the opera tickets."

This action appears to be an *incredible threat*. It supposes that if, for whatever reason, George does not buy the hockey tickets, then Lucy will, against her own self-interest, not buy the opera tickets. This is because Lucy prefers to go out to the opera rather than not go out at all, which is what would happen if she did not buy the opera tickets. However, it *is* a Nash equilibrium. If Lucy believes that George will indeed buy the tickets, this threat of not buying the opera tickets is optimal. The root of the problem is that rational learning theory has no satisfactory way to deal with zero probability events. Namely, at the equilibrium $\{B, \{DB, DB\}\}$, Lucy assigns zero probability to George's not buying the tickets. This implies that even if Lucy observes that George has not bought the hockey tickets, the strict application of Bayes's rule implies that she ignores this information.[22] Notice that the Nash equilibrium $\{DB, \{B, B\}\}$ is also problematic, but for a different reason. Now, Lucy is threatening to buy hockey tickets, even if George buys the opera tickets. In this case, the incredible threat is to purchase tickets to both events.

Selten (1975) provides the most widely accepted solution to the problem. He proceeds in two steps. The first is to recognize that if individuals are rational then their behavior is

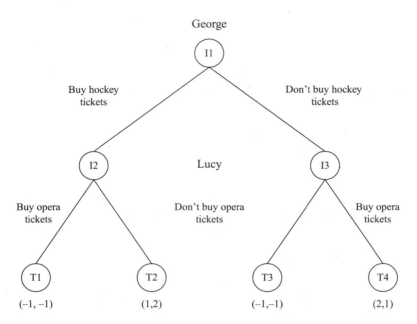

Figure 4.4
Extensive form for battle of the sexes game.

Table 4.3
Normal form for the battle of the sexes game

	Lucy			
George	{B,B}	{B,DB}	{DB,B}	{DB,DB}
DB	$(2,1)^*$	$(-1,-1)$	$(2,1)^*$	$(-1,-1)$
B	$(-1,-1)$	$(-1,-1)$	$(1,2)$	$(1,2)^*$

completely determined by their preferences. Hence, each time a person plays one should have the same outcome if this person were replaced by a new player whose preferences are the same as other players in the game with the same index. The attentive reader will notice that this assumption ensures that the set of behavioral strategies and mixed strategies are always the same.

This procedure transforms the original game into one that Selten calls the *agent normal form*. It ensures that each time a choice is made, it is done with respect to only the information available at the time the choice is made. This in turn eliminates the possibility of incredible threats. Referring back to the construction of the extensive form, the agent normal form requires that for each information set, E_{tk}, one creates a new player with the same preferences as player i_{tk}, the player who will choose an action at stage t.

Second, to deal with zero probability events, Selten requires the equilibrium to be stable against a perturbation of the game that results in all information sets being reached with strictly positive probability. This requirement ensures that players can always use Bayes's rule to update their beliefs when an information set is reached. The result is Selten's (1975)

Table 4.4
Agent normal form

	Lucy 2		Lucy 3	
George	B	DB	B	DB
DB			$(2,1,1)$	$(-1,-1,-1)$
B	$(-1,-1,-1)$	$(1,2,2)$		

concept of a *trembling hand perfect equilibrium*, also known as a *perfect equilibrium*. In our example, this would have the effect of creating two Lucys—Lucy-2 who plays when event $I2$ occurs, and Lucy-3 who plays when $I3$ occurs. In that case, the normal form of the game is shown in table 4.4.

In this game there are now three pure strategy Nash equilibria: $\{B, DB, DB\}$, $\{DB, DB, B\}$, and $\{DB, B, B\}$. Consider the equilibrium $\{B, DB, DB\}$, and suppose there is a small chance that George plays DB. In that case, Lucy-2 would optimally choose B rather than DB. That is, a small perturbation in B's strategy leads to a large change in Lucy's strategy. Therefore, this equilibrium is *not stable*. More formally, suppose that each player i chooses strategy $\gamma \in \Gamma^i$ with probability of at least $\varepsilon_\gamma^i > 0$, and let $\hat{\epsilon} = \left\{ \varepsilon_\gamma^i \right\}_{i \in N, \gamma \in \Gamma^i}$. Denote this new strategy space by $\hat{\Gamma}_{\hat{\epsilon}}^i$.

Definition 4.5 *Given any game represented by its agent normal form,* $\left\{ U^i, \Gamma^i \right\}_{i \in N}$, *then the mixed strategy* γ^* *is a* perfect equilibrium *if there exists a sequence of Nash equilibria* $\gamma_{\hat{\epsilon}_n}^*$ *for the perturbed game* $\left\{ U^i, \hat{\Gamma}_{\hat{\epsilon}_n}^i \right\}_{i \in N}$, *such that as* $\hat{\epsilon}_n \to \hat{0}$, *then* $\gamma_{\hat{\epsilon}_n}^* \to \gamma^*$.

The expression, $\gamma_{\hat{\epsilon}_n}^* \to \gamma^*$ means that the probability of each action in $\gamma_{\hat{\epsilon}_n}^*$ converges to the probability for the corresponding action in γ^* as $\hat{\epsilon}_n$ converges to $\hat{0}$. The proof of existence follows from the existence of a Nash equilibrium and the fact that the set of mixed strategies is closed. See exercise 8.

Perfect equilibria have the property that they are "close" to some Nash equilibrium in the perturbed game. Even though this concept is defined in terms of local stability, it has some rather remarkable decision theoretic properties, including the elimination of "incredible" threats. The connection between perfect equilibria and decision theory is worked out in Kreps and Wilson (1982). They introduce a number of desirable properties that an equilibrium should satisfy and show that perfect equilibria satisfy these properties.

To fix these ideas, consider the game illustrated in figure 4.5. This game has two Nash equilibria that depend upon what George believes Lucy will do, which in turn depends upon Lucy's beliefs regarding George. Suppose Lucy thinks George will play u, then the ex ante probability of Lucy's making a choice is zero. Hence, it is a Nash equilibrium for George to choose u and for Lucy to choose L.

Notice that Bayesian decision theory is of no use to Lucy because she does not expect to play, and therefore there is no way for her to update her beliefs. In particular, Lucy's decision is *inconsistent* with the hypothesis that she is a rational decision maker in Savage's sense. That is to say, suppose George does choose l or r; then Lucy will be called on to

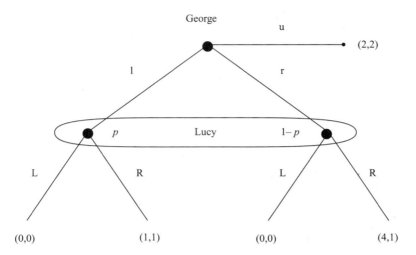

Figure 4.5
Beliefs in extensive form.

make a choice. In Savage's model, when this occurs, Lucy must first build a model of how George has decided and then choose an action.

Given this algorithm, regardless of Lucy's beliefs about George, she would always select R. The point is that rational choice, even in this relatively simple environment, entails the consideration of counterfactuals and potential outcomes, the basis of causal identification discussed in chapter 2. The building block of modern empirical analysis is the use of random noise—introduced either explicitly via an experiment or from some natural event—to identify the consequence of choice.

One might hope to be able to define rational choice without the introduction of "errors," but that seems impossible. To determine how Lucy will play in this game, George has to either explicitly experiment by not choosing u or consider what would happen if he did experiment with choices l or r. The need for random consideration of alternative choices is true even for finite, but large, games such as chess and Go. Even though these games have deterministic solutions, the best algorithms for playing them entail the introduction of random experimentation (see Silver et al. 2017).

Thus, if George believes that Lucy is rational in Savage's sense, then he must suppose that conditional upon being given a choice, Lucy must form a belief over George's play, given by p, the probability that George chose l. We call this probability Lucy's *beliefs* at this information set. Given these beliefs, she would always choose R for all beliefs $p \in [0, 1]$. Hence, George will always play r, never u or l. Given this, Lucy would rationally set $p = 0$. In this case it is easy to see that the unique perfect equilibrium occurs when George chooses r and Lucy chooses R.

More generally, let G be an extensive form game with a perfect equilibrium $\gamma^* \in \Gamma$, and suppose that $\hat{\gamma}_{\varepsilon_n}$ is the sequence of strategies in the perturbed game that is converging to γ^*. Let us suppose that it is in agent form and we index players by tk, where t is date of decision, k indexes the information sets at date t, with the utility function of agent tk given by $U^{i_{tk}}$. In addition, we now keep track of the beliefs of the players. Let μ_{tk} be a probability distribution over the nodes in E_{tk}, with the interpretation that these represent the beliefs of player tk at this information set. These are called *beliefs*. Consistent with the Nash equilibrium concept, it is assumed that the strategies of the players are common knowledge, which in turn places some structure upon beliefs.

Because the strategies $\hat{\gamma}_{\varepsilon_n}$ are completely mixed, then each node in the game occurs with positive probability. For each information set, E_{tk}, we can define the probability of a node $n \in E_{tk}$ occurring, conditional upon reaching this information set, as given by:

$$\mu_{tk}^{\varepsilon_n}(n) = \frac{\Pr(n|\hat{\gamma}_{\varepsilon_n})}{\Pr(E_{tk}|\hat{\gamma}_{\varepsilon_n})} > 0. \tag{4.10}$$

The probability distribution $\mu_{tk}^{\varepsilon_n}$ is called player i_{tk}'s beliefs at information set E_{tk}. Given that beliefs come from a compact set and there is a finite number of possible information sets, then we can take a subsequence that ensures there are limit points: $\mu_{tk} = \lim_{n\to\infty} \mu_{tk}^{\varepsilon_n}$. In general, not all information sets are reached in equilibrium; nevertheless these limit beliefs are defined for *all* information sets. Together, the strategy profile γ, and the beliefs, $\mu = \{\mu_{tk}\}_{E_{tk}\in\Phi}$ are called an *assessment*, denoted by (μ, γ).

This structure allows one to formally model how a rational person would play if there is a deviation from the equilibrium strategy. In particular, for each information set E_{tk}, one can define a "subgame" that corresponds to the occurrence of E_{tk}. Let r_{tk} define the root at which Nature plays, and select the nodes in E_{tk} with probabilities given by the probability distribution μ_{tk}. The set of nodes for the game is given by $S(E_{tk}) \cap \Sigma$, with final nodes $S(E_{tk}) \cap Z$, where the payoffs are defined as before. Consider strategies that are restricted to these nodes. Let $\mu_{tk}(z|\gamma)$ be the probability distribution over z in this restricted game; then for each information set E_{tk} let $G_{tk}(\mu) = \{\Gamma^i, U_{tk}^i\}_{i\in N}$ denote the game in normal form where:

$$U_{tk}^i(\gamma) = \sum_{z\in Z} u^i(z)\mu_{tk}(z|\gamma).$$

This allows us to define rational choice at any information set in a game.

Definition 4.6 *Given an assessment (μ, γ^*) for an extensive form game, then it is sequentially rational if for every player $i = i_{tk}$ and game $G_{tk}(\mu)$:*

$$U_{tk}^i(\gamma^*) \geq U_{tk}^i(\gamma'^i, \gamma^{-i*}), \forall \gamma'^i \in \Gamma^i.$$

Sequential rationality is the requirement that each party chooses optimally at the time they make a choice. It is stronger than the notion of a Nash equilibrium because whenever a player finds herself in a situation that is not consistent with equilibrium play, then she must, consistent with Savage's model, build a new model of the world that is consistent with the available evidence, such as finding herself at an off-equilibrium information set. She then chooses optimally given this new model of the world. It turns out that the notion of a perfect equilibrium is consistent with sequential rationality.

Proposition 4.7 *Let γ^* be a perfect equilibrium strategy profile of the game G with finite payoffs, and let $\mu = \{\mu_{tk}\}_{E_{tk}\in\Phi}$ be a set of beliefs associated with this equilibrium. Then the assessment (μ, γ^*) is sequentially rational.*

Proof. Suppose that the strategy is not sequentially rational; then there is an information set E_{tk}, player i, and associated action, a'_{tk} such that $U^i_{tk}(\gamma'^i, \gamma^{-i*}) > U^i_{tk}(\gamma^*)$, where γ'^i is the same as γ^{i*}, except at information set E_{tk} where a'_{tk} is played. Let $\delta = U^i_{tk}(\gamma'^i, \gamma^{-i*}) - U^i_{tk}(\gamma^*) > 0$. Let γ^n be the completely mixed Nash equilibrium converging to γ^* used to define the perfect equilibrium, and let ϵ^n be the associated minimum probability with which each strategy in the Agent normal form is played. Let $\tilde{\gamma}^{in}$ be a completely mixed strategy that is identical to γ^{in} except it converges to choosing a_{tk} at information set E_{tk}. Then there is an n' such that $\left| U^i_{tk}(\gamma'^i, \gamma^{-i*}) - U^i_{tk}(\tilde{\gamma}^{in'}, \gamma^{-in'}) \right| < \delta/3$ and $\left| U^i_{tk}(\gamma^{n'}) - U^i_{tk}(\gamma^*) \right| < \delta/3$. Thus, we have:

$$U^i_{tk}(\tilde{\gamma}^{in'}, \gamma^{-in'}) - U^i_{tk}(\gamma^{n'})$$

$$= U^i_{tk}(\gamma'^i, \gamma^{-i*}) - U^i_{tk}(\gamma^*) - U^i_{tk}(\gamma'^i, \gamma^{-i*}) + U^i_{tk}(\tilde{\gamma}^{in'}, \gamma^{-in'}) - U^i_{tk}(\gamma^{n'}) + U^i_{tk}(\gamma^*)$$

$$\geq U^i_{tk}(\gamma'^i, \gamma^{-i*}) - U^i_{tk}(\gamma^*) - \left| U^i_{tk}(\gamma'^i, \gamma^{-i*}) - U^i_{tk}(\tilde{\gamma}^{in'}, \gamma^{-in'}) \right| - \left| U^i_{tk}(\gamma^{n'}) - U^i_{tk}(\gamma^*) \right|$$

$$> \delta - \delta/3 - \delta/3$$

$$> 0.$$

Hence, $\gamma^{in'}$ is not a best response at E_{tk}. But since the γ^n is completely mixed, this implies that E_{ik} is reached with strictly positive probability. The payoffs for $z \notin S(E_{tk})$ have the same probabilities of occurring under $\gamma^{in'}$ and γ^{in}, from which we conclude that γ^n is not a Nash equilibrium in the perturbed game, contradicting the hypothesis that γ^* is a perfect equilibrium.   □

From this result we obtain the following corollary:

Corollary 4.8 *Suppose that the game G_{tk} defines a proper subgame in the sense that all information sets are either a successor to E_{tk} or not: for all $E \in \Phi$, $E \cap S(E_{tk}) \in \{E, \emptyset\}$. Then if γ^* is a perfect equilibrium strategy profile of the game G, it is also a Nash equilibrium strategy profile of the game G_{tk}.*

When G_{tk} is a proper subgame, then there is only one node at the root of the game; and hence all assessments assign probability 1 to this node and therefore do not need to be specified. This result can be used to eliminate some equilibria in the game between Lucy and George without resorting to the construction of a perturbed game. We can solve the game illustrated in figure 4.4 by backward induction: go to the last period, then consider a game for which each of the final period information sets is reached with probability 1. It is clear that in this case Lucy has a unique optimal strategy, namely, buy the opera tickets if and only if George has not bought the hockey tickets. Given these choices, George's unique best choice is to not buy the hockey tickets. As this is the only outcome, this is the unique perfect equilibrium of this game.

In simple normal form games, one can use dominance arguments to find the perfect equilibria. Given that perfect equilibria are constructed from games that place positive probability weights on all strategies, then any strategy with the feature that it is dominated by another strategy would not be used. Here, dominance is defined as follows:

Definition 4.9 *Given a game $G = \{U^i, \Gamma^i\}_{i \in N}$, then a strategy γ^i is weakly dominated by $\tilde{\gamma}^i$ if for every $\gamma^{-i} \in \Gamma^{-i}$ it is the case that $U^i(\tilde{\gamma}^i, \gamma^{-i}) \geq U^i(\gamma^i, \gamma^{-i})$, with strict inequality for at least one strategy profile $\gamma^{-i} \in \Gamma^{-i}$. A strategy profile γ is weakly undominated if for each player i there exists no $\tilde{\gamma}^i$ that weakly dominates player i's strategy.*

It is straightforward to show the following proposition:

Proposition 4.10 *Consider the game $G = \{U^i, \Gamma^i\}_{i \in N}$. If γ^* is a perfect equilibrium, then it is weakly undominated.*

The converse is not true; namely, in the case of three or more players, if a strategy is weakly undominated, this does not necessarily imply that it is part of a perfect equilibrium. Rather, the converse is true only in the case of two-player games:

Proposition 4.11 *Consider the two-person game $G = \{U^i, \Gamma^i\}_{i \in \{1,2\}}$. Then γ^* is a perfect equilibrium if and only if it is weakly undominated.*

See van Damme (1991, sec. 3.2) for a proof of this result.

4.6   Sequential Equilibria and Other Solution Concepts

We have shown that Selten's perfect equilibrium concept provides an elegant solution to the problem of how to model rational play in a game. We have also shown that his concept can be made consistent with Savage's theory of rational choice using the definition of assessments, μ_{tk}, via (4.10), defined for information sets E_{tk}. This in turn allowed us to define the notion of *sequential rationality*, via proposition 4.7.

Kreps and Wilson (1982) observe that perfect equilibria are difficult to compute for games with even modest complexity. Moreover, there is no accepted definition of a perfect equilibrium for games with an infinite strategy space. To address this problem, Kreps and Wilson suggest turning the tables on the definition of an equilibrium by making necessary conditions of a perfect equilibrium sufficient. In this section, we use this idea to define three widely used definitions of "self-enforcing" behavior: sequential equilibria, perfect Bayesian (Nash) equilibria, and subgame perfect (Nash) equilibria (SPNE).[23]

Kreps and Wilson's (1982) notion of a sequential equilibrium begins by making beliefs a primitive of the model rather than deriving them from the definition of a perfect equilibrium. Above it was shown that any perfect equilibrium can be used to define a probability distribution over each information set, $\mu = \mu_{tk E_{tk} \in \Phi}$. Now an equilibrium to the game is described by the pair, $\{\mu, \gamma\}$, which Kreps and Wilson call an *assessment*. They say that beliefs are *consistent* with a strategy profile γ if they are the limit point of beliefs derived via equation (4.10) from any sequence of completely mixed strategies that converges to γ. Thus we have:

Definition 4.12 *An assessment consisting of a strategy profile γ and associated beliefs μ is a* sequential equilibrium *if:*

1. *The beliefs are consistent with γ.*

2. *The strategies are sequentially rational (definition 4.6).*

The difference between a sequential equilibrium and a perfect equilibrium is that the former does not require the test sequence of completely mixed strategies used to generate the beliefs to form a Nash equilibrium in the perturbed game. Given this weaker requirement we have immediately:

Proposition 4.13 *Every perfect equilibrium of a finite game $G = \{U^i, \Gamma^i\}_{i \in N}$ is also a sequential equilibrium.*

See exercise 8 for the proof. This ensures that a sequential equilibrium exists for finite games. Kreps and Wilson (1982) also show that the two concepts do not coincide, and it is quite easy to see why. Proposition 4.11 shows that in two-person normal form games, weakly dominated strategies cannot be part of a perfect equilibrium, even though they can form a Nash equilibrium. Nash equilibria in a normal form game are sequential equilibria, which shows that perfect equilibria are a *refinement* of sequential equilibria.

Proposition 6 of Kreps and Wilson (1982) provides a weaker version of perfect equilibrium that is equivalent to a sequential equilibrium. They achieve this by using test sequences in which both the beliefs and the payoffs are perturbed. Their paper concludes with the observation that the key ingredient in their model is that by disentangling beliefs from choice, as in the Savage model, one is better able to choose between different ways to model self-enforcing behavior in strategic situations.

4.6.1   Perfect Bayesian Nash Equilibria

Even though the notion of a sequential equilibrium is in principle easier to compute than a perfect equilibrium, this does not mean that it is easy to compute! Moreover, it is not clear how to extend the definition to games with continuum strategy spaces, such as the classical Cournot quantity setting model.

The difficulty arises in determining how to construct the test sequences for beliefs that are needed in order to have well-defined beliefs for information sets that are not reached in equilibrium. Fudenberg and Tirole (1991) suggest a further weakening of the sequential equilibrium concept that is not only easier to compute, but extends naturally to situations with continuous strategy spaces:

Definition 4.14   *An assessment (μ, γ) forms a* perfect Bayesian equilibrium *in an extensive form game G if:*

1. *The strategies are sequentially rational.*

2. *For every game, G_{tk}, corresponding to information set E_{tk}, for any information set $E \subset S(E_{tk})$, if $\Pr\{E | \gamma, E_{tk}\} > 0$, then for each $n \in E$ it must be the case that:*

$$\mu_E(n) = \frac{\Pr(n | \gamma, E_{tk})}{\Pr(E | \gamma, E_{tk})}, \tag{4.11}$$

where μ_E is the belief at information set E, and $\Pr(\cdot | \gamma, E_{tk})$ is the probability measure over the nodes in $S(E_{tk})$ defined by the assessment.

At an equilibrium, beliefs should be consistent with equilibrium play whenever possible. "Whenever possible" means that at any information set that is reached with positive probability under equilibrium play, one can use Bayes's rule, (4.11), to compute the beliefs. If the probability of reaching an information set is zero in equilibrium, then the perfect Bayesian equilibrium concept places no restriction on beliefs. The construction of examples for which perfect Bayesian and sequential equilibria differ is left as an exercise.

4.6.2 Subgame Perfect Nash Equilibria

Corollary 4.8 shows that perfect equilibria have the property that they define a Nash equilibrium for every subgame of the extensive form. This property can also be used as a sufficient condition for self-enforcement.

Definition 4.15 *A strategy profile γ is a subgame perfect Nash equilibrium (SPNE) if for every information set E_{tk} that is a singleton (consists of a single node), with the property that the corresponding subgame G_{tk} is a proper subgame, then $\hat{\gamma}$ is a Nash equilibrium when restricted to the subgame G_{tk}.*

This concept was first introduced by Selten (1965) and is widely used for the study of repeated games, meaning situations in which individuals meet repeatedly to play a game in normal form. It is assumed that the outcomes from the previous plays of the game are observed by all parties. Consequently, each information set is a single node. This, combined with sequential rationality, implies that the set of sequential equilibria and SPNE coincide. This class of games is important for the theory of relational contracts reviewed in chapter 9.

4.7 Repeated Games and the Payoff Possibilities Set

This section provides a very brief introduction to repeated game theory. Rather than focus on modeling the strategy chosen by a rational player, the theory focuses on characterizing the set of *payoffs* that are *self-enforcing*. The point is that in situations in which players meet over time, there are many possible equilibrium strategies. The first step is characterizing the set of payoffs that result when parties play some self-enforcing equilibrium. The second question is which payoff will parties choose? This question can be framed as a bargaining problem, whose solution is discussed at length in chapter 5.

Keep in mind the distinction between a repeated game and a relational contract (the subject of chapter 9). The goal of game theory is to study how rational individuals choose strategies for *any* strategic game. In contrast, a contract is the *design* of a game that rational individuals would play, including the payoffs they would receive after different choices. Contract theory's goal is to achieve a particular allocation of resources, and thus it is less concerned with understanding all the behavior that is possible in a game, except to the extent that the contract needs to anticipate future behavior and ensure that parties have the incentive to perform as promised. The theory of repeated games is useful for contract design because it provides a portfolio of payoffs that can be achieved with self-enforcing behavior.

Any SPNE payoff in an infinitely or finitely repeated game with symmetric information can be achieved using strategies with the following form. First, individuals agree, either implicitly or explicitly, on payoffs and the associated choices that will generate these payoffs each period. Second, individuals are expected to follow the actions leading to these payoffs. Should an individual deviate from this agreement, then in the next period the SPNE is played that gives the lowest payoff to the person who has *breached* the implicit agreement.[24] This strategy provides necessary and sufficient conditions for the characterization of all payoffs that can be supported by some SPNE. Thus, the characterization of the set of equilibrium payoffs can be reduced to the problem of finding the SPNE that yields the lowest payoff for each player.

This result follows from the theory of dynamic programming. Optimal decision making over time can be reduced to a trade-off between current payoffs and a reduced-form representation of the future defined by a *value function*. Beginning with the work of Abreu (1988), we can apply this same kind of reasoning to games played over time when it is assumed that the game played each period is the same.

The approach here follows Abreu, Pearce, and Stacchetti (1990), who show that one can represent the future payoffs in terms of a payoff possibilities set. The notation and technical development are based upon Bergin and MacLeod (1993b), who, building on Telser (1980), view strategies in a repeated game as a self-enforcing agreement between two parties. Reaching an *agreement* means that parties have correct expectations regarding how their counterparties will play.

4.7.1   Repeated Game Payoffs

Consider a two-person normal form game, $G = \{u^i, A^i\}_{i=1,2}$, where the space A^i has n_i possible actions denoted by $a^i \in A^i = \{a_1^i, \dots, a_{n_i}^i\}, i = 1, 2$. The results of this characterization extend easily to more than two players (see Myerson 1991 for details). The game is played repeatedly in periods $t = 0, 1, 2, \dots, T-1$, where T can be finite or infinite. The following sequence of steps is played each period:

1. The history of the game, given by the sequence of plays and public randomizations, and denoted by $h^t \in H^t$, is observed by both players.

2. The players observe the common shock, $p^t \in [0, 1]$, that is uniformly distributed over $[0, 1]$ and independently drawn each period.

3. Each player chooses an action $a^{it} \in A^i$.

4. Each player realizes payoff $u^{it} = u^i(a^{1t}, a^{2t})$.

The introduction of a common shock in step 2 is a formal way to implement public randomization in the repeated game. It allows us to have a convex payoff space while avoiding the complexity that comes with the use of mixed strategies. If mixed strategies are used, then if players observe only actions, they do not know the probability that an action is chosen, and hence there are no proper subgames each period, making the analysis intractable. The use of public randomization results in a convex set of payoffs, while allowing us to restrict attention to SPNE rather than the more complex sequential equilibrium concept.

With public randomization, players can coordinate different actions for different realizations of p^t. Given that p^t and the actions chosen in period t are observed, then players are able to detect deviations from any agreement before the start of play in period $t+1$. Agreeing to different actions for different realizations of p^t allows players in expectation to realize payoffs that are convex combinations of payoffs from the one-period normal form game.[25]

The choice in period t is given by a (measurable) function:[26]

$$s^{it} : [0, 1] \to A^i.$$

Given a pair of choices, $s^t = \{s^{1t}, s^{2t}\} \in S = S^1 \times S^2$, where S^i is the set of possible choices in period t for player i, the *event* $E(a, s^t)$ that generates an action $a = \{a^1, a^2\} \in A = A^1 \times A^2$ is defined by:

$$E(a, s^t) = \left\{ p^t \in [0, 1]^2 \,|\, s^t(p^t) = a \right\}.$$

The corresponding probability that action a is chosen (and observed) is given by:

$$\lambda(a, s^t) = Pr\left\{ E(a, s^t) \right\}.$$

Without loss of generality, suppose that whenever $\lambda(a, s^t) = 0$ then $E(a, s^t) = \emptyset$.[27] The payoff for player i in period t is:

$$u^i(s^t) = \int_0^1 u^i(s^t(p)) \, dp = \sum_{a \in A} u^i(a) \, \lambda(a, s^t). \tag{4.12}$$

The set of possible payoffs is given by the convex, compact set:

$$F = conv\left(\left\{ u^1(a), u^2(a) \right\} | a \in A \right) \subset \Re^2,$$

where *conv* denotes the convexification of the set.[28] This defines all the payoff possibilities within the stage game. Players are strategic, which implies that when faced with an opponent who wishes to lower her payoff, a player can always mitigate by choosing the action that maximizes her payoff after each opponent's action. Namely, player i can always ensure that she gets at least:

$$\bar{u}^i = \min_{s^j \in S^j} \max_{s^i \in S^i} u^i\left(s^1, s^2 \right), \; j \neq i. \tag{4.13}$$

This is the amount that player i can guarantee regardless of player j's action. This is called the individually rational payoff or the minimax payoff. The definition explicitly assumes that player i correctly anticipates player j's action. Accordingly, define the set of *individually rational* payoffs for the normal form game G by:

$$\bar{F} = \left\{ u \in F | u^i \geq \bar{u}^i, \; i = 1, 2 \right\}.$$

Let A^{NE} be the set of Nash equilibrium actions when parties do not condition on the public randomization device, with payoffs given by $\{u^1(a), u^2(a)\}$, $a \in A^{NE}$. We have the following result.

Proposition 4.16 *The set of Nash equilibrium payoffs for the game G is given by:*

$$F^{NE} = conv\left\{ u^1(a), u^2(a) \,|\, a \in A^{NE} \right\} = \left\{ u^1(s), u^2(s) \,|\, s \in S^{NE} \right\} \subset \bar{F},$$

where S^{NE} is the set of Nash equilibrium choices for game G.

The proof is straightforward and left to the reader. This set is sometimes called the set of outcomes generated by *correlated equilibria* because parties can correlate their choices via the public signal p^t. Rather than introducing a new equilibrium concept, the correlation signal is part of the definition of the game, which in turn ensures that the set of Nash equilibrium payoffs is convex. Given that mixed strategies are not allowed, one needs an additional assumption to ensure that a Nash equilibrium exists:

Assumption (Existence) There exists at least one Nash equilibrium for the game G, namely $F^{NE} \neq \emptyset$.

The payoffs for the repeated game and the associated strategies can now be described. The standard repeated game model assumes that parties play at periods $t = 0, 1, \ldots, T$. If $T < \infty$, this is a finitely repeated game; otherwise, one has an infinitely repeated game. Later chapters address how information and the discount rate affect the set of possible equilibria. It is easier to think about these issues if one can distinguish between a player's discount rate and the length of time between a period. To do this, the repeated game payoffs are derived from a model of continuous time play.

Suppose the length of a period is Δ units (seconds or days) long. At the beginning of period t, the sequence of four steps described above is carried out, immediately resulting in actions a^t that are held fixed for the period after p^t is observed. This yields a *flow* payoff $u^i(a^t)$ for player i. Each player has the same interest rate given by r; thus the payoff in period t is given by:

$$\int_0^\Delta u^i(a^t) e^{-r\tau} d\tau = \frac{(1 - e^{-r\Delta})}{r} u^i(a^t).$$

The per-period discount rate is defined by $\delta = e^{-r\Delta}$. Notice that holding the interest rate, $r > 0$, fixed, which decreases the length of a period, increases the discount rate.

When the game is repeated each period, we suppose that players agree, either tacitly or explicitly, on the choices s^t to play each period. Let $s = \{s^0, s^1, \ldots, s^{T-1}\} \in S^T$ denote this agreement, where T is the number of periods, which may be infinite. The payoff under this sequence in the repeated game starting in period τ is defined by:

$$U^i(s, \tau) = \frac{(1 - \delta)}{(1 - \delta^{T-\tau})} \sum_{t=\tau}^{T-1} \delta^{t-\tau} u^i(s^t).$$

Let $U^i(s) = U^i(s, 0)$ be the payoff at the beginning of the game. The normalization factor,

$$v(r, \Delta, T - \tau) = \frac{(1 - \delta)}{(1 - \delta^{T-\tau})} = \frac{(1 - e^{-r\Delta})}{1 - e^{-(T-\tau)r\Delta}}, \tag{4.14}$$

renormalizes the payoff stream so that regardless of the values for the interest rate r, the duration of a period, Δ, or and the number of periods T, we have that $U(s) = \{U^1(s), U^2(s)\} \in F$.

In summary, a repeated game represents two parties in a relationship in which they make choices that are held fixed for $\Delta > 0$ units of time. A *period* corresponds to Δ units of time. The relationship lasts T periods, and therefore $\Delta \times T$ units of time (which might be infinite). Utility is discounted at the rate of r, and hence the one-period discount rate is given by $\delta = e^{-r\Delta}$.

The continuous time formulation illustrates that the discount rate in a repeated game is affected by two factors, which in turn can vary by the context: the length of a period (Δ) and the player's personal interest rate (r). When dealing with the case of perfect information, shortening the length of a period is equivalent to lowering the discount rate r. However, as we shall see in chapter 9, when there is uncertainty, these parameters have different effects upon the set of equilibrium payoffs.

4.7.2 Repeated Game Strategies

We have defined a choice in period t by some $s^t = \{s^{1t}, s^{2t}\} \in S$. A *repeated game strategy* for player $i \in \{1, 2\}$ is denoted by $\sigma^i = \{\sigma^{i0}, \sigma^{i1}, \ldots, \sigma^{it}, \ldots\}$ that defines the choice in period t by mapping

$$\sigma^{it} : H^t \to S^i,$$

where H^t is the set of possible histories of the game up to period t, where the first period's history is $H^0 = \emptyset$, and period t history is given by the sequence of realizations of our random shock and the action chosen by each person:

$$h^t = \left\{ \left(p^0, a^0\right), \left(p^1, a^1\right), \ldots, \left(p^{t-1}, a^{t-1}\right) \right\} \in H^t.$$

The consequence of playing a strategy pair is a sequence of choices that are determined recursively. More precisely, given strategy σ:

1. In period 0, parties observe p^0 and the strategy σ^0 determines s^0, which in turn determines the expected payoffs for the game in period 0: $u^{i0} = u^i\left(s^0\right) = E\left\{u^i\left(s^0\left(p^0\right)\right)\right\}$.

2. To work out the payoff in period 1, we need to compute the probability of $a \in A$ in period 1 under the strategy σ. This is given by finding the pairs $\{p^0, p^1\}$ that give rise to choice a:[29]

$$P[a, \sigma, t = 1] = \left\{ \left\{p^0, p^1\right\} \mid \sigma^1\left(h^1\right)\left(p^1\right) = a \right\}.$$

Because the strategies and choices are measurable functions, this is a measurable set for which the probability $\lambda(a, \sigma, 1)$ is well defined, and we can compute the probability that a is chosen in period 1. This procedure can be applied recursively to determine the probability that action a is chosen in any period t under strategy σ. Therefore, the choice in period t is well defined for each t, and we can define $\lambda(a, \sigma, t) = Pr[P[a, \sigma, t]] \in [0, 1]$ as the probability that action a is chosen in period t under strategy σ, and we get:

$$u^{it}(\sigma) = \sum_{a \in A} u^i(a)\,\lambda(a, \sigma, t). \tag{4.15}$$

Subgame perfection requires that an individual's strategy be an optimal response after any subgame. Accordingly, let $\sigma\left(h^{t^0}\right)$ denote the strategy from period t^0 onward given a history h^{t^0}, and let $\lambda\left(a, \sigma\left(h^{t^0}\right), t\right)$ be the associated probability of choosing action a in period $t \geq t^0$. We now define the payoff from a strategy σ after any subgame associated with h^{t^0} using (4.15) by:

$$U^i\left(\sigma, h^{t^0}\right) = v\left(r, \Delta, T - t^0\right) \sum_{t=t^0}^{T-1} \delta^{t-t^0} u^{it}\left(\sigma\left(h^{t^0}\right)\right).$$

As a matter of convention we let $U^i(\sigma) = U^i\left(\sigma, h^0\right)$ be the payoff at the beginning of the game. We are now in position (finally!) to define the notion of an SPNE for this game:

Definition 4.17   *A strategy profile $\sigma \in \Sigma$ is a subgame perfect equilibrium for a repeated game if:*

$$U^i\left((\sigma^i, \sigma^{-i}), h^{t^0}\right) \geq U^i\left((\tilde{\sigma}^i, \sigma^{-i}), h^{t^0}\right),$$

for every $t^0 = 0, \ldots T$, every $h^{t^0} \in H^T$, $i = 1, 2$ and every $\tilde{\sigma}^i \in \Sigma^i$. Let $\Sigma^{SPNE}(T)$ be the set of SPNE for the game that is repeated T times. When we write Σ^{SPNE} we are referring to the case $T = \infty$.

The set of possible SPNE is enormous, with many strategies that give the same payoffs to all players. For example, it is only the probability of an action a being chosen that determines the payoff, which allows parties to coordinate the public signal p^t in many ways to achieve this probability.

Observe that playing a Nash equilibrium each period—namely setting $\sigma^t\left(h^t\right) = s$ for all $t \geq 0$, $h^t \in H^t$ for some $s \in S^{NE}$—is an SPNE. Consequently the existence of a Nash equilibrium in the stage game G ensures the existence of an SPNE. In the end, rational players are interested only in payoffs and not the structure of the equilibrium per se. Thus, the goal of repeated game theory is to characterize the payoffs that are the outcome of some SPNE:

$$F^{SPNE}(T) = \left\{u \in F | u = \left(U^1(\sigma), U^2(\sigma)\right) \text{ such that } \sigma \in \Sigma^{SPNE}(T)\right\}.$$

Given that a Nash equilibrium of the stage game can be sustained as an SPNE, has the following proposition arises.

Proposition 4.18   *For all $T \geq 0$ the set of subgame perfect Nash equilibrium payoffs satisfies:*

$$F^{NE} \subset F^{SPNE}(T) \subset \bar{F}.$$

In the next section we work out the equilibria in the repeated prisoner's dilemma game to illustrate the construction of equilibria that are superior to the static Nash equilibrium. This is followed by a general characterization of the set of equilibrium payoffs.

4.7.3   Cooperation in the Repeated Prisoner's Dilemma Game

The repeated prisoner's dilemma game has received a great deal of attention as a parable about life.[30] It captures the idea that relationships may not be efficient because the temptation to cheat is stronger than the gains from sticking to an efficient agreement. If the prisoner's dilemma game is played repeatedly, there are SPNE that give payoffs that are superior to the Nash equilibrium in the one-shot game. These equilibria can be interpreted as *self-enforcing agreements*. In chapter 9 these ideas are used to build a theory of *relational contracts*.

Table 4.5
Prisoner's dilemma

	Keep quiet/cooperate	Confess/cheat
Keep quiet/cooperate	(2,2)	(−1,3)
Confess/cheat	(3,−1)	(0,0)

The payoff stream in equilibrium can be viewed as the result of an agreement or *promise* between the two parties on how they will play each period. Consider the prisoner's dilemma game in table 4.5. Suppose that player 1 has more bargaining power, and the parties agree to play (C, C) 50 percent of the time and (D, C) the rest of the time. This is implemented by supposing that (C, C) is played whenever $p^t \geq 0.5$ and (D, C) is played when $p^t < 0.5$. The expected payoff to players under this agreement leads to payoffs:

$$u^{1*} = 0.5 \times u^1 (C, C) + 0.5 \times u^1 (D, C) = 1 + 1.5 = 2.5,$$

$$u^{2*} = 0.5 \times u^2 (C, C) + 0.5 \times u^2 (D, C) = 1 - 0.5 = 0.5.$$

Observe that in the prisoner's dilemma the minimax payoffs (4.13) and the Nash equilibrium payoffs are the same and both are equal to zero. Thus the agreement to play this equilibrium each period is better than the worst that could happen to either player in the game. These points are illustrated in figure 4.6. Here, the dotted area is the set of payoffs that are individually rational.

Next, the conditions for the agreed payoffs to be an SPNE are derived. It must be the case that any deviation from the agreement will be punished. In the prisoner's dilemma, each player can guarantee getting at least zero (by playing D each period); thus a necessary condition for an equilibrium is that no player is better off deviating and then getting zero for the rest of the game—the worst possible payoff. In our example, this implies that the following conditions must be satisfied:

1. $p^t < 0.5$:
    (a) $(1 - \delta) u^1 (D, C) + \delta u^{1*} \geq (1 - \delta) u^1 (C, C) + \delta \times 0$
    (b) $(1 - \delta) u^2 (D, C) + \delta u^{2*} \geq (1 - \delta) u^2 (D, D) + \delta \times 0$
2. $p^t \geq 0.5$:
    (a) $(1 - \delta) u^1 (C, C) + \delta u^{1*} \geq (1 - \delta) u^1 (D, C) + \delta \times 0$
    (b) $(1 - \delta) u^2 (C, C) + \delta u^{2*} \geq (1 - \delta) u^2 (C, D) + \delta \times 0$

1(a) implies that player 1 cannot gain by noncooperation even though the other player is not cooperating. The necessary condition is:

$$(1 - \delta) \left(u^1 (C, D) - u^1 (D, D) \right) \geq -\delta u^{1*},$$

which implies $\delta \geq \frac{1}{3.5}$. More generally, it can be easily checked that in order to have all the inequalities satisfied we must have:

$$\delta \geq max \left\{ \frac{1}{3.5}, \frac{1}{1.5} \right\} = 2/3. \tag{4.16}$$

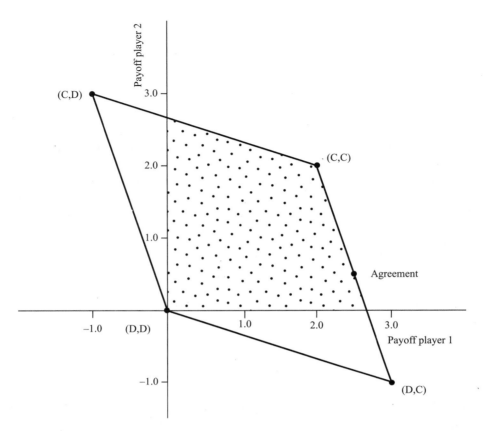

Figure 4.6
Payoffs in prisoner's dilemma game.

This condition is also *sufficient*. That is, suppose that this condition is satisfied, and players agree to play (C, C) 50 percent of the time and (D, C) 50 percent of the time. They then use the strategy of playing the agreement until there is a deviation, at which point players agree to play the static Nash equilibrium. Now, in any period, condition (4.16) ensures that they cannot gain from deviating from the agreement.

In order for strategies to form an SPNE, they must be Nash equilibria for all histories. Consider any history in which there has been a deviation; then this strategy calls for players to choose the static Nash equilibrium, which is itself an SPNE. Hence, when condition (4.16) holds then the agreement to play (C, C) 50 percent of the time and (C, D) the rest of the time can be supported by an SPNE.

The discussion thus far seems to imply that cooperation is possible because of the existence of a credible threat if there is deviation. Note that what makes cooperation possible is the *difference* in payoffs between continued cooperation and movement to a worse equilibrium. In particular, if the game is finitely repeated, then cooperation in the prisoner's dilemma is not an SPNE. In the last period of play there is no future, and therefore the unique outcome is to play (D, D) regardless of past play. Now, in the next to last period, because there is no chance to cooperate in the last period, (D, D) is again the unique equilibrium. Applying this reasoning backward implies that in a finitely repeated game there can be no cooperation.

This reasoning breaks down if there are at least two equilibria in the last period (see exercise 14). In that case one can use the choice of equilibrium in the last period to incentivize behavior in the next-to-last period. Infinitely repeated games are different because in any period there is always a chance to meet again, which in turn can be used to provide an incentive to cooperate. It is possible to provide a unified approach to the characterization of all the payoffs using the idea that it is *future* payoffs that provide incentives of performance today.

4.7.4 Characterization of the Payoffs in Repeated Games

This section characterizes the set of SPNE payoffs, F^{SPNE}, and shows how this set can be used to construct a self-enforcing agreement. The basic idea extends Bellman's principle of optimality to repeated games (see Abreu 1988 and Abreu, Pearce, and Stacchetti 1990). The idea is simple: to implement an action profile a^t today, all one needs to know are the payoffs that are potential SPNE tomorrow.

Following Abreu, Brooks, and Sannikov (2020), suppose that $W^{t+1} \subset F$ is a compact convex set representing the payoffs that are possible beginning in period $t + 1$. Under the assumption that any payoff in the set W^{t+1} is the outcome of an SPNE beginning in period $t + 1$, one can construct the set of SPNE payoffs that are possible in period t, denoted by W^t.

Next, define two functions. If player i deviates in period t, the worst payoff she might receive is given by:

$$P^i \left(W^{t+1} \right) = \min \left\{ u^i |\, \left(u^1, u^2 \right) \in W^{t+1} \right\}, \tag{4.17}$$

which always exists given that W^{t+1} is compact. Let $P \left(W^{t+1} \right) = \left\{ P^1 \left(W^{t+1} \right), P^2 \left(W^{t+1} \right) \right\}$. Next, define the most a player can gain by defecting from the agreed action pair $a \in A$:

$$h^i (a) = \max_{\tilde{a}^i \in A^i} u^i \left(\tilde{a}^i, a^{-i} \right) - u^i (a) \geq 0.$$

Let $h (a) = \left\{ h^1 (a), h^2 (a) \right\}$. Notice that $a \in A^{NE}$ if and only if $h (a) = \hat{0} = \{0, 0\}$.

Definition 4.19 *A point $v \in F$ is generated by the set W^{t+1} in a repeated game of length T if there is a payoff vector $w \in W^{t+1}$ and an action $a \in A$ such that the adding up constraint is satisfied:*

$$v = (1 - \delta) \frac{1}{1 - \delta^{T-t}} u (a) + \delta \frac{1 - \delta^{T-t-1}}{1 - \delta^{T-t}} w, \tag{4.18}$$

and the incentive constraint is satisfied:

$$h (a) \leq \frac{\delta}{(1 - \delta)} \left(1 - \delta^{T-t-1} \right) \left(w - P \left(W^{t+1} \right) \right). \tag{4.19}$$

Let $V \left(W^{t+1}, t, T \right)$ be the set of points generated by W^{t+1}. The set $V \left(W^{t+1}, t, T \right)$ is not empty given that a Nash equilibrium exists. In period $t = T - 1$, $V \left(W^{t+1}, T - 1, T \right)$ is exactly the set of Nash equilibrium payoffs of the game without the correlation device. The following result can be readily established:

Lemma 4.20 *Given that a Nash equilibrium to the static games exists ($F^{NE} \neq \emptyset$), then for every compact subset $W \subset F$ then $V(W, T-1, T)$ is a nonempty, compact subset of F. Moreover, if $W \subset W'$, then $V(W, t, T) \subset V(W', t, T)$.*

Proof. Let

$$\hat{W}(a, W) = \left\{ w \in W | h(a) \leq \frac{\delta}{(1-\delta)} \left(1 - \delta^{T-t-1} \right) (w - P(W)) \right\}$$

be the set of future payoffs that can implement action a. This set might be empty, but if not, it is compact. It is not empty for $a \in A^{NE}$. Next, let

$$V(a) = \left\{ v = (1-\delta) \frac{1}{1 - \delta^{T-t}} u(a) + \delta \frac{1 - \delta^{T-t-1}}{1 - \delta^{T-t}} w | w \in \hat{W}(a, W) \right\}$$

be the set of points generated by the action a. This is compact whenever $W(a)$ is not empty. It follows that:

$$V(W, t, T) = \cup_{a \in A} V(a)$$

is the finite union of compact sets and thus is also compact. Clearly, $\hat{W}(a, W) \subset \hat{W}(a, W')$, from which we get the final condition. $\square$

The set of points generated by W^{t+1} are payoffs associated with actions in period t that can be enforced with continuation payoffs taken from W^{t+1}. The next issue is the relationship between these payoffs and the set of SPNE.

Lemma 4.21 *Suppose each payoff in W^{t+1} can be supported by some SPNE. Then $v \in V(W^{t+1}, t, T)$ if and only if there is an SPNE from period t with payoff v and continuation payoffs taken from W^{t+1}.*

Proof. For each $w \in W^{t+1}$ there is an associated strategy σ_w that forms an SPNE starting in period $t+1$ that ignores history before period $t+1$. We now show that a point v generated by W^{t+1} can also be supported by the following SPNE. Let a_v be the strategy that defines v via the adding up constraint and that satisfies the incentive constraint and let $w(v)$ be the associated payoff in W^{t+1}. Then v is supported by the following strategy σ_v defined from period t onward:

1. In period t: $\sigma_v(h^t) = a(v)$ for all $h^t \in H^t$.

2. If both parties choose a_v or both deviate from a_v, play the SPNE strategy associated with $w(v)$.

3. If agent i deviates (and $-i$ does not), play the SPNE strategy associated with payoff $P^i(W^{t+1})$.

Under this strategy, after every history, the play in periods $\tau \geq t+1$ comprises some SPNE, and hence we know for all histories there is no incentive to deviate from the specified strategy. If player i deviates from a_v in period t, the incentive constraint ensures that she is worse off, and hence choosing a_v is optimal for both players. This shows that v is supported by this SPNE.

Next, consider the converse. Suppose there is an SPNE strategy σ that entails the choice of a in period t ($\sigma\left(h^t\right) = a$ for all h^t), and all continuation payoffs lie in W^{t+1}. Let $v = U\left(\sigma, h^t\right)$; by construction v satisfies the adding up constraint. Let $w \in W^{t+1}$ be the equilibrium continuation payoff. Because σ is an SPNE it defines an NE in period t, so it must be the case that for any action $\tilde{a}^i$ there is an associated $w\left(\tilde{a}^i\right) \in W^{t+1}$ such that:

$$v^i = (1-\delta)\frac{1}{1-\delta^{T-t}}u\left(a\right) + \delta\frac{1-\delta^{T-t-1}}{1-\delta^{T-t}}w,$$

$$\geq (1-\delta)\frac{1}{1-\delta^{T-t}}u\left(\tilde{a}^i, a^{-i}\right) + \delta\frac{1-\delta^{T-t-1}}{1-\delta^{T-t}}w^i\left(\tilde{a}^i\right),$$

$$\geq (1-\delta)\frac{1}{1-\delta^{T-t}}u\left(\tilde{a}^i, a^{-i}\right) + \delta\frac{1-\delta^{T-t-1}}{1-\delta^{T-t}}P^i\left(W^{t+1}\right). \tag{4.20}$$

This strategy must also satisfy the incentive constraint, from which we conclude that v is generated by W^{t+1}.   □

The last inequality was first pointed out by Abreu (1988); namely, one can fully characterize the set of SPNE by finding the worst SPNE that is possible for each player and using it as a threat when there is deviation from agreed play. The public randomizing device at the beginning of each period implies that the set of payoffs in period t that correspond to SPNE with continuation payoffs in W^{t+1} is exactly defined by:

$$B\left(W^{t+1}, t, T\right) = conv\left\{V\left(W^{t+1}, t, T\right)\right\}. \tag{4.21}$$

The convexification of V preserves both compactness and monotonicity properties; hence, if W is compact, then so is $B(W, t, T)$, and $B(W, t, T) \subset B(W', t, T)$ whenever $W \subset W'$. We now use this operator to characterize the set of SPNE payoffs possible for the repeated game. We begin with the case of finitely repeated games.

Proposition 4.22 *Suppose that a game is repeated $T < \infty$ times. Then the set of SPNE payoffs in period t is defined recursively by:*

$$F^{SPNE}\left(T-1\right) = F^{NE} = B\left(\{\emptyset\}, T-1, T\right)$$

$$F^{SPNE}\left(t\right) = B\left(F^{SPNE}\left(t+1\right), t, T\right), \quad t \leq T-2.$$

Lemma 4.21 implies that if $F^{SPNE}\left(t+1\right)$ consists of all SPNE payoffs in period $t+1$, then $F^{SPNE}\left(t\right)$ consists of all SPNE payoffs in period t. In the last period there is no future, and the only possible SPNE are the Nash equilibria of the one-shot game. Thus, we can define all the SPNE recursively, beginning with period $T-1$. Notice that if there is a unique Nash equilibrium, then F^{NE} is a single point w^{NE}. This implies that $w^{iNE} = P^i\left(F^{NE}\right)$, and the incentive constraint is $h\left(a\right) = 0$ every period. This in turn implies that the unique SPNE is the Nash equilibrium of the one-shot game:

Corollary 4.23 *If the Nash equilibrium of the one-shot game is unique, then repeating this action is the unique SPNE in the finitely repeated game.*

4.7.5 Infinitely Repeated Games

Infinitely repeated games have no last period and therefore this procedure for proposition 4.22 does not work. Moreover, when $T = \infty$, then the δ^T terms are zero and the $B(W, t, T)$ operator is time invariant; we denote it simply by $B(W)$. This implies that the set of SPNE payoffs is time invariant (which also explicitly depends on the discount rate δ). Moreover, the argument regarding the necessary and sufficient conditions for a point to correspond to an SPNE implies that the set of SPNE, F^{SPNE}, satisfy

$$F^{SPNE} = B\left(F^{SPNE}\right).$$

The next proposition provides an explicit way to compute F^{SPNE}.

Proposition 4.24 *The set of payoffs supported by some SPNE satisfies:*

$$F^{SPNE} = B\left(F^{SPNE}\right) = lim_{n \to \infty} B^n\left(\bar{F}\right).$$

Proof. Notice that since $F^{SPNE} \subset \bar{F}$ and $F^{SPNE} \subset B\left(F^{SPNE}\right)$, the monotonicity of the B operator implies that $F^{SPNE} \subset B^n\left(\bar{F}\right)$ for all n. Since the operator preserves compactness, we have

$$lim_{n \to \infty} B^n\left(\bar{F}\right) = \bigcap_{n=1,2,\dots} B^n\left(\bar{F}\right),$$

which converges to some compact set F' with the feature $F' = B\left(F'\right)$ and $F^{SPNE} \subset F'$. For any $w \in F'$ one can use the algorithm above to construct an equilibrium sequence of actions that are incentive-compatible each period and hence form an SPNE. This implies $F' \subset F^{SPNE}$ and $F' = F^{SPNE}$. $\square$

This provides a way to construct F^{SPNE}. Recently, Abreu, Brooks, and Sannikov (2020), building on the work of Cronshaw and Luenberger (1994) and Judd, Yeltekin, and Conklin (2003), have shown that with a finite strategy space the set of payoffs is a polytope that can be quickly computed. For the purposes of relational contract theory, the most important result is the characterization of the set of possible equilibrium payoffs in terms of the worst SPNE.

Corollary 4.25 *(Abreu 1988) Let $u_w^i = P^i\left(F^{SPNE}\right)$ (as defined in (4.17)). Then an agreement to play $s \in S$ every period in an infinitely repeated game can be supported by some SPNE if and only if for any action* a *played with positive probability:*

$$one\text{-}shot - gain = h^i(a) \leq \frac{\delta}{(1-\delta)}\left(u^i(s) - u_w^i\right) = future - loss. \tag{4.22}$$

In many contractual settings the worst payoff is generated by the threat of separation, which can often be easily computed independently of the discount rate and other features of the environment. This determines $u^i(s) - u_w^i$ in (4.22), which then allows for an elementary characterization of the set of self-enforcing agreements. Observe that in this case when the time between moves is small ($\Delta \to 0$), then $\delta \to 1$, and the right-hand side is not binding when $\left(u^i(s) - u^i_w\right) > 0$. The folk theorem for repeated games (see Fudenberg and Maskin 1986) establishes the fact that when $\delta \to 1$ then $u^i_w \to \bar{u}^i$. This result, combined with the weak inequality, implies $F^{SPNE} \to \bar{F}$ as $\delta \to 1$.

4.8 Discussion

This chapter provides a brief overview of the main themes in game theory that are relevant to the contracts and institutions to be discussed later. Game theory illustrates the importance of carefully defining the information and actions available to all participants. Risk can be introduced by viewing Nature as a player that chooses states.

The Monty Hall problem illustrates the importance of explicitly modeling the actions of agents in the environment. The Monty Hall problem seems hard because it is often approached as a problem in probability theory. It cannot be solved without making assumptions regarding the actions of Monty Hall. Game theory provides a way to systematically model and study the actions of individuals in such situations.

Though Savage's theory of rational choice includes games as a special case, it provides no guidance on how to model the probability assessments of individuals. Game theory begins with the hypothesis that individuals know that they are playing other individuals with well-defined goals. This knowledge can be used to constrain the beliefs regarding how one expects others to play. The fundamental solution concept in game theory is the notion of a Nash equilibrium. It requires that these beliefs regarding the evolution of play be correct—namely, at a Nash equilibrium each person is making an optimal decision while correctly anticipating how others will play.

Game theory differs from rational choice theory in another fundamental way. When an individual is choosing option A over option B, all players must contemplate the counterfactual: what would happen if she chooses B? The difficulty is that if at a Nash equilibrium action B is not expected, then it is assigned a probability of zero by the other players. If they observe B, Bayes's rule cannot be used, and there is no method in decision theory to guide the updating of beliefs. Depending upon the information structure of the game, game theory has a number of solutions: these include the concept of a subgame perfect Nash equilibrium (a concept that is widely used in repeated game theory) and the notion of a sequential equilibrium, which extends the notion of subgame perfection to games with asymmetric information.

In general, the theory does not produce a unique prediction for an arbitrary game. There is a long history of attempts to find a solution concept that yields a unique prediction for any game—with Kohlberg and Mertens (1986) providing possibly the most satisfactory solution. However, the project has not proven successful. Even if they had found a solution, we would be faced with the fundamental fact that given a particular game, the literature on experimental game theory has documented a large body of evidence that players vary greatly in how they act in practice (see for example Colin Camerer's [2003] review of experimental game theory).

For example, Brandts and MacLeod (1995) present an experiment in which players are helped to deal with the complexity of analyzing a given game by providing recommendations on how to play. Even then, players often deviate from the recommended play. What we do know is that when individuals are aware they are playing against another individual, they use this information to inform their choices. In later chapters, we use game theory as a way to formally model strategic interaction, particularly contract formation.

Repeated game theory answers the question of what payoffs are consistent with rational play when parties meet repeatedly. The key insight is that the set of possible informal agreements can be characterized by first finding the *worst* possible outcome for each individual. Given this information, the set of possible agreements are those that use these worst outcomes as punishments, a result that is central to the theory of relational contracts. See also the interesting work by Abreu, Brooks, and Sannikov (2020), which develops techniques for computing equilibria in complex repeated games.

Other interesting literature in decision theory builds on the idea that a person's choice is the consequence of conflict within their mind (see Minsky 1986). Gul and Pesendorfer (2001) introduce a model in which persons make choices over time, in which today's self is playing a game against tomorrow's self. Another interesting paper is Bernheim and Rangel (2004), which models preferences as being state dependent and that move between cold (rational) and hot (irrational) states. In that case, the rational person is playing a stochastic game against their potentially irrational self.

Finally, consistent with the Savage approach to rational choice, the models introduced here suppose that individuals build models of the other player's beliefs. The attentive reader might wonder why one is not building a model of the beliefs. If both players are doing this, then each has to build a model of the other's beliefs about beliefs, and so on. This leads to what is known as a hierarchy of beliefs that illustrates the challenge one faces in building a logically complete model of rational choice in social situations. Mertens and Zamir (1985) provide a mathematically consistent model of a hierarchy of beliefs and show that one can construct a finite approximation to such a model. Rubinstein (1989) cleverly shows that when communication is noisy, it may be impossible for parties to reach an agreement! Morris and Shin (2003) provide a nice review of these ideas, including the theory of global games that has been useful in macroeconomic models.

4.9   Exercises

1. Suppose that we observe a contestant refusing to change her decision in the Monty Hall problem. Can we conclude that the contestant is acting irrationally? Why or why not?

2. Suppose now that Monty Hall is free to choose whether to open a second door; how does that change the analysis?

3. Provide a simple example showing a mixed strategy that cannot be replaced by a behavioral strategy.

4. Prove that when players have perfect recall then for any mixed strategy by player i, there exists a corresponding behavioral strategy that yields the same expected payoff.

5. Prove that in a finite game of perfect information (every information set consists of a single node), there exists an equilibrium that can be found by backward induction, and that this equilibrium is perfect.

6. Prove proposition 4.10.

7. Consider the second price auction game. A single good is to be sold to one of $n \geq 2$ possible buyers at a price p. Buyer i has a value $v^i \in [0, 1]$ for the good that is drawn from the distribution $f^i(v^i)$. The distributions are common value, but each buyer knows only her valuation. After the buyers observe their valuations, they submit bids b^i for the object. The buyer with the highest bid wins and pays a price p equal to the second-highest bid, and earns utility $v^i - p$. The losers earn zero.

    (a) Describe the normal form of this game, along with the payoffs of the players.

    (b) Prove that it is a dominant strategy for player i to set $b^i = v^i$.

    (c) Suppose $f^i(v) = 1$ for all v and i. Work out the expected revenues for the seller in this game as a function of the number of players n.

    (d) For the case in (c), work out the Nash equilibrium when the price is equal to the winner's bid. What is the expected revenue in this case?

8. For any finite game $G = \{U^i, \Gamma^i\}_{i \in N}$, prove there exists a perfect equilibrium and that every perfect equilibrium is also a sequential equilibrium. This result follows from Kakutani's theorem. Let $A \subset \Re^n$, then $f : A \to A$ is a correspondence if $f(x)$ is a subset of A. In the context of games in mixed strategies, $\{U_i, \Gamma_i\}_{i \in N}$, the correspondence we have in mind is:

$$f_i(\gamma) = \arg\max_{\gamma_i \in \hat{\Gamma}_i} U_i\left(\gamma^i, \gamma^{-i}\right). \tag{4.23}$$

One can readily show that this correspondence is *upper-hemicontinuous*. Namely, the graph of f, $\{(x,y) \,|\, y \in f(x), x \in A\}$, is a closed set, and for any compact set $B \subset A$, $f(B) = \{y | y \in f(x), x \in B\}$ is compact. Then Kakutani's theorem states that if A is a compact, convex subset of $\Re^n$ and $f : A \to A$ is a upper-hemicontinuous correspondence such that $f(x)$ is convex for all $x \in A$, then there is an x^* such that $x^* \in f(x^*)$. To show the existence of a Nash equilibrium, one begins with the observation that the set of mixed strategies is a compact, convex set and that f defined in (4.23) is upper-hemicontinuous and convex-valued.

9. Provide an example of a finite game for which

$$\min_{a^2} \max_{a^1} u^1\left(a^1, a^2\right) > \max_{a^1} \min_{a^2} u^1\left(a^1, a^2\right).$$

10. Prove that we have equality in the previous exercise if we allow for mixed strategies. Hint: consider the zero-sum game where $u^2\left(a^1, a^2\right) = -u^1\left(a^1, a^2\right)$, and use the fact that a Nash equilibrium in mixed strategies exists.

11. Consider the game illustrated in figure 4.5, and find the set of sequential equilibria and perfect equilibria for the game. Now change the payoff corresponding to (l,R) to $(1, -1)$: what is the set of sequential equilibria and perfect equilibria? Specify the entire set of equilibrium assessments.

12. Consider the following final offer game. Suppose that two players have to divide a dollar. Player 1 offers player 2 an amount x. If accepted, then player 1 gets $1 - x$ and player 2 gets x. If rejected they both get zero. What are the pure strategy Nash equilibria for this game? What is the unique subgame perfect Nash equilibrium? Answer these questions when the game is played n times, where the players just add up their winnings (so the maximum gain is n dollars).

13. Consider the following three-period game. Each period, person A offers to divide a dollar, with an offer in cents, $x_t \in \{0, 0.01, 0.02, \ldots, 1\}$. If person B rejects the offer, both persons get zero, but if she accepts, she gets x_t and person A gets $1 - x_t$. Let the choice of B be $\delta_t \in \{0, 1\}$, where $\delta_t = 1$ means accept. Thus, the payoffs of the agents are:

$$U^A = \sum_{t=1}^{3} \delta_t \left(1 - x_t\right),$$

$$U^B = \sum_{t=1}^{3} \delta_t x_t.$$

Assume that parties can observe previous plays.

(a) What is the worst and best Nash equilibrium for this game for each player?

(b) What is the worst and best subgame perfect Nash equilibrium for this game for each player?

(c) Suppose the game is played n times. What is the worst and best subgame perfect Nash equilibrium payoffs for player B as a function of n?

14. Suppose that in addition to the payoffs for the prisoner's dilemma, players have the option of quitting the relationship, denoted by Q. If either player quits, then the payoff is -1 for both players. Suppose that each period they simultaneously choose $A \in \{C, D, Q\}$. Show that there are two Nash equilibria to this game. Next, characterize the payoffs when the game is repeated T times. Next, suppose the game is played over one period and that the time between moves is Δ. Characterize the set of payoffs as $\Delta \to 0$.

5 Bargaining and the Buyer-Seller Model

Thus the head clerk in a business has an acquaintance with men and things, the use of which he could in some cases sell at a high price to rival firms. But in other cases it is of a kind to be of no value save to the business in which he already is; and then his departure would perhaps injure it by several times the value of his salary, while probably he could not get half that salary elsewhere.
—Alfred Marshall ([1890] 1948, 520).

5.1   Introduction

When markets are perfectly competitive, under the appropriate assumptions, the resulting allocation of resources is uniquely determined. At a competitive equilibrium each individual is indifferent between their current choice and the next best alternative. However, many markets are characterized by what Williamson, Wachter, and Harris (1975) call *idiosyncratic* exchange. This is consistent with the above quotation from Marshall, who observes that the value of an employee to a firm may be several times his salary. This is an example of firm-specific human capital whose value can be expected to increase with a worker's tenure at the firm (Mincer 1962). The next question is: How should these quasi-rents be divided between the two parties?

Whether one is haggling with a trader in an African market or negotiating the price of a new car, the bargaining problem can be viewed as two parties attempting to achieve two goals. The first is to reach a new and better allocation of real resources, be it a new car or a job. The second is to determine the terms of trade—the allocation of the gains from trade between the two parties. In general, the outcome of bargaining can be expected to be a function of a number of factors, including the preferences of the parties, the value of alternatives to the current trade, patience in negotiating, and so on.

A useful theory of bargaining cannot be expected to include all factors that might affect a particular agreement. Rather, the bargaining theory in this chapter provides two stylized models that highlight the central aspects of the bargaining problem that connect observable features of the bargaining environment to observed outcomes.

The seminal work on bargaining theory is due to Nash (1953). In this brilliant paper he introduces two approaches to the bargaining problem that continue to be the basis for modern bargaining theories. The first approach supposes that individuals play a well-defined game in which parties make demands on how to divide the rents in a potential agreement (the Nash bargaining game). Nash shows that one can add uncertainty to this game so that there is a unique Nash equilibrium. The second approach supposes that parties reach an agreement based upon commonly accepted norms given by a set of principles or axioms. Nash shows that four axioms—efficiency, symmetry, scale invariance, and independence of irrelevant alternatives—are sufficient to uniquely determine the outcome of bargaining.

The choice of approach depends upon the problem one is trying to understand. The axiomatic approach is useful when one needs a model to *describe* the outcome of the bargaining process. For example, Svejnar (1986) and Abowd and Lemieux (1993) use the Nash bargaining solution to build empirical models of wage formation that they can take to the data. This approach does not explain why the gains from trade are divided in a particular way. See also the recent literature on wage formation and the division of rents between the worker and the firm (Card et al. 2018).

The Nash bargaining problem focuses on how to divide the gains from trade. In the second part of this chapter this idea is applied to the problem of *contract bargaining*. This adds a new layer of complexity. Axiomatic Nash bargaining applies to a one-off exchange—once the exchange is completed, the parties have no future contact. In contrast, when parties sign a contract, they regulate trade over a period of time. Even if the contract is legally binding, parties are always free to agree upon new terms. Hence, contract choice entails exploring the causal impact of some explicit counterfactuals. If parties agree upon contract k_0 today, how will they act in the future and when, if ever, will they reopen negotiations?

We study this problem in two steps. In this chapter, the question of uncertainty is put aside in favor of asking how parties will bargain over fixed contract terms that will determine trade for a period of time. Trade might be the regular delivery of a product or a service commodity, such as labor, that is supplied continuously over a period of time. In the next chapter, the model is extended to allow for uncertainty and investment in the relationship.

The contract bargaining model provides a number of insights. First, it illustrates how the right to make offers increases bargaining power. Second, in contrast to the axiomatic model, there are two distinct fallback positions during negotiation: There are the *inside options*—the payoffs that parties are receiving while negotiating. Then there are *outside options*, the payoffs parties would receive should the relationship end. It is shown that the inside options play a role similar to the threat point in Nash's axiomatic model, while the outside options act as constraints on the terms of trade. The next chapter uses this result to explain some features of observed contracts.

The agenda for the chapter is as follows. Section 5.2 outlines a general buyer-seller model that is the basis for the models in the subsequent chapters. It can represent one-off trade, exchange of commodities over time, or the supply of labor services over time. Section 5.3 introduces the Nash axiomatic bargaining model and shows how it can be used to determine the quantity and price of a commodity that is exchanged between two parties.

Section 5.4 introduces the contract bargaining model with no uncertainty, based upon Binmore, Rubinstein, and Wolinsky (1986), and the extension to contract bargaining introduced in MacLeod and Malcomson (1993).[1] It provides an explicit model of bargaining power and transaction costs. It also illustrates the sensitivity of the outcome to details of the bargaining environment and thus provides some guidance on when it is appropriate to use a reduced-form bargaining model, such as the axiomatic model of Nash.

5.2 The Buyer-Seller Model

Consider a paradigmatic buyer-seller relationship in which a buyer (B) agrees to purchase a certain quantity or quality, $q \in [0, \bar{q}]$, of a commodity from a seller (S) at a price p. The model is quite general, with the buyer representing any party that wishes to secure a good or service, such as a consumer, manufacturer, or employer. The value of this commodity to the buyer is given by the function $B(q, b)$, where b represents the characteristics of the buyer that may or may not be observed by other parties. Similarly, the seller might be a worker or producer of an intermediate good. To keep matters as simple as possible, q represents either the number of units purchased, the quality of a single unit, or the probability of trade (in which case $\bar{q} = 1$), while the cost of production is $C(q, c)$, where c denotes the characteristics of the seller that, like the buyer, may or may not be observed by others.

The discussion can be generalized to the case in which both quantity and quality are specified in a contract, though the term "quantity" is used throughout the discussion. Unless stated otherwise, it is freely interchangeable with quality. In some cases it may be desirable to have a third-party intermediary that allows the price paid by the buyer, p^B, to differ from the price received by the seller, p^S. For example, this can occur in equilibrium if there is a court case that requires parties to spend resources on legal fees. To preview results, in chapters 8 and 10, it is shown that having some third-party "budget breaker" may be a necessary condition for trade with asymmetric information.

The timeline is as follows:

1. The buyer and seller learn their own characteristics given by $b \in [b_L, b_H]$ and $c \in [c_L, c_H]$. These parameters have known densities $b \sim f(\cdot)$, with support $[b_L, b_H]$, and $c \sim g(\cdot)$, with support $[c_L, c_H]$. Let F and G be the corresponding cumulative distribution functions.[2] Let $\theta = (b, c) \in \Theta = [b_L, b_H] \times [c_L, c_H]$ denote the state of the relationship.

2. Parties bargain over contract terms $k = \{q, p^B, p^S\}$ that determine payoffs in the event of trade as a function of the benefit to the buyer ($B(q, b)$) and the cost to the seller ($C(q, c)$):

$$u^B(k|b) = B(q, b) - p^B, \tag{5.1}$$

$$u^S(k|c) = p^S - C(q, c). \tag{5.2}$$

3. If there is no trade, the buyer and seller get outside options $u^{0B} \geq 0$ and $u^{0S} \geq 0$, respectively, denoted by $\vec{u}^0 = \{u^{0B}, u^{0S}\} \geq \vec{0}$.

The contract, $k = \{q, p^B, p^S\} \in [0, \bar{q}] \times [0, \bar{p}]^2 = K$, allows the price paid to the seller to differ from the price paid by the buyer. It is assumed, unless stated otherwise, that the payoffs satisfy a "standard" set of assumptions that ensure the existence of an optimal quantity/quality. The benefit to the buyer, $B(q, b)$, and the cost to the seller, $C(q, c)$, are assumed to be twice differentiable, with $B_q, C_q, B_b, C_c \geq 0$, $B_{qq} \leq 0$, $C_{qq} \geq 0$, $B_{qb}, C_{qc} > 0$, and $B(0, b) = C(0, c) = 0$ for all $(b, c) \in \Theta$.

This basic model is quite general and can be used to illustrate a wide variety of issues that arise with the exchange of commodities. For example, when the commodity being traded is indivisible, then $q \in [0, 1]$ represents the *probability* that there is trade, in which case the expected benefit and cost are given by:

$$B(q, b) = q \times b,$$

$$C(q, c) = q \times c.$$

Thus, when parties are risk neutral, there is no formal distinction between trade of a quantity "$q \in [0, 1]$" and trade of one unit with probability "q."

The goal of this chapter is to characterize the *allocations* that parties can achieve via bargaining. Bargaining typically occurs before parties are aware of all the events that may affect the value of trade. Thus, just as an "act" in Savage's theory of exchange allows for state-contingent outcomes that affect an individual, an *allocation* is a function that describes the outcome of the meeting between the buyer and the seller given their characteristics defined by the state $\theta \in \Theta$:

$$\Xi = \{X : \Theta \rightarrow A\}, \tag{5.3}$$

where $A = \left\{ [0, \bar{q}] \times [0, \bar{p}]^2, \vec{u}^0 \right\}$ is the set of possible outcomes, and Ξ denotes the set of possible allocations between the buyer and the seller. If $X(\theta) = \vec{u}^0$, then there is no trade, and parties receive their outside options. Let $\Theta^T(X)$ be the states in which there is trade under X and $\Theta^{NT}(X)$ be the states in which there is no trade. Let $X(\theta) = \left\{ q(\theta), p^B(\theta), p^S(\theta) \right\}$. Let $u^B(X(\theta)|\theta)$ and $u^S(X(\theta)|\theta)$ denote the utilities of the buyer and seller under allocation X, given the state $(b, c) = \theta \in \Theta$.

A *feasible allocation* is one for which the price paid by the buyer is greater than or equal to the price received by the seller: $p^B(\theta) \geq p^S(\theta)$ for all $\theta \in \Theta^T(X)$. In addition, an allocation is *budget balancing* if $p^B(\theta) = p^S(\theta)$ for all $\theta \in \Theta^T(X)$.

When parties meet, they try to achieve the best outcome for themselves. Edgeworth (1881) introduced the notion of a *contract curve* to represent the outcome of a two-party exchange.[3] These are allocations with the feature that it is not possible to find another allocation that makes both parties better off. These are now known as *Pareto efficient allocations*:

Definition 5.1 *A feasible allocation X is* (ex post) Pareto efficient, *or simply* efficient, *if there exists no other allocation X' such that for all $\theta \in \Theta$:*

$$u^B\left(X'(\theta)|\theta\right) \geq u^B\left(X(\theta)|\theta\right),$$

$$u^S\left(X'(\theta)|\theta\right) \geq u^S\left(X(\theta)|\theta\right),$$

and for some $\theta' \in \Theta$, one of these inequalities is strict.

Pareto (1909) extended this concept to more than two individuals. The idea is straightforward. At a minimum, individuals should not object to changes that hurt no single individual but result in some individuals being strictly better off.

The term ex post efficiency refers to the assumption that the allocation is evaluated after all information is public. This is the weakest notion of efficiency in this context. One could evaluate payoffs before the state of nature is revealed. These are known as the set of ex ante efficient allocations that may also entail efficient risk sharing. When parties are risk averse, then the ex ante efficient allocations are a strict subset of the ex post efficient allocations.[4]

For the moment, agents are assumed to be risk neutral. This, along with the assumptions about benefits and costs, implies that the maximum gain from trade given the state θ is well defined and given by the *surplus function*:

$$S^*(\theta) = \max_{q \in [0,\bar{q}]} \left\{ B(q,b) - C(q,c), u^{0B} + u^{0S} \right\}. \tag{5.4}$$

The next proposition characterizes the set of efficient allocations.

Proposition 5.2 *An allocation $X^*(\theta) = (q^*(\theta), p^{*B}(\theta), p^{*S}(\theta))$ is (Pareto) efficient in the buyer-seller model if and only if:*

1. *For all states where there is trade, $\theta \in \Theta^T(X^*)$:*
   i. *The quantity traded, $q^*(\theta)$, satisfies:*

$$B(q^*(\theta), b) - C(q^*(\theta), c) = S^*(\theta) \geq u^{0B} + u^{0S}.$$

   ii. *The allocation is budget balancing: $p^{*B}(\theta) = p^{*S}(\theta)$.*
2. *For all states in which there is no trade, $\theta \in \Theta^{NT}(X^*)$:[5]*

$$u^{0B} + u^{0S} = S^*(\theta).$$

Let Ξ^* denote the set of efficient allocations. The proof of this proposition is left as an exercise. It shows that an efficient allocation in Ξ^* is characterized by an efficient quantity of trade when it occurs. If this generates a surplus $S^*(\theta)$ greater than the alternatives, then trade is efficient; otherwise, there is no trade. Aside from requiring that money not be paid to third parties, it places no restrictions on the trade prices. A goal of bargaining theory is to determine these prices.

5.3 Nash Bargaining Solution

This section reviews the *axiomatic* Nash bargaining model. The goal is to have a parsimonious representation of the bargaining problem and then to apply some principles, formalized as axioms, to determine a unique outcome. The buyer and seller have observed the state θ, and then they wish to agree on price and quantity terms for trade.

If parties do not reach an agreement, they get their outside or default options: $\vec{u}^0 = \{u^{0B}, u^{0S}\}$, that without loss of generality are assumed to be nonnegative. If parties agree on a contract k, then the realized payoffs are given by (5.1) and (5.2). Given that the buyer's price can be greater than the seller's price, free disposal is implicitly assumed.[6] For the rest of this chapter, the state $\theta \in \Theta$ is assumed to have been realized and to be common knowledge for the two parties. The explicit dependence upon θ is thus dropped for the rest of the discussion. The next chapter discusses in detail the relationship between the realized state and the bargained outcomes.

Let $S^* > u^{0B} + u^{0S}$ be the total surplus available for division between the two parties. The set of possible payoffs that the buyer and seller can realize is given by the set:

$$F = \left\{ \{u^B, u^S\} \in \mathfrak{R}_+^2 \mid S^* \geq u^B + u^S \right\}.$$

Observe that the free disposal assumption ensures that all payoffs between the efficient frontier and the outside options are feasible, which in turn ensures that this is a compact, convex subset of $\Re^2$.

The *static bargaining problem* is defined by $\{F, \vec{u}^0\}$, where F is a compact convex set of utilities that the two parties might agree upon, and $\vec{u}^0$ specifies the payoff they would get if there is no agreement.[7] For parties to trade, there must be some mutual gain. The assumption of a gain from trade, $S^* > u^{0B} + u^{0S}$, ensures the existence of a potential agreement $\vec{v} \in F$ such that $\vec{v} > \vec{u}^0$.[8] The question is what payoff vector in F would parties agree on?

A *bargaining solution* is a function from the set of bargaining problems to agreements in F:

$$\phi\left(F, \vec{u}^0\right) = \left\{\phi^B\left(F, \vec{u}^0\right), \phi^S\left(F, \vec{u}^0\right)\right\} \in F$$

that is assumed to have some "reasonable" properties. The properties defining the Nash bargaining solution are discussed here. The interested reader is referred to exercise 3 for a discussion of the Kalai-Smorodinsky solution.

The first requirement is that any agreement must be at least as good as each party's outside option:

Axiom(IR) A bargaining solution satisfies *individual rationality* if $\phi\left(F, \vec{u}^0\right) \geq \vec{u}^0$.

Next, rational parties should not object to outcomes that make at least one of them better off without hurting the other party:

Axiom(PE) A bargaining solution satisfies *(Pareto) efficiency* if whenever $\vec{u} \geq \phi\left(F, \vec{u}^0\right)$ and $\vec{u} \in F$, then $\vec{u} = \phi\left(F, \vec{u}^0\right)$.

In other words, given a potential agreement $\vec{u}$, it is not possible to find another agreement that makes at least one party better off without hurting the other. Next, the currency used to specify the agreement should not affect the outcome. Define an *increasing affine function* $L : \Re^2 \to \Re^2$ for $\vec{x} \in \Re^2$ by:

$$L\left(\vec{x}\right) = \left(\lambda_1 x_1 + \alpha_1, \lambda_2 x_2 + \alpha_2\right),$$

where $\lambda_1, \lambda_2 > 0$. Notice that $L^{-1}\left(x\right)$ exists and is also an increasing affine function.[9] Given this, scale independence is defined as follows:

Axiom(SI) A bargaining solution satisfies *scale independence* if for any bargaining game $\{F, \vec{u}^0\}$ and increasing affine function $L : \Re^2 \to \Re^2$ then:

$$\phi\left(L\left(F\right), L\left(\vec{u}^0\right)\right) = L\left(\phi\left(F, \vec{u}^0\right)\right).$$

One of the more controversial assumptions of the model is the independence of irrelevant alternatives (see exercise 3). This requires that adding alternatives that are no better than the existing agreement does not affect the outcome. Formally:

Axiom(IIRA) A bargaining solution satisfies *independence of irrelevant alternatives* if when $G \subset F$ and $\phi\left(F, \vec{u}^0\right) \in G$, then $\phi\left(G, \vec{u}^0\right) = \phi\left(F, \vec{u}^0\right)$.

Finally, there is the requirement of symmetry. If two individuals are the same, then they should get the same payoff. Formally, this is equivalent to saying that the names we attach to an individual (via their index) have no effect when the bargaining game is symmetric:

Axiom(S) A bargaining solution satisfies *symmetry* if whenever the bargaining set is symmetric, namely $\left\{(u^S, u^B) \mid (u^B, u^S) \in F\right\} = F$ and $u^{0B} = u^{0S}$, then $\phi^B\left(F, \vec{u}^0\right) = \phi^S\left(F, \vec{u}^0\right)$.

Nash shows that there is a *unique* bargaining solution ϕ that satisfies these assumptions. If one drops the axiom of symmetry then one has a class of rules that correspond to the *generalized Nash bargaining solution* defined by:

$$\phi^\pi\left(F, \vec{u}^0\right) = \arg\max_{\vec{u} \in F} \left(u^B - u^{0B}\right)^\pi \left(u^S - u^{0S}\right)^{1-\pi}, \tag{5.5}$$

for $\pi \in (0, 1)$. The generalized bargaining solution provides a way to model bargaining power via the coefficient $\pi \in (0, 1)$. When $\pi = 0$ or 1 we define:

$$\phi^1\left(F, \vec{u}^0\right) = \lim_{\pi \to 1} \phi^\pi\left(F, \vec{u}^0\right),$$

$$\phi^0\left(F, \vec{u}^0\right) = \lim_{\pi \to 0} \phi^\pi\left(F, \vec{u}^0\right).$$

To show that the generalized Nash bargaining solution characterizes all the solutions to the Nash axioms, we begin with the *standard bargaining problem* for which one can find a solution. One can then map this solution to all other bargaining pairs.

The standard problem is defined by $E = \left\{\vec{u} \in \Re^2 \mid u^B + u^S \leq 1\right\}$, and $\vec{u}^0 = \vec{0}$. This is the canonical problem of splitting a dollar. The outcome of no agreement has each party earning zero. A solution satisfying efficiency and individual rationality must result in a payoff on the $u^B + u^S = 1$ frontier with $u^B, u^S \geq 0$. Specifically, a solution satisfies efficiency and individual rationality if and only if it is of the form $(\pi, 1 - \pi)$. One can easily verify that the solution to the generalized bargaining solution, (5.5), for the standard bargaining problem is given by:

$$\phi^\pi\left(E, \vec{0}\right) = (\pi, 1 - \pi),$$

where π is a number in the interval $[0, 1]$. Notice that for each π we have a different solution to the bargaining problem. If we impose the requirement of symmetry this immediately implies $\pi = 1/2$. Thus:

Proposition 5.3 *For the standard bargaining problem, if ϕ satisfies efficiency and individual rationality, then $\phi = \phi^\pi$ (as defined in 5.5) for some $\pi \in [0, 1]$. If ϕ also satisfies symmetry, then $\pi = 1/2$.*

The next step is to use scale invariance and the independence of irrelevant alternatives to connect bargaining solutions for an arbitrary problem, F, to the solution for the standard problem.

Proposition 5.4 *Suppose the bargaining solution ϕ satisfies the axioms of efficiency, individual rationality, scale independence, and independence of irrelevant alternatives for all* *compact, convex bargaining sets F, and there is a $\vec{v} \in F$ such that $v > \vec{u}^0$. Then $\phi\left(F, \vec{u}^0\right)$ is given by the generalized Nash bargaining solution, $\phi^\pi\left(F, \vec{u}^0\right)$, for some $\pi \in [0,1]$.*

Proof. Let ϕ be any solution that results in division $\pi \in (0,1)$ for the standard problem E. Thus $\phi\left(E, \vec{0}\right) = \phi^\pi\left(E, \vec{0}\right)$. We now want to show that $\phi\left(F, \vec{u}^0\right) = \phi^\pi\left(F, \vec{u}^0\right)$ for any compact, convex bargaining set F. Since $\pi \in (0,1)$ then the function $V(\vec{x}) = \left(x^B - u^{0B}\right)^\pi \left(x^S - u^{0S}\right)^{1-\pi}$ is strictly concave. Since F is compact and convex there exists a unique $\vec{x}^* \in F$ that maximizes $V(\vec{x})$ on F, and hence $\phi^\pi\left(F, \vec{u}^0\right) = \vec{x}^*$. Note that since there is a $v > \vec{u}^0$, $v \in F$, then $V(\vec{x}^*) > 0$.

Let $K = \left\{\vec{x} \in \Re^2 \mid V(\vec{x}) > V(\vec{x}^*)\right\}$ and notice that this is a strictly convex, open set—the convex combination of two points results in a point in the interior. Hence $F \cap K = \emptyset$, and by the separating hyperplane theorem there is a vector, $\vec{\lambda} = \left(\lambda^B, \lambda^S\right) = \nabla V(\vec{x}^*) / V(\vec{x}^*) = \left(\frac{\pi}{(x^{*B} - u^{0B})}, \frac{(1-\pi)}{(x^{*S} - u^{0S})}\right)$, separating K from F. This implies $\vec{\lambda} \cdot (\vec{x} - \vec{x}^*) \leq 0$ for all $\vec{x} \in F$. Now consider the affine transformation $L(\vec{x}) = \left(\lambda^B\left(x^B - u^{0B}\right), \lambda^S\left(x^S - u^{0S}\right)\right)$, and observe that $L(\vec{u}^0) = (0,0)$, and $L(\vec{x}^*) = (\pi, 1-\pi) \in E$ and for $\vec{z} \in \Re^2$:

$$L^{-1}(\vec{z}) = \left(\frac{z^B}{\lambda^B}, \frac{z^S}{\lambda^S}\right) + \vec{u}^0.$$

Let $\vec{z} \in L(F)$ and $\vec{x} = L^{-1}(\vec{z})$. Using the definition of L^{-1}, we have:

$$\vec{\lambda} \cdot (\vec{x} - \vec{x}^*) \leq 0,$$

$$\vec{\lambda} \cdot \left(L^{-1}(\vec{z}) - L^{-1}((\pi, (1-\pi)))\right) \leq 0,$$

$$\left(z^B - \pi\right) + \left(z^S - (1-\pi)\right) \leq 0,$$

$$z^B + z^S \leq 1.$$

The first line follows from the definition of $\vec{\lambda}$ as the separating hyperplane. The next three lines follow from the definition of L^{-1}, which implies that $\vec{z} \in E$, and hence $L(F) \subset E$. Since $\phi\left(E, \vec{0}\right) = (\pi, 1-\pi) \in L(F)$, then independence of irrelevant alternatives implies that $\phi\left(L(F), \vec{0}\right) = (\pi, 1-\pi)$. Since $L^{-1}()$ is also an affine transformation, then the axiom of scale independence implies:

$$\phi\left(F, \vec{u}^0\right) = L^{-1}\left(\phi\left(L(F), \vec{0}\right)\right) = L^{-1}((\pi, 1-\pi)) = \vec{x}^* = \phi^\pi\left(F, \vec{u}^0\right).$$

Scale independence ensures continuity with respect to π and thus the result extends to $\pi \in [0,1]$. $\square$

The Nash bargaining solution has proven to be a useful way to *represent* the outcome of negotiation between two parties given bargaining power and a threat point. The requirements that agreements are efficient and independent of the currency in which they are negotiated are natural assumptions for rational agents.

We can apply this solution to the original buyer-seller problem to get the following result:

Proposition 5.5 *Suppose the outcome of bargaining between the buyer and the seller is given by the generalized Nash bargaining solution with the buyer having bargaining power* $\pi \in (0, 1)$. *Then parties agree to trade at the efficient level* $q^* (\theta)$ *with trade prices given by:*

$$p^\pi (\theta) = (1 - \pi) \left(B \left(q^* (\theta), b \right) - u^{0B} \right) + \pi \left(C \left(q^* (\theta), c \right) + u^{0S} \right).$$

This result provides some testable comparative static results on the effects of outside options on the trade price. In particular, $\partial p^\pi / \partial u^{0B} = - (1 - \pi) < 0$ while $\partial p^\pi / \partial u^{0S} = \pi > 0$. This implies that the sensitivity of price to outside options is a function of bargaining power. As there is a single parameter representing bargaining power, the model can be used to test for the existence of rents and the allocation of power in a bilateral relationship (see for example, Svejnar [1986] and Abowd and Lemieux [1993] for some early contributions).

In those papers, the generalized Nash bargaining model is used to provide an estimable parameter representing bargaining power. A natural question is the source of bargaining power. The next section introduces the strategic bargaining model that provides insights into the economic determinants of bargaining power. In particular, the Nash bargaining solution predicts that negotiated prices are sensitive to outside options. However, in the case of wages, they are often insensitive to market conditions. The dynamic Nash bargaining model provides a potential solution.

5.4   Contract Bargaining

This section introduces a version of the bargaining game based on Shaked and Sutton (1984), Binmore, Rubinstein, and Wolinsky (1986), and MacLeod and Malcomson (1993). It builds on the alternating offers bargaining games introduced by Ståhl (1972) and Rubinstein (1982). The goal is to provide an explicit model of the back and forth that we observe in negotiations to provide a way to explicitly link the characteristics of the bargaining parties to outcomes.

The model addresses the following questions:[10]

1. Will the parties reach an efficient agreement?

2. If efficiency is assured, how is bargaining power determined?

3. Under what conditions will an existing contract *not* be renegotiated, or if renegotiated, what will be the new terms?

The analysis begins by defining the payoffs over time as a function of the contract in place. Conceptually, trade occurs in continuous time, but bargaining occurs at discrete time intervals following an explicit protocol. Binmore, Rubinstein, and Wolinsky (1986) point out that such explicit attention to modeling the protocol can provide guidance on the external validity of different solutions to the bargaining problem, and they show that the way the external market affects bargaining outcomes is sensitive to the bargaining protocol. The strategic model used here has its roots in the arbitration model of Raiffa (1953).[11] A nice feature of that model is the assumption of symmetry. In each round of negotiation it is assumed that one party is chosen at random to make an offer given the previous offers as defaults. This in turn allows one to use a one-step dynamic programming algorithm to find the equilibria.

The next subsection outlines the payoffs in terms of a simple buyer-seller (firm-worker) model that will be used again in the following chapters. An important feature of this model is the assumption of transferable utility using money payments. This standard assumption in the law and economics literature greatly simplifies the analysis. In particular, this implies that the Pareto frontier is linear, and hence for this class of models we do not have to worry about violations of the axiom of independence of irrelevant alternatives (see exercise 8). The subsequent section outlines the strategic contract bargaining game. The key ingredient is to distinguish between the inside and outside options. Finally, the solution with frictionless bargaining is characterized.

5.4.1 The Payoffs

To capture negotiation over time, it is assumed that the buyer and the seller contract for a *flow* of services over a period of time $t \in [0, T]$. Letting the contract at time t be given by $k_t = \left(q_t, p_t^B, p_t^S \right)$ implies flow payoffs for the buyer and the seller:

$$u^B(k_t) = B(q_t) - p_t^B, \tag{5.6}$$

$$u^S(k_t) = p_t^S - C(q_t). \tag{5.7}$$

The parties have personal rates of time preference, $r_i, i \in \{B, S\}$, and trade is restricted to a fixed period of time $t \in [0, T]$. Hence the payoff for party $i \in \{B, S\}$ is given by:

$$U^i = \int_0^{t^0} u^i(k_t) e^{-r_i t} dt + \int_{t^0}^T u^{0i} e^{-r_i t} dt,$$

where t^0 is the date on which parties separate and take their outside options. To simplify matters, suppose that time is normalized so $T = 1$ and there is no discounting, so $r_i = 0$ (see exercise 9 and MacLeod and Malcomson [1995] for the general case). The model can be interpreted as employing a worker for the day or purchasing the input to a manufacturing process over a longer period.

Prices are allowed to differ to incorporate free disposal and derive efficient exchange as a result, rather than as an assumption. In particular, when we move to models with asymmetric information in later chapters, then conflict will occur in equilibrium with the consequence that the amount paid by the buyer may exceed the revenue received by the seller.

Let $s^* = \max_{q \geq 0} B(q) - C(q)$ be the flow surplus at the efficient level of trade, q^*. Without loss of generality, normalize the currency and measure output relative to the efficient level so that one can set $s^* = q^* = 1$. Parties could reach an agreement at time zero, at which point the efficient payoffs are characterized by proposition 5.2. The Pareto frontier is shown in figure 5.1.

The continuous time setup is beneficial because one can precisely describe what would happen if the parties do not reach an immediate agreement. Real-life bargaining entails parties making offers, delaying responses, making counteroffers, and so on. This chapter assumes that there is no asymmetric information; thus, any threats, such as the threat not to trade, may affect the bargaining outcome but they are not carried out in equilibrium.

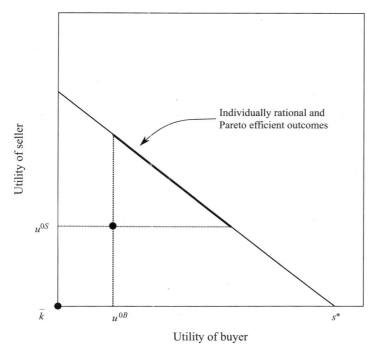

Figure 5.1
The set of individually rational and Pareto efficient outcomes.

More precisely, it is assumed that bargaining and exchange take place over a sequence of periods of length $\Delta = 1/N$, where N provides a measure of *bargaining frictions*. When N is large, parties can make many offers and counteroffers within the period. Frictionless bargaining is the outcome when N becomes large and $\Delta \to 0$. Let n denote the date of the period, starting with the first period, $n = 1$. Date n corresponds to time $t = (n-1)\,\Delta$. The contract for period n is negotiated at the beginning of the period and remains fixed for Δ units of time. Hence, contract k_n means $k_t = k_n$ for $t \in ((n-1)\,\Delta, n\Delta]$.

As a matter of convention, contract k_0 is in force before the start of negotiation. It can be a preexisting contract, or if no contract has been agreed, then $k_0 = \vec{0} = \{0, 0, 0\}$ denotes the default contract.

5.4.2 The Renegotiation Game

The early literature on strategic bargaining (Raiffa 1953; Nash 1953; Binmore, Rubinstein, and Wolinsky 1986; Ståhl 1972; and Rubinstein 1982) assumes that once an agreement has been reached the game concludes. When bargaining concludes with an immediate exchange of goods for money, this is a reasonable assumption. However, such trade tends to occur in a competitive market. Bargaining power is typically expressed in terms of a firm's supply decision to the market as a whole, with terms of trade fixed by forces of supply and demand.

Issues of bargaining power per se are more salient for exchanges over time, where events may occur that lead to changes in the terms of trade. Before exploring the effects of uncertainty (in the next chapter), one needs to work out the structure of equilibrium contracts

in the absence of uncertainty. It is assumed that bargaining always begins in the shadow
of *some* contract denoted by k_0. In the absence of an agreed contract at date 0, the default
contract, $k_0 = \vec{0} = \{0, 0, 0\}$, is in force.[12]

Any uncertainty has been resolved before negotiations begin, so that parties know the
benefit, $B(q)$, and the cost, $C(q)$, of trading q units. Bargaining begins in period $n = 1$ and
continues each period until the final period. At the beginning of period n, the contract k_{n-1}
is the contract in force from the previous period (which is contract k_0 when $n = 1$). The
protocol at the beginning of period n is:

n.0 Nature chooses the buyer (seller) with probability π $(1 - \pi)$ to be the *proposer*.

n.1 The proposer offers a new contract $\tilde{k}$.

n.2 The respondent decides between accepting the new contract, rejecting the new contract
and continuing to trade under k_{n-1}, or leaving and taking up her outside option $u^{0S}(u^{0B})$.
If the respondent does not take the outside option then trade occurs under the new contract
if it was accepted, in which case $k_n = \tilde{k}$. Otherwise, the old contract remains in force and
$k_n = k_{n-1}$.

These moves are repeated until $n = N$. The extensive form is illustrated in figure 5.2.

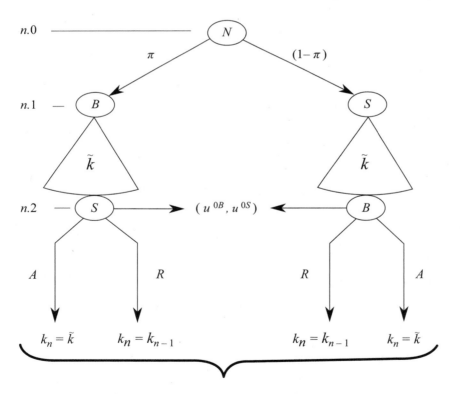

Trade and next period's round of bargaining

Figure 5.2
Bargaining game.

When parties first meet they can, if they wish, simply refuse to trade and take their outside options given by $\vec{u}^0 = \{u^{0B}, u^{0S}\} \in [0, \bar{u}]^2$, where $\bar{u} \geq 0$ is the maximum value possible for the outside option. It is also assumed that once these options are taken, parties cannot return to the bargaining table. This would be the case if the outside option entails a binding contract with another party for the good to be traded.

Parties can always renegotiate a contract by mutual assent, and therefore one cannot assume that the contract does not vary over time. It is assumed that the contract remains fixed for the duration of a single period, and k_n denotes the contract that is in force in period n. The first contract with a payoff consequence is contract k_1. It is equal to k_0 if there is no renegotiation at time 0. Given k_1, it is in force for period $n = 1$, which lasts from time $t = 0$ until $t = \Delta$.

The payoffs during negotiation are called the *inside options*. The flow payoffs from the inside options are given by equations (5.6) and (5.7). It may be that the outside options are greater than the inside options. However, parties can take their outside options only if they permanently leave the relationship at the beginning of the period. The payoffs of the buyer and seller at the beginning of period n (the time from $t_n = \Delta\,(n-1)$, until $t_{n+1} = \Delta \times n$) if they trade every period are:

$$U_n^i = \int_{t_n}^1 u^i\,(k_t)\,dt, \tag{5.8}$$

$$= \Delta \sum_{l=n}^N u^i\,(k_l),\, i \in \{B, S\}, \tag{5.9}$$

where k_l is the contract that has been agreed in period $l = n, \dots, N$. If parties have left the relationship for their outside options, then $u^i\,(k_l)$ is replaced by u^{0i} for the remainder of the bargaining game. In particular, this implies that if party i takes up the outside option in period n, then its value is given by:

$$U_n^{0i} = (1 - (n-1)\,\Delta)\,u^{0i}. \tag{5.10}$$

A significant feature of this game is that only the respondent is able to take the outside option. This implies that the proposer does not get a chance to take the outside offer until she is in a position to reject an offer in some future period. When bargaining frictions are low (N is large), this occurs quickly.

This is a significant assumption. Suppose this assumption did not hold and either party could take the outside option after a rejection. Consider a buyer who has the chance to make an offer and expects to get only his outside option the next period. Suppose the buyer makes an offer that gives the seller slightly more than the seller's outside option. In other words, the buyer tries to grab most of the surplus this period. The seller faces a problem: if she rejects this offer, then because the buyer gets his outside offer only in the next period, it makes sense for the buyer to take the outside offer on the seller's rejection. If the seller is getting some rent, then accepting the buyer's offer is better than rejecting it.

Therefore, if the buyer makes an offer and can then immediately leave upon rejection by the seller, this can result in a large increase in the buyer's power. In this case, it is interesting that the buyer's power is high because of a low future rent for the buyer that makes rejection credible.

Shaked (1994) first observed the importance of the timing in the bargaining game. He calls the case in figure 5.2 a *bazaar* because in a bazaar one can always shout out a new offer as a party walks away, and consequently it is never credible to commit to the outside option without hearing a counteroffer. In contrast, Shaked (1994) calls the case in which either party can take their outside option after rejection a *hi-tech* market. For example, if an offer for a financial asset that is made over the phone is rejected, then the rejected party can simply hang up rather than wait for a counteroffer. The equilibria in hi-tech markets are quite complex, particularly in multiperson bargaining (see Binmore [1985] for a discussion), while in the case of a "bazaar," the equilibria are generically unique, and provide a natural extensive form interpretation of the Nash bargaining solution.

5.4.3   Construction of the Bargaining Equilibrium

This section characterizes the equilibria for a "bazaar" when the bargaining friction $\left(\Delta = \frac{1}{N}\right)$ is small. Even though we allow for continuous renegotiation, the subgame perfect Nash equilibrium is characterized by immediate agreement at time $t = 0$ on a contract k^* that is never renegotiated. To find k^* one has to compute the outcome for any subgame, characterized by the current agreement in period n, given any existing contract from the previous period, k_{n-1}. This solution proceeds using backward induction as follows:

Step 1: Outcome when trade is not efficient
Consider first the case when separation is efficient: $1 < u^{0B} + u^{0S}$. If we are in period n, then regardless of the contract in force, k_{n-1}, one party is always worse off going forward with the relationship than leaving. From the perspective of the buyer making the offer (a symmetric analysis applies when the seller makes an offer), if he makes an offer that the seller accepts, this implies that he gets a payoff worse than his outside option. Hence, he only makes offers that the seller rejects, as does the seller when she gets to make an offer. Consequently, when either party receives such an offer, they would reject it and take the outside option. This implies that in all states for which no trade is efficient ($\theta \in \Theta^{NT}(X^*)$), the bargaining model predicts no trade. When $1 = u^{0B} + u^{0S}$, the equilibrium is not unique, but a modification of the previous argument implies that no trade is a possible equilibrium. In either case, the payoffs are unique, with each party getting exactly their outside option payoff.

Step 2: Efficient contracts are equilibria
A contract k is said to be *individually rational* if flow payoff is larger than the outside option:

$$u^i(k) \geq u^{0i}, i \in \{B, S\}.$$

A contract k is efficient if:

$$u^B(k) + u^S(k) = 1,$$

namely, it divides the surplus between the two parties. We now show that any individually rational and efficient contract is never renegotiated.

Consider now the case in which there are contracts that are individually rational and efficient. Suppose $1 > u^{0B} + u^{0S}$, and let $u_n^i(k_{n-1})$ denote the payoff in flow terms for player $i \in \{B, S\}$ at the beginning of period n (before we know who will make an offer in period n) as a function of the contract, k_{n-1}, in force at the end of period $n - 1$.

The analysis proceeds by deriving the equilibrium payoffs for period n given the value function for period $n + 1$. Given that the game ends in period $n = N$, we set $u_{N+1}^i(k_N) = 0$

for all k_N. The unique perfect equilibrium is computed by backward induction—given the equilibrium value function in period $n + 1$, we compute the equilibrium in period n.

Suppose $k_{N-1} = k^*$ is efficient and strictly individually rational—$u^B (k^*) > u^{0B}$ and $u^S (k^*) > u^{0S}$. Any offer the buyer makes that varies terms will make either him or the seller worse off, and hence, a new contract would never be accepted. Moreover, because the existing contract is strictly better than leaving the relationship, the seller will not leave the relationship in the final period under the terms of k^*, and hence $k_N = k^*$. A similar argument applies when the seller makes an offer.

Now, suppose $k_{N-2} = k^*$. If this contract is not renegotiated, then we know that $k_N = k^*$, and therefore no renegotiation results in an efficient allocation that is strictly better than the market alternative; hence $k_{N-1} = k^*$. Working backward we can conclude that if $k_1 = k^*$, then this contract is never renegotiated.

Next, consider the case in which k^* is efficient, but $u^S (k^*) = u^{0S}$, and suppose $k_{N-1} = k^*$. In this case, the seller is indifferent between accepting and rejecting k^*. If she threatens to reject, the buyer can always offer an efficient contract $k^{*\epsilon}$, such that $u^S (k^{*\epsilon}) = u^S (k^*) + \epsilon$ for some $\epsilon \in \left(0, (1 - u^{0B} - u^{0S})\right)$, which the seller will always choose rather than take the outside offer, and which makes both parties strictly better off than with no trade. This implies that having the seller reject can never be part of an equilibrium. However, for $\epsilon > 0$, the buyer can always choose a contract with $\epsilon / 2$, which he strictly prefers and the seller will always accept. Thus, the only subgame perfect equilibrium has the parties agreeing not to renegotiate an efficient contract, even though the seller is indifferent between accept and reject. A similar argument applies when the buyer's outside option binds.[13]

Applying the argument recursively, we find that when the gain from trade is strictly positive, then any individually rational and efficient contract is never renegotiated:

Theorem 5.6 *Suppose that there is a strictly positive gain from trade, $1 > u^{0B} + u^{0S}$, and k^* is an efficient, individually rational contract in force in period n. Then it is a subgame perfect Nash equilibrium never to renegotiate this contract ($k_l = k^*$ for $l = n, n + 1, \ldots, N$).*

This result is labeled a theorem because of its fundamental role in dynamic contract theory. It illustrates that if an enforceable agreement is efficient and individually rational, then it will never be renegotiated. The rigidity of a contract follows from a combination of enforceability and the efficiency of the agreement that leads one party or the other to block contract renegotiation. However, when an enforceable agreement is inefficient, then parties can change the terms by mutual assent.

Step 3: Efficient renegotiation
Consider now the situation for which the contract $\bar{k}$ is in force but it is not an efficient allocation, namely $u^B (\bar{k}) + u^S (\bar{k}) < 1$. In the absence of renegotiation, if the parties stay together they get the *inside options* given by $\bar{u}^B = u^B (\bar{k})$, $\bar{u}^S = u^S (\bar{k})$. To simplify the subsequent algebra, we can put the problem into standard form by subtracting the inside option payoffs from each party's payoff and outside options. Let the flows be given by:

1. Total surplus: $s^* = 1$.

2. Inside options: $\bar{u}^B = \bar{u}^S = 0$.

3. Outside options: $u^{0S}, u^{0B} \geq 0$, $u^{0S} + u^{0B} < 1$.

First, after any period $n-1$ where there has not been renegotiation, in period n parties agree to an efficient contract. We know from the analysis above that such a contract is never renegotiated. Consider first the case without outside options.

Let U_l^{*i} denote the renegotiated payoff of agent $i \in \{B, S\}$ in period l given the period length of Δ when there has been no contract renegotiation from $n = 1$ until $l - 1$. Consider first the case with no renegotiation until the last period, N. At that point the total surplus is $\Delta \times s^* = \Delta$. This is a version of the final offer game in exercise 6. When a party is chosen to make an offer, the unique subgame perfect equilibrium is to offer a contract that extracts all the surplus. Given the probability π for the buyer making the final offer, the expected value for each party at the beginning of period N is given by:

$$U_N^{*B} = \pi \times \Delta,$$

$$U_N^{*S} = (1 - \pi) \times \Delta.$$

Now suppose that renegotiation occurs in period $N-1$. If the buyer is chosen to make an offer, then he knows that in period N the seller will get a payoff of $(1 - \pi) \times \Delta$, and he must offer at least this to the seller for her to accept. When the buyer is chosen to make an offer in period $N-1$, he gets a payoff of total surplus less what the seller must get, or $2\Delta - (1 - \pi)\Delta = (1 + \pi)\Delta$. Similarly, when the seller is chosen she gets a payoff of $(1 + (1 - \pi))\Delta$. Putting this together we get:

$$U_{N-1}^{*B} = \pi \times 2\Delta,$$

$$U_{N-1}^{*S} = (1 - \pi) \times 2\Delta.$$

Each party gets a fraction of the total remaining surplus in proportion to their bargaining power/probability of making an offer. We can continue the process backward until period n. This can be converted to calendar time by observing period n begins at time $t_n = (n - 1)\Delta$. The total surplus remaining at time t is $1 - t$, and the payoff at time t is given by:

$$U_t^{*B} = \pi \times (1 - t),$$

$$U_t^{*S} = (1 - \pi) \times (1 - t).$$

When parties meet at time $t = 0$, the beginning of period 1, they agree to trade with an efficient contract that gives the buyer a π share of the gains from trade and the seller a $(1 - \pi)$ share of the gains.

5.4.4 Outside Options

We learn from the previous analysis that if the current contract is inefficient, parties will renegotiate to an efficient agreement. Because the total flow surplus is 1, the equilibrium payoff can be fully characterized by the fraction of the surplus that the buyer gets. Let this be denoted by λ. This transforms a two-dimensional problem into a one-dimension difference equation that can be explicitly solved.

The game solution proceeds by computing the buyer's share in the last period if no agreement has been reached yet. The equilibrium is then found via backward induction, and it is convenient to index from the last period to the present. Let $m = N - n + 1$ denote the *horizon* index, where n is the period index. Thus, the last period of trade occurs at $m = N - N + 1 = 1$, while $m = 2$ is the next-to-last period, and so on. Let λ_m be the share of the surplus that the buyer gets when renegotiating from the default contract $\vec{0}$ to an efficient contract when the horizon is m. Thus, the seller gets a share $1 - \lambda_m$ in period m.

We solve the game by working out the share in period $m = 1$, λ_1. Then, given λ_m, one can derive the expression for λ_{m+1}. Let $1 > u^{0i} \geq 0, i \in \{B, S\}$ denote the outside options, respectively. It is assumed that trade is efficient and hence $u^{0B} + u^{0S} < 1$.

In the standard case, both parties prefer to earn their outside options to their inside options (normalized to zero). Using the logic of the static Nash bargaining solution, it might seem that the inside options are irrelevant. As we shall see, this is not the case.

We can write the outside and inside payoffs in terms of the buyer's share. Define:

$$\lambda^{0B} = u^{0B},$$

$$\lambda^{0S} = 1 - u^{0S},$$

$$\bar{\lambda}^{B} = 0,$$

$$\bar{\lambda}^{S} = 1,$$

where $\bar{\lambda}^j$ are the inside options. For the buyer this is zero. For the seller, because she is getting zero at her inside option, this represents the buyer getting all the surplus, and hence $\bar{\lambda}^S = 1$. The assumption for this case that trade is preferred to the outside options implies:

$$1 > u^{0S} + u^{0B},$$

$$1 - u^{0S} > u^{0B},$$

$$\lambda^{0S} > \lambda^{0B}.$$

Resulting in:

$$1 = \bar{\lambda}^{S} > \lambda^{0S} > \lambda^{0B} > \bar{\lambda}^{B} = 0. \tag{5.11}$$

Consider the last period, indexed by $m = 1$, in which parties can trade for the $\Delta = 1/N$ period of remaining time. Given that there is no future after this period, both parties care only about the returns in this final period, and in particular, prefer their outside option to their inside option. Thus, when responding to an offer they will reject any offer that is less than their outside option. Therefore, in the last period the party making the offers gets the surplus, which is less than their counterparty's outside option. In this case, the buyer's expected payoff is:

$$U^{B}_{m=1} = \left(\pi \left(1 - u^{0S} \right) + (1 - \pi) u^{0B} \right) \Delta,$$

$$= \left(u^{0B} + \pi \left(1 - \left(u^{0B} + u^{0S} \right) \right) \right) \Delta. \tag{5.12}$$

This solution is exactly the generalized Nash bargaining solution with the outside options acting as threat points.

Equation 5.12 can be rewritten in buyer share terms:

$$\lambda_1 = \pi \lambda^{0S} + (1 - \pi) \lambda^{0B}. \tag{5.13}$$

This is simply another way to write the generalized Nash bargaining solution when the outside options are threat points.

The computation of λ_m given λ_{m-1} begins with the payoff of the buyer and then translates it into share terms. When the horizon is m, the total surplus is $m\Delta$. With probability π the buyer makes a take-it-or-leave-it offer of a share λ_m^B with probability π. The seller will accept if and only if her share is greater than both the outside option at horizon m and taking the inside option for one period and getting the equilibrium payoff in the next period (and using $\bar{\lambda}^S = 1$):

$$m\Delta \left(1 - \lambda_m^B\right) \geq \max \left(m\Delta \left(1 - \lambda^{0S}\right), \Delta \left(1 - \bar{\lambda}^S\right) + (m-1) \Delta \left(1 - \lambda_{m-1}\right)\right),$$

$$\geq m\Delta - \Delta \times \min \left(m\lambda^{0S}, 1 + (m-1)\lambda_{m-1}\right). \tag{5.14}$$

Because the buyer would like to give the seller the best deal for himself, (5.14) must hold with equality, and we have after division by $m\Delta$:

$$\lambda_m^B = \min \left\{ \lambda^{0S}, \frac{1}{m} + \frac{m-1}{m} \lambda_{m-1} \right\}. \tag{5.15}$$

With probability $(1 - \pi)$, the seller makes a take-it-or-leave-it offer to the buyer (which is accepted). Using a similar argument we get ($\bar{\lambda}^B = 0$):

$$\lambda_m^S = \max \left\{ \lambda^{0B}, \frac{m-1}{m} \lambda_{m-1} \right\}. \tag{5.16}$$

Thus, the expected payoff before the proposer is chosen is:

$$\lambda_m = \pi \lambda_m^B + (1 - \pi) \lambda_m^S \equiv F \left(\lambda_{(m-1)}, m\right). \tag{5.17}$$

What is particularly nice about this expression is that the length of a period has no effect on the dynamics. In other words, the share one gets is a function of only how many bargaining periods remain.

To determine the solution, we need to derive some properties of the function $F(\lambda_m, m)$ describing the bargaining dynamics. The next result shows that the solution never moves beyond the outside options.

Lemma 5.7 *For $\pi \in (0, 1)$, $\lambda_m \in \left(\lambda^{0B}, \lambda^{0S}\right)$ for all $m \geq 0$.*

Proof. From (5.11) and (5.13) we have that $\lambda_0 \in \left(\lambda^{0B}, \lambda^{0S}\right)$. Now suppose that $\lambda_{m-1} \in \left(\lambda^{0B}, \lambda^{0S}\right)$, and let us show that λ_m solves this as well. The constraints on λ_{m-1} and the fact $\bar{\lambda}^S > \lambda^{0S}$ imply:

$$\lambda^{0S} \geq \min \left\{ \lambda^{0S}, \frac{1}{m} + \frac{m-1}{m} \lambda_{m-1} \right\} = \lambda_m^B > \lambda_{m-1}$$

and a similar constraint for λ_m^S, and hence:

$$\lambda^{0S} \geq \lambda_m^B > \lambda_{m-1} > \lambda_m^S \geq \lambda^{0B}.$$

Since $\pi \in (0, 1)$, this implies that $\lambda_m \in (\lambda^{0B}, \lambda^{0S})$. $\qquad \square$

Next we want to determine the long-run equilibrium for the case in which the inside options determine the solution. Suppose that bargaining power is between the values of the outside option:

$$\pi \in (\lambda^{0B}, \lambda^{0S}).$$

Given this, we can choose M sufficiently large that $\pi \in (\lambda^{0B}, \lambda^{0S})$, so for $m \geq M$ we have:

$$\pi = F(\pi, m).$$

This implies that π is an equilibrium of (5.17).

$$\lambda^{*I} = F(\lambda^{*I}, m).$$

Observe that one has $F(\lambda, m) < \lambda$ when $\lambda > \lambda^{*I}$, and $F(\lambda, m) > \lambda$ for $\lambda < \lambda^{*I}$, and thus we have a stable equilibrium at λ^{*I}. This implies that when $\pi \in (\lambda^{0B}, \lambda^{0S})$ then:

$$\lim_{m \to \infty} \lambda_m = \pi.$$

Notice that this result does not depend on the length of a period, but only on the number of rounds of bargaining. Let the length of a period be $\Delta_m = (1 - t)/m$, and let $U^{B*}(\Delta_m)$ be the payoff to the buyer if parties have not renegotiated until $t \in [0, 1)$. Then:

$$U_t^{B*}(\Delta_m) = \lambda_m (1 - t),$$

$$U_t^{S*}(\Delta_m) = (1 - \lambda_m)(1 - t)$$

and hence:

$$\lim_{\Delta_m \to 0} U_t^{B*}(\Delta_m) = \pi(1 - t),$$

$$\lim_{\Delta_m \to 0} U_t^{S*}(\Delta_m) = (1 - \pi)(1 - t).$$

Thus, when the generalized Nash bargaining solution with threat points given by the inside options results in payoffs that are better than either outside option, then these outside options have no effect on the outcome when bargaining is frictionless.

Consider now what happens when this solution gives an outcome for the seller that is worse than her outside option (as illustrated in figure 5.3):

$$u^{0S} > (1 - \pi).$$

In terms of the share going to the buyer, this corresponds to:

$$\pi > \lambda^{0S}.$$

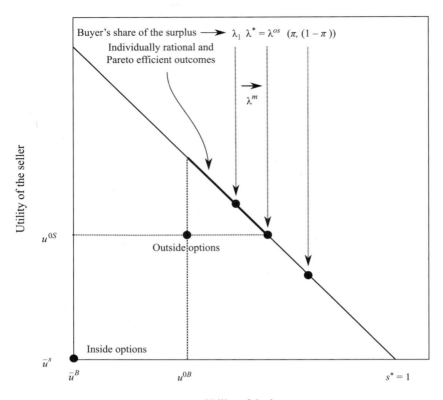

Figure 5.3
Dynamic bargaining and outside option principle.

We have already shown that $\lambda^{0S} > \lambda_m$ for all $m = 0, 1, \ldots$. In this case we claim that:

$$\lim_{m \to \infty} \lambda_m = \lambda^{0S}.$$

Suppose that this is not the case. As the share is taken from a bounded set, $\lambda_m \in \left(\lambda^{0B}, \lambda^{0S}\right)$, there must be a limit point $\lambda^* \in [\lambda^{0B}, \lambda^{0S})$. However, the fact that $\pi > \lambda^{0S}$ implies from the discussion of the stability of π that for all $m \geq M$:

$$F\left(\lambda^*, m\right) > \lambda^*,$$

and hence λ^* cannot be a limit point. Because this inequality holds for sufficiently large m for any $\lambda^* \in [\lambda^{0B}, \lambda^{0S})$, this implies that the limit point is not in $[\lambda^{0B}, \lambda^{0S})$, and hence λ^{0S} is the unique limit point of this sequence. A similar result holds when the buyer's outside option is the Nash bargaining solution based on the inside options.

The solution to the dynamic bargaining problem is illustrated in figure 5.3. The solution in terms of the buyer's share is illustrated at the top of the figure. The main insight of dynamic bargaining is that bargaining power is generated by the payoffs *while* bargaining. In the last period, the buyer's share is $\lambda_1 = \pi u^{0S} + (1 - \pi) u^{0B}$. However, as we solve the dynamic bargaining problem by backward induction, the buyer's share begins to reflect the payoffs that parties get if there is a delay in the negotiations. In the absence of outside options, the buyer's share, λ_m, converges to π. However, the seller's outside option (in buyer share terms) gives an outcome that is better than bargained for ($\lambda^{0S} < \pi$, as in figure 5.3, places an upper bound on λ_m). This constrained allocation becomes the outcome of the bargaining game in the limit.

Notice that the solution does not depend upon the length of a period, only upon the number of periods until the final period. As bargaining becomes more frequent, the solution at the beginning of the period in this example is given by $\lim_{m \to \infty} \lambda_m = \lambda^{0S}$. The next proposition summarizes this result for the general case with arbitrary inside options.

Proposition 5.8 *(Outside option principle) Given inside and outside options,*

$$\vec{U}_t, \vec{U}_t^0 \in \left\{ \left(U^B, U^S \right) | U^B, U^S \geq 0, U^B + U^S \leq (1 - t) \right\} \equiv F_t,$$

the solution to the frictionless dynamic bargaining game overflow payoffs starting at time t is given by payoffs (U_t^{B*}, U_t^{S*}) solving:

$$(U_t^{B*}, U_t^{S*}) = \arg \max_{(U^B, U^S) \in F_t} \left(U^B - \bar{U}_t^B \right)^{\pi} \left(U^S - \bar{U}_t^S \right)^{1-\pi}, \tag{5.18}$$

subject to

$$U^B \geq U_t^{0B},$$
$$U^S \geq U_t^{0S}.$$

In the simple case addressed in this section, it has been assumed that the inside options are given by no trade and no side payments. More generally, parties can set the inside option by contract. For example, one can have a penalty payment when an individual does not come to work but has not quit. That would affect his inside option and not his outside option. More generally, the fact that parties can always renegotiate a contract implies the forces described by this result are always working in the background. In the next chapter, this result forms the basis for optimal contract design where the purpose of the contract is to set terms that determine the ex post values of the inside and outside options, as well as the terms of trade.

In summary, the key insights from the dynamic bargaining model are as follows:

1. If parties have agreed upon an efficient, individually rational contract to divide the gains from trade, it is not renegotiated.

2. If the bargained outcome in the absence of an outside option is Pareto superior to the outside options, then adding those options has no effect on the negotiated payoffs. In an employment context this implies that even if a worker's outside wage rises, it will not affect the current wage until it is worthwhile to quit the firm and take the outside option.

3. If the bargained outcome based on the inside options results in a payoff for one party that is worse than her outside option, then that party gets exactly her outside option payoff. In this case any variation of the counterparty's outside option has no effect on the terms of trade.

An interesting feature of this game is that the equilibrium entails immediate agreement, so one does not observe the parties' getting payoffs generated by the inside options. This implies that with field data one may not be able to observe the payoffs that are generating the observed agreement. One way to generate evidence on the role of inside options is via an experiment in which one can set all the relevant payoffs and observe how parties behave (see Binmore, Shaked, and Sutton 1989).

5.5   Discussion

The foregoing has been an abbreviated review of bargaining theory under conditions of symmetric information. See Binmore (1998) for a more comprehensive (and entertaining) review of both the theory and the intellectual history of bargaining theory. The theory's first goal is to provide a framework to *describe* the bargaining problem. The axiomatic approach focuses on two ingredients—the set of feasible payoffs and the payoffs that parties receive if an agreement is not reached. The axiomatic approach pioneered by Nash provides a number of principles that a solution based upon this data should satisfy. Nash's approach to frame the problem in terms of a set of feasible payoffs and a threat point has endured, as have the principles of individual rationality and Pareto efficiency. In most applications it is assumed that utility is transferable with money, and hence the Pareto frontier is linear, which in turn means that we do not need to worry about the axiom of independence of irrelevant alternatives.

The most problematic assumption is symmetry. In the context of the Nash model with transferable utility, symmetry implies that the only factors that affect the bargained agreement are the threat points and the slope of the Pareto frontier. In practice, one expects that the division of the gain from trade would depend on a number of factors, including discount rates and personal characteristics of the parties. Thus today, the most widely used solution is the generalized Nash bargaining solution, in which the relative bargaining power of parties that determines the division of the gain from trade is left as a parameter that may change from case to case. This solution has proven useful in practice because it provides *descriptive* evidence of rent sharing in which one can use data to estimate the relative bargaining power of parties, as in the classic studies by Svejnar (1986) and Abowd and Lemieux (1993).

The *Coase theorem* (Coase 1960) also applies these ideas. When legal rules are clear, contracts are enforceable, and utility is transferable via money, then parties can achieve an efficient allocation of resources regardless of the allocation of property rights or the bargaining power of parties. This viewpoint has been important not so much because of the prediction of efficiency, but because it highlights that bargaining power by itself does not necessarily lead to inefficient allocations. Much of the work that goes beyond price theory tries to understand the conditions under which such an efficient agreement cannot be achieved.

The ability to estimate bargaining power does not explain its value or the factors that are likely to affect bargaining power. A goal of strategic bargaining models is to link the abstract notion of bargaining power to features of the bargaining environment. The strategic bargaining model of section 5.4 illustrates a number of points. When parties can make alternating offers over a finite horizon, then, consistent with principles of individual rationality and Pareto efficiency, parties immediately agree to a unique division of the gains from trade. The model also makes a number of new points relative to the Nash bargaining solution.

First, the bargaining power of parties depends upon how frequently they are able to make offers. The individual who can make more offers has more power. Though individual rationality is an implication of the model, the effect of outside options is different from the one envisioned by Nash. If there is one round of bargaining, then the expected payoff is exactly the generalized Nash bargaining solution, with power given by the probability that an agent is given the right to make the single offer. However, if parties negotiate over time, this result no longer holds. In that case, the appropriate threat point with repeated rounds of bargaining is the payoff individuals receive while negotiating—the inside option. If this option results in a negotiated agreement that is superior to the outside options, then small variations in the outside options have no effect on the agreement. Significant empirical implications follow. For example, it is inconsistent with the celebrated Mortensen-Pissarides model (see Mortensen and Pissarides 1999). In that model, wages are assumed to respond to market conditions. The difficulty is that it formally predicts that wages continuously adjust with market conditions, even though there is extensive evidence of wage rigidity in the short run (see for example Card and Hyslop [1997]). The model of bargaining with outside options provides a solution to this problem. In the next chapter, the holdup model is introduced, which shows that rigid wages can in some cases ensure *efficient* employment (MacLeod and Malcomson 1993).

Outside options also have an effect on outcomes because they constrain the set of possible agreements. For example, suppose a worker receives an attractive offer elsewhere. The strategic bargaining model predicts that the firm will respond by matching the offer, but not with a response that is superior to the outside offer. Over longer periods of time, this implies that wages do respond to market conditions, but less so in the short run. This highlights the point that the external validity of the models we are exploring is likely to be sensitive to the time period over which the models are being applied.

The strategic bargaining model can also be seen as an extension of the monopoly and monopsony models, in which one party, the firm, makes all the offers. The presence of a union allows workers to make meaningful and binding counteroffers, which in turn results in unions exercising bargaining power. However, such bargaining power does not necessarily imply an inefficient allocation: the symmetric information bargaining model predicts efficient outcomes, regardless of relative bargaining power.

Inefficient bargains can occur when there is asymmetric information. The introduction of asymmetric information results in a class of models in which conflict and disagreement are predicted to occur (see Kennan and Wilson [1993] and Ausubel, Cramton, and Deneckere [2002] for helpful reviews of the literature). Moreover, bargaining theory predicts that the outcome depends on individual discount rates and outside options that may not be observed by researchers. This in turn makes the empirical implementation of these ideas difficult. See Card (1990), Cramton and Tracy (1992), Currie and McConnell (1991), Machin, Stewart, and Van Reenen (1993), Currie and Ferrie (2000), and Coles and Hildreth (2000) for evidence on union-firm bargaining. Chapter 8 provides an introduction to contracting with asymmetric information and provides conditions under which inefficient conflict may occur.

There is also a literature that studies multilateral bargaining and the surplus division problem with more than two parties. Moulin (2014) provides a good review of the theory, including the important concept of a Shapley value. Gul (1989) shows that these ideas provide a strategic foundation for the Nash bargaining solution that can be extended to include the Shapley value. Flatters and MacLeod (1995) use the Shapley value to explain tax farming and corruption in developing countries. Stole and Zwiebel (1996) use these ideas to build a model of wage formation when there is imperfect competition, a result that has been quite important for trade theory (Helpman, Itskhoki, and Redding 2010).

5.6   Exercises

1. Prove proposition 5.2.

2. Here we consider a version of John Nash's (1953) *Demand Game* applied to the sales contract. After observing b and c, each party simultaneously demands a quantity and a price, $D^i = (p^i, q^i)$, $i \in \{B, S\}$. The demands are consistent if $q^B = q^S = q$ and $p^s \geq p^S$, in which case they correspond to a feasible allocation $k = (q, p^B, p^S)$. When demands are consistent, the buyer and seller get their utility under this allocation, $u^B(k|b)$ and $u^S(k|c)$, respectively. If the demands are not consistent, they obtain their outside payoffs, $\vec{u}^0 = \{u^{0B}, u^{0S}\}$. An allocation $\vec{x}$ is said to be the outcome of the Nash demand game if $\vec{x}(\theta)$ is an equilibrium of the Nash demand game for each $\theta \in \Theta$. From chapter 4 we know that the equilibria in the Nash demand game are efficient. What is the set of Nash equilibria for this game? Are they all efficient?

3. Another solution to the bargaining problem is the Kalai and Smorodinsky (1975) solution. It proceeds as follows. Let F be a convex, compact bargaining set such that $\vec{u} \geqq \vec{u}^0$ for all $\vec{u} \in F$. Define the best that party i could attain by $b_i(F) = \max \{u_i | (u_1, u_2) \in F\}$, and let $\vec{b}(F) = (b_1(F), b_2(F))$. The Kalai-Smorodinsky solution is given by:

$$\mu\left(F, \vec{u}^0\right) = \gamma^* \vec{b}(F) + \left(1 - \gamma^*\right) \vec{u}^0,$$

where $\gamma^* = \max \left\{\gamma \geq 0 | \gamma \vec{b}(F) + (1 - \gamma) \vec{u}^0 \in F\right\}$. Show that $\mu\left(F, \vec{u}^0\right)$ is well defined with $\gamma^* \leq 1$ and that the solution satisfies the axioms of efficiency, symmetry, and scale independence. Provide an example showing that it does not satisfy the axiom of independence of irrelevant alternatives. Finally, work out price and quantity for the buyer-seller agreement under the Kalai-Smorodinsky solution and compare it to the solution under the Nash bargaining solution ($\pi = 1/2$).

4. Consider the following game. There is a supplier of inputs to two firms, $i \in \{A, B\}$, who compete in the output market. Suppose that the price in the output market is given by a standard downward-sloping demand curve, $p(q_A + q_B)$, where $q_i, i \in \{A, B\}$, is the output of each firm, and $p' < 0$. You may assume that revenue is concave in quantity produced and you may add any other convenient assumptions regarding the shape of the demand curve. Firm profits are given by:

$$\pi_i(q_A, q_B, Q_i, P_i) = q_i p(q_A + q_B) - P_i, q_i \leq Q_i.$$

The quantity Q_i is the stock of the good that firms have bought from a supplier at a negotiated price P_i. The profit function of the supplier is given by:

$$\pi_S = P_A + P_B - C(Q_A + Q_B),$$

where $C(\cdot)$ is a cost function satisfying $C(0) = C'(0) = 0, C''(Q) > 0$. Suppose that each firm participates in this market only if they get at least zero profits. The "Nash in Nash" bargaining problem is one in which the supplier simultaneously engages in bargaining with each firm using the Nash bargaining solution to fix $\{Q_i, P_i\}, i \in \{A, B\}$, and then firms in the product market set output noncooperatively given the amounts $Q_i, i \in \{A, B\}$. The original "Nash in Nash" model is developed in Horn and Wolinsky (1988).[14]

(a) Draw the extensive form for this game where Nash bargaining is a black box at the market competition stage. Assume that parties have correct expectations, but each firm cannot directly observe the contract the other firm has signed with the supplier.

(b) How should you set up the threat points for the Nash bargaining solution between the supplier and the firm?

(c) In this static setup, would the firms ever choose $q_i < Q_i$?

(d) Provide a definition of an equilibrium in this market when the bargaining power of the supplier is $\pi \in (0, 1)$. Work out what happens if π goes to 1 or 0.

(e) What would happen if, after negotiation, each firm could see the contract signed by the other firm before choosing output?

5. Consider an infinite horizon bargaining game with two players. Each period $t = 0, 1, 2, \ldots$ is identical until an agreement is reached. Use this fact and the dynamic programming algorithm to find the unique subgame perfect Nash equilibrium payoffs. Perform the case $U^{A0} = U^{0B} = 0$ and discuss the relationship between these outside options and the generalized Nash bargaining solution. The stage game is as follows:

(a) At the beginning of period t, Nature chooses player A or B to make offers with probability π, $1 - \pi$, respectively.

(b) The chosen player makes an offer s to the other player. The offer $s \in [0, 1]$ is the share of a dollar that A will receive.

(c) The respondent chooses to either:
(i) Accept—then $U_t^A = \delta^t s$ and $U_t^B = \delta^t (1 - s)$, where $\delta \in (0, 1)$, and the game stops.
(ii) Reject and leave the game—then $U_t^A = \delta^t U^{0A} \geq 0$ and $U_t^B = \delta^t U^{0B} \geq 0$.
(iii) Reject and continue to bargain—move to step (a).

6. Consider the following game. Suppose that parties meet to divide a dollar. Player 1 makes an offer $x \in [0, 1]$, which player 2 can accept or reject. If accepted, player 1 gets $(1 - x)$ and player 2 gets x. Suppose that if player 2 rejects then the parties get their outside offers $u^i \in (0, 1), i = 1, 2$. Characterize the unique equilibrium payoffs as a function of the outside options. Consider the case where the offers and outside offers are constrained to be in cents $(x \in \{0, 1, 2, \ldots, 100\})$. Characterize the set of equilibria in this case, and show that they are not in unique general. Suppose this is a repeated game with discount factor δ. What are the subgame perfect equilibria in this case?

7. Consider the following variant on the contract bargaining problem for a good rather than a service. Suppose that parties are bargaining to trade at date 1. In the absence of an agreement, the parties obtain payoffs $\vec{u}^0 = (u^{0B}, u^{0S}) \geq (0, 0)$. Beginning at date 0, they

bargain using the random offers model of section 5.4. There are N periods, and at time $t_n = n/N, n = 0, 1, \ldots, N - 1$, Nature chooses the buyer (seller) with probability π $(1 - \pi)$ to offer to trade q units at date 1 at a price p. Assume there is no discounting. If no agreement is reached by time $t_{N-1} = N - 1/N$ then parties get $\vec{u}^0$. Find the unique subgame perfect Nash equilibrium payoffs as $N \to \infty$. Show that it can be an equilibrium to reach an agreement in any period.

8. Next, consider the following variation of the previous problem. Suppose parties divide one unit of a commodity so that party 1 gets q_1 with utility with Von Neumann–Morgenstern utility $u(q_1)$ and party 2 gets q_2 with utility $u(q_2)$, where $q_1 + q_2 \in [0, 1]$. Consumption occurs when parties reach an agreement (so this is bargaining with a good, not a service). Suppose $u(0) = 0$ and $u'(q) > 0$. Illustrate the Pareto set when $u'' < 0$. How would you model the strategic bargaining game in this case? What would the equilibria look like? Answer these questions when $u'' > 0$. In particular, does the principle of independence of irrelevant alternatives hold in either of these cases?

9. Work out the statement of proposition 5.8 when there is discounting: $r_j > 0$ and $r_S \neq r_B$. How does this change the Pareto frontier and the contracts that parties sign?

10. Consider yet another variant of the bargaining game of section 5.4. Suppose that if a contract offer is rejected, then the agent who offered the contract can choose to leave immediately after her counterparty rejects the contract. Shaked (1994) calls such a market "hi-tech" because the agents correspond to traders in a financial market who might hang up on a telephone call if an offer is rejected. How does this change the game? Compute one subgame perfect equilibrium for this game when there are two rounds of bargaining and compare the answer to the corresponding contract bargaining games discussed above.

6 Reliance, Holdup, and Breach

The duty to keep a contract at common law means a prediction that you must pay damages if you do not keep it—and nothing else. . . . If you commit a contract, you are liable to pay a compensatory sum unless the promised event comes to pass. . .
—Oliver Wendell Holmes (1897, 462).

6.1 Introduction

Price theory has power because it provides an elegant model of how commodities are produced and distributed in the economy. Its main insight is that relative prices represent the value of a commodity, which in turn provides signals to market participants on how much to produce and consume. A rise in price leads to an increase in supply and a corresponding fall in demand. The whole system can be viewed as a well-oiled machine that takes raw materials and labor to produce commodities that respond to supply and demand shocks over time. At the core of this system are transactions. Firms buy inputs and labor, transform them, and then, in another transaction, sell them to customers. But this story ignores that considerable time may pass between the purchase decision and final delivery and consumption of a commodity. This is where contracts come into play.

A contract is any instrument used to coordinate exchange over time.[1] For example, Jensen and Meckling (1976, 210) argue that the firm is a legal fiction that is better viewed as a "nexus of contracts" between individuals in the firm. At the time they wrote their paper, contract theory in economics was being developed as a natural extension of the Arrow-Debreu model. In *Theory of Value*, Gerard Debreu (1959) shows that one can extend the two welfare theorems of general equilibrium to allow for uncertainty over time.[2] His result is not a practical solution because it assumes trade occurs at a single point in time. It also assumes that markets are complete in the sense that there is a market for each commodity at every point in time, at every location, and for every possible state of Nature. This is clearly impossible. In practice, we observe markets for futures contracts, such as the Chicago Mercantile Exchange. Hence, one might be tempted to conclude that improving resource allocation simply entails adding more markets. But, as Hart (1975) shows, increasing the number of markets does not necessarily improve market performance, and in some cases it can make matters worse.

Contracts provide an alternative that explicitly allows parties to coordinate their supply and demand choices over time. The early contract theory literature begins with the insurance contract because it captures two necessary features for a nontrivial contract. First, there needs to be a separation in time between an agreement and contract performance. As shown in chapter 3, risk-averse individuals are willing to pay risk-neutral firms for the provision of insurance against uncertain future events, such as fire, accidents, or illness. Second, there must be an enforcement mechanism for when an adverse event occurs. Otherwise, the insurance company may not make the requested payment.

Contract design is complex because, among other things, enforcement is not always straightforward. For example, when the World Trade Center was attacked on 9/11, there was a dispute between the building owners and their insurance company over whether the attacks constituted as one or two events. There were two events if each tower that was hit by an airplane was viewed as a separate, insurable event but one event if the attack on the twin towers was coordinated. The owners' insurance contract had a per-event cap, so there was a considerable amount of money at stake in the interpretation.[3] This situation illustrates that, even detailed, well-written contracts can be incomplete.

Moreover, it is important to realize that one cannot "force" an insurance company to pay the insured. Rather, if an insurance company does not pay as required, then contract *breach* has occurred. In countries with a well-functioning rule of law, contract breach provides the harmed individual with the *right* to sue the insurance company. If the court rules in favor of the harmed party, and the insurance company does not pay, then the court can order a seizure of the insurance company's assets to enforce the judgment. This relatively complex process happens behind the scenes, and it is mostly ignored in much of the contract theory literature.[4]

Economic models typically assume that the legal process works at zero cost, so when insurance companies anticipate losing in court, they pay as required by the contract. Given this assumption, there is a large body of literature on the structure of *complete* contracts, or what is often referred to as agency theory.[5] This theory, reviewed in chapter 7, derives the pattern of payments parties use to implement trade when there is asymmetric information regarding the actions taken and the gains from trade.

Those models were developed as natural extensions of the Arrow-Debreu model of a competitive equilibrium. Because they assume that contracts are enforceable, they are not directly relevant to contract law. The economic models that reflected contract enforceability were developed soon after the agency theory was in full bloom, particularly Alchian and Demsetz (1972), Klein, Crawford, and Alchian (1978), Grout (1984), and Grossman and Hart (1986).[6] That work is more closely related to the law and economics tradition, and it is the basis for the models discussed in this chapter. The next section discusses contract law and the role of the court in enforcement. It highlights that an economic purpose of a contract is *reliance*—the ability of each party to make decisions that depend or rely upon the performance of their counterparty under the terms of the agreement.

Three sections outline the theory. Section 6.2 extends the buyer-seller model of chapter 5 to include relationship-specific investments. It describes the different possible types of investments and what constitutes an efficient allocation. The question, then, is whether a contract can be designed that implements the efficient allocation. It turns out that contract terms should depend upon both the nature of the investments that are made and the nature of the commodity being traded.

Section 6.3 works out an optimal contract when trading a "good." This is a commodity that is exchanged at a specific point in time. Exogenous shocks make the problem interesting because they may make trade inefficient before the seller is asked to perform. In that case, parties may, by mutual assent, renegotiate contract terms. Parties concerned about long term-returns will anticipate this possibility and design the initial contract to consider contract renegotiation. Section 6.3 first shows that in the absence of a contract, investment and trade may be inefficient. Then it is shown that, under the appropriate conditions, it is possible to design the initial contract to implement the efficient allocation.

Section 6.4 considers contracting for a *service*. Given that the most important and widely studied service is labor, contracts are discussed in terms of a worker-firm relationship, in which the firm is the buyer of labor services from a worker, who is in the role of a seller. As a matter of law, employment contracts are governed by a set of rules that are different from commercial contract law. This can be explained by the fundamental difference in the timing of the trade decision relative to when the buyer learns about seller quality. In the case of a good, a buyer can in principle evaluate or measure quality *before* consumption and consequently can refuse to accept defective goods.

In contrast, the quality of a worker is determined during performance of their work. This turns out to have a profound effect on the structure of the contract. In particular, the outside option principle introduced in the previous chapter on bargaining plays an important role in contract design and renegotiation. Under some natural conditions, exchange for a service entails price rigidity—contract terms may not vary in the short run, even when alternative opportunities for the buyer and seller have changed. Section 6.5 concludes the chapter with a brief discussion of the literature.

6.1.1 Contract Law and the Reliance Problem

When parties are considering entering into a contract, they must consider *why* they need a binding agreement and *what* the court may be asked to enforce. In a classic paper, Fuller and Perdue (1936) use the term *reliance interest* when referring to the investments that parties make in a relationship covered by a contract. Reliance is a form of pretrade investment that increases the value of trade relative to other potential activities.

For example, consider a concert promoter who engages a singer to perform at a venue. In advance of the performance, the promoter must invest in advertising and the cost of selling tickets, and costs can be recouped only if the singer performs as promised. Notice that the buyers of the tickets also make a pretrade investment to attend the concert on that particular night rather than make plans to go elsewhere. If the singer does not perform as promised, many parties are harmed.

If the performance contract were to be litigated in court, the first question would be whether there had been a contract breach. If breach has been shown to have occurred, the court must set the monetary damages. In this example, the nonappearance of the singer might seem to be a clear case, but this depends upon the contract terms. For example, illness is a foreseeable event, and contracts commonly include terms to deal with it that may excuse the singer from performing. Promoters can buy insurance against the costs that arise when a performer is ill, and normally the ticket will have terms and conditions that spell out the promoter's responsibilities to the concert attendee.

It would not be unusual to excuse the singer from performance should she fall ill. If the promoter has purchased insurance, the insurance company will make payments as required by the contract. However, courts might still be involved if the promoter suspects the singer is faking her illness. In that case, the insurance company might refuse to pay, and the promoter might have to sue the singer for damages. The standard remedy in common law systems, such as the United Kingdom and the United States, is *expectation damages*, which is the amount the harmed party hopes to gain had the contract been executed. In the case of the concert promoter, this would be the amount of profits he expected to earn, plus costs associated with the concert cancellation.

Fuller and Perdue (1936) observe that other remedies are possible. One is setting damages equal to the *reliance expenditures*, the amount that the promoter invested into organizing the concert. Another is *restitution*, putting the promoter back into the same position as the situation before he began to organize the concert. In practice, courts must make damages a function of measurable costs that have been submitted as evidence. Fuller and Perdue's paper is influential because it illustrates the many ways contract breach can harm a party and, in doing so, provides the court with several methods to measure damages as a function of the available evidence.

That perspective is very much ex post. Namely, it addresses the pragmatic problem of basing damages on the available evidence. It does not really provide a normative principle for setting damages before the contract is written. Since the time of Fuller and Perdue, legal scholarship has been increasingly influenced by the law and economics movement that provides explicit normative principles for setting damages. The work of Posner (1973) has been particularly influential in this regard. Building on Posner's approach, Goetz and Scott (1977) and Schwartz (1979) argue that the purpose of contract law is to enforce agreements that help parties achieve efficient exchange. Thus, rather than begin with the problems that occur after trade has begun, as in Fuller and Perdue (1936), the law and economics approach suggests that we begin with the goals of parties at the time they enter into an agreement. Should a dispute occur because of some error or missing term in the agreement, then courts should simply fill in the term in a way that is consistent with the ex ante intent of the parties.

This perspective allows us to analyze contracts under the hypothesis that courts will enforce contracts as written. The fact that Fuller and Perdue (1936) emphasize the reliance interest implies that it is one of the most important reasons for writing a contract. For example, consider the problem of renting an apartment. It seems obvious that one should sign a lease, but why? If the market is perfectly competitive, then a lease should not be necessary. The renter need only pay the market rent.

The problem is that without a lease, if the renter invests time and energy into decorating the apartment and is happy living there, then the landlord, observing the renter's happiness, can raise the rent knowing that the renter will not leave. The cost of decoration is called a *relationship-specific investment* because the return on that investment is valuable only if the renter does not move. Victor Goldberg (1976, 439) calls the landlord's rent increase "holdup":

First, once the relationship has begun, the supplier will be isolated to some degree from competition and will be in a position to "holdup" the consumer. A simple example would be the automobile mechanic who agrees to fix a car, takes it apart, and then says he will put it together again at three times the originally agreed upon price.

A long-term lease is one contractual instrument that is commonly used to reduce holdup in the rental market. Other chapters of this book discuss a number of other contractual mechanisms to deal with holdup. The behavior in Goldberg's car repair example is unlikely to occur in practice because of reputation effects and because courts would likely sanction a repair shop that behaves in this way.

However, there are many situations in which conditions change and that require the modification of terms. For example, what should happen if, after signing a lease and decorating her apartment, the renter gets a job offer that requires her to move to a new city? In such a case, neither the law nor a sensible landlord would bar the renter from breaking the lease. The issue would be the level of damages that should be paid to the landlord for breaking the lease.

When parties anticipate the possibility of such an event, they face a trade-off. If both parties expect a long relationship, they will invest more in making the relationship as efficient as possible. On the other hand, if there is a possibility of termination, then one needs to set terms for such termination, which in turn affects the level of investment in the relationship. The purpose of this chapter is to outline the basic principles for the determination of contract terms in such cases.

6.2 Production with Relationship-Specific Investments

To understand why parties enter into agreements, one must begin with the *counterfactual* of what would happen if parties traded without a formal contract. Grout (1984) provides an elegant analysis of this case (in the context of firm-union negotiation later extended by Hart and Moore [1988]). Though not discussed explicitly in Grout (1984), his model reflects English labor law, particularly the Trade Disputes Act of 1906, which was updated with the Trade Union and Labour Relations (Consolidation) Act 1992.[7] The law protects union workers from tort liability arising from industrial action. In other words, in the event of a strike, the harmed firm cannot sue the union for losses arising from the strike. The result is that labor union contracts are not legally binding because workers cannot be punished for not working. Thus, the union can renegotiate contract terms in the shadow of a strike threat whenever they feel it is reasonable and within the bounds of the law. We consider the implications of this law for the level of relationship-specific investment and then consider the consequence of adding contract law—allowing parties to enter into binding long-term contracts that, if breached, may result in the court awarding damages to the harmed party.

The buyer-seller (firm-worker) relationship is modeled as a game with a timing sequence that is similar to the buyer-seller model of chapter 5, section 5.4. The difference is that parties negotiate twice—first when they meet and agree to trade, and then later after events have occurred that may require contract renegotiation. We maintain the convention that renegotiation and trade begin at date 0, and thus the dates before trade are given by negative integers. This timing is given by a *contract bargaining game*.

Date -3: The buyer (B) and seller (S) negotiate and agree on a contract k_0. In the absence of a contract, neither party faces any future obligation from the other. This is indicated by the default contract $\vec{0}$ that sets quantity and prices to zero.

Date -2: The buyer and seller make investments (in dollars) $\vec{I} = \{I^B, I^S\} \geq 0$.

Date -1: The buyer and seller observe each other's investment and personal characteristics given by $b \in [b_L, b_H]$ and $c \in [c_L, c_H]$. Outside options are random variables $\vec{u}^0 = \{u^{0B}, u^{0S}\}$ that are correlated with investments and personal characteristics, and they are assumed to be bounded above by $u^{\max}$. The realized values of the outside options at date -1 are $\vec{u}^0 = \{u^{0B}, u^{0S}\}$. Taken together, these determine the commonly known state of Nature, $\theta = \{b, c, \vec{u}^0\} \in \Theta$.

Dates $t \in [0, 1]$: At this point, investments, $\vec{I}$, are sunk, and the state of Nature θ is known. Therefore, a complete description of the state of the relationship is given by $\omega = \{\vec{I}, \theta\} \in \Omega$. Parties, but not the courts, observe the state and then renegotiate the initial contract k_0.

This timeline captures the class of models that focus on the interplay between contract choice, investment/reliance in a relationship, and contract renegotiation and trade. A contract is needed because the investments are assumed to be noncontractible—variations in investment by one party cannot be measured or priced by the courts. We begin with the case in which the contract can specify only the amount to be traded, q, and at what price. The contract can also specify what price will be paid if one of the parties chooses not to trade. Parties are always free to mutually adjust the terms of trade in the face of new information. In particular, if a contract results in an inefficient allocation at date 0, then parties have an incentive to renegotiate terms. It is assumed that parties anticipate this behavior when choosing their investments at date -2.

The consequence of contracting, investing, revealing information, and renegotiating is an allocation denoted by $\vec{x}(\omega) = \{q(\omega), p(\omega)\}$, where $\omega \in \Omega$ describes the state with all the information needed to determine payoffs at the time of trade. The difference between this chapter and the previous one is that parties can set the terms of trade as a function of both the state of Nature, $\theta \in \Theta$, and the investments in the relationship, $\vec{I}$. Given an allocation $\vec{x}$, the ex post payoffs in the event of trade are:

$$u^B(\vec{x}, \omega) = B(q(\omega), \omega) - p(\omega), \tag{6.1}$$

$$u^S(\vec{x}, \omega) = p(\omega) - C(q(\omega), \omega). \tag{6.2}$$

Investment costs are not included in these payoffs because they are sunk and do not affect the subsequent decisions. This chapter and the next assume that price denotes a transfer from the buyer to the seller and hence, in the terminology of chapter 5, $p^B = p^S$. This assumption is relaxed when we deal with asymmetric information and relational contracts. As a matter of convention, when parties take their outside options, this is denoted by $q(\omega) = \emptyset$, and results in payoffs:

$$u^B(\{\emptyset, p(\omega)\}, \omega) = u^{0B} - p(\omega),$$

$$u^S(\{\emptyset, p(\omega)\}, \omega) = u^{0S} + p(\omega).$$

The benefits and costs satisfy the conditions that were introduced in chapter 5, and they are referred to as the "standard assumptions."[8] If we are considering a "good," then it is a commodity whose payoffs are realized at a single point in time, $t = 1$. If trade entails a service, then it is a commodity that is being continuously delivered over the period $t \in [0, 1]$.[9]

When parties initially meet to negotiate contract terms, the future state of Nature is not known. Hence, ex ante preferences are given by:

$$U^B\left(\vec{x},\vec{I}\right) = E\left\{u^B\left(\vec{x},\omega\right)\right\} - I^B, \tag{6.3}$$

$$U^S\left(\vec{x},\vec{I}\right) = E\left\{u^S\left(\vec{x},\omega\right)\right\} - I^S. \tag{6.4}$$

In the case of a service, let $\bar{t} \in [0, 1]$ denote the date on which the parties stop trading and leave the relationship. Let $\vec{x}_t = (q_t, w_t)$, $t \in [0, \bar{t}]$, denote the allocation at time t while the parties are together in the relationship, and let $\vec{X} = \{\vec{x}_t, t \in [0, \bar{t}], w_t^0, t \in (\bar{t}, 1]\}$ be the allocation between the seller and buyer at each point during service provision (the price is given by w_t given that the price plays the role of a wage in a continuing employment relationship). Their payoffs are given by:

$$u^B\left(\vec{X},\omega\right) = \int_0^{\bar{t}} \left(B\left(q_t,\omega\right) - w_t\right) dt + \int_{\bar{t}}^1 \left(u^{0B} - w_t^0\right) dt, \tag{6.5}$$

$$u^S\left(\vec{X},\omega\right) = \int_0^{\bar{t}} \left(w_t - C\left(q_t,\omega\right)\right) dt + \int_{\bar{t}}^1 \left(u^{0S} + w_t^0\right) dt. \tag{6.6}$$

The difference between a good and a service lies in the payoffs during negotiation and trade. With a good, trade is a discrete event, and there is no cost to bargaining impasses that occur before the time of trade. In contrast, with a service, the seller has the power to withhold service during the supply process in the hope of getting a better deal, but at the cost of reducing the total gains from trade. As Shaked and Sutton (1984) and MacLeod and Malcomson (1993) show, this has a significant effect on the equilibrium outcome from bargaining.

However, the difference in the cost of bargaining impasses does not affect the total gain from trade. A feature of a service, as we have defined it, is that at time $t = 0$ the efficient outcome is either to separate or to supply the good at a constant quantity/quality q. This implies that the set of efficient payoffs for goods and services is the same, and so are the efficient investment levels.

This assumption highlights that any differences in the form of the optimal contract between a good and a service arise due to differences in the available bargaining strategies and due to neither the set of feasible allocations nor the value of the outside options.

6.2.1   Characterizing Efficient Investment

The purpose of this section is to derive the first order conditions for efficient investment when parties can agree upon state-contingent transfers. The solution proceeds by backward induction. For each state $\omega \in \Omega$ (the level of investment by both parties and the shocks to inside and outside options), one determines the optimal allocation that efficiency-minded parties would choose. Given this choice, one then determines the optimal level of investment anticipating efficient trade. If the uncertainty has the feature that parties are never indifferent between trade and no-trade, then the first order condition for efficient investment takes a simple form (proposition 6.1).

Even though we are computing the optimal allocation in the absence of strategic considerations, it requires the computation of a number of counterfactuals. First, suppose parties do not have access to the market and are forced to trade with each other. In that case the optimal *inside option* is given by:

$$\bar{q}^* (\omega) = \arg \max_{q \geq 0} \{ B(q, \omega) - C(q, \omega) \}.$$

The overall level of trade includes the possibility of taking the outside option. Hence, we have:

$$q^* (\omega) = \arg \max_{q \in \{\bar{q}^*(\omega), \emptyset\}} \left\{ B\left(\bar{q}^* (\omega), \omega\right) - C\left(\bar{q}^* (\omega), \omega\right), u^{0B} + u^{0S} \right\}, \tag{6.7}$$

with the convention that $q^* = \emptyset$ if taking the outside options is efficient. We can define the *rent* from trade as the difference between the inside and outside option returns, given the efficient level of inside trade:

$$R(\omega) = B\left(\bar{q}^* (\omega), \omega\right) - C\left(\bar{q}^* (\omega), \omega\right) - \left(u^{0B} + u^{0S}\right). \tag{6.8}$$

Given that investments are sunk costs, the decision to trade is a function of the ex post rent alone. The set of states $\theta \in \Theta$ for which trade is more efficient than no trade is:

$$\Theta^T \left(\vec{I}\right) = \left\{\theta \in \Theta | R\left(\theta, \vec{I}\right) \geq 0\right\},$$

while no trade is efficient in states:

$$\Theta^{NT} \left(\vec{I}\right) = \left\{\theta \in \Theta | R\left(\theta, \vec{I}\right) \leq 0\right\}.$$

The parties are indifferent between trade and no trade in the set of states: $\Theta^I \left(\vec{I}\right) = \Theta^T \left(\vec{I}\right) \cap \Theta^{NT} \left(\vec{I}\right)$.

It is assumed that the distribution of the state $\theta = \left\{b, c, \vec{u}^0\right\}$ is realized after investments are made, characterized by the following continuous and independent probability distribution functions:

- $b \sim f(\cdot)$ and $c \sim g(\cdot)$, such that $f(b), g(c) > 0$ for $b \in [b_L, b_H]$ and $c \in [c_L, c_H]$
- $u^{0i} = U^{0i} \left(\vec{I}\right) + \epsilon^i$, where the error term has a compact support with continuous probability distribution, $\epsilon^i \sim h^i(\cdot)$, $E\left\{\epsilon^i\right\} = 0$. The function $U^{0i} \left(\vec{I}\right)$ is assumed to be differentiable, increasing, and concave in investment $\vec{I}$.

These assumptions ensure that the expected payoffs are well defined. In particular, if parties were not to trade with each other, then the ex ante total surplus from the investments is defined by:

$$U^0 \left(\vec{I}\right) = E\left\{u^{0B} + u^{0S} | \vec{I}\right\}$$

$$\equiv U^{0B} \left(\vec{I}\right) + U^{0S} \left(\vec{I}\right).$$

Parties are always free not to trade, so the decision to trade can be seen as an option to be taken if sufficiently attractive. The ex ante value of this option is given by:

$$R\left(\vec{I}\right) \equiv E\left\{\max\left\{R(\omega), 0\right\} | \vec{I}\right\} \geq 0.$$

The total value of the relationship given investment $\vec{I}$ is then:

$$W\left(\vec{I}\right) = R\left(\vec{I}\right) + U^0 \left(\vec{I}\right) - I^B - I^S.$$

Suppose that there is a unique and strictly positive optimal level of investments, $\vec{I}^* = \arg\max_{\vec{I} \geq 0} W(\vec{I})$, then it satisfies the first-order conditions:

$$\frac{\partial R(\vec{I}^*)}{\partial I^i} = 1 - \frac{\partial U^0(\vec{I}^*)}{\partial I^i}, i \in \{B, S\}. \tag{6.9}$$

The marginal return from investing in the rent from the relationship is the marginal cost of investing less the benefit from investing in the outside option. A consequence of investing in a relationship is that it changes the probability of trade. When the outside options have a continuous distribution that is independent of the inside options, then the probability of being indifferent between trade and no trade is zero. This implies that the first-order conditions take a simplified form:

Proposition 6.1 *When the probability of being indifferent between trade and no trade is zero* $(Pr[\theta \in \Theta^I(\vec{I})] = 0)$*, then for* $i \in \{B, S\}$*,*

$$\frac{\partial R(\vec{I})}{\partial I^i} = E\left\{ \frac{\partial R(\vec{I}, \theta)}{\partial I^i} | \theta \in \Theta^T(\vec{I}) \right\} P^T(\vec{I}). \tag{6.10}$$

Proof. The efficient gain from trade conditional upon the state is defined by:

$$R^*(\omega) = \max\left\{ B(\bar{q}^*(\omega), b, \vec{I}) - C(\bar{q}^*(\omega), c, \vec{I}) - (u^{0B} + u^{0S}), 0 \right\},$$

$$= \max\left\{ B(\bar{q}^*(\omega), b, \vec{I}) - C(\bar{q}^*(\omega), c, \vec{I}) \right.$$

$$\left. -(U^{0B}(\vec{I}) + \epsilon^B + U^{0S}(\vec{I}) + \epsilon^S), 0 \right\}. \tag{6.11}$$

This function is continuous and differentiable for $\theta \notin \Theta^I(\vec{I})$. Given that the errors on the outside options are bounded, we can restrict $R^*(\omega)$ to a compact domain and set an upper bound on investments so that $\vec{I} \in [0, I^{\max}]^2$. Next, take any sequence of differentiable functions $R_n^*(\omega)$ that converge uniformly to continuous function $R^*(\omega)$. The derivative of $R^*(\omega)$ with respect to investments exists everywhere, except on states in which parties are indifferent between trade and no trade. We can define the derivative of $R^*(\omega)$ everywhere by setting $\frac{\partial R^*(\omega)}{\partial I^i} = \inf\left\{ \lim_{n \to \infty} \frac{\partial R_n^*}{\partial I^i} \right\}$ for $i \in \{B, S\}$. This agrees with the derivative of R when it is defined and provides a lower bound on the directional derivatives when they are not defined. As it is not defined on a set of measure zero, we get, by the Lebesgue dominated convergence theorem that:

$$\frac{dR(\vec{I})}{dI^i} = \lim_{n \to \infty} \int_{\theta \in \Theta} \frac{dR_n^*(\omega)}{dI^i} d\mu(\theta, \vec{I}),$$

$$= \int_{\theta \in \Theta} \frac{dR^*(\omega)}{dI^i} f(b) g(c) h^B(\epsilon^B) h^S(\epsilon^S) db dc d\epsilon^B d\epsilon^S$$

$$= \int_{\theta \in \Theta^T(\vec{I})} \frac{dR(\omega)}{dI^i} f(b) g(c) h^B(\epsilon^B) h^S(\epsilon^S) db dc d\epsilon^B d\epsilon^S. \tag{6.12}$$

The second line follows from the fact that the efficient rent is zero for the states in $\Theta^{NT}\left(\vec{I}\right)$, and $R^*\left(\omega\right) = R\left(\omega\right)$ for $\omega \in \Theta^T\left(\vec{I}\right)$.

Notice that, by the envelope theorem, we have at points of differentiability:

$$\frac{dR\left(\omega\right)}{dI^i} = \frac{\partial\left(B\left(\bar{q}^*\left(\omega\right),b,\vec{I}\right) - C\left(\bar{q}^*\left(\omega\right),c,\vec{I}\right)\right)}{\partial q}\frac{\partial q^*\left(\omega\right)}{\partial I^i} + \frac{\partial R\left(\omega\right)}{\partial I^i}$$

$$= \frac{\partial R\left(\omega\right)}{\partial I^i}. \tag{6.13}$$

When the probability of trade is zero, then the return on investment is zero and consistent with (6.10). Suppose now the probability of trade is strictly positive, $P^T = Pr\left[\theta \in \Theta^T\left(\vec{I}\right)\right] > 0$. From this we obtain:

$$E\left\{\frac{\partial R\left(\vec{I},\theta\right)}{\partial I^i}|\theta \in \Theta^T\left(\vec{I}\right)\right\}$$

$$= \frac{1}{P^T}\int_{\theta \in \Theta^T\left(\vec{I}\right)}\frac{dR\left(\omega\right)}{dI^i}f\left(b\right)g\left(c\right)h^B\left(\epsilon^B\right)h^S\left(\epsilon^S\right)dbdcd\epsilon^Bd\epsilon^S,$$

and the exercise is concluded. $\square$

This result shows that the marginal return on investment is the average marginal return when there is trade times the probability of trade. Even though the level of investment affects the probability of trade, it affects these returns only at states in which one is indifferent between trade and no trade. Hence, the marginal impact is zero, and there is no term that includes the marginal effect of investment on the probability of trade. This is an application of the envelope principle to optimal matching, and the result is used later to explore conditions under which a contract fails to implement efficient investment and trade.

6.2.2 The Case of General Investments

Contract form depends on how investments affect the value of the relationship. A general investment is one that has the same marginal impact on productivity inside and outside the relationship. In the case of an employment relationship, Mincer (1958) calls such investment *general human capital*. For example, investment in education and training is expected to increase productivity equally in any future job an individual may hold.

Definition 6.2 *Investment $I^i, i \in \{B, S\}$, is general if it has the same marginal benefit inside and outside the relationship:*

$$\frac{\partial R\left(\omega\right)}{\partial I^i} = 0, \forall \omega \in \Omega, i \in \{B, S\}.$$

Even though investments do not affect the rent, the level of rent can vary with the realized state and whether parties should be trade. Thus, we can further divide the general investment case into three subcases that depend on the difference in value between the inside and outside options:

1. Perfect competition—$R(\omega) = 0, \forall \omega \in \Omega$. In this case, parties are indifferent between trading with their current partner or some other partner in the marketplace.

2. Competitive market with match-specific rents—$R(\omega)$ takes on positive and negative values, with trade occurring if and only if $R(\omega) \geq 0$.

3. Fixed turnover cost—$R(\omega) = \bar{v} > 0, \forall \omega \in \Omega$. In this case, trade is always efficient, and parties face a fixed cost to changing partners.

However, a further useful distinction can be made. A general investment is one for which the returns inside and outside the relationship are the same; it makes no statement regarding who makes the investment. For example, the US Air Force typically pays for pilot training, yet this training has value for the pilot who leaves the Air Force for a job with a commercial airline. In that case, part of the Air Force's training is general—it enhances the pilot's outside option. Training costs are so high that one cannot expect a pilot to repay the Air Force for these costs. Consequently, a typical employment contract with the Air Force requires the pilot to serve for several years in the military before being eligible to leave. Such investments by one party in the productivity of the other party are called *cooperative investments* (Che and Hausch 1999). If an investment affects only one's own payoff, then it is called a *self-investment*, for example, when one invests in a car that allows one to travel to a place of employment.

6.2.3   The Case of Relationship-Specific Investments

A relationship-specific investment arises when the investment enhances trade only with the current partner and does not affect market returns. An example is the contract between a power utility and a coal mine described in Joskow (1987). If the coal company is located near the power plant, it may be efficient for the power plant to have an exclusive supply contract with the mine. After the contract is signed, the mining company would have an incentive to invest in a transportation system, such as a rail line, that specializes in supplying the utility. These investments lower the cost of supplying the utility but may be of zero value for other potential customers.

Definition 6.3   *An investment $I^i, i \in \{B, S\}$ is relationship-specific if it has no value outside the relationship:* $\frac{\partial U^0(\vec{I})}{\partial I^i} = 0$ *for all* $\vec{I} \geq \vec{0}$.

From (6.1) we have that the first-order conditions for efficient relationship-specific investments, $\vec{I}^*$, are given by:

$$E\left\{ \frac{\partial R(\vec{I}^*, \theta)}{\partial I^i} | \theta \in \Theta^T(\vec{I}) \right\} = \frac{1}{P^{*T}}, i \in \{B, S\}. \tag{6.14}$$

Notice that the expected return of investment is a function of the probability of trade. Therefore, the assumption that the gain from trade is concave in investment implies that the efficient level of relationship-specific investment *increases* with the probability of trade.[10]

As with general investments, a *relationship-specific self-investment* is one that increases the agent's personal benefit—I^B increases $B(q, \omega)$ but does not change $C(q, \omega)$ (nor the outside options), and I^S decreases $C(q, \omega)$ but does not change $B(q, \omega)$ (nor the outside options). Another example of a self-investment would be a restaurant owner who renovates a leased space for her new restaurant. In that case, the investment does not affect the returns from other locations, and normally it does not affect the value of the property should the landlord choose to lease it to another tenant. An example of a relationship-specific *cooperative investment* would be a firm's provision of on-site day care and lunch facilities for employees. These investments affect the payoff of the employees without directly affecting the payoff of the firm. These sorts of investments may lower wages paid and possibly turnover if the services provided are highly valued by the employees and therefore may be profitable for the firm.

Achieving efficient investment may be difficult when parties cannot explicitly contract on the level of investment before trade occurs. The next two sections show that a well-designed contract may achieve efficient investment and trade by manipulating the distribution of the ex post returns between the two parties.

6.3   Contracting for a Good

This section studies the problem of contract design for simple exchange. The goal of the buyer and the seller is to exchange q units of a good for an agreed price p at date $t = 1$. As discussed above, a contract is needed because parties can make investments that increase the value of the trade. In the absence of a contract, parties may not be adequately compensated for the relationship-specific investments they make that are intended to increase the value of trade.

Contract design can be complex for two reasons. First, the level of investment made in a relationship can be difficult to measure; consequently, courts may not be able to correctly compensate parties for their losses when trade does not occur. To simplify the analysis, the literature, beginning with Grossman and Hart (1986) and Hart and Moore (1988), assumes that the level of investment cannot be observed by the courts but can be observed by contracting parties.

Second, it is assumed that parties can observe uncertain events that affect the value of trade. In any real-life exchange, there is always a risk that events occur that make trade unprofitable after a contract is agreed on but before the time specified for performance. This information is given by state of Nature, θ. Initially, it is assumed that the courts cannot observe this state, though later we consider the case in which contracts can be conditioned on the value of trade.

Exactly what constitutes a contract? The epigraph from Holmes (1897) makes clear that a contract is a set of promises, the performance of which is backed by a court of law. Holmes observes that courts do not have the power to enforce performance—all they can do is enforce monetary damages that in turn create an *incentive* to perform. In principle, courts can use injunctions (an order by the court to perform) or specific performance (the requirement that a party performance is required by the contract). If a service supplier is served an injunction, she could still refuse to perform, in which case she might face prison time. Specific performance is used when the contract involves property, in which case performance can be enforced by having a sheriff take physical possession of the property.

The economic analysis of law typically assumes parties are sensitive to monetary damages. Hence, even though these legal instruments exist, one can assume they can be replaced by monetary damages. Schwartz (1979) discusses the law regarding specific performance in detail. Aghion, Dewatripont, and Rey (1994) and MacLeod and Malcomson (1993) discuss the use of penalties to achieve specific performance.

The economic approach to contracting begins with the observation that a contract and the resulting state-contingent payments define a "game" between the buyer and the seller (Barton 1972).[11] The issue is how to design the game in such a way that investment and trade are efficient or at least more efficient than without a contract. We begin by specifying a particular sequence of moves that is sufficiently rich to capture the main elements of exchange and then provide some language that will allow us to discuss more precisely the role of a contract and court enforcement.

6.3.1   The Contract Game

The game implementing the exchange of a good starts with the stages described in section 6.2. At date -3 the default contract is $\vec{0}$. It can be negotiated to some ex ante contract k_0 (where 0 denotes the date at which the contract is in force). At this stage, the parties have symmetric information, and there have been no relationship-specific investments. It is assumed that parties reach an agreement that is consistent with the generalized Nash bargaining solution outlined in chapter 5. This process is not explicitly modeled.

In this transferable utility setting, parties will choose the contract that maximizes the total gains from trade. Given such a contract, any division of the surplus can be achieved with a side payment at date -3. Hence, we do not explicitly model contract negotiation at date -3. Rather, we focus upon the consequences of particular contract forms on the total surplus, such as no contract or a fixed-price contract. It is always implicit that the bargaining power at date -3 determines some side payments that are not explicitly modeled. This simplifies the notation and allows one to focus upon the economic consequences of the contract renegotiation that occurs at date 0.

At date -2, each party chooses how much to invest in the relationship, denoted by $I^i, i \in \{B, S\}$. At date -1, Nature chooses the shocks faced by the buyer and seller. Together these determine the state at date 0, denoted by $\omega = \{\vec{I}, b, c, \vec{u}^0\} \in \Omega$. This in turn sets the ex post gain from trade:

$$S(\omega) = \max\{R(\omega), 0\} + u^{0B} + u^{0S}. \tag{6.15}$$

Depending on the terms of the contract k_0, parties can either keep the same contract or renegotiate terms over the period $t \in [0, 1]$ and then complete exchange at date $t = 1$.

As a matter of law, parties are always free to renegotiate a privately agreed contract if there is mutual agreement on the new terms. This is modeled by supposing that from the time the state is revealed at $t = 0$ until trade at $t = 1$, parties play the contract renegotiation game as described in chapter 5, exercise 7. The time from 0 to 1 is divided into N periods. Each period, the buyer is chosen to make a contract offer with probability π; otherwise, the seller makes an offer, as illustrated in figure 6.1.

Let k be the final contract in force at date N, the last round of bargaining. It is given by the vector $k = \{q, p, \bar{p}, p^{0B}, p^{0S}\} \in K = \Re_+ \times \Re^4$, which determines the payoffs for parties, denoted by $\vec{u}(k, \omega)$. This contract implements the terms of trade as follows:

1. If the buyer cannot accept the goods, he sends a message to the seller to this effect. Parties then take their outside options and the buyer pays the seller an amount p^{0B}.

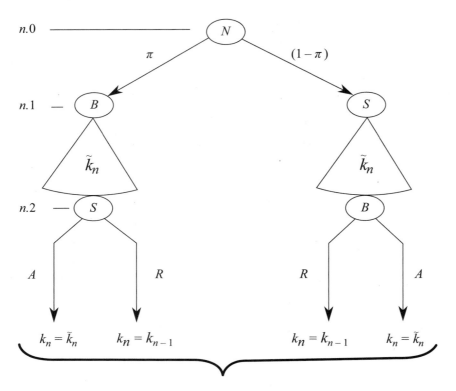

Figure 6.1
Contract game for the trade of a good.

2. If the buyer is ready to receive the goods, the seller decides to produce or not. If she cannot produce, then parties take their outside options and the buyer pays the seller p^{0S} (which can be negative, in which case it is a transfer from the seller to the buyer).

3. If the seller can deliver, then she chooses quantity/quality q' at a cost $C\left(q',\omega\right)$, and the buyer realizes the benefit $B\left(q',\omega\right)$. If $q' \geq q$, then the seller has performed (produced a quantity/quality greater than the amount in the contract, q), and the buyer pays p; otherwise, the seller has not performed, and the buyer pays $\bar{p}$.

This somewhat pedantic game form illustrates precisely the role of law in contract enforcement. Transfers are enforceable because parties can use the power of the state to seize the assets of the nonperforming party.[12] Neither the seller nor the buyer can be compelled to produce and trade. They do so voluntarily as a function of the damages that can be enforced in court. Notice that we allow separation payments to depend on who exercises the right to leave. Moreover, there are no restrictions on the signs of these payments.

The first step in determining the optimal contract is to compute the outcome under any counterfactual contract, $k_0 \in K$. From the analysis in chapter 5, we know that for any equilibrium outcome from bargaining, there is an equilibrium at which parties change the contract terms at most once to a new contract that is denoted by $k\left(k_0, \omega\right)$. This contract is efficient and divides the surplus, $S\left(\omega\right)$, between the two parties.

The determination of the equilibrium begins by determining what would happen if parties do not renegotiate until the last period and contract k_0 remains in force. At that point, Nature chooses the buyer to make an offer to the seller with probability π. If the seller rejects the buyer's offer, then contract $k_0 = \{q, p, \bar{p}, p^{0B}, p^{0S}\}$ remains in force. Choose the most efficient subgame perfect Nash equilibrium to the contract game and let it determine the default payoffs:

$$\vec{u}(k_0, \omega) = \left\{ u^B(k_0, \omega), u^S(k_0, \omega) \right\}. \tag{6.16}$$

This in turn fixes the expected payoffs before Nature moves in the last period. See exercise 6 for the explicit solution to this game. Given that parties can delay renegotiation at no cost until this point, this fixes the payoffs from the contract renegotiation at date $t = 0$:

Proposition 6.4 *For every $\omega \in \Omega$ and for every contract $k_0 \in K$ agreed on at date -3, letting renegotiation costs go to zero (time between offers over period $[0, 1]$ approaches zero) results in unique ex post payoffs:*

$$\vec{u}^*(k_0, \omega)$$

$$= \left\{ u^{B*}(k_0, \omega), u^{S*}(k_0, \omega) \right\}$$

$$\equiv \{\pi S(k_0, \omega), (1 - \pi) S(k_0, \omega)\} + \vec{u}(k_0, \omega), \tag{6.17}$$

where

$$S(k_0, \omega) = \max\{R(\omega), 0\} - \left(u^B(k_0, \omega) + u^S(k_0, \omega) \right) + u^{0B} + u^{0S}, \tag{6.18}$$

is the gain from renegotiating contract k_0.

Proof. Let $\vec{u} = \{u^B, u^S\} = \{\pi S(k_0, \omega), (1 - \pi) S(k_0, \omega)\} + \vec{u}(k_0, \omega)$. Observe $u^B + u^S = \max\{R(\omega), 0\} + u^{0B} + u^{0S}$, and these payoffs result in the optimal level of trade conditional upon the state ω. Consider first the case in which trade is optimal. The result for the case in which separation is optimal will be similar.

We proceed by supposing that there has been no renegotiation until the last period. If the buyer is making an offer, he will offer a contract that the seller will accept, with efficient quantity $q^*(\omega)$ at a price p^S that satisfies:

$$p^S - C\left(q^*(\omega), \omega\right) = u^S(k_0, \omega).$$

Because trade is efficient, we can ensure that the seller will perform by setting a no-trade price, $\bar{p}^S$, and separation payment, p^{0S}, to solve:

$$p^S - C\left(q^*(\omega), \omega\right) \geq \max\left\{\bar{p}^S - C(0, \omega), u^{0S} + p^{0S}\right\}.$$

When the seller makes an offer, she will also extract all the surplus with a contract $\{q^*(\omega), p^B, \bar{p}^B, p^{0B}, p^{0B}\}$ that satisfies:

$$B\left(q^*(\omega), \omega\right) - p^B = u^B(k_0, \omega),$$

$$B\left(q^*(\omega), \omega\right) - p^B \geq \max\left\{B(0, \omega) - \bar{p}^B, u^{0B} + p^{0B}\right\}.$$

Regardless of who is making the final contract offer, the amount traded is the same. The expected payoffs are given by $\bar{u}$. These payoffs are the expected utility for each party under k_0 if they wait until the final period to renegotiate. Because the allocation is efficient, neither can claim more. Hence, it is an equilibrium for both parties to accept a contract to trade $q^*(\omega)$ units at a price p, at date $t = 0$, that satisfies:

$$B\left(q^*(\omega),\omega\right) - p = u^B,$$

$$p - C\left(q^*(\omega),\omega\right) = u^S.$$

Next we need to set $\bar{p}$ and p^0. Because trade is efficient, we have:

$$B\left(q^*(\omega),\omega\right) - C\left(q^*(\omega),\omega\right) \geq B(0,\omega) - C(0,\omega) = 0.$$

Therefore, given p, we can find a $\bar{p}$ such that:

$$B\left(q^*(\omega),\omega\right) \geq p - \bar{p} \geq C\left(q^*(\omega),\omega\right),$$

$$B\left(q^*(\omega),\omega\right) - p \geq -\bar{p} \geq -p + C\left(q^*(\omega),\omega\right).$$

The final line implies that the buyer prefers trade at price p to no trade at price $\bar{p}$. It also implies $p - C(q^*(\omega),\omega) \geq \bar{p}$, which similarly shows that the seller prefers trade to no trade. A similar argument establishes the existence of separation fee $p^{0B} = p^{0S} = p^0$ that ensures that both parties prefer to stay together rather than separate. A similar set of arguments apply when no trade is efficient. □

Proposition 6.4 shows that regardless of the initial contract and the level of investment, renegotiation always leads to a contract k that implements efficient trade conditional on investments. Even though ex post trade is efficient, we shall see that variations in contract k_0 affect investment incentives. In particular, $u^S(k_0,\omega) + u^B(k_0,\omega)$ is not necessarily equal to the total surplus in the relationship (see exercise 8). Also, the renegotiated contract, k, is not unique, even though the renegotiated payoffs are unique (see exercise 9).

Thus, for any ex ante contract k_0, investments $\vec{I}$, and realization of the state of Nature, $\omega \in \Omega$, there are well-defined payoffs for the buyer and seller. Under the standard assumptions, this implies that the expected payoffs at the time of investment are well defined:

$$U^B\left(k_0,\vec{I}\right) = E\left\{u^{B*}(k_0,\omega)\right\} - I^B, \tag{6.19}$$

$$U^S\left(k_0,\vec{I}\right) = E\left\{u^{S*}(k_0,\omega)\right\} - I^S. \tag{6.20}$$

For any contract $k_0 \in K$, this defines an *investment game*. Given the contract k_0, parties also implicitly agree to make investments $\vec{I}(k_0)$. As investments are assumed to be noncontractible, this implies that the investment agreement, $\vec{I}(k_0)$, must be *self-enforcing*:

$$U^B\left(k_0,\vec{I}(k_0)\right) \geq U^B\left(k_0,\left\{I^B,I^S(k_0)\right\}\right), \forall I^B \geq 0, \tag{6.21}$$

$$U^S\left(k_0,\vec{I}(k_0)\right) \geq U^S\left(k_0,\left\{I^B(k_0),I^S\right\}\right), \forall I^S \geq 0. \tag{6.22}$$

In other words, $\vec{I}(k_0)$ forms a Nash equilibrium for the payoffs defined by (6.19)–(6.20). We use the term *self-enforcing* to emphasize that the principle being modeled is the requirement that parties voluntarily choose actions that have been agreed on. The different equilibrium notions for a game, such as Nash equilibrium or sequential equilibrium, are different ways to model self-enforcing behavior. It is an empirical question whether various equilibrium concepts are realistic models of actual behavior.[13]

Even though the payoffs are well defined, in general we cannot ensure the existence of a self-enforcing agreement for any contract k_0. There are cases in which the payoffs are discontinuous functions of investment, so one cannot even necessarily ensure the existence of a mixed strategy equilibrium.

However, it can be shown that in the absence of a contract $(k_0 = \vec{0})$, an equilibrium does exist, though in many cases the result is inefficient investment levels. Moreover, in many cases there exists a contract, k_0^*, that results in efficient investment levels that are self-enforcing, and hence $\vec{I}^* = \vec{I}\left(k_0^*\right)$. With such a contract in hand, there is no need to explore the properties of other contracts for which an equilibrium may not exist or may result in inefficient investment levels because rational parties would prefer a contract that results in an efficient relationship. Once such a contract has been found, then it can be used to implement ex ante any efficient, individually rational allocation with the appropriate side payments.

6.3.2 Investment with No Ex Ante Contract

Rational parties can be expected to enter into a binding agreement only when it makes them better off. A natural first question is what happens in the absence of a contract $(k_0 = \vec{0})$. A good example is an apartment lease. Imagine you have found your dream apartment, the landlord suggests you move in to see how you like it, and he says he will set a fair rent once you are settled in. Upon settling in, you make improvements so the apartment is to your liking. This increases the cost of leaving and searching for a different apartment. If the landlord can set the rent after you have made these investments, he is likely to charge a price that is higher than the price he would have given *before* investments were made. Such behavior by the landlord is known as *holdup*. It provides a fundamental motivation for entering into a long-term contract.

Whether holdup is a problem depends on the characteristics of the investments in the relationship. When there are relationship-specific investments that increase the rent $R(\omega)$, as defined in (6.8), then, in the absence of a contract, rational parties will underinvest in the relationship relative to the efficient solution. To see this, observe that even in the absence of a contract, parties might still make an investment anticipating that there will be trade at time 1. After they invest and observe the state of Nature, if trade is efficient, then proposition 6.4 implies that parties renegotiate terms to achieve ex ante payoffs for parties $i \in \{B, S\}$:

$$U^{*i}\left(\vec{I}\right) = E\left\{\alpha^i \max\left\{R(\omega), 0\right\} + u^{0i}(\omega)\right\} - I^i, \qquad (6.23)$$

where $\alpha^B = \pi$ and $\alpha^S = (1 - \pi)$ are the bargaining power parameters for the buyer and seller, respectively. Investments are *general* when they have no effect on the gains from trade:

$$\frac{\partial E\left\{R(\omega)\right\}}{\partial I^i} = 0, i \in \{B, S\}.$$

In the case of self investments then $\partial\left(u^{0B}(\omega) + u^{0S}(\omega)\right)/\partial I^i = \partial u^{0i}(\omega)/\partial I^i$. Applying these observations to (6.23) implies:

Proposition 6.5   *If parties make only general self-investments, then investment and trade are efficient under no ex ante contract.*

This result shows that with general self-investments one does not need long-term contracts nor even require perfect competition to achieve efficient investment and trade. There might be switching costs at time 1 to go to another partner, but as long as these costs do not affect the marginal benefit from investing, the relationship in the absence of a long-term contract is ex ante efficient.

Relationship-specific investments

The case that has received the most attention in the literature is one with *relationship-specific self-investments* (Rogerson 1984; Grossman and Hart 1986; Tirole 1986; and Hart and Moore 1988). In this case, the investment is assumed to have no effect upon the outside options, and therefore one may assume $U^{0i}\left(\vec{I}\right) = \bar{u}^{0i}$ is a constant. This in turn implies $E\left\{u^{0i}\right\} = \bar{u}^{0i}, i \in \{B, S\}$. From (6.23) it follows that:

$$U^{*i}\left(\vec{I}\right) = \alpha^{i} R\left(\vec{I}\right) + \bar{u}^{0i} - I^{i}, \tag{6.24}$$

where $\alpha^{B} = \pi$ and $\alpha^{S} = (1 - \pi)$. At an efficient contract it must be the case that $\frac{dR(\vec{I})}{dI^{i}} = 1$, but from (6.24) one has that agent $i \in \{B, S\}$ chooses investment to solve:

$$\frac{dR\left(\vec{I}\right)}{dI^{i}} = \frac{1}{\alpha^{i}}, i \in \{B, S\}.$$

This implies:

Proposition 6.6   *(Holdup) Under the standard assumptions, the absence of an ex ante contract results in inefficient incentives to make relationship-specific investments. A party's relationship-specific investment level increases with that party's bargaining power.*

The second condition follows from the second-order conditions for the rent. This is the classic holdup problem. Various versions of this result have been used to explain what Williamson (1975) calls *organizational failures*. He observes that two or more individuals making allocative decisions jointly can lead to *opportunism* and inefficient outcomes. The use of the term "holdup" in the context of contracts is from Goldberg (1976).[14] Klein, Crawford, and Alchian (1978) introduce the idea that the allocation of property rights, along with the bargaining power associated with ownership, can alleviate the holdup problem. Their paper is a beautiful example of an older law and economics tradition that relies on verbal argument and simple examples to make its points.

The first clear, formal statement of holdup is in Grout (1984) in the context of union-firm bargaining. In Grout's model, it is assumed that union contracts are regularly renegotiated. This results in the unions' getting some return from a firm's capital investments, which in turn leads to the firm underinvesting in plant and equipment. At the time Grout wrote this paper, UK manufacturing was in decline; his work points to labor unions as one of the possible reasons.

When considering goods production, Grossman and Hart (1986) use Grout's ideas to provide a seminal analysis of ownership and decision rights. Proposition 6.6 shows that relative bargaining power affects investment incentives. The key insight of Grossman and Hart is that the allocation of ownership and residual control rights over assets can change relative bargaining power. For example, suppose that only the buyer is making a relationship-specific investment. In that case, efficiency can be achieved by giving the buyer ownership rights over the means of production, and the seller becomes an employee who is paid a fixed wage. The next subsection discusses other solutions to the holdup problem when both the buyer and the seller make relationship-specific investments.

6.3.3 Ex Ante Efficient Contract Design

This subsection describes conditions under which it is possible for parties to sign an ex ante contract, k_0^*, that leads to self-enforcing efficient investments, along with the contracts that implement such an allocation. The characteristics of the contract that implements the optimal allocation depend upon the nature of the relationship-specific investments and the structure of the outside options. In particular, there is no "general theory." Rather, the theory shows how a number of standard contract types, or *contractual instruments*, can be used to ensure efficient investment and trade. The choice of contractual instrument varies with the characteristics of the relationship. This section focuses on two such instruments— ex ante rigid prices and the doctrine of *specific performance*. The latter is a doctrine that provides incentives for parties to deliver goods regardless of the value of the outside options.

The doctrine of specific performance is a legal concept that incentivizes parties to trade regardless of alternative opportunities. Given that courts cannot force a person to trade, in practice this means that damages are set to such a level that both parties choose to trade. Parties to the contract may ensure performance by specifying damages in the event of no trade. These are called liquidated damages. In some cases, parties may require performance but not specify damages. In this case, the courts may be called on to set damages. The court-specified damages have the benefit of having more information at the time damages are set. See Schwartz (1979) for details on the law.

The benefit of using specific performance to provide efficient investment incentives can be illustrated with a case in which there is no uncertainty regarding payoffs and the outside options are correlated. For example, the trade price might be given in nominal terms. Then, if there is unexpected inflation, the seller might wish to leave the relationship for a better nominal price somewhere else. More precisely, consider the following case with *relationship-specific self-investments*, where the $B\left(q, I^B\right)$ is the buyer's benefit, and $C\left(q, I^S\right)$ is the seller's costs satisfying the standard assumptions. Suppose that for all realizations of the outside options we have:

$$u^{0B} = \bar{u} + \gamma,$$

$$u^{0S} = \bar{u} - \gamma,$$

where γ is a random variable, with support on $[-\bar{\gamma}, \bar{\gamma}]$, and $\bar{\gamma} > 0$ is a fixed parameter that is a measure of the uncertainty of the outside option that is uncorrelated with the surplus. For example, if contracts are in nominal terms, then γ is an inflation shock.

This implies that the total value of the outside options is fixed at:

$$u^{0B} + u^{0S} = 2 \times \bar{u}.$$

Let us suppose that the rent from the relationship is strictly positive and the surplus satisfies:

$$S^* = \max_{\vec{I}} B\left(q^*\left(\vec{I}^*\right), I^{B*}\right) - C\left(q^*\left(\vec{I}^*\right), I^{S*}\right) > 2\bar{u}.$$

Thus, it is optimal for parties to trade in all states of Nature. Given an initial contract $k_0 = \left(q^*\left(\vec{I}^*\right), p^0, p^{0B}, p^{0S}\right)$, where the price p is the trade price, p^{0B} is the payment when the buyer leaves, and p^{0S} is the payment when the seller leaves, a necessary condition to avoid contract renegotiation is for the contract to be individually rational for all $\gamma \in [-\bar{\gamma}, \bar{\gamma}]$:

$$B\left(q^*\left(\vec{I}\right), I^{B*}\right) - p \geq \bar{u} + \gamma - p^{0B},$$

$$p - C\left(q^*\left(\vec{I}^*\right), I^{S*}\right) \geq \bar{u} - \gamma + p^{0S}.$$

These conditions must hold for any γ, including $\gamma = \bar{\gamma}$ and $\gamma = -\bar{\gamma}$. This implies:

$$B\left(q^*\left(\vec{I}\right), I^{B*}\right) - p \geq \bar{u} + \bar{\gamma} - p^{0B} + p,$$

$$-C\left(q^*\left(\vec{I}^*\right), I^{S*}\right) \geq \bar{u} + \bar{\gamma} + p^{0S} - p.$$

Adding these together we get:

$$S^* = B\left(q^*\left(\vec{I}^*\right), I^{B*}\right) - C\left(q^*\left(\vec{I}^*\right), I^{S*}\right) \geq 2\bar{u} + 2\bar{\gamma} + p^{0S} - p^{0B}.$$

Observe that if there is no payment when parties separate, then with sufficient uncertainty (sufficiently large $\bar{\gamma}$) it must be the case that $2\bar{u} + 2\bar{\gamma} > S^*$. Hence, for some realizations of the outside option there must be some contract renegotiation. This implies that in some states of the world there will be surplus sharing. Proposition 6.6 implies holdup reduces investment incentives.

The solution is for the parties to use a *specific performance* contract.[15] This type of contract is designed so that parties always choose to trade, regardless of the value of the outside options. This is achieved by setting the severance payments, $p^{0B} > 0$ and $p^{0S} < 0$, sufficiently large or small so that neither party wishes to leave.

The effect is illustrated in figure 6.2, where $k_0^{SP} = \{q^*, p, 0, p^{0B}, p^{0S}\}$.

The contract k_0^{SP} implements trade given by point

$$A = \left(B\left(q^*, I^{B*}\right) - p, p - C\left(q^*, I^{S*}\right)\right),$$

where

$$S^* = B\left(q^*, I^{B*}\right) - C\left(q^*, I^{S*}\right)$$

is the value of trade at the optimal output q^*. In this example, $\bar{\gamma} = \bar{u}$. Point D is the inside option in the absence of trade. Observe that as long as the price results in point A on the bold line, it gives payoffs better than the buyer's inside option. From chapter 5 we know that this implies that the inside options are not a credible threat and thus do not affect the contract price.

However, as the random shock γ varies, the outside option payoffs can lie anywhere on the diagonal line that divides the outside option surplus value, $2 \times \bar{u}$, between the two parties. For example, if $\gamma = \bar{u}$, then $u^{0B} = 2 \times \bar{u}$. This lies on the bold dashed line to the right

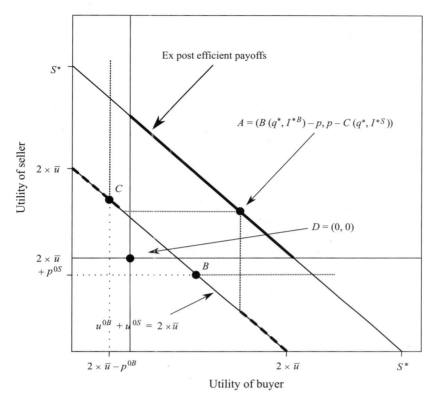

The figure shows "Ex post efficient payoffs" with a line labeled $A = (B(q^*, I^{*B}) - p, p - C(q^*, I^{*S}))$, and $D = (0,0)$. The vertical axis is "Utility of seller" with markers S^*, $2 \times \bar{u}$, $2 \times \bar{u} + p^{OS}$. Points C and B are shown. The horizontal axis is "Utility of buyer" with markers $2 \times \bar{u} - p^{OB}$, $2 \times \bar{u}$, S^*. The line $u^{OB} + u^{OS} = 2 \times \bar{u}$ is indicated.

Figure 6.2
A specific performance contract.

of the payoff from A. Thus, the buyer would leave the relationship unless there is contract renegotiation. With a payment $p^{OB} > 2 \times \bar{u}$, as illustrated in figure 6.2, the buyer would not wish to leave the relationship regardless of his realized outside option. A similar argument applies for the seller. Thus, with appropriately set separation payments, this contract ensures that neither the outside options nor the no-trade option is preferred by either party, regardless of the value of the outside option. Given there is no contract renegotiation and there is always trade, parties set investment to satisfy:

$$\frac{\partial B\left(q^*, I^{B^*}\right)}{\partial I^B} = -\frac{\partial C\left(q^*, I^{S^*}\right)}{\partial I^S} = 1.$$

Equation (6.9) and proposition (6.1) imply that parties are choosing the efficient investment levels. This is summarized with the following proposition.

Proposition 6.7 *Consider exchange under the standard assumptions and relationship-specific self-investments. Suppose there is no uncertainty regarding the inside option, trade is always efficient, and there is fixed price p such that*

$$B\left(q^*\left(\vec{I}\right), I^{B*}\right) \geq p \geq C\left(q^*\left(\vec{I}^*\right), I^{S*}\right).$$

Then there is a specific performance contract, $k_0^{SP} = \{q^*\left(\vec{I}^*\right), p, 0, p^{0B}, p^{0S}\}$, *that results in efficient investment and trade where:*

$$p^{0B} \geq u^{max},$$

$$-p^{0S} \geq u^{max}.$$

In addition to showing how specific performance can implement efficient exchange, this result also illustrates the role of a fixed price in providing appropriate investment incentives. With relationship-specific self-investments, fixed prices ensure that each party receives all the returns from their investments.

An example of a specific performance contract is the marriage contract in which, depending on the jurisdiction, divorce can be difficult and expensive. The holdup model provides a nice explanation of why such rules evolve—when divorce is expensive, the incentives to invest in the relationship increase, which in turn may be beneficial for children.[16]

An alternative to specific performance is the allocation of ex post bargaining power. In some cases, this can implement efficient investment and trade. Consider a competitive seller's market characterized by prospective sellers who make only general investments, while buyers can make both a relationship-specific investment, I^B, and cooperative investments, I^{B-S}, that lower seller costs. A nice example is the training of switchboard operators to work at telephone companies before the advent of electronic switches (see the YouTube video Operator!).[17] To simplify the analysis, suppose that the quantity traded is 0 or 1, and that efficient trade entails $q^* = 1$. Now suppose the buyer's ex post payoff after making investments $\vec{I}^B = \{I^B, I^{B-S}\}$ is:

$$u^B = \begin{cases} B\left(1, \vec{I}^B, b\right) - p, & \text{if trade,} \\ u^{0B}\left(b\right) - p^0, & \text{if no trade,} \end{cases}$$

where b is a shock that occurs after the buyer makes an investment I^B that increases the value of consumption. The buyer's cooperative investment $I^{B-S} \geq 0$ reduces the seller's costs, and thus the seller's ex post payoff at the time of trade is given by:

$$u^S = \begin{cases} p - C\left(1, I^{B-S}, I^S, c\right), & \text{if trade,} \\ u^{0S}\left(I^S, c\right) + p^0, & \text{if no trade,} \end{cases}$$

where c is the seller's shock to costs and outside option, while I^S is the investment made by the seller before the shocks b and c are observed. Since I^S is a general investment, then:

$$-\frac{\partial C\left(1, I^{B-S}, I^S, c\right)}{\partial I^S} = \frac{\partial u^{0S}\left(I^S, c\right)}{\partial I^S}, \forall c, I^{B-S}, I^S.$$

Finally, suppose there is a unique vector of efficient investments maximizing welfare, $W\left(\vec{I}\right)$:[18]

$$\vec{I}^* = \{I^{B*}, I^{B-S*}, I^{S*}\} = \arg\max_{\vec{I}} W\left(\vec{I}\right),$$

In this environment, the seller has no "skin in the game" relative to her market alternatives. Aghion, Dewatripont, and Rey (1994) show that if the contract can specify the ex post bargaining power, then one can achieve efficient investment and trade:

Proposition 6.8 *(Aghion, Dewatripont, and Rey 1994) If the market for sellers is competitive, and only the buyer makes relationship specific investments, then allocating the ex post bargaining power to the buyer (setting $\pi = 1$) and setting terms $k_0 = \vec{0}$ results in efficient investment and trade.*

Proof. Suppose that at date -3 parties can agree to give all the ex post bargaining power to the buyer. In practical terms, parties are committing themselves to having the buyer make a final take-it-or-leave-it offer to the seller. With terms $k_0 = \vec{0}$, the cost to the buyer of purchasing $q^*(\omega)$ units in state ω is given by the price that makes the seller indifferent between acceptance and rejection:

$$p(1,\omega) = u^{0S}\left(I^S,c\right) + C\left(1,I^{B-S},I^S,c\right).$$

Under this contract, the seller has ex ante payoff:

$$U^S\left(I^S\right) = E\left\{u^{0S}\left(I^S,c\right)\right\} - I^S.$$

Because investments are general, the seller chooses the efficient level of investment I^{*S}. The buyer now has ex ante payoffs:

$$U^B\left(I^B,I^{B-S}\right) = E\{\max\{B\left(1,b,I^B\right) - C\left(1,I^{B-S},I^S,c\right) \tag{6.25}$$

$$-u^{0S}\left(I^{*S},c\right),\ u^{0B}(b)\}\} - I^B - I^{B-S}$$

$$= E\{B\left(1,b,I^B\right) - C\left(1,I^{B-S},I^S,c\right) \tag{6.26}$$

$$-u^{0S}\left(I^{*S},c\right) - u^{0B}(b) - I^B - I^{B-S}\}$$

$$+E\left\{u^{0B}(b)\right\}$$

$$= E\{R(\omega)\} + E\left\{u^{0B}(b)\right\} - I^B - I^{B-S} \tag{6.27}$$

$$= W\left(I^B,I^{B-S},I^{*S}\right) - U^S\left(I^{*S}\right). \tag{6.28}$$

Because the buyer's investments do not affect the seller's outside options, the buyer has an incentive to offer the surplus-maximizing trade $q^*(\omega)$. The second term in (6.27) is not affected by the buyer's investment; hence the buyer is a residual claimant to the surplus, less a term that is independent of his investment. This in turn implies that the buyer will make efficient investment choices. □

Thus, when bargaining power can be allocated via a contract, one can achieve efficient trade under the appropriate conditions. Edlin and Reichelstein (1996) and Spier and Whinston (1995) show that one can also use penalty defaults to achieve efficient investment and trade. Evans (2008) extends this early work to show that the set of cases can be expanded to those in which efficient allocations can be implemented when there are multiple equilibria in the contract renegotiation games. Evans (2012) provides another set of conditions for which this is the case, namely when it is expensive to send messages to one's counterparty.

Aghion, Dewatripont, and Rey (1994) show that the reallocation of bargaining power can be achieved with the use of a specific performance contract. As shown in proposition 6.7, these contracts may entail payments that are greater than the loss to their counterparties. This is called a *penalty default*, though it is not enforceable in many jurisdictions.[19]

One reason for the penalty default rule is that in actual trade there may be strategies that one party can use to force the other party to leave and pay the penalty default. This problem can be resolved with payments that are independent of the identity of parties, and thus they are not viewed as a penalty. More precisely, we have the following definition.

Definition 6.9   *Trade is* voluntary *if* $p^{0B} = p^{0S}$.

In the case of a specific performance contract, it is possible that separation is efficient, but neither party wishes to invoke the penalty clause. In cases in which it is sometimes efficient for parties to separate, then specific performance contracts can lead to overinvestment in a relationship (see Rogerson 1984). Under voluntary trade, contracts have the property that if it is efficient to separate, at least one party will choose that option without the requirement of contract renegotiation. This implies that under voluntary trade, relationship-specific investments are always less than or equal to the efficient level under the standard assumptions.

The rest of the chapter deals with service contracts, particularly the employment contract. In that case, specific performance is a form of bonded labor that is illegal in most jurisdictions. Hence, for the rest of the chapter it is assumed that the separation payments do not depend on the identity of the party initiating separation.

6.4   Contracting for a Service

This section focuses upon the employment relationship to illustrate how the need to provide investment incentives can explain some puzzling features of employment contracts. In contrast to goods exchanged at a single moment, services, such as labor or the rental of a property, are continuously supplied over a period of time. Following the model of section 5.4, suppose that the efficient solution for a service entails trade beginning at date 0, continuing until date 1. If there is no trade and the outside options have not been chosen, then the flow payoffs are zero for both parties. MacLeod and Malcomson (1993) and Bolton and Whinston (1993) discuss this case.

In labor economics, it is common to view labor as a "good" that is measured by the number of hours supplied at a price represented by the wage. That perspective is extremely useful for thinking about broader labor market issues, but it suffers from the problem of not explaining important features of the employment relationship, particularly the fact that wages are relatively rigid in the short run.[20] When labor is viewed as a service commodity, then wage rigidity over time is a natural characteristic of an employment contract.

The distinction between goods and services is not only a natural economic distinction, it is also a natural legal distinction. Contract law was the starting point for employment law, but over time the distinctive features of labor services have resulted in at least three distinct and important bodies of law—*contract law* that is intended to model discrete exchanges (Farnsworth 2007), *employment law* that applies to privately negotiated agreements between a worker and a firm (Rothstein and Liebman 2007), and *labor law* that deals with contracts between a labor union and a firm (Cox et al. 2006). Our goal here is to illustrate the link between the characteristics of a commodity and efficient contract terms. The principles developed here can be applied, with suitable modifications, to each of these legal contexts.

Suppose that an *employer* (the buyer of labor services) wishes to hire an *employee* (the seller of labor services) beginning at date 0 and finishing at date 1. The *inside options* are the payoffs while the relationship is ongoing, and the *outside options* are the payoffs if parties terminate the relationship. As we saw in chapter 5, inside options formally have the same effect as the threat point in the Nash bargaining model, while outside options act as a *constraint* on the set of possible agreements. These features of bargaining for a service allow for efficient exchange over a wider range of conditions than in the case of contracting for a good.

This section begins by outlining the contracting game and the solution to the renegotiation game for any ex ante contract k_0. The next step is to find a contract k_0 that implements efficient investment and trade. Two cases are considered. In the first case, the employer is making a relationship-specific self-investment. Next, both the employer and employee are making relationship-specific self-investments. In the latter case, it is shown that efficient investment and trade may require the use of an indexed contract.

To focus on the role of contracts for investment incentives, it is assumed that performance is binary, and hence $q_t \in \{0, 1\}$. Quality is an important issue for services. However, in comparison to a good, the determination of performance can be complex. When renegotiation for a good occurs, its quality is assumed to be observable before delivery, and therefore, one can set a clear criterion for acceptable performance. In contrast, a service is supplied over time, so performance can vary while the contract is being executed. The assumption that quality is binary greatly simplifies this analysis and will be maintained in this section. The issue of how to enforce variation in performance over time is the focus of agency theory, which is reviewed in chapter 7.

6.4.1 The Contracting Game

Contracting for a service commodity follows the same timeline as in the case of a good, as outlined in section 6.2. It differs from exchange for a good in that trade occurs over the period $t \in [0, 1]$, while for a good, trade occurs only at time $t = 1$. Also, as a matter of law, specific performance employment contracts are normally not enforced because they are akin to forced work; hence, the voluntary trade condition is assumed (definition 6.9).

One reason for the voluntary trade assumption is to reduce the incentive for malfeasance by either party. For example, if the separation payment is paid only in the event of a dismissal but not when an employee quits, then the employer has an incentive to make the employee's life so difficult that she leaves voluntarily.[21]

Thus, the set of possible contracts at date -3 is given by:

$$k_0 = \left\{ w_0, \bar{w}_0, w_0^0 \right\} \in K \equiv \Re^3.$$

This contract is implemented as follows. While the relationship continues, the employee chooses whether to supply labor services. Similarly, the employer decides whether to engage the worker. Either one can block trade and force $q_t = 0$. If both agree to trade, then $q_t = 1$. When the worker supplies services ($q_t = 1$), then the employer agrees to pay a wage w_0. The ex post value of production is $B\left(I^B\right) - C\left(I^S\right)$, and it is assumed to be strictly positive for all $\vec{I} \geq \vec{0}$, while $C\left(I^S\right) > 0$ for $I^S \geq 0$.

If trade does not occur, then $q_t = 0$, the value of the relationship is zero, and the employer pays $\bar{w}_0$. If there is separation at time t^0, then the firm pays the worker w_0^0 for the period $t \in \left[t^0, 1\right]$. Total compensation for this period is $\left(1 - t^0\right) w_0^0$. We could make the separation payment explicitly time dependent, but that will not benefit either party in the stationary case being considered here.

We can suppose there are only relationship-specific investments and no uncertainty regarding the benefit or cost of trade. Thus, the only uncertainty is with respect to the outside options, $u^{0B}, u^{0S} \geq 0$, that have probability distributions:

$$u^{0B} \sim h^B\left(u^{0B}\right),$$

$$u^{0S} \sim h^S\left(u^{0S}\right).$$

It assumed now that the outside options have support $[0, \bar{u}]$ ($h^i\left(u^{0i}\right) > 0$ for $u^{0i} \in [0, \bar{u}]$, $i \in \{B, S\}$).

In terms of the inside valuations, there is no trade with cost and benefit set to zero. If $q_t = 1$, then the cost to the employee is $C\left(I^S\right)$, and the benefit of work to the employer is $B\left(I^B\right)$. These functions satisfy the standard assumptions that ensure that the efficient investment levels are unique. The simplifying assumption here is that uncertainty affects only the employee's outside option, and the efficient level of relationship-specific investment depends only on the probability of trade, as given by (6.14).

At date $t = 0$, the state of the relationship is realized. This is given by the contract k_0 that has been agreed on ex ante, and the relevant state is $\omega = \{\vec{I}, \vec{u}^0\} \in \Omega = \Re_+^4$. Given this information, the parties can renegotiate contract k_0 following the protocol in chapter 5, section 5.4. It is assumed that there are zero transaction costs, and the payoffs are determined by the limit of the discrete time bargaining game. After any offer by one party, the other party is always free to leave the relationship to take their outside option. We know from chapter 5, proposition 5.8, that the unique equilibrium payoff at time 0 has parties renegotiate to an efficient contract as a function of the realized values of the inside and outside options.

6.4.2   Solving the Contract Game for a Service

The contract game is solved by backward induction. First, the renegotiation game is solved for any contract k_0 and state $\omega \in \Omega$. This allows us to determine the expected payoffs given the contract k_0 and investments $\vec{I}$. The outcome of contract renegotiation depends on the determination of the outside and inside options given k_0. The outside options are independent of investments and defined by:

$$\vec{u}^0\left(\omega\right) = \left\{u^{0B} - w_0^0, u^{0S} + w_0^0\right\}.$$

The value of the inside options depends on whether parties choose to trade. Either party can block trade—the employee can refuse to work (e.g., strike), while the employer can refuse to allow the employee to come to work (e.g., a layoff or lockout). Necessary conditions for parties to trade at state ω are:

$$B\left(I^B\right) - w_0 \geq -\bar{w}_0,$$

$$w_0 - C\left(I^S\right) \geq \bar{w}_0.$$

Given these conditions, the effort of the employee under contract k_0 in state ω is given by:

$$q\left(k_0, \omega\right) = \begin{cases} 1, & \text{if } B\left(I^B\right) \geq w_0 - \bar{w}_0 \geq C\left(I^S\right), \\ 0 & \text{if not.} \end{cases} \tag{6.29}$$

If contract k_0 is not renegotiated, then the inside options are given by:

$$\bar{u}^B\left(k_0, \omega\right) = q\left(k_0, \omega\right)\left(B\left(I^B\right) + \bar{w}_0 - w_0\right) - \bar{w}_0, \tag{6.30}$$

$$\bar{u}^S\left(k_0, \omega\right) = \bar{w}_0 - q\left(k_0, \omega\right)\left(\bar{w}_0 - w_0 + C\left(I^S\right)\right). \tag{6.31}$$

The rent from trade (6.8) in this case is given by:

$$R\left(\omega\right) = B\left(I^B\right) - C\left(I^S\right) - \left(u^{0B} + u^{0S}\right).$$

When trade is not efficient ($\theta \in \Theta^{NT}\left(\vec{I}\right) \setminus \Theta^I\left(\vec{I}\right)$), then the rent is negative ($R\left(\omega\right) < 0$). The fact that trade is voluntary implies that at least one party is better off separating than pursuing any other strategy. Hence, when there are zero transactions costs, separation is immediate, with each party getting its outside option adjusted by the severance payment. If there is a gain from trade ($R\left(\omega\right) \geq 0$), then parties will agree to trade at date 0. Proposition 5.8 implies that the terms of trade at that point are found by maximizing the Nash production, subject to the constraints imposed by the outside options.

The renegotiated contract k solves the following program:

$$\max_{k \in K} \left(\bar{u}^B\left(k, \omega\right) - \bar{u}^B\left(k_0, \omega\right)\right)^{\pi} \left(\bar{u}^S\left(k, \omega\right) - \bar{u}^S\left(k_0, \omega\right)\right)^{1-\pi}, \tag{6.32}$$

subject to:

$$\bar{u}^B\left(k, \omega\right) \geq u^{0B} - w_0^0, \tag{6.33}$$

$$\bar{u}^S\left(k, \omega\right) \geq u^{0S} + w_0^0. \tag{6.34}$$

Denote the solution to the program by $\vec{u}\left(k_0, \omega\right) = \{u^{B*}\left(k_0, \omega\right), u^{S*}\left(k_0, \omega\right)\}$.

This is a straightforward optimization problem that can be solved explicitly; thus we have:

Proposition 6.10 *Given a contract $k_0 = \left\{w_0, \bar{w}_0, w_0^0\right\} \in K$ and a state $\omega = \left\{\vec{I}, \vec{u}^0\right\} \in \Omega$, parties renegotiate contract k_0 to some contract k that results in the following ex post payoffs:*

1. *If trade is not efficient, ($\theta \in \Theta^{NT}\left(\vec{I}\right) \setminus \Theta^{I}\left(\vec{I}\right)$), then each party gets its outside option:*

$$u^{B*}\left(k_0, \omega\right) = u^{0B} - w_0^0,$$

$$u^{S*}\left(k_0, \omega\right) = u^{0S} + w_0^0.$$

2. *If trade is efficient, ($\theta \in \Theta^{T}\left(\vec{I}\right)$), then, given the ex post surplus from renegotiation:*

$$S_0\left(k_0, \omega\right) \equiv B\left(I^B\right) - C\left(I^S\right) - \left(\bar{u}^B\left(k_0, \omega\right) + \bar{u}^S\left(k_0, \omega\right)\right),$$

   the renegotiated payoffs are:
   (a) *If $\pi S_0\left(k_0, \omega\right) + \bar{u}^B\left(k_0, \omega\right) \le u^{0B} - w_0^0$ then:*

$$u^{B*}\left(k_0, \omega\right) = u^{0B} - w_0^0,$$

$$u^{S*}\left(k_0, \omega\right) = B\left(I^B\right) - C\left(I^S\right) - u^{B*}\left(k_0, \omega\right).$$

   (b) *If $(1-\pi) S_0\left(k_0, \omega\right) + \bar{u}^S\left(k_0, \omega\right) \le u^{0S} + w_0^0$, then:*

$$u^{B*}\left(k_0, \omega\right) = B\left(I^B\right) - C\left(I^S\right) - u^{S*}\left(k_0, \omega\right),$$

$$u^{S*}\left(k_0, \omega\right) = u^{0S} + w_0^0.$$

   (c) *If neither (a) nor (b) apply, then:*

$$u^{B*}\left(k_0, \omega\right) = \pi S_0\left(k_0, \omega\right) + \bar{u}^B\left(k_0, \omega\right),$$

$$u^{S*}\left(k_0, \omega\right) = (1-\pi) S_0\left(k_0, \omega\right) + \bar{u}^S\left(k_0, \omega\right).$$

Notice that if contract k_0 is ex post efficient, then $S_0 = 0$ and contract terms are renegotiated only when one of the outside options is binding. If the employee's outside option is binding, then the employee is given a utility that is equal to her outside option, and the employer gets all the gain from trade. The reverse situation occurs when the employer's outside option is binding, in which case the employer gets his outside option, and the employee receives all the rent. When the outside options are not binding, then they have no effect on the trade price. In other words, the trade price is *rigid* in the face of market fluctuations in outside options. This follows from the outside option principle and implies that contract prices for service commodities will appear rigid relative to contract prices for goods.

If trade is efficient, and the outside options are not binding, then parties share the gains from trade as a function of their bargaining powers. These effects are illustrated in figure 6.3. Point A is the negotiated payoffs when the outside options are given by point O^A. Notice that if $k_0 = \{0, \bar{w}_0, 0\}$, then the inside option is no trade, which can move as indicated in the figure with changes in the wage with no trade, $\bar{w}_0$. If the employee has a strong outside option, as given by O^B, then her ex post payoff is constrained by the outside option, and she gets u^{0S*}.

As in the case of goods, we can now define the ex ante payoffs as a function of the ex ante contract and investments as defined by (6.19)–(6.20). Similarly, we say that the investments $\vec{I}\left(k_0\right)$ are *self-enforcing* if they satisfy (6.21)–(6.22). A general existence result

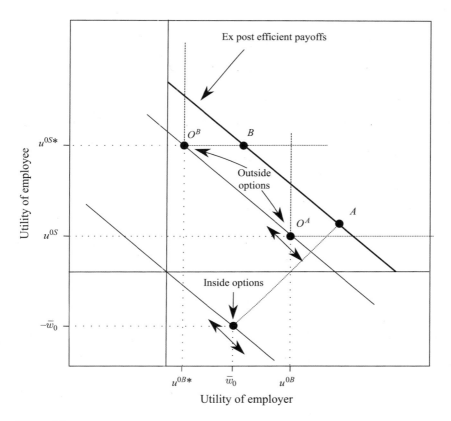

Figure 6.3
The effect of outside and inside options.

is not provided. Rather, each of the next subsections considers specific environments and shows that ex ante contracts exist that result in efficient, self-enforcing investments $\vec{I}(k_0)$.

In summary, the contract design problem consists of two interlocking elements. First, parties anticipate that any contract, k_0, signed at date -3 will be renegotiated at date 0 as a function of the specific investments and the values of the outside options. Second, when making an investment decision at date -2, both parties correctly anticipate how much investment will be made by their counterparty and how these investments will affect contract renegotiation over time.

6.4.3 Holdup and the Standard Employment Contract

Consider again the Grout (1984) model that assumes that the employer (B—buyer of labor services) makes a relationship-specific investment that enhances the productivity of the employee (S—seller of labor services) in the context of contract bargaining for a service. This section shows that this holdup model is consistent with a number of observed labor market institutions. Specifically, it is assumed that there is voluntary exchange in the sense that both the employee and the employer are free to take their outside options at any time. Also, the employee is free not to supply (i.e., go on strike) and receive contractually specified payments while not working. The employee is assumed to have available an outside option whose value is observed, but not contractible. Consistent with Grout (1984), the investments made by the employer are assumed to be noncontractible.

More precisely, the employer hires a single employee over the period $t \in [0, 1]$ and then makes a relationship-specific investment I^B before trade begins at date -2. The employer's return from trade is $B\left(I^B\right)$. It is assumed to be increasing and concave in investment $I^B \geq 0$ ($B' > 0, B'' < 0$). In addition, the return on low investment is high ($\lim_{I^B \to 0} B'\left(I^B\right) = \infty$), and the benefit, B, is bounded above.[22] For simplicity, the outside option of the employer is set to zero ($u^{0B} = 0$).

Employment begins at date 0, at which point the employee chooses contractible effort $q_t \in \{0, 1\}$, at a cost $q_t C$, where $C > 0$. Let $u^{0S} \geq 0$ be the labor market flow utility that an employee can receive if she were to leave her job after the employer invests. It is assumed that this is a random variable, with $u^{0S} \sim h^S\left(u^{0S}\right)$, and ex ante expected value $\hat{u}^{0S} = E\left\{u^{0S}\right\} > 0$. The state of the relationship at the time of contract renegotiation at date 0 is:

$$\omega = \left\{I^B, u^{0S}\right\} \in \Re_+^2 \equiv \Omega.$$

The gains from trade are deterministic, and the only uncertainty is due to the employee's outside option. The ex post bargaining powers of the employer and employee are given by π and $(1 - \pi) \in (0, 1)$. Parties are assumed to play the contract bargaining game for a service. The first step in solving the model is to determine the optimal level of investment. Because trade is efficient if and only if $B\left(I^B\right) - C \geq u^{0S}$, total welfare is given by:

$$W\left(I^B\right) = \int_0^{B(I^B)-C} \left(B\left(I^B\right) - C\right) h^S\left(u^{0S}\right) du^{0S} + \int_{B(I^B)-C}^{\bar{u}} u^{0S} h^S\left(u^{0S}\right) du^{0S} - I^B,$$
(6.35)

where the support for the outside options is given by $[0, \bar{u}]$ (as defined above).

The first term is the gain from trade, while the second term is the payoff to the employee in the market. Separation is efficient whenever $u^{0S} > B\left(I^B\right) - C$. In this case, the first-order condition for efficient investment (6.14) can be simplified to:

$$B'\left(I^{*B}\right) = \frac{1}{H^S\left(B\left(I^{*B}\right) - C\right)} = \frac{1}{P^T\left(I^{*B}\right)},$$
(6.36)

where $P^T\left(I^{*B}\right) = H^S\left(B\left(I^{*B}\right) - C\right)$ is the probability of trade at the efficient level of investment, and $H^S(\cdot)$ is the cumulative distribution function for $h^S(\cdot)$.

Ex ante, the outside options for the employer and employee are given by $U^{0B} = 0$ and $U^{0S} = E\left\{u^{0S}\right\} = \int_0^{\bar{u}} u h^S(u)\, du$. The fact that trade is efficient in some states implies that $W\left(I^{B*}\right) > U^{0S}$, so the set of feasible ex ante payoffs is given by:

$$F^* = \left\{\left(U^B, U^S\right) \mid U^B \geq 0, U^S \geq U^{0S}, U^B + U^S \leq W\left(I^{B*}\right)\right\}.$$
(6.37)

Two questions arise. First, what is the consequence of using a standard fixed wage contract that is agreed before investment? In some cases, efficiency is possible, but not in all cases. Second, does there exist a contract that implements the efficient allocation when the standard fixed wage contract cannot?

The fixed wage contract

Suppose parties agree to a fixed wage contract, denoted by $k_0 = \{w_0\}$, that is signed at date -3. This contract specifies that the employee be paid w_0 while working and zero otherwise. Employment is *at will*, namely, either party can leave the relationship when they wish at no cost. This corresponds to the standard employment contract used in common law countries, such as the United States, where employment continues at the agreed wage unless one party leaves the relationship or there is mutually agreed-upon renegotiation.

In this example, the only uncertainty is the value of the outside option that is revealed after the employer makes his relationship-specific investment. Hence, the state of the relationship at date 0 is completely defined by the existing contract and realized state, $\{w_0, \omega\} = \{w_0, u^{OS}, I^B\} \in \Re^3_+$. At this point, parties may renegotiate the wage w_0 or choose to separate. Let $\vec{U}^*(w_0, \omega) = \{U^{B*}(w_0, \omega), U^{S*}(w_0, \omega)\}$ denote the payoffs that are agreed after contract renegotiation at date 0, given the state of the relationship, ω, and the agreed wage, w_0. The payoffs depend on which of the following cases occurs:

1. Trade is not efficient:
$$B(I^B) - C < u^{OS}.$$

This occurs with probability $1 - P^T(I^B)$, where $P^T(I^B)$ is the probability of efficient trade given investment I^B. Let $\Omega^{NT} \subset \Omega$ denote this set. Notice that it is independent of the contract wage w_0. Ex post payoffs in this case are given by:

$$\vec{u}^*(w_0, \omega) = \left\{0, u^{OS}\right\}. \tag{6.38}$$

2. Trade is efficient with probability $P^T(I^B)$. The set of states for this case is denoted by $\Omega^T = \Omega \backslash \Omega^{NT}$. Let the value of trade be given by $S(I^B) \equiv B(I^B) - C \geq u^{OS}$. We now have a number of cases that depend upon the value of the contract wage w_0 and the bargaining power of parties:

(a) At wage w_0, employer and employee both prefer to trade. From (6.29) this implies $w_0 \in [C, B(I^B)]$. The inside options are therefore given by $\{\bar{u}^B, \bar{u}^S\} = \{B(I^B) - w_0 - I^B, w_0 - C\}$, leading to two subcases:

(i) The renegotiated wage is determined by the inside option when $w_0 - C \geq u^{OS}$. Because trade at the contracted wage is efficient, there is no renegotiation and the payoffs are given by:

$$\vec{u}^*(w_0, \omega) = \left\{B(I^B) - w_0, w_0 - C\right\}. \tag{6.39}$$

(ii) The employee prefers the outside option, $w_0 - C \leq u^{OS}$, and hence the outside option principle implies that the employee is paid exactly her outside option:

$$\vec{u}^*(w_0, \omega) = \left\{B(I^B) - u^{OS}, u^{OS}\right\}. \tag{6.40}$$

(b) At wage w_0, either the employer or employee prefers not to trade. From (6.29) this implies $w_0 \notin [C, B(I^B)]$, and either the current wage w_0 does not cover the employee's cost of effort or is greater than the employer's gain from trade. Thus the inside option is given by no trade that defines an inefficient threat point $\{\bar{u}^B, \bar{u}^S\} = \{0, 0\}$. The gain from renegotiation is $S(I^B)$. The outside option principle implies two subcases:

(i) The renegotiated wage is determined by the outside option when the employee's share of surplus is less than the outside option, $(1 - \pi) S (I^B) \leq u^{0S}$, and hence:

$$\vec{u}^* (w_0, \omega) = \left\{ S (I^B) - u^{0S}, u^{0S} \right\}. \tag{6.41}$$

(ii) The renegotiated wage is determined by the renegotiation of inside options when the employee's share of surplus is greater than the outside option, $(1 - \pi) S (I^B) > u^{0S}$, and hence:

$$\vec{u}^* (w_0, \omega) = \left\{ \pi S (I^B), (1 - \pi) S (I^B) \right\}. \tag{6.42}$$

The probability that these cases occur depends upon the choice of investment, I^{B*}, and the contract wage, w_0. As only the employer is making a specific investment, this implies that to achieve efficient investment incentives it is sufficient to ensure that the employer is the residual claimant on the returns to investment and there is efficient matching. Given that contract renegotiation ensures ex post efficient matching, then the fixed wage contract is efficient if and only if the firm receives all the ex post rents from investing.

When there is no trade, the ex post payoffs are given by (6.38). These are independent of investment, which ensures there is no return to the employer when there is no trade, and that in turn ensures that the probability of trade reduces investment incentives as required by (6.14). When trade is efficient, the cases corresponding to the payoffs (6.39)–(6.41) guarantee that the employer is the full residual claimant on investment returns.

The only event that results in sharing of the return from investment with the employee occurs in the case corresponding to (6.42). Consider first the situation in which there is no wage agreed ex ante and hence $w_0 = 0$. Since $u^{0S} \geq 0$, the event that $0 > u^{0S}$ occurs with zero probability. Thus, if the bargaining power of the employer is $\pi = 1$, then the event $(1 - \pi) S = 0 \leq u^{0S}$ occurs with probability 1, and the case corresponding to (6.42) never occurs. However, if $\pi < 1$ then $(1 - \pi) S (I^B) > 0$. There is a strictly positive probability that the outside option is not binding, implying that event 2(b)(ii), corresponding to expression (6.42), occurs with positive probability. This results in holdup in some states of the world, and the employer underinvests in the relationship. Hence, we have:

Proposition 6.11 *Suppose that in the Grout model, it is efficient for the employer to make a specific investment $I^{B*} > 0$ and there is no wage contract in place ($w_0 = 0$). Then the employee chooses the efficient investment level if and only if the employer has all the bargaining power ($\pi = 1$).*

Proof. The proof of sufficiency follows from our discussion before the proposition. For necessity, suppose that the bargaining power of the employer is $\pi < 1$ and $w_0 = 0$. It is efficient for some investment to be made, which implies that trade is sometimes efficient, and the efficient level of investment $S^* = B (I^{B*}) - C > 0$. Thus, the payoff of the employer at this investment level is:

$$U^B (I^{B*}) = \int_0^{(1-\pi)S^*} \left(S^* - u^{0S} \right) h \left(u^{0S} \right) du^{0S} + \int_{(1-\pi)S^*}^{S^*} \pi S^* h \left(u^{0S} \right) du^{0S} - I^{B*}. \tag{6.43}$$

Since $\pi < 1$ and $h^S\left(u^{0S}\right) > 0$ for $u^{0S} \geq 0$, this implies that the second integral occurs with positive probability. The fact that $\pi < 1$ then implies that $\frac{dU^B(I^{B*})}{dI^{*B}} < 0$, and the employee will choose investment less than I^{B*}. $\square$

This result is an extension of propositions 6.6 and 6.8 to the case of a service commodity, but there is a difference. In the case of a good, as Hart and Moore (1988) and Che and Hausch (1999) have shown, no contract may exist, aside from reallocating power ex post, that provides first-best investment incentives. Notice that the first term of expression (6.43) is the result of renegotiating the contract to make the employee indifferent between the inside and outside options. When this occurs, the employer is the full residual claimant to the returns from specific investments. This in turn implies that with the appropriate choice of wage contract, w_0, it is possible to achieve efficient investment and trade:

Proposition 6.12 *If parties agree on a contract wage that is equal to the employee's cost of effort ($w_0 = C$), then there is efficient investment and trade, and the employee has an ex ante payoff of $U^{0S} = E\left\{u^{0S}\right\}$. With a signing bonus to the employee, it is possible to achieve any division of the gains from trade.*

Proof. When $w_0 = C$, then case 2(b) never occurs. At this wage, the employee is indifferent between working and not working. However, the employee's utility is zero at this wage, the outside option is always binding, and w_0 is always renegotiated to $w = u^{0S} + C$. Thus, we get the following expression for the employer's payoff:

$$U^B\left(w_0 = C, I^B\right) = \begin{cases} -I^B, & B\left(I^B\right) < w_0, \\ \int_0^{B(I^B)-C}\left(B\left(I^B\right) - C - u^{0S}\right)h^S\left(u^{0S}\right)du^{0S} - I^B & B\left(I^B\right) \geq w_0. \end{cases}$$

Taking the first-order condition for this expression, we get (6.36), the condition for efficient investment. The fixed wage contract $w_0 = C$ induces efficient levels of investment and trade. Under this choice, the payoff of the employee is $U^{0S} = E\left\{u^{0S}\right\}$. Using a side payment at date -3 allows any payoff in the set (6.37) to be achieved. $\square$

The employer's payoff is a function of investment when the wage is set equal to the cost of production ($w_0 = C$) as illustrated in figure 6.4. With this wage, the worker is indifferent between trade and no trade, and the employer is fully internalizing the cost of production. When the employer's ex ante investment is less than I_0^B, then the employer chooses not to trade because the gain is less that the cost of production, ($B\left(I^B\right) < C$). The payoff is $-I^B$, as illustrated in figure 6.4. When investment is greater I_0^B, then trade is profitable and rises with investment until the efficient level is reached, given by $I^B = I^{B*}$.

This example illustrates a case in which a fixed wage contract can implement efficient investment and trade. It is an important example because it is often assumed that the lack of variable pay means that there are no performance incentives.[23]

Cooperative investments
The Grout model assumes that employers invest only into physical capital, yet many employers also invest into employee skills to enhance their productivity.[24] More precisely, let I^{BS}, be the investment by the employer into employee skill. This is known as a *cooperative* relationship-specific investment. The increase in productivity is modeled as a reduction

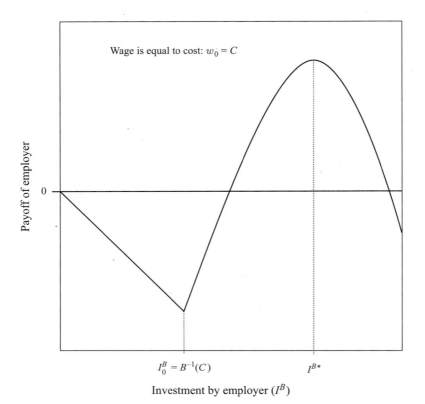

Figure 6.4
Investment returns with fixed wage contract.

in the cost of providing the service, given by $C\left(I^{BS}\right)$, where $C'\left(I^{BS}\right) \leq 0$, $C\left(I^{BS}\right) > 0$, for all $I^{BS} \geq 0$, and $-C'(0) > 1$. The last assumption implies that it is efficient to have some training $I^{BS} > 0$.

Thus, the employer's investment choices are given by the vector $\vec{I} = \left\{I^B, I^{BS}\right\}$, where I^B is the relationship-specific investment affecting the employer's value of production, $B\left(I^B\right)$, and I^{BS} is a *cooperative investment* that reduces the employee's production costs. This results in ex post payoffs when there is trade for the full period:

$$U^B = B\left(q, I^B\right) - w - I^B - I^{BS},$$

$$U^S = w - C\left(I^{BS}\right).$$

There is chance that after investment, the outside options are so attractive that trade does occur. As in the Grout model, when parties anticipate this possibility, the optimal response is to reduce investments. When the ex ante probability of trade at the efficient level of investments is P^{*T}, then the first-order conditions for efficient investment are:

$$B'\left(I^{B*}\right) = -C'\left(I^{BS*}\right) = \frac{1}{G\left(B\left(I^{*B}\right) - C\left(I^{*BS}\right)\right)} = \frac{1}{P^{*T}}.$$

At the optimal investment level, the marginal return on investment is equal to the reciprocal of the probability of trade.

The efficient level of investment can be implemented using an *option* contract as follows. Let the ex ante contract wage be set equal to the cost of production at the efficient level of cooperative investment, $w_0^* = C\left(I^{BS*}\right)$. Further, suppose that the employee has the right not to work at this wage if she wishes.

Proposition 6.12 implies that if the employer chooses an efficient level of cooperative investment, I^{BS*}, then the employer has an incentive to choose efficient investment I^{B*}. Given investment I^{B*}, if the employer chooses $I^{BS} < I^{BS*}$, then $w_0^* > C\left(I^{BS}\right)$, which in turn implies that, in the absence of renegotiation, the employee prefers to set effort $q_t = 0$. In this case, the inside options ($\bar{u}^B = \bar{u}^S = 0$) become the threat point in the contract renegotiation game, which in turn implies rent sharing between the employer and employee. Thus, for $I^{BS} < I^{BS*}$ contract renegotiation leads to an equilibrium payoff for the employer:

$$U^B\left(w_0^*, I^B, I^{BS}\right) = \int_0^{(1-\pi)S(I^B, I^{BS})} \pi S\left(I^B, I^{BS}\right) h^S\left(u^{0S}\right) du^{0S} - I^B - I^{BS} \qquad (6.44)$$

$$+ \int_{(1-\pi)S(I^B, I^{BS})}^{S(I^B, I^{BS})} \left(S\left(I^B, I^{BS}\right) - u^{0S}\right) h^S\left(u^{0S}\right) du^{0S}, \qquad (6.45)$$

where $S\left(I^B, I^{BS}\right) = B\left(I^B\right) - C\left(I^{BS}\right)$ is the gain from trade.

The employer's renegotiated payoff has two parts. The right-hand side of (6.44) shows the case for which the outside option is less than the renegotiated payoff, and thus the employer gets only a share of the surplus $\pi S\left(I^B, I^{BS}\right)$. Line (6.45) corresponds to cases in which the outside option provides a higher payoff to the employee than the renegotiated inside option, which means the employer is the full residual claimant. The fact that in some states of Nature there is rent sharing leads to underinvestment in physical capital ($I^B < I^{B*}$) by the employer.

When $I^{BS} \geq I^{BS*}$ the cost of supplying labor is less than the wage, $w_0^* = C\left(I^{BS*}\right)$, and therefore the wage is not renegotiated when trade is efficient. The payoff to the employer now satisfies:

$$U^B\left(w_0^*, I^B, I^{BS}\right) = \int_0^{w_0^* - C(I^{BS})} \left(B\left(I^B\right) - w_0^*\right) h^S\left(u^{0S}\right) du^{0S} - I^B - I^{BS} \qquad (6.46)$$

$$+ \int_{w_0^* - C(I^{BS})}^{S(I^B, I^{BS})} \left(S\left(I^B, I^{BS}\right) - u^{0S}\right) h^S\left(u^{0S}\right) du^{0S}. \qquad (6.47)$$

Comparing (6.46) with (6.44), observe that there is no rent sharing with the employee when the cooperative investment is sufficiently high. This results in a payoff with a discontinuity for the cooperative investment at $C\left(I^{BS}\right) = w_0^*$ as illustrated in figure 6.5.

For investments $I^{BS} < I^{*BS}$, $w_0^* < C\left(I^{BS}\right)$, and the employee will not supply effort until the contract wage is renegotiated. This leads to holdup and an incentive for inefficient supply of relationship-specific investments. For cooperative investments $I^{BS} \geq I^{BS*}$, the cost of effort is less than the wage w_0^*, and hence the employee always supplies effort. This implies no holdup, and renegotiation occurs only when the employee's outside option is binding. The following proposition summarizes these results:

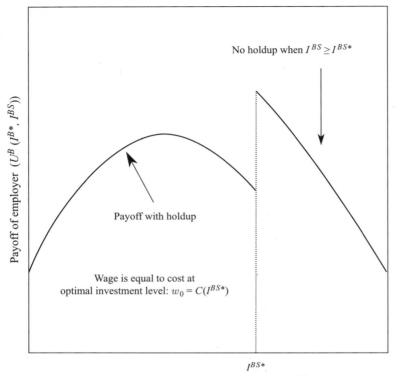

Figure 6.5
Employer payoff with cooperative investment with a fixed wage contract.

Proposition 6.13 *Suppose the employer makes relationship-specific self-investment in employee skill. Then an employment contract with an ex ante fixed wage equal to the cost of effort ($w_0^* = C\left(I^{*BS}\right)$) provides the incentive for parties to achieve efficient investment and trade.*

This result illustrates how an option-type contract can solve the holdup problem, first observed by Nöldeke and Schmidt (1995).

6.4.4   Price and Wage Indexing

Suppose now it is the employee rather than the employer who is making the specific investment that lowers the cost of production. In this case some form of fixed wage contract is still optimal, except now it needs to be tied to the value of the outside options. Such contracts are common. Labor union contracts often have terms that link wages to the inflation rate. Another example is the use of indexing for supply contracts. Joskow (1988) finds that utilities and coal suppliers enter into long-term service contracts with complex indexing formulas for the trade price. The puzzle is that these prices often closely follow the spot market price. Figure 6.6 plots coal prices from 1985, and one can see that the spot price

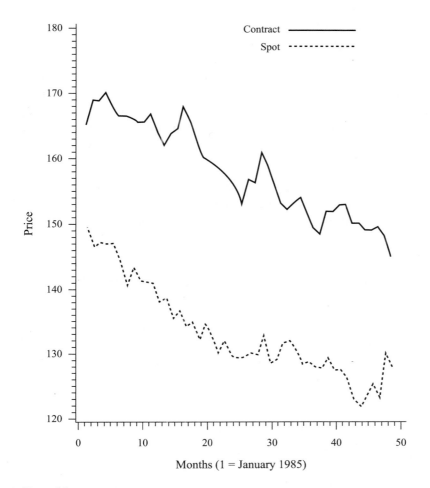

Figure 6.6
Quality weighted spot and contract prices (cents/million BTU).
Source: Wolak (1996)

and the contract price follow each other. Efficient trade is achieved with complex index formulas that ensure that shocks to the spot price get reflected in the contract price.

At the time Joskow wrote his paper, the standard economic model assumed that rigid prices are explained by an insurance motive—a more risk-averse party would prefer to be insured against uncertain future returns (see chapter 3, section 3.3). However, if contract prices are following the spot price, then they are not providing any insurance. One naturally wonders why the firms avoid writing a complex contract by agreeing to trade at the spot price?

The holdup model provides an explanation for such a contract. Joskow's (1988) data came from contracts between coal producers and electric utilities; these can be viewed as service contracts because the coal needs to be supplied continuously over time in order for the utility to operate. In this case, parties are making relationship-specific investments in the transportation system for moving the coal to the utility, while the utility is making an investment in technology that is tailored to the type of coal it will be receiving, such as installing the appropriate pollution abatement.

Suppose that the contract price cannot be conditioned on the level of investment, but it is possible to fully index the trade price as a function of the outside options. Suppose now that investments are relationship-specific self-investments, as discussed in subsection 6.3.2. In this case, the employer selects investment I^B while the employee selects investment I^S. When it is possible to index price as a function of the outside options, then there is a contract that implements the efficient solution:

Proposition 6.14 *Suppose the employer and the employee supply a service that requires relationship-specific self-investments by both parties $(\vec{I} = (I^B, I^S))$ and wages can be fully indexed as a function of the outside options $\vec{u}^0$. Then there exists an indexed wage, $w_0(\vec{u}^0)$, that ensures the first-order conditions for efficient investments are satisfied for any division $\alpha \in (0, 1)$ of the ex post surplus.*

Proof. Let $\vec{I}^*$ be the efficient effort levels. Define the rent from trade at this level of investment:

$$R\left(\vec{u}^0\right) = \left(B\left(I^{B*}\right) - C\left(I^{S*}\right) - \left(u^{0B} + u^{0S}\right)\right).$$

Here we are fixing $\vec{I}^*$ and thus assuming that this function varies only with the outside options. This is positive if and only if trade is efficient. Given a division of the rent, $\alpha \in (0, 1)$, define the wage function, $w(\vec{u}^0)$, so that the employer gets an α share of the rent (and thus the employee gets $1 - \alpha$):

$$B\left(I^{B*}\right) - w\left(\vec{u}^0\right) = \alpha R\left(\vec{u}^0\right) + u^{0B}.$$

Notice that this implies:

$$w\left(\vec{u}^0\right) - C\left(I^{S*}\right) = (1 - \alpha)\left(B\left(I^{B*}\right) - C\left(I^{S*}\right) - \left(u^{0B} + u^{0S}\right)\right) + u^{0S}.$$

Under this wage function, if parties have invested efficiently, then when trade is efficient there is no renegotiation of $w(\vec{u}^0)$. At that wage, both parties have payoffs higher than the inside option with no trade or the outside option. When trade is not efficient $(R(\vec{u}^0) < 0)$, then both parties prefer to separate and take their outside options. Define the sets when trade is efficient or not conditional upon investment:

$$\Omega^T\left(\vec{I}\right) = \left\{\vec{u}^0 | B\left(I^B\right) - C\left(I^S\right) \geq \left(u^{0B} + u^{0S}\right)\right\},$$

$$\Omega^{NT}\left(\vec{I}\right) = \left\{\vec{u}^0 | B\left(I^B\right) - C\left(I^S\right) < \left(u^{0B} + u^{0S}\right)\right\}.$$

Hence we have in an open neighborhood of $\vec{I}^*$:

$$U^B\left(w\left(\cdot\right), I^B, I^S\right) = \int_{\vec{u} \in \Omega^T\left(I^B, I^S\right)} \left(B\left(I^B\right) - w\left(\vec{u}^0\right)\right) h^B\left(u^{0B}\right) h^S\left(u^{0S}\right) du^{0B} du^{0S}$$

$$+ \hat{u}^{0B} - I^B, \cdot$$

$$U^S\left(w\left(\cdot\right), I^B, I^S\right) = \int_{\vec{u} \in \Omega^T\left(I^B, I^S\right)} \left(w\left(\vec{u}^0\right) - C\left(I^S\right)\right) h^B\left(u^{0B}\right) h^S\left(u^{0S}\right) du^{0B} du^{0S}$$
$$+ \hat{u}^{0S} - I^S,$$

where the expected value of the outside options for the buyer and seller are, respectively, $\hat{u}^{0B}$ and $\hat{u}^{0S}$.

At the efficient level of investment there is no renegotiation of the wage contract and hence:

$$\frac{\partial U^B\left(w\left(\cdot\right), \vec{I}^*\right)}{\partial I^B} = \frac{\partial U^S\left(w\left(\cdot\right), \vec{I}^*\right)}{\partial I^S} = 0.$$ □

This result is only a local result because it may be possible for one party to lower investment and gain via renegotiation. For example, suppose α is close to 0, but the employer's bargaining power is close to 1. In that case the employer can lower investment slightly so that for most values of the outside option:

$$B\left(I^B\right) - w\left(\vec{u}^0\right) < 0.$$

The employer would renegotiate to get $\pi\left(B\left(I^B\right) - C\left(I^{*S}\right)\right)$ when it is efficient to trade. (See exercise 17 for an extension of this result.)

6.5 Discussion

A contract brings together all the ingredients for choice that we have discussed in the previous chapters. First, before agreeing to trade, parties must have beliefs regarding how trade in the future will be beneficial, despite the risks of things going wrong. This is reflected in contract law with the requirement of a "meeting of the minds."[25] This is also consistent with the view that parties act using a small model of the world in the sense of Savage (1954). Of course, the goal of exchange is to create value. This chapter has focused on the case of investment incentives, when at least one party desires a contract because she would like to make investment plans that depend upon performance by the counterparty.

Contract design is challenging because it is often not possible to measure and enforce the parties' investment levels. The solution is to use property-like rules.[26] The benefit of private property is that one is able to keep any return from investments in the property that increase its value. In the case of exchange, investments are often specific to the relationship and may benefit only one party. One way to create a property-like rule is to fix the price of the product in advance. This results in the buyer's keeping any returns to investment that increase the value of consumption. Similarly, a fixed price contract provides an incentive to the seller to make cost-saving investments.

Thus, an important and often overlooked feature of fixed price contracts is that they *are* incentive contracts. In contrast to the performance pay contracts to be discussed in the next chapter, fixed price contracts provide an incentive for parties to invest in a relationship.

However, a difficulty arises when events occur that make it efficient to change the plans the parties made at the time of contract formation. Because contracts are private agreements, they can be changed by mutual assent. Consequently, an important ingredient of contract design is anticipating and planning for situations that give rise to contract renegotiation. For these cases, contract models with renegotiation build on the bargaining models discussed in chapter 5. The fact that parties make relationship-specific investments results in ex post rents that need to be divided when a contract is renegotiated. The rent division is controlled by the defaults created by the contract. This highlights the point that an essential goal of a contract is to regulate the bargaining power of parties to an agreement.

This chapter considered two cases. The first concerned goods that are exchanged at a specific point in time. This is discussed in section 6.3 where it is shown that an efficient allocation with relationship-specific self-investments can be achieved if and only if the contract is not renegotiated when there is trade. In some cases, as in Che and Hausch (1999), a contract implementing efficient investment and trade may not exist. Bajari and Tadelis (2001) show that one can view planning costs as a form of investment, which in turn illustrates the point that there is a trade-off between planning and providing efficient investment incentives. Using this model, Chakravarty and MacLeod (2009) show that the structure of the widely used American Institute of Architects form of construction contract is explicitly designed to implement efficient contract renegotiation. See Herweg and Schmidt (2019) for a recent extension of those results.

Monopoly power is often considered an important source of allocative inefficiency. Bajari, Houghton, and Tadelis (2014) find that ex post contract adaptation accounts for most of the inefficiency in highway construction contracts. Another key assumption in these models is that renegotiation occurs at no cost. Gagnepain, Ivaldi, and Martimort (2013) explore the impact of renegotiation costs in the context of transportation services. They conclude that increasing commitment can improve welfare, though the gains would accrue mainly to the service suppliers.

The second case (section 6.4) considers contract design for a service. These are commodities, such as labor, for which one contracts to have delivery over a period of time. In this environment, the seller can disrupt supply during the period of service. It is shown that this has a profound effect on the structure of the renegotiation game. In the case of a good, the market alternative acts as a threat point in the sense of the Nash bargaining solution, which in turn can lead to inefficient surplus sharing, as shown in Grout (1984). In the case of a service, as is shown in chapter 5, the market alternative acts as a *constraint* rather than a threat point leading to the *outside option principle*.

MacLeod and Malcomson (1993) show that this result provides a natural microfoundation for rigid prices. If the outside option principle does not hold, we expect a person's income to fluctuate daily with her market alternatives. Rather, the outside option principle implies that a market alternative does not affect the current contract price or wage unless the seller/worker would be better off leaving and taking the outside option.

Two empirically interesting implications flow from this. First, it implies that when both workers and firms are making relationship-specific investments, it is efficient to have nominally rigid contracts that are inflation indexed. See Altonji and Devereux (1999) for some direct evidence on this effect. Quite a bit of evidence shows that wages are nominally rigid (Card and Hyslop 1997). However, the analysis implies that it is not efficient for all employment contracts to exhibit wage rigidities. If investments in worker skills are general and firms make relationship-specific investments, then it is efficient to have worker wages priced to market (Parent 2000).

Kaufmann and Lafontaine (1994) provide evidence on contracts in franchise relationships where the rent allocation to the franchisees is controlled to provide performance incentives. Work by Cardullo, Conti, and Sulis (2015) finds evidence of holdup by trade unions consistent with the predictions of the Grout model. In contrast, Card, Devicienti, and Maida (2014), using data from the Veneto region of Italy, find little evidence that the presence of a trade union leads to underinvestment by the firm.

Such conflicting evidence is consistent with the fact that the hold-up model does not deliver a single testable implication. Rather, the theory predicts that parties have an interest in writing contracts that provide them with the appropriate incentives to invest in a relationship. The form that these contracts take is context specific and depends upon features of the relationship and how investments affect both the inside and outside options.

For example, in rural locations, markets are much thinner, and hence holdup is likely to be more important. This in turn may explain why unions are important for remote mining towns. In contrast, in cities where there are thick labor markets, investments are more likely to be general, and thus there is less benefit for long-term contracts (MacLeod and Nakavachara 2007).

In these models, the investment motive has implications for long-term contracts. However, one does not necessarily need a contract to have a return on investment, even if the investment is relationship specific. Acemoglu and Pischke (1998) show that if there is asymmetric information, firms may have an incentive to provide general trading. In their model, the existence of trading frictions leads to investment incentives. Of course, as in the case of career concerns studied in the next chapter, this does not imply there is no contracting, only that trading frictions can have an effect on the contract terms that parties choose.

Even though the theory presented here has only a few ingredients, it is sufficiently rich to explain some of the variation in observed contractual instruments, including the use of rigid prices, separation payments, indexed prices, option contracts, and specific performance contracts. The theory's real challenge is that noncontractible investment is an essential ingredient. The fact that investment is noncontractible is equivalent to saying that investment cannot be measured and thus is not available to researchers. As data quality improves we will need new ways to measure investments in order to see whether variation in contract form affects the level of investment parties make into a relationship.

6.6   Exercises

1. Prove proposition 6.1 by explicitly computing the payoffs when $B(\cdot)$ and $C(\cdot)$ do not depend upon $\theta \in \Theta$, and $u^{0B}(b)$ and $u^{0S}(c)$ are strictly increasing in b and c, respectively. Assume that, at the efficient solution, there is positive investment by both parties and that the probability of trade is strictly between zero and one.

2. Consider a two-person exchange with relationship-specific self-investments. Parties agree on the level of trade $q \geq 0$ and the price $p \geq 0$. The payoff of the buyer is:

$$u^B = \begin{cases} 0, & q = 0, \\ q - p, & q > 0. \end{cases}$$

and the payoff of the seller is:

$$u^S = \begin{cases} -I & q = 0, \\ p - I - c \times q^2/2 - \frac{F^2}{I}, & q > 0. \end{cases}$$

where I is a relationship-specific investment by the seller. The seller's types are $c \in \{1, 2\}$, where it is assumed that the probability of $c = 1$ is $\rho \in (0, 1)$. The fixed cost of production depends on $F > 0$. Notice that, if there is no investment, the fixed cost is infinite, and there is no trade. The timing is as follows:

(a) The buyer offers the seller a take-it-or-leave-it contract $k_0 = \{q, p\}$ that specifies price and quantity. Under this contract, if the seller delivers less than q, she gets zero; if she delivers q or more, she gets p. The buyer cannot refuse to accept delivery of the goods.

(b) The seller makes an investment $I \geq 0$.

(c) Nature chooses c from $\{1, 2\}$, where the probability that $c = 1$ is ρ.

(d) Assume that the buyer observes c and I and then makes a take-it-or-leave-it offer to the seller of a new contract $k = (\hat{q}, \hat{p})$. If the seller rejects the contract, then trade occurs under contract k_0.

(e) Suppose parties trade under the terms of k (which allows them to take their outside options if they wish because there is no severance penalty), and answer the following questions:

   i. Draw the extensive form of the contract bargaining game.

   ii. What is the optimal level of trade, $q^*(I, c, F)$, given the cost realization c and fixed cost F?

   iii. What is the efficient level of investment given $q^*(I, c, F)$?
For the remainder, you may assume $F = 1/8$.

   iv. What is the ex ante surplus with efficient quantity, $q^*(I, c, F)$, and efficient investment?

   v. Given an initial contract $k_0 = \{0, 0\}$, what is the equilibrium?

   vi. Find a contract $k_0 = \{q, p\}$ that results in efficient investment and trade. Discuss the properties of this optimal contract.

3. Consider the following example of investment and trade. A buyer wishes to order a specialized product of value $B = 1$ from a seller, who chooses investments I with cost of production $C(I) = \alpha^2/I$. In addition, after the seller makes investment I, the buyer has a uniformly distributed outside option $u^{OB} \in [0, 2]$. Suppose that in the event of contract renegotiation the buyer has bargaining power π.

(a) What is the optimal allocation for the model as a function of α?

(b) Find a contract that implements efficient investment and trade for each α.

(c) Under what conditions is it possible for parties to agree to a fixed price contract p that implements the efficient allocation? (Hint: consider variations in bargaining power.)

4. Provide an example with continuous payoffs where the surplus is not differentiable in investments $\vec{I}$.

5. Specify explicit functional forms for payoffs and verify formula 6.10.

6. Derive the payoffs for 6.16 given any contract k_0.

7. Consider the case of exchange of a good and define the set of feasible payoffs by:

$$F(\omega) = \left\{ \vec{u} \in \mathfrak{R}_+^2 \,|\, S^*(\omega) \ge u_1 + u_2 \ge 0 \right\}.$$

Any point in this set corresponds to an outcome that divides the returns from trade. It is defined to be a nonempty compact, convex set. Prove:

Proposition 6.15 *Under the maintained assumptions for costs and benefits, for each $\omega \in \Omega$ and for each $\vec{u}^* \in F(\omega)$ there exists a contract $k(\omega, \vec{u})$ such that $\vec{u}(k(\omega, \vec{u}), \omega) = \vec{u}^*$, where $\vec{u}(\cdot)$ is defined in subsection 6.3.1.*

8. Show that $u^S(k_0, \omega) + u^B(k_0, \omega) \ge 0$ for any contract k_0. Next, show that this "total surplus" is unbounded in the space of the contract, namely, for any M, there is a contract k_0 such that $u^S(k_0, \omega) + u^B(k_0, \omega) \ge M$. How does this affect the incentive for parties to make offers when M is greater than the total surplus in the relationship?

9. Given no ex ante contract, $k_0 = \vec{0}$, characterize the set of all contracts k that implement the efficient allocation; that is, all k such that:

$$\vec{u}(k, \omega) = \vec{u}^*(k_0, \omega)$$

in proposition 6.4, and $\vec{u}(k, \omega)$ is the solution to the contract game defined in (6.16).

10. Provide an example in which the specific performance contract for a good leads to overinvestment, even though parties efficiently renegotiate at date 0.

11. Provide details, including conditions on the second derivatives of the payoffs, for proposition 6.6. What is the effect of an increase in the buyer's bargaining power, π, on equilibrium investment? If π were a choice variable, how should it be chosen?

12. Consider a voluntary trade contract, $k_0 = \{q^*, p, 0, p^0, p^0\}$, for the exchange of a good for which is it always efficient to trade. Using the fact that at most one party's outside option is binding, derive the equilibrium payoffs for the buyer as a function of investment I^B, given the seller is choosing efficient investment, I^{*S}. Work out similar conditions for the seller. Given these expressions, work out necessary and sufficient conditions for k_0 to implement efficient investment and trade.

13. Suppose that in the case of a service commodity, parties are able to write contracts with side payments that vary with the person who chooses to leave first. How would that affect the analysis? Are there situations in which such a contract increases the social surplus?

14. Suppose that turnover costs are zero ($R(b, c) = 0$). Prove that with general self-investments, no contract is needed to obtain the first best for a service commodity.

15. Consider a situation in which trade is always efficient and there is no uncertainty, but investment is not contractible. Let the payoffs for the buyer and seller, when there is trade, be given by:

$$u^B = \bar{B} + B\left(\log\left(I^B\right) + \log\left(I^S\right)\right) - p - I^B,$$

$$u^S = p - C - I^S,$$

where $\bar{B} + 2B (\log (B) - 1) - C > u^{0B} + u^{0S}$, the total value of the outside options, and $B > 1$.

(a) What are the efficient allocations for this problem?

(b) Can an efficient allocation be achieved with a long-term contract of the form we have been using in this chapter?

(c) What is the best that can be achieved?

(d) Suppose parties can use an option contract—the seller sets the "strike" price of the good in advance, the buyer then either buys or does not buy the good, and then the game ends. What is the best that can be achieved in this case? Notice that we are explicitly dropping the requirement of efficient renegotiation ex post.

16. Consider a two-person exchange with relationship-specific self-investments. The payoffs are $u^B = bq - p$ for the buyer and $u^S = p - I^S - \frac{q^2}{I^S}$ for the seller, where the parties agree on a price p and quantity q before trade. The seller then makes an investment I^S followed by Nature, who chooses $b \in (-\infty, \infty)$, with a $N(1, \sigma^2)$ distribution. Let $\omega = (b, I^S)$ be the state just before trade. At that point the parties can renegotiate before trade. The outside options are zero for each party, and parties have equal bargaining power. Answer the following questions:

(a) Given a contract $k = \{q, p\}$ and state ω, what is the renegotiated contract?

(b) Given this contract, what investment level will the seller chose?

(c) Suppose that parties can only agree on a fixed price and quantity (indexing is not possible), and parties have equal bargaining power. What contract would they agree upon ex ante?

17. Provide some sufficient conditions under which proposition 6.14 holds globally (see MacLeod and Malcomson [1993] for one set of such conditions).

18. Provide an explicit example under which proposition 6.14 does not hold globally.

19. Suppose that trade is not discrete, and the optimal level of trade, $q^*(\omega) = \arg\max_{q \geq 0} B(q, b, \vec{I}) - C(q, c, \vec{I})$, various continuously with investments.

(a) For the optimal contracts derived in this chapter, how does allowing a continuously variable quantity affect the results?

(b) Can the efficiency results in this chapter be extended to deal with continuously variable quantities? Why or why not?

7 Insurance and Moral Hazard

I must stay here to arrange for letting my farms on long leases and I shall have to adopt a new system for this. During the past five years, despite the large reductions I have made in the rents, the arrears have increased and as a result most of my tenants have lost interest in reducing their debt because they have no hope of being able to pay off the whole; they even seize and consume the produce of the land in the belief that they will gain nothing themselves by conserving it.

I must therefore face this growing evil and find a remedy. One way would be to let the farms not for a money rent but for a fixed share of the produce, and then make some of my servants overseers to keep watch on the harvest.
—Pliny the Younger (1949, 157), letter to Valerius Paulinus, ca. 100 CE

7.1 Introduction

In addition to the reliance interest, parties also write contracts to allocate risk. Beginning with the classic work of Borch (1962), there is a voluminous literature that explores the relationship between individual attitudes toward risk and the optimal allocation of risk between these parties. As shown in chapter 3, the basic insurance contract is conceptually simple—for each future state of the world, parties agree in advance to a state contingent transfer. For example, when one has an automobile accident, the driver's insurance company agrees to pay for the loss subject to a number of conditions.

The complication that has received the most attention in optimal contract design is the presence of *moral hazard*. In the 1960s, Ken Arrow (1963) advocated for national health insurance in the United States based on the fact that health risks can be better diversified with a large pool of individuals. Pauly (1968) observes that, if individuals are fully insured, they have an incentive to seek medical care when not necessary or possibly engage in dangerous behaviors that they might avoid if they were not fully insured.

The problem of moral hazard for insurance contracts has resulted in a large and important literature that is generically known as *agency theory*.[1] The workhorse model is the "principal-agent model," in which a risk-neutral principal offers to employ a risk-averse agent under contract terms that fix payment as a function of a noisy performance measure. If effort is contractible, then the optimal contract would fix effort at the level that maximizes net output (income less cost of effort) and pay a fixed price that fully insures the agent against fluctuations in output.

Table 7.1
Holdup vs agency theory

Period/data	Holdup model		Principal-agent model	
	Buyer	Seller	Principal	Agent
Bargaining power	π	$(1-\pi)$	1	0
1. Agreement	$k_0 = \left\{p_0, p_0^0, p^{0B}, p^{0S}\right\}$		$k_0 = \{e, w(X)\}$	
2. Actions	$I^B \geq 0$	$I^S \geq 0$		$e \geq 0$
3. Nature plays	$\left\{b, u^{0B}\right\}$	$\left\{c, u^{0S}\right\}$		θ
Information observed	$\left\{\vec{I}, b, c, \vec{u}^0\right\}$		$X(e,\theta)$	$\{e, X(e,\theta)\}$
4. Settling up	Contract renegotiation/payment		Payment	
Payoffs if trade	$B\left(I^B, b\right) - p - I^B$	$p - C\left(I^S, c\right) - I^S$	$X - w(X)$	$u(w(X) - c(e))$
Payoffs if no trade	$u^{0B} - p^{0B} - I^B$	$u^{0S} + p^{0S} - I^S$	0	U^{0A}

Consider, for example, the problem of a landowner who leases land to a farmer. It is common in poor regions for the landlord to use a sharecropping contract to share production risks between himself and the farmer. When farmers are less risk averse, fixed rental contracts are used (see Eswaran and Kotwal 1985). This chapter reviews the basic theory that can explain these contract forms, as well as a number of extensions that can help us understand the structure of observed compensation contracts in a number of important contexts.

The optimal contract in an agency model results in compensation that increases with measured performance. Thus, in practice, it is common to view any form of "performance pay" as a kind of efficiency enhancing incentive pay. However, this is a misconception; when a principal is employing an agent, it can be viewed as a simple exchange in which the agent agrees to supply a specified quality of work in exchange for an agreed payment. If the quality of work can be measured and verified, there is no reason or need to agree on a performance pay contract that varies continuously with performance. It is sufficient to have a contract that pays if and only if the agent supplies the specified quality. In that case we would be in the class of models discussed in chapter 6.

Moreover, such an arrangement provides an agent who is risk averse with insurance against variation in output that is not under the control of the agent. The motivation for a performance pay contract is based on the cost of observing individual performance. This problem can be contrasted with contracts designed to deal with the problem of holdup. The differences are illustrated in table 7.1.

First, agency theory typically assumes that the principal has all the power, though, as we shall see, this does not affect the structure of the optimal contract. The two classes of models are different in that a contract in a holdup model is intended to control the relative bargaining power of parties at the renegotiation stage. In contrast, in the principal-agent model, after the agent has chosen her actions, the relationship is essentially a zero-sum game—the contract $w(X)$ specifies how much the agent will get as a function of the observable signal X.

The goal of agency theory is to work out the characteristics of the payment terms, $w(X)$, as a function of observed performance. Of particular interest is deriving the optimal contract as a function of the information held by the principal and the relative risk aversion of the agent's preferences, $u(\cdot)$.

Agency theory differs from the holdup model in another important way. In the holdup model, the role that contracts play in allocating decision rights between parties requires the law to play an essential role in contract enforcement, particularly for the determination of appropriate remedies for contract breach. In contrast, agency contracts specify payments as a function of clearly specified contingencies that are assumed to be observable. In other words, the contract clearly specifies a monetary payment, which in turn reduces the role of the courts to simply enforcing these payments. For this reason, these contracts are typically discussed with little or no explicit mention of the law. Thus, agency theory is associated with the theory of "complete contracts," while models with relationship-specific investments are often associated with the theory of "incomplete contracts."[2]

The next section introduces the details of the basic principal-agent model with contractible effort. Section 7.3 derives the optimal contract when effort is not observable and discusses in detail the general multitasking model that allows for multiple tasks and performance measures.

Section 7.4 extends the model to allow for imperfectly observed individual productivity that is revealed over time. In this case, it is shown that when career concerns are present (current performance provides information about future performance), then the optimal contract varies with the strength of these career concerns. The key finding is that career concerns and performance pay are generally not substitutes (Holmström 1999). Like the contracts in the case of holdup, this result illustrates that the design of effective agency contracts is a complex task that entails using a combination of contractual instruments that vary with the features of the environment. The chapter concludes with a brief review of the relevant literature.

7.2 Basic Agency Model

The basic agency model supposes that a principal (P) wishes to hire an agent (A) to carry out a task with a random outcome. The following sequence of moves is typical for an agency model:

1. The principal makes a take-it-or-leave-it contract offer to an agent.

2. The agent either accepts the contract or rejects the contract and then receives her market alternative.

3. If the agent accepts, then she chooses an action.

4. A random measure of output is realized, and the agent is rewarded as per the contract terms.

Most of the insights of the agency model can be illustrated using a model with constant absolute risk aversion (CARA) preferences that gives an elegant closed-form solution. Suppose that the agent is expected to work on a project whose return is given by:

$$X = e + \varepsilon, \tag{7.1}$$

where ε has a continuous distribution given by the continuous function $f(\cdot)$ with support $(-\infty, \infty)$, mean m, and variance σ^2, while e is the effort of the agent. Both the principal and the agent have preferences over money given by CARA preferences with risk-aversion parameters ρ_P and ρ_A, respectively. In addition, the cost of providing effort is $c(e)$, which satisfies $c(0) = c'(0) = 0$, $c''(e) > 0$ $\forall e \geq 0$. The preferences of the principal and agent are given by:

$$U_P(x) = -\exp(-\rho_P x),$$

$$U_A(x, e) = -\exp(-\rho_A(x - c(e))).$$

It is assumed that the agent's outside option pays a wage w^0 dollars for effort e^0, which gives her utility U^{0A} at the market alternative.

Suppose that the level of effort can be observed by the principal, in which case the contract is a pair $\{e, w(X)\}$, where e is the effort and $w(X)$ is the wage as a function of output X. The implicit assumption is if the agent chooses not to select effort e, she would face a penalty (imposed, if necessary, by the courts). Given that the principal has all the bargaining power, he offers a contract that maximizes his expected utility, subject to the agent's receiving an expected utility at least equal to her alternative U^{0A}:

$$\max_{\{e, w(\cdot)\}} E\{U_P(X - w(X)) \,|e\} \tag{7.2}$$

subject to:

$$IR: E\{U_A(w(X), e) \,|e\} \geq U^{0A}. \tag{7.3}$$

The *individual rationality* constraint, (7.3), is commonly known simply as the *IR* constraint. It requires the agent to earn at least as much as she would in her next best alternative. By altering the default utility U^{0A}, one generates all the possible efficient contracts between the principal and agent. They are characterized in the following proposition.

Proposition 7.1 *The optimal principal-agent risk sharing contract $\{e^*, w^*(x)\}$ has the form:*

$$w^*(x) = K + \frac{\rho_P}{\rho_P + \rho_A} x, \tag{7.4}$$

$$c'(e^*) = 1$$

where K is chosen to satisfy $E\left\{U_A\left(K + \frac{\rho_P}{\rho_P + \rho_A} x, e^*\right)\right\} = U^{0A}.$

Proof. This is a constrained optimization problem with Lagrangian:

$$L = \begin{array}{l} \int_{-\infty}^{\infty} -\exp(-\rho_P(\varepsilon + e - w(\varepsilon + e)))f(\varepsilon)\,d\varepsilon \\ + \lambda \int_{-\infty}^{\infty} \{-\exp(-\rho_A(w(\varepsilon + e) - c(e))) - U^{0A}\}f(\varepsilon)\,d\varepsilon \end{array} \tag{7.5}$$

$$= \int_{-\infty}^{\infty} \left\{ \begin{array}{l} -\exp(-\rho_P(\varepsilon + e - w(\varepsilon + e))) \\ -\lambda \exp(-\rho_A(w(\varepsilon + e) - c(e))) \end{array} \right\} f(\varepsilon)\,d\varepsilon - \lambda U^{0A}. \tag{7.6}$$

The expression inside the integral is concave in w, and hence for each ε, $w(\varepsilon + e)$ is chosen to maximize the term inside the integral, to yield the following first-order condition:[3]

$$-\rho_P \exp\left(-\rho_P \left(\varepsilon + e - w\left(\varepsilon + e\right)\right)\right) + \rho_A \lambda \exp\left(-\rho_A \left(w\left(\varepsilon + e\right) - c\left(e\right)\right)\right) = 0. \qquad (7.7)$$

Setting $x = \varepsilon + e$, one obtains:

$$-\rho_P \left(x - w\left(x\right)\right) + \rho_A\left(w\left(x\right) - c\left(e\right)\right) = \ln\left(\frac{\rho_A \lambda}{\rho_P}\right), \text{ or}$$

$$w\left(x\right) = \frac{1}{\rho_P + \rho_A} \ln\left(\frac{\rho_A \lambda}{\rho_P}\right)$$

$$+ \frac{\rho_A}{\rho_P + \rho_A} c\left(e\right) + \frac{\rho_P}{\rho_P + \rho_A} x.$$

Setting $K = \frac{1}{\rho_P + \rho_A} \ln\left(\frac{\rho_A \lambda}{\rho_P}\right) + \frac{\rho_A}{\rho_P + \rho_A} c\left(e^*\right)$, where λ is chosen to ensure that the IR constraint is binding, one has the optimal wage form given in equation 7.4. Differentiating the Lagrangian with respect to e and using equation 7.7, it follows that $c'\left(e^*\right) = 1$. ☐

This result illustrates that, with CARA preferences, the optimal risk sharing contract has the linear form $w\left(x\right) = a + b^* x$, where the slope $b^* = \frac{\rho_P}{\rho_P + \rho_A}$.

We make the key assumption that the support of the error term is $(-\infty, \infty)$, which in turn ensures a unique optimal linear contract. In the subsequent discussion, attention is restricted to normally distributed error terms that yield closed-form solutions.

If the principal is much more risk averse than the agent, then $b^* \simeq 1$. This corresponds to a *rental contract* under which the principal charges a fixed rent, a, that ensures the agent receives all the marginal rewards from the project. For example, farmers in North America often rent their land to neighbors using such a contract, but this was not always the case. In the past, it was common for farmers to rent land using sharecropping contracts, where the owner would share in the revenue generated from the plot of land, corresponding to a share $b^* \in (0, 1)$.

At the other extreme, if the agent is much more risk averse than the principal ($\rho_A >> \rho_P$), then the optimal contract takes the form $b^* \simeq 0$. This corresponds to a *fixed wage contract* that is independent of the outcome.

A fixed wage contract would be typical in situations in which the principal is much less risk averse. Another example of a fixed wage or price contract is in insurance, such as fire or auto insurance contracts that are not experience rated. In those cases, negative output can be interpreted as a loss, against which the agent would like to be insured, while e^* is the level of care an individual is expected to take in order to avoid the loss.

However, the contract also requires that the principal be able to enforce the efficient level of effort, e^*. Insurance companies are not usually in a position to directly observe the level of care taken by an individual to avoid an accident. Under full insurance, the agent can decrease her level of care and not suffer from the resulting increase in likelihood of an accident. For example, the homeowner may not carefully prune trees that might cause damage to a house. Individuals may demand unnecessary medical services when fully insured by their medical plan. Workers on fixed wages who are not constantly monitored may decrease effort when the supervisor is not present, a problem that Pliny the Younger complained about in his letters (see epigraph). These are examples of what Pauly (1968) calls *moral hazard*.

7.3   Moral Hazard and Agency Theory

The problem of moral hazard arises when contractible measures of effort are not possible, and thus the effort clause of the contract, $\{e^*, w^*(x)\}$, cannot be enforced. Incentives for performance are provided by making compensation conditional on imperfect measures of performance. Agency theory seeks to understand how compensation should be optimally structured as a function of the information that is available regarding performance. This section studies the basic model in which the output x doubles as both a measure of the value of the relationship and as a measure of performance. The main result illustrates the trade-off between the power of the incentives for performance, given by the slope b, and the quality of the measure of performance, given by the variance of the error term ε.

In general, the optimal contract is not a linear function of output but depends upon the detailed structure of both preferences and information. However, as discussed in chapter 3, the hypothesis of utility maximization can only approximate observed behavior, so one should be skeptical of predictions based upon the fine-grain structure of the environment. Consequently, a number of assumptions are imposed that simplify the derivation while at the same time retaining the core insights of the model.

Specifically, the stochastic disturbances are assumed to be normally distributed, $\varepsilon \sim N(0, \sigma^2)$, and preferences are assumed to be CARA. Holmström and Milgrom (1987) have shown that, under the appropriate conditions, production and compensation contracts can be assumed to be linear functions of measured performance.

Notice, given that production, $x = e + \varepsilon$, and compensation, $w(x) = a + bx$, are linear combinations of normally distributed random variables, the compensation streams to both the principal and agent are also normally distributed. A shown in chapter 3, individuals with CARA preferences can be represented by their certainty equivalents:

$$u_A(w(\cdot), e) = CE_A(a + bX - c(e)) \tag{7.8}$$

$$= E\{a + bX - c(e)\} - \frac{\rho_A}{2}\operatorname{var}\{a + bX - c(e)\}$$

$$= a + be - c(e) - \frac{\rho_A}{2}b^2\sigma^2,$$

$$u_P(w(\cdot), e) = CE_P(X - a - bX) \tag{7.9}$$

$$= E\{X - a - bX\} - \frac{\rho_P}{2}\operatorname{var}\{X - a - bX\}$$

$$= (1 - b)e - a - \frac{\rho_P}{2}(1 - b)^2\sigma^2.$$

In addition, the linear-quadratic model supposes that costs are quadratic:

$$c(e) = e^2/2\theta.$$

With this formulation, the parameter θ can be interpreted as an individual's ability or preference for work. At the optimal risk sharing contract, effort satisfies:

$$c'(e^*) = e^*/\theta = 1. \tag{7.10}$$

Thus, the optimal level of effort is given by $e^* = \theta$.

The distinguishing feature of the moral hazard problem is that effort is not observable; rather, it is assumed that the agent selects effort to maximize her payoff under the contract:

$$e \in \arg\max_{e' \geq 0} u_A\left(w(x), e'\right).\qquad(7.11)$$

This behavior is modeled as a Nash equilibrium with perfect information about the payoffs. The Nash equilibrium assumption implies that the structure of the game is common knowledge and that parties have correct expectations regarding their strategies. In particular, it implies that the principal correctly *anticipates* how the agent will respond to any compensation contract that is mutually agreed upon.

There is one caveat to this statement: for any contract $w(\cdot)$, there may be several effort levels that are optimal for the agent. Given that the agent is indifferent between these actions and that this is an explicitly contractual relationship, it is assumed that if the principal offers a contract $w(\cdot)$, then the agent upon accepting the contract also agrees to carry out any action in $\arg\max_e u_A(w(x), e)$ that is preferred by the principal. Given this assumption, then the equilibrium for the *principal-agent problem* is the solution to the following optimization problem:

$$\max_{\{e, w(\cdot)\}} u_P\left(w(\cdot), e\right)\qquad(7.12)$$

subject to:

$$IR: u_A\left(w(\cdot), e\right) \geq W^{0A},\qquad(7.13)$$

$$IC: e \in \arg\max_{e' \geq 0} u_A\left(w(\cdot), e'\right),\qquad(7.14)$$

where W^{0A} is the certainty equivalent to the agent's alternative utility: $U^{0A} = -\exp(-\rho_A W^{0A})$.

The difference between program (7.2) and (7.12) is that the principal-agent problem has an additional constraint, known as the *incentive compatibility*, or *IC* constraint (7.14), arising from the principal's inability to observe the principal's agent's action. The IC constraint is a common technique that is used repeatedly in contract theory. Information costs and asymmetries impose additional restrictions on the set of feasible contracts that in many cases, such as this one, can be expressed in terms of an additional constraint in an optimization problem. Contract theory is distinguished from game theory (and mechanism design) by contract theory's hypothesis that part of the contract specifies which effort level to play. This makes explicit that one role of a contract is the coordination of actions.

Given the restriction to linear contracts, $w(x) = a + bx$, then from (7.8) one concludes that the agent chooses effort to solve:

$$c'(e) = b,\qquad(7.15)$$

or using $c(e) = e^2/2\theta$, one concludes that the agent chooses her action $e(b) = b\theta$. An increase in b results in an increase in effort at the cost of increasing the risk faced by the agent. This cost is given by the term $-\rho_A b^2 \sigma^2/2$. To summarize:

Proposition 7.2 *The solution to the principal-agent problem (7.12)–(7.14) is given by:*

$$a^{PA} = W^{0A} + c\left(e^{PA}\right) + \frac{\rho_A}{2}\left(b^{PA}\right)^2 \sigma^2 - b^{PA} e^{PA},$$

$$b^{PA} = \frac{\theta + \rho_P \sigma^2}{\theta + (\rho_P + \rho_A)\sigma^2},$$

$$e^{PA} = b^{PA}\theta. \tag{7.16}$$

Proof. The discussion before the proposition implies that the agent chooses effort to satisfy $e^{PA} = b^{PA}\theta$. Given that the fixed term a does not affect incentives, then the principal chooses a so that the IR constraint is binding, and hence $a^{PA} = W^{0A} + c\left(e^{PA}\right) + \frac{\rho_A}{2}\left(b^{PA}\right)^2\sigma^2 - b^{PA}e^{PA}$. One can substitute for e^{PA} and a^{PA} in $u_P\left(w^{PA}\left(\cdot\right), e^{PA}\right) = \left(1 - b^{PA}\right)e^{PA} - a^{PA} - \frac{\rho_P}{2}\left(1 - b^{PA}\right)^2\sigma^2$, and then differentiate to solve for b^{PA}. $\qquad\square$

Under the optimal risk sharing contract $c'(e) = 1$, but in the case of moral hazard $c'(e) = b^{PA} < 1$ whenever $\rho_A > 0$. Hence, a risk-averse agent supplies less than the socially optimal level of effort. The addition of moral hazard results in an increased sensitivity of rewards to observed performance, with agents of higher ability facing a steeper pay/performance relationship than lower-ability agents. Finally, as the variance of the output measure, σ^2, becomes very large, the gains to risk sharing increase, and the optimal sharing rule with moral hazard, b^{PA}, approaches the solution for the pure risk sharing case. Conversely, as the level of risk falls (σ^2 approaches zero), the optimal slope, b^{PA}, approaches 1, resulting in the efficient level of effort.

Another way to think about the principal-agent problem is in terms of the agency cost to obtain effort e. For example, suppose one wishes to have the agent choose the efficient effort level e^*—how much would this cost? Grossman and Hart (1983) introduce the idea that one can think of the principal-agent problem as a two-step process. In the first step, the principal determines the cost of obtaining effort e. In the second step, he works out the optimal level of effort given this cost function. In addition to explicitly working out the cost for each effort level, the approach allows one to derive the optimal contract under a wider set of conditions.

Let us illustrate the approach under the hypothesis that the principal is risk neutral ($\rho_P = 0$). In that case, the cost of effort is simply the expected payment by the principal to the agent. Hence, the lowest cost of securing effort e from the agent is a solution to:

$$C(e) = \min_{w(\cdot)} E\{w(x)\,|e\} \tag{7.17}$$

subject to:

$$IR: u_A(w(\cdot), e) \geq W^{0A}, \tag{7.18}$$

$$IC: e \in \arg\max_{e' \geq 0} u_A(w(\cdot), e'). \tag{7.19}$$

Following the same approach as in proposition 7.2 we have:

Proposition 7.3 *The solution to (7.17) is:*

$$C^{PA}(e) = W^{0A} + c(e) + \frac{\rho_A \sigma^2}{2}\left(\frac{e}{\theta}\right)^2. \tag{7.20}$$

This cost has three components. First, there is the certainty equivalent pay at the next best job, given by W^{0A}. Next, the agent has to be compensated for the cost of effort in the task given by $c(e)$. Finally, in order to have the agent choose effort e, she must be given a bonus payment $b = e/\theta$, which then translates into the *agency cost* that arises from the additional income risk faced by the agent due to the incentive pay:

$$AC\left(e, \rho_A, \sigma^2\right) = \frac{\rho_A \sigma^2}{2} \left(\frac{e}{\theta}\right)^2. \tag{7.21}$$

This in turn leads to costly risk bearing for the agent. Under this cost function, the principal's payoff is:

$$u_P(e) = E\{X|e\} - C^{PA}(e)$$

$$= e - C^{PA}(e).$$

Taking the agent's first-order condition for effort, one has:

$$c'(e) = 1 - \frac{dAC\left(e, \rho_A, \sigma^2\right)}{de} < 1.$$

One can verify that e^{PA} solves this expression. In the absence of agency costs, the principal would choose effort $c'(e^*) = 1$ (see (7.10)). However, increasing agent effort via bonus pay results in an increase in agency costs, and therefore the optimal level of effort is less than the first best. One can see from (7.21) that marginal agency cost rises with the agent's risk aversion, ρ_A and the noise in the output measure, σ^2.

It has been assumed that reward is a linear function of measured output to provide a clear exposition of the trade-offs and to illustrate how the problem of moral hazard adds an IC constraint to the contract formation problem. In practice, many nonlinear mechanisms are used to deal with moral hazard as well. Insurance companies often use deductibles in the event of an accident (see Holmström [1979] for such a model). In addition, dynamic linkages can provide incentives. For example, individuals with poor driving records are likely to face higher insurance costs in the future. A traffic violation, even if it does not lead to an accident, can result in a higher insurance premium. The insurance company uses information about an individual's traffic violation as a signal of risky behavior.

These observations are consistent with the general message of agency theory, namely that individuals modify their behavior as a function of the link between their actions and the rewards associated with those actions. This in turn generates the prediction that a principal who changes the correlation between *observable* signals of performance and output will in turn modify behavior. However, in practice, this correlation can be difficult to predict. One reason for this is that agents typically have many ways to respond to performance pay. The next section outlines the multitasking model that extends the basic principal-agent model to allow for a more complex strategy space on the part of agents.

7.3.1 Multiple Signals and Tasks

Consider a situation in which the agent has m possible tasks, and the allocation of effort among these tasks is given by the vector $E \in \Re_+^m$. In some cases, there is a single performance measure that aggregates output from several tasks. This case is particularly important when studying team production problems, in which several individuals may contribute to a single measure of team performance. Suppose that the m tasks are linearly related to n measures of performance by the following production function:

$$X = YE + \varepsilon,$$

where Y is an $n \times m$ matrix that transforms effort into output, while ε is a multivariate normal distribution with mean $\vec{0}$ and covariance matrix Σ.[4] Depending on the context, the number of performance signals, n, may be either larger or smaller than the number of tasks, m.

Given that a major goal of agency theory is to understand the trade-off between providing incentives and insurance to the agent, the analysis of the previous section is further simplified by assuming the principal is risk neutral, while the agent's behavior is described by CARA preferences with absolute risk aversion ρ_A. Following Holmström and Milgrom (1991), attention is restricted to linear compensation schemes of the form:

$$w(X) = a + B^T X,$$

where $a \in \Re$, and $B^T = [B_1, \ldots, B_n] \in \Re^n$ is a row vector of marginal rewards for measures $1, \ldots, n$. This ensures that the returns to the agent are normally distributed, and the preferences of the agent are given by the certainty equivalent for the income stream $w(X) - c(E)$.

The cost of effort is assumed to be a multivariate quadratic:

$$c(E) = \left(E - \bar{E}\right)^T \frac{C}{2} \left(E - \bar{E}\right),$$

where C is a symmetric, positive-definite matrix.[5] As in Holmström and Milgrom (1991), the cost of effort is minimized when $E = \bar{E} > \vec{0}$. The inclusion of $\bar{E}$ ensures that the agent chooses to supply a positive amount of effort in the absence of any monetary reward for performance. The idea is that there may already be mechanisms in place to ensure a minimum level of performance, given by $\bar{E}$. For example, the agent may be intrinsically motivated to work regardless of the pecuniary rewards.[6] The issue then is how can one structure performance pay to enhance effort above the minimum quality level $\bar{E}$?

In the case of the principal, his reward is a function of agent effort, E, and the payoff from contract $w(\cdot)$. His payoff can be written as:

$$u_P(E, a, B) = E\left\{P^T X - w(X)\right\} \tag{7.22}$$

$$= P^T YE - a - B^T YE \tag{7.23}$$

$$= R^T E - a - B^T YE. \tag{7.24}$$

The vector P defines the vector of returns to each signal, which in turn can be used to define returns directly as a function of effort. This is given by $R^T = [R_1, \ldots, R_m] \equiv P^T Y \in \Re^m_+$, a (row) vector where R_i denotes the marginal value of effort allocated to task i. The second line follows from the fact that $E\{\varepsilon\} = \vec{0}$. In this formulation, it is assumed that the principal cares about X directly.

An alternative formulation that leads to the same problem supposes that the principal cares about effort directly. Because it is assumed that the principal correctly anticipates effort, then let $R^T = [r_1, \ldots, r_m]$, where r_i is the marginal value to the principal of effort i. Thus, the same model can be used for the cases in which the principal cares about the measured output X or the effort E—both lead to formulation (7.24).

It is assumed that even though effort is not observed, it contributes directly to performance. An example, considered in more detail later, is the quality of work by a building contractor. At the time the performance contract is agreed upon, the only visible sign of quality might be the speed at which the work is completed. Yet the quality of concrete used in construction is important, particularly in an earthquake zone. However, such deficiencies in quality might become known only years later, after an actual earthquake, and this in turn has implications for optimal contract design.

Let us continue to suppose that the agent has CARA preferences with risk-aversion parameter ρ_A. In that case, her payoff from contract $w(X)$ is given by:

$$u_A(E, a, B) = CE\{w(X) - c(E)\}$$

$$= E\{w(X)\} - \frac{\rho_A}{2} \text{var}(w(X)) - c(E)$$

$$= w(E) - \frac{\rho_A}{2} B^T \Sigma B - c(E).$$

It follows from (7.12) that the multitasking principal-agent problem can be written as follows:

$$\max_{E, a, B} R^T E - a - B^T Y E, \tag{7.25}$$

subject to:

$$\text{IR: } a + B^T Y E - (E - \bar{E})^T \frac{C}{2} (E - \bar{E}) - \frac{\rho_A}{2} B^T \Sigma B \geq W^{0A},$$

$$\text{IC: } E \in \arg\max_{E'} a + B^T Y E' - (E' - \bar{E})^T \frac{C}{2} (E' - \bar{E}) - \frac{\rho_A}{2} B^T \Sigma B.$$

Observe that the IC constraint can be solved explicitly using the first-order condition:

$$Y^T B - C(E - \bar{E}) = 0.$$

From this, one concludes that effort as a function of B is:

$$E = H_E(B) = \bar{E} + C^{-1} Y^T B.$$

The fixed payment a is adjusted to ensure the IR constraint is binding, and hence the payoff to the principal as a function of the rewards to performance, B, is:

$$u_P(B) = R^T H_E(B) - (H_E(B) - \bar{E})^T \frac{C}{2} (H_E(B) - \bar{E}) - \frac{\rho_A}{2} B^T \Sigma B - W^{0A}.$$

The optimal B^{PA} can be computed by maximizing $u_P(B)$ with respect to $B \in \mathfrak{R}^n$, from which one can conclude:

Proposition 7.4   *The solution to the multitasking principal-agent problem is:*

$$E^{PA} = \bar{E} + C^{-1}Y^T B^{PA}, \tag{7.26}$$

$$B^{PA} = \left[YC^{-1}Y^T + \rho_A \Sigma \right]^{-1} YC^{-1}R, \tag{7.27}$$

$$E\left(w^{PA}(X)\right) = a + \left[B^{PA}\right]^T YE^{PA} \tag{7.28}$$

$$= W^{0A} + \frac{1}{2}\left[B^{PA}\right]^T YC^{-1}Y^T B^{PA} + \frac{1}{2}\rho_A \left[B^{PA}\right]^T \Sigma B^{PA}.$$

This result is analogous to the one-dimensional case. When the agent is risk neutral, $\rho_A = 0$, and Y is invertible, then the optimal contract sets

$$B^{PA} = \left[YC^{-1}Y^T \right]^{-1} YC^{-1}R$$

$$= \left[Y^T \right]^{-1} CY^{-1} YC^{-1}R$$

$$= \left[Y^T \right]^{-1} R.$$

Conversely, as the agent becomes more risk averse, $(\rho_A \to \infty)$, we can see from (7.27) that if Σ is positive definite, then the sensitivity of income to measured performance approaches zero $(B^{PA} \to \vec{0})$. Further insight into the effect of information on the optimal structure of the incentive contract is provided by studying some applications of this general result. In many cases, what makes the multitasking problem different from the basic principal-agent model is the fact that Y may not be invertible. In that case, it may not be possible to provide performance incentives for all tasks.

Informativeness principle

Consider first the effect of an additional signal in the standard principal-agent problem. Suppose that effort is one dimensional, $C = [1]$, and marginal returns are $R = [1]$, but with two performance signals $(n = 2, m = 1)$. Hence:

$$Y = \left[\begin{array}{c} 1 \\ 1 \end{array} \right].$$

Suppose that the covariance matrix is positive definite (and hence invertible); then by proposition 7.4 the optimal B^{PA} is:

$$B^{PA} = \left[YY^T + \rho_A \Sigma \right]^{-1} Y$$

$$= \frac{1}{\gamma} \left[\begin{array}{c} \Sigma_{22} - \Sigma_{12} \\ \Sigma_{11} - \Sigma_{21} \end{array} \right],$$

where $\gamma = \Sigma_{22} + \Sigma_{11} - (\Sigma_{21} + \Sigma_{12}) + \rho_A (\Sigma_{11}\Sigma_{22} - \Sigma_{12}\Sigma_{21})$, and Σ_{ij} is the ij'th entry in the covariance matrix.

Suppose the signals are uncorrelated, then $\Sigma_{12} = \Sigma_{21} = 0$. In that case the optimal contract is:

$$B^{PA} = \frac{1}{1 + \rho_A \left(\frac{\Sigma_{11}\Sigma_{22}}{\Sigma_{22}+\Sigma_{11}} \right)} \begin{bmatrix} \frac{\Sigma_{22}}{\Sigma_{22}+\Sigma_{11}} \\ \frac{\Sigma_{11}}{\Sigma_{22}+\Sigma_{11}} \end{bmatrix}.$$

Observe that the reward to signal 1 increases with the variance of the error for signal 2. As the information content of signal 2 decreases, then the optimal contract is more dependent on signal 1. Another way to see the same result is the case in which signal 2 is simply a noisy version of signal 1. Signal 2 is still informative but does not provide any additional information over the information contained in signal 1. In that case, the error term for signal 2 is:

$$\varepsilon_2 = \varepsilon_1 + \varepsilon,$$

where ε_1 has variance σ^2, and ε has variance $\bar{\sigma}^2$, which is independent of ε_1. The covariance matrix is:

$$\Sigma = \begin{bmatrix} \sigma^2 & \sigma^2 \\ \sigma^2 & \sigma^2 + \bar{\sigma}^2 \end{bmatrix},$$

and the computed optimal pay/performance contract is:

$$B^{PA} = \begin{bmatrix} \frac{1}{1+\rho_A\sigma^2} \\ 0 \end{bmatrix}.$$

In other words, the optimal contract ignores x_2 because x_1 is a *sufficient statistic* for x_2 (see Blackwell and Girshick 1954 and Holmström 1982).

This result illustrates the lesson that the optimal contract should be a function of any signal that provides additional information regarding unobserved effort. If a signal does not provide useful information, then it should be ignored (though see exercise 4). This prediction is falsified in situations where compensation appears to be insensitive to the available information, even though it is informative relative to the other signals. This may be explained by the multidimensionality of effort itself.

Task substitution

This section addresses how to design incentive contracts when effort has several components. In that case, increasing the reward for one type of effort may cause the agent to divert effort from another valuable activity. For example, consider the problem of contracting for renovation work in a house. Suppose the two measures of interest are speed and quality, which the contractor controls through the choice of $E^T = [e_s, e_q]$, where e_s denotes the level of speed while e_q is attention to quality. The principal values both speed and quality, with marginal returns given by $R^T = [r_s, r_q]$. It is also reasonable to suppose that increasing speed increases the marginal cost of supplying quality, and vice versa. This effect is captured by supposing the cost of effort satisfies:

$$\frac{\partial^2 c(E)}{\partial e_s \partial e_q} = C_{12} = C_{21} = d > 0.$$

For simplicity, suppose that tasks have the same effort costs and thus $C_{11} = C_{22} = c$. To ensure C is strictly positive definite, it is also assumed that $c^2 - d^2 > 0$.

Next, it is assumed that while one can measure speed, the quality cannot be contractually specified. This is consistent with the assumption that the local building codes specify minimum quality standards that are incorporated into the fixed term $\bar{e}_q$. However, if the contractor faces a deadline, then he may begin to skimp on quality. In this case, it may be optimal to reduce incentives for speedy performance. To see this, suppose that the principal can observe only the completion date, and thus $Y = [1 \quad 0]$. Hence:

$$x = YE + \varepsilon,$$

where $x \in \Re$ and σ^2 is the variance of the error term.

From proposition 7.4 it follows that the optimal pay/performance slope for speedy completion is:

$$b_s = \left[YC^{-1}Y^T + \rho_A\sigma^2 \right]^{-1} YC^{-1}R,$$

$$= \frac{cr_s - dr_q}{c + \rho_A\sigma^2 \left(c^2 - d^2 \right)}.$$

In this case, increasing the value of quality via r_q results in a *lower* return to speed, b_s, under an optimal contract. If the value of quality is sufficiently high, then $cr_s - dr_q < 0$, which implies that the principal provides incentives for the agent to work more slowly. If $cr_s - dr_q = 0$, then as Holmström and Milgrom (1991) observe, the optimal contract has no incentives for performance at all, regardless of the agent's degree of risk aversion. Finally, when the tasks are substitutes ($d > 0$), then increasing the value of quality decreases b_s, but when they are complements ($d < 0$), increasing r_q increases b_s.

Relative performance evaluation

In other situations, the productivities of a group of individuals are correlated. A common example is CEO performance in a single industry. The industry's fortunes as a whole can vary over time, regardless of CEO performance, and therefore compensation that depends on firm profits has an element of risk unrelated to individual performance but common to all individuals in the same industry. Incentives can be improved by filtering out industry shocks from a CEO's compensation. This is achieved by basing compensation on a company's stock market performance relative to other firms in the same industry.

Consider two individuals, indexed by $i \in \{1, 2\}$, each of whom selects an effort level $e_i \in \Re_+$. The extension to several individuals is straightforward. For each individual, the principal can observe the firm's stock market price, which is assumed to have the form:

$$x_i = e_i + \alpha + \varepsilon_i,$$

where $\{\alpha, \varepsilon_1, \varepsilon_2\}$ are independent, normally distributed random variables with mean zero. The term α is a shock with variance σ^2 that is common to the two agents representing general economic conditions, while ε_i are idiosyncratic shocks with variance $\bar{\sigma}^2$. Letting $\gamma_i = \alpha + \varepsilon_i$ and E be the vector of efforts for the two agents, the performance measure is the vector of market performance for the two firms:

$$X = E + \gamma,$$

where $\gamma \sim N(0, \Sigma)$, and

$$\Sigma = \left[\begin{array}{cc} \sigma^2 + \bar{\sigma}^2 & \sigma^2 \\ \sigma^2 & \sigma^2 + \bar{\sigma}^2 \end{array} \right].$$

Compensation is assumed to be a linear function of X, and hence agent i receives:

$$w_i(X) = a_i + B_i^T X,$$

where $B_i^T = [b_{i1}, b_{i2}]$. The principal is assumed to be risk neutral, and the agents have ability parameters θ_i and absolute risk aversion ρ_i. The payoffs in terms of certainty equivalents for the principal and agent as a function of effort and the contracts are given by:

$$u_P = P^T E - \sum_{i \in \{1,2\}} \left(a_i + B_i^T E \right),$$

$$u_A^i = a_i + B_i^T E - e_i^2/2\theta_i - \frac{\rho_i}{2} B_i^T \Sigma B_i, \ \ i \in \{1, 2\}.$$

The principal-agent problem is now the same as in the one-agent case, except now one has IR and IC constraints for each agent. Agent i's IC constraint implies:

$$e_i(b_{ii}) = \theta_i b_{ii}.$$

Let W_i^0 denote agent i's alternative wage; then the binding IR constraint for each agent implies that the principal's payoff is:

$$u_P = \sum_{i \in \{1,2\}} \left(p_i e_i - e_i^2/2\theta_i - \frac{\rho_i}{2} B_i^T \Sigma B_i - W_i^0 \right).$$

The contribution of each agent is independent of the other, and hence for each $i = 1, 2$, one can solve for B_i by maximizing $p_i e_i - e_i^2/2\theta_i - \rho_i B_i^T \Sigma B_i/2 - W_i^0$ with respect to B_i. The first-order condition is:

$$\left[\begin{array}{c} p_i \theta_i - \theta_i b_{ii} \\ 0 \end{array} \right] - \rho_i \Sigma B_i = \left[\begin{array}{c} 0 \\ 0 \end{array} \right],$$

from which we conclude for $i \neq j$:

$$b_{ii} = p_i \theta_i \frac{\sigma^2 + \bar{\sigma}^2}{\theta_i \left(\sigma^2 + \bar{\sigma}^2 \right) + \rho_i \bar{\sigma}^2 \left(2\sigma^2 + \bar{\sigma}^2 \right)},$$

$$b_{ij} = -p_i \theta_i \frac{\sigma^2}{\theta_i \left(\sigma^2 + \bar{\sigma}^2 \right) + \rho_i \bar{\sigma}^2 \left(2\sigma^2 + \bar{\sigma}^2 \right)}.$$

Even though agent i's measure depends only on her effort, the optimal contract also depends on performance measure x_j, $j \neq i$. Letting $\beta(\theta_i, \rho_i) = \left(\sigma^2 + \bar{\sigma}^2 \right) + \frac{\rho_i \bar{\sigma}^2}{\theta_i} \left(2\sigma^2 + \bar{\sigma}^2 \right)$, then compensation for agent i can be written in the form:

$$w_i(X) = a_i + \frac{p_i}{\beta(\theta_i, \rho_i)} \left(\bar{\sigma}^2 x_i + \sigma^2 \left(x_i - x_j \right) \right).$$

Thus agent i's compensation has two components: a direct incentive effect, $\frac{p_i\bar{\sigma}^2}{\beta_i(\theta_i,\rho_i)}x_i$, and a component that depends on her performance compared to agent j, $\frac{p_i\sigma^2}{\beta_i(\theta_i,\rho_i)}\left(x_i - x_j\right)$. The weight that the comparative evaluation takes in the optimal contract depends on correlation between signals 1 and 2, as parameterized by σ^2.

The optimal contract varies with the agent's ability, θ_i, and attitude toward risk, ρ_i; consequently, a single contract that is suitable for all worker types does not exist. Relative performance contracts raise the concern that low-ability agents may become discouraged. However, one attractive feature of this contract is that the agent's incentives for performance are *independent* of the performances of other agents, since:

$$\frac{\partial w_i(X)}{\partial e_i} = \frac{p_i}{\beta_i(\theta_i,\rho_i)}\left(\bar{\sigma}^2 + \sigma^2\right).$$

This implies that, regardless of the effort of the other agent, the return to effort does not change. Holmström and Milgrom (1987) use this idea to explain the widespread use of linear contracts. In their model, agents allocate effort over time in a way that is unobservable to the principal. If contracts are not linear, then the agents inefficiently allocate time to periods with high personal returns. They show linear contracts are optimal in this context because the agents face the same marginal returns to effort in every period, regardless of their past performance.

The agency literature has also considered the case of a *tournament*. In a tournament, the performances of the two agents are compared, and the one with the higher performance receives a bonus. The optimal contract in that case is derived in exercise 8. If both agents have the same preferences, the prize can be chosen to elicit efficient effort. However, because the contract imposes additional risk, it is not efficient when agents are risk averse. Moreover, in contrast to the relative performance contract derived above, if agents differ greatly in their abilities, then the low-ability agent may give up and choose low effort, defeating the purpose of the tournament.

Tournaments do have the desirable property that they are implementable even if the outcome of the tournament is private information to the principal. With a tournament, the principal can commit in advance to paying the prize to the best performer. In that case, the cost of rewarding the agents is not sensitive to who is chosen, and the principal has no reason to distort the ranking (see Carmichael 1983 and Malcomson 1984).

7.3.2   The Lake Wobegone Effect: Penalties and the Probability of Detection

A ubiquitous feature of many observed contracts is the *Lake Wobegone Effect*, named after the fictional hometown of Garrison Keillor, who each week would end his monologue on American NPR radio with "Well, that's the news from Lake Wobegone, where all the women are strong, all the men are good-looking, and all the children are above average."[7] Under a "Lake Wobegone contract" all performance is graded the same (i.e., above average), except the worst performance. This is consistent with the well-known observation among compensation consultants that managers are reluctant to give poor performance evaluations to employees and end up sanctioning only the worst performers (Milkovich and Newman 2005).

This observation seems to be inconsistent with the celebrated principal-agent result that predicts that pay varies monotonically with performance (proposition 7.2). However, Mirrlees (1974) has shown that, under the appropriate conditions, one can achieve close to the *first best* using a Lake Wobegone contract, or more precisely, a *penalty* contract that pays a fixed amount and imposes a penalty if performance falls below a low threshold (in other words, most people are above average and do not get penalized).

A standard principal-agent model consisting of a risk-neutral principal and a risk-averse agent illustrates this point. In the Mirrlees model, it is assumed that given agent effort e, the distribution of output X has a density $f(x|e)$, with support $[\underline{x}, \bar{x}]$ that does not depend on effort e.[8] It is typically assumed that increasing e increases the mean of X, though for the analysis that follows this is not strictly necessary. It is also assumed that $f(x|e)$ is a continuous function of e.

Given a sharing rule $s(X)$, the preferences of the principal and agent are given by:

$$U_P(X - s(X)) = \int_{\underline{x}}^{\bar{x}} (x - s(x)) f(x|e)\, dx,$$

$$U_A(s(X), e) = \int_{\underline{x}}^{\bar{x}} u(s(x)) f(x|e)\, dx - g(e),$$

where $u(\cdot)$ is the agent's Bernoulli utility function satisfying $u' > 0$, $u'' < 0$ on $(\underline{x}, \bar{x})$, and $g(\cdot)$ is the cost of effort satisfying $g' > 0$ and $g'' > 0$ on $[0, \bar{e})$, and $\lim_{e \to \bar{e}} g(e) = \infty$. The latter assumption implies that $\bar{e}$ represents an upper physical constraint on the efforts of the agent. If effort were observable, the optimal contract $\{s^*(\cdot), e^*\}$ would solve:

$$\max_{\{s(\cdot), e\}} \int_{\underline{x}}^{\bar{x}} (x - s(x)) f(x|e)\, dx,$$

$$\text{subject to:} \quad \int_{\underline{x}}^{\bar{x}} u(s(x)) f(x|e)\, dx - g(e) \geq U^{0A},$$

where U^{0A} is the alternative utility available to the agent.

Given that the principal is risk neutral, we know that optimal risk sharing implies that there is some fixed payment x^* such that $s^*(x) = x^*, \forall x \in [\underline{x}, \bar{x}]$. The assumptions of the model ensure that optimal effort exists. It is further assumed that effort is strictly positive, and let:

$$e^* \in \arg\max_{e \geq 0} \int_{\underline{x}}^{\bar{x}} x f(x|e)\, dx - g(e) > 0.$$

At the optimum, the individual rationality constraint is binding, and therefore one may conclude:

$$u(x^*) - g(e^*) = U^{0A}, \text{ or}$$

$$x^* = u^{-1}\left(U^{0A} + g(e^*)\right).$$

Hence, the principal's first-best utility is given by:

$$U_P^* = \int_{\underline{x}}^{\bar{x}} xf\left(x|e^*\right) dx - x^*.$$

Suppose that a solution to the first-best problem exists with $x^* \in (\underline{x}, \bar{x})$, and now consider how one can construct a contract close to the first best when there is moral hazard. In this case, a fixed wage contract provides no incentive to perform. Mirrlees observed that one can achieve the first best if two additional conditions exist. First, a payoff must exist that gives the agent an arbitrarily low utility. Second, there is a signal that occurs with very low probability with the feature that an increase in effort results in a large proportional increase in the probability of this signal occurring. These ideas are captured with the following assumptions:

A1 $\lim_{x \to \underline{x}} u(x) = -\infty.$

A2 $\lim_{x \to \underline{x}} \frac{f_e(x|e)}{f(x|e)} = -\infty$, for all $e \in [0, \bar{e})$.

A3 There is a $K > \underline{x}$ such that $F_{ee}(x|e) > 0$, for all $x \in (\underline{x}, K)$ and $e \in [0, \bar{e})$.

Condition A1 ensures that the principal can provide an arbitrarily strong punishment by choosing a payment close to the lower bound for the payoffs, $\underline{x}$.[9] Condition A2 is a likelihood ratio property that requires the probability of getting a value close to the lower bound of the support, $\underline{x}$, to approach zero more quickly than the size of the effect of effort on x (recall that $f_e(x|e) < 0$ means that increasing effort decreases the likelihood of x occurring). Finally, condition A3 ensures that the density function, $F(x|e) = \int_{\underline{x}}^x f(x|e)\, dx$, is convex in e for low values of x, allowing one to characterize the optimal choice by a first-order condition.

Mirrlees's idea is that one can provide incentives to perform by punishing agents that realize very low outputs. Define a *penalty* sharing rule as follows:

$$s\left(X|\underline{s}, \bar{s}, \hat{x}\right) = \begin{cases} \underline{s} & \text{if } X < \hat{x} \\ \bar{s} & \text{if } X \geq \hat{x} \end{cases}.$$

Two issues must be considered. The first is whether such a scheme can induce the efficient level of effort. The second is whether it can be made to approximate full insurance for the agent. It is first shown that the first-best effort can be achieved with $\hat{x}$ arbitrarily close to $\underline{x}$. Second, it is shown that the expected penalty in that case approaches zero as $\hat{x}$ approaches zero.

Proposition 7.5 *Suppose conditions A1–A3 are satisfied. Then for every $\hat{x} \in (\underline{x}, K)$, there is a sharing rule $s\left(X|\underline{s}, \bar{s}, \hat{x}\right)$ such that*

$$e^* \in \arg \max_{e \in (0, \bar{e})} U_A\left(s\left(X|\underline{s}, \bar{s}, \hat{x}\right), e\right), \tag{7.29}$$

and

$$U_A\left(s\left(X|\underline{s}, \bar{s}, \hat{x}\right), e^*\right) = U^{0A}. \tag{7.30}$$

Letting $\bar{s}(\hat{x})$ and $\underline{s}(\hat{x})$ be the upper and lower bounds of payoffs given $\hat{x}$ that solve (7.29)–(7.30), then as $\hat{x}$ approaches $\underline{x}$ the sharing rule approaches the first best:

$$\lim_{\hat{x} \to \underline{x}} \bar{s}(\hat{x}) = x^*, \tag{7.31}$$

$$\lim_{\hat{x} \to \underline{x}} \underline{s}\left(\hat{x}\right) = \underline{x}, \tag{7.32}$$

$$\lim_{\hat{x} \to \underline{x}} U_A\left(s\left(X|\underline{s}, \bar{s}, \hat{x}\right), e^*\right) = u(x^*) - g(e^*). \tag{7.33}$$

Proof. First notice:

$$U_A\left(s\left(X|\underline{s}, \bar{s}, \hat{x}\right), e\right) = \left[u\left(\underline{s}\right) - u\left(\bar{s}\right)\right] F\left(\hat{x}|e\right) + u\left(\bar{s}\right) - g\left(e\right). \tag{7.34}$$

If $\bar{s} > \underline{s}$, then by A3 this payoff is concave in e when $\hat{x} < K$. Hence the optimum is characterized by the first-order condition. In particular, we can choose the sharing rule such that:

$$\left[u\left(\underline{s}\right) - u\left(\bar{s}\right)\right] F_e\left(\hat{x}|e^*\right) - g'\left(e^*\right) = 0. \tag{7.35}$$

In addition, the optimum must satisfy the individual rationality constraint. Hence we have:

$$\left[u\left(\underline{s}\right) - u\left(\bar{s}\right)\right] F\left(\hat{x}|e\right) + u\left(\bar{s}\right) - g\left(e\right) = U^{0A}. \tag{7.36}$$

Fixing the cutoff $\hat{x} < K$, we can solve equations (7.35) and (7.36) for $\underline{s}$ and $\bar{s}$:

$$\underline{s}\left(\hat{x}\right) = u^{-1}\left(U^{0A} + g\left(e^*\right) + g'\left(e^*\right) \frac{1 - F\left(\hat{x}|e^*\right)}{F_e\left(\hat{x}|e^*\right)}\right), \tag{7.37}$$

$$\bar{s}\left(\hat{x}\right) = u^{-1}\left(U^{0A} + g\left(e^*\right) - g'\left(e^*\right) \frac{F\left(\hat{x}|e^*\right)}{F_e\left(\hat{x}|e^*\right)}\right). \tag{7.38}$$

This shows that for each $\hat{x} \in (\underline{x}, K)$ we can find a sharing rule that satisfies individual rationality and the incentive constraint in the first part of the proposition. The next step is to show that, as $\hat{x} \to \underline{x}$, we get the first-best risk sharing. By l'Hopital's rule and condition A2, one has:

$$\lim_{\hat{x} \to \underline{x}} \frac{F\left(\hat{x}|e^*\right)}{F_e\left(\hat{x}|e^*\right)} = \lim_{\hat{x} \to \underline{x}} \frac{f\left(\hat{x}|e^*\right)}{f_e\left(\hat{x}|e^*\right)} = 0.$$

This implies:

$$\lim_{\hat{x} \to \underline{x}} \bar{s}\left(\hat{x}\right) = \lim_{\hat{x} \to \underline{x}} u^{-1}\left(U^{0A} + g\left(e^*\right) - g'\left(e^*\right) \frac{F\left(\hat{x}|e^*\right)}{F_e\left(\hat{x}|e^*\right)}\right)$$

$$= u^{-1}\left(U^{0A} + g\left(e^*\right)\right)$$

$$= x^*.$$

By construction $U_A\left(s\left(X|\underline{s}, \bar{s}, \hat{x}\right), e\right) = U^{0A}$, and it follows that the risk faced by the agent satisfies:

$$\lim_{\hat{x} \to \underline{x}} \left[u\left(\underline{s}\left(\hat{x}\right)\right) - u\left(\bar{s}\left(\hat{x}\right)\right)\right] F\left(\hat{x}|e^*\right) = \lim_{\hat{x} \to \underline{x}} U^{0A} - \left(u\left(\bar{s}\left(\hat{x}\right)\right) - g\left(e^*\right)\right)$$

$$= \lim_{\hat{x} \to \underline{x}} \left(u\left(x^*\right) - g\left(e^*\right)\right) - \left(u\left(\bar{s}\left(\hat{x}\right)\right) - g\left(e^*\right)\right)$$

$$= 0.$$

This implies (7.33). Finally, notice that $\lim_{\hat{x}\to\underline{x}} F_e\left(\hat{x}|e^*\right) = 0$. Thus, to satisfy the first-order condition for effort, it must be the case that $\lim_{\hat{x}\to\underline{x}} u\left(\underline{s}\left(\hat{x}\right)\right) = -\infty$, from which we conclude $\lim_{\hat{x}\to\underline{x}} \underline{s}\left(\hat{x}\right) = \underline{x}$. $\qquad\qquad\qquad\qquad\qquad\qquad\qquad\qquad\qquad\qquad\square$

For cutoffs close to $\underline{x}$, the agent receives with probability almost 1 the payoff x^*. She is deterred from reducing effort because this would increase the probability of her receiving a bad outcome in utility terms. The key idea here is that very low values provide high-quality information concerning the probability that the agent has selected low effort. This idea can be immediately applied also in a case in which the agent's effort affects the *support* of the output distribution.

For example, suppose that the support of $F(x|e)$ is $\left(\underline{x}(e), \bar{x}(e)\right)$, where it is assumed that $\underline{x}(0) = \underline{x}$, $\frac{\partial \underline{x}(e)}{\partial e} > 0$, and $f(x|e) > k > 0$ for $x \in \left(\underline{x}(e), \underline{x}(e) + \varepsilon\right)$, for some small ε. In this case, if we set $\hat{x} = \underline{x}(e^*)$ and $\bar{s} = x^*$, then for $\underline{s}$ sufficiently close to $\underline{x}$ the agent will choose $e = e^*$. Thus, with a moving support one obtains the first best because if we observe any $x \in [\underline{x}, \underline{x}(e^*))$, then we can conclude that the agent must have shirked with probability 1.

In a famous paper, Becker and Stigler (1974) introduce the idea of optimal enforcement. They argue that one way to reduce enforcement costs is to combine a reduction in the probability of enforcement with an increase in the punishment. The Mirrlees result shows that this idea can be implemented within a principal-agent framework. This leaves open the question of why it is not used more widely. In practice, we see lots of examples of malfeasance that make little sense given the penalties. Missing from the model is the element of learning.

The next section introduces career concerns into a learning model that is widely used in labor economics. Called the career concerns model, it illustrates the point that learning and reputation effects can reduce the link between incentive pay and performance. However, it is only a beginning—much work remains to fully integrate human learning into agency theory (see Kahneman and Thaler 2006).

7.4 Career Concerns

The agency models considered thus far suppose that the principal constructs an incentive contract based on observed performance. Fama (1980) has argued that the market can also provide a solution to the incentive problem when performance is publicly available. Such incentive effects are common. For example, a young athlete on a sports team may be on a fixed salary, but good performance may lead to lucrative offers in the future. The effect of effort on future income is called a *career concern*.

In an important paper, Holmström (1999) shows that, in general, career concerns provide incentives for increased performance. However, he also shows that Fama was not correct in claiming that market incentives alone are sufficient to induce the first best. Holmstrom finds that career concerns can work only if there is some uncertainty regarding a person's true ability. If an individual's ability is known perfectly by the market, there is no reason for compensation to vary with time, and thus there is no way for current effort to result in higher income in the future.[10] In a market setting, income rises with a good outcome due to a *learning effect*—the market revises upward its beliefs regarding an individual's ability.

Therefore, when a person is young and there is great uncertainty regarding her ability, she works hard to create a favorable impression. As her true ability becomes better known, the incentive to work decreases. Gibbons and Murphy (1992) explore the consequence of adding agency contracts to counterbalance the effect of career concerns. They show that individuals need to be given more powerful incentive contracts as they age to counterbalance the decreasing effect of career concerns. This prediction is consistent with the pattern of contracts offered to CEOs of major corporations.

7.4.1   Market Wage Determination

Consider an infinitely lived agent, with time indexed by $t = 0, 1, 2, \ldots$. Each period, the agent chooses effort $a_t \geq 0$ and produces output:

$$y_t = \eta + a_t + \varepsilon_t,$$

where η denotes the *ability* of the agent, with prior distribution $N\left(m_\eta, \sigma_\eta^2\right)$, while ε_t is an independent and identically distributed sequence of error terms with distribution $N\left(0, \sigma_\varepsilon^2\right)$. In the subsequent development, it is convenient to use *precision* as a parameter. It is defined by the reciprocal of the variance: $\rho_\eta = 1/\sigma_\eta^2$ and $\rho_\varepsilon = 1/\sigma_\varepsilon^2$. The market for agents is assumed to be perfectly competitive: each period the agent receives her expected output, and all labor market participants observe this output. Information is assumed to be *symmetric*, that is, both the agent and the principals in the market have the same beliefs regarding worker ability. These beliefs are updated each period as a function of the observed output, y_t.

The timing of decisions in each period is as follows:

1. At the beginning of period t, two principals offer the agent a wage w_t as a function of information based upon previous periods' output. If the principal does not employ the agent, profits are zero.

2. The agent selects effort a_t.

3. The output y_t is paid to the principal who employs the agent, and it is observed by all market participants.

Let r be the interest rate, and Δ be the length of one period. Hence, if I_t is income in period t, then the present value of this income is given by:

$$\int_{t\Delta}^{(t+1)\Delta} I_t e^{-r\tau} \, d\tau = I_t \frac{\left(1 - e^{-r\Delta}\right) e^{-r\Delta t}}{r}. \tag{7.39}$$

Let $\delta = e^{-r\Delta}$ be the discount factor per period, and suppose that the agent is risk averse but has an intertemporal rate of substitution equal to her discount rate. We can use the approximation that for small Δ, $\frac{(1-\delta)}{r} \cong \Delta$ and hence agent preferences are given by:

$$U = E\left\{-\exp\left\{-\rho_A \Delta \sum_{t=0}^{\infty} (w_t - g(a_t)) \delta^t\right\}\right\},$$

where ρ_A is the absolute risk aversion of the agent, δ is the discount rate per period, and $g(\cdot)$ is the disutility of effort, satisfying the assumptions $g(0) = g'(0) = 0$ and $g'(a)$,

$g''(a), g'''(a) > 0$, for $a > 0$. Letting δ approach 1 is equivalent to supposing that there is more frequent measurement of performance as $\Delta \to 0$. It is assumed that the principals are risk neutral and there are no long-term contracts: each period, the agent is free to work for either principal, and hence competition between the principals implies that the expected return of each principal is zero each period.

Market participants are assumed to correctly anticipate the effort of the agent each period (this is true for both the fixed wage contract and the performance pay contract). Let $\hat{a}_t$ denote this effort in period t. This implies that, at the end of the period, the market observes a signal of agent ability given by:

$$x_t = y_t - \hat{a}_t = \eta + \varepsilon_t.$$

Given the hypothesis of perfect competition between the principals each period, the wage offered to the agent will be:

$$w_t = m_t + \hat{a}_t,$$

where $m_t = E\{\eta|x_0, x_1, \ldots, x_{t-1}\}$ is the expected ability of the agent in period t. Since the prior distribution of η is normal with mean m_η and precision ρ_η, the posterior distribution of η is also normal with mean and precision at the beginning of date t given by:[11]

$$m_t = \frac{\rho_\eta m_\eta + \rho_t \bar{x}_t}{\rho_\eta + \rho_t}, \tag{7.40}$$

$$\rho_t = t\rho_\varepsilon, \tag{7.41}$$

where $\bar{x}_t = \frac{1}{t}\sum_{s=0}^{t-1} x_s$ is the mean productivity of the individual in the past at dates $t \geq 1$, and $\sigma^2 = \frac{1}{\rho_t}$ is the variance of this estimate. Thus, the market's estimate of an individual's ability is the weighted average of prior estimate, m_η, and the on-the-job estimate, $\bar{x}_t$. With more experience, observed performance becomes the main determinant of an individual's expected future productivity.

Due to the time invariance of the payoffs in the model, effort in subsequent periods has the same relationship between beliefs and effort, except that prior beliefs are more precise. Therefore, it is sufficient to determine the optimal effort in period 0 given η, and then this formula can be appropriately adjusted to determine effort in future periods.

To solve for expected effort, one applies the Nash equilibrium concept (see chapter 4). A Nash equilibrium has the feature that even though a party cannot observe the action of its counterparty, it correctly anticipates their counterparty's optimal choice. In order for a choice to be an equilibrium, it must be the case that a deviation is not profitable.

In equilibrium, the market expects the agent to choose effort $\hat{a}_0$ in period 0. In order for this to be an equilibrium, it must be the case that the agent cannot gain by choosing a different effort, a_0. If she chooses a_0, then the signal of performance at the end of period 0 is:

$$x_0 = y_0 + \hat{a}_0 + (a_0 - \hat{a}_0).$$

In other words, choosing an action different from $\hat{a}_0$ causes the signal observed by the principal to be *biased*, resulting in the estimated ability being biased by an amount $(a_0 - \hat{a}_0)$. This bias affects beliefs in all future periods as a function of the weight placed on the first period's information. Therefore, the expected wage in period t as a function of first-period effort is:

$$w_t(a_0) = \frac{\rho_\eta m_\eta + \rho_t \bar{x}_t}{\rho_\eta + \rho_t} + \hat{a}_t + \frac{\rho_\varepsilon}{\rho_\eta + \rho_t}(a_0 - \hat{a}_0).$$

Notice that this deviation does not affect the variance of future wages, only the mean. Hence, the individual maximizes expected utility by choosing a_0 to maximize the expected discounted future income less the cost of effort. The payoff in certainty equivalents is thus:

$$u_0(a_0) = \Delta\left\{E\left\{\sum_{t=0}^{\infty}(w_t(a_0) - g(\hat{a}_t))\delta^t\right\} - \frac{\rho_A}{2}\text{var}\left\{\Delta\sum_{t=0}^{\infty}w_t(a_0)\delta^t\right\}\right\}$$

$$= \frac{m_\eta - \rho_A\left(\frac{1}{\rho_\eta} + \frac{1}{\rho_\varepsilon}\right)/2}{r} + \Delta\sum_{t=1}^{\infty}(\hat{a}_t - g(\hat{a}_t))\delta^t$$

$$+ \Delta\left(CC\left(\frac{\rho_\eta}{\rho_\varepsilon}, \delta\right)(a_0 - \hat{a}_0) - g(a_0)\right),$$

where:

$$CC(x, \delta) = \sum_{\tau=1}^{\infty}\frac{1}{x + \tau}\delta^\tau \tag{7.42}$$

is the *career concerns effect* at date 0.[12] This is the effect that increasing effort in the first-period of work has upon the discounted present value of future income. Thus, the first-order condition for optimal effort in period 0 is:

$$g'(\hat{a}_0) = CC(\rho_\eta/\rho_\varepsilon, \delta). \tag{7.43}$$

In period 0, the precision of prior beliefs is ρ_η, while in subsequent periods it is given by $\rho_\eta + t \times \rho_\varepsilon$. If we plug this into the career concerns expression, we get the first-order condition for effort for all periods:

$$g'(\hat{a}_t) = CC(\rho_\eta/\rho_\varepsilon + t, \delta), \forall t \geq 0. \tag{7.44}$$

The career concerns effect, $CC(\rho_\eta/\rho_\varepsilon + t, \delta)$, is the marginal benefit from effort due to the effect of the current performance signal on the discounted value of future income. As the precision of the noise term goes to 0, $\rho_\varepsilon \to 0$, then the amount of information that the market obtains from observing output falls as does the career concerns effect, with the following limit:

$$\lim_{\rho_\varepsilon \to 0} CC(\rho_\eta/\rho_\varepsilon + t, \delta) = 0. \tag{7.45}$$

Conversely, when the prior becomes less precise, $\rho_\eta \to 0$, then it provides very little information regarding agent ability. In this case, career concerns rise with ρ_η, which explains why early output matters more when there is little information regarding ability.

The model also generates predictions over time. In that case, learning increases the precision of estimated ability over time, which in turn lowers effort incentives, leading to a fall in the career effect:

$$\lim_{t \to \infty} CC(\rho_\eta/\rho_\varepsilon + t, \delta) = 0. \tag{7.46}$$

These results can be summarized in the following proposition.

Proposition 7.6 *Given a discount rate, $\delta \in (0, 1)$, when individual effort arises purely from career concerns, then effort rises with uncertainty regarding individual ability and falls over time.*

Finally, it is interesting to consider the effect of the discount rate. When $\delta = 0$, the agent is not concerned about the future, and thus the career concern effect is zero. Now consider the effect when the agent is more patient and $\delta \to 1$. In that case we have:

$$\lim_{\delta \to 1} CC \left(\rho_\eta / \rho_\varepsilon + t, \delta \right) = \sum_{\tau=1}^{\infty} \frac{1}{(\rho_\eta / \rho_\varepsilon + \tau)} = \infty. \tag{7.47}$$

For a patient agent, the career effect provides high-powered incentives to perform.

Depending on the discount rate, career concerns can lead to effort that is lower or higher than the first best. This result implies that, in this employment model, parties cannot rely on a person's concern for her reputation to provide efficient effort incentives. A solution to this problem is to provide additional incentives (or disincentives) via performance pay.

7.4.2 Incentive Contracts with Career Concerns

Given that reputation effects cannot be relied on to ensure efficient effort, the principal may wish to combine career concerns with performance pay. Given that the agent has CARA preferences, without loss of generality, performance pay may be assumed to take a linear form:

$$w_t (y_t) = c_t + b_t y_t.$$

It is assumed that all participants can observe this contract (or correctly anticipate its use), and therefore the market correctly anticipates the effort chosen by the agent each period. This, combined with the hypothesis of perfect competition among firms, implies that expected income each period satisfies:

$$E \{w_t\} = m_t + \hat{a}_t = c_t + b_t \left(m_t + \hat{a}_t \right), \tag{7.48}$$

where m_t is the expected ability in period t, given observed performance in the previous period. This in turn implies:

$$c_t = (1 - b_t) \left(m_t + \hat{a}_t \right).$$

The next step is the determination of b_t and $\hat{a}_t$. Effort now affects both current income (through the incentive contract) and future income (via career concerns). In this additive model, ability affects only income level, not the marginal cost of providing effort, and therefore the slope parameter b_t will not depend upon m_t. This implies that the introduction of performance pay does not affect career concern incentives, nor does individual effort affect future income risk. Consequently, an individual's choice of effort in period t solves:

$$g' (a_t (b_t)) = b_t + CC \left(\rho_\eta / \rho_\varepsilon + t \right). \tag{7.49}$$

The contract is negotiated at the beginning of period t, at which point b_t affects only the risk and the level of effort; hence it is chosen to maximize the payoff of the agent in period t:

$$\max_{b_t} \left\{ m_t + a_t (b_t) - g (a_t (b_t)) - \frac{\rho_A}{2} b_t^2 (\sigma_t + \sigma_\varepsilon) \right\},$$

where $\sigma_t = \frac{1}{\rho_\eta + t\rho_\varepsilon}$ is the variance of the agent's ability at date t. Taking the first-order conditions and then using (7.49) to determine $\partial a_t / \partial b_t$ one has:

$$\left(1 - g'\left(a_t\left(b_t\right)\right)\right) \frac{da_t\left(b_t\right)}{db_t} - \rho_A \left(\sigma_t + \sigma_\varepsilon\right) b_t = 0. \tag{7.50}$$

Taking the derivative of (7.49) with respect to b_t, and using the facts regarding g, including $g''' > 0$, we have $\frac{da_t(b_t)}{db_t} > 0$. Taking the derivative of (7.49) and substituting into (7.50), combined with (7.49) we get:

$$\left(1 - b_t - CC\left(\rho_\eta / \rho_\varepsilon + t\right)\right) \left(\frac{1}{g''\left(a_t\left(b_t\right)\right)}\right) = \rho_A \left(\sigma_t + \sigma_\varepsilon\right) b_t, \tag{7.51}$$

which in turn implies:

Proposition 7.7 *Suppose that $g(a)$ is twice continuously differentiable, with $g(0) = g'(0) = 0$ and $g'(a), g''(a), g'''(a) > 0,$ for $a > 0$. There is a unique b_t^* and corresponding action $\hat{a}_t\left(b_t^*\right) \geq 0$ that solves:*

$$b_t = \frac{1 - CC\left(\rho_\eta / \rho_\varepsilon + t\right)}{1 + \rho_A \left(\sigma_t + \sigma_\varepsilon\right) g''\left(a_t\left(b_t\right)\right)}.$$

Proof. Let $f\left(b_t\right) = b_t(1 + \rho_A \left(\sigma_t + \sigma_\varepsilon\right) g''\left(a_t\left(b_t\right)\right))$ and notice that the assumptions on g ensure that f is increasing with b_t, $|f| \geq |b_t|$, and $f(0) = 0$. Hence, there is a unique $f\left(b_t\right) = 1 - CC\left(\rho_\eta / \rho_\varepsilon + t\right)$. □

When the agent is risk neutral, $\rho_A = 0$, then $b_t = 1 - CC\left(\rho_\eta / \rho_\varepsilon + t\right)$. Then from (7.50) effort is set at the first-best level with $g'(a_t) = 1$ for all $t \geq 0$.

We already know that career concerns can take on any positive value, and therefore it is possible that the optimal reward is negative. We do not normally envisage employers paying workers to work slowly, though it is not uncommon for employers to ask employees to reduce hours so they do not get "burned out."

With experience, the career concerns effect and the amount of risk individuals face become smaller, which together imply that b_t is *increasing* with time. Gibbons and Murphy (1992) find this implication is consistent with the observed performance pay slope as a function of time for their sample of CEOs.

7.5   Discussion

Formal agency theory in economics begins with the observation that parties have an incentive to take less care when fully insured against risks. From this observation has developed an enormously rich and important field of study. In a nutshell, the principal's problem is to design a contract that the agent will accept and that aligns the agent's interests with those of the principal. The agency contract has the feature that the agent voluntarily makes decisions that are valued and rewarded by the principal.

The theory shows that, as the quality of information increases, one can design contracts with better risk sharing while ensuring the agent acts as she has promised. The basic model predicts that there is a trade-off between risk and incentives. The multitasking model illustrates the point that when the agent has several dimensions of effort, providing incentives for one dimension can divert effort from other dimensions.

The subsequent literature builds on this idea to derive the optimal contract for a number of cases. It is not possible to do justice to the many contributions in this area, so instead we will focus on several papers that illustrate the direction of the recent literature. The interested reader is invited to explore the many other contributions that are cited in these works.

An important early paper by Baker (1992) illustrates the problems of incentive design when the principal and agent have different goals. In his model the agent is able to choose effort after observing some information. Increasing performance pay increases the agent's effort, but in the wrong direction, due to the divergence in goals. Hence, the trade-off is between total effort and effort in a direction that furthers the goals of the agent rather than the principal.

For this problem, Lazear and Rosen (1981) and Mookherjee (1984) suggest using relative performance pay. Murphy (2000) shows that firms can partially solve the problems raised by Baker through the use of external performance standards.

Holmström and Milgrom (1987) made the important observation that when there is performance over time, but measured performance is an imperfect summary statistic, then the agent may respond to rewards with intertemporal substitution of effort. Holmström and Milgrom assume that agents have constant absolute risk aversion. Building on this work, Sannikov (2008) provides a characterization of the optimal contract for more general agent preferences. The result is a rich set of predictions regarding compensation over time that are consistent with some of the observed features of employment contracts, including pay that is deferred to the future, training combined with promotion, and an optimal retirement date.

In those models, agents choose the *intensity* of their effort per period of time. Another important class of problems is innovation and project choice, where the only way a person can learn is by experimenting with different options. However, experimentation is risky, and thus risk-averse agents may engage in too little exploration of possible projects. Manso (2011) introduces an elegant model of contract design for this case. Rather than assuming the agent is risk averse, it assumes that she faces a limited liability constraint, and therefore all payments are bounded from below.

Manso's paper illustrates that limited liability can be used as another way to capture risk aversion, which may lead to more tractable models. In this case, when the outside option is low enough to make the minimum liability constraint binding, then to induce high effort, the principal must offer expected compensation that is higher than the outside option. In the case of experimentation, Manso (2011) shows that to encourage productive exploration, the principal may have to reward early failure, particularly when followed by success.

Halac and Prat (2016) study an important, and underexplored question, namely the effect of endogenous monitoring of performance by the principal. They find that recognition of good performance may lead to declining performance by the agent because she comes to believe that she is not being watched. This effect does not occur when monitoring is independent of effort or in response to bad performance. Georgiadis and Szentes (2020) study how much information to collect before rewarding the agent. They show that the optimal contract takes the form of a simple two-point distribution, namely a fixed wage with a bonus.

This literature illustrates that there are a wide variety of environments that lead to contracts that have features, such as simple bonus pay, that are consistent with observed contracts. A challenge is not only to explain observed contracts but also to understand the consequences of counterfactual contract choices.

These papers do not address how to explicitly test the predictions. The reviews by Gibbons (1997) and Prendergast (1999) show that there is overwhelming evidence that individuals respond to incentives and that information plays a key role. The economics literature for the most part has avoided considering the nitty-gritty details of how this information is collected and used. Bushman and Smith (2001) review the accounting and corporate governance literatures from the perspective of agency theory and outline an agenda for research that is still relevant today. Edmans, Gabaix, and Jenter (2017) provide a more recent review of CEO compensation. They highlight that one of the open issues is how to best model the goals of firms and CEOs.

For the most part, agency theory assumes that parties are motivated mainly by pecuniary rewards. Yet, as we know from our daily experiences, individuals are often motivated to act based on intrinsic preferences (see Deci [1972] for some seminal experimental work). Benabou and Tirole (2003) show that these preferences can be integrated into agency theory, while Koszegi (2014) provides a comprehensive review of the literature that applies insights from behavioral economics to contract theory.

The behavioral economics work does not change the approach outlined in this chapter, which is concerned with the optimal design of rewards to align the goals of the principal and the agent. We learn from behavioral economics that given a particular context, the optimal contract is likely to vary not only with the information regarding performance, but also with how the agent values monetary rewards relative to other potential rewards, such as status and intrinsic preferences toward one's work. For example, Ash and MacLeod (2015) find that when the workload of US judges is decreased, they write longer, better-cited opinions, suggesting that they get satisfaction from doing a better job.

The challenge is that, in practice, it is difficult to observe the details of the environment that lead to a particular contract form. One way to deal with this issue is to use laboratory experiments that allow one to fix the environment and then to see how changes to the environment affect observed behavior (see Charness and Kuhn [2011] for a review of laboratory methods in labor economics).

Finally, a common feature of all the models we have discussed is the assumption that principals understand their environment and, moreover, correctly anticipate how agents will respond to the contracts that are chosen by the principal. In a classic management paper, Kerr (1975) discusses a number of examples where management implemented rewards mechanisms that were intended to improve performance, but where agents did not act as expected. Despite the vast amount of work since then, it is not difficult to find such examples today. In other words, principals have imperfect information regarding the preferences of their agents. This naturally leads to the question of contract design with asymmetric information.

7.6   Exercises

1. Suppose that parties have Von Neumann–Morgenstern preferences over positive income given by:
$$U^i(x_i) = \rho_i \ln(x_i + 1),$$
and total income is given by $x \sim f(x)$ with support $\Re_+ = \{x \in \Re | x \geq 0\}$. What is the optimal risk sharing formula when parties have bargaining power $\pi_1 = \pi$ and $\pi_2 = 1 - \pi$? Assume the default payoff in the absence of an agreement is zero.

2. Suppose now that parties have CARA preferences with risk-aversion parameters ρ_1 and ρ_2. Again, suppose that, in the absence of an agreement, each gets zero. However, suppose that *after* an agreement, party 2 has limited liability—she cannot pay more than $L \geq 0$—while party 1 has unlimited liability. How does this affect the agreement? Does limited liability make person 2 more or less risk averse?

3. Verify the expressions in proposition 7.4.

4. Provide an example for which the optimal contract for a principal-agent problem has compensation depend on a signal that is unrelated to performance.

5. Consider the principal-agent problem with a risk-neutral principal and CARA preferences for the agent, $-\exp(-\rho(w - c(e)))$, $c(0) = c'(0) = 0, c'' > 0$, with an outside option of U^0. Suppose that the signal is:
$$x = e + \epsilon,$$
where $\epsilon \sim f(\epsilon)$, and $f(\epsilon)$ has support $[e, e + \gamma]$, where $\gamma > 0$ is a fixed parameter and $f(\epsilon) \geq M > 0$ on its support. Does an optimal contract exist? If not, does one close to the optimum exist? Answer the question when the support is $[-e, e]$. Discuss the differences in your solutions.

6. Consider two parties, A and B, with CARA preferences, with risk parameters r_A and r_B, respectively. Suppose that they wish to share the returns x from a project, with a continuous probability distribution function $f(x)$ with support $\Re$ and $E\{x\} = m > 0$ and var$\{x\} = \sigma^2 > 0$.

   (a) Suppose that parties bargain over the risk sharing contract—they have equal bargaining power and earn an income of zero if there is no agreement. What is the optimal risk sharing formula on which they would agree?

   (b) Now suppose $x \sim N(m, \sigma^2)$ for the rest of the question. Express your answer in certainty equivalent terms.

   (c) Is there is a level of risk, holding m constant, at which there will be no agreement?

7. Consider the following multitasking problem, as in section 7.3.1. The principal hires two agents and has payoff given by:
$$U^P = E\{y - w\},$$
where y is the total output given by:
$$y = e_1 + e_2 + \epsilon_y,$$

where $\epsilon \sim N\left(0, \sigma^2\right)$, and $w = w_1 + w_2$ is the total payments to agents $i \in \{1, 2\}$. The agents have CARA preferences with certainty equivalent payoffs:

$$u_i = E\{w_i\} - \frac{e_i^2}{2\theta_i} - \frac{\rho_i}{2} \text{var}\left(w_i\right).$$

The agents have outside options fixed at $u_i^0, i \in \{1, 2\}$, while the principal's outside option is 0. Answer the following:

(a) Suppose effort is observable. What is the optimal contract? Here, make sure to explore how the outside option affects the optimal contract and provide conditions under which the principal hires two, one, or zero agents.

(b) Now work out the optimal contract under the hypothesis that agent effort is known only to the agent choosing the effort.

(c) Now suppose that the principal observes signals:

$$x_i = e_i + \epsilon_i,$$

where $\Sigma = \text{cov}\left(\{\epsilon_y, \epsilon_1, \epsilon_2\}\right)$. Work out the formula for the optimal contract.

(d) Explore the optimal contract for special cases of Σ. For example, what happens in the i.i.d. case when $\Sigma_{22} \to \infty$? How about when $\Sigma_{yy} \to 0$?

(e) What happens when $\epsilon_i = \epsilon_y + \epsilon$, where $\epsilon \sim N(0, 1)$?

(f) Suppose that agent 1 gets to observe agent 2's action before choosing her action. How would this affect the analysis?

8. Consider the principal and two-agent problem. Suppose that the agents are risk neutral, and their performance measures are independent of each other. Derive the optimal compensation contract with the feature that the principal's performance evaluation for each agent is private information, yet the principal is truthful in equilibrium. (See Carmichael [1983] and Malcomson [1984] on this point.)

9. Now consider a problem with a single principal and $N \geq 2$ agents. The N agents work in a team and produce $y(e_1, e_2, \ldots, e_N) \in \Re^1$, where e_i is the effort of member i. The production function, $y(\cdot)$, is deterministic and concave in e_i. To produce this output, each agent has an increasing and convex cost of effort given by $c_i(e_i)$. Every agent observes her own effort and total output. The wage schedule of the team members is given by $w_i(y)$, $i \in \{1, 2, \cdots, N\}$. For the first two parts, assume away the principal, that is, the agents form a team and divide the output among themselves.

(a) Write the budget balancing condition for this problem. Find the first-best solution.

(b) Can the team achieve the first-best solution?

(c) Can a principal who does not add to the effort of the team, but is entitled to transfers help achieve the first best? (See Holmström 1982.)

10. Consider the following principal-agent problem. Suppose a principal who is risk neutral is hiring a risk-averse agent. Suppose that output is given by:

$$x = e \times \epsilon,$$

where $e \geq 0$ is effort, and $\log(\epsilon) \sim N(0,1)$. For this problem, the goal is to find the lowest-cost contract that implements effort e. It is also assumed that the minimum payment is given by w^0. Suppose that the contract offered is given by:

$$w(x|k) = \begin{cases} \bar{w}, & x \geq \bar{x} \\ \underline{w}, & x < \bar{x} \end{cases},$$

where $k = \{\bar{w}, \underline{w}, \bar{x}\}$. The problem that the principal solves is the following:

$$C^*(e) = \min_k E\{w(x|k)\},$$

$$U^A(w(x|k), e) = E\{\log(w(x|k)) \,|e\} - g(e) \geq U^{0A}, \tag{7.52}$$

$$U^A(w(x|k), e) \geq U^A(w(x|k), e'), \forall e' \geq 0, \tag{7.53}$$

$$\bar{w}, \underline{w} \geq w^0.$$

It is assumed that the cost of effort is $g(e) = e^2/2$ and that the outside option, U^{0A}, is sufficiently low (less than zero) to ensure that employment is always optimal.

(a) Show that a solution exists, and use proposition 7.2 to show that the lower bound w^0 is always binding. Characterize $\bar{w}$ as a function of e.

(b) What is the effect of increasing w^0? In particular, show that for w^0 sufficiently high, the individual rationality constraint, (7.52), is not binding. Notice that this can be interpreted as an *efficiency wage*.

(c) Suppose that the principal's payoff is:

$$u^P = p \times x - E\{w(x|k)\,|e\}.$$

Characterize the optimal principal-agent contract and work out how changes in the minimum wage, w^0, affect contracted effort.

11. Let us continue with the same structure as in the previous question, except now production is over two periods, $t \in \{1, 2\}$. Here we have in mind that the output is the return on investment. Suppose that end-of-the-period output is:

$$x = e_1 \times \epsilon_1 \times e_2 \times \epsilon_2,$$

and the principal can only use contract $w(x|k)$. The agent can observe ϵ_1 when choosing effort e_2, and hence her period 2 effort choice is a function, $e_2(\epsilon_1)$, with payoff:

$$U_2^A(e_1, e_2, \epsilon_1) = E\{E\{\log(w(x|k)) \,|e_1, e_2, \epsilon_1\} - g(e_2)\} - g(e_1).$$

(a) Suppose the principal can observe effort and end-of-the-period output; how will it set effort and compensation?

(b) What is the optimal decision rule for the agent given contract $w(x|k)$? Can the principal implement effort given in (a)?

(c) Suppose that the principal uses a sharing contract, $w(x) = \alpha x$. What are the agents' efforts in this case, and what is the optimal sharing rule?

(d) Discuss the costs and benefits of each contract form.

12. Suppose that a worker's log output in period t is:

$$y_t = \alpha + e_t + \epsilon_t,$$

where the prior belief on work ability is given by $\alpha \sim N\left(m^0, 1/\tau^0\right)$, $\epsilon_t \sim N\left(0, 1/\tau\right)$ is an i.i.d. noise process, and e_t is effort. Suppose that the utility function of the worker is given by:

$$U\left(I\right) = \sum_{t=1}^{\infty} \left\{ E\left\{w_t | I\right\} - \frac{e_t^2}{2} - \frac{r}{2} \text{var}\left(w_t | I\right) \right\} \delta^{t-1}.$$

Further suppose that $w_t = E\left\{y_t | y_1, y_2, \ldots, y_{t-1}\right\}$.

(a) What is the efficient effort level?

(b) The worker is assumed to choose effort to maximize utility, and the market is assumed to have correct expectations regarding worker effort. Show, depending on the parameter values, that the worker may choose e_1 larger or smaller than the efficient effort level.

(c) What is $\lim_{t \to \infty} e_t$?

8 Trade with Asymmetric Information

When you run up against someone else's shamelessness, ask yourself this: Is a world without shame-lessness possible?
No.
—Marcus Aurelius (2002, 127), ca. 170 CE

8.1 Introduction

The Coen Brothers' film *Fargo* has a scene in which the main character, a car salesman named Jerry Lundegaard, deals with an irate customer whom he has charged $500 for rust proofing that he did not want on a car the customer intended to buy. Jerry promises to discuss the issue with his boss and walks to another office. There, rather than discuss the rust proofing issue, he talks with his boss about hockey. He comes back and tells the irate customer the boss has approved a $100 reduction, but no more. The customer is upset and calls him a liar, but in the face of all this Jerry is calm. Eventually the customer relents and buys the car rather than go to a different dealer.

The scene encapsulates many features of contract and trade with asymmetric information. The parties had a deal, which Jerry violated, but the cost of proving that to a court is not worth the trouble. However, the customer knows that he is being heldup and reacted by losing his temper, which in turn secured a $100 reduction in price. The dialogue makes clear that the customer anticipated that auto salespersons cannot be trusted, but still could not design a contract to achieve the desired outcome.

The movie dramatizes the frustration individuals feel when they believe they are treated unfairly. One view of such behavior is that it is *irrational*. Losing one's temper simply makes things worse for all parties. The field of behavioral economics begins with the fact that observed behaviors are not consistent with the hypothesis that individuals have stable preferences over goods and services. Rather, individuals often make decisions based upon the gains of others (Fehr and Schmidt 2006). Conditional upon these preferences, this implies that observed outcomes may be different from the predictions of price theory.

This chapter reviews the theory of trade with asymmetric information and shows that in some cases losing one's temper is a *rational* response. The result is important because it implies that violence is not simply a feature of human behavior that can be easily modified.

As long as parties care about the allocation of resources and there is uncertainty regarding the value of these resources, then conflict may be part of an optimal mechanism.

Although the theory predicts that conflict may be part of an optimal mechanism, this conflict does not necessarily have to occur via violence. One can view disputes that arrive in courts of law as a nonviolent form of rent dissipation. Hence, costly court proceedings may be part of an optimal mechanism to allocate resources when there is asymmetric information.

This chapter consists of six sections. The first section introduces the mechanism design approach to the trade of goods with asymmetric information, based upon D'Aspremont and Gerard-Varet (1979) and Myerson and Satterthwaite (1983). As shown in chapter 4, the timing of information revelation can have a profound effect upon the observed outcomes. The goal of the mechanism design approach is to find the set of possible allocations that are determined by fundamental information and resource constraints. Using the revelation principle, one can transform the exchange problem into one in which the price and quantity traded are functions of the private information, subject to the constraint that each party truthfully reveals their information. The basic model and the revelation principle are outlined in section 8.2.

How should one evaluate allocations in the face of asymmetric information? When parties are asymmetrically informed, there may not be common knowledge regarding the set of efficient allocations. Section 8.3 outlines the approach based on Holmström and Myerson (1983). They use the revelation principle to define an efficient allocation under asymmetric information at three stages: the *ex ante stage* before parties acquire information, the *interim* stage after parties receive their private signals, and the *ex post stage* when all information is revealed. The main insight is that, at the interim *stage*, parties cannot necessarily agree upon an efficient allocation, which in turn illustrates the main theme of this chapter—private information can lead to trading failures.

Section 8.4 characterizes the set of implementable allocations for these three cases. D'Aspremont and Gerard-Varet (1979) show that when parties know ex ante that it is efficient to trade (though maybe not the level of trade), and they have available to them specific performance contracts, then there are many implementable allocations, including the efficient allocation.[1] Specific performance may be needed to increase the rents in the relationship that are used to ensure truth-telling by parties. This implies that even though ex ante parties to the trade may get payoffs greater than their outside options, in some cases their ex post payoff, after learning their type, may be less than their outside option.

The second part of this section considers the case of voluntary trade, in which parties are free to leave the relationship after they have observed their private information and before they have committed themselves to trade. We begin by proving Lazear's (1990) observation that severance pay does not affect the efficiency of the job match. This implies that employment at will and employment with severance pay result in the same level of employment. Next, the Myerson-Satterthwaite theorem is introduced. It provides necessary conditions for the implementation of allocations when parties are free to leave a relationship after they have observed their private information. This theorem implies that there may be bargaining breakdowns. Even though trade at the realized payoffs is efficient, the agreement may require separation.

The last case considers the problem of implementing trade that is ex post efficient. Williams (1999) shows that any efficient and incentive-compatible mechanism is payoff equivalent to a *Groves mechanism*. Williams uses this result to extend the Myerson-Satterthwaite theorem to the case of many parties. In addition, Williams's work shows that subsidies to trading parties may increase the efficiency of trade and may explain why governments use subsidies to encourage private projects to locate in their jurisdiction.

Finally, section 8.5 discusses the relationship between power and asymmetric information. When there is one-sided asymmetric information (one party is informed, but the other party is not), if decision rights can be allocated to the informed party, efficient exchange is possible. However, a classic buyer-seller exchange, in which the buyer has private information and the seller has all the power, is a typical monopoly situation that leads to output that is less than efficient. The optimal nonlinear price for the monopolist is derived. In addition, this section has a result showing that the optimal mechanism can be approximated by a finite number of bundled quantity-price combinations.

Similarly, where the seller has the private information while the buyer has all the bargaining power, it is a classic monopsony. The buyer corresponds to a firm that has market power over privately informed sellers/workers. As in the monopoly case, this leads to employment that is lower than the efficient level. This point is illustrated using the example of ride-hailing services such as Uber and Lyft. We consider why these services have been successful and the implications of these services for the welfare of taxi drivers. The chapter concludes with a brief summary and discussion of relevant literature.

8.1.1   Trade with Asymmetric Information

One goal of a noncooperative foundation for the Nash bargaining solution is to help us better understand the conditions under which parties reach an efficient agreement. One only has to glance at the front pages of the morning papers (or your phone) to see many examples of bargaining breakdowns. The next two sections discuss some reasons that rational, self-interested individuals may not reach an efficient agreement.

The challenge is to find some generic reasons for bargaining breakdowns. The use of a formal, strategic model faces the problem that each bargaining game is in a sense unique. Consider the following example from my personal experience. While living in Boston many years ago, I needed to purchase a new car. I had already decided to buy a bottom-of-the-line Honda Accord. At the time, Internet sales did not exist, and car dealers were unwilling to provide prices over the phone.

To solve this problem, I decided to buy the car on a Wednesday and I went to a number of dealers. I informed each one that I intended to buy a car today, so they had the chance to make an immediate sale. However, I also asked them to give me a quote and told them if they were the best deal, I would buy the car from them at the end of the day.

The first dealer was nice and happy to sell me a car. The salesman explained all the features of the car and why I should buy it then gave me a quote. When I got up to leave, he seemed upset that I was not buying the car immediately. He reiterated he was giving me a good deal. I thanked him for his time and said that if the price was indeed good, then I would be back. As I left the dealership, a manager chased after me and asked what happened. I explained my strategy, and he immediately provided a new quote that was $1500 less than the previous quote. I was stunned, but went to the next dealer. In the end, this dealership's price was not the lowest, but I did end the day with a car.

This tale has several interesting features. At the beginning of the search, I was not sure what a good price would be, so I was operating under asymmetric information. However, notice that the relationship with the salesperson can be complex. My strategy likely puzzled the first salesman, so he was not sure how to react. This example illustrates why it is difficult for one to specify in advance exactly the game that will be played. Neither the buyer nor the seller can be expected to know all the possible strategies. This implies that we have a game of *incomplete* information, which does not neatly fall into the framework described in chapter 4.

A second, more subtle point is the extent to which I could rely upon a dealer honoring its quote. If I did return to a dealer, then it would know that they must have the lowest price, and they might try to renegotiate the price upward or invent add-ons to increase the price. As a matter of practice, many, if not most, firms honor such agreements. If the offer is written, then under the US Uniform Commercial Code, the terms are binding for up to three months.

Finally, the story highlights the extent of asymmetric information between the parties. In my example, the salesperson might have concluded that I was eager to buy a car and would be happy to reach an agreement immediately rather than continuing my search. In effect, he made a bet on my unobserved characteristics. Once I started to leave, he had to revise his beliefs. In countries where parties traditionally always negotiate prices, the threat of leaving is often used. If the seller thinks I am bluffing, then his optimal strategy is to wait for me to return.

Rather than attempting to formally model this complex strategic interaction (for which there is no known solution at the moment), this section answers a different question. Suppose that we can design any game we wish; does asymmetric information preclude efficient transactions? The answer to this question would seem to be a more formidable task than solving a particular game, but it turns out to be analytically much more tractable.

8.2   The Base Model

Consider the buyer-seller model of section 5.2, where payoffs satisfy the standard conditions that ensure they are well defined, continuous functions of the parameters of the model, and the optimal level of trade is unique. Suppose that each agent can observe only their own type, but not the type of the other agent. The probability distributions are common knowledge and agree with the ex ante probability distributions chosen by Nature. Hence, $b \sim f()$ with support $[b_L, b_H]$, and $c \sim g()$ with support $[c_L, c_H]$, with the states given by $\omega = \{b, c\} \in \Omega = [b_L, b_H] \times [c_L, c_H]$. Let F and G be the corresponding cumulative distribution functions.

Regardless of how parties negotiate, suppose that the process must end at some date with an allocation denoted by $\vec{x}(\omega) = \{q(\omega), p(\omega)\}$, similar to equation 5.3. For the moment, it is assumed that $p(\omega)$ is a transfer as a function of types from the buyer to the seller. Below we allow the buyer and seller to have personalized transfers. As a matter of convention, $q(\omega) = \emptyset$ means that parties have taken their outside options. With this convention we can define the events with trade and no trade:

$$\Omega^T(\vec{x}) = \{\omega \in \Omega | q(\omega) \neq \emptyset\},$$

$$\Omega^{NT}(\vec{x}) = \{\omega \in \Omega | q(\omega) = \emptyset\}.$$

Given the allocation $\vec{x} \in \Xi$, the payoffs for the buyer and the seller conditional upon their types are:

$$u^B(\vec{x}(\omega), b) = \begin{cases} B(q(\omega), b) - p(\omega), & q(\omega) \neq \emptyset, \\ u^{0B} - p(\omega), & q(\omega) = \emptyset. \end{cases} \tag{8.1}$$

$$u^S(\vec{x}(\omega), c) = \begin{cases} p(\omega) - C(q(\omega), c), & q(\omega) \neq \emptyset, \\ u^{0S} + p(\omega), & q(\omega) = \emptyset. \end{cases} \tag{8.2}$$

In these expressions the parties receive their *outside options* $\vec{u}^0 = \{u^{0B}, u^{0S}\}$ when there is no trade ($q(\omega) = \emptyset$). Notice that the types b and c are differentiated from the state ω. This difference is used when we come to the revelation principle, where $\omega = \{\hat{b}, \hat{c}\}$ represents the reports of the buyer and the seller, which can be different from the realized values of b and c that fix the benefit and cost functions. Let $q^*(b, c)$ denote the optimal level of trade given types:

$$q^*(b, c) = \arg\max_q (B(q, b) - C(q, c)) I_{q \neq \emptyset} + \left(u^{0B} + u^{0S}\right) I_{q = \emptyset},$$

where $I_{q \neq \emptyset}$ is 1 if $q \neq \emptyset$ and 0 otherwise, and $I_{q = \emptyset} = 1 - I_{q \neq \emptyset}$ is 1 when $q = \emptyset$. Recall that Ξ^* denotes the set of efficient allocations when agents' types are known.

The bargaining process can either be an agreed upon protocol or it may be defined by the environment under which the parties negotiate terms at the beginning of the relationship. Given that payoffs are continuous, and the type space is bounded, then one may suppose that the quantity traded is bounded, and therefore the parties follow strategies that, at the end of the period, result in an outcome in the set of possible outcomes: $A = \{[0, \bar{q}] \times \Re, \vec{u}^0\}$, where $\bar{q} > 0$ is some upper bound on the quantity to be traded.

This formulation is quite general and can be used to think about any economic institution that determines quantity and price. As an example, consider a standard price-setting monopolist who sets the price of a good after observing her costs but before she knows the buyer's valuation. This problem can be set up as a principal-agent problem as follows. For each seller/monopoly type $c \in [c_L, c_H]$, the monopolist chooses a price per unit, P. Given the unit price, P, the buyer chooses demand $Q(P, b)$ to maximize her payoff:

$$Q(P, b) = \arg\max_{q \geq 0} B(q, b) - P \times q.$$

Optimal demand is $Q^*(P, b) = Q(P, b)$ if $B(Q(P, b), b) - P \times Q(p, b) \geq u^{0B}$, otherwise $Q^*(P, b) = 0$. The seller/monopolist does not observe the buyer's type and sets her price policy, $P^*(c)$, based upon the expected payoff:

$$P^*(c) = \arg\max_{P \in \Re} \left(\begin{array}{c} \int_{b_L}^{b_H} (P \times Q^*(P, b) - C(Q^*(P, b), c)) I_{Q^* > 0} f(b) \, db \\ + \int_{b_L}^{b_H} u^{0S} I_{Q^* = 0} f(b) \, db \end{array} \right). \tag{8.3}$$

The outcome of this relationship can be written as an allocation that is a function of types:

$$\vec{x}^{monopoly}(b,c) = \left\{ q^*(b,c), p^*(b,c) \right\}, \tag{8.4}$$

where $q^*(b,c) = Q^*(P^*(c),b)$ and $p^*(b,c) = P^*(c) \times Q^*(P^*(c),b)$, given types $\{b,c\} \in \Omega$. The monopoly problem is an example of a *mechanism*—a method by which parties provide information to an impartial third party that translates the data on types, $\{b,c\}$, into an allocation, $\vec{x}(b,c)$.

8.2.1   Revelation Principle

The monopoly problem is an example of a two-stage contract with messaging. In the first stage, the seller observes her private information, c, and then sends a message to the buyer containing the price. Given the price, $P^*(c)$, the buyer sends a message with his demand $Q^*(P^*(c),b)$. In the second stage, the exchange is executed—the seller delivers the quantity desired and the buyer pays the agreed price.

Now consider the following thought experiment. Rather than choosing price and quantity, suppose that parties hire an escrow firm whose job is to implement the contract terms. Next, suppose that the contract, rather than being written in terms of a fixed price, asks the parties to report their private valuations to the escrow firm. Because their valuations are private, there is no way to verify the truth of their report. Let the seller's reported type be $\hat{c} \in [c_L, c_H]$, and let the buyer's report be $\hat{b} \in [b_L, b_H]$. After the reports are made, the contract is enforced with terms given by $x^{monopoly}\left(\hat{b},\hat{c}\right)$, as defined in (8.4). In other words, the escrow firm implements the monopoly solution given their *reported* types and not their actual types. The question then is whether parties will be truthful.

Consider first the case in which the parties agree to trade in all states. When they do not agree to trade in all states, the argument is similar. Suppose that the buyer expects the seller to be truthful, then, since $Q^*(P^*(c),b)$ is the optimal quantity given types, we have:

$$u^B\left(x^*(b,c)|b\right) = B\left(Q^*\left(P^*(c),b\right),b\right) - P^*(c) \times Q^*\left(P^*(c),b\right),$$

$$\geq B(q,b) - P^*(c) \times q, \forall q \geq 0.$$

The second line follows from the fact that the quantity under the contract is the one that maximizes the buyer's payoff given his type b. In particular, reporting a different type, $\hat{b} \neq b$, simply results in a quantity that may be different from $Q^*(P^*(c),b)$ and that leads to lower profits. Thus, the buyer's payoff as a function of his report $\hat{b}$ satisfies:

$$u^B\left(x^*(b,c)|b\right) \geq u^B\left(x^*(\hat{b},c)|b\right), \forall \hat{b} \in [b_L, b_H]. \tag{8.5}$$

In other words, under this contract it is optimal for the buyer to truthfully report his type to the escrow company.

Next, consider the problem from the seller's perspective. Let us suppose that the seller expects the buyer to be truthful. In that case, for every price p, a buyer of type b chooses her optimal quantity $Q^*(p,b)$. Suppose the seller now considers reporting a type $\hat{c}$ that is different from her true type. As in the case of the buyer, this simply means that she is setting a price $P(\hat{c})$ that may be different from her optimal price $P^*(c)$. Thus, from (8.3):

$$E\left\{u^{S}\left(\vec{x}\left(b,c\right),c\right)|c\right\}\geq E\left\{u^{S}\left(\vec{x}\left(b,\hat{c}\right),c\right)|c\right\}, \forall\hat{c},c\in[c_{L},c_{H}], \tag{8.6}$$

and it follows that the optimal strategy for the seller is to be truthful regarding her type c. Notice that the escrow firm does not need to know anything about either party. It simply sets price and quantity according to the contract specified by $x^{*}\left(\omega\right)$. Thus, it is possible to implement the monopoly solution using a contract in which parties reveal their private information to an independent escrow firm, which in turn determines the price and quantity to be traded.

In the monopoly example, it is assumed that the seller fixes the price and the buyer chooses quantity. A natural question is whether the seller could find some other mechanism that results in higher profits. The revelation principle provides an answer to this question. It states that for any mechanism or game that implements an allocation, there exists a direct mechanism, such as the one we derived for the monopoly problem. Under the mechanism, the final allocation is expressed in terms of the private information alone, with the feature that it is in each party's interest to be truthful. This turns a potentially intractable problem into a tractable optimization problem.

More precisely, a mechanism is a nonstrategic mediator that translates messages from parties to allocations. When the buyer observes his type $b\in[b_{L},b_{H}]$, he sends a message $m_{B}\left(b\right)\in M_{B}$ to the mediator. Similarly, when the seller observes her type $c\in[c_{L},c_{H}]$, she sends a message $m_{S}\left(c\right)\in M_{S}$ to the mediator. The mediator represents a function $\mathcal{M}$ that maps messages to an allocation:

$$\mathcal{M}:M_{B}\times M_{S}\to A. \tag{8.7}$$

A *mechanism* is denoted by the triple $\Gamma=\{M_{B},M_{S},\mathcal{M}\}$ that specifies both the set of messages and the mapping between messages and outcomes. This induces a game between the buyer and the seller, with payoffs defined as follows:

$$u^{B}\left(m_{B},m_{S}\left(\cdot\right)|b,\Gamma\right)=\int_{c_{L}}^{c_{H}}u^{B}\left(\mathcal{M}\left(m_{B},m_{S}\left(c\right)\right)|b\right)dG\left(c\right),$$

$$u^{S}\left(m_{B}\left(\cdot\right),m_{S}|c,\Gamma\right)=\int_{b_{L}}^{b_{H}}u^{S}\left(\mathcal{M}\left(m_{B}\left(b\right),m_{S}\right)|c\right)dF\left(b\right).$$

Behavior is assumed to be determined by a Bayesian Nash equilibrium, at which each party correctly anticipates the strategies of the other individual. If an allocation $\vec{x}\left(b,c\right)$ can be achieved as the equilibrium outcome of some mechanism, then this allocation can be *implemented*. More precisely:

Definition 8.1 *An allocation $\vec{x}\left(b,c\right)$ is* implemented *(with a Bayesian Nash equilibrium) by a mechanism $\{M_{B},M_{S},\mathcal{M}\}$ if $\vec{x}\left(b,c\right)=\mathcal{M}\left(m_{B}^{*}\left(b\right),m_{S}^{*}\left(c\right)\right)$, where $\{m_{B}^{*}\left(\right),m_{S}^{*}\left(\right)\}$ satisfy*

$$m_{B}^{*}\left(b\right)\in\arg\max_{m_{B}\in M_{B}}u^{B}\left(m_{B},m_{S}^{*}\left(\cdot\right)|b\right),$$

$$m_{S}^{*}\left(c\right)\in\arg\max_{m_{S}\in M_{S}}u^{S}\left(m_{B}^{*}\left(\cdot\right),m_{S}|c\right),$$

for every $\{b,c\}\in[b_{L},b_{H}]\times[c_{L},c_{H}].$[2]

This definition corresponds to what is sometimes called *weak implementation* because it requires the allocation to correspond to some equilibrium of the mechanism. Strong implementation denotes the case in which *every* equilibrium of the mechanism gives the same allocation. Given that this is a more restrictive condition, any negative results for weak implementation also apply for strong implementation. Conversely, there are many situations in which an efficient, weakly implementable allocation exists, but no efficient, strongly implementable allocations exist.

A mechanism does not explicitly require an entity that plays the role of a "mediator." For example, if parties bargain over time, their behaviors are represented by some equilibrium strategies, as defined in chapter 4. In that case, the direct mechanism corresponds to the *mapping* from individual types to the strategies played over time.

The requirement that the outcome of a mechanism be a Bayesian Nash equilibrium is a minimal condition for an equilibrium. This perspective is helpful because it can be used to describe all the allocations that are possible equilibria, which in turn can be used to show that, in some cases, it is not possible for parties to reach an efficient agreement with *any* mechanism.

The revelation principal is the main tool for the analysis of general mechanisms. It's derivation begins with the observation that, for any environment, it is always possible to define a *direct mechanism*. A direct mechanism is one for which the message space is set equal to the type space, $M_B = [b_L, b_H]$ and $M_S = [c_L, c_H]$. In that case, the strategy is to report one's type. Because types are private information, parties may not wish to reveal their true type, but may use reporting strategies, $\hat{b}(b)$ for the buyer and $\hat{c}(c)$ for the seller. In this case:

$$\mathcal{M}^D\left(\hat{b}, \hat{c}\right) = \vec{x}\left(\hat{b}, \hat{c}\right).$$

An allocation can be implemented with a direct mechanism if truthfully reporting one's type ($\hat{b}^*(b) = b, \hat{c}^*(c) = c$) forms a Bayesian Nash equilibrium.

The next step is to observe that any mechanism can be used to define a direct mechanism. To see this, suppose mechanism $\Gamma = \{M_B, M_S, \mathcal{M}\}$ implements allocation $\vec{x}(b, c)$ with strategies $\vec{m}^*(b, c) = \{m_B^*(b), m_c^*(c)\}$, $b \in [b_L, b_H]$, $c \in [c_L, c_H]$. This mechanism defines the following direct mechanism, $\vec{x}\left(\hat{b}, \hat{c}\right) = \mathcal{M}\left(\vec{m}^*\left(\hat{b}, \hat{c}\right)\right)$, where $\left(\hat{b}, \hat{c}\right)$ are the reports by the buyer and seller. This is illustrated in figure 8.1.

Given a mechanism Γ, let Γ^D be the corresponding direct mechanism as defined in figure 8.1, and let $b(\cdot)$ and $c(\cdot)$ denote truth-telling strategies: $b(b) = b$ and $c(c) = c$. Suppose that mechanism Γ implements the allocation $\vec{x}(b, c)$ with the Bayesian Nash strategies $\left(m_B^*(\cdot), m_S^*(\cdot)\right)$; then we have for all $b, \hat{b} \in [b_L, b_H]$:

$$u^B\left(b, c(\cdot) \,|b, \Gamma^D\right) = u^B\left(m_B^*(b), m_S^*(\cdot) \,|b, \Gamma\right),$$

$$\geq u^B\left(m_B^*\left(\hat{b}\right), m_S^*(\cdot) \,|b, \Gamma\right),$$

$$= u^B\left(\hat{b}, c(\cdot) \,|b, \Gamma^D\right).$$

In other words, if an allocation can be implemented by some mechanism, it can be implemented by a direct mechanism. If the buyer has observed b, he cannot gain from

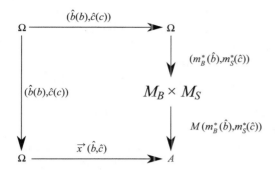

Figure 8.1
Direct mechanism = indirect mechanism.

any deviation from the equilibrium message $m_B^*(b)$, and in particular he cannot gain by pretending to be type $\hat{b} \neq b$ and sending the message $m_B^*\left(\hat{b}\right)$.

Similarly, for the seller, we have:

$$u^S\left(b\left(\cdot\right), c | c, \Gamma^D\right) = u^S\left(m_B^*\left(\cdot\right), m_S^*\left(c\right) | c, \Gamma\right)$$

$$\geq u^S\left(m_B^*\left(\cdot\right), m_S^*\left(\hat{c}\right) | c, \Gamma\right)$$

$$= u^S\left(b\left(\cdot\right), \hat{c} | c, \Gamma^D\right).$$

Thus, if an allocation can be implemented, then one can define a mechanism using agent types as the message space under which it is a Bayesian Nash equilibrium to be truthful.

Define the payoffs under a direct mechanism by:

$$u^B\left(\vec{x} | b, \hat{b}\right) \equiv \int_{c_L}^{c_H} u^B\left(\vec{x}\left(\hat{b}, c\right), b\right) dG\left(c\right), \tag{8.8}$$

$$u^S\left(\vec{x} | c, \hat{c}\right) \equiv \int_{b_L}^{b_H} u^S\left(\vec{x}\left(b, \hat{c}\right), c\right) dF\left(b\right). \tag{8.9}$$

Then, since a direct mechanism *is* a mechanism, we have:

Theorem 8.2 *(Revelation principle) An allocation $\vec{x}\left(b, c\right)$ can be implemented if and only if:*

$$u^B\left(\vec{x} | b, b\right) \geq u^B\left(\vec{x} | b, \hat{b}\right), \tag{8.10}$$

$$u^S\left(\vec{x} | c, c\right) \geq u^S\left(\vec{x} | c, \hat{c}\right), \tag{8.11}$$

for all $\hat{b}, b \in [b_L, b_H]$ and $\hat{c}, c \in [c_L, c_H]$.

Let $\Xi^{IC} \subset \Xi$ denote the set of incentive-compatible allocations.

When an allocation satisfies (8.10) and (8.11), we say that it is *(Bayesian) incentive compatible*. Typically, we leave off the qualifier "Bayesian" as it is usually implied by the context. Even though the revelation principle is almost an immediate consequence of the definition of an implementable mechanism, it is a powerful tool because it shows that expanding the message space beyond the set of possible types cannot increase the set of implementable allocations. However, observe that the analysis applies only for situations in which parties reveal their information once, and then the mechanism is implemented. If there is information revelation over time, then things are more complex (see Myerson 1986).

Above, it is shown that the monopoly problem can be viewed as a direct mechanism that results in an inefficient allocation. Consider now the case in which the seller's costs are known and only the buyer's valuations are not observed. In that case, monopoly pricing results in an inefficient allocation. However, one can use the revelation principle to design a contract that achieves the first best.

To see this, suppose that the seller's cost is given by

$$C(q,c) = q\bar{c} + k,$$

where $\bar{c}$ is a constant and known in advance—there is no uncertainty regarding costs—and k is a fixed cost that must be paid in advance. Suppose that, under no trade, both parties get zero. In this example, the efficient level of supply to the buyer is $q^*(b)$, given by the solution:

$$B_q\left(q^*(b),b\right) = \bar{c}. \tag{8.12}$$

Suppose that the gains from trade at the efficient solution are positive, namely:

$$S^* = E\left\{B\left(q^*(b),b\right) - \bar{c}q^*(b) - k\right\} > 0.$$

In other words, the buyer would be willing in advance to contract with the seller to pay for the fixed costs k before knowing her type b.

Now consider the contract:

1. The buyer agrees to pay a down payment $p^0 > k$ to secure the services of the seller.

2. The seller agrees to supply whatever quantities the buyer wishes at a price per unit of $\bar{c}$.

This contract has no explicit mention of buyer type; however, we can easily map the consequences of this contract into a direct revelation mechanism. Observe that under the terms of this agreement, a buyer of type b would choose to buy the efficient quantity $q^*(b)$ because the buyer's cost is equal to the marginal cost of production. Thus, under this contract, the allocation parties would choose is given by:

$$\vec{x}(b) = \left\{q^*(b),p^*(b)\right\} \in \Xi^{IC},$$

where $p^*(b) = \bar{c}q^*(b) + p^0$.

Under this allocation the payoff of the seller is the fixed amount $p^0 - k$, so the seller's incentive-compatibility constraint (8.11) is satisfied. Similarly, for a buyer with type b, since $q^*(b)$ is the optimal quantity given marginal cost $\bar{c}$, then we have:

$$B\left(q^*(b),b\right) - \bar{c}q^*(b) - p^0 \geq B(q,b) - \bar{c}q - p^0, \forall q \geq 0.$$

This inequality is also satisfied when q is replaced by $q^*\left(\hat{b}\right)$, therefore the buyer's incentive-compatibility constraint is satisfied.

This mechanism works because the contract is designed so the price paid by the buyer reflects the true cost of the good, so the buyer has an incentive to select the efficient level of consumption. This mechanism corresponds to a more general class of pricing mechanisms known as *Groves mechanisms*.

Notice there are a number of ways to implement this allocation. If binding contracts are available, the buyer need not pay the fixed price in advance, but merely upon delivery of the good. This also corresponds to a direct mechanism and reiterates the point we made in chapter 6, that the theory cannot deliver a unique prediction regarding the timing of payments over time.

8.3   The Normative Evaluation of Allocations under Asymmetric Information

The essence of a contract is that both parties voluntarily agree to trade if and only if terms are preferable to their alternatives. The presence of asymmetric information at the time parties negotiate greatly complicates matters because one party may not know how the other party values her alternative options. This section outlines the approach introduced by Holmström and Myerson (1983) on how to evaluate the efficiency of an allocation in the presence of asymmetric information.

The revelation principle allows us to restrict attention to the set of all possible *direct mechanisms*, given by $\vec{x} \in \Xi = \{\vec{x}(\cdot) | x : \Omega \to A\}$. The subset of such mechanisms that are *incentive compatible* is denoted by the set $\Xi^{IC} \subset \Xi$.

Consider the problem of bargaining ex ante over the choice of an allocation. If types are observed, then parties are free to choose any allocation from the set Ξ. The introduction of asymmetric information is viewed as restricting parties to choose from the set of incentive-compatible allocations, Ξ^{IC}. The difficulty is that the evaluation of an allocation depends upon what information is known at the time the parties reach an agreement. Holmström and Myerson (1983) consider three distinct dates on which parties can evaluate an allocation— the ex ante, interim, and ex post dates.

When parties meet at the ex ante date, it is assumed to be before they have acquired any private information. Under the hypothesis that the distribution of private information is known to both parties, then the ex ante payoffs from an allocation $\vec{x}$ are defined for the buyer and seller respectively by:

$$u_A^B(\vec{x}) = E\left\{u^B(\vec{x}(b,c),b)\right\},$$

$$u_A^S(\vec{x}) = E\left\{u^S(\vec{x}(b,c),c)\right\}.$$

An allocation is efficient if it is not possible for both parties to be better off.

Definition 8.3 *An allocation $\vec{x} \in \Xi$ $(\vec{x} \in \Xi^{IC})$ is* ex ante efficient *(respectively* ex ante incentive efficient*) if there does not exist $\vec{x}' \in \Xi$ $(\vec{x}' \in \Xi^{IC})$ such that $u^B(\vec{x}') \geq u^B(\vec{x})$ and $u^S(\vec{x}') \geq u^S(\vec{x})$ where at least one inequality is strict.*

An allocation is not efficient if both the buyer and the seller are better off with some other allocation. Let $\Xi_A \subset \Xi$ denote the set of ex ante efficient allocations, while $\Xi_A^{IC} \subset \Xi^{IC}$ denotes the set of ex ante incentive efficient allocations.

From a normative point of view, the ex ante perspective has desirable properties. John Rawls (1971) famously argued that allocations should be evaluated under the "veil of ignorance," namely, before individuals learn of their situations in life. As individuals learn of their capabilities, they are more likely to wish to protect any advantage they may have. A second benefit of an ex ante efficient allocation is requiring allocations to be incentive compatible does not restrict the set of ex ante efficient payoffs:

Proposition 8.4 *Suppose that there is a well defined efficient level of trade for all types, given by $q^*(b, c)$, and courts enforce specific performance. Then every ex ante efficient allocation is payoff equivalent to some ex ante incentive* efficient *allocation with a price function given by:*

$$p^*\left(\hat{b}, \hat{c}\right) = \int_{b_L}^{b_H} B\left(q^*(b, \hat{c}), b\right) dF(b) + \int_{c_L}^{c_H} C\left(q^*\left(\hat{b}, c\right), c\right) dG(c) + \bar{p}, \qquad (8.13)$$

where $q^*(b, c)$ is the ex ante efficient quantity as a function of individual types.

Proof. If the incentive constraints are not binding, then parties would always agree to trade with an *ex post* efficient quantity $q^*(b, c)$. If $q^*(b, c)$ were not *ex post* efficient, then we could find a q' that would increase total surplus at (b, c) and not reduce it elsewhere. Hence, every ex ante efficient allocation trades at some efficient quantity $q^*(b, c)$ in state (b, c).

Consider the case in which the buyer is truthful, and the seller observes c, but contemplates reporting $\hat{c} \neq c$:

$$\int_{b_L}^{b_H} \left(p^*\left(\tilde{b}, c\right) - C\left(q^*\left(\tilde{b}, c\right), c\right)\right) dF\left(\tilde{b}\right) = \int_{b_L}^{b_H} \left(B\left(q^*\left(\tilde{b}, c\right), \tilde{b}\right)\right.$$

$$\left. + \int_{c_L}^{c_H} C\left(q^*\left(\tilde{b}, \tilde{c}\right), \tilde{c}\right) dG\left(\tilde{c}\right) - C\left(q^*\left(\tilde{b}, c\right), c\right)\right) dF\left(\tilde{b}\right) + \bar{p}$$

$$= \int_{b_L}^{b_H} \left(B\left(q^*\left(\tilde{b}, c\right), \tilde{b}\right) - C\left(q^*\left(\tilde{b}, c\right), c\right)\right) dF\left(\tilde{b}\right) + K$$

$$\geq \int_{b_L}^{b_H} \left(B\left(q^*\left(\tilde{b}, \hat{c}\right), \tilde{b}\right) - C\left(q^*\left(\tilde{b}, \hat{c}\right), \hat{c}\right)\right) dF\left(\tilde{b}\right) + K.$$

The constant is given by: $K = \int_{b_L}^{b_H} \int_{c_L}^{c_H} C\left(q^*\left(\tilde{b}, \tilde{c}\right), \tilde{c}\right) dG\left(\tilde{c}\right) dF\left(\tilde{b}\right) + \bar{p}$. The third line is the total surplus plus a constant, and $q^*(b, c)$ maximizes this expression, which in turn implies that one cannot gain by being untruthful. At the ex ante stage, parties care only about the expected payment, which can be set to any level by the appropriate choice of $\bar{p}$. Hence, any ex ante efficient payoffs can be achieved with an incentive-compatible allocation.   □

This result requires specific performance in the sense used in chapter 6: after the contract is signed, parties cannot leave the relationship. When that is the case, one can define a price function that internalizes the effect of their decisions upon the other agent's payoffs. This idea originates with the work of Clarke (1971) and Groves (1973). The formulation here is in terms of a Bayesian game that follows from D'Aspremont and Gerard-Varet (1979). They were the first to show that one can construct a budget balancing mechanism to implement the efficient quantity using a direct revelation game. Williams (1999) shows that this result is also sufficient, even at the interim stage. The resulting price functions are examples of a *Groves Mechanism* (Groves 1973; see proposition 8.14 below)—namely, the mechanism is designed so that each party is a full residual claimant to the consequences of their decisions for the total gain from trade. Notice that this result does not imply that $\Xi_A = \Xi_A^{IC}$; see exercise 2.

Specific performance blocks contract renegotiation after parties learn their types. In many cases, parties are negotiating trade knowing their own types but not the other parties' types. Formally, these are agreements that occur at the *interim* stage in the three-period-trading timeline.

Definition 8.5 *An allocation $\vec{x} \in \Xi$ ($\vec{x} \in \Xi^{IC}$) is* interim *efficient (respectively* interim incentive efficient) *if there does not exist $\vec{x}' \in \Xi$ ($\vec{x}' \in \Xi^{IC}$) such that $u^B\left(\vec{x}' \mid b, b\right) \geq u^B\left(\vec{x} \mid b, b\right)$ and $u^S\left(\vec{x}' \mid c, c\right) \geq u^S\left(\vec{x} \mid c, c\right)$ for every $\{b, c\} \in \Omega$, with at least one inequality that is strict, where the payoffs are defined by (8.8) and (8.9).*

The set of *interim efficient allocations* and *interim incentive efficient allocations* are denoted by $\Xi_I \subset \Xi$ and $\Xi_I^{IC} \subset \Xi^{IC}$, respectively. These definitions present the challenge that parties know only their own type at the interim stage, so the bilateral negotiation is a potentially complex game with asymmetric information that varies with agent type. Holmström and Myerson (1983) (theorem 1) and Kobayashi (1980) explicitly address this issue and show that an incentive-compatible decision rule is interim incentive efficient if and only if there does not exist any common-knowledge event such that the decision rule is interim dominated given this information by another incentive-compatible decision rule. This provides some justification for the hypothesis that parties at the interim stage would always agree on interim efficient allocations.

Holmström and Myerson (1983) also introduce the notion of a "durable decision rule" to model the potential renegotiation of decision rules at the interim stage. The recent literature has moved away from these issues, in part because it is not known how to empirically implement these ideas. Card 1990, and Cramton and Tracy 1992 are examples of early work testing contract models with asymmetric information using data from labor disputes. This research was not entirely successful partially because the structure of bargaining with asymmetric information is extremely complex, and these simple models may not capture the wide variety of strategies parties may use in practice (see Ausubel, Cramton, and Deneckere 2002).

That there is no obvious way to define an efficient allocation at the interim stage is consistent with the fact that we observe so many conflicts and bargaining breakdowns in practice. The rest of this book sidesteps the issue of bargaining at the interim stage and instead takes a mechanism design approach. Two issues will be addressed. First, we will use the mechanism design approach to determine how parties would choose the quantity and price functions ex ante given that the mechanism must be incentive compatible at the interim stage. Second, we will consider the minimum cost of achieving an ex post efficient allocation. Cramton (1992) observes that, even though there is asymmetric information, parties can eventually reach an ex post efficient level of trade with sufficient delay of the time of trade. The costly delay results in a separation of types that can eventually result in *ex post* efficient exchange.

This ex post efficient exchange is possible because at the ex post stage, there is a dramatic increase in the set of efficient allocations. In this case, the definition from chapter 6 can be restated for the current context:

Definition 8.6 *An allocation $\vec{x} \in \Xi$ ($\vec{x} \in \Xi^{IC}$) is ex post efficient (respectively ex post incentive efficient) if there does not exist $\vec{x}' \in \Xi$ ($\vec{x}' \in \Xi^{IC}$) such that $u^{B}\left(\vec{x}'(b,c),b\right) \geq u^{B}\left(\vec{x}(b,c),b\right)$ and $u^{S}\left(\vec{x}'(b,c),c\right) \geq u^{S}\left(\vec{x}(b,c),c\right)$ for every $(b,c) \in \Omega$, where at least one inequality is strict.*

The set of *ex post* efficient allocations and *ex post* incentive efficient allocations are denoted by $\Xi_{P} \subset \Xi$ and $\Xi_{P}^{IC} \subset \Xi^{IC}$, respectively. The next proposition shows that these notions of efficiency can be ranked in terms of the extent to which they constrain the set of feasible allocations.

Proposition 8.7 *Let $\Xi_{A}, \Xi_{I}, \Xi_{P}$ and $\Xi_{A}^{IC}, \Xi_{I}^{IC}, \Xi_{P}^{IC}$ denote the set of ex ante, interim, and ex post efficient, and ex ante, interim, and ex post incentive efficient allocations. If allocations are constrained to be continuous, then:*

$$\Xi_{A} \subset \Xi_{I} \subset \Xi_{P} \text{ and } \Xi_{A}^{IC} \subset \Xi_{I}^{IC} \subset \Xi_{P}^{IC}, \tag{8.14}$$

$$\Xi_{A} \cap \Xi^{IC} \subset \Xi_{A}^{IC}, \tag{8.15}$$

$$\Xi_{I} \cap \Xi^{IC} \subset \Xi_{I}^{IC}, \tag{8.16}$$

$$\Xi_{P} \cap \Xi^{IC} \subset \Xi_{P}^{IC}. \tag{8.17}$$

Proof. If an allocation $\vec{x}$ is ex ante efficient, but not interim efficient, there is an allocation $\vec{x}'$ that is strictly better than $\vec{x}$ for some states either for the buyer or for the seller, and no worse than for the other agent. Suppose the state is better for the buyer. Then the continuity of the allocation implies:

$$E\left\{u^{B}\left(\vec{x}',b\right)\right\} > E\left\{u^{B}\left(\vec{x},b\right)\right\},$$

$$E\left\{u^{S}\left(\vec{x}',c\right)\right\} \geq E\left\{u^{S}\left(\vec{x},c\right)\right\},$$

and hence $\vec{x}$ is not ex ante efficient. A similar argument applies for the other cases (8.14). Cases (8.15)–(8.17) follow immediately from the definitions.   □

If parties reach an ex ante incentive efficient agreement, the agreement remains incentive efficient at the interim and ex post stages. From proposition 8.4, parties can, without loss of generality, choose allocations at the ex ante stage that are also both interim and ex post efficient. Thus, by itself, asymmetric information does not necessarily imply inefficient exchange, nor conflict. A necessary condition for this result is that specific performance is an enforceable legal rule that binds parties to each other at both the interim and ex post stages. In general, most relationships provide conditions under which parties may leave.

8.4   Characterizing the Set of Incentive-Compatible Allocations

This section provides some results on the structure of the incentive-compatible allocations in the set Ξ^{IC}. Three cases are considered. First, suppose that parties can bind themselves to trade, as in proposition 8.4. If the quantity to be traded is monotonic in type (increasing in the buyer's type b and decreasing in the seller's type c), then the requirement that the allocation be incentive compatible does not constrain the set of ex ante payoffs.

The next question is what happens when trade is voluntary and parties can terminate the relationship at will after learning their types, modulo some previously agreed termination fee. The answer is provided by the celebrated Myerson-Satterthwaite theorem, which implies that, if the gains from trade at the interim stage are not sufficient, then some ex ante efficient allocations may not be implementable. Specifically, it is not always possible to implement ex post efficient trade for some types.

The final subsection considers the reverse question. Suppose the level of trade is required to be efficient. What are the implications for the transfer function? This subsection shows that a necessary and sufficient condition for the implementation of efficient trade is that the transfer function, $p(\omega)$, takes the form of a Groves mechanism—the mechanism that ensures each party faces the full marginal return from their choices. This result is applied to the question of how much one should subsidize a project to ensure that the level of trade is *ex post* efficient.

8.4.1   The Set of Incentive-Compatible Allocations with Specific Performance

Consider the problem of implementing an allocation with asymmetric information when parties can be forced to trade at the interim period. Specific performance means that if parties agree to an allocation ex ante, they cannot then back out of the deal even if the *ex post* payoff (after getting their private information) is less than their outside option. Attention is restricted to what we call the *standard* case under which the buyer's type, b, indicates an increase in the marginal return to trade, while an increase in the seller's type, c, indicates an increase in marginal costs:

Definition 8.8   *The standard payoffs are assumed to have the following properties. Benefit, $B(q, b) \geq 0$, and cost, $C(q, c) \geq 0$, are twice differentiable. It is efficient to trade a positive quantity q $(B_q(0, b_L) > C_q(0, c_H) \geq 0)$. Payoffs are normalized so that $B(0, b) = C(0, c) = 0$. For all interior types, $\{q, b, c\} \in \Re_+ \times [b_L, b_H] \times [c_L, c_H]$:*

1. *Benefits and costs rise with quantity:*

$$B_q, C_q > 0. \tag{8.18}$$

2. *The net benefit is strictly concave and increasing:*

$$B_{qq} < 0, C_{qq} > 0. \tag{8.19}$$

3. *Private valuations increase the marginal benefit and cost:*

$$B_{qb}, C_{qc} > 0. \tag{8.20}$$

4. *Private valuations increase the concavity/convexity:*

$$B_{qqb} \leq 0, C_{qqc} \geq 0. \tag{8.21}$$

With standard payoffs, concavity (8.19) ensures that for each pair of types, $\{b, c\}$, there is a unique optimal quantity, $q^*(b, c) > 0$, uniquely defined by:

$$B_q\left(q^*(b,c), b\right) - C_q\left(q^*(b,c), c\right) = 0.$$

The effect of types upon marginal costs and benefits (8.20) implies:

$$\frac{\partial q^*}{\partial b} > 0, \frac{\partial q^*}{\partial c} < 0. \tag{8.22}$$

This subsection addresses whether it is possible to agree on an incentive-compatible allocation $\vec{x} = \{q(b,c), p(b,c)\}$ with the feature that the agreed quantity, $q(b,c)$, is increasing with b and decreasing with c. With standard payoffs, this case includes agreements to trade at the efficient level.

By the revelation principle, such an allocation can be implemented if and only if there is a price function such that each party is willing to truthfully reveal its private information. Without loss of generality, the revelation principle allows one to restrict attention to direct mechanisms under which the buyer reports his type as $\hat{b} \in M_B = [b_L, b_H]$, while the seller reports her type $\hat{c} \in M_S = [c_L, c_H]$. The payoffs and payments as a function of types, $\{b, c\}$, and messages, $\{\hat{b}, \hat{c}\}$, can be defined by:

$$u^B\left(b, \hat{b}\right) = \hat{B}\left(b, \hat{b}\right) - P^B\left(\hat{b}\right), \tag{8.23}$$

$$u^S\left(c, \hat{c}\right) = P^S\left(\hat{c}\right) - \hat{C}\left(c, \hat{c}\right), \tag{8.24}$$

with:

$$\hat{B}\left(b, \hat{b}\right) = \int_{c_L}^{c_H} B\left(q\left(\hat{b}, c\right), b\right) dG(c),$$

$$P^B\left(\hat{b}\right) = \int_{c_L}^{c_H} p\left(\hat{b}, c\right) dG(c),$$

$$\hat{C}\left(c, \hat{c}\right) = \int_{b_L}^{b_H} C\left(q\left(b, \hat{c}\right), c\right) dF(b),$$

$$P^S\left(\hat{c}\right) = \int_{b_L}^{b_H} p\left(b, \hat{c}\right) dF(b).$$

At an implementable allocation, both parties tell the truth, and hence the equilibrium payoffs are given by:

$$u^{B*}(b) = u^B(b, b) = \max_{\hat{b}} u^B\left(b, \hat{b}\right), \tag{8.25}$$

$$u^{S*}(c) = u^S(c, c) = \max_{\hat{c}} u^S\left(c, \hat{c}\right). \tag{8.26}$$

Suppose that the payoffs are differentiable in type. For the buyer's truth-telling constraint to be satisfied, (8.25) implies:

$$u_{\hat{b}}^B(b,b) \equiv \left.\frac{\partial u^B\left(b,\hat{b}\right)}{\partial \hat{b}}\right|_{\hat{b}=b} = 0, \partial\left\{\hat{B}(b,\hat{b}-P^B(\hat{b})\right\}. \tag{8.27}$$

By (8.23):

$$u_b^B(b,b) \equiv \left.\frac{\partial u^B\left(b,\hat{b}\right)}{\partial b}\right|_{\hat{b}=b} = \left.\frac{\partial \hat{B}\left(b,\hat{b}\right)-P^B\left(\hat{b}\right)}{\partial b}\right|_{\hat{b}=b}$$

$$= \left.\frac{\partial \hat{B}\left(b,\hat{b}\right)}{\partial b}\right|_{\hat{b}=b}$$

$$= \int_{c_L}^{c_H} B_b\left(q\left(b,c\right),b\right)g\left(c\right)dc,$$

$$\equiv \hat{B}_b\left(b,b\right).$$

Thus, the equilibrium payoff for the buyer, (8.25), satisfies the following differential equation:

$$\frac{du^{B*}(b)}{db} = u_b^B(b,b) + u_{\hat{b}}^B(b,b) = \hat{B}_b(b,b). \tag{8.28}$$

By the fundamental theorem of calculus, the incentive-compatible payoff to the buyer is:

$$u^{B*}(b) = u^{B^0}(b) + u_L^B, \tag{8.29}$$

where:

$$u^{B^0}(b) \equiv \int_{b_L}^{b}\int_{c_L}^{c_H} B_b\left(q\left(b',c\right),b'\right)g\left(c\right)dcdb', \tag{8.30}$$

is the payoff for the buyer when the value of the lowest type is fixed at zero ($u_L^B = 0$).

This result is useful because it shows that the requirement of truthful revelation completely determines the utility of the buyer conditional on the agreement $q(b,c)$, up to a constant. This in turn completely determines the price the buyer expects to pay given his reported type:

$$P^B\left(\hat{b}\right) = \hat{B}\left(\hat{b},\hat{b}\right) - u^{B^0}\left(\hat{b}\right) - u_L^B. \tag{8.31}$$

Even though the first-order condition yields unique payoffs (up to a constant), one needs to ensure that the truthful revelation is optimal. The second-order condition for the buyer is:

$$\left.\frac{\partial^2 u^B\left(b,\hat{b}\right)}{\partial \hat{b}\partial \hat{b}}\right|_{\hat{b}=b} = u_{\hat{b}\hat{b}}^B(b,b) \leq 0.$$

One can write:

$$u^B\left(b,\hat{b}\right) = \hat{B}\left(b,\hat{b}\right) - \hat{B}\left(\hat{b},\hat{b}\right) + u^{B*}\left(\hat{b}\right).$$

Taking the second derivative and using (8.28) implies:

$$u^B_{\hat{b}\hat{b}}\left(b,b\right) = -\hat{B}_{\hat{b}b}\left(b,b\right),$$

$$= -\int_{c_L}^{c_H}\left(B_q\left(q\left(b,c\right),b\right)q_b\left(b,c\right) + B_b\left(q\left(b,c\right),b\right)\right)dG\left(c\right).$$

It is assumed that $B_q\left(q,b\right), B_b\left(q,b\right) \geq 0$; hence, the assumption that $q_b\left(b,c\right) \geq 0$ for all b,c implies:

$$\left.\frac{\partial^2 u^B\left(b,\hat{b}\right)}{\partial\hat{b}\partial\hat{b}}\right|_{\hat{b}=b} = u^B_{\hat{b}\hat{b}}\left(b,b\right) \leq 0, \partial\left\{\hat{B}(b,\hat{b} - P^B(\hat{b})\right\}.$$

Therefore, the second-order condition for truth-telling ($\hat{b} = b$) to be optimal is satisfied.

A similar argument applies to the seller for which a sufficient condition for the existence of an implementable allocation is that $q_c(b,c) \leq 0$. Following the argument used for the buyer, the seller's payoff under an incentive-compatible allocation is given by:

$$u^{S*}\left(c\right) = \int_c^{c_H}\int_{b_L}^{b_H}C_c\left(q\left(b,c'\right),c'\right)f\left(b\right)dbdc' + u^S_H, \tag{8.32}$$

$$= u^{S^0}\left(c\right) + u^S_H, \tag{8.33}$$

where u^S_H is utility at the highest cost realization c_H. In this case, the price function is:

$$P^S\left(\hat{c}\right) = \hat{C}\left(\hat{c},\hat{c}\right) + u^{S^0}\left(\hat{c}\right) + u^S_H. \tag{8.34}$$

Finally, the quantity function determines the total surplus possible:

$$S\left(q\left(\cdot\right)\right) = \int_{b_L}^{b_H}\int_{c_L}^{c_H}\left(B\left(q\left(b,c\right),b\right) - C\left(q\left(b,c\right)c\right)\right)g\left(c\right)f\left(b\right)dcdb,$$

a quantity that is independent of the price function. One can use (8.29) and (8.32) to compute the expected utility for the buyer given the quantity traded and payoff at the buyer's lowest valuation. Use this result and an equivalent relationship for the seller to write the surplus as:

$$S\left(q\left(\cdot\right)\right) = E\left\{u^{B*}\left(b\right)\right\} + E\left\{u^{S*}\left(c\right)\right\}$$

$$= M\left(q\left(\cdot\right)\right) + u^B_L + u^S_H, \tag{8.35}$$

where

$$M\left(q\left(\cdot\right)\right) \equiv \int_{b_L}^{b_H}\int_{b_L}^{b}\int_{c_L}^{c_H}B_b\left(q\left(b',c\right),b'\right)g\left(c\right)dcdb'f\left(b\right)db +$$

$$\int_{c_L}^{c_H} \int_{c}^{c_H} \int_{b_L}^{b_H} C_c\left(q\left(b,c'\right),c'\right) f\left(b\right) db dc' g\left(c\right) dc,$$

$$= E\left[\frac{1-F\left(b\right)}{f\left(b\right)} B_b\left(q\left(b,c\right),b\right) + \frac{G\left(c\right)}{g\left(c\right)} C_c\left(q\left(b,c\right),c\right)\right].$$

This implies that, given any quantity that is a monotonic function of types, the gain from trade at an implementable allocation is unique up to the value of the buyer's lowest payoff and the seller's highest possible payoff.[3] This result is used in the next proposition to establish the existence of an implementable allocation.

Proposition 8.9 *Suppose parties have standard payoffs, and the quantity allocation, $q\left(b,c\right)$, is differentiable, increasing with the buyer's valuation, b, and decreasing with the seller's cost, c. Further, suppose that the buyer and the seller can be bound to trade in all states, and their ex ante outside options, u^{0B} and u^{0S}, satisfy:*

$$S\left(q\left(\cdot\right)\right) \geq u^{0B} + u^{0S}.$$

Then there exists an implementable allocation $\vec{x}\left(b,c\right) = \{q\left(b,c\right), p\left(b,c\right)\}$, and associated payoffs $\left\{u^{B*}\left(b\right), u^{S*}\left(c\right)\right\}$, given by (8.29) and (8.32), that satisfy:

1. *The payoffs are* ex ante *individually rational:*

$$E\left\{u^{B*}\left(b\right)\right\} \geq u^{0B},$$

$$E\left\{u^{S*}\left(c\right)\right\} \geq u^{0S}.$$

2. *The* ex post *gain from trade satisfies:*

$$u^{B*}\left(b\right) + u^{S*}\left(c\right) \geq u^{B*}\left(b_L\right) + u^{S*}\left(c_H\right) = S\left(q\left(\cdot\right)\right) - M\left(q\left(\cdot\right)\right), \tag{8.36}$$

$$\forall b \in [b_L, b_H], \forall c \in [c_L, c_H].$$

Proof. We need to demonstrate the existence of a price function $p\left(b,c\right)$ that implements the allocation $q\left(\cdot\right)$. Let $u^{B*}\left(b\right), u^{S*}\left(c\right)$ be the payoffs at an incentive-compatible allocation given u_L^B; hence, $u_H^S = S\left(q\left(\cdot\right)\right) - M\left(q\left(\cdot\right)\right) - u_L^B$. Using the price definitions (8.31) and (8.34), without loss of generality, we can set:

$$p\left(b,c\right) = P^B\left(b\right) + P^S\left(c\right) + p^0, \tag{8.37}$$

which yields an incentive-compatible allocation $\vec{x}^*\left(b,c\right) = \{q\left(b,c\right), p\left(b,c\right)\}$ where:

$$P^B\left(b\right) = \hat{B}\left(b,b\right) - \left(u^{B^0}\left(b\right) + u_L^B\right),$$

$$P^S\left(c\right) = \hat{C}\left(c,c\right) + u^{S^0}\left(c\right) + u_H^S.$$

Set p^0 so that:

$$\int_{c_L}^{c_H} P^S\left(c\right) g\left(c\right) dc + p^0 = 0,$$

which ensures that:

$$\int_{c_L}^{c_H} p(b,c) g(c) dc = P^B(b).$$

One can verify, using the definition of u_L^B, that for the seller one has:

$$\int_{b_L}^{b_H} p(b,c) f(b) db = P^S(c).$$

Note that for any $\bar{p}$, the allocation $\vec{x}(\cdot) = \{q(\cdot), p(\cdot) + \bar{p}\}$ is also incentive compatible. Since

$$S(q(\cdot)) = E\{B(q(b,c),b) - C(q(b,c),c)\} = E\left\{u^B(b) + u^S(c)\right\},$$

one simply sets $\bar{p}$ so that:

$$E\left\{u^B(b)\right\} - \bar{p} \geq u^{0B},$$

$$E\left\{u^S(c)\right\} + \bar{p} \geq u^{0S}.$$

Finally, observe that $u^{B*}(b)$ is increasing in b and $u^{S*}(c)$ is decreasing in c. This combined with expression (8.35) implies (8.36). □

When parties can bind themselves to trade, the restriction that incentive compatibility places upon the quantity traded is slight—it needs only be decreasing in the seller's cost parameter c and increasing in the buyer's valuation parameter b. In particular, for the standard payoffs (8.22), this implies that the optimal quantity, $q^*(b,c) = \arg\max_q B(q,b) - C(q,c)$, is increasing in b and decreasing in c. This result provides an alternative proof to proposition 8.4:

Corollary 8.10 *For the standard payoffs, if it is efficient for parties to trade ex ante in all states, there exists a price function that implements an efficient allocation when parties can bind themselves to trade.*

In summary, if parties can bind themselves to trade regardless of their private information, then under the relatively mild condition that quantity is monotonic with respect to types, it is possible to implement an arbitrary allocation. Note that this is *Bayesian* implementation, which requires both parties to reveal their information privately, without knowing the characteristics of the other.

It is natural to wonder what would happen if parties could mutually observe their types. There is a large literature on this question that explores a number of different models of equilibrium behavior, such as Nash Implementation (see Maskin's [1999] original work on this problem), or dominant strategy implementation (see Jackson [2001] for a helpful review). The main result is that efficient allocations can be implemented only under rather restrictive conditions. It was D'Aspremont and Gerard-Varet (1979) who first showed that Bayesian implementation allows one to implement allocations under a wider set of conditions than possible under dominant strategy or Nash implementation. The next subsection addresses the problem of implementing an incentive-compatible allocation when parties have the right to leave the relationship after observing their private information.

8.4.2 Voluntary Exchange

When it is always efficient to trade and courts enforce specific performance, a contract exists that implements the efficient level of trade for all buyer and seller types. As was discussed in chapter 6, such contracts are not always enforceable. In particular, it is the norm for an employer to give an employee the right to leave at will. For example, at the interim stage, after the employee has agreed to start work, she might acquire information about a more attractive market alternative and leave the employer. The purpose of this section is to characterize the set of implementable contracts when parties may choose to separate at the interim stage.

As discussed in chapter 6, by voluntary exchange we mean that transfers associated with taking the outside option do not depend on who chooses to separate. Voluntary exchange ensures that, if it is efficient to separate, one party will always wish to exercise that option. In the context of a labor market, there are often mandated severance payments that the buyer/firm must pay to the seller/worker. An allocation has a *fixed severance pay* $\bar{p}$ if this is paid whenever there is no trade, $q(\omega) = \emptyset$. More precisely the allocation satisfies:

$$p(\omega) = \bar{p}, \forall \omega \in \Omega^{NT}(\vec{x}).\tag{8.38}$$

In general, as Lazear (2000) has observed, the existence of such payments does not affect the set of implementable allocations but merely shifts the set of possible allocations along a Pareto frontier. Given this, interim individual rationality is defined as follows:

Definition 8.11 *An allocation $\vec{x} \in \Xi$ is interim individually rational *with a fixed severance pay $\bar{p}$ if:*

$$u^B(\vec{x}, b) \geq u^{0B} - \bar{p},\tag{8.39}$$

$$u^S(\vec{x}, c) \geq u^{0S} + \bar{p},\tag{8.40}$$

for all $(b, c) \in [b_L, b_H] \times [c_L, c_H]$.

In other words, an allocation is interim individually rational if each party, regardless of its private information, prefers trade under the agreed allocation over the outside option or status quo point net of the transfer. The proof of proposition 8.9 implies that adding a fixed transfer does not affect the incentive-compatibility constraints. More precisely:

Proposition 8.12 *(Lazear 1990) Suppose the allocation $\vec{x}(\omega) = \{q(\omega), p(\omega)\}$ satisfies (8.38) and is incentive compatible and interim individually rational with severance pay $\bar{p}$, then the allocation $\vec{x}^0(\omega) = \{q(\omega), p(\omega) - \bar{p}\}$ is also incentive compatible and satisfies:*

$$u^B\left(\vec{x}^0, b\right) \geq u^{0B},\tag{8.41}$$

$$u^S\left(\vec{x}^0, c\right) \geq u^{0S},\tag{8.42}$$

for all $(b, c) \in [b_L, b_H] \times [c_L, c_H]$.

Thus, there is no loss in generality in restricting attention to the individual rationality constraints (8.41)–(8.42). This is another example showing that a variety of contracts with different terms can give rise to the same level of trade. The purpose of severance pay is to move payoffs along the Pareto frontier. By combining proposition 8.9 with the interim individual rationality constraint, one obtains:

Theorem 8.13 *(Myerson and Satterthwaite 1983) Suppose parties have standard payoffs, and the quantity allocation, $q(b,c)$, is differentiable, increasing with the buyer's valuation, b, and decreasing with the seller's costs, c. A quantity allocation, $q(\cdot)$ that has trade in all states can be implemented with an allocation, $\vec{x}(b,c) = \{q(b,c), p(b,c)\}$, that is interim individually rational and incentive compatible if and only if:*

$$S(q(\cdot)) - M(q(\cdot)) \geq u^{0B} + u^{0S}. \tag{8.43}$$

Proof. Suppose the allocation $q(\cdot)$ satisfies (8.43); then, by proposition 8.9 one can construct an incentive-compatible price term, $p(\cdot)$, so that $u_L^B = u^{0B} - \bar{p}$. Since $u^{B*}(b)$ is increasing in b, this ensures $u^{B*}(b) \geq u^{0B} - \bar{p}, \forall b \in [b_L, b_H]$. Next, we have:

$$u_H^S = S(q(\cdot)) - M(q(\cdot)) - u_L^B = S(q(\cdot)) - M(q(\cdot)) - u^{0B} + \bar{p} \geq u^{0S} + \bar{p}.$$

Since $u^{S*}(c)$ is decreasing with c, this implies $u^{S*}(c) \geq u_H^S \geq u^{0S} + \bar{p}, \forall c \in [c_L, c_H]$. Thus the allocation is interim individually rational and incentive compatible.

Now suppose that one has an incentive compatible and interim individually rational allocation. This implies that by proposition 8.9 and interim individual rationality:

$$S(q(\cdot)) - M(q(\cdot)) = u_L^B + u_H^S \geq u^{0B} + u^{0S}. \qquad \square$$

When $M(q(\cdot)) > 0$, the last inequality of the proof implies that a necessary condition to implement $q(\cdot)$ is that the gain from trade be *strictly* larger than value of the outside options. Thus, the *combination* of asymmetric information and interim incentive constraints implies that some ex ante efficient allocations may not be implementable. See Williams (1999) for an extension of this result to many agents (see also the discussion in Ausubel, Cramton, and Deneckere 2002). The next three examples illustrate this result.

Example 1 Consider the case in which parties agree to trade a fixed amount q at a price p. This allocation is clearly incentive compatible because it does not change with the reported types. In this case, one has:

$$M(q) = S(q) - (B(q, b_L) - C(q, c_H)). \tag{8.44}$$

This implies that an allocation can be implemented if and only if the lowest social surplus possible is at least as desirable as the outside options:

$$B(q, b_L) - C(q, c_H) \geq u^{0B} + u^{0S}.$$

When this condition does not hold, parties may agree to trade, but trade will occur only when both parties prefer trade to no trade, namely when:

$$B(q, b) - p \geq u^{0B}, \tag{8.45}$$

$$p - C(q, c) \geq u^{0S}.$$

Increasing the price increases the lowest value, b, at which the buyer will trade while increasing the highest cost c at which the seller will trade. See exercise 3.

Example 2 Myerson and Satterthwaite (1983) provide the following example that illustrates the impossibility of efficient trade. Let b, c be uniformly distributed over $[0, 1]$, $q \in [0, 1]$, $B(q, b) = bq$ and $C(q, c) = cq$. This corresponds to the trade of a single indivisible good, where $q \in [0, 1]$ represents the probability of trade. In this case the efficient allocation requires:

$$q^*(b, c) = \begin{cases} 1, & \text{if } b \geq c, \\ 0, & \text{if not.} \end{cases}$$

For these payoffs, choosing $q = 0$ gives a total payoff of zero, and thus, in the absence of penalties, one must have $u_L^B + u_H^S \geq 0$. Though this is not a differentiable function, Myerson and Satterthwaite (1983) show that proposition 8.9 still holds in this case. At the optimal contract one has $S(q^*(\cdot)) = 1/6$, but:

$$M(q^*(\cdot)) = \int_0^1 \int_0^b [(1 - b) + c]\, dc\, db$$

$$= 1/3.$$

Thus a necessary condition to implement the efficient allocation is:

$$0 \leq u_L^B + u_H^S = S(q^*(\cdot)) - M(q^*(\cdot)) = -\frac{1}{6}.$$

This leads to a contradiction, and hence efficient trade with an incentive-compatible allocation is impossible.

Example 3 In practice, trade is determined by the actions of individuals who are playing a bargaining game. In such games, individuals with different types may choose different bargaining strategies that are optimal within the context of the bargaining game they are playing. The revelation principle implies that, at any equilibrium, the optimal type-dependent strategies can be used to define an incentive-compatible direct mechanism in which parties are simply asked to reveal their private information.

To illustrate this point, suppose that the payoffs are as in example 2, but now the buyer makes a take-it-or-leave-it offer to the seller at a price p after he learns his type b. If the seller accepts, the good is delivered for the price p; otherwise there is no trade. In this case, the seller would accept the offer if and only if $p \geq c$, and hence, from the buyer's perspective, the offer will be accepted with probability $Pr\{c \leq p\} = p$ since the distribution of c is uniform on $[0, 1]$. The profit for the buyer as a function of the price charged is the gain from trade times the probability of trade:

$$u^B(p|b) = (b - p)\, p.$$

The optimal strategy for the buyer as a function of b is:

$$p(b) = b/2. \tag{8.46}$$

We can use these strategies to define an incentive-compatible allocation that gives the same payoff as the bargaining game:

$$q(b,c) = \begin{cases} 0, & \text{if } b < 2c, \\ 1, & \text{if } b \geq 2c, \end{cases} \tag{8.47}$$

$$p(b,c) = q(b,c) \times b/2. \tag{8.48}$$

One can verify that this allocation is indeed incentive compatible and interim individually rational (see exercise 4). However, it is not *ex post* efficient because there is no trade for types $b \in [c, 2c)$.

8.4.3 Implementing Ex Post Efficient Trade

The Myerson-Satterthwaite theorem (theorem 8.13) implies that bargaining at the interim stage, after one learns one's type, may result in an inefficient allocation. The purpose of this section is to discuss the situations in which this possibility can be avoided and parties can nevertheless implement efficient trade. These cases can be mapped to specific economic institutions such as the allocation of decision rights and the use of bonds or other methods to relax the participation constraints.

Proposition 8.4 shows that with commitment, there is an *ex ante* mechanism with price given by (8.13) that implements an efficient mechanism. This transfer function is a Groves mechanism (Groves 1973) because each party gets the full marginal return or cost of the other party. Williams (1999) shows that the converse also holds. Namely, any interim efficient mechanism that is continuous with respect to types, with $b_H > b_L$ and $c_H > c_L$, must take the form of a Groves mechanism.[4]

To see this, let $q^*(b,c)$ be the efficient level of trade, where $q^*(b,c) = 0$ implies no trade is efficient. As a matter of convention, set the costs and benefits to the outside options when there is no trade:

$$-C(0,c) = u^{0S}, \forall c \in [c_L, c_H],$$

$$B(0,b) = u^{0B}, \forall b \in [b_L, b_H].$$

Under this assumption, one has $B_q(q^*(b,c),b) = C_q(q^*(b,c),c)$, except upon a set of measure zero. Total surplus is a continuous function of types b and c, and payoffs are differentiable almost everywhere. Suppose that a mechanism exists that implements the efficient level of trade; then, from (8.23):

$$0 = \left. \frac{\partial u^B(b,\hat{b})}{\partial \hat{b}} \right|_{b=\hat{b}} = \left. \frac{\partial \left(\hat{B}(b,\hat{b}) - P^B(\hat{b}) \right)}{\partial \hat{b}} \right|_{b=\hat{b}}.$$

This implies the following differential equation:

$$\frac{dP^B\left(\hat{b}\right)}{d\hat{b}} = \int_{c_L}^{c_H} \left(B_q\left(q^*\left(\hat{b},c\right),\hat{b}\right) \frac{\partial q^*\left(\hat{b},c\right)}{\partial \hat{b}} g\left(c\right) \right) dc,$$

$$= \int_{c_L}^{c_H} \left(C_q\left(q^*\left(\hat{b},c\right),c\right) \frac{\partial q^*\left(\hat{b},c\right)}{\partial \hat{b}} g\left(c\right) \right) dc,$$

$$= \frac{d\int_{c_L}^{c_H}\left(C\left(q^*\left(\hat{b},c\right),c\right)g\left(c\right)\right) dc}{d\hat{b}}.$$

The second line follows from the fact that q^* is efficient.[5] From this, it follows that the price function satisfies (up to a constant):

$$P^B\left(\hat{b}\right) = \int_{c_L}^{c_H} \left(C\left(q^*\left(\hat{b},c\right),c\right)g\left(c\right) \right) dc + \bar{p}^B,$$

$$= C^*\left(\hat{b}\right) + \bar{p}^B, \tag{8.49}$$

where $C^*\left(b\right)$ is the expected cost of the good at the efficient level of trade, when the buyer's true type is b. Notice that $C^*\left(b\right)$ is an increasing function. An analogous argument implies that the seller's price function up to a constant satisfies:

$$P^S\left(\hat{c}\right) = \int_{b_L}^{b_H} \left(B\left(q^*\left(b,\hat{c}\right),b\right)f\left(b\right) \right) db + \bar{p}^S,$$

$$= B^*\left(\hat{c}\right) + \bar{p}^S, \tag{8.50}$$

where $B^*\left(c\right)$ is the expected value of efficient exchange for the buyer, given the seller's true type c. If the price function is also required to be budget balancing, then the implementable price function must satisfy (8.37) and one has:

Proposition 8.14 *(Williams 1999) For the standard buyer-seller model, there is a budget balancing incentive-compatible mechanism implementing ex post efficient trade if and only if the price function has the form:*

$$p\left(b,c\right) = C^*\left(b\right) + B^*\left(c\right) + \epsilon\left(b,c\right), \tag{8.51}$$

for some $\epsilon\left(b,c\right)$ satisfying

$$E\left\{\epsilon\left(b,c\right)|b\right\} = E\left\{\epsilon\left(b,c\right)|c\right\} = \bar{p},$$

$\forall b \in [b_L, b_H]$, $\forall c \in [c_L, c_H]$ *and some constant $\bar{p}$. Any price function satisfying these conditions is called a Groves mechanism.*

Proof. The assumptions on $\epsilon\left(b,c\right)$ ensure that:

$$E\left\{p\left(b,c\right)|b\right\} = C^*\left(b\right) + \hat{B}^* + \bar{p}, \quad \forall b \in [b_L, b_H],$$

$$E\{p(b,c)\,|c\} = \hat{C}^* + B^*(c) + \bar{p}, \; \forall c \in [c_L, c_H],$$

where $\hat{B}^* = E\{B^*(b)\} = E\{B^*(c)\}$ is the *ex ante* expected benefit and $\hat{C}^* = E\{C^*(b)\} = E\{C^*(c)\}$ is the *ex ante* expected cost. By construction, this ensures that the price mechanism satisfies the incentive constraints for truth-telling.

For the converse, let $p(b,c)$ be any incentive-compatible mechanism. Define:

$$\epsilon(b,c) = p(b,c) - \big(C^*(b) + B^*(c)\big).$$

Since $p(b,c)$ is incentive compatible, then, from the discussion before the proposition, one has:

$$
\begin{aligned}
E\{\epsilon(b,c)\,|b\} &= E\big\{p(b,c) - \big(C^*(b) + B^*(c)\big)\,|b\big\} \\
&= \big(C^*(b) + \bar{p}^B\big) - \big(C^*(b) + \hat{B}^*\big) \\
&= \bar{p}^B - \hat{B}^*,
\end{aligned}
$$

and

$$
\begin{aligned}
E\{\epsilon(b,c)\,|c\} &= E\big\{p(b,c) - \big(C^*(b) + B^*(c)\big)\,|c\big\} \\
&= \big(B^*(c) + \bar{p}^S\big) - \big(\hat{C}^* + B^*(c)\big) \\
&= \bar{p}^S - \hat{C}^*.
\end{aligned}
$$

Next:

$$\int_{b_L}^{b_H} \int_{c_L}^{c_H} \epsilon(b,c)\, g(c) f(b)\, dc\, db = \int_{c_L}^{c_H} \int_{b_L}^{b_H} \epsilon(b,c) f(b) g(c)\, db\, dc$$

$$\int_{b_L}^{b_H} E\{\epsilon(b,c)\,|b\} f(b)\, db = \int_{c_L}^{c_H} E\{\epsilon(b,c)\,|c\} g(c)\, dc$$

$$\bar{p}^B + \hat{B}^* = \bar{p}^S - \hat{C}^*.$$

Thus $\epsilon(b,c)$ satisfies the conditions of the proposition with $\bar{p} = \bar{p}^S - \hat{C}^* = \bar{p}^B + \hat{B}^*$. $\quad\square$

The $\epsilon(b,c)$ term can be viewed as potentially adding noise to the transfer. Since b and c are independently distributed, then adding any term of the form

$$\epsilon(b,c) = h(b) k(c) + \bar{\epsilon},$$

where $h(b)$ and $k(c)$ are arbitrary functions of b and c with the properties: $E\{h(b)\} = E\{k(c)\} = 0$, and $E\{\bar{\epsilon}\} = \bar{p}$ will not affect the incentive constraints.

The Groves mechanism is defined by (8.51). It has the feature that any change in the buyer's report affects the true costs via $C^*\left(\hat{b}\right)$, which in turn creates the incentive to optimally trade off the benefit against the cost of trade. There is a similar effect for the seller who is rewarded with $B^*\left(\hat{c}\right)$. This result also provides another perspective on the Myerson-Satterthwaite theorem. If an interim incentive-compatible allocation exists, then the interim payoffs satisfy for all b and c:

$$U^{*B}(b,\bar{p}) = B^*(b) - \hat{B}^* - C^*(b) - \bar{p} \geq u^{0B}, \tag{8.52}$$

$$U^{*S}(c,\bar{p}) = B^*(c) + \bar{p} - \left(C^*(c) - \hat{C}^*\right) \geq u^{0S}, \tag{8.53}$$

where $\hat{B}^* = E\{B^*(b)\} = E\{B^*(c)\}$ is the *ex ante* expected benefit and $\hat{C}^* = E\{C^*(b)\} = E\{C^*(c)\}$ is the *ex ante* expected cost. Given that the expected surplus increases with the buyer's type and decreases with the seller's type, we have the following proposition:

Proposition 8.15 *Efficient trade can be implemented with an interim efficient allocation if and only if:*

$$S^*(b_L) + S^*(c_H) - (u^{0B} + u^{0S}) \geq S^*, \tag{8.54}$$

where $S^*(t)$ is the total surplus conditional upon knowing type t (equal to b or c), and S^* is the total ex ante *gain from trade under the efficient allocation.*

Proof. Since the gains from trade increase with the buyer's type, one has for all $b \in [b_L, b_H]$:

$$U^{*B}(b,\bar{p}) \geq U^{*B}(b_L,\bar{p}) \geq u^{0B}.$$

Similarly, since the gains from trade fall with the seller's type, then for all $c \in [c_L, c_H]$:

$$U^{*S}(c,\bar{p}) \geq U^{*S}(c_H,\bar{p}) \geq u^{0S}.$$

Thus, there is a $\bar{p}$ such that the participation constraints are satisfied for all types if and only if:

$$U^{*B}(b_L,\bar{p}) + U^{*S}(c_H,\bar{p}) \geq u^{0S} + u^{0B}.$$

Expressions (8.52)–(8.53) together imply (8.54). $\qquad\square$

This result allows for a generalization of the Myerson-Satterthwaite result on the impossibility of efficient trade. The key ingredient is the fact that, for the lowest buyer or highest seller type, no trade is common knowledge:

Corollary 8.16 *(Myerson and Satterthwaite 1983) Suppose that for the low-value buyer ($b = b_L$) or for the high-cost seller ($c = c_H$), it is not efficient to trade and $S^* > \max\{S^*(c_H), S^*(b_L)\}$; then, there is no interim incentive efficient and individually rational mechanism that implements the efficient allocation $q^*(b,c)$.*

Proof. If it is not efficient to trade at $b = b_L$, then $S^*(b_L) = u^{0B} + u^{0S}$. The fact that $S^* > S^*(c_H)$ implies $S^* - S^*(c_H) > 0 = S^*(b_L) - (u^{0B} + u^{0S})$, and hence condition (8.54) cannot hold. A similar argument applies when $S^*(c_H) = u^{0B} + u^{0S}$. $\qquad\square$

One can reinterpret this result in terms of common knowledge, as in Ausubel, Cramton, and Deneckere (2002). Suppose that it is not efficient to trade when $b = b_L$ but $S^* > \max\{S^*(c_H), S^*(b_L)\}$. This implies that, for some seller type c, trade may or may not be efficient. In particular, if $b = b_L$ then the buyer knows trade is not efficient but the seller does not. Thus, this condition is equivalent to supposing that whether trade is efficient is not common knowledge. In summary, a budget balancing and individually rational mechanism that implements the efficient allocation exists if and only if it is common knowledge for all types whether trade is efficient.

Subsidies

In general, one cannot expect parties to reach efficient agreements when there is two-sided asymmetric information and the conditions for corollary 8.16 are not satisfied. Is there a practical solution? An example of a pragmatic solution is to subsidize trade so that it is common knowledge that it is always efficient to trade. Suppose a third party is able to subsidize the buyer with a subsidy to be paid if and only if there is trade. If this amount is set as follows:

$$Subsidy = \max \left\{ \left(S^* + u^{0B} + u^{0S} \right) - \left(S^* \left(c_H \right) + S^* \left(b_L \right) \right), 0 \right\},$$

then condition (8.54) is satisfied.

Specifically, the following Groves mechanism implements the efficient allocation. First, set the transfer price so the seller always wishes to participate:

$$\bar{p} = u^{0S} - S^* \left(c_H \right) - \hat{C}^*.$$

Next, set the payment from the buyer to:

$$p^B \left(b, c \right) = C^* \left(b \right) + B^* \left(c \right) + \bar{p} - Subsidy.$$

This ensures that the buyer's participation constraint is satisfied when $b = b_L$.

Since $\min \left\{ S^* \left(c_H \right), S^* \left(b_L \right) \right\} \geq u^{0B} + u^{0S}$, it follows that the subsidy is bounded by the gain from trade:

$$S^* - \left(u^{0B} + u^{0S} \right) \geq Subsidy \geq 0,$$

with $Subsidy = S^* - \left(u^{0B} + u^{0S} \right)$ whenever it is not efficient for parties to trade when $c = c_H$ and $b = b_L$.

The literature on spatial economics (Moretti 2011) tends to view the use of subsidies as an income transfer that at best has a positive effect upon equity. A classic reason for the use of subsidies is to encourage local employment. When there is asymmetric information between parties, the Myerson-Satterthwaite theorem implies that subsidies to parties may improve resource allocation. However, given that the necessary subsidy may be as large as the potential gains from trade, the transaction costs associated with the transfer of public funds may result in costs that outweigh any potential benefit from better matching.

Conflict

Another manifestation of asymmetric information is conflict. Chapter 10 deals in some detail with a principal-agent model in which each party has a subjective evaluation of agent performance. This subjective evaluation is equivalent to each party's having private information regarding agent performance. If there is imperfect correlation in signals, then the provision of effort incentives necessarily entails conflict between parties. Chapter 10 provides a complete characterization of the optimal contract in that case.

Another way conflict is manifested in practice is via bargaining delay and strikes. When a firm and union meet, they may not have common knowledge regarding the value of the work, or the extent to which the union is willing to fight for a wage increase. Cramton (1985) and Cramton (1992) show that delay in a bargaining game can be used as a screening mechanism for unobserved types. He builds on this work to develop the implications for strike behavior in Cramton and Tracy (1992).

An alternative way to think about conflict, which is also explored in chapter 10, is to suppose that one of the parties is able to impose costs upon the other. For example, Mas (2006) shows that police unions that are not satisfied with the outcome of bargaining may reduce effort, resulting in an increase in crime. Similarly, Mas (2008) shows that the quality of machines produced during difficult labor negotiations is lower than when there is contract in force. These are actual examples of one party punishing another when they feel they have been unfairly treated.

A shorthand way to model this is to suppose that the seller (union) can impose a cost $K \geq 0$ at the interim stage should the buyer (firm) attempt to renege on an agreement, where the types b and c are private information to the firm and union. The level of trade $q(\omega)$ can represent the level of employment, while $p(\omega)$ is the transfer from the firm to the union. Suppose that it is efficient to trade in all states at level $q^*(\omega)$, and u^{0B} and u^{0S} are the outside options for the firm and union that satisfy:

$$S^* > u^{0B} + u^{0S} > S^* - M\left(q^*(\omega)\right).$$

Proposition 8.14 implies that any incentive-compatible transfer function that implements $q^*(\omega)$ must be a Groves mechanism given by (8.51). Thus set $p(b,c) = B^*(c) + C^*(b)$. This ensures both parties are telling the truth. Using (8.52)–(8.53), define $\bar{p}^B$ and $\bar{p}^S$ by

$$U^{*B}\left(b_L, \bar{p}^B\right) = u^{0B},$$

$$U^{*S}\left(c_H, \bar{p}^S\right) = u^{0S}.$$

Since $u^{0B} + u^{0S} > S^* - M(q^*(\omega))$, then it follows that $\bar{p}^S > \bar{p}^B$, and the price paid by the firm is less than the price paid by the union.

There are two possibilities. One is for the union to have a credible strike threat unless $\bar{p}^S = \bar{p}^B$. This can be enforced with a threat of size $K = \bar{p}^S - \bar{p}^B > 0$. In this case, the union is in effect enforcing a specific performance contract. Another possibility is that union workers extract rents from the firm in terms of shirking, or on-the-job theft, that impose a cost K. In that case, the union is paid a lower wage but the firm suffers from more organizational inefficiency. In practice, unions are often associated with both types of behavior. The model illustrates that such behaviors may have their roots in asymmetric information between the firm and the union.

8.5 Power and Asymmetric Information: Monopoly and Monopsony

As shown in chapter 6, contracts can play a role in controlling the *ex post* bargaining power of parties. For example, in the absence of a contract, if a buyer has all the *ex post* bargaining power, the seller's incentive to make relationship-specific investments is reduced. Bargaining power also has significant allocative effects in the presence of asymmetric information. In particular, if markets are complete, in principle parties should be able to bargain to an efficient allocation, regardless of the ex ante allocation of bargaining power.[6] This section shows that in the presence of asymmetric information the allocation of power ex post can affect the efficiency of exchange.

When parties can negotiate ex ante, and the contractual instrument of specific performance is available, then under the appropriate conditions one can use a Groves mechanism to achieve efficient trade. However, the classic monopoly and monopsony problems assume trade occurs at the interim stage and that trade is voluntary. In the case of monopoly, the buyer is free not to purchase from the seller, who does not know the buyer's private valuation. Similarly, in the case of monopsony, workers are free to reject wage offers by the firm that depend on observed outside options.

This section follows Mussa and Rosen (1978), who work out the optimal contract when the seller's costs are known but buyers are characterized by a continuum of unobserved valuations for the good. The results from the previous section are used to characterize the optimal monopoly contract. The properties of the optimal nonlinear pricing are found by working out the optimal contract with a discrete number of quantities, as is typically observed in a store where firms sell a few different sizes (such as small, medium, and large) at different per unit prices.

The final subsection applies these ideas to the problem of monopsony. In that section it is shown that the technology introduced by Uber and Lyft more effectively screens for driver types and hence they are able to provide ride services at a lower cost than a traditional taxi.

8.5.1   Informed Seller and Efficient Monopoly

Consider the case in which the seller's cost parameter is known and given by $\bar{c}$, but the buyer's valuation is private information. Let $C(q)$ denote the seller's cost function given $\bar{c}$. As before, suppose that payoffs satisfy the standard conditions. Let $b_L = 0$, $u^{0B} = 0$, $u^{0S} > 0$, and suppose that for low buyer types it is not efficient to trade but for high types trade is efficient. Let $\underline{b}$ denote the type in a direct mechanism at which the seller agrees to sell to the buyer and suppose that sales are positive for $b > \underline{b}$. The surplus for type b is given by:

$$S(q, b) = B(q, b) - C(q).$$

The efficient allocation is given by $\{q^*(b), \underline{b}^*\}$ and characterized by:

$$B_q(q^*(b), b) = C_q(q^*(b)), b \in [\underline{b}^*, b_H]. \tag{8.55}$$

The lowest type, $\underline{b}^*$, at which trade is efficient is defined by:

$$B(q^*(\underline{b}^*), \underline{b}^*) - C(q^*(\underline{b}^*)) = u^{0S}.$$

The *ex ante* total gain from trade is thus:

$$S^* = \int_{\underline{b}^*}^{b_H} S(q^*(b), b) f(b) \, db + F(\underline{b}^*) \times u^{0S}. \tag{8.56}$$

Under these assumptions, whether parties trade depends on the buyer's private information b.

Consider two cases. In the first case, the buyer has all the bargaining power and offers to the seller a take-it-or-leave it contract, $\{p, q\}$, that may vary with the buyer's information. In this case, the first best can be achieved. Next, reverse the tables and suppose that the seller makes an offer to the buyer. Given that the seller does not know the buyer's type, she increases her returns by allowing the quantity traded to vary with the buyer's report of his type, $\hat{b}$. By the revelation principle one can suppose that the seller offers a type-dependent contract of the form $\left\{q\left(\hat{b}\right), p\left(\hat{b}\right)\right\}$, with the property that the buyer has an incentive to truthfully reveal his private information.

In this case, the seller has an incentive to reduce output relative to the first best. When buyer types are sufficiently evenly distributed on $[0, b_H]$, quantity and price increase monotonically with buyer type. However, when there are groups of different types, for example if the distribution of types is bimodal, then it is optimal for the seller to bunch the contracts and offer the same quantity to a set of types. We show how to construct a step function that approximates the optimal selling rule. This explicitly illustrates the trade-off the seller faces between extracting rents from a type and providing the optimal quantity that generates the greatest surplus.

The next two subsections present the details for the derivation of the optimal contract for each case—buyer power and seller power.

Buyer power case

Suppose the buyer observes his valuation $b \geq 0$, and then makes a take-it-or-leave-it offer $\{q, p\}$ to the seller, who can accept or reject. As we know from chapter 5, this game has a unique equilibrium at which the seller accepts the offer if and only if:

$$p - C(q) \geq u^{0S} = 0. \tag{8.57}$$

Hence the equilibrium offer, $\vec{x}^{B-\textit{offer}}(b)$, satisfies:

$$\vec{x}^{B-\textit{offer}}(b) \in \arg\max_{\{q,p\}} \{B(q, b) - p\}$$

subject to (8.57).

It is immediate that the solution to this problem has the buyer offering a contract that results in efficient trade and gives all the rents to the buyer:

$$\vec{x}^{B-\textit{offer}}(b) = \begin{cases} \{q^*(b), p^*(b) = C(q^*(b))\}, & \text{if } b \geq \underline{b}^*, \\ \vec{0}, & \text{if } b < \underline{b}^*. \end{cases}$$

Therefore, when the buyer has all the bargaining power, and the seller's costs are known, parties can reach an efficient level of trade. Notice that, because the allocation is *ex post* efficient, there are no gains to renegotiation after the seller learns the buyer's type (as given by the quantity demanded, $q^*(b)$).

Seller power case

Let us turn the tables and suppose that the seller now has all the bargaining power and makes a take-it-or-leave-it offer to the buyer. Here we have two subcases that depend on when parties negotiate terms and the contractual instruments that are available. In the first case it is assumed that the seller can manipulate the ex post power of the buyer during the renegotiation stage. The second case supposes that the seller sets terms after the buyer has observed his type and is restricted to setting price as a function of the buyer's demand.

Contractible power case   Suppose that negotiation occurs *before* the buyer learns his type and there are no liquidity constraints. In this case, the seller can offer to the buyer the mechanism $\vec{x}^{B-offer}$ at a price equal to the expected surplus S^* given by (8.56). In other words, ex ante the seller agrees to cede to the buyer all the bargaining power at the interim stage. Because the buyer is risk neutral and this mechanism is ex post efficient, then the buyer is willing to accept it at any price $p \leq S^*$. As long as the price is paid before the buyer learns his type, the individual rationality constraints for both parties are satisfied ex ante and ex post.

The form construction contracts sold by the American Institute of Architects (AIA) are examples of contracts that manipulate bargaining power in this way.[7] Typically, the builder (the person who is paying for the project) begins with a set of plans for a project, then asks contractors to bid for construction rights. The bids reveal the low-cost contractor and bind the contractor to a specific contract renegotiation procedure.

After construction begins new information is often revealed, such as problems with the site or events that lead the builder to desire a change to the plans. The AIA contracts have specific rules dealing with each of these contingencies. First, the contractor has decision rights over how to complete the project. This is efficient under the sensible hypothesis that she knows her costs and how best to proceed. However, the builder is the final consumer of the project, and his preferences determine the ultimate value of the project. Consequently, the AIA contracts give the builder the unilateral right to change the plans and design of the building, consistent with the builder's having private information regarding the value of the project. Such changes may lead to an increase in costs. To deal with this problem, the AIA contracts require parties to maintain high-quality accounting records to reduce asymmetric information regarding the cost of any changes to the plans ex post. This data is used to assess the cost of any changes ordered by the builder and makes the builder fully liable for these costs. This in turn leads to efficient ex post changes to the project.

Thus, the AIA contracts are an example of a contractual instrument that is consistent with the theory of trade under asymmetric information. Power is allocated ex post to the informed party, which is combined with recording requirements that help ensure that asymmetric information is on one side only.

Monopoly pricing: Power is noncontractible   In many cases, contracts are agreed *after* the buyer learns his valuation. For example, the standard monopoly problem is one in which the seller chooses a price schedule and then the buyer selects the quantity and price based upon his private valuation of the good sold. In this case, the mechanism that has the buyer pay S^* no longer works because that is the average gain from trade. There are many types for which the gain from trade is less than S^*, and some parties will refuse to participate after they have learned their valuation.

The optimal mechanism for the seller in such cases is found using the revelation principle. The seller offers a mechanism of the form $\kappa = \{\underline{b}, p(b), q(b)\}$, which the buyer can accept or reject. This mechanism is implemented as follows. Buyers with types $b \in [0, \underline{b})$ choose not to buy the good. Second, buyers $b \in [\underline{b}, b_H]$ purchase $q(b)$ units at price $p(b)$. In addition to satisfying the buyer's participation constraint, it must also be the case that the buyer truthfully reports his type. A buyer of type b who reports $\hat{b}$ under mechanism κ has a payoff:

$$U^B\left(b, \hat{b}, \kappa\right) = \begin{cases} B\left(q\left(\hat{b}\right), b\right) - p\left(\hat{b}\right), & \hat{b} \geq \underline{b}, \\ 0, & \hat{b} < \underline{b}. \end{cases} \tag{8.58}$$

Let K denote the set of possible mechanisms. Because the seller has all the power, she chooses to offer a mechanism $\kappa^M \in K$ to the buyer that maximizes her payoff subject to the buyer's participation constraint (8.59) and truth-telling constraint (8.61):

$$U^{S-offer} = \max_{\kappa \in K} \int_{\underline{b}}^{b_H} (p(b) - C(q(b))) f(b) \, db + F\left(\underline{b}\right) \times u^{0S}, \tag{8.59}$$

subject to :

$$U^B(b, b, \kappa) \geq 0, \forall b \in [0, b_H], \tag{8.60}$$

$$U^B(b, b, \kappa) \geq U^B\left(b, \hat{b}, \kappa\right), \forall b, \hat{b} \in [0, b_H]. \tag{8.61}$$

Under the standard assumptions, the analysis in the previous section implies that the buyer's payoff is continuously increasing with his type. Next, observe that type $\underline{b}$ must be indifferent between trade and no trade; otherwise a type b close to but not equal to $\underline{b}$ would choose to report $\underline{b}$. A similar argument also implies that quantity is nondecreasing in type and the incentive-compatibility constraint implies (8.29). Thus, we can apply (8.30)–(8.31) with $u_L^B = 0$ and use the fact that the seller's cost is known to determine price as a function of the quantity function:

$$p(b) = B(q(b), b) - \int_{\underline{b}}^{b} B_b\left(q\left(b'\right), b'\right) db'. \tag{8.62}$$

This allows us to rewrite the seller's problem (8.59) in terms of the quantity schedule $q(b)$ and $\underline{b}$:

$$U^{S-offer} = \max_{\{q(b), \underline{b}\}} \int_{\underline{b}}^{b_H} \left(S(q(b), b) - \int_{\underline{b}}^{b} B_b\left(q\left(b'\right), b'\right) db'\right) f(b) \, db + u^{0S} F\left(\underline{b}\right). \tag{8.63}$$

Mirrlees (1971) observes that we can further simplify (8.63) via integration by parts using $d(1 - F(b))/db = -f(b)$, to imply:

$$\left[\int_{\underline{b}}^{b} B_b\left(q\left(b'\right), b'\right) db' (1 - F(b))\right]_{\underline{b}}^{b_H} = -\int_{\underline{b}}^{b_H} \int_{\underline{b}}^{b} B_b\left(q\left(b'\right), b'\right) db' f(b) \, db$$

$$+ \int_{\underline{b}}^{b_H} B_b(q(b), b)(1 - F(b)) \, db.$$

The first term is zero ($F(b_H) = 1$ and $\int_{\underline{b}}^b db = 0$). Hence, substituting this back into (8.63) gives us:

$$U^{S-\text{offer}} = \max_{\{q(b), \underline{b}\}} \int_{\underline{b}}^{b_H} J(q(b), b) f(b) \, db \tag{8.64}$$

$$+ u^{0S} F(\underline{b}), \tag{8.65}$$

where

$$J(q, b) = S(q, b) - \frac{1 - F(b)}{f(b)} B_b(q, b) \tag{8.66}$$

is called the *virtual surplus*. This result is helpful because one can find the optimal quantity by taking the pointwise maximum of $J(q, b)$. However, a necessary condition for a nonlinear price, $q(b)$, to be incentive compatible is that it increases with type. To ensure this, one can impose the following condition:

Definition 8.17 *The monopoly problem is* monotone *if $J_{qq} < 0$ and $J_{bq} > 0$.*

This assumption ensures that there is a unique and increasing nonlinear price function, $q^M(b)$, that maximizes (8.64), and it is characterized by the first-order condition:

$$J_q(q^M(b), b) = 0. \tag{8.67}$$

Given that it maximizes pointwise the integrand of (8.64), the nonlinear supply function also maximizes (8.63). Since $S_q > 0$ for $b < b_H$, it follows that the monopoly output is less than the efficient output ($q^M(b) < q^*(b)$), except for $b = b_H$, where the efficient output is supplied. The number of types served is also found by differentiating (8.64) with respect to $\underline{b}$ to get:

$$J(q^M(\underline{b}^M), \underline{b}^M) = u^{0S}. \tag{8.68}$$

We are assured of a solution as there is no distortion in the quantity supplied at $b = b_H$, and it is efficient to trade in some states. At the efficient solution, $S(q^*(\underline{b}^*), \underline{b}^*) = u^{0S}$ and (8.68) implies that $\underline{b}^M > \underline{b}^*$. Thus, monopoly pricing results in some lower types not being served, even though their valuation of the good is greater than the cost.

Finally, from (8.62), we get the optimal price mechanism for $b \in [\underline{b}^M, b_H]$:

$$p^M(b) = B(q^M(b), b) - \int_{\underline{b}^M}^b B_b(q^M(b'), b') \, db'.$$

These observations are summarized in the following proposition:

Proposition 8.18 *Consider a buyer-seller exchange with standard preferences where the seller's type is known, the buyer's type is not known, and the buyer's outside option is independent of his type. If terms of trade are determined after the buyer learns his type then:*

1. If the buyer has all the bargaining power, the result is efficient trade with the buyer receiving all the gains from trade.

2. *If the seller has all the bargaining power and the problem is monotone, then she maximizes her profits by offering the buyer a nonlinear price schedule $P(q)$, for $q \in \left[q^M \left(\underline{b}^M \right), q^* (b_H) \right]$ defined by:*

$$P(q) = p^M \left((q^M)^{-1} (q) \right), \tag{8.69}$$

where $q^M (\cdot)$ satisfies (8.67), $\underline{b}^M$ satisfies (8.68), and price is given by:

$$p^M (b) = B \left(q^M (b), b \right) - \int_{\underline{b}^M}^{b} B_b \left(q^M (b'), b' \right) db'.$$

This proposition illustrates an application of the revelation principle to the problem of nonlinear pricing. The revelation principle is beneficial because it allows one to set up the monopoly problem as a constrained optimization problem with a closed-form solution.

In order to obtain a closed form solution, it is assumed that the monopoly problem is monotone, but as Rochet and Chone (1998) observe, this does not hold generically. For example, suppose $C(q) = q^2/2$, $b_H = 1$, $B(q, b) = q \times b$ and $u^{0S} = 0$. In this case, the optimal quantity is:

$$q^* (b) = b,$$

and the virtual surplus is given by:

$$J(q, b) = \left(q \times b - q^2/2 \right) - \frac{(1 - F(b))}{f(b)} q.$$

If the distribution of buyer types is uniform, then $f(b) = 1$ and $F(b) = b$. In this case, the optimal selling schedule is

$$q^{M1}(b) = \begin{cases} 0, & b \in [0, \frac{1}{2}), \\ 2b - 1, & b \in [1/2, 1]. \end{cases}$$

Thus, the consumers with types $b < 1/2$ are not served, and type $b = 1$ receives the efficient quantity.

However, suppose that the distribution of types is bimodal, with most consumers located at the lower-end distribution function:

$$f^2 (b) = \begin{cases} 3, & b \in [0, 1/4], \\ 0, & b \in (1/4, 3/4), \\ 1, & b \in [3/4, 1]. \end{cases}$$

One can suppose that $f^2 (b) \sim \epsilon$ for $b \in (1/2, 3/4)$ to ensure the virtual surplus is defined. One need only observe that we require $q \geq 0$ and hence, for this distribution function, we have:

$$q^{M2}\,(b) = \begin{cases} 0, & b \in [0, 1/6), \\ 2b - 1/3, & b \in [1/6, 1/4], \\ 0, & b \in (1/4, 3/4), \\ 2b - 1, & b \in [3/4, 1]. \end{cases}$$

The fact that the distribution of types is bimodal results in q^{M2} that is not monotonic. This is due to the large number of low-value buyers that the seller would like to serve. However, when the number of buyers is very low (or zero) in the region $(1/4, 3/4)$, the seller would prefer to set quantity equal to zero and then start selling again for types $b \geq 3/4$.

However, incentive compatibility requires the quantity schedule to be monotonic. The ϵ types in the interval $(1/4, 3/4)$ have an incentive to report a type at which they trade a positive amount of the good. Thus, the optimal *incentive-compatible* price scheme takes the form:

$$q^{M2*}\,(b) = \begin{cases} 0, & b \in [0, 1/6), \\ 2b - 1/3, & b \in [1/6, 1/4], \\ 1/6, & b \in (1/4, 3/4), \\ 2b - 1, & b \in [3/4, 1]. \end{cases}$$

Here for $b \in (1/4, 3/4)$ the seller offers the quantity $1/6$ at the price $p\,(1/4)$. Neither the higher or lower types who are served under $q^{M2}\,(b)$ would choose this allocation (except for $b = 1/4$), and hence this allocation is incentive compatible and optimal.

Figure 8.2 illustrates this. The optimal quantity is the diagonal line $(q = b)$. The bimodal density $f^2\,(b)$ is illustrated at $1/4$ scale. The optimal monopoly quantity is illustrated by $q^{M2}\,(b)$. The dashed line is the quantity that is created by the incentive constraint that requires the quantity traded to be nondecreasing in type.

Both Mussa and Rosen (1978) and Maskin and Riley (1984) discuss the problem of deriving the optimal nonlinear price when the optimal quantity maximizing the virtual surplus is not monotonic. Rochet and Chone (1998) provide a general existence result when buyer types are multidimensional. Toikka (2011) shows that it is possible to define the virtual surplus via a convexification procedure that allows one to compute the optimal selling mechanism via a pointwise maximization of a modified/virtual surplus function.

In practice, firms do not know the true distribution of buyer types and typically use a finite number of standardized quantities. For example, Starbucks sells coffee, at different prices per milliliter, in short, tall, grande, and venti cup sizes. Similarly, laundry or dishwasher detergent comes in a limited number of sizes. The next section discusses the problem of choosing the optimal mechanism for any buyer distribution when the seller is restricted to n possible quantities and groups of buyer types. In addition to providing additional insight into the continuous problem, the section provides a way to explicitly compute the optimal selling strategy using standard computational algorithms. By letting the number of groups increase, one can approximate the optimal strategy as closely as one wishes.[8]

Optimal bundling

Suppose that, due to transactions costs, there is a fixed cost to providing the consumer with different quantities. For example, the good must be shipped in containers of predetermined sizes (say small, medium, and large). This restricts the seller to choosing a finite number

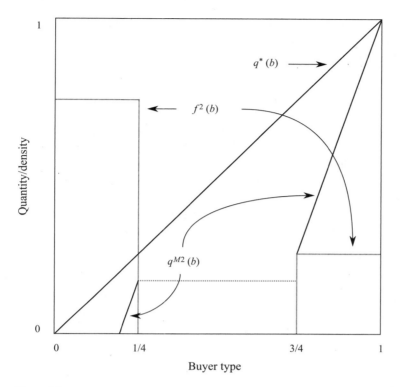

Figure 8.2
Optimal nonlinear price.

of quantities and prices for each bundle of goods. By the revelation principle, the problem is equivalent to partitioning the set of types into n groups, given by $\vec{b} = \{b_0, b_1, \ldots, b_n\}$, where $b_0 = b_L, b_n = b_H$ and $b_{i+1} \geq b_i$. Let the interval $I_i = [b_i, b_{i+1})$ denote group i who will be offered a quantity q_i at price p_i.[9] Suppose $b_L = 0$ and that $u^{0S} > 0$ and hence group 0, $b \in [0, b_1)$ is assigned $q_0 = p_0 = 0$.

Let $\kappa = \left\{ \vec{b}, \vec{q}, \vec{p} \right\} \in K = \Re^{3n}$ denote the set of possible mechanisms. Under this mechanism, the only information required is a buyer's group membership. Define the function $i(b) = i$, where $b \in I_i$. Hence, the payoff for a buyer of type b who reports $\hat{b}$ is given by:

$$U^B \left(b, \hat{b}, \kappa \right) = B \left(q_{i(\hat{b})}, b \right) - p_{i(\hat{b})}. \tag{8.70}$$

In order for mechanism κ to satisfy the truth-telling constraints, it must be the case that $U^B(b, b, \kappa) \geq U^B \left(b, \hat{b}, \kappa \right)$, $\forall b, \hat{b} \in [0, b_H]$. Given that the allocation does not change within a group, one has the following result:

Lemma 8.19 *The mechanism κ satisfies the truth-telling constraint if and only if:*

$$p_i - p_{i-1} = B(q_i, b_i) - B(q_{i-1}, b_i), i = 1, \ldots, n-1, \tag{8.71}$$

where $p_0 = q_0 = 0$, and $q_i \geq q_{i-1}$.

Proof. Suppose that the cutoffs b_i are distinct. If they are not, then, without loss of generality, one can drop the empty groups.

Suppose (8.71) holds and $q_i \geq q_{i-1}$. The buyer's returns satisfy $B_{qb} > 0$, and hence for $j \geq i$ and for b such at $i(b) = j$ then:

$$B(q_j, b) - B(q_i, b) \geq 0 \geq p_{i-1} - p_j.$$

Therefore, type b would not gain by reporting $\hat{b} < b$. A similar argument applies for $j \leq i$.

Conversely, suppose the mechanism satisfies the truth-telling constraints. Observe that for $b_i, i = 1, \ldots, n-1$, condition (8.71) must hold. If $p_{i-1} - p_i > B(q_{i-1}, b_i) - B(q_i, b_i)$, then types b just below b_i would choose q_i. If the inequality is reversed, then types slightly higher than b_i would choose group $i-1$.

Given $p_{i-1} - p_i = B(q_{i-1}, b_i) - B(q_i, b_i)$, notice that if $q_i < q_{i-1}$ then, since $B_{qb} > 0$, types slightly larger than b_i would choose q_{i-1}. Thus, it must be the case that $q_i \geq q_{i-1}$.   □

Given this result, the seller's problem is given by:

$$U^S(n) = \max_{\kappa \in K} \sum_{i=1}^{n-1} (p_i - C(q_i))(F(b_{i+1}) - F(b_i)) + u^{0S} F(b_1) \tag{8.72}$$

subject to for $i = 1, \ldots, n-1$:

$$p_i - p_{i-1} + B(q_{i-1}, b_i) - B(q_i, b_i) = 0,$$

$$q_i - q_{i-1} \geq 0,$$

$$b_H \geq b_i \geq b_{i-1} \geq 0. \tag{8.73}$$

The payoff is the number of buyers in interval $[b_i, b_{i+1})$, given by $(F(b_{i+1}) - F(b_i))$ times the profit over that interval $(p_i - C(q_i))$. For group $i = 0$, there are no sales and the seller gets her outside option u^{0S} times the number of buyers who are not served, $F(b_1)$. The objective function and constraints are continuous and, without loss of generality, mechanism choice can be restricted to a compact subset $\bar{K} \subset K$ of the feasible mechanisms. Thus, a solution always exists. Let $\kappa^n = \{q^n(b), p^n(b)\}$ denote a solution when the group size is n, where:

$$q^n(b) = q^*_{i(b)},$$

$$p^n(b) = p^*_{i(b)}.$$

Proposition 8.20 *For the standard payoffs and for each $n \geq 1$ there exists a solution $\kappa^{*n} = \left\{\vec{b}^{*n}, \vec{q}^{*n}, \vec{p}^{*n}\right\}$ to program (8.72). Moreover, if $U^S(n)$ is the solution where there are n groups, then $U^S(n)$ is increasing in n and $\lim_{n \to \infty} U^S(n) = U^{*S}$ is the optimal solution for the seller with quantity and price strategies given by $\lim_{n \to \infty} q^n(n) = q^{*M}(b)$ and $\lim_{n \to \infty} p^n(n) = p^{*M}(b)$.*

Proof. For each n, observe that the constraints are feasible—the seller is free to offer a single quantity at a fixed price, which automatically satisfies the truth-telling constraints.

Next, given that the problem with n groups includes $n' < n$ groups as a special case, then $U^S(n) \geq U^S(n')$, and $U^S(n)$ is a sequence that is increasing in n and bounded from above and hence has a limit. Similarly, since $q^n(n)$ and $p^n(n)$ are monotonic functions that are bounded above and below, they can uniformly approximate continuous monotonic functions. $\square$

Next, it is shown that the optimal solution converges to the first-order conditions defined by the virtual surplus. Because the payoff and constraints are differentiable, the optimal seller strategy can characterize the properties of the solution from the first-order conditions for the Lagrangian for program (8.72).

$$L = \sum_{i=1}^{n-1} (p_i - C(q_i))(F(b_{i+1}) - F(b_i)) + u^{0S}F(b_1)$$

$$+ \sum_{i=1}^{n-1} \lambda_i (B(q_i, b_i) - p_i - B(q_{i-1}, b_i) + p_{i-1}). \tag{8.74}$$

The constraint $q_i \geq q_{i-1}$ is not explicitly included but will be used when deriving the first-order conditions. Consider first prices and observe that $\partial L / \partial p_i = 0$ implies:

$$\lambda_i = \lambda_{i+1} + (F(b_{i+1}) - F(b_i)),$$

except for $i = n - 1$, where:

$$\lambda_{n-1} = 1 - F(b_{n-1}).$$

This can be solved recursively to get:

$$\lambda_i = 1 - F(b_i).$$

Thus, the shadow value of the i'th constraint is given by the number of buyers with type greater than or equal to b_i. The next step is to derive the first-order conditions for the b_i. For $i = 1$ the first-order condition $\partial L / \partial b_i = 0$ implies exactly the same first-order condition as in the continuous case:

$$J(q_1, b_1) = u^{0S}. \tag{8.75}$$

This implies that $q_1 < q^*(b_1)$, and hence $b_1 > \underline{b}^*$, leaving some types unserved who would be served under the efficient allocation. For $i > 1$, the equality constraints and $\partial L / \partial b_i = 0$ imply:

$$J(q_{i-1}, b_i) = J(q_i, b_i).$$

Given that quantity is nondecreasing in type, given $J_q(q^M(b), b) = 0, J_{qq}(q^M(b), b) < 0$, one has:

$$q_{i-1} < q^M(b_i) < q_i < q^M(b_{i+1}). \tag{8.76}$$

Next consider the first-order condition $\partial L / \partial q_i = 0$ for quantity q_i. This implies:

$$-C_q(q_i)(F(b_{i+1}) - F(b_i)) + (1 - F(b_i))B_q(q_i, b_i) - (1 - F(b_{i+1}))B_q(q_i, b_{i+1}) = 0. \tag{8.77}$$

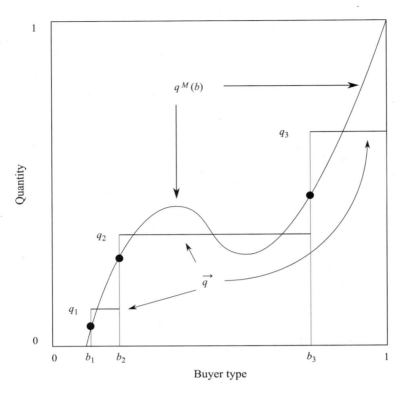

Figure 8.3
Optimal contracting with three groups of buyers.

One can take the derivatives of the second two terms with respect to b to get the following expression:

$$\int_{b_i}^{b_{i+1}} J_q\left(q_i, b\right) f\left(b\right) db = 0. \tag{8.78}$$

From condition (8.76), one has $J_q\left(q_i, b_{i+1}\right) > 0 = J_q\left(q_i, b\right) > J_q\left(q_i, b_i\right)$, and for some $b \in (b_i, b_{i+1})$. If $q^M\left(b\right)$ is an increasing function of $b \in (b_i, b_{i+1})$ then more surplus can be extracted by increasing n and reducing the size of the groups I_i. Suppose that $q^M\left(b\right)$ is the optimal solution that is increasing in b. Then as n gets large one has: $b_i \to b_{i+1}$, and $q_i \to q^M\left(b_i\right)$.

An example when $q^M\left(b\right)$ is not monotonic is illustrated in figure 8.3. Beginning with the first group, one has $q_1 > q^M\left(b_1\right) > 0$, where $q^M\left(b_1\right)$ is represented by the large dot. For group 2 given by $[b_2, b_3)$, the quantity that maximizes the virtual surplus is nonlinear in b. In particular, since $q^M\left(b_3\right) > q_2 > q^M\left(b_2\right)$, then it is not possible to have either b_3 or b_2 located between the local maximum and local minimum in the figure. Finally, q_3 maximizes the virtual surplus on the interval $[b_3, 1]$.

8.5.2 Monopsony and Uber Economics

The classic monopsony model is one in which the buyer/firm has market power relative to many sellers/workers. For example, consider a monopsonistic firm facing a supply of workers, represented by a labor supply curve, $H^S(w)$, where w is the wage offered by the firm. Suppose that H^S is upward sloping and differentiable; then the firm's profit as a function of the wage w offered to workers is given by:

$$U^B(w) = Y\left(H^S(w)\right) - H^S(w)\,w,$$

where $Y(H)$ is the revenue from H hours of labor. The monopsonistic firm maximizes profits with a wage w^M that satisfies:

$$MR = w^M\left(1 + \frac{1}{\epsilon^S}\right),$$

where $\epsilon^S > 0$ is the elasticity of labor supply at wage w^M and marginal revenue is given by $MR = Y'\left(H^S\left(w^M\right)\right)$.[10] Thus, the marginal return of an hour is greater than the market wage, and we have $H^M < H^*$, where H^* is the efficient labor supply ($Y'(H^*(w^*)) = w^*$).

In this classical formulation of the monopsony problem, as described by Ashenfelter, Farber, and Ransom (2010), the model is in terms of the number of workers who are willing to work rather than the number of hours. Ashenfelter, Farber, and Ransom (2010) argue that such a model is controversial because it supposes there is an unlimited supply of workers at the going wage and an upward-sloping labor supply curve so, one needs some sort of market imperfection to explain observed wages. For example, Currie, Farsi, and MacLeod (2005) show that when contracts are incomplete, firms may use work conditions to exert monopsony power. They find that hospitals are able to use their increased market power to increase workloads for nurses without lowering wages.

These results teach us that understanding the effect of power in the labor market requires an explicit model of market imperfections. The rest of this chapter is devoted to using the model of trade with asymmetric information to understand the recent rise in ride sharing programs such as Lyft and Uber. These programs have been criticized for exerting monopsony power over drivers and reducing work for traditional taxis. The goal is not to completely analyze this case but to illustrate how the buyer-seller model with asymmetric information can be applied to a current policy issue and can explain some features of this market.

Next, this model is extended to compare the consequences of a standard taxi market with a market dominated by an Uber or Lyft ride sharing technology. The key ingredient is modeling the unobserved variation in a driver's labor supply curve. The purpose of the example is to illustrate how a ride sharing technology can more effectively utilize the variation in labor supply across drivers.

Labor supply

Let one unit of time correspond to a twelve-hour shift. This is the system New York City taxis use. Yellow cabs are leased on a twelve-hour basis to individual drivers. Once a driver has a car, he may work as long as he wishes up to the twelve-hour limit. For simplicity, it is assumed that a driver cannot physically work longer than one shift; hence each driver supplies $h \in [0, 1]$ hours.[11]

As the number of drivers increases, this increases total supply to the market, which in turn reduces the earnings of drivers via reduced rides per hour. Even though the price per ride might be fixed, the time between fares can vary depending upon total supply of drivers. Suppose that the total hours supplied during a period is H. If each driver works the full shift, then H equals the number of drivers.

In the taxi business, the total revenue earned depends upon the number of drivers supplying services. Let w be the "wage" or average income per shift. Total revenue is given by:

$$R(w) = H^D(w) \, w,$$

where $H^D(w)$ is a differentiable downward-sloping demand curve for labor given the wage $w \geq 0$.

Suppose the characteristics of a driver are given by $c \in [c_L, c_H]$, where $c \sim f(c), f(c) > 0$ is density function, and $F(c)$ is the corresponding cumulative density function. A driver of type c has a payoff of:

$$U^S = wh - C(h, c), \tag{8.79}$$

with the driver's alternative normalized to zero. It is assumed that $\forall c \in [c_L, c_H]$ costs satisfy:

$$C(0, c) = C_h(0, c) = 0, \tag{8.80}$$

$$C_h(h, c), C_{hh}(h, c), C_{hc}(h, c) > 0, h \in (0, 1), \tag{8.81}$$

$$\lim_{h \to 1} C(h, c) = \infty. \tag{8.82}$$

The first assumption ensures that at zero hours the driver faces no costs. Setting $C_h(0, c) = 0$ implies that all potential drivers would like to supply some hours at any positive wage. This simplifies the analysis and saves having to keep track of the marginal driver who enters the market, and it can be relaxed without changing the main results. The second set of conditions ensures that for each $c \in [c_L, c_H]$ there is a well-defined amount of labor supplied by the driver, $h(w, c)$, satisfying:

$$C_h(h(w, c), c) = w, \tag{8.83}$$

with the properties:

$$h_w > 0, h_c < 0.$$

Consequently, hours supplied increase with wage but fall with driver type. Moreover, these assumptions imply that $C_c(h, c) > 0$ for $h > 0$ and, at the optimal labor supply for $w > 0$, one has:

$$dU^S(h(w, c), c)/dc < 0. \tag{8.84}$$

Condition (8.82) is the requirement that drivers face a physical limit and cannot work more than one unit of time (a twelve-hour shift).

A taxi monopsony

Consider first a taxi monopsony in which the taxi company supplies the taxis and charges a fixed rental fee R for each shift. Let $\bar{k} > 0$ be the cost per shift for a taxi cab. If N is the number of drivers, then the payoff to the company is given by:

$$U^B = (R - \bar{k}) N.$$

Determining the number of drivers who enter given the rental rate R requires determining the labor supply curve as a function of the rental rate, R, and the market wage, w. From this, one can determine the market equilibrium wage and the number of drivers who enter given the rental rate.

Given a wage w, the payoff of the driver before paying the rental charge is given by:

$$U^S (w, c) = wh (w, c) - C (h (w, c), c).$$

Notice that the assumptions on costs and (8.84) imply:

$$\partial U^S / \partial w > 0, \partial U^S / \partial c < 0. \tag{8.85}$$

A driver is willing to enter the market if and only if $U^S (w, c) \geq R$.

Because their payoff is strictly decreasing in c, then from the revelation principle one can suppose that the taxi company chooses $\bar{c}$ so that all drivers with $c \leq \bar{c}$ are employed. This is incentive compatible if and only if $U^S (w, \bar{c}) = R$. If the company charged a higher rent, then type $\bar{c}$ would not enter. Similarly, if the company charged a lower rent, then types higher than $\bar{c}$ would choose to enter. This fixes the rent as a function of the wage and marginal type to be employed.

The next step is to determine the wage given $\bar{c}$. The labor supply given $\bar{c}$ is:

$$H^S (w, \bar{c}) = \int_{c_L}^{\bar{c}} h (w, c) f (c) dc.$$

Thus the market price as a function of the cutoff $\bar{c}$ is determined by the market-clearing condition:

$$H^D (w (\bar{c})) = H^S (w (\bar{c}), \bar{c}).$$

Notice that $\frac{dw(\bar{c})}{d\bar{c}} < 0.$[12] Putting this all together, the payoff of the taxi company as a function of the type $\bar{c}$ is:

$$U^B (\bar{c}) = \left(U^S (w (\bar{c}), \bar{c}) - \bar{k} \right) F (\bar{c}). \tag{8.86}$$

The self-selection constraint fixes $R = U^S (w (\bar{c}), \bar{c})$, and the number of drivers is given by the cumulative distribution function $F (\bar{c}) = \int_{c_L}^{\bar{c}} f (c) dc$.

In this setup, the surplus maximizing solution when rent is the only instrument is given by c^* defined by $U^S (w (c^*), c^*) = \bar{k}$. This provides the lowest fare and highest supply of services subject to the constraint that each driver earns nonnegative returns. The rent that a monopsonist would charge is characterized in the following proposition:

Proposition 8.21 *Suppose $U^S (w (c_L), c_L) > \bar{k} > U^S (w (c_H), c_H)$; then there is a driver type $c^M \in (c_L, c^*)$, where c^* defines the efficient cutoff type, such that the taxi company* *maximizes profits by charging a rent $R^M = U^S\left(w\left(c^M\right), c^M\right)$ per shift for a taxi. All drivers with type $c \in \left[c_L, c^M\right]$ work for the company and c^M satisfies:*

$$U^S\left(w\left(c^M\right), c^M\right) = \bar{k} - \frac{dU^S\left(w\left(c^M\right), c^M\right)}{dc^M} \frac{F\left(c^M\right)}{f\left(c^M\right)} > \bar{k}. \tag{8.87}$$

Proof. Observe that the standard assumptions on payoffs, combined with the fact that the labor demand curve is differentiable and downward sloping, ensure that $U^S\left(c\right) \equiv U^S\left(w\left(c\right), c\right)$ is differentiable and decreasing for $c \in [c_L, c_H]$. The intermediate value theorem ensures the existence of c^* such that $U^S\left(c^*\right) = \bar{k}$. This defines the efficient solution given that cars are rented for the full twelve-hour period. The choice of rent is the only instrument. Observe that $U^B\left(c_L\right) = 0$, $U_c^B\left(c_L\right) > 0$ and $U^B\left(c\right) \leq 0, c \in [c^*, c_H]$. Thus, by the continuity of $U^B\left(c\right)$, there exists a $c^M \in \left(c_L, c^*\right)$ solving $\max_{c \in [c_L, c_H]} U^B\left(c\right)$. Condition (8.87) follows from differentiating $U^B\left(c\right)$.   □

This proposition establishes the existence of an optimal rent for the taxi company at which employment is lower than the efficient level. The first-order condition (8.87) is necessary but, without further assumptions regarding the distribution function $f\left(c\right)$, it is not necessarily sufficient.

The proposition also illustrates that unobserved worker characteristics are at the heart of the monopsony problem. If the taxi company could write individualized, type-specific contracts with drivers, then the efficient allocation could be achieved. When renting taxis by shift, it is optimal to choose drivers who prefer to work long hours at the existing wage. They ensure that the taxis are more efficiently utilized each shift.

Uber

Uber introduces an innovation into this market—drivers are permitted to use their own cars. This means that when not driving for Uber, the driver can use her own car for private consumption. To highlight the effect this has upon selection, let us suppose that the cost per shift of a car is the same in both cases and thus the only difference is the payment technology. Given that we have normalized a shift to one unit, the capital cost for a driver who works an h'th of a shift is $h \times \bar{k}$. If the driver works a full shift then $h = 1$, and the capital cost is the same as the taxi company's cost. Thus, one can immediately see that one cost advantage of Uber is the more effective utilization of the cars used for transportation.

A second difference between Uber and a traditional taxi company is the way it charges for its service. Uber provides a mobile phone application that connects passengers looking for a ride with drivers willing to transport them. A fraction of the Uber fare is used to support the back-office costs of the application, as well as providing insurance and other services. Let us ignore these costs and suppose that Uber keeps the fixed fee f as profit. Under this system a driver of type c has a payoff:

$$U^S = \left(w - f - \bar{k}\right) h - C\left(h, c\right).$$

The driver chooses hours to maximize her payoff. The labor supply function is derived above and given by $h\left(\hat{w}, c\right)$, with $\hat{w} = w - f - \bar{k}$. It is assumed that labor supply is always positive as long as $\hat{w} > 0$, and thus, in contrast to the taxi case, in this market *all* drivers will choose to participate, with the amount of participation determined by a driver's type c.

Labor supply under Uber is given by:

$$H^S(w-f) = \int_{c_L}^{c_H} h\left(w-f-\bar{k},c\right)f(c)\,dc.$$

Notice that $H_w^S = -H_f^S > 0$ whenever $H^S > 0$. Given the fee f, the equilibrium wage as a function of the fee, $w(f)$ is the unique solution (when it exists) to:

$$H^D(w(f)) = H^S(w(f)-f). \tag{8.88}$$

Putting all this together, Uber's profit is given by:

$$U^B(f) = f \times H^D(w(f)). \tag{8.89}$$

The right-hand side is continuous, and we can establish an upper bound, f_H, for which profits are driven back to zero; therefore, the continuity of the payoff function ensures the existence of a fee, $f^U > 0$, that maximizes profits (8.89). From (8.88)–(8.89) one can derive the following characterization of the optimal fee:

Proposition 8.22 *Given conditions (8.80)–(8.82) on costs, for a monopsonistic Uber service, there is an optimal fee $f^U > 0$ that satisfies:*

$$f^U = w^U \left(\frac{1}{\epsilon^D} + \frac{1}{\epsilon^S}\right), \tag{8.90}$$

where $\epsilon^D, \epsilon^S > 0$ are the (absolute) wage elasticities of labor demand and supply respectively, and w^U is the equilibrium wage in the monopsonistic market.

Proof. Condition (8.80) implies that, at a positive wage, all drivers supply some labor time. Therefore, the monopsonist can make strictly positive profits with a small fee. This, combined with (8.82), ensures the existence of an optimal fee $f^U > 0$. From (8.88) we get:

$$\frac{dw(f)}{df} = \frac{\epsilon^S}{\epsilon^D + \epsilon^S} \in (0,1).$$

The first-order condition for f^U is:

$$f \times H_w^D(w(f)) \times \frac{dw(f)}{df} + H^D(w(f)) = 0.$$

Substituting the expression for dw/df and rearranging the expression implies (8.90). $\quad\square$

A necessary condition for an optimal fee is that $f^U < w - \bar{k}$, which in turn implies that the supply and demand elasticities must be greater than 1.

Discussion

The explosive growth of ride sharing companies such as Uber and Lyft has led to the question of why they have been so successful entering the market. The simple asymmetric information model provides some insight into this question. Notice that the optimal rental policy for the monopsonistic taxi company leaves no rent to the marginal worker with type $\bar{c}$. More generally, all drivers with types $c \geq \bar{c}$ do not enter and hence get zero in this market.

In contrast, in an Uber market, under assumption (8.80) *all* drivers provide some labor hours to the market.

Proposition 8.23 *Under the assumptions of propositions 8.21 and 8.22, there is a driver type $c^U < c^M$, such that all types $c > c^U$ are strictly better off in an Uber monopsony than in a taxi monopsony.*

This result follows immediately from two facts. First, drivers of type c^M get zero under a taxi monopsony, but positive payoffs under an Uber monopsony. Second, the monotonicity and continuity of payoffs in types, implies that there are types less than c^M that are strictly better off with Uber. We can let c^U be the infimum of such types.

These facts imply that if Uber were to enter a market with an existing taxi service, some taxi drivers would prefer to become Uber drivers because of the extra control over their hours. This provides another perspective on the point made above that efficiency is enhanced when an informed party is provided with control rights. The theoretical point is consistent with the results in Chen et al. (2017), who find that the welfare gains to these additional control rights are quite large. This observation is also consistent with the evidence in Angrist, Caldwell, and Hall (2017), who find that many drivers resist changing to lease contracts from fee-per-ride contracts.

Control over hours of work is important in other areas as well. Goldin and Katz (2011) document the importance of control over hours of work for women. Because women tend to be responsible for a greater share of childcare, it is costly for them to enter professions with inflexible hours. Goldin and Katz (2011) find that professional positions such as pharmacist, optometrist, and veterinarian that allow for more flexibility of hours have seen much more entry by women relative to professions such as law and business.

The evidence in Goldin and Katz (2011) provides a set of examples for which the allocation of control rights due to unobserved individual characteristics has significant implications for the observed allocation of resources. There is a growing theoretical literature that explores the use of control rights to efficiently manage exchange with asymmetric information. For example, see, Aghion and Tirole (1997) and Dessein (2002). Clean tests of these models are very difficult. A solution is to use field experiments. Bandiera et al. (2021) carried out an innovative experiment with procurement officers in Pakistan. They find that increasing autonomy can enhance performance without increasing costs.

8.6   Discussion

This chapter provides a brief introduction to the vast literature on trade with private information. The starting point of the theory is in explicitly thinking about how the benefits and costs of trade vary with information that is held by each party to an exchange. The revelation principle extends the ideas developed for agency models to the case of asymmetric information. The allocation problem can be viewed as a constrained optimization exercise in which the final allocation is a function of the private information, subject to the constraint that under the allocation rule parties have an incentive to be truthful. This turns out to be a powerful tool because it allows one to solve for the optimal terms of trade in the face of asymmetric information.

The main results from this approach can be summarized as follows:

1. If parties can agree on terms of trade before they observe their private information, then efficient trade is possible, and the optimal mechanism must have the feature that payments result in each party internalizing the other party's payoff—the buyer's cost must vary with the true cost of trade while the seller's payment must vary with the true benefit of trade for the buyer.

2. The previous result implies that the terms of trade ex post vary a great deal with the private information, so that in some cases even though trade is efficient ex ante, some types may be worse off under the efficient contract ex post than they would have been had they not entered into an agreement. This implies that if parties meet and trade *after* they have learned their private information there can be bargaining breakdowns—parties may choose not to trade, even though it is in their best interests to do so.

The Myerson-Satterthwaite theorem provides precise conditions under which conflict may occur. An implication of this result is that in some states of the world, even though parties are fully rational, they may not agree on what constitutes efficient exchange. The fact that asymmetric information can lead to a failure in trade was observed in Akerlof's (1970) seminal paper "The market for 'lemons' " (see exercise 7). Rothschild and Stiglitz (1976) observe that this can also arise in the competitive insurance market, while Greenwald (1986) applies these ideas to the labor market. Chiappori and Salanié (2000) provide a seminal empirical study on asymmetric information in insurance markets.

3. In contrast to the principal-agent model, the allocation of power matters when there is asymmetric information. When costs are known and the valuation of the buyer is his private information, the buyer having all the bargaining power results in a Pareto efficient allocation. This is not the case when the seller has all the power, as in a monopoly. In that case, rather than selling at a fixed price, the seller prefers to provide quantity discounts and to inefficiently exclude low-value buyers. The monopsony problem is similar, but with the tables turned. In that case, it is the seller/worker who has private information regarding her willingness to work. If the buyer has power then employment is lower than the efficient level. In the Uber example, increasing worker discretion and power by letting workers choose their hours can increase the welfare of workers who prefer to supply fewer hours.

The mechanism design approach illustrates how information costs alone can constrain the set of possible allocations. In practice, the parties are not free to set price or quantity as they wish, but face constraints regarding the set of feasible instruments. The taxi example illustrates how these ideas can also be used in situations in which transaction costs limit the set of feasible instruments. Armstrong (2016) provides a review of the literature on the monopoly pricing problem, including the problem of pricing when types are multidimensional. Recent work by Bergemann, Brooks, and Morris (2015) provides an elegant analysis of monopoly pricing when there is different information regarding different market segments. The insights of the Myerson-Satterthwaite theorem have also been widely used to study the problem of bargaining with asymmetric information (Ausubel, Cramton, and

Deneckere 2002; Abreu and Pearce 2007), including the issues of strikes and bargaining breakdowns (Kennan and Wilson 1993; Cramton and Tracy 1992).

A very active area of research combines the insights of agency theory with the problem of asymmetric information. Freixas, Guesnerie, and Tirole (1985) provide a useful model of the "ratchet effect." When there is uncertainty regarding the productivity of an agent, the agent may shade effort down in order to maintain a higher wage in the future. Gibbons (1987) shows that such uncertainty about job difficulty can lead to conflict and inefficient supply of effort. Kanemoto and MacLeod (1992) show that if the uncertainty is about worker ability rather than job difficulty, then under the appropriate conditions efficient contracting is possible. These results reinforce the theme of this book that the form of observed contractual instruments and their performance are sensitive to the details and timing of actions and information revelation in the exchange relationship.

These results have been extended and applied to many important issues. Lewis and Sappington (1989) provide some interesting results when the outside options of parties vary with their types. Laffont and Tirole (1993) provide a comprehensive application of these ideas to the problem of regulating public firms. Laffont and Martimort (2002) provide a review of the interplay between agency theory and problems of asymmetric information.

There is also an extensive literature that studies markets in which parties compete with contracts, bringing together the problems of competition, performance incentives, and information revelation. This literature requires extensions and modifications of the revelation principle. Bernheim and Whinston (1986) introduce the idea of a common agency in which principals offer competing contracts to the same agent (for example two manufacturers offering contracts to a single retailer). Laffont and Martimort (2000) extend these ideas to a mechanism design model with collusive agents. Bester and Strausz (2001) provide a new approach to Akerlof's lemon problem based on competing mechanisms. Martimort and Stole (2002) provide an extension of the revelation principle to the common agency problem. Attar, Mariotti, and Salanié (2011) and Calzolari and Denicolo (2013) discuss the implications of these ideas for exclusive-dealing contracts and competition policy. There is also a literature on competitive equilibria in markets with asymmetric information that builds on the seminal contributions of Roschild and Stigliz (1976) and Riley (1979). Recent contributions include Dubey and Geanakoplos (2002), Guerreiri, Shimer, and Wright (2018), and Azevedo and Gottlieb (2017).

Finally, Malcomson (2016) paper explores the effect of private information on relational contracts. However, before discussing these results, we need to review the theory of relational contracts, which is the subject of the next chapter.

8.7   Exercises

1. Suppose we introduce a third-party intermediary at the *ex ante* stage who has unlimited liability. Show that she can offer a contract to the buyer and seller that results in efficient trade and is *interim incentive efficient.*

2. Provide an example of an allocation that is *ex ante* incentive efficient, but is not *ex post* incentive efficient.

3. Derive equation (8.44). Work out the optimal fixed price and quantity contract with voluntary participation and discuss how the outside options affect the optimal quantity and the probability of trade when the probability of trade is less than 1.

4. Verify that the allocation given in (8.47)–(8.48) is indeed incentive compatible and interim individually rational.

5. Provide the details for proposition 8.18.

6. Consider a buyer-seller model in which the buyer's types are uniformly distributed on $b \in [1, 2]$, with payoffs:
$$U^B = b \times \log (q + 1) - p.$$
The seller has payoffs $U^S = p - q$. The outside options for both parties are fixed at zero. Answer the following:

(a) What is the efficient allocation as a function of buyer types?

(b) Suppose parties can negotiate terms before they learn their private valuations. Does a contract exist that implements the efficient allocation? If so, what is the contract?

(c) Work out the equilibrium allocations at the interim stage for the cases in which the buyer has all the power and then when the seller has all the power.

(d) Suppose that the seller is a price-setting monopolist (she sets the price and the buyer chooses his consumption). What is the equilibrium price?

(e) Compare the allocative and distributive consequences of these solutions.

7. Consider the following buyer-seller problem. A seller has a car for sale that is either a lemon, $t = L$, or good, $t = H$. Suppose $Pr\,[t = H] = \rho \in (0, 1)$. The seller knows her type but the buyer does not. Let level of trade be given by $q_t \in [0, 1]$ and the price be p_t. We use a direct mechanism, so the buyer's payoff is:
$$U^B = \rho\,(q_H v_H - p_H) + (1 - \rho)\,(q_L v_L - p_L)\,.$$

Now, the payoff of the seller with type $t \in \{H, L\}$ is:
$$U^S\,(\hat{t}, t) = p_{\hat{t}} - q_{\hat{t}} \bar{v}_t,$$

where $\bar{v}_t$ is the value of the car to the owner, and $\hat{t}$ is the seller's report of quality. Answer the following questions for these three cases:

Case 1: Suppose that $v_H > \bar{v}_H > \bar{v}_L > v_L$.

Case 2: Suppose that $v_H > \bar{v}_L > \bar{v}_H > v_L$.

Case 3: Suppose that $v_H > \bar{v}_H > v_L > \bar{v}_L$.

(a) What are the efficient allocations in these cases? Assuming specific performance, for each case provide a mechanism that implements an *ex ante* incentive efficient allocation (if possible).

(b) Suppose that the buyer is able make a take-it-or-leave-it offer of a nonlinear price schedule after the seller's learns her type. If the seller rejects, she keeps the car, while the buyer gets a payoff of zero. For each case, what is the buyer's optimal pricing strategy?

8. Consider a game in which the buyer's valuation takes one of two values, b_H or b_L, and the probability of b_H is ρ. The seller's costs are either c_H with probability γ or c_L with probability $1 - \gamma$. The utilities of the buyer and seller are given by $qv_t - p$ and $p - qc_s$, where $q \in [0, 1]$ is the probability that one unit is traded. Suppose $b_H > c_H > b_L > c_L$. Suppose that bargaining occurs at the interim stage, and if no agreement is reached, then agents receive zero. You may assume that the bargaining game is one round of the random proposer game.

    (a) What is the optimal incentive allocation when the buyer makes a take-it-or-leave-it offer at the interim stage? Work this out for the seller.

    (b) Suppose that before bargaining, parties can agree to a default contract of $\{p, 1\}$ or $\{p, 0\}$ if renegotiation fails. Which would they choose? (See McKelvey and Page 2002.)

    (c) Suppose that at the ex ante stage parties can choose a default contract and who has all the ex post power. What would they agree on?

9. (Signaling game: see Spence 1973 and Cho and Kreps 1987). The purpose of this exercise is to explore screening versus signalling. Consider a buyer and two-seller problem (equivalently, an employer and two employees) with the following characteristics. The sellers produce products with qualities $\theta_g > \theta_b > 0$, for sellers $t \in \{g, b\}$. These qualities are not observed by the buyer, who believes that $t = g$ with probability $\rho \in (0, 1)$. If the buyer purchases the commodity from seller t at price p_t he gets utility $U_t^B = \theta_t - p_t$. The cost of production for seller $t \in \{g, b\}$ is:

$$C_t(s) = k_t + c_s/\theta_t,$$

where $s \in \{H, L\}$, and $c_H > c_L$ is a costly observable *signal*, such as advertising. It is assumed that the buyer cannot observe the seller's fixed cost of production, $k_g > k_b$ and hence cannot directly see whether the seller is of high or low quality. The buyer does observe the signal $s \in \{H, L\}$.

The sellers have a default payoff of zero and a payoff if there is trade:

$$U_t^S(s) = p_t - C_t(s).$$

In Spence's education model it is assumed that high-ability individuals face a lower cost of acquiring an education, and therefore more years of education (higher c_s) signal a higher ability. In a production context, the assumption is that the high-quality producer is more efficient, and, for example, can have a higher-intensity advertising campaign (higher c_s) at a lower cost. In the context of the Akerlof market for lemons, the signal s may be the cleanliness of the car.

For each case outlined below, work out sufficient conditions on the parameters to get trade with both types and a pooling equilibrium (both seller types are paid the same price) and trade with both types at a separating equilibrium (different types are paid different prices). Draw the extensive form for each case and describe carefully the sequential equilibrium that implements each outcome.

    (a) Suppose the buyer makes a take-it-or-leave-it offer of contract $k = \{(p_1, s_1), (p_2, s_2)\}$. This contract pays the seller p_i if they choose s_i, $i \in \{1, 2\}$. Work out the set of incentive-compatible offers given the conditions you place on the parameter values, and then work out the utility-maximizing solution for the buyer.

(b) Suppose Nature moves first and selects seller $t = g$ with probability ρ. The seller then chooses $s \in \{H, L\}$ (observed by the buyer), and then makes a take-it-or-leave-it offer to the buyer to purchase the good at price p. Be sure to carefully describe the beliefs held by the buyer when working out the equilibria for this game.

9 Relational Contracts

Glass, China, and Reputation, are easily crack'd, and never well mended.
—Poor Richard's Almanack, Saunders (1750).[1]

9.1 Introduction

Successful exchange over time requires sellers to provide commodities as promised and buyers to pay as promised. It is quite easy to suppose that part of the success of advanced market economies is the existence of a well-functioning legal system. In 1963, Stewart Macaulay (1963) put this idea to a test. He carried out a series of interviews with businessmen in Wisconsin to see to what extent they relied on careful planning and legal enforcement in their business dealings. Macaulay found that legal enforcement is rare and it is called on only in the most extreme cases. Moreover, parties continue to trade even while not respecting contract terms laid out in the purchase orders that clearly specify requirements for the exchange. Thus, he demonstrated that, in the United States, a great deal of trade is carried out based on the promise of future exchange and the expectation that each party behaves appropriately, without resorting to legal enforcement. This work was the beginning of a literature on "relational contracts"—agreements to trade that are enforced by the promise of future trade and goodwill.

The goal of this chapter is to provide a brief introduction to the microeconomic foundations of this large literature. The focus of the review is the *enforcement problem*. The contract models of the previous chapters can be viewed as theories of reward or reinforcement. In the holdup problem, prices remain fixed so that parties are able to enjoy the fruits of their investment in a relationship. In the case of agency theory, the goal of the contract is to reward the seller for allocating her effort appropriately. Finally, asymmetric information models are designed to ensure that sellers reveal private information that is relevant for determining the level of trade.

In contrast, relational contract theory is about ensuring parties do not breach their promise to perform. Breach is not merely a legal issue, it is also an emotional one. When a seller delivers a defective product, the disgruntled buyer can respond with a sanction. The theory aims to predict the level of trade as a function of the information available and the nature of the possible sanctions. The contract is relational because the sanction is assumed to occur during the periods after trade. The sanction can take a variety of forms, including stopping trade, nonpayment of a bonus, or the dissemination of negative information regarding the seller.

The chapter is divided into six sections. The next section discusses the timeline for contract execution and the importance of the breach event. Section 9.3 introduces the formal model used in this chapter. The model is an extension of the repeated game model introduced in chapter 4 (proposition 4.15) to include imperfect information. This model includes the efficiency wage model of Shapiro and Stiglitz (1984) as a special case. In the classical efficiency wage model, it is assumed that output is a Poisson process for which low effort increases the frequency with which "defects" or "accidents" occur. These are called *normal commodities* because they correspond to the common situation in which the seller usually delivers a satisfactory product but, in some cases, delivers a substandard product that leads to a capital loss.

When the noisy signal is about *good news*, this is represented by a Poisson process in which the observation of a positive signal means that the seller or employee was successful in producing a high-quality product. These are called *innovative commodities*, such as a hit movie or a successful new drug. In this situation there is little output in the short run while research is undertaken for the new product. With effort, there is a high probability of eventually producing a large reward. The reason for distinguishing between normal and innovative commodities follows from an important result due to Abreu, Milgrom, and Pearce (1991). They show that with a normal commodity, increasing the frequency of trade leads to more efficient equilibria. In contrast, with an innovative commodity, increasing the frequency of trade can *reduce* the efficiency of equilibria. In this case, efficiency may be enhanced by delaying the provision of rewards.

Section 9.4 details the role the value of trade plays in relational contract theory. In that section, it is assumed the seller's effort can be observed, and hence performance can be defined in terms of effort rather than output. The level of trade possible under a relational contract is determined by the value of future trade with one's current trading partner. The theory makes predictions regarding the maximum level of trade that can be sustained, though it is silent regarding the division of the gains from trade. A necessary condition for efficient trade is the existence of a *self-enforcing social norm* within which parties play a subgame perfect Nash equilibrium that deters parties from breaching contract terms.

Playing the "punishment" equilibrium can result in both parties being harmed. In such cases, bargaining theory (chapter 5) predicts that parties would try to renegotiate to a more efficient allocation. But if the renegotiation is anticipated, it undermines the incentive to play the efficient subgame perfect Nash equilibrium. This is known as the problem of renegotiation in repeated games and is discussed in subsection 9.4.1.

Section 9.5 extends the theory of relational contracts to agency models with moral hazard developed by Levin (2003). In this case, effort is not observed, so performance incentives are provided by defining breach in terms of the observed output. One begins with the analysis from chapter 7 to derive the terms for optimal one-period compensation. Given that parties are assumed to be risk neutral, there are many optimal compensation contracts. These contracts are a combination of two extreme contract forms. The first is a bonus contract that rewards the seller or employee when there is a good signal of performance. The second is a penalty contract that punishes the seller or employee in the event of a negative performance signal.

The rest of the chapter looks at the implementation of these generic contract forms using relational contracts. The classic efficiency wage model of Shapiro and Stiglitz (1984), as well as the reputation model of Klein and Leffler (1981), show that markets can act as an informal discipline device, an idea that goes back to Friedman (1962). Friedman argued that one does not need to regulate competitive markets because participants care about their reputation which, if lost, can lead to a loss of demand in the market. This approach to enforcing relational contracts is called the "market mechanism." Subsection 9.5.2 on market mechanisms shows that the threat of losing market share or employment can serve as an incentive to produce a high-quality commodity. In general, it is not the most efficient way to manage the relationship. Therefore, market-based reputation mechanisms by themselves cannot be relied on to ensure efficient trade.

Subsection 9.5.3 outlines the theory of *efficient* relational contracts in the case of moral hazard. It is shown that an essential ingredient in efficient contracting is the *design* of the breach event. Specifically, when the seller does not perform, then under the market mechanism this behavior is considered a breach of contract and results in termination. An alternative, more efficient approach is to make pay vary with performance, which acknowledges that output can be stochastic. In this case, breach of contract occurs when the buyer or employer does not appropriately reward good performance with higher compensation. When this occurs, it is the buyer or employer who has breached the agreement, and this subsequently leads to termination of the relationship by the seller or employee.

These results illustrate the point that two important ingredients in contract design are specifying the breach event and identifying who is responsible for performance. This approach has spawned a large literature, some of which is briefly discussed in section 9.6.

9.2 Breach and Contract Design

Humans have been using relational contracts in commercial exchange for millennia.[2] This fact has led some legal scholars to question the usefulness of formal theory. For example, Macaulay (2000) describes the application of economics to the law as a "desert" that is not capable of explaining the complexity of observed contractual relationships.[3] He is certainly correct when he describes observed contracts as complex and varied. It is exactly this complexity that makes objective analysis difficult and interesting.

Yet, contracts are used precisely because trade is *idiosyncratic*. The goods or services to be provided need to be tailored to the characteristics of the trading parties. This uniqueness makes forming and testing hypotheses difficult. Contract law can help with this task because one of its goals is to codify elements that are common to all contracts. Of particular importance is the notion of contract breach.

Economics ignores the breach event for the most part. In the introduction to their book, *Contract Theory*, Bolton and Dewatripont (2005) explicitly rule out the breach event as central to the economics of contract theory. Rather, they assume that there is a well-functioning legal system to enforce agreements. When well-defined performance measures exist, as is assumed in chapter 7, then the goal of the analysis is to explain the relationship between observed performance and enforceable payment contracts.

As a matter of law, there is no obligation for parties to agree to performance pay. For example, a legally binding sales contract may require only that the seller agree to provide goods at a future date in exchange for a fixed price. Should the seller not perform, she is in breach of contract. When a breach occurs, the buyer now has the *right* to seek damages from the seller in a court of law. In other words, breach gives the buyer some additional power to seek a remedy in a court.

Relational contracts have exactly the same structure. The difference is that when breach occurs, the buyer cannot resort to a court but instead uses a *self-help* mechanism, such as terminating his relationship with the seller or posting negative comments on a public website.

Part of contract design is specifying what events give rise to breach and the sanctions to be applied to the breaching party. For example, if a waiter accidentally spills some wine or food on a customer at a restaurant table, this would normally be viewed as a breach of the implicit agreement to provide good service. In that case, the patrons may reasonably expect compensation.

By contrast, it would not be considered a breach of contract if one's computer is not functioning on delivery. That event would be covered by the consumer warranty, and the customer would simply return the computer for a replacement. In that case, breach of contract would occur only if the firm did not replace the machine as required by the warranty contract.

In these two examples, it is the seller who might breach the agreement. However, contracts can also be designed to move the locus of the breach decision to the buyer. Suppose the buyer is an employer and the seller is an employee. The parties might agree to a contract under which the employer pays a bonus if and only if the employee has performed well. Contract breach would occur if the employee performed well but the employer did not pay the promised bonus. In this case, the tables are turned and it is the employee/seller who sanctions the employer/buyer for contract breach.

In this chapter, sanctions are restricted to termination by either party. In the case of termination, the timing of choices in a relational contract can be illustrated with the timeline shown in figure 9.1. After parties reach an agreement, the seller (or employee) is typically the first to perform. If her performance is not consistent with her obligations under the contract, then the buyer or employer may terminate the relationship.

The relational contract might also include discretionary payment terms from the buyer to the seller. If the buyer does not make a promised payment, then he has breached the agreement, which may lead to the seller's terminating the relationship.

The theory developed below illustrates that the choice of breach events depends on the type of commodity being traded. Two extreme cases are considered. The first concerns "normal commodities," that feature a high probability of high quality. For these commodities, it is shown that the optimal relational contract entails placing the performance obligation on the seller. In the case of "innovative commodities," the optimal relational contract entails rewarding the seller/employee with a bonus when performance is high. The buyer/employer has breached the agreement if they do not pay the bonus when it has been earned.

9.3   The Production Environment

This section introduces the payoffs of parties in a relational contract based on the framework of Levin (2003) and extended to include the information structure introduced by Abreu, Milgrom, and Pearce (1991). The model includes as special cases the continuous-time

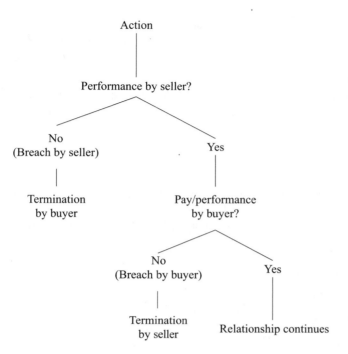

Figure 9.1
Relational contract.

efficiency wage model of Shapiro and Stiglitz (1984) as well as the discrete time, symmetric information models of Telser (1980) and MacLeod and Malcomson (1989). The additional generality of this approach allows predictions about how the structure of relational contracts varies with characteristics of the commodities being traded.

Consider a buyer/employer and a seller/employee who are infinitely lived and risk neutral, and who discount income with a common interest rate r. Performance occurs in continuous time, while decisions are made at discrete time intervals. As in the case of the strategic bargaining games introduced in chapter 5, using discrete time for modeling decisions ensures that the information available when a choice is made is unambiguous and can be modeled using the notion of a perfect Bayesian Nash equilibrium.[4] The use of continuous time for the payoffs allows for a clear distinction between stocks and flows, as well as allowing information arrival to be a Poisson process.

Decisions are made at fixed time intervals indexed by periods $t = 0, 1, 2, \ldots$. It is assumed the environment is stationary, and hence in each period there is always the potential for future trade. Depending on past behavior, parties may choose to stop the relationship. The last period is denoted by T, which is potentially infinite. In general T is a random variable that can depend on the history of choice. The length of a period is $\Delta > 0$, and hence the *frequency of trade* is defined by $f = \frac{1}{\Delta}$. Time is given by $\tau \in [0, \infty)$ and choices at the beginning of period t occur at times $\tau(\Delta, t) \equiv \Delta \times t$.[5]

The following sequence of events occurs in period t:

1. At the beginning of period t, the buyer and seller observe output $y_{(t-1)}$ and income $w_{(t-1)}$ from the previous period.

2. The seller observes a cost parameter, c_t, an i.i.d. random variable with stationary distribution $c_t \sim g(\cdot)$ with support $[c_L, c_H]$. She then chooses effort $e_t \in [0, 1]$, that has a flow cost of $v(e_t, c_t)$ to the seller that is a twice differentiable function satisfying $v(0, c) = v_e(0, c) = 0$, $v_e(\cdot), v_{ee}(\cdot), v_{ec}(\cdot) > 0$ for $e \in (0, 1]$, $c \in [c_L, c_H]$.

3. In the symmetric information case, the buyer observes both the cost, c_t, and the effort chosen by the seller, e_t. In the case of moral hazard, the buyer observes neither cost nor effort.

4. At the end of the period, the buyer realizes a flow payoff from effort, $y_t = y(e_t)$, and makes a flow payment w_t to the seller.

The next two sections detail the exact functional form for the payoff, $y(e_t)$. It is assumed that the payoff is a Poisson process whose expected realized value varies with effort and the length of a period. Two extreme cases correspond to a normal or an innovative commodity.[6] These are discussed in turn.

9.3.1 Normal Commodities

A normal commodity corresponds to the case in which the purpose of effort is to avoid a negative signal that entails a capital loss. This loss might come from an accident, a product defect, or a failure. For example, a new computer might not work, or food that is delivered might be spoiled. In the canonical efficiency wage model of Shapiro and Stiglitz (1984), the negative signal is the employer observing shirking by the worker.

Normal commodities are modeled using a Poisson process that supposes that the probability of the adverse event occurring is approximated with a linear time effect, $\Delta \gamma^B(e_t)$, that results in an expected return in period t:

$$\Delta y_t \equiv \Delta y(e_t) = \Delta \bar{y} - \Delta \gamma^B(e_t) L, \tag{9.1}$$

where Δ is the length of a period, $\bar{y}$ is the output per unit of time, and L is a capital loss that occurs when there is a bad event. It is assumed that $\gamma^B(e_t)$ is differentiable, positive, strictly decreasing, and convex in effort e_t. It is also assumed that, for the values of interest, $0 \le \Delta \gamma^B(e_t) < 1$, and hence $\Delta \gamma^B(e_t)$ represents the probability of the bad event happening in one period. It is also assumed that the length of a period is sufficiently small that we can ignore the possibility of two losses in a single period.[7]

In this case, when the adverse event occurs, the loss can be much larger than the gain in the current period:

$$L \ggg \Delta \bar{y}.$$

For example, in an employment context, the driver of a truck produces a flow of services while driving, yet a driving error that occurs in less than a second could result in a catastrophic loss due to a traffic accident. Given that all parties are risk neutral and they value income in the same way, the flow return from trade is:

$$s^N(e_t, c_t) \approx \bar{y} - \gamma^B(e_t) L - v(e_t, c_t).$$

This in turn implies that the efficient level of effort is *independent* of the length of a period and satisfies:

$$e^N(c, L) = \arg\max_{e \geq 0}\left(-\Delta\gamma^B(e)L - \Delta v(e, c)\right),$$

$$= \arg\max_{e \geq 0}\left(-\gamma^B(e)L - v(e, c)\right), \tag{9.2}$$

and it is the unique solution to:

$$\frac{dv\left(e^N(c, L), c\right)}{de} = -\frac{d\gamma^B\left(e^N(c, L)\right)}{de}L. \tag{9.3}$$

These assumptions imply that efficient effort, e^N, is increasing in the value of the loss, L, and decreasing in the difficulty of the job, c:

$$\frac{\partial e^N}{\partial c} < 0, \frac{\partial e^N}{\partial L} > 0.$$

9.3.2 Innovative Commodities

The polar opposite of normal commodities are "innovative commodities." These have the feature that even if the seller works hard, the probability of a *positive* signal of performance over a short period of time is low. For example, consider research to produce a new drug. In that case, there is no marketable product or outcome until an effective compound is discovered, at which point there may be a large payoff or reward, denoted by $G > 0$. Innovative commodities can also be modeled as a Poisson process where the random signal is now *good news*, and the Poisson parameter represents the success rate over time.

Let $\gamma^G(e_t)$ be the positive Poisson rate that is a differentiable, increasing, and strictly concave function of effort e_t. In this case the payoff in period t is given by:

$$\Delta y_t \equiv \Delta y(e_t) = \Delta\bar{y} + \Delta\gamma^G(e_t)G, \tag{9.4}$$

and the flow surplus is:

$$s^I(e_t, c_t) \approx \bar{y} + \gamma^G(e_t)G - v(e_t, c_t).$$

Thus, the efficient effort for the production of an innovative good is the unique solution to:

$$\frac{dv\left(e^I(c, G), c\right)}{de} = \frac{d\gamma^G\left(e^I(c, G)\right)}{de}G. \tag{9.5}$$

As in the case for a normal good, the effect of effort costs and returns to innovation satisfy:

$$\frac{\partial e^I}{\partial c} < 0, \frac{\partial e^I}{\partial G} > 0.$$

9.3.3 Discounted Expected Payoffs

For the rest of the chapter, let $y(e_t)$ denote the expected flow output in period t, which can be either a normal or an innovative commodity. When the nature of the commodity is relevant to the discussion, two cases are denoted by $y^N(e_t)$ and $y^I(e_t)$ for the payoff from a normal and innovative commodity respectively. In either case, there is always an implicit dependence on the length of a period, Δ, and the cost of effort, c_t.

Given this definition, an allocation is defined in terms of the effort choices and payments to the seller: $\vec{x} = \{x_0, x_1, \ldots, x_{T-1}\}$, where $x_t = \{e_t, w_t\}$ defines the effort and wage at date t, while $T \geq 1$ denotes the date at which the relationship terminates.[8] Because effort can depend on the cost, and the wage in period t can depend on both effort and the realized outcome, then effort e_t and wage w_t are in general random variables. However, it is explicitly assumed that these random variables are independent of each other. Hence, one can let $\vec{x}(t) = \{x_t, x_{t+1}, \ldots, x_{T-1}\}$ be the allocation starting at date t (and hence $\vec{x} = \vec{x}(0)$), and this is well defined and independent of the events that have occurred before date t.

This construction allows us to deal with both the classic relational contract model and the moral hazard model introduced by Levin (2003). If a contract includes performance pay, then it produces independent and identically distributed (i.i.d.) random payoffs that are captured by this definition of an allocation. Relational contracting adds the possibility that parties agree to move from one allocation to another depending on observed behavior.

When termination occurs at date T, each party receives its outside option, given by Π^0 and U^0 for the buyer/employer and seller/employee, respectively. These can be allowed to be random variables, though for this chapter we can take them as exogenous and fixed. Thus, the discounted present value of trade for each party is given by:

$$\Pi(\vec{x}) = E\left\{\sum_{t=0}^{T-1} \delta^t \Delta \left(y(e_t) - w_t\right) + \delta^T \Pi^0\right\}, \tag{9.6}$$

$$U(\vec{x}) = E\left\{\sum_{t=0}^{T-1} \delta^t \Delta \left(w_t - v(e_t, c_t)\right) + \delta^T U^0\right\}, \tag{9.7}$$

where $\delta = e^{-r\Delta}$ is the one-period discount rate. When writing the discounted payoffs in this way, it is assumed that the length of a period is sufficiently small that the discounted present value of returns over a period of length Δ is approximately Δ:

$$\int_0^\Delta e^{-rt} dt = \frac{(1 - e^{-\Delta r})}{r} \cong \Delta. \tag{9.8}$$

The total surplus is defined by:

$$S(\vec{x}) = \Pi(\vec{x}) + U(\vec{x}) = E\left\{\sum_{t=0}^{T-1} \delta^t \Delta s(e_t, c_t) + \delta^T S^0\right\}, \tag{9.9}$$

where $S^0 = \Pi^0 + U^0$ is the surplus under no trade, and $s(e_t, c_t) = y(e_t) - v(e_t, c_t)$ is the flow surplus in period t. Notice that the total surplus is independent of the terms of trade defined by the wages $\{w_0, \ldots, w_{T-1}\}$.

9.3.4   Feasible Allocations

Relational contracts are defined in terms of the flow output to the buyer and payments to the seller. Bargaining theory predicts that rational parties care only about how the gains from trade are divided between them. Given that actions and payment can change over time, it is not obvious how to translate flow returns to a specific division of the surplus each period.

This section shows that any agreed division of the gains from trade can be implemented by an allocation that specifies effort and the wage each period.

A necessary condition for an allocation, $\vec{x}$, to be agreed on by rational parties is the requirement of individual rationality:

Definition 9.1 *An allocation $\vec{x}$ is* individually rational *if and only if for all $t = 0, 1, 2, \ldots$*:

$$\Pi\left(\vec{x}\left(t\right)\right) \geq \Pi^0,$$

$$U\left(\vec{x}\left(t\right)\right) \geq U^0.$$

This implies that the gain from trade satisfies:

$$S\left(\vec{x}\left(t\right)\right) \geq S^0 = \Pi^0 + U^0, \forall t = 0, 1, 2, \ldots$$

The efficient level of effort gives rise to a flow return at the beginning of the period before the seller's cost of effort, c_t, is known:

$$s^* = E\left\{\max_{e \geq 0}\left(y\left(e\right) - v\left(e, c\right)\right)\right\}$$

$$= \int_{c_L}^{c_H}\left(y\left(e^*\left(c\right)\right) - v\left(e^*\left(c\right), c\right)\right)g\left(c\right)dc, \tag{9.10}$$

where $e^*\left(c\right)$ is the optimal effort choice given effort costs, solving either (9.2) or (9.5). Let $S^* = \frac{\Delta}{(1-\delta)}s^* \approx \frac{s^*}{r}$ be the maximum possible surplus.

As parties care only about their payoffs rather than contract terms per se, then a natural way to think about the relationship is in terms of the short-run payoffs versus the long-run returns, and the share of those future returns one will receive. For every individually rational allocation $\vec{x}$ there exists a corresponding surplus sequence $\vec{S}\left(\vec{x}\right) = \{S_0, S_1, \ldots\} \in \left[S^0, S^*\right]^\infty \equiv \mathscr{S}$, where $S_t = S\left(\vec{x}\left(t\right)\right) \geq S^0$ is the surplus computed starting in period t. This in turn defines the gain from trade or rent $R\left(t\right) = \left(S_t - S^0\right) \geq 0$. Let $\alpha_t \in [0, 1]$ be the fraction of the gain going to the buyer, defined by:

$$\alpha_t R\left(t\right) = \left(\Pi\left(\vec{x}\left(t\right)\right) - \Pi^0\right), \forall t = 0, 1, \ldots. \tag{9.11}$$

When the rent from trade is strictly positive $\left(R\left(t\right) > 0\right)$, then α_t is uniquely defined by (9.11); otherwise it can take any value in $[0, 1]$. Let $\vec{\alpha}\left(\vec{x}\right) = \{\alpha_0, \alpha_1, \ldots\}$ denote any sequence satisfying (9.11).

If parties are rational in the sense of the bargaining models discussed in chapter 5, then they are concerned only with their returns and not with contract terms per se. Therefore, one can view the division of the surplus as a primitive and ask if there are relational contract terms that implement allocation $\vec{x}$. The next proposition answers this question.

Proposition 9.2 *A surplus sequence $\vec{S} \in \mathscr{S}$ and corresponding division of returns $\vec{\alpha} \in [0, 1]^T$ are the result of some individually rational allocation $\vec{x}$ if and only if:*

$$S_t = S\left(\vec{x}\left(t\right)\right) \in \left[S^0, \Delta s^* + \delta S_{t+1}\right], t = 0, 1, 2, \ldots. \tag{9.12}$$

Proof. Let $\vec{x}$ be an individually rational allocation. By definition this implies $S(\vec{x}(t)) \in [S^0, S^*]$, $\forall t = 0, 1, \ldots$. The assumption that the allocation at date t is independent of events before date t implies that we can write:

$$S(\vec{x}(t)) = \Delta \int_{c_L}^{c_H} (y(e(c)) - v(e(c), c)) g(c) \, dc + \delta S(\vec{x}(t+1)).$$

The fact that $\int_{c_L}^{c_H} (y(e(c)) - v(e(c), c)) g(c) \, dc \leq s^*$, implies $S(\vec{x}(t)) \leq \Delta s^* + \delta S(\vec{x}(t+1)) \leq S^*$ and hence (9.12) is satisfied. The corresponding division of returns is defined by (9.11).

Conversely, suppose $\vec{S} \in \mathcal{S}$ satisfies (9.12). Given that the cost of effort is unbounded above, for each date t we can find an $e_t = h_t(c_t)$, where h_t is some measurable function, such that:

$$\Delta E\{y(h_t(c_t)) - v(h_t(c_t), c_t)\} = S_t - \delta S_{t+1} \leq \Delta s^*.$$

Next, it is assumed that there are no limits on payments, and thus w_t can be defined to satisfy:

$$w_t = E\{y(h_t(c_t))\} + \frac{1}{\Delta}\left(-\Pi^0 + \delta \alpha_{t+1} R(t+1) - \alpha_t R(t)\right),$$

where $R(t) = S_t - S^0$ is the gain or rent from trade in period t. Notice that we cannot bound w_t, and it can take on both negative and positive values depending on the division of the surplus changes from period to period. This ensures $S(\vec{x}(t)) = S_t, t = 0, 1, \ldots$. $\square$

This result implies that we can think about a relational contract via its terms (effort and wage sequences) or in terms of how the gains from trade are divided. The formalism provides one way that parties can "think" about an agreement, $k(t)$, at the beginning of period t. First, parties take as data the future gains from trade, S_{t+1}, and the current outside options, U^0 and Π^0. Given this, the agreed effort for the period, e_t, determines the flow surplus, s_t. Parties can then agree on a wage, w_t, that ensures condition (9.12) is satisfied. This procedure determines the set of feasible, individually rational allocations that implement any agreed division of the gain from trade.

Note that it is not assumed that wages are deterministic. Rather, allocations represent agreements to divide the gains from trade. As a relationship evolves, parties may mutually agree to change the allocation. It is crucial that any agreement between two parties necessarily entails agreement on how the gains from trade are divided over time and are not simply based on the current wage or effort. This perspective follows from Abreu (1988), who introduced the idea that strategies in a repeated game can be viewed as transitions between sequences of choices, which in our case correspond to allocations.

Abreu also emphasizes the link between repeated game theory and dynamic programming to show that, in each period, the only information one needs to check is whether current actions are optimal given the current within-period rewards and the discounted expected future payoffs that follow from each action. In this way, he extended Blackwell's (1965) principle of optimality for dynamic decision making to repeated games.

9.4 Relational Contracts with Symmetric Information

This section reviews the "classic" relational contract model (Telser 1980; and MacLeod and Malcomson 1989) in which both cost of effort and effort are assumed to be observed by both parties in the relationship. However, in contrast to agency theory, relational contract theory begins with the hypothesis that promises are not enforceable in a court of law. As Macaulay's (1963) evidence shows, the lack of enforceability does not necessarily stem from the absence of a legal system. Relational contracts are useful whenever the value of the transaction is smaller than the cost of pursuing damages for breach of contract in court.

The symmetric information assumption means that whether the seller works in a given period is verifiable, as are any monetary payments. Hence, a fixed wage contract that pays a seller if and only if she arrives for work is legally enforceable. Similarly, separation payments are assumed to be enforceable.

Performance pay contracts that explicitly link seller effort with compensation, though, are not enforceable. However, if compensation is independent of effort, then agency theory predicts that the seller will exert no effort. This is solved by parties agreeing to performance pay that is supported by a *self-enforcing social norm*. Self-enforcing means that the agreed actions form a perfect Bayesian Nash equilibrium. The term "norm" highlights the fact that there are many possible equilibria that may characterize behavior in a relationship. A relational contract is one in which parties explicitly select one of these equilibria, and then parties agree, either explicitly or implicitly, to abide by the norm.

The classic relational contract model considers two norms. The first is the potential for the buyer to reward effort with bonus pay. In the absence of third-party enforcement, the buyer has an incentive to renege. He is deterred from this behavior by the possibility the seller will terminate the relationship. The second norm is the mechanism that promises the buyer will continue employing the seller at a high wage as long as her effort is acceptable. The second norm corresponds to the classic efficiency wage model.

The formal game is defined in terms of dates and steps. The dates correspond to periods of production, while the steps occur within a single period and precisely define the information held by each party before each action. At the beginning of period t, both parties observe the history of the game $h_{t.0} \in \mathcal{H}(t.0)$, where $\mathcal{H}(t.s)$ denotes the set of possible histories at the beginning of date t and step s, while $\mathcal{H}$ is the set of all possible histories. The assumption of symmetric information implies that, at each step, both parties can observe previous events as follows:

Step 0: The buyer (or principal) offers a contract $k(t) = \left\{ \bar{w}_t, b_t = \phi_t^P(m_t^P), e_t(c_t) \right\}$ to be in place for period t. If $k(t) = \emptyset$, then the buyer has dismissed the seller, and both parties take their outside options.

Step 1: The seller (or agent) accepts $(a_t = 1)$ or rejects $(a_t = 0)$ the offer. If rejection occurs, the outside options are taken. If accepted, $\bar{w}_t$ is paid and the cost of effort c_t is realized.

Step 2: The seller chooses e_t for the duration of the period to produce output $y(e_t)$.

Step 3: The buyer sends a message $m_t^P \in M^P$ that determines the bonus $b_t = \phi_t^P(m_t^P)$ paid to the seller.

Table 9.1
Timing for the relational contract game

Period	Public information	Buyer choice	Seller choice	Transfers
$t.0$	$h_{t.0} = h_{t-1.3} \cup \{m^P_{t-1}\}$	Offers contract $k(t)$		
$t.1$	$h_{t.1} = h_{t.0} \cup \{k(t)\}$		Accepts ($a_t = 1$) or leaves ($a_t = 0$)	If $a_t = 1$ buyer pays $\bar{w}_t$
$t.2$	$h_{t.2} = h_{t.1} \cup \{b_t, c_t\}$		Chooses effort $e_t \geq 0$	Buyer realizes output y_t
$t.3$	$h_{t.3} = h_{t.2} \cup \{e_t, y_t\}$	Message m^P_t sent to determine bonus pay		$b_t = \phi^P(m^P_t)$

Notice that the contract is designed to have minimal reliance on legal enforcement. If it is certain that the seller will arrive at work, then the amount $\bar{w}_t$ can be paid at the beginning of the period. For most firms the enforcement of agreed wages is rarely an issue.

At the end of the period, the buyer agrees to pay a bonus, $b_t = \phi^P_t(m^P_t)$, as a function of a message, $m^P_t \in M^P$, where M^P is a finite message space. These messages can be viewed as the buyer's evaluation of the work. For example, the message may simply be that the work is acceptable. In that case this term is equivalent to giving the buyer the discretion to pay $b_t \in \{0, \bar{b}\}$, where the payment of a bonus $\bar{b} > 0$ explicitly means that the work is acceptable.

In other cases, for example, when the seller is a manufacturer and the product is substandard, the seller may have to pay the buyer. In that case the payment is a "damages" payment, $d_t = -b_t = -\phi^P_t(m^P_t) > 0$, to compensate the buyer for the seller's "breach" of the agreement to supply high quality. Notice that one can always reframe the contract as a bonus payment for high quality by redefining the wage as $\bar{w}'_t = \bar{w}_t + \min_{m \in M^P} \phi^P_t(m)$ and setting the discretionary payment to $\phi^{P'}_t(m) = \phi^P_t(m) - \min_{m \in M^P} \phi^P_t(m)$.

Parties are assumed to be risk neutral and to face no liquidity constraints. Thus, without loss of generality, it can be assumed:

$$\min_{m \in M^P} \phi^P_t(m) = 0. \tag{9.13}$$

The timing of choices and definitions of histories are illustrated in table 9.1. Let $A^P(h)$ and $A^A(h)$ be the actions available to the buyer and seller given a history $h \in \mathcal{H}$. A legally enforceable term is one of which parties can seek court enforcement. In this model, the wage payment and the bonus rule $\phi^P_t(m^P_t)$ are enforceable. When we say that $\phi^P_t(m^P_t)$ is enforceable, this means that when the buyer sends a message m^P_t, the payment $\phi^P_t(m^P_t)$ is made. For example, the message might be "pay a bonus," which is then enforced. The message sent is not enforceable.[9]

Though this model is quite stark, it admits a large set of possible behaviors. Rather than suppose that parties "discover" efficient behavior as in Axelrod (1981), the term *relational contract* explicitly means that parties understand their formal and informal obligations that stem from behavioral norms. More precisely, a relational contract defines for each history $h \in \mathcal{H}$ the actions of party $i \in \{P, A\}$ by a function $\sigma^i(h) \in A^i(h)$, for all $h \in \mathcal{H}$. Notice that the initial explicit terms are given by $k(0) = \sigma^P(h(0.0))$, where $h(t.s)$ denotes the history at date $t = 0, 1, \ldots$, and step $s = 0, 1, 2, 3$. Let $\sigma = \{\sigma^P, \sigma^A\} \in \Sigma^P \times \Sigma^A$ denote the relational contract between parties, where $\Sigma \equiv \Sigma^P \times \Sigma^A$ denotes all possible contracts.

Every relational contract determines recursively an allocation $\vec{x}(\sigma)$ (see chapter 4). The expression $\vec{x}(\sigma | h_{t.s})$ means that the allocation is determined by $h_{t.s}$ up to date $t.s$, and then from that point, the relational contract σ determines the actions and payoffs. A relational contract is called *self-enforcing* if at no point parties wish to deviate from their agreement.

Definition 9.3 *A relational contract $\sigma \in \Sigma$ is* self-enforcing *if for every $h \in \mathcal{H}$, $\tilde{\sigma}^i \in \Sigma^i$, and $i = P, A$:*

$$E\{\Pi(\vec{x}(\sigma)) | h\} \geq E\left\{\Pi\left(\vec{x}\left(\tilde{\sigma}^P, \sigma^A\right)\right) | h\right\}, \tag{9.14}$$

$$E\{U(\vec{x}(\sigma)) | h\} \geq E\left\{U\left(\vec{x}\left(\sigma^P, \tilde{\sigma}^A\right)\right) | h\right\}. \tag{9.15}$$

When information is symmetric, self-enforcement is the requirement that the relational contract forms a subgame perfect Nash equilibrium. The next section allows for some asymmetric information, in which case this definition corresponds to a perfect Bayesian Nash equilibrium. We use the term "self-enforcing," rather than a particular game theoretic equilibrium concept because the equilibrium concept depends on the context.

Note that agency/contract theory has a perspective different from game theory. Game theory begins with a precisely specified game and then applies the theory to make a prediction. In contrast, agency/contract theory takes the perspective of two parties who wish to reach a deal and who wish to design terms (namely the game to be played) in a way that neither party breaches the agreement. This pragmatic perspective views self-enforcement as a constraint rather than a solution concept. Parties are free to choose the solution concept they believe best captures the requirement that the agreement is self-enforcing.

Given that information is symmetric, one can use the results of Abreu (1988) to characterize the set of allocations and corresponding payoffs that can be supported by some self-enforcing agreement. Abreu shows that finding subgame perfect Nash equilibrium payoffs in a repeated game begins with finding an equilibrium that yields the worst possible payoff for each party. The other equilibria can be characterized as promises to play a sequence of actions where deviation/breach leads to the parties' playing the equilibria that is worst for the breaching party. MacLeod and Malcomson (1989) show the same logic can be applied to relational contracts. Under the appropriate conditions, the outside option payoffs, Π^0 and U^0, can be supported by some self-enforcing payoff for each party:

Proposition 9.4 *Suppose trade is not efficient under no effort ($y(0) < s^0$); then there exists a self-enforcing agreement $\sigma^0 = \{\sigma^{0P}, \sigma^{0A}\}$ that results in parties' getting their outside option payoffs at the beginning of each period. That is, for all $t = 0, 1, \ldots$, and all histories $h_{t.0} \in \mathcal{H}(t.0)$:*

$$E\{\Pi(\vec{x}(\sigma)) | h_{t.0}\} = \Pi^0,$$

$$E\{U(\vec{x}(\sigma)) | h_{t.0}\} = U^0.$$

Proof. The proof proceeds by induction. The worst self-enforcing relational contract σ^0 is defined as follows. The buyer offers no contract at the beginning of period t: $k(t) = \emptyset$.

The seller's strategy is to accept a contract $k\,(t)$ if and only if:

$$\bar{w}_t > s^0.$$

That is, the seller plans never to put in any effort and hence would accept only contracts that provide an effort-independent wage that is higher than her outside flow. Given that the bonus is nonnegative, this ensures that the behavior is sequentially rational. Finally, the buyer always sends the message that results in the lowest payoff regardless of the seller's effort.

Such a contract results in a payoff of Π^0 and U^0 for parties at the beginning of each period, regardless of previous play because neither party expects future trade to be worthwhile, and thus, not trading is always optimal for at least one party.

To show that it is a subgame perfect Nash equilibrium, it is sufficient to show that, at each stage, there is no one-shot gain from deviation. At step $t.3$, the buyer expects there to be no trade in the following period, and consequently his report m_t^B has no effect on future returns. Therefore it is optimal to send the message giving the lowest payoff. At step $t.2$ the seller faces a similar situation—regardless of her choice, she will get no bonus and then move to the market payoff; hence $e_t = 0$ is optimal.

At step $t.1$, the seller computes the income stream and accepts the contract if and only if it gives her a payoff with no effort that is strictly better than her market alternative. The seller's choice is optimal because to ensure subgame perfection, we need to have the seller accept contracts that make her strictly better off. Thus there is zero effort for any contract offered by the buyer at date $t.0$, and, because this payoff is worse than the outside options, it is optimal to offer $k\,(t) = \emptyset$.   □

Given that parties can ensure they get their outside option by not entering into an agreement, this result shows that their outside option is exactly the worst subgame perfect equilibrium payoff for each party when zero effort makes trade inefficient. At one level, this result seems obvious—if I do not expect the other party to cooperate, then I should not enter into the deal. Yet, as discussed in more detail below, it runs counter to the ideas underlying the Nash bargaining model. Rational parties should seek to achieve efficient allocations, so why would they agree to play the worst outcomes?

The key ingredient here is that behavior is driven by *expectations*. When each party expects the other party not to perform, then cooperation breaks down. This shows that, in a relational contract, observed behavior cannot be explained only by the set of possible payoffs—expectations are a key part of the equilibrium agreement. The potential for a breakdown in the relationship creates the incentive to perform. Given that the payoff possibility set is the same each period (in expected value), consider now the problem of finding the self-enforcing contracts that implement a gain from trade, $\bar{S} \in (S^0, S^*]$, that is between the value of the outside options ($S^0 = U^0 + \Pi^0$) and the maximum surplus possible (S^*). Without loss of generality attention is restricted to stationary contracts of the following form:

$$\bar{k} = \left\{ \bar{w}, \bar{e}\,(c), \bar{b}\,(c) \right\},$$

with the following interpretation. The term $\bar{w}$ is the fixed wage, and $\bar{e}\,(c)$ is the effort the seller promises to supply as a function of the effort cost c. The term $\bar{b}\,(c) \geq 0$ is a bonus that the buyer promises to pay to the seller at date $t.3$ if $e_t \geq \bar{e}(c)$. If not, then the seller gets zero. Should either party breach the agreement (the seller chooses low effort or the buyer does not pay the bonus when he should) then parties separate as soon as possible. In this risk-neutral setup, such a one-step contract is sufficient to implement all the payoffs that can be supported by some self-enforcing contract. Let $\bar{\sigma} = \{\bar{\sigma}^P, \bar{\sigma}^A\}$ be the corresponding stationary relational contract. Since $\bar{S} \in (S^0, S^*]$, we know that $\bar{e}(c)$ can be defined so that:

$$\bar{S} = S(e(\cdot)) \equiv \frac{\Delta}{1-\delta}(\hat{y} - \hat{v}), \qquad (9.16)$$

where $\hat{y} = E\{y(\bar{e}(c))\}$ and $\hat{v} = E\{v(\bar{e}(c), c)\}$ are the respective flow income and effort costs. The corresponding equilibrium payoffs for the buyer and seller are:

$$\bar{\Pi} = \frac{\Delta}{1-\delta}\left(\hat{y} - \hat{w} - \hat{b}\right),$$

$$\bar{U} = \frac{\Delta}{1-\delta}\left(\hat{w} + \hat{b} - \hat{v}\right),$$

where $\hat{b} = E\{\bar{b}(c)\}$.

From Abreu (1988) and proposition 9.4, the relational contract $\bar{\sigma}$ is self-enforcing if and only if at no point can a party gain by deviating from the equilibrium. That is, on a deviation at date $t-1$, the parties will separate at date t. This corresponds to the following necessary and sufficient conditions for the stationary relational contract $\bar{\sigma}$ to be self-enforcing:

1. The contract $\bar{\sigma}$ is individually rational:

$$\bar{\Pi} \geq \Pi^0,$$

$$\bar{U} \geq U^0.$$

2. The seller prefers to choose effort $\bar{e}(c)$ rather than zero effort:

$$\Delta\left(\bar{w} + \bar{b}(c) - v(\bar{e}(c), c)\right) + \delta\bar{U} \geq \Delta\bar{w} + \delta U^0, \forall c \in [c_L, c_H].$$

3. The buyer prefers paying the bonus over not paying it:

$$\Delta\left(-\bar{b}(c)\right) + \delta\bar{\Pi} \geq \delta\Pi^0, \forall c \in [c_L, c_H].$$

The first condition ensures that parties gain by accepting the contract $\bar{k}$. Implicit in this condition is that if the buyer in period t attempts to offer a contract that is different from the contract $\bar{k}$ and better for the buyer, then the seller views this as breach of the agreement and expects termination the following period. This leads to playing the worst equilibrium described above, and thus it is part of equilibrium play to offer $\bar{k}$ each period.

If the seller shades her effort, then she believes the buyer will not pay the bonus. The best she can do then is zero effort, followed by no bonus and separation, which generates the second condition. Finally, the buyer has to decide whether to pay the bonus. If he does not pay the bonus when it is expected, then the relationship goes "bad" and the parties play the worst equilibrium for the buyer in the next period.

Notice that we can add conditions 2 and 3 and, since $\bar{S} = \bar{\Pi} + \bar{U} = S(\bar{e}(\cdot))$, we get the following inequality:

$$\Delta v(\bar{e}(c), c) \leq \delta R(\bar{e}(\cdot)), \forall c \in [c_L, c_H], \tag{9.17}$$

where

$$R(\bar{e}(\cdot)) \equiv S(\bar{e}(\cdot)) - S^0 \tag{9.18}$$

is the future reputational rent from the agreement given effort. Note the reputational rent depends on the effort that is a *function* of the future possible realizations of costs c, while the inequality 9.17 must hold for every possible realization of c on the left-hand side.

This argument shows that (9.17) is a necessary condition for the existence of a self-enforcing relational contact. It is also sufficient:

Proposition 9.5 *(MacLeod and Malcomson 1989; Levin 2003) There exists a self-enforcing, individually rational relational contract with agreed effort, $\bar{e}(c), c \in [c_L, c_H]$, each period if and only if incentive constraint (9.17) is satisfied.*

Proof. The discussion before (9.17) shows the condition is necessary. To prove sufficiency we need to show that, if this expression is satisfied, then there exists an individually rational self-enforcing contract, denoted by $\bar{\sigma}$, that implements effort $\bar{e}(c)$. Condition (9.17) ensures that, for any agreement to a division of the surplus $\alpha \in [0, 1]$, there is an allocation $\vec{x}^\alpha$ with effort function $\bar{e}(c)$ and wage w^α each period such that:

$$\frac{\Delta}{1-\delta}\left(E\{y(\bar{e}(c))\} - w^\alpha\right) = \bar{\Pi}^\alpha = \alpha\left(\bar{S} - S^0\right) + \Pi^0,$$

$$\frac{\Delta}{1-\delta}\left(w^\alpha - E\{v(\bar{e}(c), c)\}\right) = \bar{U}^\alpha = (1-\alpha)\left(\bar{S} - S^0\right) + U^0.$$

Define $\bar{\sigma}$ as follows. If breach (to be defined) has not occurred in any previous period, the buyer offers the contract $k^\alpha = \{\bar{w}, \bar{b}(c), \bar{e}(c)\}$ with the following interpretation. If the seller agrees to choose $e_t \geq \bar{e}(c_t)$, then she has "performed," and the buyer agrees to pay a bonus $\bar{b}(c_t)$ in addition to the wage $\bar{w}$. Moreover, parties continue to trade, following the same pattern in the next period.

Should the seller choose $e_t < \bar{e}(c_t)$, then she has *breached* the agreement, and the buyer pays no bonus. In terms of the formal model, the message space consists of the effort level and whether there is breach: $M^P = \{(\text{performed}, c_t)_{c_t \in [c_L, c_H]}, \text{breach}\}$ where $\phi^P(\text{performed}, c_t) = \bar{b}(c_t)$, and $\phi^P(\text{breach}) = 0$. When breach has occurred, then both parties separate the following period. Similarly, if the seller chooses $e_t \geq \bar{e}(c_t)$ and the buyer does not pay the bonus, then the buyer has breached the contract. Regardless of who is responsible for contract breach, the breach leads to both parties' separating in the following period.

Let us now show the existence of a k^α that ensures this contract is self-enforcing and individually rational. By proposition 9.4, no trade is an equilibrium, and any agreement to separate after some history h is self-enforcing. Now consider the choice of the buyer. He has an incentive to pay $\bar{b}(c)$ only if the return from paying is greater than not paying and then separating. Hence, $\forall c_t \in [c_L, c_H]$, we have:

$$-\bar{b}(c_t) + \delta\bar{\Pi} \geq \delta\Pi^0. \tag{9.19}$$

For the seller we have a similar condition. She must be better off by choosing $\bar{e}(c_t)$ than shirking. Because she gets the same punishment whether she chooses e_t slightly less than $\bar{e}(c_t)$ or $e_t = 0$, then, if she decides to breach, the optimal choice of effort is to set $e_t = 0$. Therefore, for the contract to be self-enforcing we must have $\forall c_t \in [c_L, c_H]$:

$$-v(\bar{e}(c_t), c_t) + \bar{b}(c_t) + \delta \bar{U} \geq \delta U^0. \tag{9.20}$$

A solution $\bar{b}(c_t) \geq 0$ to both (9.19) and (9.20) exists if and only if $\forall c_t \in [c_L, c_H]$:

$$\delta\left(\bar{\Pi} - \Pi^0\right) \geq \bar{b}(c_t) \geq v(\bar{e}(c_t), c_t) - \delta\left(\bar{U} - U^0\right) \geq 0. \tag{9.21}$$

The requirement of individual rationality ensures the right-hand inequality; hence, if this condition is satisfied, we automatically have $\bar{b}(c_t) \geq 0$. Bonus pay that satisfies this inequality exists if and only if:

$$\delta\left(\bar{\Pi} - \Pi^0\right) \geq v(\bar{e}(c_t), c_t) - \delta\left(\bar{U} - U^0\right),$$

which is equivalent to (9.17). Let $\bar{b}^\alpha(c)$ be any bonus pay that satisfies (9.21), which ensures the contract is self-enforcing. The final step is to choose $\bar{w}^\alpha$ to satisfy:

$$\frac{\Delta}{1-\delta}\left(\bar{w}^\alpha + E\left\{\bar{b}^\alpha(c) - v(\bar{e}(c), c)\right\}\right) = \bar{U}^\alpha.$$

The budget constraint ensures that the equilibrium payoff for the buyer is $\bar{\Pi}^\alpha$. □

This is the central result of relational contract theory. It immediately provides conditions under which an efficient contract exists.

Corollary 9.6 *There exists a individually rational, self-enforcing relational contract resulting in efficient effort each period if and only if:*

$$f \times R(e^*(c)) \geq \max_{c \in [c_L, c_H]} v(e^*(c), c)/\delta,$$

where $f = \frac{1}{\Delta}$ is the frequency of trade.

Notice that if $R(e^*(c))$ is strictly positive, then by making trade sufficiently frequent, this condition is always satisfied. This can explain why for small, frequent transactions there is little need to rely on court-enforced agreements when performance/effort is *observable*.

The next issue is what happens when the future gains from trade are not sufficient to implement the efficient allocation. In that case, trade is still possible but at a reduced level of output. Given that condition (9.17) is both necessary and sufficient, then the optimal stationary level of effort that can be enforced with a relational contract can be found as the solution to the following fixed-point problem.

Let R^* be the level of rent at the optimal contract. At a stationary solution, the maximum surplus possible is the solution to the following problem:

$$RR\left(R^0\right) = \max\left\{\max_{e(\cdot) \geq 0} R(e(\cdot)), 0\right\} \tag{9.22}$$

subject to:

$$v(e(c),c) \leq \frac{\delta}{\Delta}R^0, \forall c \in [c_L, c_H]. \tag{9.23}$$

The function $RR(R^0)$ defines the maximum stationary rent that can be supported by a relational contract given future rent R^0. Let $e(c, R^0)$ be the effort function that solves program (9.22). Proposition 9.5 implies that effort $e(c, R^0)$ can be supported by some self-enforcing relational contract if and only if $R^0 \leq RR(R^0)$ (see exercise 4).

Notice that $RR(0) = 0$ corresponds to the self-enforcing contract with no trade. The optimal self-enforcing contract is the one that maximizes the relational rent subject to the self-enforcement constraint:

$$R^* = \max\{R^0 | R^0 \leq RR(R^0)\}. \tag{9.24}$$

The result can be used to generate predictions on what will happen when the relational rent is not sufficiently large to support efficient trade. Figure 9.2 illustrates the effect of future rent, R^0, on the cost of effort, $v(e^0(c), c)$, and the effort, $e^0(c)$, that can be supported by a self-enforcing relational contract.[10] The cost of effort is constrained by $\frac{\delta}{\Delta}R^0$, which in turn reduces effort when the cost of effort c is low.

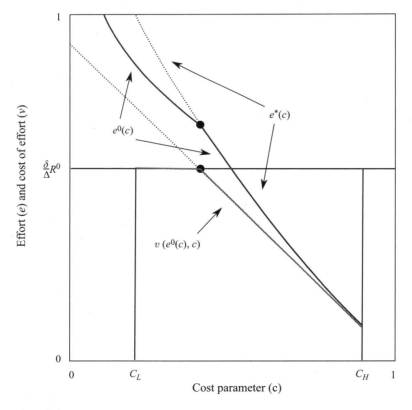

Figure 9.2
Effect of future rent (R^0) on effort.

For high effort costs (low optimal effort) the self-enforcement constraint is not binding, and it is possible to implement efficient effort. The self-enforcement constraint reduces performance when effort costs are *low* and the optimal effort choice is high. Thus, the use of relational contracts is predicted to have a dampening effect on performance.

Another implication of the model is the effect of competition. In a perfectly competitive market, there are no rents—each party is paid exactly their outside option, which in turn implies there can be no effort incentives. This does not necessarily mean no output—parties can be compensated based on observable performance measures.[11] The interplay between competition and relational incentives also has implications for output over the business cycle (MacLeod, Malcomson, and Gomme 1994).

A challenge to directly testing the implications of relational contracts is finding situations in which there are exogenous shocks to the future surplus. Macchiavello and Morjaria (2015) have a clever solution to this problem. They consider the market for flowers grown in Kenya and sold to buyers in Europe. As a proxy for the value of future relationships, they use variation in domestic unrest and violence, which makes it difficult for sellers to export their product. The authors show that reputations are important. They also find evidence that learning is important, an implication that is discussed in more detail below.

In addition to the impact the level of future rents has on performance, the allocation of those rents has some sharp implications for contract form. In particular, if the market for sellers is perfectly competitive ($\bar{U} = U^*$), then (9.21) implies that any self-enforcing contract *necessarily* entails a bonus. Conversely, if the buyer's market is perfectly competitive (and for example, the seller is a monopolist), then bonus pay is necessarily zero, and parties use a fixed price contract.

Finally, the conditions for self-enforcement do not require the contract to be stationary. Suppose that parties agree on effort $\bar{e}(c)$, yielding total return $\bar{S}$ that satisfies the necessary condition for the existence of a self-enforcing agreement. Let $\alpha_t \in [0, 1]$ be any agreed sequence of rent division. Proposition 9.2 implies that a price w_t can be chosen each period to achieve this allocation. Thus, we have:

Corollary 9.7 *Suppose that $\bar{e}(c)$ satisfies (9.17); then for any sequence $\vec{\alpha} = \{\alpha_0, \alpha_1, \alpha_2, \ldots\}$ there exists a self-enforcing contract $\sigma = \{\sigma^P, \sigma^A\}$ such that the equilibrium payoffs and contracts in period t satisfy:*

$$\bar{\Pi}_t = \alpha_t \bar{R}/\delta + \Pi^0,$$

$$\bar{U}_t = (1 - \alpha_t)\,\bar{R}/\delta + U^0,$$

and the equilibrium bonus pay satisfies:

$$\alpha_{t+1}\delta\bar{R} \geq \bar{b}(c_t) \geq v(\bar{e}(c_t), c_t) + (1 - \alpha_{t+1})\,\delta\bar{R}, \tag{9.25}$$

where $\bar{R} = R(\bar{e}(\cdot)) = S(\bar{e}(\cdot)) - S^0$ is the reputational rent from effort $\bar{e}(\cdot)$ (9.18).

This result is an immediate consequence of proposition 9.5.

9.4.1 Renegotiation

Relational contracts suffer from the following logical inconsistency. Proposition 9.5 builds on Abreu's (1988) insight that the set of subgame perfect Nash equilibria are characterized by the worst equilibrium payoff that can be imposed on a party. Yet, the notion of a relational contract begins with the idea that parties agree to choose efficient equilibria when these are feasible.

The difficulty is that in the time-stationary version of the model, the set of equilibria at date t is the same as at date $t + 1$. Thus, if one party breaches the agreement at date t, this is a sunk cost that does not affect the set of feasible payoffs in the future. At the beginning of date $t + 1$, the breaching party could claim she made a mistake, and they should restart with an efficient agreement. If such a claim were believed, then one would have endless breach—each period one (or both parties) would breach, then try to make up in the next period, which would lead to continual "cheating."

Is it possible to make relational contracts resistant to such behavior?[12] One solution proposed in the literature is to make the contract *renegotiation-proof*. van Damme (1989) shows that in a repeated prisoner's dilemma game a contract can be made renegotiation-proof by choosing equilibria that are always Pareto efficient in every subgame, even after contract breach. This is achieved by using punishments that vary the *division* of the rent as a function of the history of play. Suppose parties agree on setting effort at $e(c)$ each period to produce a total surplus $\bar{S}$ that satisfies (9.17). From proposition 9.5, there exists a relational contract, σ^1, that sets $\alpha_t = 1$ for all $t \geq 0$, and another, σ^0, that sets $\alpha_t = 0$ for all $t \geq 0$ that implement effort $\bar{e}(c)$.

Now, consider a relational contract σ that implements $e(c)$ each period with the feature that when the seller breaches an agreement, parties play contract σ^1. When the buyer breaches, then contract σ^0 is used. Such a contract uses the most severe punishment possible for the breaching party while ensuring trade continues. This motivates the following definition.

Definition 9.8 *A self-enforcing and individually rational relational contract σ is renegotiation-proof if for every period $t \geq 0$ and every history $h_{t,0} \in \mathcal{H}$ under which the buyer is able to make a contract offer, there does not exist another self-enforcing and individually rational relational contract, σ', such that:*

$$\Pi\left(\sigma'|h_{t,0}\right) > \Pi\left(\sigma|h_{t,0}\right),$$

$$U\left(\sigma'|h_{t,0}\right) > U\left(\sigma|h_{t,0}\right).$$

This definition requires parties to agree a contract with the feature that, at the beginning of any period, the buyer cannot offer a new relational contract that makes both parties better off. In particular, the contract defined in proposition 9.5 is *not* renegotiation-proof. If breach occurs, parties separate, leaving an unexploited surplus on the table.[13]

It has already been shown that, for any effort allocation that satisfies (9.17), any division of the surplus can be supported by some self-enforcing contract. Thus, the trick to making such a contract renegotiation-proof is to make breach affect the division of the surplus and not the efficiency of trade:

Proposition 9.9 *Suppose there exists an individually rational self-enforcing contract that entails trade every period; then there exists a renegotiation-proof contract resulting in an effort allocation $e^{RP}(\cdot)$ that maximizes reputational rent subject to the incentive constraint:*

$$e^{RP}\left(\cdot\right) \in \arg\max_{e(\cdot)} R\left(e\left(\cdot\right)\right) \qquad (9.26)$$

subject to :

$$v\left(e^{RP}\left(c\right),c\right)/\delta \leq f \times R\left(e\left(c\right)\right), \forall c \in [c_L, c_H]. \qquad (9.27)$$

In period 0, any division of the surplus $S\left(e^{RP}\left(c\right)\right)$ can be supported by some individually rational renegotiation-proof contract.

Proof. Given that the payoffs are time invariant, then, if a renegotiation-proof contract exists, it must give the same total surplus S^{RP} in each period. In order to be self-enforcing, the contract must satisfy (9.27). Because the same constraint applies every period, the optimal renegotiation-proof contract is an effort profile that satisfies (9.26) subject to the incentive constraint. If the effort profile does not satisfy this condition, then one could find another that would lead to greater surplus, which in turn implies that the contract is not renegotiation-proof.

Next we show the existence of a solution. For $x \in \Re_+$, let $e^{RP}(c,x)$ maximize the reputational rent subject to:

$$v\left(e^{RP}\left(c,x\right),c\right)/\delta \leq f \times x, \forall c \in [c_L, c_H].$$

It is assumed that a self-enforcing contract with trade each period exists. Since the payoffs are concave in effort, there exists a self-enforcing contract with trade every period and the same effort function, $e\left(\cdot\right)$, every period. Let $\bar{R}_t \geq 0$ be the reputational rent under this contract for some period t. It must be the case that:

$$R\left(e^{RP*}\left(c,\bar{R}_t\right)\right) \geq \bar{R}_t.$$

This proves that the program (9.26) is feasible. The reputational rent function $R\left(\cdot\right)$ is bounded, say by $\bar{x} > 0$. For $x \in [0,\bar{x}]$ let:

$$F\left(x\right) = R\left(e^{RP}\left(\cdot,x\right)\right).$$

The function $F : [0,\bar{x}] \to [0,\bar{x}]$ is continuous; hence, by Brouwer's fixed-point theorem we have a solution R^{RP}:

$$F\left(R^{RP}\right) = R^{RP},$$

which in turn solves (9.26).

To show the solution is indeed renegotiation-proof, notice the maximum rent for a self-enforcing contract in period t is increasing in the rent available in period $t+1$. The maximum rent in each period is the same, which implies the most efficient self-enforcing contract is time stationary, and therefore it solves (9.26).

The contract implementing a rent division of $\alpha \in [0, 1]$ is constructed as follows:

$t.0$ Until a breach event, each period the buyer offers the contract $k = \left\{w, e^{RP}\left(c\right), b\left(c\right)\right\}$ that implements $e^{RP}\left(c\right)$, and the buyer gets a share α of the surplus, as described in proposition 9.5 and corollary 9.7.

$t.1$ The seller accepts this contract.

t.2 The seller chooses effort $e^{RP}(c_t)$.

t.3 The buyer pays $b(c_t)$ if the seller performs, 0 if the seller does not.

In the next period, if the seller breaches the agreement then, in addition to not paying the bonus, the buyer offers a contract in the next period that gives the buyer all the surplus ($\alpha = 1$). Should the seller perform and the buyer does not pay the promised bonus, then in the next period the buyer offers a contract that gives the seller all the surplus ($\alpha = 0$).

Should the buyer deviate from this behavior, then the seller chooses the best of the following two options:

1. Accept the contract, set effort to zero, and plan to get all the surplus in the next period.

2. Reject the contract and take the outside option.

One can verify this is indeed self-enforcing and renegotiation-proof.   □

The central idea here comes from Levin (2003), who observed that, in a contracting environment, the existence of side payments allows one to apply van Damme's (1989) existence proof for renegotiation-proof equilibria to relational contracts.

Notice that renegotiation-proofness as defined here does not require efficiency after every history, but only at the end of each period of play.[14] The requirement of efficiency for any history is very strong—it cannot hold for general games.[15] As we can see from exercises 7 and 10 in chapter 5, there are various approaches to model bargaining that may give rise to an efficient allocation. Rather than require bargaining itself to be efficient, the concept of renegotiation has the natural requirement that the outcome of bargaining must be efficient, not the outcome after every action.

The notion of renegotiation-proofness has a number of interesting implications for observed contracts. Schmidt and Schnitzer (1995) show that technological changes that make some aspects of performance enforceable can undermine relational contracts. As MacLeod (2007b) observes, this can undermine the use of relational contracts and lead to an interesting trade-off between the quality of law and the use of reputational enforcement. Better-quality legal institutions improve market performance that in turn reduce the rent from a relationship and ultimately reduce the ability of relational contracts to enforce agreements.

More generally, the fact that the threat to terminate is not renegotiation-proof implies that contract breach may not lead to termination but to contract renegotiation and a continuation of the relationship. The next section shows that a request to mitigate is an optimal response to quality uncertainty. Finally, the theory has some helpful implications for effort as a function of job difficulty. Exercise 3 asks the reader to derive the optimal renegotiation-proof contract as a function of the gain from trade. One will discover that the optimal effort function has pooling for both high and low realizations of job difficulty.

9.5   Relational Contracts with Moral Hazard

In the classic relational contract model, there is clear division of duty between incentives and rent allocation. The value of future trade determines the size of the incentive effect, while the size of the bonus pay determines how much of this value is shared with the seller.

The introduction of moral hazard into relational contracts significantly modifies these insights. Moral hazard means the buyer cannot observe effort, e_t, nor task difficulty c_t. Hence, compensation can only be conditioned on the observed output, y_t. In contrast to the agency model of chapter 7, this compensation cannot be legally enforced; thus parties have to rely on relational contracts to implement performance pay.

This section characterizes the self-enforcing contracts with moral hazard in three parts. Section 9.5.1 discusses the payoff structure, the possible contracts, and the first-best allocation when contracts are legally enforceable. Subsection 5.2.2 discusses relational contracts that rely only on the threat to terminate the relationship for contract enforcement. This is called the *market mechanism* because the threat entails parties leaving the relationship to trade with a different party in the market. Milton Friedman in his book *Capitalism and Freedom* (Friedman 1962) suggested that this mechanism is sufficient to ensure the efficient supply of complex commodities. Friedman realized that measuring the performance of complex services, such as health or education, is very difficult. One solution to this is regulation. Friedman explicitly argued that government regulation is not necessary because markets can rely on parties' concern for their reputation to enforce promises. Healthcare suppliers or schools that provide substandard services would be punished with a negative market reputation which would lead to lower demand and profits. Consequently, reputational concerns provide some performance incentives. Klein and Leffler's (1981) seminal model of this effect shows that a concern for reputation does indeed enhance performance. However, in general it does not achieve the first best.

As performance evaluations are noisy, sellers who do not breach their agreement to perform may still find themselves dismissed. The solution to this problem is outlined in subsection 9.5.3, using a model that builds on the work of Levin (2003).

9.5.1 Contracts for Normal and Innovative Commodities

Consider first the case of a normal commodity. Suppose the seller has chosen effort e_t in period t. At the end of the period, the buyer realizes a total output of $\Delta \bar{y}$ with probability $1 - \Delta \gamma^B(e_t)$ and $\Delta \bar{y} - L$ with probability $\Delta \gamma^B(e_t)$. When the cost of effort is observable, then, from the buyer's perspective, breach is associated with changes in the *expected* return given by $\Delta y(e_t)$. Variation in effort leads to perceived variation that is of order of magnitude Δ, which is assumed to be small relative to the value of the relationship. As a consequence, bonus pay in period t is given by a flow b_t whose capital value is $\Delta b_t << L$, much less than the loss associated with the negative signal.

In contrast, when effort is not observed, the buyer is not aware of shirking until there is a capital loss $L >> \Delta$. Given that compensation cannot be adjusted until such a loss is observed, this implies from (9.3) that to provide efficient incentives the seller should pay the capital loss at the time it occurs. This is achieved with a stationary incentive contract denoted by $k^N = \{\bar{w}, D\}$ with the following interpretation. In each period, the buyer pays the seller a flow payment $\bar{w}$. If, in period t, a negative signal is observed, then the seller must make the lump-sum payment D to the buyer. Under such a contract the payoffs of parties are:

$$\Pi^N(\vec{e}, k^N) = E \left\{ \sum_{t=0}^{T-1} \delta^t \Delta \left(\bar{y} - \gamma^B(e_t)L - (\bar{w} - \gamma^B(e_t)D) \right) + \delta^T \Pi^0 \right\}, \qquad (9.28)$$

and

$$U^N(\vec{e}, k^N) = E\left\{\sum_{t=0}^{T-1} \delta^t \Delta\left((\bar{w} - \gamma^B(e_t)D) - v(e_t, c_t)\right) + \delta^T U^0\right\}. \qquad (9.29)$$

The vector $\vec{e}$ is the (random) sequence of effort levels chosen by the seller, and k^N is the contract for a normal commodity. In the absence of enforcement issues, (9.2) implies that the first best can be implemented with a contract that sets $D = L$, and employment continues indefinitely.

Consider now an innovative commodity. Observe that one could also use damages to incentivize the seller. The probability of a negative signal in period t with an innovative good is $1 - \Delta\gamma^G(e_t)$. To provide efficient incentives, the damages have to be set so that the marginal benefit from effort is equal to the marginal cost:

$$-\frac{d\left(1 - \Delta\gamma^G(e^*(c))\right)}{de}D = v_e\left(e^*(c), c\right) \qquad (9.30)$$

$$= \frac{d\gamma^G(e^*(c))}{de}G. \qquad (9.31)$$

This in turn implies the optimal damage level is:

$$D = \frac{G}{\Delta}. \qquad (9.32)$$

Thus, in principle, one can use fixed damage payments to incentivize sellers to choose effort optimally in the case of an innovative commodity. However, as the frequency of trade increases, the optimal damage payment becomes unbounded. This (as is shown below) increases the cost of using relational contracts. To solve this problem, parties use a bonus contract that rewards the seller when there is a positive signal. Thus, for innovative goods, contracts are assumed to take the form $k^I = \{\bar{w}, B\}$, resulting in payoffs:

$$\Pi^I(\vec{e}, k^I) = E\left\{\sum_{t=0}^{T-1} \delta^t \Delta\left(\bar{y} + \gamma^G(e_t)G - (\bar{w} + \gamma^G(e_t)B)\right) + \delta^T \Pi^0\right\}, \qquad (9.33)$$

$$U^I(\vec{e}, k^I) = E\left\{\sum_{t=0}^{T-1} \delta^t \Delta\left((\bar{w} + \gamma^G(e_t)B) - v(e_t, c_t)\right) + \delta^T U^0\right\}. \qquad (9.34)$$

From (9.5) it follows that the first best can be implemented with the contract $k^I = \{\bar{w}, G\}$ that pays a bonus equal to G whenever there is a good signal.

In summary, if enforceable contracts are possible and there is some gain from trade, then the efficient contracts are $k^N = \{\bar{w}, L\}$ and $k^I = \{\bar{w}, G\}$ for normal and innovative commodities respectively. These contracts ensure that the seller has an incentive to choose effort efficiently each period. The wage $\bar{w}$ can then be set to divide the surplus between the two parties. Consider now the use of relational contracts to enforce these contract terms.

9.5.2 The Market Mechanism and Efficiency Wages

This subsection explores the use of the *market mechanism* to implement self-enforcing contracts when there is moral hazard. The model comes from Klein and Leffler (1981), whose goal is to capture the implications of Milton Friedman's (1962) idea that the threat of buyers shunning sellers who supply low-quality goods can provide the appropriate incentive for quality.

Klein and Leffler consider a situation in which the buyer cannot rely on a court-enforced contract to ensure a seller delivers a product with the agreed on quality. The market mechanism works as follows. The seller agrees to supply a high-quality good for a price above her cost. This arrangement continues until the buyer observes a defect in the supplied commodity. At that time, the buyer transmits this information to the market and the seller loses her "reputation for quality." Consequently, the market no longer believes the seller will continue to offer high quality, and buyers are no longer willing to pay a price above cost.

One can map this situation into a relational contract by viewing the market as fulfilling the role of buyer and the seller maintaining its role as a seller. Next, as trade of goods continues until the buyer observes a defect, this model is most appropriate for *normal* commodities, and therefore the flow value of the commodity at date t is $y(e_t) = \bar{y} - \gamma^B(e_t) L$, where L is the loss when the commodity is defective. Suppose that $y(0) > 0$; hence, one can identify low-quality sellers as those who engage in no effort and who sell the commodity at the competitive price:

$$w^L = v(0, c_t) = 0.$$

This in turn fixes the outside option for the sellers at $U^0 = 0$, while the market's consumption of the low-quality commodity yields a payoff of $\Pi^0 = y(0)/r$.

One can view the seller's entering into a relational contract with the market as follows. Under the market mechanism, only the seller is punished, and one does not need to consider intertemporal payoff effects for different buyers in the market. The only decision for a buyer is whether to purchase a high-quality or a low-quality product from seller with either a good or a tarnished reputation.

The Klein and Leffler (1981) strategy supposes that a prospective high-quality (untarnished) seller enters and agrees to supply to the market a high-quality good at high price, $w^H > w^L$. Under this contract, it is assumed that once a defect is observed then the market believes the seller will choose low effort ($e_t = 0$) from that point forward. Consequently, the market is willing to pay only the price w^L to such a "tarnished" seller. This ensures that the default payoff for a tarnished seller is $U^0 = 0$. Here one is relying on proposition 9.4, which ensures that once a seller is tarnished by producing a defective product, then there is a self-enforcing agreement making it impossible for her to recover her reputation.

The next question is whether it can be an equilibrium for a seller to enter and charge a price w^H and to supply positive effort, $e_t > 0$. The crucial assumption of the market mechanism is that price in period t *does not* depend on quality in period t. This is the explicit noncontractible assumption of Klein and Leffler (1981). For example, individuals may choose a college based on publicly observable reputation measures, but one cannot enter into a contract requiring the college to deliver an agreed level of "educational services."[16] Rather, effort affects the probability of a defect, which in turn determines whether the seller becomes "tarnished" by nonperformance and then loses the future rent from charging w^H. It is this rent that Klein and Leffler (1981) associate with a seller's return to her reputation.

Consider a stationary equilibrium at which the untarnished seller chooses the same effort choice given costs, c_t each period, and charges a price w^H until she loses her reputation. The seller's payoff as a function of the price is given by $U\left(w^H\right)$—this payoff is determined jointly with the equilibrium effort. If the seller delivers a defective good then she has tarnished her reputation and gets the default payoff $U^0 = 0$ from that point on.

This payoff is determined by the seller's optimal effort choice. A seller with an untarnished reputation chooses effort after observing costs, and her effort choice satisfies:

$$e\left(c_t, \delta U\left(w^H\right)\right) = \arg\max_{e \geq 0} E\{\Delta\left(w^H - v\left(e, c_t\right)\right)$$

$$+ \delta\left(\left(1 - \Delta\gamma^B\left(e\right)\right) U\left(w^H\right) + \Delta\gamma^B\left(e\right) U^0\right)\}$$

$$= \arg\max_{e \geq 0} E\left\{-v\left(e, c_t\right) - \gamma^B\left(e\right) \delta U\left(w^H\right)\right\}. \tag{9.35}$$

The first line takes into account the possibility that the good is defective, leading to a tarnished reputation. Since the utility of a tarnished seller is normalized to zero ($U^0 = 0$), this implies the second line. The future payoff can be identified with the reputational rent from being untarnished—let this rent be defined by $R = U\left(w^H\right)$. The equilibrium given the price w^H is found by computing effort as a function of the rent, and then using a fixed-point argument to determine effort and the equilibrium price.

Given rent R, effort is uniquely determined by:

$$\frac{\partial v\left(e^M\left(c, \delta R\right), c\right)}{\partial e} = -\frac{\partial \gamma^B\left(e^M\left(c, \delta R\right)\right)}{\partial e} \delta R,$$

an expression that is independent of the frequency of trade.

From this, it immediately follows that effort rises with the value of the seller's future reputation given by:

$$\frac{\partial e^M\left(c, \delta R\right)}{\partial R} > 0.$$

The equilibrium payoff is found using an argument that is similar to expression (9.24). The reputational rent R determines the effort of the seller and her present value of trade at price w^H:

$$F\left(w^H, \delta R\right) = \Delta\left(w^H - \bar{v}^M\left(R\right)\right) + \left(1 - \Delta\bar{\gamma}^M\left(R\right)\right) \delta R,$$

where $\bar{v}^M\left(R\right) = E\left\{v\left(e^M\left(c, \delta R\right), c\right)\right\}$ is the expected cost of effort as a function of the future rent, and $\bar{\gamma}^M\left(R\right) = E\left\{\gamma^B\left(e^M\left(c, \delta R\right)\right)\right\}$ is the probability of a defect under the optimal effort given the future rent R. When the rent is zero there is no effort, and hence $\bar{v}^M\left(0\right) = 0$. This, combined with the envelope theorem, implies:

$$\frac{\partial F\left(w^H, \delta R\right)}{\partial R} = \delta\left(1 - \Delta\bar{\gamma}^M\left(R\right)\right) \in (0, 1), \tag{9.36}$$

$$F\left(w^H, 0\right) = \Delta w^H. \tag{9.37}$$

Moreover, since $\bar{\gamma}^M\left(R\right)$ is decreasing with R, $F\left(w^H, \delta R\right)$ is a convex function of R.

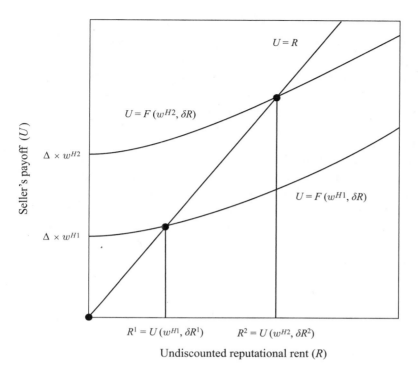

Figure 9.3
Equilibrium in Klein-Leffler model.

If $U\left(w^H\right)$ is the stationary payoff for a seller with an untarnished reputation, then it must solve:

$$U\left(w^H\right) = F\left(w^H, \delta U\left(w^H\right)\right). \tag{9.38}$$

From (9.36)–(9.37) it follows that there exists a unique solution to (9.38) that determines the equilibrium payoff under the market mechanism.

The solution is illustrated in figure 9.3. On the bottom axis is the undiscounted rent, R, from the relationship in the following period, that determines utility $F\left(w^H, \delta U\left(w^H\right)\right)$. When the reputational rent is zero, then the seller has no incentive to input effort, and her utility is given by the price she receives in the first period. As the rent rises, so does her discounted payoff and her effort. The point at which the rent is equal to the future payoff with reputation intact defines the solution (9.38).

For any price w^H, there is an equilibrium effort choice with the feature that the expected utility of the seller is equal to her reputational rent. Possible prices are illustrated by w^{H1} and w^{H2} in figure 9.3. This price is called an *efficiency wage* when the seller is a worker because it has the feature that an increase in the price/wage leads to an increase in effort. Thus, an increase in the price/wage leads to an increase in seller/worker "efficiency." These results are summarized as follows:

Proposition 9.10 *For each price $w^H > 0$, there exists a self-enforcing relational contract under the market mechanism resulting in payoff $U\left(w^H\right) > U^0$ satisfying (9.38) that is increasing in price w^H, with effort $e^M\left(c, \delta U\left(w^H\right)\right)$ that is also increasing in price w^H.*

This result shows there is a one-to-one relationship between the offered price and equilibrium effort by the untarnished sellers. It is common for these models to be solved using only the participation and incentive constraints. However, the fact that there can be many prices supporting different effort levels implies there is a need for a commonly held social norm. Entrants expect to be paid w^H and expect to lose customers when the product is defective. This behavior does not follow from any price-theoretic considerations because all firms are identical, and there is no technical reason why firms who are tarnished cannot produce high-quality goods.

The interlocking behaviors that punish the sellers are necessary under the hypothesis of a fixed price to ensure high effort. Thus, the market mechanism and the equivalent efficiency wage model illustrate a situation in which social norms play a central role, consistent with Akerlof's (1980) emphasis on the importance of social norms for labor market performance.

The next question is: Which norm will the market select? A unique market equilibrium can be determined if it is assumed that buyers can choose the profit-maximizing price, where the profit as a function of the price w^H is:

$$\pi^M\left(w^H\right) = \bar{y} - \bar{\gamma}^M\left(\delta U\left(w^H\right)\right) L - w^H, \tag{9.39}$$

where $\bar{\gamma}^M\left(\delta U\left(w^H\right)\right)$ is defined to be the Poisson parameter for failure when the seller gets a future rent $U\left(w^H\right)$. Let $w^{H*} \geq w^L$ be the price that maximizes this expression. If the firm sets the price equal to w^L there is no rent, the seller selects zero effort, and buyer payoffs are:

$$\pi^M\left(w^L\right) = \bar{y} - \bar{\gamma}^M\left(\delta U\left(w^L\right)\right) L = \bar{y} - \gamma\left(0\right) L > 0.$$

Whether there is a price $w^{H*} > w^L$ such that $\pi^M\left(w^{H*}\right) > \pi^M\left(w^L\right)$ depends on the parameter values. When the frequency of trade is very low, then $\delta \to 0$ and the cost of eliciting effort rises to the point where paying a high price for effort is no longer profitable (see exercise 5). We can summarize as follows:

Proposition 9.11 *If $w^{H*} > w^L$, then under the market mechanism there exist self-enforcing strategies for buyers and sellers that result in the supply of commodities whose quality is above the minimum quality offered in the market. Generically, the first best is not achieved with the market mechanism.*

Proof. The first part of this proposition follows from the discussion above. The generic result means the efficient allocation is implemented at best on a measure zero set of parameter values. This result follows immediately from the observation that efficient effort is independent of the frequency of trade. However, equilibrium quality, and hence wage, changes continuously with the length of a period Δ, and thus there is at most a single value of Δ that results in efficient production. $\square$

The model of Klein and Leffler (1981) has a number of attractive features that can help explain why it has been so influential. First, it captures well the Friedman intuition that high-quality sellers can charge premiums that in turn provide an incentive to perform above the minimum quality level. Second, given that high-quality sellers are earning rents, the puzzle is how this is possible in a competitive market. Klein and Leffler observe that there must be some mechanism that leads to a dissipation of these rents. They suggest that the market mechanism may explain why we observe excessive advertising by high-quality sellers. For example, in 2016, firms selling mechanical watches spent about $5 billion on advertising mechanical watches that in many cases tell worse time than a $10 quartz watch. Similarly, the model can explain why high-end fashion shops on Fifth Avenue in New York may have few items that take up a great deal of floor space. In both cases, these expenditures help dissipate the rents that accrue to high-reputation sellers.

This idea has also been used to explain why competitive labor markets may be inefficient. Shapiro and Stiglitz (1984) observe that one way to enhance worker productivity is to pay a high wage and combine it with the threat of dismissal to ensure high effort. They argue that, in this case, rent dissipation occurs via unemployment—workers who lose their "reputations" by being fired must spend some time unemployed before finding new work. The model in their paper belongs to the class of "efficiency wage" models, a concept that goes back to the work of Leibenstein (1957). He observes that employers in developing countries may offer above-market clearing wages because this increases worker productivity.[17]

The early evidence on efficiency wages tended to be indirect because one cannot directly observe effort and the strategies of market participants. The early work of Krueger and Summers (1988) finds evidence of unexplained differences in wages across industries, a result that is potentially consistent with an efficiency wage model. However, work beginning with Gibbons and Katz (1991), Abowd, Kramarz, and Margolis (1999), and most recently Card et al. (2016) suggests that high wages are the result of rent sharing between the workers and the firms and not necessarily due to efficiency wages. The best evidence comes from experimental studies using human subjects in a laboratory setting. For a good review see Fehr and Gächter (2008).

The theory implies that if workers are paid a rent and the probability of dismissal is correlated with effort then workers will work harder. The empirical challenge is that one cannot easily disentangle effort from ability; the evidence of Gibbons and Katz (1991) suggests that workers at high-wage firms have higher quality, consistent with the implications of the relational contract model. However, we cannot conclude that firms *choose* high wages to induce higher effort.

Those data are based on labor market dynamics. An alternative approach is internal labor market economics developed by Doeringer and Piore (1971) for US firms and Dore's (1973) classic study that compares UK and Japanese firms. Their work is based on case studies of practices within the firm that highlight the role of job assignments and promotions in providing performance incentives. Waldman (1984) introduces a model of job assignment to illustrate the role of worker ability in generating a hierarchy within the firm.

MacLeod and Malcomson (1988) combine Waldman's idea with relational contracting to generalize the market mechanism to include an internal labor market. The model predicts that young workers choose high effort in order to be promoted. However, this generates a "Peter Principle."[18] When a worker reaches his final level, effort drops. This implies there is a tenure effect, with older workers receiving a rent. There is still an open question about the extent to which performance incentives, rent sharing, and sorting by ability can explain observed wage patterns in firms.

Finally, proposition 9.11 implies that even if the market mechanism is at work in the marketplace, it is far from perfect. Financial markets provide a good example. Though he did not cite Friedman, Greenspan (1998) explicitly uses Friedman's argument that the market mechanism would be sufficient to police the trade in over-the-counter securities. Ten years later, Greenspan admitted that he had made a mistake (Greenspan 2008).

9.5.3   Efficient Relational Contracts with Moral Hazard

The market mechanism is a simple, ad hoc institution that creates performance incentives by providing sellers/workers with rents that they may lose when the market observes low performance. However, as shown in proposition 9.11, this does not in general lead to an efficient level of trade. This is for two reasons.

First, competition may lead to a level of rents that depends on the options available to parties and not the marginal cost of effort. Hence, the level of rents can be either above or below the level that induces efficient effort. This is similar to the earlier result on career concerns in chapter 7 where reputation effects may result in too little or too much effort. Second, because the signal of performance is imperfect, there is a positive probability of sanctioning the seller, even though the efficient effort level is supplied. This in turn leads to inefficient separations.

Levin (2003) shows that relational contracts with performance pay can solve this problem. The key insight is that inefficient separations are eliminated by conditioning reputation loss on events that both parties observe without error. In the case of moral hazard, effort is not observed, but the output, y_t, is observed by both parties, as is any bonus pay by the buyer or damage payments by the seller.

Under a performance pay contract, the seller's pay varies with output, and thus there is no specific performance obligation—the seller chooses effort as she wishes. The link between effort and pay creates an incentive for the seller to choose the agreed effort level, as in the principal-agent model of chapter 7.

When the contract calls for bonus pay, the buyer has an obligation to pay the mutually agreed bonus pay whenever there is a good signal. As both the buyer and seller can observe the signals, then enforcement can be based on the classic relational contract theory discussed in section 9.4. To see this, consider a seller who agrees to supply effort $e(c)$ every period when task difficulty is c. The gain from trade or rent from continuing the relationship is given by:

$$R(e(\cdot)) = \delta \left(E\{y(e(c)) - v(e(c),c)\} \frac{\Delta}{1-\delta} - \Pi^0 - U^0 \right). \qquad (9.40)$$

This rent defines the maximum penalty that can be imposed on either party via the threat of separation. Given that there are only two signals—good or bad—the agreed contract in period t can be assumed to take the form:

$$k_t = \{\bar{w}_t, B_t, D_t, \bar{e}(c_t)\},$$

where $\bar{w}_t$ is a payment per unit of time to the seller, B_t is a bonus payment to the seller if the good signal occurs, while D_t is the *damage* payment from the seller to the buyer if the bad signal occurs. The contract also includes the seller's performance obligation in period t, given by $\bar{e}(c_t)$, the effort she agrees to choose as a function of task difficulty c_t.

The key idea in Levin (2003) is that a bad signal does not trigger an end to the relationship, as it would with the market mechanism. Rather, as in the classic principal-agent problem, the optimal contract entails the use of pay linked to commonly observed performance measures. *Contract breach* occurs if there is a good signal and the buyer does not pay an agreed bonus to the seller, in which case the buyer should face a sanction. Conversely, in the event of a bad signal, if the seller does not pay the promised damages to the buyer, then she faces a sanction. In both cases, as the observed breach is common knowledge, punishments can be coordinated. Hence, one can directly apply proposition 9.5 to moral hazard in relational contracts:

Proposition 9.12 *Under moral hazard, parties can agree to an individually rational, self-enforcing contract with the seller choosing effort $\bar{e}(c_t)$ each period if and only if there is a constant $K \geq 0$ such that:*

1. *For all $c \in [c_L, c_H]$ effort satisfies:*
   (a) *For normal commodities:* $\frac{\partial v(e(c),c)}{\partial e} = -\frac{\partial \gamma^B(e(c))}{\partial e}K,$
   (b) *For innovative commodities:* $\frac{\partial v(e(c),c)}{\partial e} = \frac{\partial \gamma^G(e(c))}{\partial e}K.$
2. $K \leq \delta R(e(\cdot)).$

Moreover, if the future payoffs in each period do not vary with observed seller performance, then the explicit terms, $k_t = \{\bar{w}_t, B_t, D_t, \bar{e}(c)\}$, satisfy:

$$B_t + D_t = K.$$

Proof. We consider the case of a normal commodity; the proof for an innovative commodity is similar. Suppose that a constant K satisfying the conditions of the proposition exists. Choose any $B, D \geq 0$ such that $B + D = K$. Each period, the buyer offers the contract $k = \{\bar{w}, B, D, \bar{e}(\cdot)\}$ with the flow wage chosen so that the seller gets equilibrium utility $U^* = U^0 + D$ each period. The second condition implies that the payoff to the buyer is

$$\Pi^* = S(\bar{e}(\cdot)) - U^0 - D$$

$$\geq \Pi^0 + B.$$

These conditions ensure the contract is individually rational. In order to enforce terms, the seller promises to pay D when the adverse event occurs. If she does not, then the contract calls for her to get U^0 in the next period, either via separation or by using a renegotiation-proof contract, as described in section 9.4. Because the seller has a gain of D from continuing the relationship, it is optimal for her to pay when there is a bad outcome rather than breach the agreement.

Similarly, if the good event occurs, then the contract requires the buyer to pay a bonus B to the seller. Again, as the buyer's gain from continuing the relationship is greater than B, there is no incentive to breach.

Finally, since $B + D = K$, then by condition 1 it is optimal for the seller to choose effort $\bar{e}(c)$ when job difficulty is c.

For the converse, let U_{t+} denote the equilibrium payoff to the seller immediately after the performance signal is observed, given the history up to period t. Notice that this can take on only two values depending on whether there is a good or bad outcome: $E\{U_{t+}|y_t = \bar{y}\}$ and

$E\{U_{t+}|y_t = \bar{y} - L\}$. Given that the probability of a loss L does not depend on job difficulty, then $K = E\{U_{t+}|y_t = \bar{y}\} - E\{U_{t+}|y_t = \bar{y} - L\}$ is independent of c, and thus effort must solve condition 1. The second condition follows from the arguments in proposition 9.5. The case of an innovative good is similar.

Finally, if future utility does not depend on the realized outcome, then it must be the case that performance pay is the sole source of effort incentives. This in turn implies $B_t + D_t = K$. Notice that if $K < \delta R(e(\cdot))$, then it is possible for these payments to vary over time, while having time-invariant payoffs for both parties. $\qquad\Box$

This result shows that the introduction of a noisy performance measure does not necessarily imply endogenous separation under a relational contract. It also is consistent with evidence from the Indian software industry in Banerjee and Duflo (2000), who find, contrary to what they had expected, that the delivery of a substandard product did not immediately imply the end of a relationship.[19] Rather, firms would ask their counterparties to correct any defects. This behavior is also consistent with American rules for commercial exchange under the UCC, which requires sellers to remedy the delivery of defective goods with either a price reduction or with the delivery of conforming goods.[20] In both cases, notice that from proposition 9.9 one can use a self-enforcing contract that is renegotiation-proof.

Having characterized the set of self-enforcing, individually rational contracts, the next stage is to derive the relational contract on which the parties would agree. This can be viewed as a two-step procedure. If parties are rational, then we would expect them to agree to an arrangement that maximizes the joint surplus subject to their participation and the incentive constraints. Any contract that satisfies this is simply called a *constrained efficient relational contract*. The second step is to determine the share of the surplus as a function of the relative bargaining powers of the two parties.

Given that the environment is stationary, without loss of generality we can restrict attention to contracts that require the same effort as a function of costs in each period. Next, from proposition 9.12, it follows that any constrained efficient relational contract for a normal commodity maximizes the future rent (9.40) subject to the self-enforcement and incentive constraints:

$$\max_{e(\cdot)\geq 0, K\in\Re} R(e(\cdot)), \tag{9.41}$$

subject to:

$$0 \leq K \leq \max\{\delta R(e(\cdot)), 0\}, \tag{9.42}$$

$$\frac{\partial v(e(c), c)}{\partial e} = -\frac{\partial \gamma^B(e(c))}{\partial e} K, \forall c \in [c_L, c_H]. \tag{9.43}$$

In the case of an innovative commodity, the term $-\frac{\partial \gamma^B(e(c))}{\partial e}$ is replaced by $\frac{\partial \gamma^G(e(c))}{\partial e}$.

Proposition 9.13 *There exists a unique solution, $\{K^{R*}, e^{R*}(\cdot)\}$, to the program (9.41). Moreover, the efficient effort level in the absence of self-enforcement constraints, $e^{R*}(\cdot) = e^*(\cdot)$, is a part of a constrained efficient relational contract if and only if $\delta R(e^*(\cdot)) \geq L$ in the case of a normal commodity, and $\delta R(e^*(\cdot)) \geq G$ in the case of an innovative good.*

Proof. Since $v_{ee}(e,c) > 0$ and $v_e(0,c) = 0$, the solution to (9.43) is unique. Let it be denoted by $e(c,K)$, and observe that $e(c,0) = 0$ and $e(c,K) > 0$ iff $K > 0$. Since $e(c,0) = 0$, it follows that $\{0,0\}$ is a feasible solution. Next, observe that $e(c,K)$ is a strictly increasing continuous function of K, which in turn implies that $R(e(\cdot,K))$ is a continuous function of K. This ensures that the set of K solving (9.42) is compact and, combined with the continuity of $R(e(\cdot,K))$, it ensures the existence of a solution. If, in the case of a normal good, $R^*(e^*(\cdot)) < L$, then there is not enough surplus to support a self-enforcing contract that implements the efficient effort, while if $R^*(e^*(\cdot)) \geq L$ then one can achieve efficient effort with $K = L$. A similar argument applies in the case of an innovative good.

To show uniqueness, there are two cases. First, suppose constraint (9.42) is not binding. This implies that

$$\frac{\partial R(e(\cdot,K))}{\partial K} = 0;$$

in other words, K defines a global optimum, which in turn implies $K = L$ for a normal good, or $K = G$ for an innovative good. The second case supposes constraint (9.42) is binding. If the solution is not unique, then there must be two solutions, K^1 and some $K^2 > K^1$. Both have to be binding for (9.42); otherwise, one has a unique global solution. But if both are binding, $K^i = R(e(\cdot,K^i))$, $i = 1, 2$, which in turn implies that K^2 has a higher surplus, and hence K^1 cannot be part of a constrained optimal relational contract. $\square$

This result shows the existence and uniqueness of a constrained efficient relational contract with effort $e^{R*}(\cdot)$ and associated penalty: $D = K^{R*}$ for a normal good and bonus pay, $B = K^{R*}$ for an innovative good. In cases where $R(e^{R*}(\cdot)) < 0$, then it must be the case that $K^{R*} = e^{R*}(0,0) = 0$ and parties would choose not to trade. This can occur even though there are gains from trade—$R(e^*(\cdot)) \geq 0$ (see exercise 6). This result characterizes the payoffs that are possible but not the contract terms. These depend in part on how the gain from trade is divided between parties in each period, as is the case for self-enforcing contracts with symmetric information. The case that provides the strongest and possibly the most interesting result supposes that parties agree to the same division of the gain from trade each period. Again, consider first the case of a normal commodity, and suppose that the buyer is able to get a share α of the gains from trade. Let $\vec{\kappa}^{R*} = \{K^{R*}, e^{R*}(\cdot)\}$ denote the optimal terms for effort and the incentive level and let $R^{R*} = R(e^{R*}(\cdot)) > 0$ be the corresponding gain from trade.

We know that with a normal commodity, if incentives are provided only with bonus pay, then the wage term becomes unbounded as the frequency increases. Hence, for normal commodities, attention is restricted to contracts under which the seller pays the buyer damages $D^{R*} = K^{R*}$ whenever there is a defect. Let $w(\alpha, \vec{\kappa}^{R*})$ be the wage that gives the buyer a share α, then it must solve:

$$\Pi(\alpha, \vec{\kappa}^{R*}) = \Pi^0 + \alpha R^{R*} = \frac{\Delta}{1-\delta} E\{\bar{y} - \gamma^B(e^{R*}(c))(L - D^{R*}) - w(\alpha, \vec{\kappa}^{R*})\}.$$

This implies a wage:

$$w(\alpha, \vec{\kappa}^{R*}) = E\{\bar{y} - \gamma^B(e^{R*}(c))(L - D^{R*})\} - \frac{1-\delta}{\Delta}(\Pi^0 + \alpha R^{R*}).$$

Under this wage payment, the seller receives a payoff in each period:

$$U\left(\alpha, \vec{\kappa}^{R*}\right) = (1-\alpha)\, R^{R*} + U^{0}.$$

The difficulty with this contract is that when the seller's share of the rent, $(1-\alpha)$, is sufficiently small, the seller is better off shirking, getting the wage $w(\alpha, \vec{\kappa}^{R*})$, and quitting to get the outside option U^{0}. To solve this problem, the contract has to be supplemented with a *severance penalty* $P\left(\alpha, \vec{\kappa}^{R*}\right)$ from the seller to the buyer should the seller decide to leave the relationship.

Consider the case at date $t.3$ in which parties observe that low signal. In this case, the seller is called on to pay to the buyer an amount D^{R*}. If she does not, then the buyer terminates the relationship. For this behavior to be self-enforcing we must have:

$$D^{R*} = K^{R*} \leq (1-\alpha)\,\delta R^{R*} + P\left(\alpha, \vec{\kappa}^{R*}\right).$$

It must also be the case that the buyer does not have an incentive to take advantage of the seller by forcing separation, and hence we have:

$$\Pi\left(\alpha, \vec{\kappa}^{R*}\right) \geq \Pi^{0} + P\left(\alpha, \vec{\kappa}^{R*}\right),$$

from which we get the following proposition:

Proposition 9.14 *Suppose it is efficient to trade a normal commodity under terms $\vec{\kappa}$, and the buyer receives a share α from the gains from trade in each period; then this allocation can be implemented with a relational contract with stationary price terms $\vec{k}\left(\alpha, \vec{\kappa}^{R*}\right) = \{\bar{w}, D, P\}$:*

$$\bar{w} = E\left\{\bar{y} - \gamma^{B}\left(e^{R*}(c)\right)\left(L - K^{R*}\right)\right\} - \frac{1-\delta}{\Delta}\left(\Pi^{0} + \alpha R\left(e^{R*}(\cdot)\right)\right),$$

$$D = K^{R*},$$

$$P \in \left[K^{R*} - (1-\alpha)\,\delta R\left(e^{R*}(\cdot)\right), \alpha\delta R\left(e^{R*}(\cdot)\right)\right],$$

where $\bar{w}$ is the flow payment from the buyer to the seller each period, D is the damage payment from the seller to the buyer whenever a low signal is observed, and P is the payment from the seller to the buyer whenever there is separation.

The damage payment under this contract is set to the optimal level, given by K^{R*}. If the seller receives a rent that is less than K^{R*} ($K^* > (1-\alpha)\delta R\left(e^{R*}(\cdot)\right)$), then to ensure the seller will pay the promised damages the contract requires the seller to pay damages P when there is dismissal. This damage payment ensures that the contract is both individually rational and self-enforcing. The fact that $K^{R*} \leq \delta R\left(e^{R*}(\cdot)\right)$ ensures that P can be set so the buyer does not terminate the relationship in order to collect P. A similar contract works in the case of an innovative good. In that case the incentive payment goes from the buyer to the seller, and it is the buyer who must pay the severance pay if the relationship is terminated.

Corollary 9.15 *Suppose it is efficient to trade an innovative commodity under terms $\vec{\kappa}$, and the buyer receives a share α from the gains from trade in each period; then*

this allocation can be implemented with a relational contract with stationary price terms
$\vec{k}\left(\alpha, \vec{\kappa}^{R*}\right) = \{\bar{w}, B, P\}$:

$$\bar{w} = E\left\{\bar{y} + \gamma^G\left(e^{R*}(c)\right)\left(G - K^{R*}\right)\right\} - \frac{1-\delta}{\Delta}\left(\Pi^0 + \alpha R\left(e^{R*}(\cdot)\right)\right),$$

$$B = K^{R*},$$

$$P \in \left[K^{R*} - \alpha\delta R\left(e^{R*}(\cdot)\right), (1-\alpha)\,\delta R\left(e^{R*}(\cdot)\right)\right],$$

where $\bar{w}$ is the flow payment from the buyer to the seller in each period, B is a bonus payment from the buyer to the seller whenever a high signal is observed, and P is the payment from the buyer to the seller whenever there is separation.

For both contracts, the fixed payments are bounded as the frequency of trade increases, and from these expressions, one can compute the corresponding self-enforcing continuous-time contract (see exercise 7).

In summary, extending relational contract theory to the case of moral hazard provides a number of new insights relative to agency theory. The key trade-off in agency theory is between the quality of information regarding performance and an agent's aversion toward risk. In contrast, relational contracts deal with risk-neutral parties, and the predictions follow from potentially observable features of the trading environment rather than unobserved risk aversion.

Finally, the folk theorem for repeated games (Fudenberg and Maskin 1986) suggests that when the frequency of trade increases, generically the set of possible self-enforcing contracts should increase. However, the results of Abreu, Milgrom, and Pearce (1991) imply that this outcome is sensitive to the information structure. In particular, the threat to terminate a relationship when performance is low is not effective for innovative commodities. In this case, efficient trade is achieved with a bonus pay contract, which may explain why bonus pay is more commonly associated with highly skilled workers (Lemieux, MacLeod, and Parent 2009). See Fuchs (2007) and Manso (2011) for results on the optimal design of contracts for innovative goods.

9.6 Discussion

The goal of relational contract theory is to understand how parties are able to enforce agreements when they cannot rely on court enforcement, either because the courts cannot observe the relevant information or because they are not an effective institution. A key insight is that agreements are more effective when they define breach events that are common knowledge for both the buyer and the seller. The difference between a relational contract and a legally enforceable contract depends on what happens when contract breach occurs.

A legally enforceable contract is one for which breach gives the harmed party the right to seek remedies in court. In contrast, a relational contract is one for which breach gives rise to informal "self-help" remedies, such as choosing not to continue a relationship. Malcomson (1981) argues that this can occur because worker performance is not easily verifiable and enforceable, which in turn can lead to the use of an efficiency wage.

The theory of self-enforcing contracts models this idea as the equilibrium of a dynamic game. Efficient equilibria exist if and only if the short-run gain from breach is less than the long-run return from continuing the relationship (MacLeod and Malcomson 1989). Section 9.5 shows that this result extends to the case with moral hazard, when the buyer cannot observe effort but both parties observe a common performance signal (Levin 2003). It is shown that the form of the contract (bonus pay versus a warranty or damage payment) depends on the nature of the good—a normal or innovative commodity (MacLeod 2007b).

The literature on relational contracts has developed a number of interesting empirical implications of the basic relational contract model. Baker, Gibbons, and Murphy (1994) explores the implications when parties can add to a relational contract enforceable performance pay terms, such as commission payments or piece-rate payments. If the introduction of a piece rate increases the value of continued exchange, then it enhances performance. However, as Schmidt and Schnitzer (1995) show, it can also have the effect of increasing the value of not using a relational contract, which in turn may reduce the future gain from trade using a relational contract. One can view the ability to use enforceable performance pay contracts as a measure of the quality of the legal system. In that case, this result implies that increasing the quality of law may reduce the quality of output in some cases (see table 2, MacLeod 2007b).

Pearce and Stacchetti (1998) extend these results to the case of risk-averse parties. Bernheim and Whinston (1998) observe that the need to generate a future gain from trade to support cooperation can explain why parties may choose incomplete contracts.

Ramey and Watson (2002) were the first to highlight that common observability of the breach event enhances cooperation. Specifically, they point out that a way to solve this problem is through the use of arbitration. In international agreements it is more difficult to use courts to enforce an agreement. However, parties may request an arbitrator to settle a dispute. This can add value precisely because the arbitrator's ruling is common knowledge to the parties. This in turn makes the breach event common knowledge, thereby enhancing the performance of relational contracts.

The idea that a decrease in the future value of a relationship can undermine performance goes back to the work on exit and voice by Hirschman (1970). He argues that an important ingredient for successful civic institutions, such as schools, is citizen participation. Parents fleeing a school that is having difficulty leads to a downward spiral in performance. MacLeod (1984) uses this idea in the context of a repeated game with exit to show that imposing exit fees can enhance the performance of a labor cooperative, consistent with the observation that many successful labor cooperatives have some form of exit cost.[21] Rayo (2007) nicely extends these ideas to characterize the set of relational contracts in teams.

Greif (1994) uses relational contract theory to help explain the existence and form of social norms and relationships in medieval Europe. A key ingredient in his studies is the control of group membership, which in turn translates into a higher level of long-distance commercial exchange.

Kranton (1996) presents a formal model of reciprocal exchange in a market setting. She shows that the insight of Schmidt and Schnitzer (1995) applies here—namely, that the introduction of markets can undermine efficient cooperation. Carmichael and MacLeod (1997) show that the institution of gift exchange can act as a substitute for the existence of a future gain from trade. In their model, a gift is any cost that is sunk at the beginning of a relationship, such as the time spent in having meals and ritualistic meetings when starting a new business partnership.[22] Sobel (2006) shows how formal institutions can help support exchange in random matching environments. Okuno-Fujiwara and Postlewaite (1995) explore the role of norms in sustaining cooperation in market environments. Ramey and Watson (1997) show that uncertainty regarding future returns to trade can undermine the ability of parties to enter into long-term binding agreements.

MacLeod and Malcomson (1998) discuss the role of social norms in supporting efficiency wage and performance pay equilibria. Specifically, there is a link between market expectations regarding an unemployed person's ability and the type of employment contract they had in their previous job.[23] Chassang (2010) models norm formation as a process of routine building, which in turn results in path-dependent outcomes.

Another strand of literature applies relational contract theory to the theory of the firm. Baker, Gibbons, and Murphy (1999) show that the theory can be used to understand the informal allocation of authority. Halonen (2002) illustrates that the allocation of ownership rights can shape the nature of optimal relational contracts. Tadelis (2002) supposes that reputation can be attached to brand names, which in turn allows parties to "trade" the future returns from a relationship. Halac (2015) extends Halonen (2002) to the case in which values are uncertain, and consequently, the efficiency of the relationship varies with bargaining power.

Halac (2012) and Li and Matouschek (2013) explore the implications of persistent private information regarding the value of trade and show that this private information requires parties to manage their conflict. Miller and Watson (2013) show how these ideas can be extended to a new theory of disagreement; this work has been extended in Watson, Miller, and Olsen (2020) to deal with environments with partial contractual enforcement. Another extension is made by Malcomson (2016), who explores the ratchet effect in relational contracts.

Another developing branch of literature is that on empirical relational contracts. A weakness of the theoretical literature is that it typically assumes that players live forever. This assumption captures the way people *reason* about the environment—namely, they do not breach an agreement today because of the negative consequences of breach tomorrow. Logically, this form of reasoning has to break down in the long run; the issue is whether it is a reasonable working model of *observed* behavior.[24] Dal Bo (2005) shows directly that if parties believe the relationship will continue, they cooperate more.

Fehr, Gächter, and Kirchsteiger (1997) show that cooperation in finite repeated games can be viewed as a taste for reciprocity. This result is extended by Fehr and Falk (1999) to explain why parties are reluctant to cut wages, a result that has recently been shown to hold in more realistic field experiments by Kaur (2019). MacLeod (2007a) shows that one needs only a small amount of trust to support a high level of trade, which is consistent with Johnson, McMillan, and Woodruff (2002), who find that even though legal institutions in transition economies are weak, they can help support a high level of exchange.

Yet another growing literature explores the empirical properties of observed contracts. Corts and Singh (2004) show that relational contracts can affect the choice of high-power incentive contracts. Kalnins and Mayer (2004) find that parties are more likely to use low-power contracts when they have an existing relationship. Sloof and Sonnemans (2011) provide direct experimental evidence on how relationships affect the use of performance pay contracts. Gil and Marion (2013) find that relationships are associated with more effective contracts in California highway procurement. Zanarone (2013) has evidence from Italy showing that franchisers use relational contracts to bypass rigid legal rules.

A challenge for all field studies is to find convincing random variation that can be used to estimate the causal effect of a change in the environment on contract form and performance. Macchiavello and Morjaria (2015) uses civil conflict as a random shock to the future gain from trade. They find the value of a relationship increases with time, and it falls if there is a negative productivity shock. These results, they argue, can be explained by a relational contract model in which the value of trade increases with the value of a continued relationship.

9.6.1   What Is Reputation?

The model of self-enforcing relational contracts relies on the theory of infinitely repeated games. The benefit of this approach is that the strategic problem in each period is identical, which in turn allows for closed-form solutions of the stationary equilibria. It captures a basic type of reasoning—at least one party values continuing the relationship, while the other party can punish breach with the threat of termination.

The threat of termination imposes a cost because when an adverse event occurs, the harmed party believes the breaching party will continue to breach, while the breaching party, given the anticipated response, has no incentive to perform. These self-reinforcing beliefs nicely capture how a reputation is lost and why it is hard to regain (as in the chapter's epigraph, taken from Poor Richard's Almanack, and popularly attributed to Benjamin Franklin).

In addition, the theory highlights the point that contract design is closely linked to two features of the environment. First, is the frequent signal good or bad (the distinction between a normal and innovative good)? Second, who is the party that holds the reputation? When buyers are considered reputable, the optimal contract places payment obligations on the buyer—the buyer is relied on to compensate the seller appropriately after delivery. If this is not done, the buyer loses her reputation and is excluded from the market.

In contrast, if the seller holds the reputation, then the buyer must pay in advance and may claim damages from the seller should the quality of the good be substandard. Empirical work by Startz (2016) illustrates this effect well. She studies the market for consumer goods in Nigeria, where small merchants travel to China to make in-person purchases, and finds that the cost of travel, and hence the cost of forming long-term relationships, has a significant impact on the efficiency of trade. She also observes that the performance obligation rests with the large Chinese firms rather than the smaller Nigerian traders. This is consistent with the hypothesis that large firms face a larger reputation loss from nonperformance.

Antras and Foley (2015) provide direct evidence on the link between financing terms and the quality of law. In their model, it is assumed that in trade between two regions, the probability that a contract is enforced varies. The insight is that terms are defined so that the party in the region with the better law is relied on to perform. Their results provide direct evidence on the relationship between contract enforceability and contract form.

Their model also illustrates that there are a number of ways to model relational contracts. In their case, quality of law is represented by the probability of performance. This approach is also used in game theoretic models of reputation that build on the work of Kreps et al.

(1982), who suppose there is a positive probability that some individuals always play tit-for-tat (TFT) in a repeated prisoner's dilemma.[25] This idea builds on Axelrod (1981), who discusses the benefits of TFT as a general strategy for cooperation. The implication is that since TFT is generally a good strategy, then for a specific repeated game some individuals may choose TFT rather than play the Nash equilibrium. If this is common knowledge, then participants would take this into account when playing the game.

Kreps et al. (1982) provide some lower bounds on the payoffs that are supported by any sequential equilibria of the repeated prisoner's dilemma game, and they show that these are above the payoff under the Nash equilibrium in the full information game that entails defect in each period. Sobel (1985) explicitly shows this approach can be used to model individual reputations with the features that individuals can build their reputation by being trustworthy, while in other cases they can "milk" their reputation when the short-run gain is greater than the long-run benefit.[26]

An extensive literature explores equilibria in reputation games in which players update beliefs over the preferences of their counterparties. Tadelis (1999) illustrates how reputation can be viewed as a tradable asset. Mailath and Samuelson (2001) extend this work to a model in which firms are long-lived but of two types—inept and competent. They face short-run incentives to shirk on quality when selling to a sequence of short-lived buyers.

Horner (2002) explores a model with reputation and perfect competition. He assumes that sellers are of two unobservable types and that consumers are infinitely lived. In his model, sellers enter the market and fix prices, then buyers choose a firm and demand based on their past experiences with that firm. Under the appropriate assumptions, the model exhibits some fascinating dynamics, in particular that high-quality sellers eventually milk their reputations.

Board and Meyer-ter Vehn (2013) extend this line of work to explore the effect on reputation dynamics of the quality of information, similar to our dichotomy between normal and innovative goods. They find that the effect of reputation on performance incentives depends on whether learning is done via a Poisson process of good or bad signals.

Both Horner (2002) and Board and Meyer-ter Vehn (2013) suppose that contingent contracts are not possible. Hence, they do not consider the possibility of parties investing in information technologies; a key message of the classic principal-agent model is the importance of information in contract design. It remains an open question on how best to think about and measure the interplay between reputation building and investment into information systems. Better information would allow parties to use performance pay contracts rather than rely upon a counterparty's reputation.

This chapter has focused on the understanding of the structure of equilibrium *norms*. These are interlocking, self-enforcing behaviors that, with the appropriate design of the breach event and sufficient future gains from trade, give rise to efficient exchange. In practice, many norms are possible, particularly in large, diverse economies.

The empirical work of Antras and Foley (2015) and Macchiavello and Morjaria (2015) shows that both relational contract terms and reputation effects are likely important in practice. An open question remains as to how best to integrate contract design and learning into a comprehensive theoretical framework that simultaneously remains tractable. Even more challenging is integrating asymmetric information into relational contract theory. The next chapter addresses this question from the perspective of the classic agency model.

Finally, there is exciting research in neuroeconomics exploring the relationship between individual characteristics and behavior in a repeated game. King-Casas et al. (2008) show that individuals with borderline personality disorder have greater difficulty cooperating in a repeated prisoner's dilemma. Knoch et al. (2009) report results on how building a good reputation depends on the performance of the right prefontal cortex of the brain. See Ruff and Fehr (2014) for a review of these developments.

Of course, most economic data do not have information regarding individual brain performance. This research emphasizes a need to have models that allow for heterogeneity in behavior. For simplicity, it is often assumed that parties to a relational contract have similar preferences. An open question for the theory is how to introduce heterogeneity into the model in a way that can be measured with population-level data.

Another open question for economics is how to better understand conflict in relational contracts. The next chapter turns to this question and shows that one can build a model of "rational conflict" in a relational contract based on the fact that parties have different information regarding contractual performance.

9.7 Exercises

1. Prove proposition 9.2.

2. Suppose c takes on a single value. Work out the continuous-time version of the relational contract model. Specifically, let $\Delta \to 0$, and derive the expressions for the stationary payoffs when choosing optimally and when shirking. Use the fact that the rewards are a Poisson process controlled by the seller's effort.

3. Consider the symmetric information relational contract model for an innovative commodity. Suppose the cost of effort function is given by:

$$v(e, c) = \frac{(e + 1)^2}{2c},$$

where $c \in [1, 2]$ is uniformly distributed on $[1, 2]$. Let $\Delta, r > 0$ be the length of a period and the interest rate. Let the flow output be given by:

$$y(e) = B \times \log(e + 1),$$

where the probability of a good outcome in a period is given by $\Delta \log(e + 1)$. Suppose that the outside options are normalized at $\Pi^0 = U^0 = 0$. Answer the following:

(a) What is the efficient effort function $e^*(c, B, \Delta)$ as a function of the reward $B \geq 0$ and the length of a period?

(b) Work out the unique renegotiation-proof effort profile $e^{RP}(c, B, \Delta)$. In particular, derive the lower bound $\underline{B}(\Delta)$ such that for $B < \underline{B}(\Delta)$ there is no trade.

(c) What happens when the frequency of trade increases while holding all other parameters fixed? Namely, derive $\lim_{\Delta \to 0} e^{RP}(c, B, \Delta)$.

4. Show that $e(c, R^*)$ solves (9.22) and is well defined and unique. Next, prove that proposition 9.5 implies that effort $e(c, R^*)$, defined in (9.22), can be supported by some

self-enforcing relational contract if and only if $R^* \leq RR(R^*)$. Provide an example for which there are several solutions to $RR(R^*) = R^*$.

5. For the market mechanism, work out the expressions for the payoffs and the equilibrium wage w^{H*} when the frequency of trade is high ($\Delta \to 0$). Provide sufficient conditions under which $w^{H*} > w^L$. Conversely, show that when Δ is large, high-quality exchange is not possible.

6. Provide an example of a relational contract with moral hazard under which it is efficient to trade but parties choose not to trade.

7. Derive the conditions implied by proposition 9.14 and corollary 9.15 when the frequency of trade is increased, holding all other parameters fixed. How does the contract derived here compare to the corresponding contract for the market mechanism, and in particular, the efficiency wage contract derived in Shapiro and Stiglitz (1984)?

10   Opportunism and Conflict in Agency Relationships

This chapter is coauthored with Teck Yong Tan.[1]

[The farmer] should be civil in dealing with his tenants, should show himself affable, and should be more exacting in the matter of work than of payments, as this gives less offense yet is, generally speaking, more profitable.
—Columella (1941, 79), 4 CE

10.1   Introduction

Agency theory describes contract design as if it were a well-oiled machine. The theory supposes that principals can design contracts that ensure agents respond in predictable ways. In such a world, there is no conflict and relationships proceed harmoniously. Even a mildly skeptical reader might wonder if such a theory is of any practical use. In a classic contribution to the management literature, Steven Kerr (1975) provides a number of examples in which large private companies implement dysfunctional incentives. Moreover, like the children in Garrison Keillor's fictional town of Lake Woebegone, there is evidence that supervisors have a tendency to rank most employees as above average.[2] The purpose of this chapter is to show that when agency theory is extended to include *subjective* evaluation, the result has the potential to explain some of these observations in the rough-and-tumble world of contract design in the wild.

Agency theory's starting point is a situation in which the principal can observe or evaluate the agent. It is assumed that this evaluation is enforceable in the sense that the principal can promise payments as a function of measured performance, and the agent can expect this promise to be enforced, either in court or via a relational contract, as discussed in chapter 9.

The essence of a "subjective" evaluation is that the principal's information is private, so there is no way to contractually link a principal's evaluation to compensation. Of course, the principal can say what he thinks, but our everyday experiences teach us that humans do not easily reveal what they truly think. For example, a husband might not like the clothes that his wife is wearing, but many husbands keep this evaluation private. More generally, the fact that managers are loath to give employees low evaluations is generally viewed as a serious problem in human resource management because it may reduce overall organizational effectiveness.

The classic relational contract model reviewed in the previous chapter is often interpreted as a model of subjective evaluation because agent performance is assumed to be unobserved by outside parties, such as courts. For example, a supervisor might catch an employee napping, and they both know the nap took place. However, in the absence of physical evidence, such as a video of the employee sleeping, there is no way to prove it. An insight of the relational contract model is that if punishments are triggered by mutually observed breach events, then in equilibrium punishments are never triggered. In the napping example, the employer may not recommend a bonus for the employee, which the employee would have to admit is fair.

The main implication of the classic relational contract model is that when events of material importance cannot be observed by third parties, enforcement of contract terms based on these events relies on the existence of a rent from continuing the relationship. When the breach event is mutually observed, the contract can be designed so that breach never occurs in equilibrium.

However, matters are not always so clear-cut. Suppose the principal is the maître d' at a restaurant who offers a contract to an agent (the chef) that promises a bonus if and only if the maître d' believes that the performance (meal quality) is acceptable. The catch is that the evaluation of the maître d' is subjective and hence private information.

Different individuals may honestly have different evaluations of whether the food at a restaurant is good. Moreover, there is no way to prove at the time of consumption that one's subjective evaluation is truthful. Because the subjective evaluation of the maître d' has financial consequences, there is a natural tendency for the evaluator to shade the evaluation to lower costs.

Principals worry about a countervailing incentive. If the agent believes the evaluation is unfair, she can take a number of actions. If the agent believes she did a good job, then a negative evaluation can be discouraging, which can cause her to lower future performance. Alternatively, disgruntled employees may use a variety of retaliation strategies, such as displaying passive-aggressive behavior, or in some cases, committing real malfeasance, such as theft.

It is exactly these sorts of responses that make principals reluctant to give low evaluations. Although the exact nature of the responses can vary, they have a common source—disagreement regarding the quality of the commodity supplied by the agent. Technically, this is the same phenomena discussed in chapter 8 on exchange with asymmetric information. With two-sided asymmetric information, it may simply be impossible to have terms of trade that lead to efficient exchange in all possible states.

As the potential for conflict creates an incentive for the principal to give a positive evaluation, the optimal contract requires a delicate balance between conflicts and rewards. If there is no threat of conflict, then the principal will shade bonuses downward, leading to lower performance by the agents. Conversely, if the threat of conflict is too high, then the principal always pays a bonus, also breaking the link between performance and reward. Thus, the optimal contract is one in which the level of conflict is calibrated to make the principal indifferent between reporting good or bad performance, which in turn makes truthful revelation an equilibrium.

The next section illustrates this point using the two-signal model introduced in MacLeod (2003). After the agent chooses effort, there is output that may be high or low. This performance is not observed directly; rather, each party receives a private signal on whether the output is high or low. It is assumed that the signals are positively correlated with the output. The two-type setup allows one to obtain a complete closed-form solution for the optimal bonus payment that illustrates the role that correlation in beliefs plays in determining the optimal contract (proposition 10.1).

The extension to the general case is quite interesting because it turns out that the timing of information revelation plays a key role. The two-type case is an example of an *authority contract*. It has the feature that the agent's compensation is determined solely by the principal's evaluation, while the agent's evaluation is used only to punish the principal who has not rewarded her "fairly." The form of this contract is fixed by the assumption that the principal reveals his information first.

When the order of information release is reversed, compensation is determined by the agent's subjective evaluation, with the principal responding with conflict when he believes the compensation demanded by the agent is "unfair." This is called a *sales contract* because it is consistent with market exchange where the seller/agent sets the terms. For example, for professional services such as legal services, it is common for the professional to send a bill after the work has been performed. In theory, the bill is based on the number of hours worked, but as the hours are set by the professional, as a practical matter, the seller/agent is setting compensation after the service has been provided.

A sales contract has the interesting feature that the set of incentive constraints is more complex than in the case of an authority contract. In an authority contract, after an agreement is reached, the principal has only one action—to reveal his private information. Therefore, for a contract to be incentive compatible, one need only check that he has no incentive to misrepresent his information, given the subsequent choices by the agent. In contrast, under a sales contract, the agent first chooses her effort and then reveals her information. Because her effort affects the distribution of the signals, incentive compatibility requires that the agent has no incentive to do a "double deviation"—jointly modify her effort and misrepresent her information.

The decision to modify effort in order to affect the information the principal receives is a form of "guile." This corresponds precisely to Oliver Williamson's (1975) notion of "opportunism"—self-interest seeking combined with guile. This case also provides the conditions under which employment relationships characterized by employer-set compensation are more efficient than arm's length contracts between self-employed entities.

The agenda for the chapter is as follows. The next section presents an example illustrating the main point. Section 10.3 outlines the general framework. Section 10.4 characterizes the set of authority contracts, and sales contracts are discussed in section 10.5. The chapter concludes with a discussion of the literature.

10.2   A 2 × 2 Example

Consider the following principal-agent relationship, which is similar to the basic model in chapter 7 except that now it is assumed that both the principal and the agent are risk neutral. The timing and information structure are as follows:

1. The principal offers to the agent a contract $\psi = \{w, b, \delta\}$, where w is a fixed wage and b is a discretionary bonus paid if the principal believes the performance to be acceptable (A), while δ is a cost the agent imposes on the principal if she believes the pay is unacceptable.

2. The agent either rejects and gets her outside option of U^0, or accepts. If she accepts, then we move to step 3.

3. The agent chooses effort $\lambda \in [0, 1]$ at a cost $V(\lambda)$, where $V'(\lambda), V''(\lambda) > 0$ for $\lambda > 0$, and $V(0) = V'(0) = 0$. Effort represents the probability that the output is high, $o = H$, while the probability that the output is low, $o = L$, is $(1 - \lambda)$. This in turn determines the payoff $y \in \{y^H, y^L\}$, where $y^H > y^L \geq 0$. Let $B = y^H - y^L$ be the increase in output due to successful agent effort.

4. After the effort is chosen and the output is realized, the principal and agent observe private signals $t, s \in \{A, U\}$, respectively, which are interpreted as an acceptable performance (A) or an unacceptable performance (U). Neither party can directly observe the output o nor the payoff y. The probabilities of these signals are:

$$\Gamma_{ts}^o = Pr[ts|o],$$

where $o \in \{L, H\}$ is the realized output.[3]

5. The principal pays the agent the wage w and a discretionary bonus $\hat{b} \geq 0$.

6. Finally, the agent, after observing her signal, s, and the principal's bonus, $\hat{b}$, imposes a cost $\hat{\delta} \geq 0$ on the principal. This results in end-of-period payoffs:

$$U^A = w + \hat{b} - V(\lambda), \tag{10.1}$$

$$U^P = y^L + \lambda B - w - \hat{b} - \hat{\delta}. \tag{10.2}$$

The difference between this case and the standard principal-agent model is the hypothesis that there is no directly verifiable signal of effort λ. Even if the parties always see the same signal (i.e., $t = s$), these evaluations are assumed to be private information which that are not observed by others.

The goal of this model is to provide a way to apply the ideas from relational contract theory to a standard principal-agent framework. Like relational contracts, the contract $\psi = \{w, b, \delta\}$ consists of both enforceable and self-enforcing elements. The wage term w is enforceable, and it is paid to the agent on the acceptance of the contract, regardless of performance. What makes the contract legally enforceable is that the agent must appear for work and choose some (unobserved) effort $\lambda \in [0, 1]$.

The self-enforcing terms are b and δ. The principal is free to pay any positive bonus $\hat{b}$ that he wishes but, under the terms of the agreement, he pays b if the performance is deemed acceptable. Given that the principal's information is private, it is not possible to make this payment enforceable by a third party. Rather, the agent decides whether she is being fairly treated based on her own private information. Specifically, it is assumed that the signals are correlated, and when the agent observes $s = H$, she believes that she should get the bonus. In this case, she imposes a cost δ on the principal if she did not get the bonus. In a relational contract, this cost is the consequence of playing a perfect equilibrium that punishes the principal for a deviation.

As one can see from (10.1)–(10.2), the agent can impose a cost on the principal at no cost to herself. It is assumed that she chooses the amount that is given in the contract— this is consistent with the standard assumption in agency theory that when one party is indifferent between two choices, the contractually agreed choice is made. This conflict term is a reduced-form representation of the conflict that can occur in any relationship. For example, in the relational contract model considered in chapter 9, the conflict term can be implemented with a bonus pay contract under which the agent threatens to leave if she is unfairly treated. Such a behavior is optimal if she is indifferent between staying and leaving.

Notice that all the efficient relational contracts considered in the previous chapter share the feature that the threat to punish is never carried out in equilibrium. As a consequence, the existence of a relational contract depends on the existence of sufficient gains from continued trade (9.5) that may be lost if the relationship terminates. Thus, much of the focus of the literature has been on the effect that the size of the future potential gain from trade has on the efficiency of trade. Here, we take the opposite approach, namely, it is assumed that there is no limit to the amount of surplus destruction. However, the presence of asymmetric information implies that there is conflict in equilibrium, which in turn implies that the parties have an incentive to minimize the magnitude of δ.

If the parties set the conflict to zero, then there would be no consequence for the principal of not paying the bonus, leading to no bonus payment, and hence no incentive for the agent to perform. In this 2×2 example, closed-form solutions for the optimal contract can be derived to illustrate this trade-off using the approach pioneered by Grossman and Hart (1983). They observe that the principal-agent problem can be solved in two steps. In the first step, the principal computes the cost of hiring an agent to supply at least λ units of effort, denoted by $C^*(\lambda)$. The second step is to choose the contracted upon effort (λ) that maximizes profit.

Grossman and Hart (1983) show that this approach results in a well-defined, continuous cost function which is increasing in λ. For each $\lambda \in [0, 1]$, there is an optimal contract $\psi^*(\lambda)$ that implements this effort. Given the optimal cost function, the principal chooses effort to solve:

$$\lambda^* = \arg \max_{\lambda \in [0,1]} \lambda y^H + (1 - \lambda) y^L - C^*(\lambda)$$

$$= \arg \max_{\lambda \in [0,1]} \lambda \left(y^H - y^L \right) - C^*(\lambda).$$

The contracted performance depends on the marginal benefit from high output, $B \equiv y^H - y^L$, and the marginal cost of obtaining effort with an incentive-compatible contract, $C^*(\lambda)$. The rest of the chapter focuses on the computation of this cost function and the associated optimal contract $\psi^*(\lambda)$ as a function of the primitives of the model.

To make the example a bit more stark, suppose, as in Shapiro and Stiglitz (1984), that when there is low output, it is commonly observed by both parties; formally, the probability that both parties observe unacceptable performance is 1 ($\Gamma_{UU}^L = 1$). Because conflict in this contract exists to provide incentives to the principal to pay the bonus whenever he observes the high signal, it can be assumed that conflict occurs on the equilibrium path only when the principal observes the unacceptable signal while the agent observes the acceptable signal. When this happens, the agent imposes a cost δ on the principal. Given these assumptions, the principal's cost under contract ψ for the provision of effort λ is:

$$C(\lambda, \psi) = w + \lambda b \left(\Gamma_{AA}^H + \Gamma_{AU}^H \right) + \lambda \Gamma_{UA}^H \delta. \tag{10.3}$$

The principal is assumed to choose a contract that minimizes cost subject to the agent's participation constraint, which is also known as the individual rationality (IR) constraint, as well as the incentive compatibility constraints (IC) for both players. The agent's payoff and participation constraint are given by:

$$U(\lambda, \psi) = w + \lambda b \left(\Gamma_{AA}^H + \Gamma_{AU}^H \right) - V(\lambda) \geq U^0. \qquad (10.4)$$

At the optimal contract, this constraint is binding, and thus the cost of effort function can be written as:

$$C(\lambda, \psi) = U^0 + V(\lambda) + \lambda \Gamma_{UA}^H \delta.$$

This is the cost of hiring the agent given her outside option (U^0), the cost of effort ($V(\lambda)$), and the cost due to conflict ($\lambda \Gamma_{UA}^H \delta$). The agent must voluntarily wish to provide effort. The agent's payoff in (10.4) is differentiable and concave in effort; hence, differentiating (10.4) with respect to effort gives the first-order condition, which implies that the bonus pay must satisfy the following IC:

$$b = \frac{V'(\lambda)}{\left(\Gamma_{AA}^H + \Gamma_{AU}^H \right)}. \qquad (10.5)$$

In particular, if $\lambda > 0$, then it must be the case that the bonus pay is strictly positive. In that case, when the principal observes $t = A$, he must prefer to pay the bonus b. At that point, the wage w is sunk, and hence the principal's IC is:

$$E\{\text{wage} + \text{bonus}, t = A\} \leq E\{\text{wage} + \text{conflict}, t = A\}$$

$$w + b \leq w + \delta \frac{\Gamma_{AA}^H}{\Gamma_{AA}^H + \Gamma_{AU}^H}$$

$$\delta \geq b \left(1 + \frac{\Gamma_{AU}^H}{\Gamma_{AA}^H} \right). \qquad (10.6)$$

Notice that the level of conflict is increasing with the size of the bonus. Moreover, the level of conflict must be higher than the bonus by a factor of $\frac{\Gamma_{AU}^H}{\Gamma_{AA}^H}$. In relational contracts in chapter 9, a breach is assumed to be common knowledge, in which case $\Gamma_{AU}^H = 0$, and the level of potential conflict is exactly equal to the bonus.

If the conflict is too high and there is a risk of misunderstanding, then the principal may choose to pay the bonus even when $t = U$ in order to avoid facing the cost δ. Thus, one has the constraint:

$$E\{\text{wage} + \text{conflict}, t = U\} \leq E\{\text{wage} + \text{bonus}, t = U\}$$

$$w + \delta \frac{\lambda \Gamma_{UA}^H}{\Gamma_U(\lambda)} \leq w + b$$

$$\delta \leq b \frac{\Gamma_U(\lambda)}{\lambda \Gamma_{UA}^H}, \qquad (10.7)$$

where $\Gamma_U(\lambda) = \lambda\left(\Gamma_{UA}^H + \Gamma_{UU}^H\right) + (1-\lambda)$ is the probability of the principal observing a low signal. Notice that this function is decreasing in effort; hence the constraint is more binding for a higher effort. The existence of an optimal contract requires the existence of a feasible solution. Together, (10.6)–(10.7) imply:

$$\frac{\Gamma_U(\lambda)}{\lambda\Gamma_{UA}^H} \geq \left(1 + \frac{\Gamma_{AU}^H}{\Gamma_{AA}^H}\right). \tag{10.8}$$

For a solution to exist for all effort levels, (10.8) should hold for $\lambda = 1$, which in turn implies the following necessary condition for a feasible solution:

$$\Gamma_{AA}^H\Gamma_{UU}^H - \Gamma_{AU}^H\Gamma_{UA}^H \geq 0.$$

This is the natural requirement that signals are positively correlated. In this model, the only social cost arises from the existence of conflict, and thus in an optimal contract, we expect conflict to be set as low as possible, which in turn implies that (10.6) is binding.

Proposition 10.1 *For the 2 × 2 contracting problem, suppose that it is common knowledge when the output is low ($\Gamma_{UU}^L = 1$), and the performance signals when the output is high are positively correlated ($\Gamma_{AA}^H\Gamma_{UU}^H - \Gamma_{AU}^H\Gamma_{UA}^H > 0$).[4] Then the lowest cost contract $\psi^*(\lambda)$ implementing effort λ,*

$$C^*(\lambda) = \min_{\psi \in \Psi} C(\lambda, \psi),$$

subject to (10.4)–(10.7)

is unique and defined by:

1. *The bonus satisfies $b = V'(\lambda) / \left(\Gamma_{AA}^H + \Gamma_{AU}^H\right)$.*
2. *The conflict satisfies $\delta = V'(\lambda) / \Gamma_{AA}^H$.*
3. *The wage satisfies $w = U^0 + V(\lambda) - \lambda V'(\lambda)$.*
4. *The cost function is $C^*(\lambda) = U^0 + V(\lambda) + \lambda\frac{\Gamma_{UA}^H}{\Gamma_{AA}^H}V'(\lambda)$.*

The result has an intuitive interpretation. The bonus is paid if and only if the principal believes the work is good. The agent is upset and imposes a cost on the principal if and only if she feels that her work is of high quality but she is not paid the bonus (i.e., agent observes $s = A$ and principal observes $t = U$). When a conflict occurs, the size is increasing with the marginal cost of effort, $V'(\lambda)$ and decreasing with the probability that the parties' subjective evaluations concur regarding high performance, which is given by Γ_{AA}^H.

In contrast to the standard agency models, costs arise not from the trade-off between risk and incentives but between conflict and incentives. The expected agency cost under the contract to provide effort λ is given by:

$$AC^{SE}(\lambda) = \lambda\frac{\Gamma_{UA}^H}{\Gamma_{AA}^H}V'(\lambda).$$

As the cost of effort function is convex, agency costs are increasing with the desired effort. The other key parameter is the likelihood ratio between the unacceptable and acceptable signals, conditional on the agent observing the acceptable signal: $\left(\frac{\Gamma_{UA}^H}{\Gamma_{AA}^H}\right)$. This ratio measures the extent to which parties agree that there has been a breach.

When the probability of disagreement is zero ($\Gamma_{UA}^H = 0$), there are no agency costs—this corresponds to the case of relational contracts studied in proposition 9.12. In both cases, when the principal observes an unacceptable signal ($t = U$), the result is the nonpayment of a bonus. When there is symmetric information, the agent provides incentives to the principal for payment via the threat of terminating the relationship if the agent is not fairly compensated. The main empirical implication of the relational contract model is that the size of the bonus pay is constrained by the value of continuing to trade. In equilibrium, the threat to terminate trade is never carried out and hence the counterfactual to nonperformance by the principal is never observed, which in turn makes it challenging to test the model empirically.

The subjective evaluation model relaxes the assumption that a breach by the principal is common knowledge. When disagreement is possible ($\Gamma_{UA}^H > 0$), it is possible for the principal to believe the performance is unacceptable while the agent believes it is acceptable. This in turn implies that conflict is observed in equilibrium. To focus on the implications of asymmetric information, it is assumed that both parties have sufficient punishment ability to enforce any agreement. Thus, the form of the optimal contract is a trade-off between the provision of incentives to ensure that the agent chooses effort $\lambda > 0$ and the resulting agency cost $AC^{SE}(\lambda)$. The rest of the chapter considers a general version of this model that allows for variation in the number of signals, the signal quality, and the timing of information release. It concludes with a formal model of "opportunism" that can explain the choice between employment and the contracting out of services.

10.3   Modeling Subjective Evaluation

This section extends the example in the previous section in two directions. First, there is no limit to the number of signals that the parties are able to observe. This extension allows us to determine how to optimally combine subjective measures of performance. Second, we consider two contract forms that depend on the timing of information revelation. It is common for models with asymmetric information to suppose that parties reveal information simultaneously (as in chapter 8). It is shown that the timing of information revelation has a significant impact on contract design and cost.

Contracts in which the principal reveals his private information after which the agent reveals hers are called *authority contracts*. Under this timing, it is the principal who evaluates the agent and then decides on her compensation. In contrast, a contract in which the agent sets the price, which is followed by the principal's response, is called a *sales contract*. This terminology is chosen because price setting is an activity typically associated with a seller. The seller is assumed to choose price as a function of her perception of quality.

The variation in timing has implications for the observed contract form. Specifically, under an authority contract, only the information held by the principal affects the agent's compensation. The converse is not the case with a sales contract. A discussion of the relationship between these results and the literature is deferred to section 10.6.

10.3.1 The Environment

Consider a principal-agent model with risk-neutral parties. Both players have a zero outside option and unlimited liability. The agent privately chooses effort $\lambda \in [0, 1]$. The performance is binary: $o \in \{L, H\}$. Under λ, the probability of getting H is λ, and the probability of getting L is $1 - \lambda$. The outcome H represents a success that generates revenue $B > 0$ to the principal. On the other hand, L is a failure that generates no revenue. The agent's cost of exerting effort λ is $V(\lambda)$, which is assumed to be a function:

$$V : [0, 1] \to \Re_+,$$

which is twice differentiable and strictly convex such that $V(0) = 0$, $V'(0) \geq 0$.

Let λ^{FB} be the efficient effort level. If $B \geq V'(1)$, then $\lambda^{FB} = 1$; otherwise, it is uniquely defined by $V'(\lambda^{FB}) = B$. Hence, the first-best surplus is:

$$\text{surplus}^{FB} = \lambda^{FB} B - V(\lambda^{FB}), \tag{10.9}$$

which is assumed to be strictly positive. The parties' ability to achieve the first-best surplus surplus^{FB} is constrained by the availability of information regarding effort.

It is assumed that the outcome is not directly observable.[5] Instead, the principal and the agent each receives a *private* signal about the outcome,[6] which is denoted, respectively, by $t, s \in S = \{1, 2, \ldots, n\}$, where S is a finite set with $n \geq 2$ elements. These signals have the same "meaning" to the two parties. For example, if $s = 10$ means that the good is excellent according to the agent, the principal will have the same interpretation for $t = 10$. However, he may perceive the quality differently when he receives a signal of, say, $t = 8$, which means that the good is satisfactory but not excellent. The two parties can then reasonably disagree regarding the quality of performance. This provides a precise notion of subjective evaluation where the extent to which the parties' signals are correlated provides a measure of the subjectivity level (or the lack of it); when signals are perfectly correlated, the judgments are objective, and we are back in the standard principal-agent framework.

The joint-realization ts is known as the *state*. Let the probability of getting state ts under outcome $o \in \{L, H\}$ be given by

$$Pr[ts|o] = \Gamma_{ts}^o.$$

If the principal correctly anticipates the effort λ exerted by the agent, both parties will have the same ex ante unconditional probability of state ts:

$$\Gamma_{ts}(\lambda) = \lambda \Gamma_{ts}^H + (1 - \lambda) \Gamma_{ts}^L$$

$$= \Gamma_{ts}^L + \lambda \hat{\Gamma}_{ts},$$

where

$$\hat{\Gamma}_{ts} = \Gamma_{ts}^H - \Gamma_{ts}^L$$

is the marginal effect of effort λ on the probability of state ts.

It will be useful to exploit the linear structure of the problem by representing the probability distribution as a $1 \times n^2$ row vector. We take the convention of lexicographically ordering states ts by the agent's signal s first and then the principal's signal t. Hence, $\vec{\Gamma}^o$ is the probability vector for outcome o with:[7]

$$\vec{\Gamma}^o = \left[\underbrace{\Gamma^o_{11}, \Gamma^o_{21}, \ldots, \Gamma^o_{n1}}_{s=1}, \underbrace{\Gamma^o_{12}, \Gamma^o_{22}, \ldots, \Gamma^o_{n2}}_{s=2}, \ldots, \underbrace{\Gamma^o_{1n}, \Gamma^o_{2n}, \ldots, \Gamma^o_{nn}}_{s=n} \right].$$

The vector $\vec{\hat{\Gamma}}$ is defined analogously for the $1 \times n^2$ vector of $\hat{\Gamma}_{ts}$. The unconditional probability vector of states can be written as:

$$\vec{\Gamma}(\lambda) = \vec{\Gamma}^L + \lambda \vec{\hat{\Gamma}} \in \Re^{n^2}.$$

10.3.2 Contracts

From the revelation principle (chapter 8), it is sufficient to consider only contracts with the feature that the parties are truthful in equilibrium. In addition, both the principal and the agent can impose a deadweight loss on each other at no personal cost. This assumption is a way to represent costs that are observed in all organizations. For example, a purchasing officer may consciously slow the processing of an order that comes from a person who had treated him poorly in the past.[8]

The extent to which such conflicts occur depends on the context. For example, if the principal has to make a payment that is more than his perceived value of the commodity he receives from the agent, then he might retaliate by harming the agent's reputation on social media.[9] Alternatively, if the agent receives a payment that is less than what she perceives to be deserving of her performance, she might retaliate with lower-quality services in the future or, likewise, try to harm the reputation of the principal. Such conflicts can be viewed as "behavioral" responses that are implemented when the parties disagree on their evaluations of the performance level.[10]

This behavior is modeled by letting c_{ts} denote the principal's cost and w_{ts} the agent's wage when the reported state is ts. The potential for conflict is introduced via the *relaxed budget constraint* (RBC):

$$c_{ts} \geq w_{ts}, \forall ts \in S^2. \tag{10.10}$$

The agent's income is paid by the principal, and hence this condition must always be satisfied. When a conflict occurs, resources are destroyed, so that the income received by the agent is strictly less than the costs faced by the principal. The deadweight loss due to the conflict at state ts is:

$$\delta_{ts} = c_{ts} - w_{ts} \geq 0. \tag{10.11}$$

This social loss is the sum of conflicts imposed by the principal on the agent and by the agent on the principal. It is crucial that these conflicts are pure losses—they are not transfers.[11] The next issue is *who* is responsible for imposing the deadweight loss. The next result shows that this responsibility can be allocated in any way we wish without affecting the set of feasible outcomes.

Lemma 10.2 *In the absence of constraints on the size of the conflict δ, it is without loss of generality to consider contracts in which only one party (the principal or the agent) is inflicting the conflict.*

Proof. Consider a contract where at state $ts \in S^2$, x_{ts} is what the principal pays out before conflict takes place, and let $d^A_{ts} > 0$ and $d^P_{ts} > 0$ be the conflicts inflicted by the agent and the principal, respectively. Under this contract, $c_{ts} = x_{ts} + d_{ts}^A$, $w_{ts} = x_{ts} - d_{ts}^P$, and $\delta_{ts} = c_{ts} - w_{ts} = d_{ts}^A + d_{ts}^P$. Next, consider a contract where $x'_{ts} = x_{ts} + d_{ts}^A$, $d_{ts}^{P'} = d_{ts}^A + d_{ts}^P$, and $d_{ts}^{A'} = 0$; this contract has only the principal inflicting all the conflicts. It is readily verified that under this contract, $c'_{ts} = x'_{ts} + d_{ts}^{A'} = c_{ts}$, $w'_{ts} = x'_{ts} - d_{ts}^{P'} = w_{ts}$, and $\delta'_{ts} = d_{ts}^{A'} + d_{ts}^{P'} = \delta_{ts}$, and hence, the social loss and both parties' payoffs are left unchanged. A contract that has only the agent inflicting all the conflicts can be constructed analogously. $\square$

This result can be viewed as an accounting identity: given any allocation of conflict costs, δ_{ts}, between the two parties, one can redefine compensation, c_{ts} and w_{ts}, to leave each party's payoff unchanged.

Analogous to the vector representation for the probability distribution, we denote $\vec{c}$, $\vec{w}$, and $\vec{\delta}$ as the vector representations of the cost, wage, and conflicts terms, respectively, with the same ordering as previously (i.e., s first and then t lexicographically). As a matter of convention, these variables are $n^2 \times 1$ column vectors so that for $\vec{x} \in \left\{ \vec{c}, \vec{w}, \vec{\delta} \right\}$, we can write the expectation of x as the inner product: $\vec{\Gamma}(\lambda)\vec{x} = \sum_{ts \in S^2} \Gamma_{ts}(\lambda) x_{ts}$.[12]

We will see later that the problem is convex, and hence there is no gain from randomization. A contract implementing effort $\lambda \in [0, 1]$ is defined by:

$$\psi = \{\lambda, \vec{c}, \vec{w}\} \in \Psi \equiv [0, 1] \times \Re^{n^2} \times \Re^{n^2}, \tag{10.12}$$

which specifies the agent's effort obligation λ, together with the principal's cost and the agent's wage at each reported state under the restriction of the RBC (10.10). The conflict term in the contract is given by $\vec{\delta} = \vec{c} - \vec{w}$. Effort λ is not directly contractible because it is privately exerted by the agent, so the wage term $\vec{w}$ has to provide incentives for the agent to adhere to the effort obligation.[13]

Regarding information revelation, consider first the authority contract in which the principal reports his private signal and then the agent reports her signal. The second case is called a sales contract in which the agent reports her private signal, s, first and then the principal, on observing the agent's report, reports his signal t. The heuristic sequence of moves for the contracting game is shown in table 10.1.

Table 10.1
Contract formation and enforcement

Period	Actions	
1.	Principal offers a contract $\psi \in \Psi$ to the agent.	
2.	Agent "accepts" or "rejects." If "reject," the relationship ends.	
3.	Agent privately selects effort λ.	
4.	Nature selects outcome $o \in \{L, H\}$. This in turn generates private signals t and s for the principal and the agent, respectively.	
	Authority contract	**Sales contract**
5.	Principal reports $\hat{t}$ regarding his signal t.	Agent reports $\hat{s}$ regarding her signal s.
6.	Agent observes report $\hat{t}$ and then reports $\hat{s}$ regarding her signal s.	Principal observes report $\hat{s}$ and then reports $\hat{t}$ regarding his signal t.
	Enforceable contract terms	
7.	Principal pays $c_{\hat{t}\hat{s}}$ and the agent receives $w_{\hat{t}\hat{s}}$.	

When the parties abide by the conditions of the contract and report their signals truthfully, the expected payoffs of the principal and the agent are, respectively:

$$U^P(\psi) = \lambda B - \vec{\Gamma}(\lambda)\,\vec{c}, \tag{10.13}$$

$$U^A(\psi) = \vec{\Gamma}(\lambda)\,\vec{w} - V(\lambda). \tag{10.14}$$

Following Grossman and Hart (1983), the problem is framed in terms of finding a contract $\psi \in \Psi$ that implements an agreed effort obligation λ at the lowest cost, where costs are given by:

$$C(\lambda, \psi) = \vec{\Gamma}(\lambda)\,\vec{c} = \vec{\Gamma}(\lambda)\left[\vec{w} + \vec{\delta}\right]. \tag{10.15}$$

The existence of a nondegenerate optimal contract is ensured by requiring the full support assumption that all states occur with strictly positive probability under λ:

Definition 10.3   *The effort obligation λ satisfies the* full support *condition at λ if* $\Gamma_{ts}(\lambda) > 0, \forall ts \in S^2$.

Combining (10.14) and (10.15), the principal's costs when the agent's participation constraint binds is given by:

$$C(\lambda, \psi) = V(\lambda) + \vec{\Gamma}(\lambda)\,\vec{\delta} + U^0. \tag{10.16}$$

Namely, costs consist of three components: the agent's payoff in the next best alternative (U^0), the cost of effort in this task ($V(\lambda)$), and the cost of ensuring that the parties are truthful, ($\vec{\Gamma}(\lambda)\,\vec{\delta}$).

Matters can be simplified further if effort costs satisfy a condition that ensures an interior solution ($\lambda \in (0, 1)$):

Definition 10.4   *Effort costs satisfy the* interior condition *if $V(0) = V'(0) = 0$, $V''(\lambda) > 0$ for $\lambda \in [0, 1)$ and* $\lim_{\lambda \to 1} V(\lambda) = \infty$.

This condition ensures that an arbitrarily small amount of reward leads to positive effort. However, the agent would never choose effort $\lambda = 1$ because the cost of perfection ($\lambda = 1$) is unbounded. One can allow $\lambda \in [0, 1]$, with the understanding that when this condition holds, the agent would never choose $\lambda = 1$.

10.4   The Authority Contract

This section explores the properties of an optimal authority contract—a contract under which the principal reveals his information first, followed by the agent revealing her information. More precisely, as described by table 10.1, at step 5, the principal makes a report $\hat{t}$ regarding his signal t first. Then at step 6, on observing the principal's report $\hat{t}$, the agent gives her report $\hat{s}$ on her signal s.

The principal faces the problem of choosing a contract $\psi = \{\lambda, \vec{c}, \vec{w}\}$ that maximizes his payoff subject to the constraints that the agent chooses the agreed effort, and both parties reveal their private information truthfully. The problem is solved via backward induction. In the last period, the agent knows her own effort, λ, and the report $\hat{t}$ set by the principal.[14] Suppose that the agent has observed s. The requirement that she truthfully reports this signal implies that for all $\hat{t}, \hat{s} \in S$, we have:

$$w_{\hat{t}s} - V(\lambda) \geq w_{\hat{t}\hat{s}} - V(\lambda). \tag{10.17}$$

Under the full support assumption, all $t, s \in S$ occur with a strictly positive probability and hence all signals are possible. Thus, for a contract to be incentive compatible, (10.17) implies that the agent's truth-telling constraint is:

$$w_{\hat{t}s} \geq w_{\hat{t}\hat{s}}, \quad \forall \hat{t}, s, \hat{s} \in S. \tag{10.18}$$

This immediately implies:

Lemma 10.5 *In an authority relationship in which the principal reports his signal $\hat{t}$ first, the agent's truthful-telling constraint (10.18) requires that $w_{\hat{t}s} = w_{\hat{t}\hat{s}}$, $\forall \hat{t}, s, \hat{s} \in S$. Therefore, without loss of generality, the wage contract can be written in the form $w_{\hat{t}}^A$ and $\vec{w}^A = \{w_1^A, \ldots, w_n^A\}$.*

This lemma implies that the agent's net compensation is completely determined by the principal's evaluation; thus, one can ensure that constraint (10.18) is satisfied by setting $w_{ts} = w_t^A$, where $\vec{w}^A \in \Re^n$ represents payments as a function of only t. Although this result is simple, it is important in practice because it illustrates the value of separating information revelation from pecuniary rewards. For example, the employment of expert advisers, such as lawyers or physicians, often entails compensation based on time rather than the advice per se, to reduce their incentive to misrepresent their private information.

Consider now the problem faced by the principal. He cannot observe effort, so at the time when compensation is determined, the only information available is the contract, ψ, which has been agreed, and his private assessment, $t \in T$, of the agent's performance. The contract is assumed to satisfy (10.18), and the principal believes the agent will be truthful. The principal can be truthful if and only if:

$$B \times Pr[o = H | \lambda, t] - \vec{\Gamma}(\lambda, t) \vec{c}_t \geq B \times Pr[o = H | \lambda, t] - \vec{\Gamma}(\lambda, t) \vec{c}_{\hat{t}}, \forall t, \hat{t} \in S, \tag{10.19}$$

where $\vec{c}_t = \{c_{t1}, c_{t2}, \ldots, c_{tm}\}^T$ is the column vector of agreed costs when given the signal $t \in S$ and $\vec{\Gamma}(\lambda, t)$ is a $1 \times n$ row vector, where each entry,

$$\Gamma_s(\lambda, t) = Pr[s | t, \lambda] = \frac{\Gamma_{ts}(\lambda)}{\sum_{s' \in S} \Gamma_{ts'}(\lambda)}$$

is the probability that the agent observes $s \in S$ given that the principal has observed t. The left-hand side of (10.19) is the principal's payoff conditional on his signal t when reporting truthfully, while the right-hand side is the payoff if he reports $\hat{t}$ instead.

The RBC implies that $c_{ts} \geq w_t^A$ for all $t, s \in S$, and thus we can replace the RBC by:

$$\delta_{ts} \geq 0, \tag{10.20}$$

where $\delta_{ts} = c_{ts} - w_t^A$ is the level of conflict in state $ts \in S^2$. Using this, we can rewrite (10.19) as:

$$w_t^A - w_{\hat{t}}^A \leq \sum_{s \in S} \Gamma_{ts}(\lambda) \left(\delta_{\hat{t}s} - \delta_{ts}\right), \forall t, \hat{t} \in S. \tag{10.21}$$

Suppose that the principal at t has an incentive to report performance $\hat{t}$ (when $w_t - w_{\hat{t}} > 0$); then the right-hand side of (10.21) must be positive, which in turn implies:

Lemma 10.6 *Suppose that the performance evaluations are purely subjective. If the agent's pay varies with performance t under an authority contract, then there must be some states $ts \in S^2$ at which $\delta_{ts} > 0$.*

This result shows that when evaluations are purely subjective, contracts with a pay-for-performance component *necessarily* entail conflict. The next step is to determine how much performance pay is needed to enforce an agreed effort level.

This result allows us to write the authority contract in the following form:

$$\psi^A = \left\{ \vec{\delta}, \vec{w}^A \right\} \in \Psi^A \equiv \Re_+^{n^2} \times \Re^n, \tag{10.22}$$

where we replace the cost vector by the mutually agreed conflict at each state. Given that the agent's effort is her private information, the contract must be *self-enforcing*—namely, under the payment terms, the agent has the incentive to choose the principal's desired effort level. Let

$$\Gamma_t (\lambda) = \sum_{s \in S} \Gamma_{ts} (\lambda) \tag{10.23}$$

be the probability that state t occurs given effort λ. Under the hypothesis that the principal is truthful, in period 3, the agent chooses effort to maximize her expected payoff:

$$\lambda = \arg\max_{\lambda \geq 0} \sum_{t \in S} \Gamma_t (\lambda) w_t^A - V (\lambda).$$

The first term is linear in effort, while the second term is strictly concave. Therefore, under the interior effort assumption, the agent's effort is uniquely determined by the incentive constraint for effort (ICE):

$$\sum_{t \in S} \hat{\Gamma}_t w_t^A = V' (\lambda), \tag{10.24}$$

where $\hat{\Gamma}_{ts} = \Gamma_{ts}^H - \Gamma_{ts}^L$ and $\hat{\Gamma}_t = \sum_{s \in S} \hat{\Gamma}_{ts}$. Notice that if the wage does not vary with the principal's evaluation—say $w_t^A = w^A, \forall t \in S$, then we have:

$$V' (\lambda) = \sum_{t \in S} \hat{\Gamma}_t w^A$$

$$= w^A \sum_{t \in S} \hat{\Gamma}_t$$

$$= w^A \sum_{t \in S} \left(\Gamma_t^H - \Gamma_t^L \right)$$

$$= 0.$$

The last line follows from the fact that the probabilities have to add up to 1. Thus, if the wage does not vary with the principal's evaluation, then effort is necessarily zero. This, combined with lemma 10.6, implies that in order to have positive effort, there must be some conflict.

Finally, for the agent to accept a contract ψ^A in period 2, the contract must also satisfy the agent's *participation constraint* (PC):

$$U^A\left(\lambda|\psi^A\right) = \sum_{t\in S} \vec{\Gamma}_t(\lambda)\,\vec{w}_t^A - V(\lambda) \geq U^0. \tag{10.25}$$

Together, these constraints determine the conditions for arriving at the optimal authority contract chosen by the principal in period 1:

Definition 10.7 *An authority contract $\psi^{A*} = \{\delta, w^A\} \in \Psi^A$ implements effort λ if it satisfies the RBC (10.20), the principal's truth-telling constraint (10.21), and the agent's ICE and PC (10.24 and 10.25). Let $\Psi^{A*}(\lambda)$ be the set of contracts implementing λ. ψ^{A*} is an optimal authority contract if it solves:*

$$C^A(\lambda) \equiv C\left(\lambda, \psi^{A*}\right) = \min_{\psi^A \in \Psi^{A*}(\lambda)} C\left(\lambda, \psi^A\right). \tag{10.26}$$

The participation constraint (10.25) ensures that the costs are bounded from below. Because the constraints conditional on effort λ are linear, the set of feasible contracts is a convex set. Hence, the existence of an optimal contract depends on only whether a contract implementing effort λ exists.

Proposition 10.8 *Suppose that the interior condition and the full support condition at $\lambda \in (0, 1)$ holds. Then there exists an optimal authority contract, ψ^{A*}, that implements λ if and only if there exists some $t \in S$ such that $\hat{\Gamma}_t = \sum_{s\in S} \hat{\Gamma}_{ts} \neq 0$.*

Proof. First, suppose $\hat{\Gamma}_t = 0$ for all $t \in S$. Since $\lambda > 0$, the interior condition implies $V'(\lambda) > 0$, hence ICE (10.24) cannot be satisfied, and there is no contract that can implement λ. Conversely, suppose $\hat{\Gamma}_{t'} \neq 0$. Since $\sum_{t\in S} \hat{\Gamma}_t = 0$, this implies that there is some $\bar{t} \in S$ such that $\hat{\Gamma}_{\bar{t}} > 0$. Let $b = \frac{V'(\lambda)}{\hat{\Gamma}_{\bar{t}}}$ be a bonus that is paid if and only if the principal observes $\bar{t}$. The agent is assumed to impose a cost b if and only if the bonus is not paid—namely, $\delta_{ts} = b$ if $t \neq \bar{t}$ and zero otherwise. Under this strategy, the principal is always indifferent between paying and not paying the bonus; therefore, the truth-telling constraint from the principal is satisfied.

Given this bonus policy, the principal can offer a fixed wage that ensures the agent's participation constraint is satisfied. Consequently, there exists some implementable contract $\psi^A \in \Psi^{A*}$ resulting in costs $\bar{c} = C\left(\lambda, \psi^A\right)$. The fact that the constraints are linear, combined with the FSC implies that:

$$\bar{\Psi}^{A*}(\lambda) = \left\{ \psi^A \in \Psi^{A*}(\lambda) \,|\, C(\lambda, \psi) \leq \bar{c} \right\}$$

is a compact and convex set, and hence there exists an optimal authority contract. □

Under an authority contract, the truth-telling constraint for the agent implies that only the principal can modulate the rewards the agent receives. Hence, the principal can provide performance incentives if and only if he has signals that provide information on effort, which is a requirement that corresponds to $\sum_{s \in S} \hat{\Gamma}_{ts} \neq 0$ for some signal $t \in S$. The requirement for truth-telling by the principal imposes a cost that equals the value of the bonus when a bonus is not paid. This makes the principal indifferent between paying and not paying, thus ensuring that the principal's truth-telling constraint is satisfied.

10.4.1   Relational Contracts

We can view the model with subjective evaluation as a generalization of the relational contracts model of the previous chapter of the case of contracting with asymmetric information. To see this, consider the case in which there is a perfect correlation between the principal's and the agent's signals. More precisely, suppose:

$$\Gamma_{ts}^H = \Gamma_{ts}^L = 0, t \neq s, t, s \in S. \tag{10.27}$$

Under this assumption, the principal and the agent get exactly the same signal. Further, suppose that the signals satisfy the monotone likelihood condition:

$$\hat{\Gamma}_{t+1,t+1} > \hat{\Gamma}_{tt}, \quad t = 1, \ldots, n-1. \tag{10.28}$$

Under this condition, a higher signal indicates a higher likelihood of high output. In this case, as in the case of relational contracts, there can be many implementable contracts. More precisely, we have:

Proposition 10.9   *Suppose that the effort cost satisfies the interior condition, and the signals are perfectly correlated (10.27) and satisfy the monotone likelihood condition (10.28). Then for any $\bar{t} \in S$ such that $\hat{\Gamma}_{\bar{t}\bar{t}} > 0$, there exists an optimal authority contract ψ^{A*} which pays a bonus $b = \frac{V'(\lambda)}{\hat{\Gamma}_{\bar{t}}}$ if and only if $t = \bar{t}$, there is no conflict in equilibrium ($\delta_{tt} = 0, \forall t \in S$), and the principal's cost from the contract is given by:*

$$C\left(\lambda, \psi^{A*}\right) = U^0 + V\left(\lambda\right).$$

The proof of this proposition is left as exercise 3. The result follows from the fact that because the parties are risk neutral, the agent can be incentivized to provide effort λ by paying a bonus that is based on any signal that is informative. Given that there is a perfect correlation between the parties' signals, the principal has an incentive to be truthful with any punishment that satisfies $\delta_{tt} = 0$ for $t \in S$ and $\delta_{ts} > b_t$ for $s \neq t$.

Given that the principal is always truthful, the punishments are never used in equilibrium. This is also the case for the relational contracts studied in the previous chapter. There, it is assumed that when one party breaches the contract, the other party can observe the breach, which in turn allows for coordinated punishment. In the context of proposition 10.9, contract performance by the principal corresponds to the principal's reporting his true valuation $t = s$. Breach of contract occurs if he reports $\hat{t} \neq t$, in which case the agent observes $s \neq \hat{t}$. Consequently, the agent punishes the principal for contract breach by imposing a cost $\delta_{\bar{t}s} > 0$ on the principal. In the context of a relational contract, this punishment corresponds to the play of an inefficient perfect equilibrium. Thus, this model provides a reduced-form representation of the relational contract by adding a constraint on the size of the loss $\delta_{\bar{t}s}$ that the agent can impose on the principal. See exercise 5.

The effect of noise

A benefit of the subjective evaluation model relative to the relational contract model is that it explicitly allows for errors and misunderstandings. The introduction of misunderstandings also restricts the set of optimal contracts and increases the empirical context of the theory relative to the relational contract model. To see this, begin with the case of perfect correlation, and then suppose that there is small chance ϵ that the parties disagree. We then ask which contract is chosen as $\epsilon \to 0$.

More precisely, when misunderstanding occurs, we suppose that these beliefs are given by $\Gamma_{ts}^{\text{noise}} > 0, t, s \in S$, which is assumed to have full support. In the event of a misunderstanding, the parties entertain the possibility that any signal might have occurred. Hence, the perturbed beliefs are given by:

$$\Gamma_{ts}^{o\epsilon} = (1 - \epsilon)\,\Gamma_{ts}^{o} + \epsilon \Gamma_{ts}^{\text{noise}}, o \in \{H, L\}. \tag{10.29}$$

This in turn defines $\Gamma^{\epsilon}(\lambda) = (1 - \lambda)\,\Gamma^{L\epsilon} + \lambda \Gamma^{H\epsilon}$ and $\hat{\Gamma}^{\epsilon} = \Gamma^{H\epsilon} - \Gamma^{L\epsilon}$. Since $\hat{\Gamma}_{ts}^{o} > 0$ for some observations $t, s \in S$, then there is some number $\bar{\epsilon} > 0$ such that for all $\epsilon \in (0, \bar{\epsilon})$ the conditions of proposition 10.8 are satisfied, and there exists a contract implementing any effort $\lambda \in (0, 1)$.

Let us begin with a *simple bonus contract* that rewards the agent with a bonus $\bar{b}$ if and only if the principal observes $\bar{t}$. When $\epsilon = 0$, such a contract can be optimal if $\hat{\Gamma}_t > 0$, so we restrict attention to signals with this property. If the agent observes t and the principal does not pay the bonus, it is assumed that the agent chooses the minimum punishment δ that provides the principal with an incentive to be truthful. In addition, the agent is paid a fixed wage w^0. Let $\psi = \{\lambda, w^0, \bar{t}, \bar{b}, \bar{\delta}\}$ denote an arbitrary simple bonus contract. The cost of the contract is given by:

$$C^{\epsilon}(\lambda, \psi) = w^0 + \sum_{s \in S} \Gamma_{\bar{t}s}^{\epsilon}(\lambda)\,b_{\bar{t}} + \sum_{t,s \in S} \Gamma_{ts}^{\epsilon}(\lambda)\,\bar{\delta}_{ts}. \tag{10.30}$$

The agent's IC determines the bonus given the signal, $\bar{t}$, that is used to reward the agent. The assumption that the probability of a misunderstanding is independent of effort implies $\hat{\Gamma}_{\bar{t}}^{\epsilon} = (1 - \epsilon)\,\hat{\Gamma}_{\bar{t}}$ and hence (10.24) implies that the bonus satisfies:

$$b_{\bar{t}} = \frac{V'(\lambda)}{(1 - \epsilon)\,\hat{\Gamma}_{\bar{t}}}. \tag{10.31}$$

The fixed wage can be set to ensure that the PC (10.25) is binding, and hence:

$$w^0(\lambda, \bar{t}, \bar{b}) = U^0 + V(\lambda) - \sum_{s \in S} \Gamma_{\bar{t}s}^{\epsilon}(\lambda)\,\bar{b} \tag{10.32}$$

$$= U^0 + V(\lambda) - \sum_{s \in S} \Gamma_{\bar{t}s}^{\epsilon}(\lambda)\,\frac{V'(\lambda)}{(1 - \epsilon)\,\hat{\Gamma}_{\bar{t}}}.$$

Given that we have chosen to reward the agent when signal $\bar{t}$ is observed, the next step is to determine the conflict required to ensure that the principal keeps his promise to pay when he observes signal $\bar{t}$. When ϵ is small, without loss of generality, we can suppose that there is no punishment when the principal reports $\bar{\imath}$, so we can set $\delta_{\bar{\imath}s}^* = 0$ because when the correlation is sufficiently high, the principal will not have an incentive to pay the bonus to avoid punishment in other states. Given this, the only binding constraint on truth-telling is to ensure that the principal pays the bonus whenever he observes $\bar{\imath}$. Thus, constraint (10.21) implies that for all reports $\hat{\imath} \in S \setminus \{\bar{\imath}\}$ we have:

$$\Gamma_{\bar{\imath}}^{\epsilon}(\lambda) \, b_{\bar{\imath}} \leq \sum_{s \in S} \Gamma_{\bar{\imath}s}^{\epsilon}(\lambda) \, \delta_{\hat{\imath}s} \tag{10.33}$$

$$\leq \left((1 - \epsilon) \, \Gamma_{\bar{\imath}}(\lambda) + \epsilon \Gamma_{\bar{\imath}\bar{\imath}}^{\text{noise}} \right) \delta_{\bar{\imath}\bar{\imath}} + \epsilon \sum_{s \in S \setminus \{\bar{\imath}\}} \Gamma_{\bar{\imath}s}^{\text{noise}} \delta_{\bar{\imath}t}. \tag{10.34}$$

The term for $\delta_{\bar{\imath}\bar{\imath}}$ is of order $O(1)$ while the terms $\delta_{\bar{\imath}t}$ for $t \neq \bar{\imath}$ are of order $O(\epsilon)$. Therefore, for small ϵ, it is efficient to set $\delta_{\bar{\imath}t} = 0$ for $t \neq \bar{\imath}$, and thus we get:

$$\delta_{\bar{\imath}\bar{\imath}} = \frac{R(\epsilon, \bar{\imath})}{\hat{\Gamma}_{\bar{\imath}}} V'(\lambda), \tag{10.35}$$

where

$$R(\epsilon, \bar{\imath}) = 1 + \frac{\epsilon}{1 - \epsilon} \frac{1 + \sum_{s \in S \setminus \{\bar{\imath}\}} \Gamma_{\bar{\imath}s}^{\text{noise}}}{\left((1 - \epsilon) \, \Gamma_{\bar{\imath}}(\lambda) + \epsilon \Gamma_{\bar{\imath}\bar{\imath}}^{\text{noise}} \right)} > 1$$

is a term that approaches 1 for small ϵ. The terms in conditions (10.30)–(10.35) imply that the cost of conflict when using signal $\bar{\imath}$ to reward the agent is given by:

$$C^{\epsilon}(\lambda, \bar{\imath}) = \epsilon R(\epsilon, \bar{\imath}) \frac{V'(\lambda)}{SN(\bar{\imath})},$$

where:

$$SN(\bar{\imath}) = \frac{\hat{\Gamma}_{\bar{\imath}}}{\sum_{\hat{\imath} \in S \setminus \{\bar{\imath}\}} \Gamma_{\bar{\imath}\bar{\imath}}^{\text{noise}}}$$

is the signal-to-noise ratio for signal $\bar{\imath}$. The numerator is a measure of how likely the high outcome has occurred given signal $\bar{\imath}$. The ϵ times the denominator is the ex ante probability that the principal observes signal $\bar{\imath}$ while the agent observes a different signal. Given that $\lim_{\epsilon \to 0} R(\epsilon, \bar{\imath}) = 1$, we have the following proposition:

Proposition 10.10 *Suppose that the beliefs satisfy the noisy signal condition (10.29), and the signal-to-noise ratios, $SN(\bar{\imath})$, are distinct for all $t \in S$. For sufficiently small ϵ, the optimal contract entails paying a bonus if and only if the principal observes the signal with the highest signal-to-noise ratio.*

The discussion above provides a sketch of the proof, with details left as exercise 6. Intuitively, when there is close to perfect correlation in the signals for the principal and agent, then one should use the most cost-effective signal to reward the agent. In the generic case in which signals vary in their signal-to-noise ratios, it never pays to use two or more signals. As the payoffs and the constraints are linear, one can lower the costs by increasing the bonus for the more effective signal and decreasing the bonuses for other signals while maintaining the agent's IC and also adjusting the size of the penalties.

10.4.2 Efficiency Wage Contracts

The model of subjective evaluation can be applied to the efficiency wage model discussed in chapter 9, section 9.5. The distinctive feature of the efficiency wage model is the assumption that the agent's signal provides no information regarding performance, and therefore it is not possible for agents to punish principals for misreporting their signals. This, combined with lemma 10.5, implies that incentive-compatible contracts must entail paying the agent a fixed wage w that does not vary with the performance.

Thus, suppose that only the principal receives a signal $t \in S$:

$$Pr[t|\lambda] = \gamma_t(\lambda)$$

$$= (1 - \lambda)\gamma_t^L + \lambda\gamma_t^H$$

$$= \gamma_t^L + \lambda\hat{\gamma}_t,$$

where it is assumed that $\gamma_t^o > 0$ is the probability of signal t given outcome $o \in \{L, H\}$. For convenience, the probabilities are indexed by the informativeness $(\hat{\gamma}_t = \gamma_t^H - \gamma_t^L)$ of signal t:

$$\hat{\gamma}_{t+1} > \hat{\gamma}_t, t = 1, \ldots, n - 1. \tag{10.36}$$

This ensures that each signal is either good news $(\hat{\gamma}_t > 0)$, bad news $(\hat{\gamma}_t < 0)$, or uninformative $(\hat{\gamma}_t = 0)$ regarding performance.

Given that the agent has no information, then to ensure truth-telling by the principal, the principal's payoff must be independent of his signal, and hence the principal's payoff is:

$$U^P = \lambda B - w.$$

Incentives are provided in the Shapiro and Stiglitz (1984) model via the dismissal costs faced by the worker. The firm has a *dismissal policy* that defines the set of unsatisfactory performance evaluations $S^U \subset S$. If the principal observes $t \in S^U$, then the agent is dismissed and must look for another job. This is assumed to impose a cost with reduced form $d \times (w - w^0)$, where $d > 0$ discounts the future value of the job relative to the market wage of w^0. Hence, the payoff of the agent is:

$$U^A = w - V(\lambda) - \sum_{t \in S^U} \gamma_t(\lambda) d\left(w - V(\lambda) - w^0\right). \tag{10.37}$$

When the worker is paid a market wage $(w = w^0 + V(\lambda))$, she is indifferent between being dismissed or not. Thus, she would choose effort $\lambda = 0$ and then end up with a utility above the market-clearing wage. To elicit positive effort, the principal must pay an above-market-clearing wage $w > w^0 + V(\lambda)$ and have a dismissal policy that punishes low effort. Differentiating (10.37) with respect to effort, one can immediately derive the wage as a function of the desired effort and dismissal policy S^U:

$$w\left(\lambda, S^U\right) = -\frac{V'(\lambda)}{d\sum_{t \in S^U} \hat{\gamma}_t} + w^0 + V(\lambda). \tag{10.38}$$

Under this contract, the principal has to pay a wage premium of $\frac{V'(\lambda)}{-d\sum_{t\in S^U}\hat{\gamma}_t}$ above the market-clearing wage. The optimal contract is one that minimizes this premium. One can immediately see by inspection that this quantity is minimized by using all signals with bad news ($\hat{\gamma}_t < 0$). Hence, we have:

Proposition 10.11 *Suppose that the conditions of proposition 10.8 for the existence of an authority contract hold, the agent has no information regarding the performance, and firms can dismiss workers at no cost. Then the optimal employment contract is an efficiency wage contract denoted by $k^{EW} = \left(w^{EW}, S^{EW}\right)$, where the wage satisfies (10.38) and the principal dismisses the agent when the principal receives bad news: $t \in S^{EW} = \left\{t | \hat{\gamma}_t < 0\right\}$.*

Given this result, one can also derive the optimal effort level. The efficient level of effort is one at which the marginal cost of effort is equal to the marginal benefit ($V'(\lambda^*) = B$). Under an efficiency wage contract, the optimal effort is given by:

$$V'\left(\lambda^{EW}\right) = B - \frac{V''\left(\lambda^{EW}\right)}{-d\sum_{t\in S^{EW}}\hat{\gamma}_t} < B,$$

and hence, the effort is less than first best.

This example illustrates how the subjective evaluation model provides a natural framework for efficiency wage models. It explains why wages may not vary with the observed performance. Notice that it does not predict rigid wages over time, but only explains why wages may be fixed in advance when it is expensive for the principal and the agent to have common beliefs regarding performance. This model is consistent with wages adjusting to business cycle fluctuations via their effects on the reservation wage w^0. Notice as well that an efficiency wage contract is very much an authority relationship—employment determination is in the hands of the principal. It turns out that the question of whether one should use an authority contract can also be viewed through the lens of information flows.

10.5   The Sales Contract with Subjective Evaluation

The only difference between the sales contract and the authority contract is the timing of information release. In an authority contract, there is a natural division of duty—the agent provides the effort and the principal sets the reward. Potential conflict is needed to ensure that the principal is truthful. Under a sales contract (with subjective evaluation),[15] the agent sets both effort and compensation, which corresponds in practice to cases in which one has an expert, such as a physician or lawyer, selling her services. As we shall see, the analysis of the optimal sales contract is more complex than an authority contract, which raises a natural question of whether there are situations in which the sales contract is preferred.

From proposition 10.8, we know that a necessary and sufficient condition for the existence of an authority contract is that the principal has some useful information regarding the agent's performance. The next section presents an example in which the principal has no information regarding the agent's performance, but nevertheless there exists a sales contract that can implement a positive effort using only information held by the agent. This example shows there are situations in which a sales contract may be strictly preferred to an authority contract because it can more effectively use the information held by the agent.

However, sales contracts do come at a cost that is not present in an authority contract. Under an authority contract, the agent's truth-telling incentives are unaffected by her effort. Thus, it is without loss of generality that the truth-telling constraints are required to be satisfied at only the agreed effort. This is no longer the case for the sales contract. The agent's effort affects the distribution of signals received by the principal and the agent. Because the agent chooses her effort and reporting strategy before the principal has a chance to choose his reporting strategy, there may be cases in which the agent is tempted to deviate from the agreed effort and then mislead the principal regarding the true state.

This is known as a "double deviation"—the agent shirks and lies—a phenomenon which is all too common in human affairs.[16] For example, a stockbroker may not carry out due diligence in researching a stock, but she might nevertheless recommend the stock to a client to obtain the sales commission. The remainder of the section discusses the analysis of this case and provides a general existence result and conditions under which one does not have to worry about a double deviation.

10.5.1   Contracting with an Uninformed Principal

Under a sales contract, the agent chooses effort and then reveals her information, followed by the principal revealing his information (as in table 10.1). This subsection presents an example featuring an uninformed principal, so by proposition 10.8 one cannot implement effort $\lambda > 0$ with an authority contract. However, it will be possible to implement positive effort under a sales contract. An example then shows that this can arise only in the case of three or more signals, illustrating the danger of relying on only two signal examples to develop intuition regarding contracting with subjective evaluation.

Consider the following information structure with three signals, $S = \{0, 1, 2\}$. Suppose that the principal draws $t = 0, 1$, or 2 with equal probability. This ensures that the principal's signal by itself contains no information regarding the agent's performance. Moreover, under a sales contract, the terms of trade for the principal do not depend on his signal, so one can assume the principal is always truthful. Next, consider the agent's information:

1. If $t = 0$ then:
   (a) $Pr[s = 0 | t = 0] = 0$.
   (b) $Pr[s = 1 | t = 0, o = H] = \pi$, where $\pi > 1/2$ is a fixed probability.
   (c) $Pr[s = 1 | t = 0, o = L] = (1 - \pi)$.
2. If $t = 1$ then:
   (a) $Pr[s = 1 | t = 1] = 0$.
   (b) $Pr[s = 2 | t = 1, o = H] = \pi$, where $\pi > 1/2$ is a fixed probability.
   (c) $Pr[s = 2 | t = 1, o = L] = (1 - \pi)$.
3. If $t = 2$ then:
   (a) $Pr[s = 2 | t = 2] = 0$.
   (b) $Pr[s = 0 | t = 2, o = H] = \pi$, where $\pi > 1/2$ is a fixed probability.
   (c) $Pr[s = 0 | t = 2, o = L] = (1 - \pi)$.

Since $Pr[s=t]=0$, the contract can specify an arbitrarily large value of $\hat{\delta}=\delta_{00}=\delta_{11}=\delta_{22}$, which, given that the principal is truthful, implies that the agent always tells the truth. Next, let $\delta_{01}=\delta_{12}=\delta_{20}=0$, and set $\delta_{02}=\delta_{10}=\delta_{21}=\bar{\delta}$ to satisfy:

$$\bar{\delta}=\frac{V'(\lambda)}{(2\pi-1)}.$$

In this case, the truth-telling constraints are automatically satisfied regardless of effort, and the agent is rewarded with less conflict if she works harder. Finally, the payment $\bar{c}$ is fixed to satisfy the participation constraint with equality. In this example, there are many optimal contracts because the full support assumption is not satisfied. With the introduction of some noise, this would dramatically reduce the number of optimal contracts, as it did for the case of relational contracts in subsection 10.4.1.

This example does not work in the case of binary signals, $S=\{0,1\}$. It is worthwhile to see why and also to illustrate some of the new issues that arise when dealing with sales contracts. The distribution of signals $t,s\in S$ is as follows:

1. A fair coin is flipped, and the principal draws $t=0$ if heads and $t=1$ if tails.
2. If $t=0$ then:
   (a) $Pr[s=0|t=0,o=H]=\pi$, where $\pi>1/2$ is a fixed probability.
   (b) $Pr[s=0|t=0,o=L]=(1-\pi)$.
3. If $t=1$ then:
   (a) $Pr[s=0|t=1,o=H]=(1-\pi)$.
   (b) $Pr[s=0|t=1,o=L]=\pi$.

One can verify that this results in signal matrices:

$$\Gamma^L=\begin{bmatrix} (1-\pi)/2 & \pi/2 \\ \pi/2 & (1-\pi)/2 \end{bmatrix},$$

$$\Gamma^H=\begin{bmatrix} \pi/2 & (1-\pi)/2 \\ (1-\pi)/2 & \pi/2 \end{bmatrix}.$$

In this example, the meaning of the signal s depends on the realization of t, though the signal t itself contains no information regarding the productivity of the agent—it merely provides information on how to interpret s. When both parties get the same signal, the probability of a high output is π; however, when they get different signals, the probability of a high output is $1-\pi$. The fact that $\pi>1/2$ means that a high output is more likely when the principal and the agent get the same signal. In other words, getting the same signal is good news, while having different signals is bad news. In this case, the marginal effect of effort on signals is given by:

$$\hat{\Gamma}=\frac{(2\pi-1)}{2}\begin{bmatrix} 1 & -1 \\ -1 & 1 \end{bmatrix}.$$

Similarly, the signal s, like the signal t, cannot by itself provide good or bad news.

As before, let the effort costs be given by a twice differential and convex function $V(\lambda)$, where $V(0)=0$.

The contract

From lemma 10.5, we know that to ensure truth-telling, the information revealed by the last mover cannot affect their payoff. This implies that the price paid by the principal cannot vary with his information. From lemma 10.2, we are free to decide who allocates the conflict costs, and without loss of generality we can suppose that the principal imposes these costs (for example, by posting a negative review online regarding a financial adviser). Without loss of generality, the sales contract can be assumed to be of the following form:

$$w_{ts} = c_s - \delta_{ts}, t, s \in S, \tag{10.39}$$

where c_s is the cost to the principal and δ_{ts} is the conflict cost imposed by the principal on the agent.

For the current example, neither the principal's nor the agent's signal provides any information, so for this example, we can suppose without loss of generality that the principal's costs do not vary with s, and we let $c_s = \bar{c}, s \in \{0, 1\}$, where $\bar{c}$ is a constant. This constant does not affect incentives and can be chosen to ensure that the participation constraint is satisfied with equality. Therefore, we can take it as a proxy for the agent's outside option and focus on the determination of the conflict, δ_{ts}, given $\bar{c}$.

The problem is symmetric in the sense that the signal label 0 or 1 provides no information, resulting in payoffs varying in a useful way only with the information of whether the two signals are the same. We can restrict ourselves to payoffs that are a function of whether parties agree, $\delta_{00} = \delta_{11} = \delta_A$, or disagree, $\delta_{01}^S = \delta_{10}^S = \delta_D$. Let $\psi = \{\bar{c}, \delta_A, \delta_D\} \in \Psi = \Re \times \Re_+^2$ denote the contract with these terms, and let Ψ be the corresponding set of possible contracts. By construction, the principal's payoff does not vary with his signal; thus, we may suppose that he is always truthful. Before the principal chooses, the agent's strategy is given by her unobserved effort, λ, and the signal that she sends to the principal. We can again appeal to symmetry and observe that if it is optimal to lie about state $s = 0$, then it is also optimal to lie about state $s = 1$. Therefore, at the price-setting stage, the agent chooses a reporting strategy $R \in \{T, L\}$, where $R = T$ is truth-telling ($\hat{s} = s$) and $R = L$ is lying ($\hat{s} = (1 - s)$), thus implying a payoff function:

$$U^A(\lambda, R|\psi) = \begin{cases} \bar{c} - \pi \delta_D - (1 - \pi) \delta_A - \lambda (2\pi - 1)(\delta_D - \delta_A) - V(\lambda), & \text{if } R = T, \\ \bar{c} - \pi \delta_A - (1 - \pi) \delta_D - \lambda (2\pi - 1)(\delta_A - \delta_D) - V(\lambda), & \text{if } R = L. \end{cases} \tag{10.40}$$

Notice that under this contract, the cost to the principal is simply $\bar{c}$. Given that the participation constraint is always binding at an optimal contract, we have from (10.16):

$$C(\lambda, \psi) = \pi \delta_D + (1 - \pi) \delta_A + \lambda (2\pi - 1)(\delta_D - \delta_A) + V(\lambda) + U^0 = \bar{c}. \tag{10.41}$$

The goal of the principal is now to choose ψ to minimize $C(\lambda, \psi)$ subject to the two remaining incentive constraints—the agent should choose effort λ and truthfully report her private information.

The incentive constraint

Because the agent chooses these actions *before* the principal reports his information, it is possible for the agent to coordinate these choices. Taking the first-order condition for effort (10.40), we get:

$$\partial U^A / \partial \lambda = \begin{cases} (2\pi - 1)(\delta_D - \delta_A) - V'(\lambda), & \text{if } R = T, \\ (2\pi - 1)(\delta_A - \delta_D) - V'(\lambda), & \text{if } R = L. \end{cases}$$

If we want a positive effort, then one necessarily needs to set $\delta_D - \delta_A > 0$. But this implies that if $R = L$, then $\frac{\partial U^A}{\partial \lambda} < 0$. In other words, at the time when the agent chooses her effort, if she plans to lie in the next period, then her optimal effort choice is to set $\lambda = 0$.

More generally, under a sales contract, at the time when effort is chosen, the agent can also decide on her reporting strategy, and this ensures that her effort is optimal conditional on the information revelation choice. Let $\lambda^*(R, \psi)$ denote the optimal effort given the reporting strategy R. When $\delta_D - \delta_A \geq 0$, then $\lambda^*(L, \psi) = 0$ and $\lambda^*(T, \psi)$ is the solution to:

$$V'\left(\lambda^*(T, \psi)\right) = (2\pi - 1)(\delta_D - \delta_A). \tag{10.42}$$

Notice that the information revelation strategies have the opposite effects on incentives whenever $(\delta_D - \delta_A) \neq 0$. This might seem like an example in which the revelation principle does not apply, but that is not quite correct because one has to define the revelation constraint for the complete set of strategies available to the agent at the beginning of the game. In the case of the authority contract, the agent's reporting strategy is not affected by her effort, and the truth-telling constraints could be applied after her effort is chosen. In this case, the agent's signal necessarily provides effort incentives, and the revelation principle has to be used at the beginning of the game. To implement effort λ, there must be a contract ψ such that $\lambda = \lambda^*(T, \psi)$ and

$$U^A\left(\lambda^*(T, \psi), T | \psi\right) \geq U^A\left(\lambda^*(L, \psi), L | \psi\right). \tag{10.43}$$

For this 2×2 case, there is no solution (see exercise 8) because we are short of an instrument—the difference, $\delta_D - \delta_A$, has the double duty of providing incentives for both truth-telling and effort provision, which in this case move in opposite directions.

10.5.2 Optimal Sales Contracts

In this section, the examples from the previous section are extended to general information structures. Starting with a general contracting model, the revelation principle can be used to transform the problem into a standard constrained optimization problem with truth-telling constraints. This is an illustration of the revelation principle applied to a problem with moral hazard.

The timing of the contracting game is given in table 10.1. The principal offers the agent a contract that asks the agent to produce effort $\lambda \in [0, 1]$, under the terms $\psi = \left\{c_{m_t m_s}, \delta_{m_t m_s} | \{m_t, m_s\} \in M_t \times M_s\right\}$, where M_t, M_s are message spaces of finite sizes that may include revealing their true observations taken from the set S. We already know that we can allocate the task of imposing conflict to either party. In the case of the sales contract, it is more convenient to have the principal, who moves last, impose conflict on the agent, and one can set:

$$w_{m_t m_s} = c_{m_t m_s} - \delta_{m_t m_s}, \forall \{m_t, m_s\} \in M_t \times M_s.$$

Thus it is assumed that the set of possible contracts takes the form:

$$\hat{\Psi}^S = \left\{c_{m_t m_s}, \delta_{m_t m_s} | \delta_{m_t m_s} \geq 0, \{m_t, m_s\} \in M_t \times M_s\right\}.$$

Let $\Psi^S \subset \hat{\Psi}^S$, where Ψ^S is the set of contracts with the message space restricted to the parties reporting their private information: $M_t = M_s = S$.

Given a contract $\hat{\psi} \in \hat{\Psi}^S$, the payoffs as a function of the actions by the principal and the agent are given by:

$$U\left(\lambda, \hat{m}_t\left(\cdot\right), \hat{m}_s\left(\cdot\right) \mid \hat{\psi}\right) = \sum_{t,s \in S} \Gamma_{ts}\left(\lambda\right)\left(c_{m_t(t),m_s(s)} - \delta_{m_t(t),m_s(s)}\right) - V\left(\lambda\right), \qquad (10.44)$$

$$C\left(\lambda, \hat{m}_t\left(\cdot\right), \hat{m}_s\left(\cdot\right) \mid \hat{\psi}\right) = \sum_{t,s \in S} \Gamma_{ts}\left(\lambda\right) c_{m_t(t),m_s(s)}, \qquad (10.45)$$

where $\hat{m}_t\left(\cdot\right) \in \hat{M}_t = \left\{\hat{m}_t : S \to M_t\right\}$ and $\hat{m}_s\left(\cdot\right) \in \hat{M}_s = \left\{\hat{m}_s : S \to M_s\right\}$. Consistent with the full support assumption regarding the signals, suppose that the contract specifies the set of possible signals such that all messages are observed with strictly positive probability.[17] As this in turn allows one to suppose that the principal never observes an "off equilibrium" event, his beliefs can be set equal to the equilibrium strategies implementing the contract. Given that the agent chooses both her effort and reporting strategy, we do not need to suppose that her effort choice is part of her information set when she chooses her reporting strategy. However, as effort does affect the probability distribution of states, we do have to suppose that the effort and the message are chosen jointly. Thus, we have the following definition of an implementable contract.

Definition 10.12 *A sales contract $\hat{\psi} \in \hat{\Psi}^S$ implements effort λ if there exist reporting strategies $\left\{\hat{m}_t\left(\cdot\right) \hat{m}_s\left(\cdot\right)\right\}$ such that:*

$$U\left(\lambda, \hat{m}_t\left(\cdot\right), \hat{m}_s\left(\cdot\right) \mid \hat{\psi}\right) \geq U\left(\bar{\lambda}, \hat{m}_t\left(\cdot\right), \bar{m}_s\left(\cdot\right) \mid \hat{\psi}\right), \forall \bar{\lambda} \in [0, 1], \forall \bar{m}_s\left(\cdot\right) \in \hat{M}_s, \qquad (10.46)$$

$$C\left(\lambda, \hat{m}_t\left(\cdot\right), \hat{m}_s\left(\cdot\right) \mid \hat{\psi}\right) \leq C\left(\lambda, \bar{m}_t\left(\cdot\right), \hat{m}_s\left(\cdot\right) \mid \hat{\psi}\right), \forall \bar{m}_t\left(\cdot\right) \in \hat{M}_t, \qquad (10.47)$$

Let $\hat{\Psi}\left(\lambda\right)$ denote the set of sales contracts that implement effort λ.

The possibility of a "double deviation" is created by the fact that the agent can coordinate her effort strategy with her reporting strategy before the principal chooses.[18] When contemplating a deviation from the equilibrium, the agent considers changing both her effort and her reporting strategy. It is this possibility that distinguishes the authority contract from the sales contract. In the former, we were able to consider the effort and reporting incentives independently, while in the sales contract, effort and reporting incentives are combined into a single constraint (10.46).

This constraint can be simplified as follows. Suppose that a contract $\hat{\psi}$ can be implemented with $\{\lambda, \hat{m}_t\left(\cdot\right) \hat{m}_s\left(\cdot\right)\}$. Hence:

$$U\left(\lambda, \hat{m}_t\left(\cdot\right), \hat{m}_s\left(\cdot\right) \mid \hat{\psi}\right) \geq U\left(\bar{\lambda}, \hat{m}_t\left(\cdot\right), \hat{m}_s\left(\cdot\right) \mid \hat{\psi}\right), \forall \bar{\lambda} \in [0, 1].$$

In other words, a necessary condition for implementation by $\{\lambda, \hat{m}_t\left(\cdot\right) \hat{m}_s\left(\cdot\right)\}$ is that effort λ is optimal given the reporting strategies. Regardless of the reporting strategies, strict convexity of $V\left(\lambda\right)$ implies that the utility is strictly concave in effort, which enables us to define a unique optimal payoff:

$$\lambda^* \left(\hat{m}_t \left(\cdot \right), \hat{m}_s \left(\cdot \right), \hat{\psi} \right) = \arg \max_{\lambda \in [0,1]} U \left(\lambda, \hat{m}_t \left(\cdot \right), \hat{m}_s \left(\cdot \right) \mid \hat{\psi} \right). \tag{10.48}$$

Given that the number of reporting strategies is finite, the set of implementable contracts is characterized with a finite number of inequalities, which in turn implies the revelation principle.

Proposition 10.13 *Suppose that the interior condition and the full support condition at $\lambda \in (0,1)$ hold. The contract $\hat{\psi} \in \hat{\Psi}(\lambda)$ can implement effort $\lambda \in (0,1)$ if and only if there exists a direct revelation contract $\psi \in \Psi$ of the form $\{c_s, \delta_{ts}\}$ that satisfies:*

$$\sum_{t,s \in S} \Gamma_{ts} \left(\lambda \right) \left(w_{ts} - w_{t\hat{s}(s)} \right) \geq V \left(\lambda^* \left(t \left(\cdot \right), s \left(\cdot \right), \psi \right) \right) - V \left(\lambda^* \left(t \left(\cdot \right), \hat{m} \left(\cdot \right), \psi \right) \right), \forall \hat{m} \left(\cdot \right) \in \hat{M},$$
$$\tag{10.49}$$

where $w_{ts} = c_s - \delta_{ts}$, $\hat{M} = \left\{ \hat{m} : S \to S \right\}$ is the set of reporting strategies using the signal space S as the message space, and $t \left(\cdot \right), s \left(\cdot \right) \in M$ represent truthful reporting.

Proof. Suppose a truth-telling contract ψ that satisfies (10.49) exists. By construction, it ensures that the principal's payoff does not vary with his report, so truth-telling is optimal. It follows from the discussion before the proposition that satisfying (10.49) implies truth-telling is optimal and that choosing effort $\lambda \in (0,1)$ is optimal for the agent.

For the converse, let $\hat{\psi}$ be a contract implementing $\lambda \in (0,1)$ that uses reporting strategies $\left\{ \hat{m}_t \left(t \right), \hat{m}_s \left(s \right) \right\} \in \hat{M}_t \times \hat{M}_s$. Define a direct revelation contract from this contract denoted by $\psi = \{c_{ts}, \delta_{ts}\}_{t,s \in S}$:

$$c_{ts} = c_{\hat{m}_t(t), \hat{m}_s(s)},$$

$$\delta_{ts} = \delta_{\hat{m}_t(t), \hat{m}_s(s)}.$$

The FSC implies that if $c_{\hat{m}_t(t), \hat{m}_s(s)} > c_{\hat{m}_t'(t), \hat{m}_s(s)}$, then when s is observed, the principal would always choose $\hat{m}_t'(t)$ over $\hat{m}_t(t)$. This immediately implies that costs cannot vary with the principal's report. Consequently, we may suppose that the contract takes the form $\hat{\psi} = \left\{ c_{\hat{m}_s(s)}, \delta_{\hat{m}_t(t), \hat{m}_s(s)} \right\}$ and hence $\psi = \{c_s, \delta_{ts}\}$. Moreover, since δ_{ts} does not affect the principal's payoff, then the principal's truth-telling constraint is automatically satisfied, and we now need to consider only the incentives faced by the agent.

By construction:

$$\lambda = \lambda^* \left(t \left(\cdot \right), s \left(\cdot \right), \psi \right) = \lambda^* \left(\hat{m}_t \left(\cdot \right), \hat{m}_s \left(\cdot \right), \hat{\psi} \right),$$

and if the parties are truthful under the direct mechanism, then effort λ is implemented. The final step is to show that the agent has no incentive to deviate from truth-telling. Suppose that the agent considers using the strategy $\hat{s} \left(\cdot \right) \in \hat{M}$. Then the state-dependent payoffs must satisfy:

$$c_{\hat{s}(s)} = c_{\hat{m}_s(\hat{s}(s))},$$

$$\delta_{t\hat{s}(s)} = \delta_{\hat{m}_t(t(\cdot)), \hat{m}_s(\hat{s}(s))},$$

and we have:

$$U\left(\lambda^*\left(t\left(\cdot\right),\hat{s}\left(\cdot\right),\psi\right),t\left(\cdot\right)\hat{m}_s\left(\cdot\right)|\psi\right)=U\left(\lambda^*\left(\hat{m}_t\left(\cdot\right),\hat{m}_s\left(\hat{s}\left(\cdot\right)\right),\hat{\psi}\right),\hat{m}_t\left(\cdot\right),\hat{m}_s\left(\hat{s}\left(\cdot\right)\right)|\hat{\psi}\right)$$

$$\leq U\left(\lambda^*\left(\hat{m}_t\left(\cdot\right),\hat{m}_s\left(\cdot\right),\hat{\psi}\right),\hat{m}_t\left(\cdot\right),\hat{m}_s\left(\cdot\right)|\hat{\psi}\right)$$

$$=U\left(\lambda^*\left(t\left(\cdot\right),s\left(\cdot\right),\psi\right),t\left(\cdot\right)s\left(\cdot\right)|\psi\right).$$

This in turn implies that the direct revelation contract satisfies (10.49). □

This result suggests that, without loss of generality, we may restrict the study of sales contracts implementing effort level λ to direct revelation mechanisms that satisfy condition (10.49), denoted by $\Psi^S\left(\lambda\right)\subset\Psi^S$. Let $\psi^{S*}\left(\lambda\right)$ denote an optimal sales contract implementing λ that satisfies:

$$C\left(\lambda|\psi^{S*}\left(\lambda\right)\right)=\min_{\psi^S\in\Psi^S\left(\lambda\right)}C\left(\lambda|\psi^S\right).$$

In principle, the agent can choose to deviate to any effort level when planning to misrepresent her information in the final period. An important implication of proposition 10.13 is that one needs to consider only a finite number of constraints—for each potential reporting strategy, the agent needs to consider only the consequence of choosing the optimal effort conditional on her reporting strategy. This, combined with the convexity assumptions for effort costs, implies that $\Psi^S\left(\lambda\right)$ is a closed set.

Finally, under a sales contract, the principal can, in an incentive-compatible manner, impose arbitrary punishments on the agent. Using an argument similar to proposition 10.8 it follows:

Proposition 10.14 *Under the conditions of proposition 10.8, for all $\lambda\in\left(0,1\right)$, there exists an optimal sales contract $\psi^{S*}\in\Psi^S\left(\lambda\right)$.*

Proof. Under the conditions of proposition 10.8, it is possible for the principal to incentivize the agent using just his signal. In particular, suppose that the state-contingent bonus $\vec{b}=\{b_t\}_{t\in S}\geq\vec{0}$ provides the agent with the incentive to select effort $\lambda\in\left(0,1\right)$. We can define a corresponding sales contract that implements effort λ as follows. Let $\bar{\delta}=\max_{t\in S}b_t$. Next, set the cost/conflict that the principal imposes on the agent to $\delta_t=\bar{\delta}-b_t$. Now the principal agrees to pay the agent a fixed wage w^0 given by:

$$w^0=U^0+V\left(\lambda\right)+\sum_{t\in S}\Gamma_t\left(\lambda\right)\delta_t,$$

where $\Gamma_t\left(\lambda\right)$ is the probability of the principal's observing state t given effort λ. Under the contract, the agent's information has no effect on her payoff. Similarly, because the principal moves last, the contract satisfies the principal's incentive constraints. This shows that $\Psi^S\left(\lambda\right)\neq\emptyset$. From the argument in proposition 10.8, it follows that contract choice can be restricted to a nonempty compact subset of Ψ^S, and thus a cost minimizing sales contract exists. □

This result shows that an optimal sales contract exists whenever an optimal authority contract exists. This leads naturally to the question of whether parties should use a sales contract or an authority contract when both are feasible.

10.5.3   Opportunism and Contract Complexity

One way to think about the choice between a sales or an authority contract is in terms of Oliver Williamson's notion of *opportunism:*

Opportunism is a variety of self-interest seeking but extends simple self-interest seeking to include self-interest seeking with guile. It is not necessary that all agents be regarded as opportunistic in identical degree. It suffices that those who are less opportunistic than others are difficult to ascertain ex ante and that, even among the less opportunistic, most have their price.[19]

Within the context of the models reviewed in this book, the statement is puzzling—all agents have been assumed to be self-interested. Williamson himself is quite careful to distinguish the transaction cost theory, for which opportunism is a central component, from the formal agency theory. This key difference is the use of the term "guile" which, according to the Merriam-Webster dictionary, means "deceitful" and "cunning." Agency theory does not in general explicitly allow for principals to be unaware of such behaviors. The multitasking model (chapter 7, section 7.3.1) can be used to understand some of the dysfunctional behavior observed in organizations. For example, Lincoln Electric Company is the basis for a case widely studied in business school for the successful use of performance pay. However, as Irrgang (1972) observes, it was not always successful. He describes the case in which secretaries were rewarded based on the number of keystrokes produced by their typewriter. This led one enterprising person to hit the same key on her typewriter while eating lunch.

Kerr (1975) documents many other cases of incentive systems that led to behaviors that the principals did not anticipate. In his examples, the agents are acting in a self-interested way, but not with guile. In the secretary example, the company is directly rewarding keystrokes, so the secretary is acting in a perfectly rational, self-interested way by supplying more keystrokes. What these examples illustrate is not so much irrational behavior on the part of agents, but that the principals cannot always correctly anticipate the agent's responses. This is consistent with the hypothesis that bounded rationality on the part of principals is a potentially important transaction cost, but this does not necessarily imply "guile" on the part of the agent.

A sales contract presents a situation in which in addition to supplying effort, the agent is always asked to provide information regarding the quality of the service that she is providing. This situation can more easily be characterized as "guile." Examples include stockbrokers who recommend stocks to increase trading by their client (on which they receive a fee) or physicians who recommend unnecessary but costly procedures. In these cases, the agents may be characterized as using "guile" to manipulate the payments from the principal, thereby increasing their personal gain. The question then is whether the transaction costs associated with implementing an authority contract differ substantially from those of a sales contract.

One way to think about this is in terms of the complexity of the principal's optimization problem as measured by the number of signals, n, that are used in the incentive contract. In order for an authority contract to implement an effort λ, the principal needs to ensure that the

Table 10.2
Number of constraints for the authority and sales contracting problems

Number of signals	Authority contract	Sales contract
2	3 cents	3 cents
5	21 cents	31 dollars
10	1 dollar	100 million dollars

incentive constraint (10.24) and the n truth-telling constraints (10.21) are satisfied. For each possible signal, the principal must not gain by misreporting. Thus, there are $1 + n(n-1)$ conditions to check.[20] In contrast, for the sales contract, the agent can coordinate her reports with her effort choice. She begins by computing her payoff when she chooses the agreed effort and reports truthfully. Next, she needs to check that this payoff is higher than from choosing a different reporting strategy and then selecting an effort that is optimal for that reporting strategy (constraint 10.49). A reporting strategy is a function $\sigma : S \to S$, and for each strategy, the agent must compute her optimal effort $\lambda^*(\sigma)$. Given that the principal's report has no effect on his payoff, the principal's truth-telling constraint is automatically satisfied. Hence, there are $n^n - 1$ conditions that need to be checked. Checking each of these constraints requires time and effort. For purposes of illustration, suppose it costs 1 cent of time per constraint that needs to be checked. The cost of checking that a single contract is implementable given this cost as a function of the number of states is presented in table 10.2.

As is evident, it is *much* more expensive to find an implementable sales contract. This observation may explain Williamson's intuition that opportunism—self-interest plus guile—is a more significant transaction cost than the transaction costs that arise from self-interest seeking alone. Agency theory implies that transaction costs are lower when the parties have better information. However, even if the agent has better-quality information, the complexity considerations may lead the parties to use an authority contract instead. The next subsection discusses a case in which this intuition applies.

10.5.4   Effort-Neutral Information Systems

The complexity of the sales contract arises from the fact that the agent's effort can affect the quality of the information received by the principal. Now suppose that the principal's information is not affected by the agent's effort but only by the agent's information. In that case, one no longer needs to consider double deviations. More precisely:

Definition 10.15   *An information structure is* effort neutral *if the distribution of the principal's signals is not dependent on effort:*

$$Pr\,[t|s, \lambda] = Pr[t|s], \forall \lambda \in [0, 1] \text{ and } t, s \in S.$$

Observe that this implies:

$$\Gamma_{ts}(\lambda) = Pr\,[ts|\lambda]$$

$$= Pr\,[t|s, \lambda] \times Pr\,[s|\lambda]$$

$$= Pr\,[t|s] \times Pr\,[s|\lambda], \forall \lambda \in [0, 1], t, s \in S. \tag{10.50}$$

Under the full support assumption, we can let $r_{ts} = Pr\,[t|s] > 0$, and then from (10.50), we can set $\Gamma_{ts}^o = \beta_s^o r_{ts}$, $\forall t, s \in S$, where $\beta_s^o = \sum_{t \in S} \Gamma_{ts}^o$, $o \in \{H, L\}$. Thus, when information is effort neutral, the agent, conditional on her signal, cannot manipulate the principal's signal by changing effort. Consequently, the truth-telling constraints for the sales contract now take the same form as for an authority contract.

Proposition 10.16 *Suppose that the interior condition and the full support condition at $\lambda \in (0, 1)$ hold. Then when the information structure is effort neutral, a sales contract $\psi = \{c_s, \delta_{ts}\}_{s,t \in S}$ can implement effort $\lambda \in (0, 1)$ if and only if the incentive constraint for effort:*

$$\sum_{s \in S} \left(\left(\beta_s^H - \beta_s^L \right) w_s \right) = V'\,(\lambda) \tag{10.51}$$

and the truth-telling constraint:

$$c_s - \sum_{t \in S} r_{ts} \delta_{ts} \ge c_{\bar{s}} - \sum_{t \in S} r_{ts} \delta_{t\bar{s}}, \forall s, \bar{s} \in S \tag{10.52}$$

are satisfied, where $w_{s\bar{s}} = c_{\bar{s}} - \sum_{t \in S} r_{ts} \delta_{t\bar{s}}$ is the wage in state s when the agent reports $\bar{s}$ and $w_s = w_{ss}$ is the wage when truthful.

Proof. Suppose that the sales contract $\psi = \{c_s, \delta_{ts}\}_{s,t \in S}$ can implement effort $\lambda \in (0, 1)$. It must be the case that choosing effort λ is optimal, which implies the first-order condition (10.51). Implementation requires that truth-telling is optimal at the agreed effort and hence (10.49) implies that all reporting strategies $\hat{m} : S \to S$ satisfy:

$$\sum_{t,s \in S} \beta_s\,(\lambda)\,r_{ts}\,(c_s - \delta_{ts}) - V\,(\lambda) \ge \sum_{t,s \in S} \beta_s\,(\lambda)\,r_{ts} \left(c_{\hat{m}(s)} - \delta_{t\hat{m}(s)} \right) - V\,(\lambda)\,, \forall t, s, \bar{s} \in S. \tag{10.53}$$

The FSC implies that $\beta_s\,(\lambda) > 0$, $\forall s \in S$. This combined with (10.53) implies (10.52).

For the converse, suppose that (10.51) and (10.52) hold. The interior condition implies that (10.51) ensures that the agent chooses λ if there is no incentive to misrepresent information after effort λ. Given that the principal's payoff is not affected by his report, then he can be assumed to report truthfully. By contrast, suppose that the direct revelation contract ψ is not implementable; hence, there exists a reporting strategy $\hat{m}\,(s)$ and effort choice $\hat{\lambda}$ such that:

$$U\,(\lambda|\psi) < U\left(\hat{\lambda}, \hat{m}(s)|\psi \right)$$

$$\le U\left(\hat{\lambda}|\psi \right)$$

$$\le U\,(\lambda|\psi)\,.$$

The second inequality follows from (10.52) and the fact that $\beta_s\,(\lambda)\,r_{ts} \ge 0$. The final inequality follows from the fact that λ is an optimal effort choice when both parties tell the truth. This leads to a contradiction, and hence ψ implements effort choice λ. $\square$

Thus, "opportunism" is a binding transaction cost only in cases in which the agent's effort affects the conditional probability of observed signal t given signal s. This makes the notion of "guile" very precise.

Notice that when an information system is effort neutral, it necessarily implies that the agent has better-quality information regarding the performance than the principal. From agency theory, we know that the parties should use the most informative signal to set compensation (see chapter 7, subsection 7.3.1), which in turn might suggest that the sales contract is more efficient than an authority contract in this case. As it turns out, this intuition is false in both directions. This result is explored in exercise 9.

The trade-off depends on which type of reward is most efficient. Under an authority contract, the principal is punished for not rewarding the agent, so the efficiency of the contract depends on cost of deterring the principal's incentive to underreport his evaluation. In contrast, under a sales contract, the agent has an incentive to overstate her performance, so enforcement costs depend on the ability of the principal to detect this overreporting. Exercise 9 explores these effects in the context of binary signals and reiterates the point that the optimal contract form is a potentially complex function of the information structure and may explain why incentive design is so difficult.

10.6 Discussion

This chapter introduces a model of subjective evaluation to illustrate the trade-off between incentives and organizational conflict. This is achieved by introducing a new strategy into the principal-agent model—the ability of each party to costlessly impose a deadweight loss on the other party. In relationships with two-sided asymmetric information, the ability to impose such a cost is a *necessary* condition for truth-telling. When information is private and there is no screening mechanism, one party must be able to costlessly punish the other when they feel that party has been untruthful.[21] The level of conflict needed to ensure performance is increasing with the effort desired by the principal and inversely related to the correlation between the performance assessments of the relevant parties.

This perspective on organizational conflict is quite different from the traditional approaches. For example, March (1962) views the differences in goals as the driver of conflict. Yet, in a principal-agent relationship, the agent would like higher compensation while the principal would like to pay less; therefore, their preferences at this level are diametrically opposed. However, these opposing preferences would not always result in a conflict. Pondy (1967) argues that a conflict may be good or bad without actually explaining why it arises. He views conflict as a complex dynamic process that can have positive effects by increasing interaction between individuals in an organization. Both approaches highlight that conflicts in organizations are ubiquitous phenomena that require managerial attention.

The early economic models of conflict focused on union-firm disputes to explain the incidence of strikes. The Ashenfelter and Johnson (1969) model provides a seminal analysis of strike incidence and duration based on the idea that firms make wage offers that trade off the benefits of a lower wage against the cost of tolerating a longer strike that sufficiently softens the union's stand against accepting the lower wage. The subsequent literature has shown that strikes can be viewed as a bargaining breakdown in the face of asymmetric information.[22]

Lazear's (1989) article is an early contribution to the economics of conflict. He begins with a discussion of the previous evidence supporting the hypothesis that increasing performance pay increases organizational conflict and proceeds to provide an economic model to explain this observation. He points out that cooperation between employees enhances organizational performance, but it is difficult to measure. If one rewards only the measured performance but not cooperation, then increasing the performance pay may cause employees to sabotage their colleagues' work, thus resulting in higher levels of organizational conflict. Hence, optimal contracting entails some wage compression for workers within the same reference group to reduce dysfunctional conflict.

The use of group incentives, such as profit sharing or team compensation is another way to reduce the costs associated with subjective performance evaluations. However, group rewards have a number of intractable problems. First, any rule that divides the returns from team production suffers from free-riding—there is always an incentive for one party to choose an effort that is less than the efficient level (Holmström 1982). One solution to the free-riding problem is to use a relational contract. MacLeod (1984) suggests this solution, but he also observes that implementing it requires some form of exit cost; if there are no exit costs, then one party always has an incentive to shirk and quit. The previous chapter provides a complete analysis of this case in a bilateral exchange problem. Rayo (2007) shows that when there are objective performance measures, an optimal team contract uses a combination of profit sharing and relational incentives.

Building on Malcomson (2009) and Gromb and Martimort (2007), Deb, Li, and Mukherjee (2016) show that any team-based incentive scheme is susceptible to gaming when team members have private information about each other. These are examples of "guile" in a team context. This in turn can help explain why organizational design also entails the management of interpersonal relationships.

This observation is consistent with Alchian and Demsetz's (1972) theory of the firm, which emphasizes the importance of allocating the right to monitor and reward employees to the owner/manager/principal. When the evaluations are noncontractible, Carmichael (1983) and Malcomson (1984) show that employers can use a comparative reward system. The rewards are fixed in advance and then the principal gives a "prize" to the agent whom the principal believes is the highest performer. If the principal has precommitted the prize, then he has no incentive to misrepresent his private information. However, as Eswaran and Kotwal (1984) observe, an incentive remains for the principal to collude with one of the agents to share the prize in return for promising the prize to that agent.

The literature on the interaction between objective and subjective evaluation begins with Baker, Gibbons, and Murphy (1994) and includes work such as Rajan and Reichelstein (2006) and Zabojnik (2014). Recently Taylor and Yildirim (2011) studied subjective evaluation in a nonagency setting and considered the value of "blind review."

Prendergast and Topel (1996) observe that another way in which subjectivity manifests itself in organizations is via favoritism. They show that the use of subjective performance evaluation entails a trade-off between the benefits of performance pay and the costs introduced by favoritism. Rahman (2012) has a clever take on this problem and shows that information systems have been implemented that provide principals with incentives to monitor the workers accurately.

However, that solution relies on having some verifiable signals. Thus, the literature is consistent with the hypothesis that when there is private information, one cannot avoid conflict. The relational contract models discussed in the previous section show that the threat of conflict can be part of the equilibrium behavior. However, in those models, conflict is an unrealized threat. Levin (2003) introduces subjective evaluation to the relational contracting theory and shows that conflict cannot be avoided when rewarding based on subjective evaluations. The literature on repeated games with private information (Kandori and Matsushima 1998 and Compte 1998) has shown that incentives can be (imperfectly) improved on by delaying the release of information using "T-period review contracts"—that is, contracts that evaluate the worker only after $T > 1$ periods. Such a contract improves the quality of the signal by pooling the evaluations and lowers the probability that satisfactory work is punished.

Fuchs (2007) shows that this idea can be applied to the models of MacLeod (2003) and Levin (2003) by using T-period review contracts combined with wage compression to improve the efficiency of contracting with subjective evaluation. This builds on an idea developed in Abreu, Pearce, and Stacchetti (1990), who provide a solution to deter shirking in the provision of innovative commodities (discussed in the previous chapter). If one waits T periods before punishment, then, in every period before that time, the agent is deterred from shirking because of the threat of punishment at date T. Thus, the threat of a punishment at a single date is being "reused" in every period before that date. Manso (2011) discusses a number of features of contracts for innovative commodities whose quality is difficult to observe.

Maestri (2012) shows that when the players' beliefs are correlated, contracts with bonus pay provide further improvement. Lang (2019) has an interesting model in which managers can justify their evaluations at a cost. He shows that because justification is costly, an optimal contract entails justification if and only if the performance is low. Finally, Zhu (2018) introduces an equilibrium refinement that imposes the requirement of common knowledge at each stage and shows that the efficiency wage contracts are optimal in that case.

Other literature explores the impact of uncertainty regarding the value of a relationship. In chapter 8, section 8.5, we saw that the allocation of power has allocative implications when there is asymmetric information. Halac (2012) applies this observation to relational contract theory to show how the principal's distortion of his private information regarding his outside value is affected by the agent's power. An interesting result is that when the principal receives good information, he may follow a strategy that leads to an inefficient turnover that would not have occurred in a bad state. Malcomson (2016) provides a general analysis of relational contracts with persistent private information. He shows that full revelation of information is inconsistent with continuation payoffs being on the Pareto frontier, and therefore it generalizes the observation that asymmetric information leads to conflict in relational contracts. Miller and Watson (2013) explore a similar set of issues in the context of relational bilateral bargaining. Again, they find that with asymmetric information there can be bargaining impasses in equilibrium.

Halac and Prat (2016) make the important observation that the quality of managerial information is endogenous. They study a relational contract in which the principal must invest in the technology to observe the agent's performance. If the agent receives no positive feedback from the principal for a period of time, then this can lead to a gradual decrease in the agent's effort and eventually to the breakdown of the relationship. Interestingly, these deteriorating dynamics do not arise when the principal's observation is about the agent's bad performance.

Martimort, Semenov, and Stole (2017) explore bilateral exchange in a dynamic buyer-seller model with limited contract enforcement. When there is one-sided moral hazard, as we saw in the previous chapter, one can always design a contract that achieves the first best, though the terms will of course vary with the bargaining power of the parties. The paper shows that with learning over time, self-enforcement constraints bind only at the beginning of the relationship. This interesting result is consistent with earlier work on relational contracts that find that relationships have to "start small" to allow the parties to gradually resolve their asymmetric information (Ghosh and Ray 1996; Watson 1999; and Watson 2002).

There is a related literature on sender-receiver games with the feature that the sender can at no cost send a message to the receiver, who then takes an action. In this case, the sender is an interested party because the receiver's action can affect the sender's payoff. There are two problems with sending meaningful messages. First, game theory by itself cannot ensure that the messages have meaning. As in the relational contract models of the previous chapter, parties need a common understanding regarding the meaning of the messages. Second, conflicts of interest between the buyer and the seller can limit the amount of information that can be credibly transmitted (see exercise 10). A common theme of this literature is that in complex contractual relationships, there is always a chance the parties do not have full information regarding the production possibilities set, their preferences, and the preferences of the party with whom they are trading. The seminal papers are by Crawford and Sobel (1982) and Kamenica and Gentzkow (2011). Other contributions include Alonso and Matouschek (2008) on optimal delegation and Kartik (2009) on the effect of lying costs.

This theoretical research highlights that the introduction of asymmetric information to the agency model has the potential to help us understand a rich set of empirical phenomena. For example, when evaluations are subjective, biases may limit the effectiveness of the employment relationship and explain a source or income inequality. (See Lang and Lehmann [2012]; Heywood and Parent [2012]; and Giuliano, Levine, and Leonard [2009] for a literature review and evidence on the interaction between race and performance pay.)

At the center of behavior that triggers conflict is what is perceived as "fair." The importance of fairness in labor markets is now addressed in work such as Mas (2006) and Card et al. (2012). See Fehr, Goette, and Zehnder (2009) for a review.

A growing empirical literature, such as Jacob and Lefgren (2008) and Liberti and Mian (2009), explores the organizational implications of subjective evaluations, while Bloom and Van Reenen (2011) provide a comprehensive review of the literature. Other rapidly expanding literature uses experiments, both in the laboratory and in the field, to explore the effect of evaluation and compensation on performance (List and Rasul 2011 and Charness and Kuhn 2011).

10.7 Exercises

1. Consider the 2×2 case from section 10.2. Given that $\Gamma^L_{UU} = 1$, the agency cost to implement effort λ^* is $\lambda^* \frac{\gamma_{UA}}{\gamma_{AA}} V'(\lambda^*)$, whose level is determined by the parameter $\alpha = \frac{\gamma_{UA}}{\gamma_{AA}}$, called the *perceived bias* in the relationship. Derive the cost function and the optimal effort level as a function of the perceived bias and show that $\partial \lambda^* / \partial \alpha \leq 0$.

2. Continue with the 2×2 case with $\Gamma^L_{UU} = 1$, and let p be the probability that the principal observes acceptable performance A, given that a good outcome occurs. If the principal were completely unbiased, then $p = 1$; otherwise, there is some chance that even though performance is acceptable, the principal feels the quality is unacceptable. Correlation in beliefs is modeled by letting ρ be the probability that the agent has the same evaluation (or equivalently knows the evaluation) of the principal. With probability $(1 - \rho)$, the agent has her own independent observation of performance, under which the probability she observes a good signal is q. This parameter can be viewed as the agent's *self-confidence*, namely the probability that she feels her performance is acceptable when she is not able to observe the principal's evaluation. Given these parameters, derive the perceived bias as a function of p, q, and ρ. Work out how the optimal effort and conflict vary with these parameters. Discuss the implications of your results for discrimination policy.

3. Prove proposition 10.9.

4. Consider now the information structure of proposition 10.9, but now suppose that the agent is risk averse, where preferences are given by:

$$U^A\left(\lambda, \psi^A\right) = \sum_{t \in S} \Gamma_t(\lambda) u(w_t) - V(\lambda),$$

where $u(w) = -\exp(-rw)$ and r is the agent's coefficient of absolute risk aversion. Write the program to determine the optimal cost function in this case and solve it. Contrast the solution with the one in proposition 10.9. In particular, notice that in this case, the payments w_t are uniquely defined.

5. Consider the relational contract case from section 10.4.1. Suppose that punishments are bounded by $\bar{\delta}$. Derive the set of optimal contracts as a function of $\bar{\delta}$. In particular, for each λ, derive $\delta^*(\lambda)$, the lowest level of conflict such that effort λ can be implemented (namely, for $\delta < \delta^*(\lambda)$, there exists a self-enforcing contract implementing effort (λ). What are the properties of $\delta^*(\lambda)$ as a function of λ?

6. Provide the details for the proof of proposition 10.10.

7. Consider the efficiency wage model of section 10.4.2, in which the principal offers an efficiency wage contract of the $k^{EW} = \left\{\lambda^{EW}, w^{EW}, S^{EW}\right\}$ and the agent has utility:

$$U^A = \sum_{t \notin S^{EW}} \gamma_t(\lambda) u(w - V(\lambda)) + \sum_{t \in S^{EW}} \gamma_t(\lambda) u\left((1 - d)(w - V(\lambda)) + dw^0\right),$$

where $d \in (0, 1)$ represents a discount factor and $u(w) = -\exp(-rw)$ is a Von Neumann–Morgenstern utility function. The agent gets payoff $u(w^0)$ if the contract is rejected. Derive the optimal efficiency wage contract and its properties as a function of the discount factor d and risk-aversion coefficient r.

8. Show that there is no feasible solution to the optimal contracting problem given by (10.43).

9. Suppose that the parties have binary signals $t, s \in S$. The agent is assumed to observe perfectly whether there is high or low performance $(Pr[s = H|\lambda] = \lambda)$, and the principal's information satisfies $Pr\,[t = H|s = H] = q \in (1/2, 1)$ while $Pr\,[t = H|s = L] = 1 - p \in (0, 1/2)$. In other words, the agent's and principal's signals are positively correlated, but the probability that the principal observes a high signal can vary with the agent's signal. Derive the optimal sales and authority contracts for the provision of effort $\lambda \in (0, 1)$ as a function of p and q. Which contract form is more efficient? Carry out the same exercise with the tables turned—the principal observes output perfectly and $Pr\,[s = H|t = H] = q \in (1/2, 1)$ while $Pr\,[s = H|t = L] = 1 - p \in (0, 1/2)$.

10. Consider a situation in which a stockbroker (S) is providing advice to an investor (I) on whether to buy a stock (B) or hold (H). The game is as follows:

(a) Nature chooses state high (H) with probability p and state low (L) with probability $(1 - p)$.

(b) Broker (S) observes state $\omega \in \{L, H\}$ and sends message $m \in m_H, m_L$ to investor (I).

(c) Investor (I) does not observe the state, but receives the message and decides to either buy $(d(m) = B)$ or hold $(d(m) = H)$).

(d) The state of Nature is revealed and parties get the following payoffs $\vec{u} = \{u_I, u_S\}$:

	State of Nature	
Decision	High (H)	Low (L)
$d = $ Buy (B)	$(1 - k_H, k_H)$	$(-1 - k_L, k_L)$
$d = $ Hold (H)	$(0, 0)$	$(0, 0)$

The payment k is a commission that can depend on the outcome of the trade. Answer the following:

(a) Draw the extensive form for this game.

(b) Work out the sequential equilibria when $k_H = k_L > 0$. In this case, do there exist equilibria in which the investor acts on the message? (Notice that this answer depends on the value of k—work out the different cases.)

(c) Are there conditions on the payoffs to the broker that result in the investor following the advice of the broker? Are the sequential equilibrium payoffs unique?

(d) Suppose, instead of observing the state of Nature $\omega \in \{L, H\}$, the broker observes a signal $s \in \{L, H\}$ such that:

$$Prob[s = \omega] = \rho \in (1/2, 1).$$

The broker sends a message based on this signal. Answer the previous questions for this case.

11 Summary

Well I think I've been in the top 5% of my age cohort all my life in understanding the power of incentives, and all my life I've underestimated it. And never a year passes but I get some surprise that pushes my limit a little farther.
—Charles Munger (1995)

One of the challenges for microeconomic theory is connecting the often complex mathematical models to empirical phenomena. This book features citations to both theoretical and empirical papers to illustrate the potential applications of the models in each chapter. The goal of this chapter is to briefly discuss the main empirical takeaway points from each chapter of the book.

All the models reviewed here predict that market opportunities act as constraints on observed contracts. Therefore, the competitive model is *always* a good first-order model of wages and prices. The issue is the level of precision. Over a period of years and decades we can expect wages and prices to respond to the forces of supply and demand. However, as we move to more high-frequency data—days and hours—we need better models, such as the ones reviewed in this book, to explain the dynamics of wages and prices over time. Models provide useful, simple representations of data for a limited range of situations. For example, the models used in physics to explain the structure of stars are different from those used to design solid-state electronic devices.

In other words, all models have a limited scope. The challenge is to select the right model or set of models for a particular question. This summary chapter outlines the main features of the models in this book so that a researcher can more easily find the best model for the job at hand and then review the relevant chapter for details. The various models are differentiated mainly by the relative timing of information revelation and choices. These differences are illustrated below with figures of the choice sequence for individuals in a transaction. In particular, as no single model is likely to organize all the data regarding a class of transactions, much more research is needed to help quantify the relative importance of different features of the environment in explaining the characteristics of observed exchange. The fundamental question is not which is the true model; the purpose of a model is to provide a simplified representation of the evidence. Rather, the question is what is the best model and finding better and more elegant models of the phenomena discussed in this book.

To keep the narrative as clear as possible, there are no citations to the literature in this chapter—interested readers are asked to return to the chapters themselves for the references.[1]

11.1 Price Theory and the Role of Evidence

Chapter 1: Introduction

Chapter 1 begins with a discussion of price theory. In economics, price theory plays a role similar to the one played by Newton's laws of motion in physics. With the development of relativity theory and quantum mechanics, we know that Newton's laws are "false." Nevertheless, they make a very good first-order model of physical behavior that is sufficient for many, if not most, practical applications.

Price theory builds on two ideas that go back to the work of Adam Smith, Léon Walras, and Knut Wicksell. The first idea is that resources are scarce, so individuals must make decisions given these resource constraints. Second, task specialization creates economies of scale. The combination of comparative advantage with voluntary exchange is one of the reasons the world has experienced an exponential growth in economic output in the last two centuries.

The Arrow-Debreu model provides a formal starting point for modern price theory. In that model, commodities are allocated in a competitive market, where prices provide a signal of the resource cost of a commodity that guides the decisions made by consumers and firms. This in turn implies that the use of markets for the allocation of commodities can lead to a more efficient outcome and greater output. The fall of the Soviet Union and the rise of China as an economic powerhouse provide tangible evidence that markets can increase output relative to a planned economy. One might conclude that the success of market economies provides empirical support for the welfare theorems of general equilibrium theory. That would be a mistake.

Market economies are far from perfect, and we observe a great deal of variation in performance across different countries. Economies can be compared to a mechanical watch. Like the parts of a watch, a modern market economy requires a complex set of interlocking components to function well. Institutions, like courts, and other government systems, such as welfare programs and pollution regulation, work together to produce the output that is observed today. Like a watch, even when all the pieces are assembled, there can be variations in performance.

Some markets perform poorly because market prices do not necessarily reflect the true "economic" price. When commodities are well defined and consumers can easily differentiate between high and low quality, markets work extremely well, as we see today with the abundant supply of high-quality, technically sophisticated products.

At the same time, many markets do not work as well, such as the markets for education and health services. These markets share the feature that consumers cannot easily observe or anticipate the quality of the service before consumption. For example, the return on college education is realized years after attending college. In the case of health care, there is always a possibility that an operation will go badly or the physician will be unable to correctly diagnose a patient's illness. When an incorrect diagnosis occurs, it is difficult to determine whether this is due to the complexity of the case or poor performance by the physician.

In an Arrow-Debreu economy, this uncertainty is resolved by having a complete set of futures markets that set prices for each of the future outcomes that result from consuming education or health services. For example, in the case of education, if markets were complete then a student would, before entering college, enter into contracts that would provide education and set wages for her future labor services to future employers, and whose terms would depend on events that may occur, such as whether she becomes ill. Although this seems incredible, this type of trade is what the theory requires to make the claim that competitive labor markets lead to an efficient allocation.

Chapter 2: Evidence, Models, and Decision Making

Chapter 2 briefly outlines how science helps us develop better institutions. There are two steps. The first step is to build a *model* that connects actions to outcomes. The second step is to make a choice given the model one has constructed. The seminal paper by Skinner on learning in pigeons is discussed in chapter 2 because it clearly shows that even pigeons build models of their environment and use these models to make food foraging decisions. Skinner also shows that these models can be quite poor and easily manipulated. A model of the process that generates the observed behavior is necessary in order to understand expressed behavior.

Humans share with pigeons the need to build models and beliefs about our environment and use these to guide our choices. This makes designing contracts and institutions difficult because one needs to understand how individuals with a particular set of beliefs and preferences are going to respond to changes in their environment.

What makes economics a science is a system that formalizes the process of model building and testing to create knowledge that has a clear and unambiguous meaning that can be passed on from one person to another and from one generation to another. All sciences feature models that are domain and problem specific. Chapter 2 illustrates this point using two maps of New York City. The first is a street map drawn to scale. With this map, one can find named locations or the best bicycle route from the Upper West Side to Wall Street. The street map is extremely useful, but it is not a "true" representation of New York City. For example, it provides no information on the topology of the city, so our cyclist cannot use it to avoid hills.

A point about the map that is particularly relevant for economic models is that the street layout is not static. Over time streets are renamed and modified. The usefulness of the map is highest at the time it is created but falls over time due to human-created change. Technically, the ability of a map or model to provide useful information in the future is called the *external validity* of a map or model.

Finally, the chapter asks how models are evaluated. In the case of the street map, its quality depends on its accuracy and whether a person can use it to find a particular location in New York. However, if the question is to find the best subway route from one stop to another, even if the information in the detailed map is available, it may not be the most appropriate model. The chapter's second map is of the subway, and it allows a user in hurry to work out an efficient route in time to get on an approaching subway car. The second map is a less accurate (or more false) model, but it is actually more useful for making route choices on a subway.

This point is true of all sciences, including economics. For example, when building a skyscraper, the engineer is concerned about the steel having the right properties as she designs the building. When making those choices, she is not particularly concerned with the solid-state physics that cause iron and carbon to produce steel with particular properties.

Similarly, an economist who advises a firm on compensation policy is not concerned with how an employee spends his income. Rather, she begins with measures of job performance defining the potential outcomes, such as the quality and speed of work completed. The next question is the counterfactual question. What will be the causal effect of an increase in bonus pay on quality and speed of performance?

In practice, this can be a difficult question because it may not be possible to conduct an experiment. The empirical literature cautions against using firm-level data on the relationship between bonus pay and performance because it may not be a causal relationship. This is where theory can play an important role in helping to measure such effects. If the data are from firms that have made optimal decisions, then a positive relationship between bonus pay and performance may be because more-skilled workers are paid a bonus and not because the bonus pay *caused* the higher performance. The recent empirical literature in economics has focused on techniques and models that can help disentangle the difference between correlation and causation in such situations.

As the science progresses, individuals are able to rely on better-quality models to make better decisions. However, in many (maybe most) situations, individuals have to make choices in the absence of clear evidence to guide those choices. The next chapter addresses how one makes rational choices in those cases.

11.2   Decision and Game Theory

Chapter 3: Decision Theory

Chapter 3 introduces Savage's ([1954] 1972) model of rational choice. This approach solves a longstanding problem in statistics, namely what do we mean by probability? Savage introduces the idea of a "personal probability" that allows for integration of science into everyday decision making. His model of rational choice builds on the idea of counterfactuals discussed in chapter 2. For example, when deciding whether to bring an umbrella to work, one has to think about whether it will rain and the cost of being caught in the rain without an umbrella. Savage realized that one does not need to be a meteorologist to think about the likelihood of rain. Rather, given that a choice *must* be made, Savage shows that with the appropriate conditions on preferences, one can back out a person's subjective assessment of the probability of rain from observing a person's choice.

Thus, linking choice to probability, and not the other way around, provides a conceptual framework to think about how individuals process and use information. If good evidence is available, individuals are free to incorporate that information into their personal probability. Therefore, if the forecast is for rain, then an individual can appropriately update her beliefs and make sure she brings an umbrella.

Savage's model does not require beliefs to be correct, but his model does connect beliefs to actions. As I write this in the winter of 2021, we have certainly witnessed a great deal of misinformation in the United States that has led individuals to make poor choices regarding the COVID–19 pandemic. From the perspective of the Savage model, if we know that individuals believe the virus is not dangerous, then their behavior to ignore public health recommendations is rational.

This is not a new problem. During the early twentieth century's Progressive Era in the United States, many unsuspecting individuals were part of a large market for home remedies, such as "snake oil" to cure all illnesses. These examples teach us that understanding beliefs *is* an economic question—individual beliefs determine the market demand for "snake oil," and thus its price. It has proven difficult to ensure that a population is well informed. In the end, the problem of fraudulent remedies was solved by the government regulation of the quality of food and drugs.

One might be tempted to conclude from this example that the rational choice model is false and should be abandoned. But as stated earlier, models are simplified representations of the world that in turn allow for better decision making. Chapter 3 also illustrates the point that the rational choice model is a *simple* model of choice. At its core is the hypothesis that individuals prefer more rather than fewer resources, an assumption that is consistent with thousands of years of human history.

There is nothing in rational choice theory that requires beliefs to be correct. In the case of "snake oil," if the consumer believes it will help him, then it is completely rational for him to purchase some. As the field of behavioral economics develops, better models will be constructed that will capture how individuals make choices in practice and that can be used to improve the models outlined in this book.

Chapter 4: Game Theory

Chapter 4 provides an overview of game theory from the perspective of the Savage model of choice. The goal is to provide a framework to study exchange between interested parties. Even when there is a gain from trade, individuals may try to "game" contract terms to their personal advantage. The goal of game theory is to model the outcome of strategic decision making when it is common knowledge that all parties are making choices that are consistent with their goals and beliefs. This leads to the notions of a Nash equilibrium and a sequential equilibrium that are used throughout the book.

The original goal of game theory was to provide a model that could predict how rational players would make choices in any game. Consistent with the evidence for the rational choice model, there is much evidence that individuals are strategic in the sense that when making choices they think about and model the actions of their counterparties. However, observed choices are sensitive to the details of the game, and parties often make mistakes in their choices. Consequently, at the moment there is no general theory that can accurately predict observed choice by individuals for any strategic situation.

In particular, when the Nash equilibrium of a game is not unique, then parties need some sort of device to coordinate their actions. For the purposes of the models in this book, it is assumed that the coordination of actions is part of the model. More precisely, when parties trade, it is assumed that they agree on self-enforcing choices. This is modeled using a Nash equilibrium (each person is making her preferred choice, correctly anticipating the actions of her counterparty) combined with a market norm that coordinates the actions or includes an explicit agreement on how each party will behave. In this way, game theory can be viewed as a building block for a theory of institutions and organizations, where the latter plays an explicit role in coordinating the actions of individuals.

Chapter 5: Bargaining and the Buyer-Seller Model

Chapter 5 turns to a question at the core of every exchange relationship: How does one divide the gains from trade? If markets are perfectly competitive, then there is always an alternative partner who will give the same return as the current partner. Hence, the surplus is zero and the terms of trade are uniquely determined.

In practice, there are always costs to changing partners, particularly in long-term relationships, where there may be large relationship-specific investments. In the absence of an existing contract, parties need to agree upon the terms of trade to divide the surplus from mutual trade. The first part of the chapter develops the generalized Nash bargaining solution that supposes parties trade efficiently and set the terms of trade based on a single parameter that is interpreted as the parties' relative bargaining power.

This solution is a useful, reduced-form model of exchange that has been used to estimate relative bargaining power, but it does not explain the source of such power. The second part of the chapter addresses this question using an explicit dynamic bargaining model. In that model, relative bargaining power is determined by the relative frequency at which individuals can make offers. In particular, it shows that one party's ability to block listening to offers from its counterparty can lead to an increase in power.

This model also provides an explanation for wage and price rigidity. When parties agree on a wage or price, there is no legal impediment to renegotiating terms as a function of shocks to the value of the relationship. The dynamic bargaining model highlights two sources of the rents. The first is due to the "inside options"—the payoffs if parties stay together but do not trade. The second, "outside options," are the payoffs they receive if they leave the relationship. It is shown that the generalized Nash bargaining model can be mapped to the payoffs determined by the inside options. The outside options have no effect if they are worse than the payoffs negotiated based on the inside options alone.

The practical implication is that even if a worker's outside wage were to go up due to lower unemployment, if that wage is less than her current wage it will have no effect on the current bargain. This simple model predicts that business-cycle fluctuations affect the wages only of workers who would be strictly better off if they left their current jobs.

Thus, the dynamic bargaining model provides predictions of the terms of trade given the inside and outside options. In relationships that extend over time, the value of these options can be set by contracts that fix wage and price terms over time, including severance payments. The model also provides an explanation for wage and price rigidity in the short run. The next part of the book explores the factors that determine contract terms.

11.3   The Theory of Exchange

The next three chapters of the book deal with the microeconomics of bilateral exchange. In economics, this is commonly called "contract theory." This term can be confusing to noneconomists because it is quite different from the legal notion of a "contract." The economics of contracts deals with any feature of the exchange relationship that can affect the terms of trade. This includes contract law as a special case. In contrast, contract law is restricted to agreements that in principle can be enforced by a court of law. For example, contract law is not relevant for informal agreements between employers and employees where the principle of forbearance applies.[2] Such agreements are an important topic in the economics of contracts because they can determine on-the-job performance.

The fact that the law, and contract law in particular, has evolved to solve the practical problem of resolving disputes between individuals that are brought before the courts. Hence, the solutions are often tailored to the specifics of the case. In a common law system, these solutions are recorded and can be used again in the future. Thus, contract law, particularly in a common law jurisdiction, can be viewed as providing a large set of solutions to specific exchange problems that courts have seen in the past.

In contrast, economic models proceed from first principles. Given the technology of production, and the information available, the theory derives solutions that best further the goals of the transacting parties. The theory's goal is to create categories of problems within which the solutions are similar.

In these chapters, exchange is categorized along two dimensions. The first is whether the commodity to be traded is a good or service. A good is a physical commodity that can be inspected by the buyer before trade occurs. In contrast, a service is a commodity that is consumed at the time of production, which means there can be no refusal to trade. For example, a firm cannot observe a worker's output before employment. Rather, after employing the worker, the firm may vary compensation based on realized performance or it may decide to terminate the employment relationship.

The second dimension of an exchange is the timing of actions and information flows. This is where game theory plays an important role in modeling the actions of parties as a function of the events during the relationship. Each chapter considers a different set of exchange conditions, which in turn lead to a different set of contractual solutions or instruments.

The timing of information release in the exchange relationship differentiates the models of each chapter. One or two figures for each chapter illustrate this. The key takeaway is that the efficient regulation of an exchange relationship depends not only on the resource constraints (i.e., price theory) but also on the information parties have at each stage of the relationship.

Chapter 6: Reliance, Holdup, and Breach

Chapter 6 concerns what legal scholars call the "reliance interest." The reliance interest provides one of the classic motivations for parties to enter into a binding contract. All commodities take time to be produced, and in many cases these commodities are produced to order. For example, a museum would like to build a new gallery. For such a specialized commodity it needs to hire a construction firm that decides how to devote resources to the museum's production, and the construction firm needs to be assured it will be compensated at the time of final delivery. Similarly, the museum must be assured that the gallery will meet certain specifications. Moreover, the museum may wish to have the project finished by a certain time in order to book events in advance. In these types of exchanges, both parties are making *relationship-specific* investments that cannot be recouped if the counterparty does not perform its end of the bargain.

For the current discussion, the term "contract" refers to any agreement whose goals are to manage the reliance interest and relationship-specific investments. The next chapter deals with performance pay and the principal-agent model. In that case, the term "agency contract" will be used. The contracts described in chapter 6 are sometimes referred to as

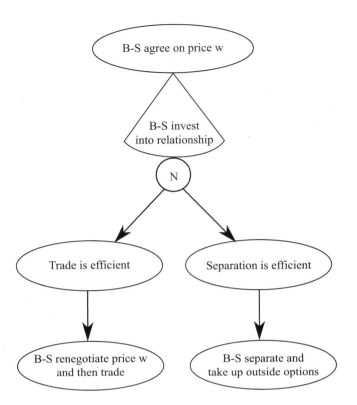

Figure 11.1
Contract timing with holdup.

exhibiting the "property rights" approach. The reason for this terminology is that when one owns property, one is the full residual claimant on any returns to that property.

Fixed price contracts are a way to generate property-type incentives. For example, when a restaurant signs a five-year lease, it has an incentive to renovate the property to maximize the return on sales. What makes the design of such contracts difficult is that nothing is forever. The restaurant may go out of business in six months, resulting in a loss on the investment in renovation. The generic timing for a contract is illustrated in figure 11.1. Party *B* refers to the buyer or employer, and party *S* refers to the seller or potential employee. After parties agree upon a price (or wage), they make investments anticipating the value of future trade. Next, Nature moves and determines whether trade is efficient and whether the contract price should be renegotiated. If the price is not renegotiated and parties trade as planned, then the contract has an incentive that mimics a property right. The fixed price implies that the seller gets to keep the returns from any investment that reduces costs. Similarly, the buyer is able to keep any returns from investments that increase the value of the commodity to the buyer.

But there is a catch. Events may occur that require renegotiating contract terms or abandoning the trade altogether. In either case, if parties anticipate these possibilities, the investment incentives are reduced. Chapter 6 aims to describe a variety of solutions to this problem that depend on the form of the specific investments.

Chapter 6's main insight is that an essential feature of a high-quality contract is the management of bargaining power and decision rights. For example, in an employee-employer contract, if only the employer invests in machinery and employee training, then it is efficient for the employer to have all the bargaining power, and thus employment at will may be optimal.

Conversely, if the machinery is a general investment and the employee is making specific investments, then a long-term fixed wage contract may be efficient. An example of this is the academic tenure given to research scientists at a university. Scientists must make large investments in building up a laboratory, and security of employment creates an incentive for them to do so, which in turn enhances the quality of research desired by the university. Research effort incentives are provided by the scientists' desire for professional recognition outside of the university.

Employment at will and tenure are *contractual instruments* that can enhance the efficiency of a relationship. The choice of instrument is a function of who is making the relationship-specific investment. The chapter describes a number of other contractual instruments that enhance exchange performance, including severance payments, option contracts, inflation-indexed wage contracts, and specific performance contracts.

Chapter 7: Insurance and Moral Hazard

Chapter 7 introduces the canonical principal-agent model. This model and its extensions have resulted in a large and important literature that is known simply as "agency theory." The principal-agent model is built on two ingredients. The first is the insurance motive. For example, a poor farmer who lives off the land will have returns that vary with the weather. In a bad harvest year, the family may suffer great harm. If shocks to the harvest are idiosyncratic (bad harvest years do not correspond to general economic downturns), then welfare can be enhanced with an insurance contract against a poor harvest.

In this case, the optimal agency contract is one that ensures that the risk averse farmer gets the same income each year. The difficulty is that farm output also depends on effort by the farmer. If the farmer is insured against income risk, it may lead to a decrease in effort and lower output. The key point of agency theory is that compensation should be linked to independent measures of effort, such as direct monitoring of daily work. With improved information regarding effort, one can simultaneously improve both risk sharing and effort incentives.

A sharecropping contract provides a compromise solution. Insurance is imperfect, but the farmer does share in increased output when effort is increased. One of the reasons for the rise of modern manufacturing is that bringing artisans into factories simultaneously allowed for fixed wage compensation and a more efficient organization of tasks via performance monitoring. However, the presence of relationship-specific investments also created a balance in bargaining power, which in turn led to the rise of the modern trade union movement.

Figure 11.2 illustrates the timing of events in an agency contract. The key ingredient is that effort is not directly observable (and hence not contractible). Rather, the agent is paid a bonus above a fixed wage if and only if high output is observed. When effort is highly correlated with measured output, the agent can avoid the low output with close to probability 1, and thus ensure she gets the bonus.

The key prediction of this model is that an increase in bonus pay leads to increased effort. When there are other costly actions available to the agent that are not rewarded, increasing

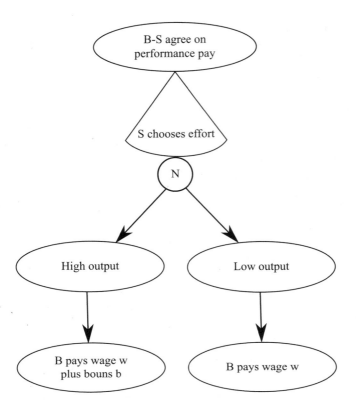

Figure 11.2
Agency contract timing.

rewards for one action can lead to a reduction in effort for the unrewarded actions. In both cases, rewards increase the risk borne by the agent. This risk can be reduced by increasing the quality of information received by the principal, which in turn should lead to an increase in the level of exchange.

The final section of the chapter explores the impact of using reputation, rather than performance pay, to set compensation in a perfectly competitive market. A worker's reputation is defined as the expected ability of the individual conditional on measures of her past performance. In general these measures are imperfect, with the consequence that the individual may work hard to make a good impression and thereby increases the market's perception of her ability. This is called a career concern.

There is less information regarding a younger worker's skill, so variation in past performance has a larger impact on her future compensation than it would for an older worker. The empirical implication is that in markets where compensation is based on reputation, younger workers make greater effort than older workers. There is evidence to support this hypothesis for CEOs of corporations. Specifically, the model predicts that one should use more performance pay for older workers as the market's assessment of a worker's ability becomes more precise.

The important implication of this result is that one cannot rely on reputation alone to ensure efficient performance in a market economy.

Chapter 8: Trade with Asymmetric Information

Chapter 8 takes effort as either fixed or observed and then studies the problem of exchange when there is asymmetric information regarding the value of trade. This occurs when the buyer and seller have private information regarding the benefit and cost of the commodity to be exchanged. Naturally, they would like to conceal their private information in order to get the best deal.

The first result is the revelation principle. It shows that regardless of the potential complexity of exchange, negotiation can always be modeled as a strategic game with the feature that each party has an incentive to truthfully reveal its private information. In practice, parties use a variety of messages to communicate their private information. For example, a monopolist chooses the price to charge as a function of costs, while the buyer chooses the quantity to buy as a function of the value of consumption.

Within the context of exchange that is modeled as a game, one can compute the price and demand as a function of the strategies by each party that, in turn, are a function of their private information. Conceptually, this implies that one can replace this game and associated equilibrium strategies with a *mechanism* that simply mimics the optimal strategies as a function of a party's private information. Under the mechanism, each party reports its valuation, and then the mechanism sets the price and quantity. As the mechanism is simply mimicking the optimal strategy, it is optimal for the parties to reveal their information truthfully. This process is illustrated in figure 11.3, where "Negotiation" represents the mechanism that is used in practice, such as monopoly pricing or give-and-take negotiation.

The revelation principle has the empirical implication that allocation mechanisms do not require a message space that is more complex than the underlying private information. The revelation principle allows one to characterize all the allocations that are possible when parties have private information. In particular, the model can be used to characterize a monopolist's optimal nonlinear pricing rule.

The situation illustrated in figure 11.3 is one in which parties negotiate after they have observed their private information. If trade is voluntary, then in some cases the right to leave the relationship may make it impossible to achieve an efficient allocation. This idea is used in chapter 10 to explain why conflict is ubiquitous in organizations. In those cases, if parties can meet and make a *binding* agreement, then efficient trade is possible. This result, as well as a similar result on specific performance from chapter 6, shows that efficient agreements may entail allocations that make one party worse off ex post than in their next best alternative. In such cases the courts may be called on to enforce a contract that is ex ante efficient but which places one party in a worse position ex post than they were before entering into the contract.

The need for specific performance arises when both parties are making relationship-specific investments or both parties have private information. Chapter 6 shows that in the case of one-sided relationship-specific investment, efficiency can be achieved by allocating to the investing party all the ex post bargaining power. There is a similar result here. When there is one-sided asymmetric information, one can achieve the first best by allocating the ex post bargaining power to the informed party.

This result can help explain the explosive growth of ride sharing services such as Lyft and Uber. In those cases, the asymmetric information is whether a person has spare time to

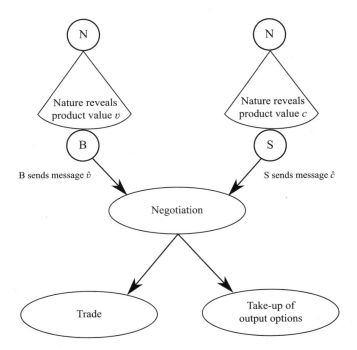

Figure 11.3
Trade with asymmetric information.

use their private car to provide rides to individuals. The ride sharing application allows an individual driver to decide when and for how long she wants to work. These applications released a large volume of rides to the market. As price theory would predict, this increase in supply decreased the demand for taxi services and resulted in a large drop in the value of a New York City taxi medallion.

11.4   Relational Contracts and Social Norms

The final two chapters introduce some behavioral elements into the exchange process. Chapter 9 reviews the classic relational contract model that is appropriate when there is limited or costly contract enforcement. Chapter 10 extends this model to situations in which the evaluation of performance is subjective. These models illustrate the importance of reputations, social norms, and conflict for understanding repeated exchange relationships.

Chapter 9: Relational Contracts

The classic relational contract model is for situations in which a buyer and seller, or employer and employee, enter into a trading relationship over time. It is assumed that there is a well-defined performance criterion with the feature that both parties observe the criterion, but it is impossible (or too expensive) to rely on court-enforced payments.

In this case, contract enforcement requires the use of *self-enforcing agreements*. The basic model takes two forms. The first of these corresponds to the classic efficiency wage

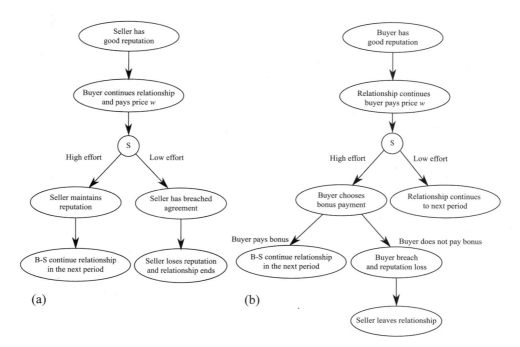

Figure 11.4
The timeline for a relational contract.

model that is illustrated in figure 11.4. In that case there is a social norm based on the seller or employee having an incentive to maintain her reputation to perform as specified by the social norm.

Reputation here is different from the career concerns model discussed in chapter 7. There, reputation referred to the expected ability of a person. In this case, reputation is concerned with expected *behavior*, particularly whether a party can be trusted to perform as promised.

In each period, parties agree to trade at a fixed price. In exchange, the seller agrees to choose high effort in order to provide a high-quality commodity. This in turn produces a high- or low-quality product that is assumed to be observed by the buyer or employer. If high effort is observed, then the reputation of the seller remains high and the relationship continues. If the seller chooses low effort, then she has breached her agreement. This results in reputation loss and the consequence that the buyer refuses to trade with her in the future. Two conditions are necessary for this to be self-enforcing. The first is that low effort is also a self-enforcing social norm. Specifically, once the seller breaches the agreement, the buyer believes that breach will occur in the future with this seller. This belief is consistent with the seller's future behavior. Because she has lost her reputation, the seller no longer gives high effort because she believes she will be dismissed in any case. Thus, the loss of reputation can be viewed as a set of interlocking and mutually consistent expectations regarding future behavior.

The second condition is that there is a sufficient gain from future trade. If markets are perfectly competitive, and the seller is paid a competitive price or wage, then she will get the same payoff in the future regardless of whether the relationship ends. Hence, for there to be a rent, the future value of continuing the relationship must be greater than the value from leaving the relationship.

The literature has identified a number of market institutions that create such a rent. They include efficiency wages (paying a future wage that is above the market rate), sunk investments in inefficient advertising that requires sellers to charge above market prices (for example, expensive advertising for Swiss mechanical watches that keep time worse than an inexpensive quartz watch), and the requirement of upfront "gifts" to start a new relationship. The latter may correspond to costly, get-to-know-each-other meetings and dinners between potential trading partners.

The size of the future rent needed for relational enforcement depends on the potential gain to the seller from breach. This rent is lower when there is frequent monitoring. Relational contracts can also be used to enforce agreements with imperfect monitoring. However, this comes at a cost.

When the seller performs as promised, but the buyer observes low output due to uncertainty in the production, an unfair separation can occur. Consequently, efficiency wage type relational contracts are inefficient (high wages combined with dismissal when there is low observed output).

However, there is a solution. If the output is mutually observed, then parties can agree to a bonus contract in which the buyer agrees to pay if and only if the output is high. This contract is illustrated in figure 11.4b. In this case, the social norm is to have the buyer hold the reputation. His reputation will be lost if he does not pay the bonus whenever there is high output. Even if effort is not directly observable, the fact that output can be observed implies that relational contracting can implement efficient performance by the seller.

Figure 11.4(b) illustrates the case of the buyer paying a bonus, but it can be reversed. An example of this is the warranties that large manufacturers regularly supply for their products. Technically, these warranty contracts are legally enforceable, but in practice no one is likely to bring a legal case for a $500 loss. Rather, consumers rely on performance due to the manufacturer's concern for its reputation in producing high-quality commodities and making good on warranty repairs.

Chapter 9 shows that reputation is an endogenous feature of contract form. Contracts can be designed so that either the buyer or the seller holds the reputation for performance. The party holding the reputation is the one who moves last to make a payment—bonus pay when the buyer holds the reputation or a warranty payment when the seller holds the reputation. Finally, the event that triggers breach is also endogenous. Contractual performance is higher when parties can condition breach on events that both parties can observe with certainty. When the breach event is private information, then we have a situation characterized by subjective evaluation, the case considered in chapter 10.

Chapter 10: Opportunism and Conflict in Agency Relationships

In many trading relationships, performance evaluation is subjective. Such subjective performance evaluations can be found in consumer commodities such as wine or restaurant meals or the employment of individuals providing services. Employment examples include researchers who are working on long-term projects for which there is little to show in the

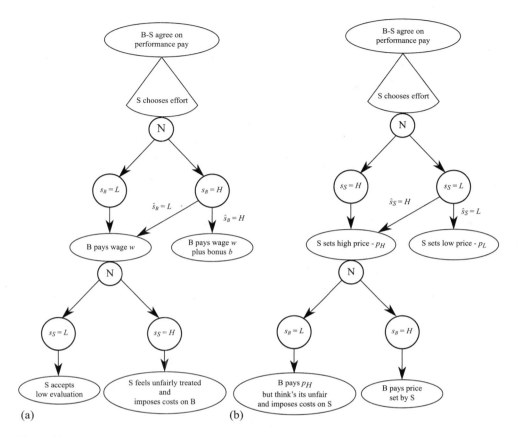

Figure 11.5
The timeline for a contract with subjective evaluation.

short run, customer service employees whose behavior can affect the customer experience, and members of a creative work team developing software or proposing a product launch.

In these cases, the buyer/employer may have a view of performance that is different from the individual who is providing the service. The goal of chapter 10 is to understand how to efficiently manage such relationships. This is accomplished with the explicit introduction of a behavioral element into the model that builds on a combination of relational contract theory (chapter 9), contracting with asymmetric information (chapter 8), and agency theory (chapter 7). As in the case of relational contracting, there are two cases to consider. The situations vary with the timing of information revelation.

These cases are illustrated in figure 11.5. To keep matters simple, each party receives a signal on whether the performance is high or low. The crucial assumption is that the signals are *private* information and hence represent a subjective evaluation of performance. The figures have very similar structures but different implications for contract formation due to the differences in the timing of the information revelation and how that information is used to determine actions and rewards.

The first case, illustrated in figure 11.5a, is called an *authority contract* because it corresponds to a paradigmatic agency relationship in which the buyer (principal or employer) evaluates the quality of the commodity produced and then decides whether to reward the seller (agent or employee). The issue is that the seller does not observe the buyer's signal, so the buyer has a financial incentive to claim that the seller performed poorly and therefore no bonus need be paid.

The challenge is to ensure that the buyer does not misrepresent his private information. Suppose that the subjective signal the seller gets is correlated with the buyer's signal. If she imposes a cost on the buyer whenever she observes a high signal and the buyer does not pay the bonus, this will punish the buyer for not rewarding the seller. The balance is delicate because if the punishment is too large, then the buyer will always pay the bonus, in which case the seller has no incentive to perform. If the punishment is too low, then the buyer will never pay the bonus. The punishment must be calibrated to the size of the bonus pay and the probability of an error, so that ex post the buyer is indifferent between paying and not paying. In that case, he can be truthful and pay the bonus if and only if he observes high performance.

This delicate dance between the buyer and seller provides some insights into the problem of organizational design. The first observation is that with subjective evaluations, potential conflict is a necessary ingredient for effective performance pay. When individuals feel unfairly treated, they may submit negative reviews online or, in an employment context, they may become demoralized and reduce performance. Both of these behavioral responses provide incentives for the buyer to be truthful.

At the same time, the fact that the negative responses need to be calibrated implies that the balance is delicate. This is consistent with the fact that we observe in practice lots of variation in organizational effectiveness that cannot be explained by the physical characteristics of the environment. Hence, a high-performance organization should provide rewards that vary with the buyer's evaluations, while tolerating an "optimal" level of conflict to ensure truthful behavior.

A necessary condition for effective bonus pay is that the buyer's signal is informative. However, this assumption is not always satisfied. For example, in the case of professional services, where the seller might be a doctor or lawyer, the buyer is by construction uninformed. The reason they are seeking a professional is to get advice. In that case, it may still be possible to have incentive pay, where the price charged reflects the seller's information.

This case is illustrated in figure 11.5b, corresponding to what is called a "sales contract with subjective evaluation." In this case, it is still possible to have an incentive contract. The key assumption is not whether the buyer has information on performance but whether the buyer's signal is *correlated* with the seller's signal. For example, the buyer might detect cheating from the tone of the seller's voice. In the case of a recommended medical procedure, the physician may provide some test results that support the decision. Even though the patient cannot interpret the results, their existence may lead the patient to follow the doctor's recommendation. In either case, as long as the buyer's information is correlated with the signal (as opposed to the effort of the seller), then an incentive contract implementing efficient effort may exist.

There is, however, a catch. Suppose that the buyer imposes exactly the right amount of conflict costs to make the seller indifferent between being truthful or not. In the case of an authority contract this is efficient. The problem now is that the seller could follow a strategy of shirking (and hence increase her return) and simultaneously report the high state to get undeserved bonus pay. There are situations in which this strategy may be optimal. The behavior corresponds exactly to what Oliver Williamson calls "opportunism"—self-interest seeking combined with guile.

In the previous chapters, all the contracts assume that individuals make choices consistent with their preferences. None of those models captures the notion of "guile" because in a standard principal-agent model, the principal correctly anticipates how the agent will choose effort. There is no misperception of performance. The combination of effort choice and information revelation leads to a formal model of guile because of the incentive that the agent has to mislead the principal. Sales contracts with subjective evaluation not only provide a formal model of opportunism, they also imply that finding optimal contracts in the face of opportunistic behavior is an order of magnitude more complex than in the basic authority contract with subjective evaluation. Thus, the model is consistent with Williamson's intuition that opportunism may be a significant constraint on organizational performance.

Finally, the main message of this chapter is that when there are differences of opinion, then conflict plays a useful role in optimal incentive design. The chapter also highlights that the source of the conflict is the existence of different views regarding the same activity.

Appendix

This appendix provides a brief outline of constrained optimization and the welfare theorems for general equilibrium. The purpose is to illustrate conditions under which prices reflect the true opportunity cost of resources and to provide a refresher on constrained optimization. The close connection between competitive equilibria and optimal allocations provides the foundation for the widespread use of markets for the allocation of resources. At the same time, the conditions for efficiency are rather stringent. In particular, this short outline discusses the computation of an efficient allocation and the empirical relevance of the assumptions.

A.1 Constrained Optimization Theory

The fundamental problem studied in economics is the efficient allocation of scarce commodities. The starting point of all economic models is the problem of constrained optimization. Here, I present the basic result from nonlinear optimization theory, the Karush-Kuhn-Tucker (KKT) conditions for the convex optimization problem. For a beautiful presentation of the theory, see Boyd and Vanderberghe (2004). The result presented here is taken from chapter 5 of their book, suitably modified as a maximization problem. This result is used throughout this book and corresponds to what I have called *the standard case,* namely the case in which first-order conditions are sufficient to characterize the optimal solution.

Consider the following constrained optimization problem:

$$\begin{aligned} \text{maximize} \quad & f_0(\vec{x}) \\ \text{subject to} \quad & f_i(\vec{x}) \le 0, \quad i = 1, \dots, m, \end{aligned} \tag{A.1}$$

where $\vec{x} \in \Re^n$ with domain $D = \cap_{i=0}^m dom\, f_i$. It is assumed that f_0 is concave ($-f_0$ is convex) and differentiable, while f_i are convex and differentiable. Given this problem, and $\vec{\lambda} \in \Re^n_+$, we define the *Lagrangian*:

$$L\left(\vec{x}, \vec{\lambda}\right) = f_0(\vec{x}) - \sum_{i=1}^m \lambda_i f_i(\vec{x}). \tag{A.2}$$

Suppose that problem (A.1) has a solution given by $v^* = f_0(\vec{x}^*)$. The functions $f_i, i = 1, \ldots, m$ represent resource constraints, while the Lagrange multipliers, $\vec{\lambda}$, represent the cost or *price* of each resource constraint. From the Lagrangian we can define a *primal function* $h : D \to \Re \cup \{-\infty\}$ and a *dual function* $g : \Re_+^m \to \Re \cup \{\infty\}$:

$$h\left(\vec{x}\right) = \inf_{\vec{\lambda} \in \Re_+^n} L\left(\vec{x}, \vec{\lambda}\right), \tag{A.3}$$

$$g\left(\vec{\lambda}\right) = \sup_{\vec{x} \in \Re^n} L\left(\vec{x}, \vec{\lambda}\right). \tag{A.4}$$

Notice that for all $\vec{\lambda} \in \Re_+^m$ we have:

$$g\left(\vec{\lambda}\right) \geq v^* \geq h\left(\vec{x}\right). \tag{A.5}$$

For feasible $\vec{x}$ then $-\lambda_i f_i(\vec{x}) \geq 0$, and hence $L\left(\vec{x}, \vec{\lambda}\right) \geq v^*$ for feasible values. Thus if $\vec{x}^*$ is feasible we have:

$$g\left(\vec{\lambda}\right) = \sup_{\vec{x} \in \Re^n} L\left(\vec{x}, \vec{\lambda}\right) \geq L\left(\vec{x}^*, \vec{\lambda}\right) \geq v^*.$$

We also have $h(\vec{x}) = -\infty$ when $\vec{x}$ is not feasible. When $\vec{x}$ is feasible, then $h(\vec{x}) = f_0(\vec{x})$. From this we get the right-hand side of (A.5). The set of feasible choices is a lower bound, from which we get the left-hand side of (A.5). Since v^* is a lower bound on $g\left(\vec{\lambda}\right)$, we have the following *dual* problem:

$$d^* = \inf_{\vec{\lambda} \in \Re_+^m} g\left(\vec{\lambda}\right) \geq v^*. \tag{A.6}$$

The difference, $d^* - v^*$, is the duality gap, and if $\vec{\lambda}^*$ is a solution, it is called the *dual solution*. For the convex problem we have described, when a feasible solution exists, the duality gap is zero. More precisely, suppose the duality gap is zero, $\vec{x}^*$ is a solution to (A.1), and $\vec{\lambda}^*$ is the dual solution minimizing $g\left(\vec{\lambda}\right)$; then we have for all $\vec{x} \in D$ and $\vec{\lambda} \in \Re^*$:

$$g\left(\vec{\lambda}\right) \geq L\left(\vec{x}^*, \vec{\lambda}\right) \geq L\left(\vec{x}^*, \vec{\lambda}^*\right) = f_0(\vec{x}^*) \geq L\left(\vec{x}, \vec{\lambda}^*\right) \geq h(\vec{x}). \tag{A.7}$$

This is the central insight of price theory. The inequalities on the right show that if we get the "price" of resources correct ($\vec{\lambda}^*$), then the optimal choice for the constrained optimization problem (A.1) can be transformed into an *unconstrained* optimization problem, as given by condition (A.4).

Suppose that the solution to this unconstrained problem exists and can be described by the function $\vec{x}^*\left(\vec{\lambda}\right)$. Observe that by the envelope theorem we have:

$$\frac{\partial g\left(\vec{\lambda}\right)}{\partial \lambda_i} = -f_i\left(\vec{x}^*\left(\vec{\lambda}\right)\right).$$

Prices $\vec{\lambda}$ are set to minimize $g()$; hence when f_i is positive, then it is optimal to set λ_i arbitrarily large. When f_i is negative, then it is optimal to set $\lambda_i = 0$, and hence we can obtain a optimal positive price only when $f_i = 0$. While it is true the prices can decentralize decision making, the goal to set prices to minimize $g\left(\vec{\lambda}\right)$ is quite unstable in the neighborhood of $f_i = 0$—when we cross the $f_i(\vec{x}) = 0$, the first-order conditions push prices arbitrarily high or low. This provides some intuition as to why prices in markets can sometimes be very unstable. This potential instability, combined with lack of knowledge on some of the production functions, is one of the reasons institutions are needed to supplement market forces.

For the convex problem, the KKT conditions provide necessary and sufficient condition for an optimum. The necessary conditions hold under more general conditions than we have assumed here. The assumption that the problem is convex is needed to ensure sufficiency.

Proposition A.1 *The choice $\vec{x}^*$ is a solution to the convex primal problem (A.1) and $\vec{\lambda}^*$ is a solution to the dual, with duality gap zero, if and only if:*

$$
\begin{aligned}
f_i(\vec{x}^*) &\leq 0, & i &= 1,\ldots,m \\
\lambda_i^* &\geq 0, & i &= 1,\ldots,m \\
\lambda_i^* f_i(\vec{x}^*) &\geq 0, & i &= 1,\ldots,m \\
\nabla f_0(\vec{x}^*) &= \sum_{i=1}^{m} \lambda_i \nabla f_i(\vec{x}^*),
\end{aligned}
$$

where $\nabla f = \begin{bmatrix} \partial f/\partial x_1 \\ \vdots \\ \partial f/\partial x_m \end{bmatrix}$ is the gradient of f.

See Boyd and Vanderberghe (2004, sec. 5.5.3). Here we have made assumptions that allow for a simple characterization of an optimal solution. Boyd and Vanderberge (2004) address a large number of special cases and show how algorithms to find optimal solutions vary from case to case. This issue is analogous to the economic theory of institutions. Economic institutions can be viewed as solving specific resource allocation problems when market institutions are insufficient to ensure an efficient allocation.

A.2   Pareto Optimal Allocations in an Exchange Economy

The purpose of this section is to introduce a formal exchange model along the lines of Debreu (1959) and to characterize the efficient allocations. This section shows that there is a one-to-one mapping between a single constrained optimization problem and the set of Pareto-efficient allocations. This approach is widely used to study nonmarket institutions.

Let us suppose that there are $n \geq 2$ commodities in an economy and that each of $i \in I = \{1,\ldots,\bar{i}\}$, $\bar{i} \geq 2$ persons wishes to consume a bundle $\vec{x}_i \in \Re_+^n$, where $x_{ik} \geq 0, i \in I, k \in K = \{1,\ldots,n\}$. The first assumption is that the level of trade and consumption is observable and measurable. Next, it is assumed that each person's preferences can be represented by a concave and differentiable utility function:

$$ u_i : \Re_+^n \to \Re. $$

The concavity assumption is restrictive, but it allows us to use first-order conditions to characterize efficient allocations. In particular, the use of first-order conditions is ubiquitous in economics, in part because it allows one to have comparative static results that in turn generate testable predictions from the theory. It is also assumed:

Definition A.2 *Preferences are* strictly monotonic *if for* $\vec{x} \geq \vec{y} > \vec{0}$ *and* $\vec{x} \neq \vec{y}$ *then* $u(\vec{x}) > u(\vec{y})$.

Without lost of generality, it is assumed that $u\left(\vec{0}\right) = 0$, and hence $u(\vec{x}) \geq 0$ for all $\vec{x} \in \mathfrak{R}_+^n$.[1] This is the essence of a "good"—more is always better. This ensures we have a well defined resource allocation problem. As more is always better, individuals are never satisfied. In particular, this assumption excludes individuals who are happy to live within their means. While it may seem to be an innocuous assumption, it is not. If a person is happy living within her means, then one cannot use additional financial rewards to motivate or change her behavior.

The next step is production. Notice that one can include labor supply by setting one of the commodities to be leisure. This ensures that there are some individuals in the economy with a nonzero endowment. Similarly, one can suppose that individuals own the other inputs to production, such as minerals, water, and so on. The initial allocation of endowments is given by $\omega_i \in \mathfrak{R}_+^n$. Let $\omega = \sum_{i \in I} \omega_i$ denote the total endowment in the economy. We do not require this to be nonzero for each commodity, but we allow for production.

Firms are indexed by $j \in J = \left\{1, \ldots, \bar{j}\right\}, \bar{j} \geq 1$. The production plan for firm j is given by $\vec{y}_j \in \mathfrak{R}^n$. When $y_{jk} > 0$, this represents the production of commodity $k \in \{1, \ldots, n\}$. When $y_{jk} < 0$, this is an input to production. For simplicity, it is assumed that firms (and individuals) can freely dispose of a commodity. Commodities are all valued so this will not occur at a competitive equilibrium, but it does make the analysis a bit easier. Given free disposal, the production possibilities set for a firm are given by:

$$Y_j = \left\{\vec{y} \in \mathfrak{R}^n | f_j(\vec{y}) \leq 0\right\},$$

where $f_j : \mathfrak{R}^n \to \mathfrak{R}$ is a convex, differentiable function describing the production frontier. A vector $\vec{y}_j \in Y_j$ represents a feasible production plan for firm j. It is assumed that the plant can shut down, and hence $f_j\left(\vec{0}\right) = 0$, which in turn implies $\vec{0} \in Y_j$. Total production capacity is given by:

$$Y = \left\{\sum_{j \in J} \vec{y}_j | \vec{y}_j \in Y_j\right\}.$$

Since the Y_j are convex and closed, then so is Y.

Definition A.3 *Production satisfies* no free lunch *if* $Y \cap \mathfrak{R}_+^n = \vec{0}$.

This ensures that it is not possible to produce an unlimited amount of any commodity. Notice that production can be defined without any reference to price at all.

Definition A.4 *An* allocation *is denoted by* $\vec{z} = \left\{\{\vec{x}\}_{i \in I}, \{\vec{y}_j\}_{j \in J}\right\} \in \mathfrak{R}_+^{n \times \bar{i}} \times \mathfrak{R}^{n \times \bar{j}}$. *An allocation is* feasible *if:*

1. $\vec{y}_j \in Y_j, j \in J$,

2. $\sum_{i \in I} \vec{x}_i \leq \sum_{i \in I} \vec{w}_i + \sum_{j \in J} \vec{y}_j$.

Let $Z \subset \mathfrak{R}_+^{n \times \bar{i}} \times \mathfrak{R}^{n \times \bar{j}}$ be the set of feasible allocations.

Thus, an allocation is feasible if total consumption is less than or equal to the output that can be produced with the available endowments and production technologies. An economy is said to be *productive* if there exists $z \in Z$ such that $\vec{x}_i >> \vec{0}$ for $i \in I$. It is common to use an equality constraint for property 2, and this will not change the results. Monotonicity ensures that consumers always want more, and hence in any efficient allocation condition 2 will always be satisfied with equality. However, using an inequality will sign the Lagrange multiplier, and the free-disposal property implies that the multiplier on the resource constraints is always nonnegative. For the rest of the appendix, all the assumptions we have made are assumed to hold.

An efficient allocation is defined as follows:

Definition A.5 *A feasible allocation $\vec{z}^* \in Z$ is* Pareto efficient *if there does not exist another feasible allocation $\vec{z} \in Z$ such that:*

1. *$u_i(\vec{x}_i) \geq u_i(\vec{x}_i^*)$, for all $i \in I$.*
2. *There is an $i \in I$ such that: $u_i(\vec{x}_i) > u_i(\vec{x}_i^*)$.*

A Pareto-efficient allocation is one that is possible with the current technology and where there is no other allocation that makes at least one person better off without harming the others. The next question is how to find such an allocation.

Proposition A.6 *The set of Pareto-efficient allocations, $Z^* \subset Z$ is not empty. Moreover, an allocation $\vec{z}^*$ is Pareto efficient if and only if there is a nonzero vector of weights $\vec{\lambda} \in \Re_+^n$ such that $\vec{z}^*$ solves:*

$$\max_{\vec{z} \in Z} \sum_{i \in I} \lambda_i u_i(\vec{x}_i).\tag{A.8}$$

Proof. The first step is to show existence. Both Y and $\Re_+^n$ are closed, convex sets. By the no-free-lunch assumption, $\vec{0}$ is their only point of intersection. Hence, by the separating hyperplane theorem, there is a vector $\vec{p} \in \Re^n$ such that $\vec{p} \cdot \vec{x} > 0$ for $\vec{x} \in \Re_+^n \setminus \vec{0}$. This implies that $p_i > 0, i \in I$. The set of feasible vectors must satisfy:

$$\sum_{i \in I} \vec{x}_i \leq \sum_{i \in I} \vec{\omega}_i + \sum_{j \in J} \vec{y}_j,\tag{A.9}$$

$$\sum_{i \in I} \vec{x}_i \leq \vec{\omega} + \vec{y},$$

where $\vec{\omega} = \sum_{i \in I} \vec{\omega}_i \in \Re_+^n$ and $\vec{y} = \sum_{j \in J} \vec{y}_j \in Y$. Since the economy is productive, this implies that $\vec{\omega} \neq \vec{0}$, and since $\vec{p} \cdot \vec{w} > 0$ and $\vec{x}_i \in \Re_+^n$ we have:

$$\vec{p} \cdot \sum_{i \in I} \vec{x}_i \leq \vec{p} \cdot \vec{w} + \vec{p} \cdot \vec{y} \leq \vec{p} \cdot \vec{w}.$$

From this we conclude that the set of feasible consumption bundles, $X = \sum_{i \in I} \vec{x}_i \in X \equiv \Re_+^n \cap (\vec{w} + Y)$, is a nonempty compact, convex subset of $\Re_+^n$. Thus, the continuity of payoff functions ensures the existences of a solution $\vec{z}^*$ to problem (A.8).

Suppose that $\vec{z}^*$ is not Pareto optimal. Then there is another feasible allocation, $\vec{z}^0$, that makes at least one party strictly better off, say i^0. If $\lambda_{i^0} > 0$, the allocation $\vec{z}^0$ gives a higher payoff, and hence $\vec{x}^*$ is not a solution. If $\lambda_{i^0} = 0$, then the monotonicity of preferences implies that consumer i^0 is getting zero utility at $\vec{z}^*$. Thus, we can take some of the allocation at $\vec{z}^0$ and give it to another consumer with $\lambda_i > 0$ to make them strictly better off, resulting in a feasible allocation that gives a higher value to A.8. Thus $\vec{z}^*$ could not have been a solution. So all solutions to (A.8) are Pareto efficient.

For the converse, let $\vec{z}^*$ be a Pareto-efficient allocation, and $\vec{u}^* = \vec{u}(\vec{x}^*)$ the corresponding payoff. Next, define:

$$U = \left\{ \vec{u} | \vec{u} \le \left\{ u_1(\vec{x}_1), \dots, u_{\bar{\imath}}(\vec{x}_{\bar{\imath}}) \right\}, \vec{z} \in Z \right\},$$

and observe that the convexity of Z and the concavity of u_i imply that this is a closed, convex set. Next, define:

$$V(\vec{u}^*) = \left\{ \vec{u} \in \mathfrak{R}^n | \vec{u} \ge \vec{u}^* \right\}$$

the convex set of utilities that is superior to the payoff at the efficient allocation. The convexity of U and the definition of Pareto optimality implies:

$$U \cap V(\vec{u}^*) = \vec{u}^*.$$

Hence by the separating hyperplane theorem there is a nonzero vector $\vec{\lambda} \in \mathfrak{R}^n$ such that for all $\vec{u} \in U$ and $\vec{v} \in V(\vec{u}^*)$:

$$\max_{\vec{u} \in U} \vec{\lambda} \cdot \vec{u} \le \vec{\lambda} \cdot \vec{u}^* \le \min_{\vec{v} \in V(\vec{u}^*)} \vec{\lambda} \cdot \vec{v}.$$

Since U is unbounded below, and $V(\vec{u}^*)$ is unbounded above, it follows that $\vec{\lambda}_i \ge 0$.   □

Observe that if all consumers are getting more than the lower bar on utility ($u(\vec{0}) = 0$), then it must be that $\lambda_i > 0$ for all $i \in I$. Also observe that one may give individuals the right to their endowments, so one must add the constraints $u_i(\vec{x}_i) \ge u_i(\vec{\omega}_i)$. In that case, the program A.8 still generates a Pareto-optimal allocation, but now when the weight on person i is zero ($\lambda_i = 0$), they get their endowment payoff rather than zero.

A.3   The Welfare Theorems of General Equilibrium Theory

The first section shows that in a convex problem one can change a constrained optimization problem into an unconstrained problem with the right "prices" for each constraint. This is followed by showing that the set of Pareto-efficient allocations can be found as the solution to a constrained optimization problem. The insight of general equilibrium theory is to show that when market prices reflect the opportunity cost of resource constraints, then competitive equilibria are efficient. This is the first welfare theorem.

Conversely, suppose that society has weights for each person, as given in proposition (A.6). Then there exists a reallocation of endowments and ownership shares such that this efficient allocation is a competitive equilibrium.

More precisely, let $\vec{p} = \{p_1, \dots, p_n\} \in \mathfrak{R}^n_+$ be a real vector of positive prices for commodity x_k, $k = 1, \dots, n$. To reduce complexity we consider allocations for which all products have positive prices. This can be relaxed at the cost of a having to check a number of corner cases. Firms in the market are assumed to maximize profits:

$$\pi_i\left(\vec{p}\right) = \max_{\vec{y}_j} \vec{p} \cdot \vec{y}_j$$

subject to:

$$f_j\left(\vec{y}_j\right) \leq 0.$$

The consequence is a unique supply function:

$$S_j\left(\vec{p}\right) = \left\{ y_j^* \in \Re^n | \vec{p} \cdot \vec{y}_j^* \geq \vec{p} \cdot \vec{y}_j, f_j\left(y_j^*\right), f_j\left(\vec{p}\right) \leq \vec{0} \right\}.$$

The components of supply, $S_{jk}, k \in K$, have a negative sign for inputs and a positive sign for output.

It is assumed that each consumer $i \in I$ has an endowment $\omega_i \in \Re_+^n$. In addition, consumer i owns a share $\theta_{ij} \in [0, 1]$ of firm $j \in J$ with the feature:

$$\sum_{i \in I} \theta_{ij} = 1.$$

Let $\Omega = \left\{ \left\{ \omega_i, \left\{ \theta_{ij} \right\}_{j \in J} \right\}_{i \in I} \right\}$ denote the initial endowment. Given a feasible allocation, $\vec{z}$, price vector $\vec{p}$, and endowment Ω, the wealth of consumer i is given by:

$$W_i\left(\vec{p}\right) = \vec{p} \cdot \left(\sum_{j \in J} \theta_{ij} y_j + \omega_i \right).$$

The demand by consumer i is given by:

$$D_i\left(\vec{p}\right) = \left\{ \vec{x}^* \in \Re_+^n | u_i\left(\vec{x}^*\right) \geq u_i\left(\vec{x}\right), \vec{p} \cdot \vec{x} \leq \vec{p} \cdot \vec{x}^* = W\left(\vec{p}\right), \forall \vec{x} \in \Re_+^n \right\}.$$

Definition A.7 *An allocation $\vec{z} \in Z$ is a* competitive equilibrium *if there exists a price $\vec{p} \in \Re_+^n$ such that:*

$$\sum_{i \in I}(\vec{x}_i - \omega_i) \leq \sum_{j \in J} y_j,$$

$$\vec{y}_j \in S_j\left(\vec{p}\right), j \in J,$$

$$\vec{x}_i \in D_i\left(\vec{p}\right), i \in I.$$

Proposition A.8 *Suppose $\vec{z} \in Z$ is a competitive equilibrium for a productive economy, with price vector $\vec{p}$, then:*

1. $\vec{p} \gg \vec{0}$.

2. $\vec{z}$ is Pareto efficient.

Proof. If $p_i = 0$, then since preferences are monotonic, consumers will buy an infinite quantity of commodity i, and hence demand cannot be feasible. Next, the fact that preferences are monotonic implies that the resource constraints bind and we have:

$$\vec{p} \cdot \left(\sum_{i \in I} \omega_i + \sum_{j \in J} y_j - \sum_{i \in I} \vec{x}_i \right) = 0.$$

Next, suppose the allocation $\vec{z}$ is not efficient; then there is feasible allocation $\vec{z}^*$ such that $u_i (\vec{x}_i^*) \geq u_i (\vec{x}_i)$ for all $i \in I$, and an i^* for which this is strict. It must be the case that $\vec{p} \cdot \vec{x}_i^* \geq \vec{p} \cdot \vec{x}_i$; otherwise, by monotonicity the consumer can buy a small amount of any good to get an allocation $\vec{x}_i^{**}$ that is strictly preferred to $\vec{x}_i$, and hence $\vec{x}_i$ is not on the demand curve.

Similarly, for $\vec{x}^*$ it must be the case that

$$\vec{p} \cdot \vec{x}_{i^*}^* > \vec{p} \cdot \vec{x}_{i^*},$$

otherwise consumer i^* would be able to afford a strictly superior good. Since y_i^* is feasible, then the profits at that price cannot be greater than at the original allocation y_j. Thus we get:

$$0 = \vec{p} \cdot \left(\sum_{i \in I} \omega_i + \sum_{j \in J} y_j - \sum_{i \in I} \vec{x}_i \right)$$

$$> \vec{p} \cdot \left(\sum_{i \in I} \omega_i + \sum_{j \in J} y_j^* - \sum_{i \in I} \vec{x}_i^* \right).$$

Hence, the new allocation is not feasible, and there is no allocation that Pareto dominates the original allocation. $\qquad\square$

This is a very strong result in the sense that little is required to ensure that competitive equilibria are efficient. The key assumptions are the existence of an equilibrium and monotonicity of preferences. The fact that parties are optimizing with respect to positive prices ensures that the budget constraints are binding. This implies that any superior allocation requires violating at least one budget constraint.

The converse is the second welfare theorem:

Proposition A.9 *Suppose that $z^* \in Z$ is a Pareto-efficient allocation; then initial endowments and firm ownership shares can be allocated so that the allocation z^* is a competitive equilibrium at some price $\vec{p}$.*

Proof. Since z^* is Pareto efficient, there are weights $\vec{\lambda} \in \Re_+^i, \vec{\lambda} \neq \vec{0}$ such that the allocation is a solution to (A.8). If any $\lambda_i = 0$, then these individuals get no commodities and have zero utility. They can therefore be dropped, and without loss of generality we can suppose that $\lambda_i > 0$. Similarly, to keep matters simple, suppose that $x_{ik}^* > 0$ and $\vec{y}_j^* \neq \vec{0}$, and leave the more general case as an exercise for the reader. Problem (A.8) can be written in the form:

$$\max_{\vec{x} \in R^n} \sum_{i \in I} \lambda_i u_i (\vec{x}_i),$$

subject to:

$$x_{ik} \geq 0, i \in I, k \in K,$$

$$\sum_{i \in I} (x_{ik} - w_{ik}) - \sum_{j \in J} y_{jk} \leq 0, k \in K,$$

$$f_j(y_j) \leq 0, j \in J.$$

The simplifying assumptions imply that the constraints $x_{ik} \geq 0$ are not binding, while the constraints $f_j \leq 0$ are binding. Let $\vec{p} \in \mathfrak{R}^n_{++}$ and $\vec{\mu} \in \mathfrak{R}^i_{++}$ be the multipliers for the Lagrangian:

$$L = \sum_{i \in I} \lambda_i u_i (\vec{x}_i) - \vec{p} \cdot \left(\sum_{i \in I} (\vec{x}_i - \vec{w}_{ik}) - \sum_{j \in J} \vec{y}_j \right) - \sum_{j \in J} \mu_j f_j (\vec{y}_j).$$

Since the problem is convex, then from the KKT theorem the solution $(\vec{x}^*, \vec{y}_j)$ maximizes L and satisfies the first-order conditions:

$$\lambda_i \nabla u_i (\vec{x}_i^*) = \vec{p}, i \in I,$$

$$\mu_j \nabla f_j (\vec{y}_j) = \vec{p}, j \in J.$$

Since the profit function is scale independent, then the first-order condition implies that $\vec{y}_j$ is profit maximizing given price $\vec{p}$, and hence $\vec{y}_j \in S_j(\vec{p})$. For the consumers, their first-order condition implies that there is a wealth level W_i that generates a Lagrange multiplier equal to λ_i such that $\vec{x}_i^*$ solves:

$$\max_{\vec{x}_i \in \mathfrak{R}^n_{++}} u_i (\vec{x}_i)$$

subject to:

$$\vec{p} \cdot \vec{x}_i \leq W_i.$$

It must be the case that $\sum_{i \in I} W_i = \vec{p} \cdot \sum_{i \in I} \vec{x}_i^* = \vec{p} \cdot \left(\sum_{i \in I} \vec{w}_{ik} + \sum_{j \in J} \vec{y}_j \right)$, otherwise the resource constraint for the Pareto-optimal problem is not satisfied. Letting

$$\theta_i^* = \frac{W_i}{\sum_{i \in I} W_i}$$

and providing each consumer with an initial endowment $\vec{w}_i^* = \theta_i^* \vec{w}$ and profit share $\theta_{ij} = \theta_i^*$ ensures that $\vec{x}_i \in D_i(\vec{p}), i \in I$. Hence, for this initial endowment and ownership shares, $\vec{p}$ forms a competitive equilibrium. □

This result plays an important role in normative policy. It explicitly recognizes that competitive equilibria are not necessarily normative ideals. However, with the appropriate redistribution, one can rely on competitive markets to allocate resources both fairly and efficiently.

The derivation relies on a large number of assumptions, many of which cannot be expected to hold in practice. One of the most important of these is that there exists a market for all commodities. One might be tempted to conclude that adding markets would improve matters, but Hart (1975) shows that this is not the case.

However, an important feature of a market is the voluntary nature of participation that allows parties to conceal their personal valuations. They need only to reveal their desire to trade. When parties can gain a great deal from trade, they may have an incentive to distort their gain from trade, which in turn leads to inefficient allocations. There is now a large literature on how to design market-like mechanisms that encourage individuals to provide information that leads to more-efficient allocations (Roth 2002; 2018). There is also a large literature on auction theory and how to design trading mechanisms to efficiently allocate commodities when valuations are private (see Krishna [2010] for a book-length review).

Notes

Chapter 1

1. Here the term *efficient* is always in the sense of Pareto efficiency: there is no other allocation that makes everybody as well off and some people strictly better off.

2. For a discussion of economic institutions and commodification over time, see Allen (2012).

3. The term *agentic* is also used in the context of Milgram's (1974) theory. He supposes that individuals who follow orders are in an agentic state. One might wonder what is the alternative. See MacLeod (2016) for a discussion of skill and human capital where choices are pattern-based rather than outcome-based.

4. One commodity has to be given a numeraire price of 1 against which all the others are measured.

5. See Katz and Autor (1999) for a review of how the supply demand framework can explain the pattern of wage changes in the United States.

6. See Card (2001) on the returns to education and Acemoglu and Autor (2011) for a discussion of inequality and the returns to skill.

7. See Rogerson, Shimer, and Wright (2005).

8. See Gibbons and Katz (1991) and Schmieder and von Wachter (2010).

9. See Blinder and Choi (1990).

10. See Akerlof and Yellen (1986) for a collection of the important papers in the area.

11. The common law rule for contract breach is the awarding of "expectation damages"—an amount that ensures the promisee receives the value agreed to by the promisor.

12. UCC refers to the US Uniform Commercial Code, a default set of legal rules covering trade. All countries have a similar set of rules, though enforcement can vary from country to country.

13. The term moral hazard is from Pauly (1968), who observed that if a person has full health insurance, this may lead to the overconsumption of health services.

14. In economics, Mincer (1962) discusses the implications of investments that are job specific and have no value on the market. Klein, Crawford, and Alchian (1978) discuss the implications of relationship-specific investments for vertical integration.

15. See Currie and MacLeod (2014) for an application of Savage's model to tort law.

16. See Kreps and Wilson (1982) for a model that integrates Savage's model of decision making into game theory.

Chapter 2

1. Fisher's comment is about how to clarify the step from association to causation. See Rosenbaum (2017, pages 118–119) for a discussion of William G. Cochran's 1945 interview with R. A. Fisher. The quotation comes from that interview on the step from association to causation.

2. See the articles by Deaton (2010), Heckman (2010), and Imbens (2010).

3. Adams (1979).

4. This book was in the final stages of editing during the 2020 SARS-CoV-2 pandemic, another example of an unanticipated event with major social impacts.

5. See Joskow (1987) on the value of long-term contracts.

6. The problem of foreseeability is an important part of modern contract law. See Farnsworth (2004, sec. 3B).

7. In a large market, there will always be some individuals who seem to do well, even if they are simply lucky. See exercises 1 and 2.

8. See Hamilton (1994) for an excellent review of the literature on time series and predictions based on past observations.

9. See the files on his case at http://www.justice.gov/usao/nys/madoff.html.

10. This is achieved by using color filters to split the image into three separate images that are recorded by three separate sensors, a process used in professional cameras. In consumer cameras, the three colors are recorded by different pixels on a single sensor.

11. See www.jpeg.org for more information about ISO/IEC IS 10918-1 | ITU-T Recommendation T.81, or more simply the JPEG standard.

12. See Peierls (1960, 186): "Quite recently, a friend showed him the paper of a young physicist, which he suspected was not of great value but on which he wanted Pauli's views. Pauli remarked sadly, 'It is not even wrong.' " Though this remark was quite cryptic, it did imply that good models should be making falsifiable predictions.

13. Street map, New York City, St. Louis, MO: Diversified Map Corporation, 1964. Retrieved from the Library of Congress, https://www.loc.gov/item/2007630435.

14. Created by Jake Berman, and uploaded to wikicommons 20:23, September 26, 2009 (UTC) at https://commons.wikimedia.org/wiki/File:NYC_Subway_map_stations.svg.

15. See Currie (2009).

16. See http://www.bls.gov/nls for more information.

17. Recall $R^2 = 1 - \frac{SE}{TSS}$, where $TSS = \Sigma_{i \in I} w_i^2$ is the total sum of squares.

18. See Angrist and Krueger (1999) for a good discussion.

19. See Rosenbaum (2010) and Imbens and Rubin (2015) for recent reviews. The discussion here follows Deaton (2010) and MacLeod (2017).

20. Labor market experience does increase with age. Angrist and Krueger control for this possibility by looking at workers from forty to forty-nine years of age where one quarter of experience would have a small effect upon earnings. See Angrist and Krueger (1999) for a further discussion.

21. Unit homogeneity is discussed in section 4.2 of Holland (1986). This is a standard assumption in physics where one assumes that the laws of physics do not change over time.

22. $X = \cup_{k=1}^{n} X_k$ and $X_k \cap X_l = \emptyset$, for $k \neq l$.

Chapter 3

1. See Camerer (2006) and Koszegi (2014) for reviews of the literature. See also MacLeod (2016) for a further discussion of how to view human capital as another way to think about behavioral economics.

2. See de Finetti (1974) for discussion and review of the history of the concept of probability

3. On unit homogeneity, see definition 2.2. Time invariance is similar, except one is assuming the effect on a unit does not change with time, as opposed to comparing the effect across different units.

4. The notation 2^A denotes the set of functions mapping from A to the set $\{0, 1\}$. Each function corresponds to the subset B of A where the function takes on the value of 1 (and hence has a value of 0 on the complement, B^c). Such functions are called *correspondences* when viewed as a mapping from 2^A to A.

5. See definition 3.12 below.

6. Here the limits are defined with the topology induced by the standard Euclidean norm.

7. See Vaughan (1997) for a discussion of how traders in the first and second millennia BCE entered into risk sharing agreements. See Hintze et al. (2015) for a recent paper that discusses an evolutionary approach to risk aversion.

8. The discussion here is taken from Savage ([1954] 1972).

9. A sequence of random variables X_n converges to x almost surely if $Pr\{\lim_{n \to \infty} X_n = x\} = 1$.

10. Savage was well aware of the difficulties—see Savage ([1954] 1972, chap. 4) on shortcomings of the personalistic view.

11. For a full discussion of measure theory, see any standard book on real analysis, such as Ash (1972). The main point here is that the discussion of measurability in mathematics texts can often seem very abstract but in fact corresponds rather naturally to the amount of information available.

Chapter 4

1. See Ayres and Talley (1995), who apply King Solomon's clever solution to the law of property.

2. See Harbaugh, Krause, and Vesterlund (2007) for evidence.

3. Harbaugh, Krause, and Berry (2001) find that college students are no more rational than eleven year olds.

4. See Govindan and Wilson (2016) for a discussion of the literature on refinements of the Nash equilibrium concept.

5. Classic references include von Neumann and Morgenstern (1944) and Luce and Raiffa (1957), and they are still worth reading. Myerson (1991) and van Damme (1991) provide good reviews of the different solution concepts used in game theory.

6. See Rabin (1998), Camerer (2003), and DellaVigna (2009).

7. Mertens and Zamir (1985) show mathematically that it is possible to create a *universal type space* that captures the characteristics of all the players in the game.

8. See https://en.wikipedia.org/wiki/Monty_Hall_problem.

9. For example, in the case of chess, Z consists of the set of board positions that correspond to checkmate or stalemate.

10. See Mas-Colell, Whinston, and Green (1995, 277).

11. In a famous paper, Chase and Simon (1973) prove that part of chess-playing skill entails memorizing strong board positions. Hence, skill is not simply the ability to think logically. Because these games are very complex but have clear rules of play, there is an extensive literature on building "artificially intelligent" programs to play chess. See Silver et al. (2016) for citations to the earlier literature and for a description of how to build a strong program to play the game of Go.

12. This assumption is relaxed when we address the topic of repeated games.

13. See Selvin (1975).

14. See Schelling (1980) for an excellent discussion of this issue. At the time he wrote the first version of his book the Cold War between the United States and the Soviet Union was in full swing, and there was a real threat of nuclear war. The open question for policymakers was determining the conditions under which the Soviet Union might use its weapons.

15. See Luce and Raiffa (1989, sec. 5.3). Many well-known examples in game theory come from this classic text.

16. See Luce and Raiffa (1989, sec. 5.4). See also Axelrod (1981) for an extended discussion of how the prisoner's dilemma can be applied to politics.

17. See Lewis (1967) for a more formal definition and discussion.

18. The careful reader might observe that we have not strictly applied Savage's model to this situation. That would require expanding the state space to include Lucy's beliefs as explicit states. But if the hypothesis that they are rational is common knowledge, then Lucy would have to form states that would include George's beliefs regarding Lucy's beliefs and so on. This implies a hierarchy of beliefs, greatly complicating the analysis. See Myerson (1991, chap. 2) for a further discussion. Mertens and Zamir (1985) provide a formal analysis of such a state space.

19. See Binmore (1994) and Binmore (1998) for an entertaining wide range of discussions on the foundations of game theory.

20. See the discussion in Schelling (1980, chap. 5) explicitly linking the notion of a Nash equilibrium to the concept of an agreement.

21. Self-interest does not mean that parties do not behave altruistically, only that if they are altruistic, this should be reflected in their preferences.

22. See Diaconis and Zabell (1982) for a discussion and a formal solution to the problem.

23. "Nash" is in parentheses because it is often left out of the term, so that one may say perfect Bayesian equilibrium or subgame perfect equilibrium without the "Nash" qualifier.

24. If more than one player deviates in any period then there is no punishment. The notion of a Nash equilibrium only considers deviations by single players. We come back to this issue when we discuss renegotiation.

25. One could make the mixed strategy observable via a process known as *strategy purification*. One can suppose that players observe a private shock p^{it} and then choose their action, and that p^{it} becomes commonly observable after actions are chosen. Requiring agents to coordinate on a commonly observed event is rather natural in contract theory. For example, wage contracts are often indexed with the rate of inflation.

26. This book avoids using measure theory as much as possible and for the most part relies upon intuitive arguments. Here, measurable means that there is a well-defined set of subsets of [0, 1], denoted by Ω, and that for each action $a^i \in A^i$, $s^{it}(a^i)^{-1} \in \Omega$. Normally, Ω is the set of Lebesgue measurable sets. See Ash (1972) for an excellent introduction to measure and probability theory.

27. Without this assumption, one would have to worry about zero probability events where players might choose nonequilibrium play, leading to unnecessary complications.

28. For $A \subset \Re^n$ then

$$conv(A) = \left\{ \sum_{i \in I} \lambda_i x_i \middle| I \text{ is finite set, } \lambda_i \in [0, 1], x_i \in A, \sum_{i \in I} \lambda_i = 1 \right\}.$$

29. Recall that $\sigma^1 \left(h^1 \right) \in S$, which is a function from $[0, 1]$ to A, and $\sigma^1 \left(h^1 \right) \left(p^1 \right)$ is the action chosen when p^1 is realized.

30. Axelrod (1984) is an early example. Greif (1989) uses this game to study medieval trade, while Dixit (2003) applies the prisoner's dilemma game to the problem of trade enforcement with asymmetric information.

Chapter 5

1. Shaked and Sutton (1984) is the seminal paper that introduces the idea that one can use a bargaining game to model labor market equilibria.

2. The support of f is defined by support $(f) = \{b \in \Re | f(b) > 0\}$.

3. See Edgeworth (1881, 28) on a Robinson Crusoe economy.

4. This follows immediately from our discussion in section 3.3.

5. Notice that in some states parties are indifferent between trade and no trade. We suppose that these states occur with zero probability.

6. Free disposal implies that one can credibly destroy resources at no cost. For example, it implies that if there is an unequal allocation, it can be made equal simply by having the person with more resources destroy enough resources to equalize utilities.

7. The utilities in the bargaining problem are normally assumed to be Von Neumann–Morgenstern preferences, and hence convexity can also be achieved for any finite set of outcomes through the use of lotteries.

8. For $y, z \in \Re^n$ the expression $y \geqq z$ means that $y_i \geq z_i$ for $i = 1, \ldots, n$. Similarly, $y > z$ means $y_i > z_i$ for $i = 1, \ldots, n$.

9. An affine function $L : \Re^n \rightarrow \Re^m$ is any function of the form:

$$L(\vec{x}) = A\vec{x} + \vec{b},$$

where $A \in \Re^{m \times n}$ is a matrix and $\vec{b} \in \Re^m$ is some constant. An inverse exists if and only if A is invertible.

10. The development here closely follows MacLeod and Malcomson (1995).

11. Sjöström (1991) has shown the equivalence between the Raiffa model and a strategic model based on the Ståhl (1972) bargaining model.

12. It is worth emphasizing that, as a matter of law, all trade in developed market economies occurs in the shadow of a complex set of obligations. For example, in the United States, simple exchange occurs in the shadow of the Uniform Commercial Code (UCC). See American Law Institute and National Conference of Commissioners on Uniform State Laws (2009) for details.

13. Notice that this step does not work in the case of a hi-tech market.

14. See Gaynor, Ho, and Town (2015) for a discussion of the application of this model to healthcare markets. It is assumed that the supplier has separate negotiation teams that do not communicate with each other during negotiations. Recent applications include Crawford and Yurukoglu (2012) and Ho and Lee (2017).

Chapter 6

1. Notice that this definition implies that simultaneous trade, for example at a retail store, is not a contract given that one directly observes the quality of the good and immediately pays. If one did not pay, this would be an event covered by criminal law, not contract law.

2. In short, competitive equilibria are efficient and, conversely, under the appropriate conditions every efficient allocation forms a competitive equilibrium with the appropriate reallocation of initial endowments.

3. In the end, the court ruled that one event had occurred: *SR International Business Insurance Company Ltd. v. World Trade Center Properties, LLC, et al.*, 467 F.3d 107 (2d Cir. N.Y. 2006).

4. See Kornhauser and MacLeod (2012) for a discussion of contract law and enforcement.

5. See Eisenhardt (1989).

6. The earliest formal paper on contract theory is Simon (1951).

7. See http://www.legislation.gov.uk/ukpga/1992/52/contents.

8. From chapter 5, we have $B_q, C_q, B_b, C_c > 0$, $B_{qq} < 0$, $C_{qq} > 0$, $B_{qb}, C_{qc} > 0$. To this is added the assumption that benefits and costs are differentiable in investments, with $M \geq \frac{\partial(B(q,\omega)-C(q,\omega))}{\partial I^i} \geq 0$ for all $I^S, I^B \geq 0$, and some constant $M > 0$. It is also assumed that the surplus is concave in $\bar{I} = \left\{ I^B, I^S \right\}$. Without loss of generality, one may suppose that there is an upper bound I^{max} to the investments made by parties.

9. Note $\int_0^1 u^i(\bar{x}, \omega)\, dt = u^i(\bar{x}, \omega)$, $i \in \{B, S\}$.

10. For example, suppose that the buyer's efficient level of investment is I^B and the returns are concave in I^B, then:

$$dR\left(I^B\right)/dI^B \times p^T = 1,$$

hence:

$$\frac{dI^B}{dp^T} = -\frac{dR\left(I^B\right)/dI^B}{d^2 R\left(I^B\right)/dI^B dI^B \times p^T} > 0.$$

11. The formal law and economic analysis begins with Barton (1972), who introduces a game theoretic model of contract performance. Goetz and Scott (1977) provide a seminal, graphical analysis of liquidated damages and the penalty doctrine. They argue that courts should enforce contracts, including liquidated damages, as intended by the contracting parties. Diamond and Maskin (1979) look at the interplay between contract damages and search behavior. Shavell (1980) and Rogerson (1984) provide early analysis of contract damages and the holdup problem.

12. See Kornhauser and MacLeod (2012, sec. 3). When a party is insolvent, they are "judgment proof." In practice, commercial parties solve this problem by requiring counterparties to purchase insurance. An insurance requirement is common in the case of construction, where contracts are often small and potentially judgment proof. See Sweet (2000) for an excellent discussion of these and other practical issues in contract law.

13. There is a large literature on this question, beginning with Flood (1952). Some other examples include Cooper et al. (1992), Brandts and MacLeod (1995), Roth (1995a), Erev and Roth (1998), Roth (2002), and Camerer (2003).

14. Goldberg (1976, 439) states: "Generally, after the consumer has entered into the relationship with the producer, he will find himself vulnerable to price increases or the threat of termination; the producer will be in a position to price discriminate in an attempt to capture the 'ex post consumer surplus.' In addition to protection from being held up, the consumer will want protection from arbitrary and capricious behavior."

15. See Schwartz (1979).

16. See Currie and Moretti (2003) for a discussion of the importance of maternal inputs for children that can explain why we have divorce laws. Friedberg (1998) shows, using variation in divorce law across states, that in fact we do not get efficient dissolution of marriages. Stevenson and Wolfers (2006) also show increasing the cost of divorce can lead to more violence. Chiaporri and Mazzocco (2017) provide a review of family economics illustrating the theoretical importance of intertemporal resource allocation choices. Lafortune and Low (2017) empirically show a positive relation between the marriage contract and the acquisition of assets in a marriage. Given that marriage contracts often entail specific performance (parties cannot separate unless both agree), this result is consistent with the hypothesis that specific performance can enhance investment into a relationship.

17. See "AT&T Archives: Operator! (1938)," July 18, 2011, YouTube video, https://www.youtube.com/watch?v=IOEOM4S6vgA.

18. See (6.4.3) for the definition of welfare, with the appropriate modification to deal with cooperative investments.

19. See Farnsworth (2004, sec. 12.18).

20. This has been documented in many studies. See for example Bewley (1999), McLaughlin (1994), and Schmieder and von Wachter (2010).

21. This is called a constructive discharge and is not normally allowed in most jurisdictions. See Rothstein and Liebman (2007) and the case of *Pennsylvania State Police v. Suders*, 542 U.S. 129 (2004) for details.

22. In the Grout model it is assumed that the investment is in capital. In this case, because the employer can bargain with only a single union, capital investment is effectively a relationship-specific self-investment by the employer.

23. See in particular see the the National Academy report by Milkovich and Wigdor (1991) for a discussion of the goals of performance pay.

24. There is a huge literature on employee training beginning with Mincer (1962).

25. Farnsworth (2004, sec. 3.6).

26. It is worth emphasizing that property, and its protection, is a feature of all human societies, regardless of their level of development. See Boas (1920, chap. 9).

Chapter 7

1. See Baker, Jensen, and Murphy (1988) and Eisenhardt (1989) for critical reviews of the early literature. For excellent reviews of the theory, see also Laffont and Martimort (2002) and Salanié (2005).

2. See Tirole (1999) for a discussion of incomplete versus complete contracts.

3. Technically, this is an infinite-dimension problem. This first-order condition follows from the Gateaux derivative with respect to the contract choice. See Luenberger (1969).

4. Notice that one can transform the model $X = Y(E + \varepsilon)$ into this form by letting the covariance matrix $\Sigma = cov\{Y\varepsilon\}$.

5. That is, $C^T = C$ and $E^T C E > 0$, for every $E \neq \vec{0}$.

6. There is a significant literature on intrinsic motivation, including Deci, Koestner, and Ryan (1999), Kreps (1997), Prendergast (2008), Gneezy, Meier, and Rey-Biel (2011), and Ash and MacLeod (2015).

7. See https://en.wikipedia.org/wiki/Lake_Wobegon.

8. Recall that the support of a random variable is the set of x such that $f(x|e) > 0$. If the support moves monotonically with effort, it is possible to implement the first best quite easily. Why?

9. It is possible to have a different lower bound. Making the support of the output to be the same as the support of the payoffs makes the notation a bit easier. The analysis can be easily extended to the case in which the support of the payoffs for the agent is different from the support of observed output.

10. This is not the case if worker and firm play a repeated game, a case considered in greater detail in chapter 9. The point here is that the market merely rewards an individual based upon their expected productivity.

11. See DeGroot (1972).

12. To get this expression, observe that $E\left\{\frac{\rho_\eta m_\eta + \rho_t \bar{x}_t}{\rho_\eta + \rho_t}\right\} = \frac{\rho_\eta m_\eta + \rho_t m_\eta}{\rho_\eta + \rho_t} = m_\eta$.

Chapter 8

1. See chapter 6 for a discussion of specific performance contracts.

2. Several possible equilibrium strategies can be used. It is assumed, unless mentioned otherwise, that the perfect Bayesian Nash equilibrium concept is used, which implies subgame perfect Nash equilibria when there is no asymmetric information.

3. Notice that all we need is monotonicity. If $q(b, c)$ is decreasing in b, then we just define $\bar{b} = -b$, and perform the analysis in terms of $\bar{b}$.

4. See also Ausubel, Cramton, and Deneckere (2002) for a review of this class of models.

5. Notice that we do not require q^* to be differentiable for these expressions to hold; it is sufficient that q^* is almost everywhere differentiable.

6. This point was first made by Coase (1960) in the context of the allocation of legal rights. His point is that in the absence of transactions costs, parties can always bargain around any initial allocation of rights. The allocation of rights does affect inequality but not the efficiency of trade.

7. See Chakravarty and MacLeod (2009) for a full discussion.

8. See Belloni, Lopomo, and Wang (2010) for a computational approach to the general, multidimensional monopoly pricing problem.

9. We set $I_{n-1} = [b_{n-1}, b_H]$, though it not strictly necessary because what happens at a single type does not affect profits.

10. $\epsilon^S = \frac{dH^S(w^M)}{dw} \times \frac{w^M}{H^S(w^M)}$.

11. See Farber (2015) for a good discussion of the New York taxi industry.

12. $w_c(c) = \frac{H_c^S}{H_w^D - H_w^S} = \frac{h(w,c)f(c)}{H_w^D - H_w^S} < 0$.

Chapter 9

1. This appears to be the source of a quotation widely attributed to Benjamin Franklin: "It takes many good deeds to build a good reputation, and only one bad one to lose it."

2. We can see evidence of relational contracts in Roman times for construction (Vitruvius 1914) and the management of agricultural estates (Columella 1941). Greif (1989) explicitly connects the trading practices of medieval traders to relational contract theory.

3. See the discussion in Macaulay (2000, 783).

4. See Bergin and MacLeod (1993a) for a discussion of how to extend repeated games to continuous time. It is shown that in general, continuous time games are not well defined but should be described as the limit of a well-defined discrete time game.

5. The period corresponding to time τ is defined by $t(\tau, \Delta) = \lfloor \frac{\tau}{\Delta} \rfloor$, where $\lfloor x \rfloor = \max\{z \in Z | z \leq x\}$ is the floor function that returns the largest integer less than or equal to x.

6. The terminology is based on MacLeod (2007b).

7. In Shapiro and Stiglitz (1984), if the worker chooses high effort ($e_t = 1$), there is no loss $\left(\gamma^B(e_t) = 0\right)$. However, if the seller shirks ($e_t = 0$), there is chance q that she will be caught $\left(\gamma^B(0) = q\right)$. It is assumed that when shirking is detected, there is no output. This corresponds to setting the loss equal to the value of production with no shirking ($L = \bar{y}$).

8. Parties are risk neutral and have no liability constraint, and hence the expected wage is a sufficient statistic for compensation in period t. If the relationship terminates in period T, this occurs *before* production at date T.

9. If messages could be verified, then as a matter of law parties are required to be truthful. This is known as the good faith exception to employment at will, as established in the case of *Woolley v. Hoffmann-La Roche, Inc.*, 99 A.2d 284 (1985).

10. In this example, it is assumed that $y(e) = log(e + 1)$ and $v(e, c) = c \times e$.

11. See Baker, Gibbons, and Murphy (1994) for some results on the interplay between implicit relational contract terms and explicit agency contracts.

12. See Pearce (1992) for a discussion and literature review.

13. Levin (2003) calls this condition "strong optimality."

14. See Goldlücke and Kranz (2013) for a recent discussion of renegotiation proofness, along with a characterization of strong and weak renegotiation proof equilibria in a repeated game with side payments.

15. See Bergin and MacLeod (1993b) for an approach that integrates various approaches to the problem of renegotiation. When the efficient frontier is not linear, then the concept is not well defined.

16. In fact, a couple did sue a New York kindergarten for nonperformance. See Associated Press, "Peeved NYC mom sues, says preschool's 'a playroom,' but failed," *Wall Street Journal*, March 14, 2011.

17. See Akerlof and Yellen (1986) for a collection of classic papers in this area.

18. See Peter and Hull (1969).

19. This is based on a private discussion with Abhijit Banerjee.

20. See American Law Institute and National Conference of Commissioners on Uniform State Laws (2009, part 6).

21. This discussion paper was eventually published as two papers, MacLeod (1987, 1988). See Vanek (1970) for seminal work on labor cooperatives and Bonin, Jones, and Putterman (1993) for a review of the early empirical literature.

22. See Mauss's (1990) pioneering study showing the importance of gift exchange in human societies.

23. See also MacLeod and Malcomson (1988), who provide a formal model of "job titles" and an explanation of the "Peter Principle."

24. See Roth and Murnighan (1978) for a discussion of the early literature, and see the introduction to Kagel and Roth (1995) for a discussion of the finite horizon issue. See also Rubinstein (1991) for a discussion of how to interpret equilibria in repeated games.

25. A tit-for-tat player is one who always plays the strategy of her opponent the previous period and begins by cooperating. As long as one party cooperates, the TFT player continues to cooperate. As Axelrod (1981) observes, the benefit of TFT is that in an environment with different strategies, it is easy for an opponent to learn that he is facing a TFT player, in which case it is optimal to cooperate until the last period, when a rational player will defect.

26. See also Watson (1999), who studies reputation building in a partnership model.

Chapter 10

1. College of Business, University of Nebraska-Lincoln.

2. This was part of a weekly dialogue on *A Prairie Home Companion*, which appeared on National Public Radio from 1974 to 2016. See https://en.wikipedia.org/wiki/A_Prairie_Home_Companion, and above, chapter 7, section 7.3.2. See Milkovich and Newman (2005) for a discussion of evidence on ranking systems.

3. An example of this type of relationship is hiring an academic whose research is considered good, but it is not yet known if she will receive a Nobel Prize. Another example might be the making of a film, where the producer might pay a bonus to the staff at the end of production if she thinks the film will be a success. In both cases, current effort is being rewarded for output that will have its value realized in the future.

4. Notice that this assumption is equivalent to the assumption that the signals are *informative*: $\Gamma_{AA}^H \Gamma_{UU}^H - \Gamma_{AU} \Gamma_{UA} \neq 0$. If $\Gamma_{AA}^H \Gamma_{UU}^H - \Gamma_{AU} \Gamma_{UA} < 0$, then we can simply relabel A as U and U as A, and we satisfy the condition of the proposition.

5. For concreteness, one can think of B as some future payoff in which the value is not immediately realized.

6. This asymmetry in information on the outcome prohibits the principal from efficiently "selling the firm" to the agent.

7. Formally, we index each state by an index function $\mathcal{I}: S^2 \to \{1, \dots, n^2\}$ where $\mathcal{I}(ts) = (n \times (s-1)) + t$. Thus for vector $\vec{x} \in \Re^{n^2}$, x_{ts} refers to the $\mathcal{I}(ts)$-th entry of vector $\vec{x}$.

8. There is a large literature on aggression and conflict in organizations and how to reduce conflict. See, for example, March and Simon (1958), Pondy (1967), and Neuman and Baron (1998).

9. Banerjee and Duflo (2000) and Macchiavello and Morjaria (2015) provide evidence on the value of reputation in relationships with repeated interactions.

10. One could also view these conflicts as the level of aggrievement, in the sense of Hart and Moore (2007).

11. In some cases, employment can be organized so that these losses are implemented as a transfer to other workers (see Malcomson 1984 and Carmichael 1983). In this case, these losses are then no longer social losses. However, this arrangement introduces the problem of collusion among agents and contracts will then have to be designed to be collusion proof, which adds further complexity to the contract design.

12. All multiplications between vectors refer to the inner product.

13. In defining the contract this way, we are implicitly assuming that the players are contracting on a joint payment of $\delta_{ts} = c_{ts} - w_{ts}$ to a third party at each reported state ts. This interpretation is convenient from a modeling perspective, but it might not be obvious to readers that this also fits our interpretation of δ as a reduced-form punishment in the relationship, especially when it might be difficult to imagine that the level of conflict can be contracted upon. To reconcile this, one can take the interpretation that the only contractible term in the contract is a price term, p_{ts}, that the principal must pay to the agent at each reported state ts. On top of that, the contract also specifies a set of punishment *recommendations* $\left(d_{ts}^A, d_{ts}^P\right)$ for each reported state ts. d_{ts}^A is the recommended deadweight loss that the agent should be imposing upon the principal in reported state ts, and likewise d_{ts}^P is the recommended deadweight loss that the principal should be imposing on the agent. Like effort λ, the punishment recommendations have to be incentive compatible in the sense that it is the best response of the players to obey these punishment recommendations. Because it is assumed that it is costless to the inflicting party to inflict deadweight loss on the other party, obeying the punishment recommendations will always be a best response. The principal's cost term in the contract in (10.12) is then given by $c_{ts} = p_{ts} + d_{ts}^A$ and the agent's wage term is $w_{ts} = p_{ts} - d_{ts}^P$.

14. Keep in mind that the report might be in the form of the pay, which is the consequence of having observed a given level of performance t, rather than an actual rating. Thus the information might only be in the form of $t \geq \bar{t}$, where $\bar{t}$ is some threshold for getting a bonus.

15. For the rest of this section, sales contract refers to a situation with subjective evaluation, to differentiate it from the sales contracts of chapter 6.

16. See Malcomson (2009) for an analysis and an extensive discussion of the previous literature.

17. One can extend the analysis to zero probability events, as we saw in the case of relational contracts. That analysis is best done case by case.

18. See Deb, Li, and Mukherjee (2016).

19. See Williamson (1979, 234n3).

20. One needs to check the 1 IC for effort, and for each of the n signals, there are $n-1$ deviations, leading to $1 + n(n-1)$ conditions to check.

21. A screening mechanism is a signal whose cost is correlated with the party's private information. For example, a monopolist can use the fact that buyers with different valuations desire different quantities of a good to effectively discriminate over price. If all the buyers wish to buy only one unit of the good, then the best the monopolist can do is to charge a single take-it-or-leave-it price, which in turn can lead to a social loss that is interpreted as a "conflict cost" in an organizational context.

22. See Kennan and Wilson (1993) for a review of the earlier literature and Ausubel, Cramton, and Deneckere (2002) for an update on bargaining with asymmetric information.

Chapter 11

1. Unfortunately, the literature is so vast that I have certainly missed some important papers, and I apologize to those authors. To complete a review, it is recommended that the reader use Web of Science, Scopus, and Google Scholar, in that order. As Meho and Yang (2007) find, Web of Science is more efficient, while Google Scholar allows one to find technical reports that are not yet published in an academic journal.

2. Forbearance is the principle that parties to an agreement within an organization cannot appeal to a court of law for enforcement. It is the responsibility of the management in the organization to adjudicate disputes that arise from disagreements. This does not apply to the employment contract since it is agreed between an individual and an employer before the individual has joined the organization.

Appendix

1. If this were not the case, we could always define a new utility function, $u(\vec{x}) - u(\vec{0})$, with exactly the same properties.

References

Abowd, J. M., F. Kramarz, and D. N. Margolis (1999). High wage workers and high wage firms. *Econometrica 67*(2), 251–333.

Abowd, J. M., and T. Lemieux (1993). The effects of product market competition on collective bargaining agreements: The case of foreign competition in Canada. *Quarterly Journal of Economics 108*(4), 983–1014.

Abreu, D. (1988). On the theory of infinitely repeated games with discounting. *Econometrica 56*(2), 383–396.

Abreu, D., B. Brooks, and Y. Sannikov (2020). Algorithms for stochastic games with perfect monitoring. *Econometrica 88*(4), 1661–1695.

Abreu, D., P. Milgrom, and D. Pearce (1991). Information and timing in repeated partnerships. *Econometrica 59*(6), 1713–1734.

Abreu, D., and D. Pearce (2007). Bargaining, reputation, and equilibrium selection in repeated games with contracts. *Econometrica 75*(3), 653–710.

Abreu, D., D. Pearce, and E. Stacchetti (1990). Toward a theory of discounted repeated games with imperfect monitoring. *Econometrica 58*(5), 1041–1063.

Acemoglu, D., and D. Autor (2011). Skills, tasks and technologies: Implications for employment and earnings. In O. Ashenfelter and D. Card (Eds.), *Handbook of Labor Economics*, vol. 4B, 1043–1171. Elsevier.

Acemoglu, D., and J.-S. Pischke (1998). Why do firms train? Theory and evidence. *Quarterly Journal of Economics 113*(1), 79–119.

Adams, D. (1979). *The Hitch-hikers Guide to the Galaxy*. Pan.

Aghion, P., M. Dewatripont, and P. Rey (1994). Renegotiation design with unverifiable information. *Econometrica 62*(2), 257–282.

Aghion, P., and J. Tirole (1997). Formal and real authority in organizations. *Journal of Political Economy 105*(1), 1–29.

Akerlof, G. A. (1970). The market for "lemons": Quality uncertainty and the market mechanism. *Quarterly Journal of Economics 84*(3), 488–500.

Akerlof, G. A. (1980). A theory of social custom, of which unemployment may be one consequence. *Quarterly Journal of Economics 94*(4), 749–775.

Akerlof, G. A., and J. L. Yellen (1986). *Efficiency Wage Models of the Labor Market*. Cambridge University Press.

Alchian, A., and H. Demsetz (1972). Production, information costs, and economic organization. *American Economic Review 62*(5), 777–795.

Allen, D. W. (2012). *The Institutional Revolution*. University of Chicago Press.

Alonso, R., and N. Matouschek (2008). Optimal delegation. *Review of Economic Studies 75*(1), 259–293.

Altonji, J. G., P. Bharadwaj, and F. Lange (2012). "Changes in the characteristics of American youth: Implications for adult outcomes." *Journal of Labor Economics 30*(5), 783–828.

Altonji, J. G., and P. J. Devereux (1999). The extent and consquences of downward rigidity. Technical Report 7236, NBER.

American Law Institute and National Conference of Commissioners on Uniform State Laws (2009). *Uniform Commercial Code: Official Text and Comments*. Westlaw.

Angrist, J., P. Azoulay, G. Ellison, R. Hill, and S. F. Lu (2017). Economic research evolves: Fields and styles. *American Economic Review 107*(5), 293–297.

Angrist, J. D., S. Caldwell, and J. V. Hall (2017). Uber vs. taxi: A driver's eye view. Working Paper 23891, National Bureau of Economic Research.

Angrist, J. D., and A. B. Krueger (1991). Does compulsory school attendance affect schooling and earnings? *Quarterly Journal of Economics 106*(4), 979–1014.

Angrist, J. D., and A. B. Krueger (1999). Empirical strategies in labor economics. In O. Ashenfelter and D. Card (Eds.), *Handbook of Labor Economics*, vol. 3A, 1278–1357. Elsevier.

Angrist, J. D., and J.-S. Pischke (2009). *Mainly Harmless Econometrics: An Empiricist's Companion*. Princeton University Press.

Anscombe, F. J., and R. J. Aumann (1963). A definition of subjective probability. *Annals of Mathematical Statistics 34*(1), 199–205.

Antras, P., and C. F. Foley (2015). Poultry in motion: A study of international trade finance practices. *Journal of Political Economy 123*(4), 853–901.

Armstrong, M. (2016). Nonlinear pricing. *Annual Review of Economics 8*, 583–614.

Arrow, K. J. (1958). Utilities, attitudes, choices: A review article. *Econometrica 26*(1), 1–23.

Arrow, K. J. (1963). Uncertainty and the welfare economics of medical care. *American Economic Review 53*(5), 941–973.

Ash, E., and W. B. MacLeod (2015). Intrinsic motivation in public service: Theory and evidence from state supreme courts. *Journal of Law and Economics 58*(4), 863–913.

Ash, R. B. (1972). *Real Analysis and Probability*. Academic Press.

Ashenfelter, O., H. Farber, and M. Ransom (2010). Labor market monopsony. *Journal of Labor Economics 28*(2), 203–210.

Ashenfelter, O., and G. E. Johnson (1969). Bargaining theory, trade unions, and industrial strike activity. *American Economic Review 59*(1), 35–49.

Attar, A., T. Mariotti, and F. Salanié (2011). Nonexclusive competition in the market for lemons. *Econometrica 79*(6), 1869–1918.

Ausubel, L. M., P. Cramton, and R. J. Deneckere (2002). Bargaining with incomplete information. In R. J. Aumann and S. Hart (Eds.), *Handbook of Game Theory with Economic Applications*, 3:1897–1945, Elsevier Science.

Axelrod, R. (1981). The emergence of cooperation among egoists. *American Journal of Political Science 75*(2), 306–318.

Axelrod, R. (1984). *The Evolution of Cooperation*. Basic Books.

Ayres, I., and E. Talley (1995). Solomonic bargaining: Dividing a legal entitlement to facilitate Coasean trade. *Yale Law Journal 104*(5), 1027–1117.

Azevedo, E. M., and D. Gottlieb (2017). Perfect competition in markets with adverse selection. *Econometrica 85*(1), 67–105.

Bajari, P., S. Houghton, and S. Tadelis (2014). Bidding for incomplete contracts: An empirical analysis of adaptation costs. *American Economic Review 104*(4), 1288–1319.

Bajari, P., and S. Tadelis (2001). Incentives versus transaction costs: A theory of procurement contracts. *RAND Journal of Economics 32*(3), 387–407.

Baker, G. P. (1992). Incentive contracts and performance measurement. *Journal of Political Economy 100*(3), 598–614.

Baker, G. P., R. Gibbons, and K. J. Murphy (1994). Subjective performance measures in optimal incentive contracts. *Quarterly Journal of Economics 109*(439), 1125–1156.

Baker, G. P., R. Gibbons, and K. J. Murphy (1999). Informal authority in organizations. *Journal of Law Economics and Organization 15*(1), 56–73.

Baker, G. P., M. C. Jensen, and K. J. Murphy (1988). Compensation and incentives: Practice vs. theory. *Journal of Finance 43*(3), 593–616.

Bandiera, O., M. C. Best, A. A. Khan, and A. Prat (2021). The allocation of authority in organizations: A field experiment with bureaucrats. *Forthcoming Quarterly Journal of Economics*. Available as NBER working paper 26733.

Bandura, A. (2001). Social cognitive theory: An agentic perspective. *Annual Review of Psychology 52*, 1–26.

Banerjee, A. V., and E. Duflo (2000). Reputation effects and the limits of contracting: A study of the Indian software industry. *Quarterly Journal of Economics 115*(3), 989–1017.

Bartling, B., E. Fehr, and H. Herz (2014). The intrinsic value of decision rights. *Econometrica* 82(6), 2005–2039.

Barton, J. H. (1972). The economic basis of damages for breach of contract. *Journal of Legal Studies* 1(2), 277–304.

Becker, G. S. (1962). Investment in human capital: A theoretical analysis. *Journal of Political Economy* 70(5, 2), 9–49.

Becker, G. S. (1976). *The Economic Approach to Human Behavior*. University of Chicago Press.

Becker, G. S., and G. J. Stigler (1974). Law enforcement, malfeasance, and compensation of enforcers. *Journal of Legal Studies* 3(1), 1–18.

Belloni, A., G. Lopomo, and S. Wang (2010). Multidimensional mechanism design: Finite-dimensional approximations and efficient computation. *Operations Research* 58(4, 2, SI), 1079–1089.

Benabou, R., and J. Tirole (2003). Intrinsic and extrinsic motivation. *Review of Economic Studies* 70(3), 489–520.

Bergemann, D., B. Brooks, and S. Morris (2015). The limits of price discrimination. *American Economic Review* 105(3), 921–957.

Bergin, J., and W. B. MacLeod (1993a). Continuous time repeated games. *International Economic Review* 34(1), 21–37.

Bergin, J., and W. B. MacLeod (1993b). Efficiency and renegotiation in repeated games. *Journal of Economic Theory* 61(1), 42–73.

Bernheim, B. D. (1984). Rationalizable strategic behavior. *Econometrica* 52(4), 1007–1028.

Bernheim, B. D., and A. Rangel (2004). Addictions and cue-conditioned cognitive processes. *Amercian Economic Review* 94(5), 1558–1590.

Bernheim, B. D., and M. D. Whinston (1986). Common agency. *Econometrica* 54(4), 923–942.

Bernheim, B. D., and M. D. Whinston (1998). Incomplete contracts and strategic ambiguity. *American Economics Review* 68(4), 902–932.

Bernoulli, D. (1738). Specimen theoriae de mensura sortis. *Commentarii Academiae Scientarum Imperialis Petropolitanae* 5, 175–192.

Bernstein, L. (1992). Opting out of the legal system: Extralegal contractual relations in the diamond industry. *Journal of Legal Studies* 21(1), 115–157.

Bernstein, L. (2001). Private commercial law in the cotton industry: Creating cooperation through rules, norms, and institutions. *Michigan Law Review* 99, 1724–1790.

Bernstein, L. (2014). Merchant law in a modern economy. In G. Klass, G. Letsas, and P. Saprai (Eds.), *Philosophical Foundations of Contract Law*, 238–271. Oxford University Press.

Bester, H., and R. Strausz (2001). Contracting with imperfect commitment and the revelation principle: The single agent case. *Econometrica* 69(4), 1077–1098.

Bewley, T. F. (1999). *Why Wages Don't Fall during a Recession*. Harvard University Press.

Binmore, K. G. (1985). Bargaining and coalitions. In A. E. Roth (Ed.), *Game-Theoretic Models of Bargaining*. Cambridge University Press.

Binmore, K. G. (1994). *Game Theory and the Social Contract*. Vol. 1, *Playing Fair*. MIT Press.

Binmore, K. G. (1998). *Game Theory and the Social Contract*. Vol. 2, *Just Playing*. MIT Press.

Binmore, K. G., A. Rubinstein, and A. Wolinsky (1986). The Nash bargaining solution in economic modeling. *RAND Journal of Economics* 17(2), 176–188.

Binmore, K. G., A. Shaked, and J. Sutton (1989). An outside option experiment. *Quarterly Journal of Economics* 104(4), 753–770.

Blackwell, D. (1965). Discounted dynamic programming. *Annals of Mathematical Statistics* 36(1), 226–235.

Blackwell, D., and M. A. Girshick (1954). *Theory of Games and Statistical Decisions*. John Wiley.

Blinder, A. S., and D. H. Choi (1990). A shred of evidence on theories of wage stickiness. *Quarterly Journal of Economics* 105(4), 1003–1015.

Bloom, N., and J. Van Reenen (2011). Human resource managment and productivity. In O. Ashenfelter and D. Card (Eds.), *Handbook of Labor Economics*, vol. 4B, 1697–1767. Elsevier.

Board, S., and M. Meyer-ter Vehn (2013). Reputation for quality. *Econometrica* 81(6), 2381–2462.

Boas, F. (1920). The social organization of the kwakiutl. *American Anthropologist* 22(2), 111–126.

Bolton, P., and M. Dewatripont (2005). *Contract Theory*. MIT Press.

Bolton, P., and M. D. Whinston (1993). Incomplete contracts, vertical integration, and supply assurance. *Review of Economic Studies* 60(202), 121–148.

Bonin, J. P., D. C. Jones, and L. Putterman (1993). Theoretical and empirical studies of producer cooperatives: Will ever the twain meet? *Journal of Economic Literature 31*(3), 1290–1320.

Borch, K. H. (1962). Equilibrium in a reinsurance market. *Econometrica 30*(3), 424–444.

Boyd, S., and L. Vanderberghe (2004). *Convex Optimization*. Cambridge University Press.

Brandts, J., and W. B. MacLeod (1995). On the strategic stability of equilibria in experimental games. *Games and Economics Behavior 11*, 36–63.

Bushman, R. M., and A. J. Smith (2001). Financial accounting information and corporate governance. *Journal of Accounting and Economics 32*(1), 237–333.

Calvo, G. (1979). Quasi-Walrasian theories of unemployment. *American Economic Review 69*(2), 102–107.

Calzolari, G., and V. Denicolo (2013). Competition with exclusive contracts and market-share discounts. *American Economic Review 103*(6), 2384–2411.

Camerer, C. F. (2003). *Behavioral Game Theory: Experiments in Strategic Interaction*. Russell Sage Foundation.

Camerer, C. F. (2006). Behavioral economics. In R. Blundell, K. N. Whitney, and T. Persson (Eds.), *Advances in Economics and Econometrics*. Vol. 2, *Theory and Applications*, 181–214. Cambridge University Press.

Camerer, C. F., G. Loewenstein, and M. Rabin (2004). *Advances in Behavioral Economics*. Princeton University Press.

Card, D. (1990). Strikes and wages: A test of an asymmetric information model. *Quarterly Journal of Economics 105*(3), 625–659.

Card, D. (2001). Estimating the return to schooling: Progress on some persistent econometric problems. *Econometrica 69*(5), 1127–1160.

Card, D., A. R. Cardoso, J. Heining, and P. Kline (2016). Firms and labor market inequality: Evidence and some theory. Working Paper 22850, National Bureau of Economic Research.

Card, D., A. R. Cardoso, J. Heining, and P. Kline (2018). Firms and labor market inequality: Evidence and some theory. *Journal of Labor Economics 36*(1), S13–S70.

Card, D., F. Devicienti, and A. Maida (2014). Rent-sharing, holdup, and wages: Evidence from matched panel data. *Review of Economic Studies 81*(1), 84–111.

Card, D., and D. Hyslop (1997). Does inflation "grease the wheels of the labor market"? In C. D. Romer and D. H. Romer (Eds.), *Reducing Inflation: Motivation and Strategy*, 71–122, University of Chicago Press.

Card, D., A. Mas, E. Moretti, and E. Saez (2012). Inequality at work: The effect of peer salaries on job satisfaction. *American Economic Review 102*(6), 2981–3003.

Cardullo, G., M. Conti, and G. Sulis (2015). Sunk capital, unions and the hold-up problem: Theory and evidence from cross-country sectoral data. *European Economic Review 76*(C), 253–274.

Carmichael, H. L. (1983). The agents-agents problem: Payment by relative output. *Journal of Labor Economics 1*(1), 50–65.

Carmichael, H. L., and W. B. MacLeod (1997). Gift giving and the evolution of cooperation. *International Economic Review 38*(3), 485–509.

Chakravarty, S., and W. B. MacLeod (2009). Contracting in the shadow of the law. *RAND Journal of Economics 40*(3), 533–557.

Charness, G., and P. Kuhn (2011). Lab labor: What can labor economists learn from the lab? In O. Ashenfelter and D. Card (Eds.), *Handbook of Labor Economics*. Vol. 4A, 229–330, Elsevier.

Chase, W. G., and H. A. Simon (1973). Perception in chess. *Cognitive psychology 4*(1), 55–81.

Chassang, S. (2010). Building routines: Learning, cooperation, and the dynamics of incomplete relational contracts. *American Economic Review 100*(1), 448–465.

Che, Y.-K., and D. B. Hausch (1999). Cooperative investments and the value of contracting. *American Economic Review 89*(1), 125–147.

Chen, M. K., J. A. Chevalier, P. E. Rossi, and E. Oehlsen (2017). The value of flexible work: Evidence from Uber drivers. Working Paper 23296, National Bureau of Economic Research.

Chiaporri, P.-A., and M. Mazzocco (2017). Static and intertermporal household decisions. *Journal of Economic Literature 55*(3), 985–1045.

Chiappori, P., and B. Salanié (2000). Testing for asymmetric information in insurance markets. *Journal of Political Economy 108*(1), 56–78.

Cho, I.-K., and D. M. Kreps (1987). Signaling games and stable equilibria. *Quarterly Journal of Economics 102*(2), 179–222.

Clarke, E. H. (1971). Multipart pricing of public goods. *Public Choice 11*, 17–33.

Coase, R. A. (1960). The problem of social cost. *Journal of Law and Economics 3*, 1–44.

Coles, M., and A. Hildreth (2000). Wage bargaining, inventories, and union legislation. *Review of Economic Studies 67*(2), 273–293.

Columella, L. J. M. (1941). *On Agriculture: Books 1–4*. Edited by H. Boyd, translated by H. B. Ash. Harvard University Press.

Compte, O. (1998). Communication in repeated games with imperfect private monitoring. *Econometrica 66*(3), 597–626.

Cooper, R., D. V. DeJong, R. Forsythe, and T. W. Ross (1992). Communication in coordination games. *Quarterly Journal of Economics 107*(2), 739–771.

Cooper, Z., S. V. Craig, M. Gaynor, and J. Van Reenen (2019). The price ain't right? Hospital prices and health spending on the privately insured. *Quarterly Journal of Economics 134*(1), 51–107.

Corts, K. S., and J. Singh (2004). The effect of repeated interaction on contract choice: Evidence from offshore drilling. *Journal of Law Economics and Organization 20*(1), 230–260.

Cournot, A. A. ([1838] 1974). *Recherches sur les principes mathématiques de la théorie des richesses*. Calmann-Lévy.

Cox, A., D. C. Bok, R. A. Gorman, and M. W. Finkin (2006). *Labor Law*. 14th ed. Foundation Press.

Cramton, P. C. (1985). Sequential bargaining mechanisms. In A. E. Roth (Ed.), *Game-Theoretic Models of Bargaining*, 149–180. Cambridge University Press.

Cramton, P. C. (1992). Strategic delay in bargaining with two-sided uncertainty. *Review of Economic Studies 59*(1), 205–225.

Cramton, P. C., and J. S. Tracy (1992). Strikes and holdouts in wage bargaining: Theory and data. *American Economic Review 82*(1), 100–121.

Crawford, G. S., and A. Yurukoglu (2012). The welfare effects of bundling in multichannel television markets. *American Economic Review 102*(2), 643–685.

Crawford, V. P. (1988). Long-term relationships governed by short-term contracts. *American Economic Review 78*(3), 485–499.

Crawford, V. P., and J. Sobel (1982). Strategic information-transmission. *Econometrica 50*(6), 1431–1451.

Cronshaw, M. B., and D. G. Luenberger (1994). Strongly symmetrical subgame perfect equilibria in infinitely repeated games with perfect monitoring and discounting. *Games and Economic Behavior 6*(2), 220–237.

Currie, J. (2009). Healthy, wealthy, and wise: Socioeconomic status, poor health in childhood, and human capital development. *Journal of Economic Literature 47*(1), 87–122.

Currie, J., and S. McConnell (1991). Collective-bargaining in the public sector: The effect of legal structure on dispute costs and wages. *American Economic Review 81*(4), 693–718.

Currie, J., and E. Moretti (2003). Mother's education and the intergenerational transmission of human capital: Evidence from college openings. *Quarterly Journal of Economics 118*(4), 1495–1532.

Currie, J. M., M. Farsi, and W. B. MacLeod (2005). Cut to the bone? Hospital takeovers and nurse employment contracts. *Industrial and Labor Relations Review 58*(3), 471–493.

Currie, J. M., and J. Ferrie (2000). The law and labor strife in the United States, 1881–1894. *Journal of Economics History 60*(1), 42–66.

Currie, J. M., and W. B. MacLeod (2014). Savage tables and tort law: An alternative to the precaution model. *University of Chicago Law Review 81*(1), 53–82.

Dal Bo, P. (2005). Cooperation under the shadow of the future: Experimental evidence from infinitely repeated games. *American Economic Review 95*(5), 1591–1604.

d'Aspremont, C., and L.-A. Gerard-Varet (1979). Incentives and incomplete information. *Journal of Public Economics 11*(1), 25–45.

Deaton, A. (2010). Instruments, randomization, and learning about development. *Journal of Economic Literature 48*(2), 424–455.

Deb, J., J. Li, and A. Mukherjee (2016). Relational contracts with subjective peer evaluations. *RAND Journal of Economics 47*(1), 3–28.

Debreu, G. (1954). Representation of a preference ordering by a numerical function. In R. M. Thrall, C. H. Coombs, and R. L. Davis (Eds.), *Decision Processes*, 159–165. John Wiley.

Debreu, G. (1959). *Theory of Value*. Yale University Press.

Deci, E. L. (1972). Effects of contingent and noncontingent rewards and controls on intrinsic motivation. *Organizational Behavior and Human Performance 8*(2), 217–229.

Deci, E. L., R. Koestner, and R. Ryan (1999). A meta-analytic review of experiments examining the effects of extrinsic rewards on intrinsic motivation. *Psychological Bulletin 125*(6), 627–668.

de Finetti, B. (1974). *Theory of Probability*. 2 vols. John Wiley.

DeGroot, M. H. (1972). *Optimal Statistical Decisions*. McGraw-Hill.

DellaVigna, S. (2009). Psychology and economics: Evidence from the field. *Journal of Economic Literature 47*(2), 315–372.

Dessein, W. (2002). Authority and communication in organizations. *Review of Economic Studies 69*(4), 811–838.

Diaconis, P., and S. L. Zabell (1982). Updating subjective probability. *Journal of American Statistical Association 77*(380), 822–830.

Diamond, P. A., and E. Maskin (1979). An equilibrium analysis of search and breach of contract, I: Steady states. *Bell Journal of Economics 10*(1), 282–316.

Dixit, A. (2003). On modes of economic governance. *Econometrica 71*(2), 449–481.

Doeringer, P., and M. Piore (1971). *Internal Labor Markets and Manpower Analysis*. Lexington.

Dore, R. (1973). *British Factory, Japanese Factory: The Origins of National Diversity*. Allen and Unwin.

Dubey P., and J. Geanakoplos (2002). Competitive pooling: Rothschild-Stiglitz reconsidered. *Quarterly Journal of Economics*, 117(4), 1529–1570.

Duflo, E., R. Glennerster, and M. Kremer (2008). Using randomization in development economics research: A toolkit. In T. P. Schultz and J. A. Strauss (Eds.), *Handbook of Development Economics*, vol. 4, 3895–3962. Elsevier.

Edgeworth, F. Y. (1881). *Mathematical Psychics*. Kegan Paul.

Edlin, A. S., and B. E. Hermalin (2000). Contract renegotiation and options in agency problems. *Journal of Law, Economics and Organization 16*(2), 395–423.

Edlin, A. S., and S. Reichelstein (1996). Holdups, standard breach remedies, and optimal investment. *American Economic Review 86*(3), 478–501.

Edmans, A., X. Gabaix, and D. Jenter (2017). Executive compensation: A survey of theory and evidence. Working Paper 23596, National Bureau of Economic Research.

Eisenhardt, K. M. (1989). Agency theory: An assessment and review. *Academy of Management Review 14*(1), 57–74.

Epstein, L. G. (1992). Behavior under risk: Recent developements in theory and applications. In J.-J. Laffont (Ed.), *Advances in Economic Theory: Sixth World Congress*, vol. 2, 1–63. Cambridge University Press.

Erev, I., and A. E. Roth (1998). Predicting how people play games: Reinforcement learning in experimental games with unique, mixed strategy equilibria. *American Economic Review 88*(4), 848–881.

Eswaran, M., and A. Kotwal (1984). The moral hazard of budget-breaking. *RAND Journal of Economics 15*(4), 578–581.

Eswaran, M., and A. Kotwal (1985). A theory of contractual structure in agriculture. *American Economic Review 75*(3), 352–367.

Evans, R. (2008). Simple efficient contracts in complex environments. *Econometrica 76*(3), 459–491.

Evans, R. (2012). Mechanism design with renegotiation and costly messages. *Econometrica 80*(5), 2089–2104.

Fama, E. F. (1980). Agency problems and the theory of the firm. *Journal of Political Economy 88*(2), 288–307.

Farber, H. S. (2015). Why you can't find a taxi in the rain and other labor supply lessons from cab drivers. *Quarterly Journal of Economics 130*(4), 1975–2026.

Farnsworth, E. A. (2004). *Contracts*. 4th ed. Aspen.

Farnsworth, W. (2007). *The Legal Analyst*. University of Chicago Press.

Fehr, E., and A. Falk (1999). Wage rigidity in a competitive incomplete contract market. *Journal of Political Economy 107*(1), 106–134.

Fehr, E., and S. Gächter (2008). Wage differentials in experimental efficiency wage markets. In C. R. Plott and V. L. Smith (Eds.), *Handbook of Experimental Economics Results*, vol. 1, 120–126. Elsevier.

Fehr, E., S. Gächter, and G. Kirchsteiger (1997). Reciprocity as a contract enforcement device: Experimental evidence. *Econometrica 65*(4), 833–860.

Fehr, E., L. Goette, and C. Zehnder (2009). A behavioral account of the labor market: The role of fairness concerns. *Annual Review of Economics 1*(1), 355–384.

Fehr, E., and K. Schmidt (2006). The economics of fairness, reciprocity and altruism-experimental evidence and new theories. In S.-C. Kolm and J. M. Ythier (Eds.), *Handbook on the Economics of Giving, Altruism and Reciprocity*, vol. 1, 615–691. Elsevier.

Feynman, R. P., R. B. Leighton, and M. Sands (1963). *The Feynman Lectures on Physics*. 3 vols. Addison-Wesley.

Flatters, F., and W. B. MacLeod (1995). Administrative corruption and taxation. *International Tax and Public Finance 2*(3), 397–417. Reprinted in G. Fiorentini and S. Zamagni (Eds.), *The Economics of Corruption and Illegal Markets*. Edward Elgar, 1999.

Flood, M. M. (1952). Some experimental games. Research Memorandum RM-789, RAND Corporation.

Fourcade, M., E. Ollion, and Y. Algan (2015). The superiority of economists. *Journal of Economic Perspectives 29*(1), 89–113.

Freixas, X., R. Guesnerie, and J. Tirole (1985). Planning under incomplete information and the ratchet effect. *Review of Economic Studies 52*(2), 173–191.

Friedberg, L. (1998). Did unilateral divorce raise divorce rates? Evidence from panel data. *American Economic Review 88*(3), 608–627.

Friedman, M. (1953). The methodology of positive economics. In *Essays in Positive Economics*, 3–43. University of Chicago Press.

Friedman, M. (1962). *Capitalism and Freedom*. University of Chicago Press.

Fuchs, W. (2007). Contracting with repeated moral hazard and private evaluations. *American Economic Review 97*(4), 1432–1448.

Fudenberg, D., and E. Maskin (1986). The folk theorem in repeated games with discounting or with incomplete information. *Econometrica 54*(3), 533–556.

Fudenberg, D., and J. Tirole (1991). Perfect Bayesian equlibrium and sequential equilibrium. *Journal of Economics Theory 52*(2), 236–260.

Fuller, L. L., and W. Perdue (1936). The reliance interest in contract damages: 1. *Yale Law Journal 46*(1), 52–96.

Gagnepain, P., M. Ivaldi, and D. Martimort (2013). The cost of contract renegotiation: Evidence from the local public sector. *American Economic Review 103*(6), 2352–2383.

Gaynor, M., K. Ho, and R. J. Town (2015). The industrial organization of health-care markets. *Journal of Economic Literature 53*(2), 235–284.

Georgiadis, G., and B. Szentes (2020). Optimal monitoring design. *Econometrica 88*(5), 2075–2107.

Ghosh, P., and D. Ray (1996). Cooperation in community interaction without information flows. *Review of Economic Studies 63*(3), 491–519.

Gibbons, R. (1987). Piece rate incentive schemes. *Journal of Labor Economics 5*(4, 1), 413–429.

Gibbons, R. (1997). Incentives and careers in organizations. In D. M. Kreps and K. F. Wallis (Eds.), *Advances in Economics and Econometrics: Theory and Applications*, 1–37. Cambridge University Press.

Gibbons, R., and L. F. Katz (1991). Layoffs and lemons. *Journal of Labor Economics 9*(4), 351–380.

Gibbons, R., and K. J. Murphy (1992). Optimal incentive contracts in the presence of career concerns. *Journal of Political Economy 100*(3), 468–505.

Gil, R., and J. Marion (2013). Self-enforcing agreements and relational contracting: Evidence from California highway procurement. *Journal of Law Economics and Organization 29*(2), 239–277.

Giuliano, L., D. I. Levine, and J. Leonard (2009). Manager race and the race of new hires. *Journal of Labor Economics 27*(4), 589–631.

Gneezy, U., S. Meier, and P. Rey-Biel (2011). When and why incentives (don't) work to modify behavior. *Journal of Economic Perspectives 25*(4), 191–209.

Goetz, C. J., and R. E. Scott (1977). Liquidated damages, penalties and just compensation principle: Some notes on an enforcement model and a theory of efficient breach. *Columbia Law Review 77*(4), 554–594.

Goldberg, V. P. (1976). Regulation and administered contracts. *Bell Journal of Economics 7*(2), 426–448.

Goldin, C., and L. F. Katz (2011). The cost of workplace flexibility for high-powered professionals. *Annals of the American Academy of Political and Social Science 638*(1), 45–67.

Goldlücke, S., and S. Kranz (2013). Renegotiation-proof relational contracts. *Games and Economic Behavior 80*, 157–178.

Govindan, S., and R. B. Wilson (2016). Nash equilibrium, refinements of. In *The New Palgrave Dictionary of Economics*, 1–14. Palgrave Macmillan.

Greenspan, A. (1998). The regulation of OTC derivatives. *Hearing before the Committee on Banking and Financial Services*, U.S. House of Representatives, 105th Cong. (Testimony of Alan Greenspan, Chairman, Federal Reserve Board), July 24.

Greenspan, A. (2008). *Hearing before the Committee on Oversight and Government Reform*, House of Representatives, 110th Cong. (Testimony of Alan Greenspan, Chairman, Federal Reserve Board).

Greenwald, B. C. (1986). Adverse selection in the labor-market. *Review of Economic Studies 53*(3), 325–347.

Greif, A. (1989). Reputation and coalitions in medieval trade: Evidence on the Maghribi traders. *Journal of Economic History 49*(4), 857–882.

Greif, A. (1994). Cultural beliefs and the organization of society: A historical and theoretical reflection on collectivist and individualist societies. *Journal of Political Economy 102*(5), 912–950.

Greif, A., P. Milgrom, and B. R. Weingast (1994). Coordination, commitment, and enforcement: The case of the merchant guild. *Journal of Political Economy 102*(4), 745–776.

Gromb, D., and D. Martimort (2007). Collusion and the organization of delegated expertise. *Journal of Economic Theory 137*(1), 271–299.

Grossman, S. J., and O. D. Hart (1983). An analysis of the principal-agent problem. *Econometrica 51*(1), 7–45.

Grossman, S. J., and O. D. Hart (1986). The costs and benefits of ownership: A theory of vertical and lateral integration. *Journal of Political Economy 94*(4), 691–719.

Grout, P. (1984). Investment and wages in the absence of binding contracts: A Nash bargaining approach. *Econometrica 52*(2), 449–460.

Groves, T. (1973). Incentives in teams. *Econometrica 41*(4), 617–631.

Guerrieri, V., R. Shimer, and R. Wright (2010). Adverse selection in competitive search equilibria. *Econometrica*, 78(6), Art. no. 6, 1823–1862.

Gul, F. (1989). Bargaining foundations of Shapley value. *Econometrica 57*(1), 81–95.

Gul, F., and W. Pesendorfer (2001). Temptation and self-control. *Econometrica 69*(6), 1403–1435.

Halac, M. (2012). Relational contracts and the value of relationships. *American Economic Review 102*(2), 750–779.

Halac, M. (2015). Investing in a relationship. *RAND Journal of Economics 46*(1), 165–185.

Halac, M., and A. Prat (2016). Managerial attention and worker performance. *American Economic Review 106*(10), 3104–3132.

Halonen, M. (2002). Reputation and the allocation of ownership. *Economic Journal 112*(481), 539–558.

Hamilton, J. D. (1994). *Time Series Analysis*. Princeton University Press.

Harbaugh, W. T., K. Krause, and T. R. Berry (2001). Garp for kids: On the development of rational choice behavior. *American Economic Review 91*(5), 1539–1545.

Harbaugh, W. T., K. Krause, and L. Vesterlund (2007). Learning to bargain. *Journal of Economic Psychology 28*(1), 127–142.

Harless, D. W., and C. F. Camerer (1994). The predictive utility of generalized expected utility theories. *Econometrica 62*(6), 1251–1289.

Hart, O. D. (1975). On the optimality of equilibrium when the market structure is incomplete. *Journal of Economic Theory 11*(3), 418–443.

Hart, O. D., and J. Moore (1988). Incomplete contracts and renegotiation. *Econometrica 56*(4), 755–785.

Hart, O. D., and J. H. Moore (2007). Contracts as reference points. *Quarterly Journal of Economics 123*(1), 1–48.

Heckman, J. J. (2010). Building bridges between structural and program evaluation approaches to evaluating policy. *Journal of Economic Literature 48*(2), 356–398.

Helpman, E., O. Itskhoki, and S. Redding (2010). Inequality and unemployment in a global economy. *Econometrica 78*(4), 1239–1283.

Herweg, F., and K. M. Schmidt (2019). Procurement with unforeseen contingencies. *Management Science 66*(5), 2194–2212.

Hey, J. D., and C. Orme (1994). Investigating generalizations of expected utility theory using experimental data. *Econometrica 62*(6), 1291–1326.

Heywood, J. S., and D. Parent (2012). Performance pay and the white-black wage gap. *Journal of Labor Economics 30*(2), 249–290.

Hintze, A., R. S. Olson, C. Adami, and R. Hertwig (2015). Risk sensitivity as an evolutionary adaptation. *Scientific Reports 5*(1), 8242.

Hirschman, A. O. (1970). *Exit, Voice, and Loyalty: Responses to Declines in Firms, Organizations, and States*. Harvard University Press.

Ho, K., and R. S. Lee (2017). Insurer competition in health care markets. *Econometrica 85*(2), 379–417.

Holland, P. W. (1986). Statistics and causal inference. *Journal of the American Statistical Association 81*(396), 945–960.

Holmes, O. W. (1897). The path of the law. *Harvard Law Review 10*(8), 457–478.

Holmström, B. (1979). Moral hazard and observability. *Bell Journal of Economics 10*(1), 74–91.

Holmström, B. (1982). Moral hazard in teams. *Bell Journal of Economics 13*(2), 324–340.

Holmström, B. (1999). Managerial incentive problems: A dynamic perspective. *Review of Economic Studies 66*(1), 169–182.

Holmström, B., and P. Milgrom (1987). Aggregation and linearity in the provision of intertemporal incentives. *Econometrica 55*(2), 303–328.

Holmström, B., and P. Milgrom (1991). Multi-task principal-agent analyses: Incentive contracts, asset ownership, and job design. *Journal of Law, Economics, and Organization 7*(SI), 24–52.

Holmström, B., and R. Myerson (1983). Efficient and durable decision rules with incomplete information. *Econometrica 51*(6), 1799–1819.

Horn, H., and A. Wolinsky (1988). Bilateral monopolies and incentives for merger. *RAND Journal of Economics 19*(3), 408–419.

Horner, J. (2002). Reputation and competition. *American Economic Review 92*(3), 644–663.

Imbens, G. (2010). Better LATE than nothing: Some comments on Deaton (2009) and Heckman and Urzua (2009). *Journal of Economic Literature 48*(2), 399–423.

Imbens, G. W., and D. B. Rubin (2015). *Causal Inference for Statistics, Social, and Biomedical Sciences*. Cambridge University Press.

Irrgang, W. (1972). *The Lincoln incentive management program*. In Lincoln Lecture Series. Arizona State University, 1–23.

Jackson, M. O. (2001). A crash course in implementation theory. *Social Choice and Welfare 18*(4), 655–708.

Jacob, B. A., and L. Lefgren (2008). Can principals identify effective teachers? Evidence on subjective performance evaluation in education. *Journal of Labor Economics 26*(1), 101–136.

Jeffrey, R. C. (1965). *The Logic of Decision*. McGraw-Hill.

Jensen, M., and W. Meckling (1976). Theory of the firm: Managerial behavior, agency costs and ownership structure. *Journal of Financial Economics 3*(4), 305–360.

Johnson, S., J. McMillan, and C. Woodruff (2002). Courts and relational contracts. *Journal of Law, Economics, and Organization 18*(1), 221–277.

Joskow, P. (1987). Contract duration and relation-specific investments: Empirical evidence from coal markets. *American Economic Review 77*(1), 168–185.

Joskow, P. L. (1988). Price adjustment in long-term-contracts: The case of coal. *Journal of Law and Economics 31*(1), 47–83.

Judd, K. L., S. Yeltekin, and J. Conklin (2003). Computing supergame equilibria. *Econometrica 71*(4), 1239–1254.

Kagel, J. H., and A. E. Roth (1995). *The Handbook of Experimental Economics*. Princeton University Press.

Kahneman, D., and R. H. Thaler (2006). Anomalies: Utility maximization and experienced utility. *Journal of Economic Perspectives 20*(1), 221–234.

Kahneman, D., and A. Tversky (1979). Prospect theory: An analysis of decisions under risk. *Econometrica 47*(2), 263–292.

Kalai, E., and M. Smorodinsky (1975). Other solutions to Nash's bargaining problem. *Econometrica 43*(3), 513–518.

Kalnins, A., and K. J. Mayer (2004). Relationships and hybrid contracts: An analysis of contract choice in information technology. *Journal of Law Economics and Organization 20*(1), 207–229.

Kamenica, E., and M. Gentzkow (2011). Bayesian persuasion. *American Economic Review 101*(6), 2590–2615.

Kandori, M., and H. Matsushima (1998). Private observation, communication and collusion. *Econometrica 66*(3), 627–652.

Kanemoto, Y., and W. B. MacLeod (1992). The ratchet effect and the market for secondhand workers. *Journal of Labor Economics 10*(1), 85–98.

Kartik, N. (2009). Strategic communication with lying costs. *Review of Economic Studies 76*(4), 1359–1395.

Katz, L. F., and D. H. Autor (1999). Changes in the wage structure and earnings inequality. In O. Ashenfelter and D. Card (Eds.), *Handbook of Labor Economics*, vol. 3A, 1463–555. Elsevier.

Kaufmann, P., and F. Lafontaine (1994). Costs of control: The source of economic rents for McDonalds franchisees. *Journal of Law and Economics 37*(2), 417–453.

Kaur, S. (2019). Nominal wage rigidity in village labor markets. *American Economic Review 109*(10), 3585–3616.

Kennan, J., and R. Wilson (1993). Bargaining with private information. *Journal of Economic Literature 31*(1), 45–104.

Kerr, S. (1975). On the folly of rewarding A, while hoping for B. *Academy of Management Journal 18*(4), 769–783.

King-Casas, B., C. Sharp, L. Lomax-Bream, T. Lohrenz, P. Fonagy, and P. R. Montague (2008). The rupture and repair of cooperation in borderline personality disorder. *Science 321*(5890), 806–810.

Klein, B., R. Crawford, and A. Alchian (1978). Vertical integration, appropriable rents, and the competitive contracting process. *Journal of Law and Economics 21*(2), 297–326.

Klein, B., and K. Leffler (1981). The role of market forces in assuring contractual performance. *Journal of Political Economy 89*(4), 615–641.

Knight, F. H. (1921). *Risk, Uncertainty, and Profit*. Hart, Schaffner, and Marx.

Knoch, D., F. Schneider, D. Schunk, M. Hohmann, and E. Fehr (2009). Disrupting the prefrontal cortex diminishes the human ability to build a good reputation. *Proceedings of the National Academy of Sciences of the United States of America 106*(49), 20895–20899.

Kobayashi, T. (1980). Equilibrium contracts for syndicates with differential information. *Econometrica 48*(7), 1635–1665.

Kohlberg, E., and J.-F. Mertens (1986). On the strategic stability of equilibria. *Econometrica 54*(5), 1003–1037.

Kornhauser, L., and W. B. MacLeod (2012). Contracts between legal persons. In R. Gibbons and J. Roberts (Eds.), *Handbook of Organizational Economics*, 918–957. Princeton University Press.

Koszegi, B. (2014). Behavioral contract theory. *Journal of Economic Literature 52*(4), 1075–1118.

Kranton, R. (1996). Reciprocal exchange: A self-sustaining system. *American Economic Review 86*(4), 830–851.

Kreps, D. M. (1997). Intrinsic motivation and extrinsic incentives. *American Economic Review 87*(2), 359–364.

Kreps, D. M., P. Milgrom, J. Roberts, and R. Wilson (1982). Rational cooperation in the finitely repeated prisoners' dilemma. *Journal of Economic Theory 27*(2), 245–252.

Kreps, D. M., and R. B. Wilson (1982). Sequential equilibria. *Econometrica 50*(4), 863–894.

Krishna, V. (2010). *Auction Theory*. 2nd ed. Academic Press.

Krueger, A. B., and L. H. Summers (1988). Efficiency wages and the inter-industry wage structure. *Econometrica 56*(2), 259–294.

Krugman, P. (2014). The dismal science "Seven Bad Ideas," by Jeff Madrick. *New York Times Sunday Book Review*, September 25.

Laffont, J.-J., and D. Martimort (2000). Mechanism design with collusion and correlation. *Econometrica 68*(2), 309–342.

Laffont, J.-J., and D. Martimort (2002). *The Theory of Incentives*. Princeton University Press.

Laffont, J.-J., and J. Tirole (1993). *A Theory of Incentives in Procurement and Regulation*. MIT Press.

Lafortune, J., and C. Low (2017). Tying the double-knot: The role of assets in marriage commitment. *American Economic Review 107*(5), 163–167.

Lang, K., and J.-Y. K. Lehmann (2012). Racial discrimination in the labor market: Theory and empirics. *Journal of Economic Literature 50*(4), 959–1006.

Lang, M. (2019). Communicating sujective evaluations. *Journal of Economics Theory 179*, 163–199.

Lazear, E. P. (1989). Pay equality and industrial politics. *Journal of Political Economy 97*(3), 561–580.

Lazear, E. P. (1990). Job security provisions and employment. *Quarterly Journal of Economics 105*(3), 699–726.

Lazear, E. P. (2000). Performance pay and productivity. *American Economic Review 90*(5), 1346–1361.

Lazear, E. P., and S. Rosen (1981). Rank-order tournaments as optimal labor contracts. *Journal of Political Economy 89*(5), 841–864.

Leibenstein, H. (1957). *Economic Backwardness and Economic Growth*. Wiley.

Leibenstein, H. (1958). Underemployment in backward economies: Some additional notes. *Journal of Political Economy 66*(3), 256–258.

Lemieux, T., W. B. MacLeod, and D. Parent (2009). Performance pay and wage inequality. *Quarterly Journal of Economics 124*(1), 1–49.

Levin, J. (2003). Relational incentive contacts. *American Economic Review 93*(3), 835–857.

Lewis, D. (1967). *Convention: A Philosophical Study*. Harvard University Press.

Lewis, T. R., and D. E. Sappington (1989). Countervailing incentives in agency problems. *Journal of Economic Theory 49*(2), 294–313.

Li, J., and N. Matouschek (2013). Managing conflicts in relational contracts. *American Economic Review 103*(6), 2328–2351.

Liberti, J. M., and A. R. Mian (2009). Estimating the effect of hierarchies on information use. *Review of Financial Studies 22*(10), 4057–4090.

List, J. A., and I. Rasul (2011). Field experiments in labor economics. In O. Ashenfelter and D. Card (Eds.), *Handbook of Labor Economics*, vol. 4, 103–228.

Low, A. W., and J. Hasanhodzic (2010). *The Evolution of Technical Analysis*. John Wiley.

Luce, R. D., and H. Raiffa ([1957] 1989). *Games and Decisions*. Dover.

Luenberger, D. G. (1969). *Optimization by Vector Space Methods*. John Wiley.

Luenberger, D. G., and Y. Ye (2008). *Linear and Nonlinear Programming*. Springer.

Macaulay, S. (1963). Non-contractual relations in business: A preliminary study. *American Sociological Review 28*(1), 55–67.

Macaulay, S. (2000). Relational contracts floating on a sea of custom? Thoughts about the ideas of Ian Macneil and Lisa Bernstein. *Northwestern University Law Review 94*(3), 775–804.

Macchiavello, R., and A. Morjaria (2015). The value of relationships: Evidence from a supply shock to kenyan rose exports. *American Economic Review 105*(9), 2911–2945.

Machin, S., M. Stewart, and J. Van Reenen (1993). The economic effects of multiple unionism: Evidence from the 1984 workplace industrial relations survey. *Scandinavian Journal of Economics 95*(3), 279–296.

MacLeod, W. B. (1984). A theory of cooperative teams. Working paper, Université Catholique de Louvain, CORE Discussion Paper 8441.

MacLeod, W. B. (1987). Behavior and the organization of the firm. *Journal of Comparative Economics 11*(2), 207–220.

MacLeod, W. B. (1988). Equity, efficiency and incentives in co-operative teams. In D. C. Jones and J. Sveijnar (Eds.), *Advances in the Economic Analysis of Participatory and Labor-Managed Firms*, vol. 3, 5–23. JAI.

MacLeod, W. B. (2002). Complexity, bounded rationality and heuristic search. *Contributions to Economic Analysis and Policy 1*(1), 1–52.

MacLeod, W. B. (2003). Optimal contracting with subjective evaluation. *American Economic Review 93*(1), 216–240.

MacLeod, W. B. (2007a). Can contract theory explain social preferences? *American Economic Review 97*(2), 187–192.

MacLeod, W. B. (2007b). Reputations, relationships and contract enforcement. *Journal of Economics Literature 45*(3), 595–628.

MacLeod, W. B. (2011). Great expectations: Law, employment contracts, and labor market performance. In O. Ashenfelter and D. Card (Eds.), *Handbook of Labor Economics*, vol. 4B, 1591–1696.

MacLeod, W. B. (2016). Human capital: Linking behavior to rational choice via dual process theory. SOLE/EALE conference issue 2015. *Labour Economics 41*, 20–31.

MacLeod, W. B. (2017). Viewpoint: The human capital approach to inference. *Canadian Journal of Economics 50*(1), 5–39.

MacLeod, W. B., and J. M. Malcomson (1988). Reputation and hierarchy in dynamic models of employment. *Journal of Political Economy 96*(4), 832–854.

MacLeod, W. B., and J. M. Malcomson (1989). Implicit contracts, incentive compatibility, and involuntary unemployment. *Econometrica 57*(2), 447–480.

MacLeod, W. B., and J. M. Malcomson (1993). Investments, holdup, and the form of market contracts. *American Economic Review 83*(4), 811–837.

MacLeod, W. B., and J. M. Malcomson (1995). Contract bargaining with symmetric information. *Canadian Journal of Economics 28*(2), 336–367.

MacLeod, W. B., and J. M. Malcomson (1998). Motivation and markets. *American Economic Review 88*(3), 388–411.

MacLeod, W. B., J. M. Malcomson, and P. Gomme (1994). Labor turnover and the natural rate of unemployment: Efficiency wage versus frictional unemployment. *Journal of Labor Economics 12*(2), 276–315.

MacLeod, W. B., and V. Nakavachara (2007). Can wrongful discharge law enhance employment? *Economic Journal 117*, F1–F62.

Maestri, L. (2012). Bonus payments versus efficiency wages in the repeated principal-agent model with subjective evaluations. *American Economic Journal: Microeconomics 4*(3), 34–56.

Mailath, G. J., and L. Samuelson (2001). Who wants a good reputation? *Review of Economic Studies 68*(2), 415–441.

Malcomson, J. M. (1981). Unemployment and the efficiency wage hypothesis. *Economic Journal 91*(364), 848–866.

Malcomson, J. M. (1984). Work incentives, hierarchy, and internal labor markets. *Journal of Political Economy 92*(3), 486–507.

Malcomson, J. M. (2009). Principal and expert agent. *B.E. Journal of Theoretical Economics 9*(1), 1–36.

Malcomson, J. M. (2016). Relational incentive contracts with persistent private information. *Econometrica 84*(1), 317–346.

Manso, G. (2011). Motivating innovation. *Journal of Finance 66*(5), 1823–1860.

March, J. G. (1962). The business firm as a political coalition. *Journal of Politics 24*(4), 662–678.

March, J. G., and H. A. Simon (1958). *Organizations*. John Wiley.

Marcus Aurelius (2002). *Meditations*. Edited by G. Hays. Modern Library.

Marshall, A. ([1890] 1948). *The Principles of Economics*. 8th ed. Macmillan.

Martimort, D., A. Semenov, and L. Stole (2017). A theory of contracts with limited enforcement. *Review of Economic Studies 84*(2), 816–852.

Martimort, D., and L. Stole (2002). The revelation and delegation principles in common agency games. *Econometrica 70*(4), 1659–1673.

Marx, K. (1981). *Capital: A Critique of Political Economy*. Penguin.

Mas, A. (2006). Pay, reference points, and police performance. *Quarterly Journal of Economics 121*(3), 783–821.

Mas, A. (2008). Labour unrest and the quality of production: Evidence from the construction equipment resale market. *Review of Economic Studies 75*(1), 229–258.

Mas-Colell, A., M. D. Whinston, and J. R. Green (1995). *Microeconomic Theory*. Oxford University Press.

Maskin, E. (1999). Nash equilibrium and welfare optimality. *Review of Economic Studies 66*(1), 23–38.

Maskin, E., and J. Riley (1984). Monopoly with incomplete information. *RAND Journal of Economics 15*, 171–96.

Mauss, M. (1990). *The Gift*. W. W. Norton.

McKelvey, R. D., and T. Page (2002). Status quo bias in bargaining: An extension of the Myerson-Satterthwaite theorem with an application to the Coase theorem. *Journal of Economic Theory 107*(2), 336–355.

McLaughlin, K. (1994). Rigid wages. *Journal of Monetary Economics 34*(3), 383–414.

McMillan, J., and C. Woodruff (1999). Interfirm relationships and informal credit in Vietnam. *Quarterly Journal of Economics 114*(4), 1285–1320.

Meho, L. I., and K. Yang (2007). Impact of data sources on citation counts and rankings of lis faculty: Web of Science versus Scopus and Google Scholar. *Journal of the American Society for Information Science and Technology 58*(13), 2105–2125.

Mertens, J.-F., and S. Zamir (1985). Formulation of Bayesian analysis for games with incomplete information. *International Journal of Game Theory 14*(1), 1–29.

Milgram, S. (1974). *Obedience to Authority: An Experimental View*. HarperCollins.

Milkovich, G. T., and J. M. Newman (2005). *Compensation*. 8th ed. MacGraw-Hill.

Milkovich, G. T., and A. K. Wigdor (1991). *Pay for Performance: Evaluating Performance and Appraisal Merit Pay*. National Academy Press.

Miller, D. A., and J. Watson (2013). A theory of disagreement in repeated games with bargaining. *Econometrica 81*(6), 2303–2350.

Mincer, J. (1958). Investment in human capital and personal income distribution. *Journal of Political Economy 66*(4), 281–302.

Mincer, J. (1962). On-the-job training: Cost, returns, and some implications. *Journal of Political Economy 70*(5), 50–79.

Minsky, M. L. (1986). *The Society of Mind*. Simon and Schuster.

Mirrlees, J. A. (1971). Exploration in theory of optimum income taxation. *Review of Economic Studies 38*(114), 175–208.

Mirrlees, J. A. (1974). Notes on welfare economics, information and uncertainty. In M. Balch, D. McFadden, and S.-Y. Wu (Eds.), *Essays on Economic Behavior under Uncertainty*, 243–258. North-Holland.

Mookherjee, D. (1984). Optimal incentive schemes with many agents. *Review of Economic Studies 51*(3), 433–446.

Moretti, E. (2011). Local labor markets. In O. Ashenfelter and D. Card (Eds.), *Handbook of Labor Economics*, vol. 4B, 1237–1313. Elsevier.

Morris, S., and H. S. Shin (2003). Gobal games: Theory and applications. In M. Dewatripon, L. Hansen, and S. Turnovsky (Eds.), *Advances in Economics and Applications*, 56–144. Cambridge University Press.

Mortensen, D. T., and C. A. Pissarides (1999). New developments in models of search in the labor market. In O. Ashenfelter and D. Card (Eds.), *Handbook of Labor Economics*, vol. 3B, 2567–2627. Elsevier.

Moulin, H. (2014). *Cooperative Microeconomics*. Princeton University Press.

Munger, C. (1995). The psychology of human misjudgement. Speech at Harvard Law School.

Murphy, K. (2000). Performance standards in incentive contracts. *Journal of Accounting and Economics 30*(3), 245–278.

Mussa, M., and S. Rosen (1978). Monopoly and product quality. *Journal of Economic Theory 18*(2), 301–317.

Myerson, R. B. (1986). Multistage games with communication. *Econometrica 54*(2), 323–58.

Myerson, R. B. (1991). *Game Theory*. Harvard University Press.

Myerson, R. B., and M. A. Satterthwaite (1983). Efficient mechanisms for bilateral trading. *Journal of Economic Theory 29*(2), 265–281.

Nash, J. F. (1950). Equilibrium points in N-Person games. *Proceedings of the National Academy of Sciences of the United States of America 36*(1), 48–49.

Nash, J. F. (1953). Two-person cooperative games. *Econometrica 21*(1), 128–140.

Neuman, J. H., and R. A. Baron (1998). Workplace violence and workplace aggression: Evidence concerning specific forms, potential causes, and preferred targets. *Journal of Management 24*(3), 391–419.

Newell, A., and H. Simon (1972). *Human Problem Solving*. Prentice-Hall.

Nöldeke, G., and K. M. Schmidt (1995). Option contracts and renegotiation: A solution to the hold-up problem. *RAND Journal of Economics 26*(2), 163–179.

Nöldeke, G., and K. M. Schmidt (1998). Sequential investments and options to own. *RAND Journal of Economics 29*(4), 633–653.

Okuno-Fujiwara, M., and A. Postlewaite (1995). Social norms and random matching games. *Games and Economic Behavior 9*(1), 79–109.

Organisation for Economic Co-operation and Development (OECD) (1994). *The Jobs Study: Evidence and Explanations*. OECD.

Palacios-Huerta, I. (2003). Professionals play minimax. *Review of Economics Studies 70*, 395–415.

Parent, D. (2000). Industry-specific capital and the wage profile: Evidence from the National Longitudinal Survey of Youth and the Panel Study of Income Dynamics. *Journal of Labor Economics 18*(2), 306–323.

Pareto, V. (1909). *Manuel d'économie politique*. V. Giard et E. Briere.

Pauly, M. V. (1968). The economics of moral hazard: Comment. *American Economics Review 58*(3), 531–537.

Pearce, D. G. (1984). Rationalizable strategic behavior and the problem of perfection. *Econometrica 52*(4), 1029–1050.

Pearce, D. G. (1992). Repeated games: Cooperation and rationality. In J.-J. Laffont (Ed.), *Advances in Economic Theory: Sixth World Congress*, vol. 1, 132–174. Cambridge University Press.

Pearce, D. G., and E. Stacchetti (1998). The interaction of implicit and explicit contracts in repeated agency. *Games and Economic Behavior 23*(1), 75–96.

Peierls, R. E. (1960). Wolfgang Ernst Pauli, 1900–1958. *Biographical Memoirs of Fellows of the Royal Society 5*, 175–192.

Peter, L. J., and R. Hull (1969). *The Peter Principle*. William Morrow.

Pliny the Younger (1949). *Letters Books VIII–X and Panegyricus*. Edited and translated by B. Radice. Harvard University Press.

Pondy, L. R. (1967). Organizational conflict: Concepts and models. *Administrative Science Quarterly 12*(2), 296–320.

Popper, K. R. ([1957] 2002). *The Poverty of Historicism*. Routledge.

Popper, K. R. (1963). *Conjectures and Refutations: The Growth of Scientific Knowledge*. Basic Books.

Posner, R. A. (1973). *Economic Analysis of Law*. Little, Brown.

Prendergast, C. (1999). The provision of incentives in firms. *Journal of Economic Literature 37*(1), 7–63.

Prendergast, C. (2008). Intrinsic motivation and incentives. *American Economic Review 98*(2), 201–205.

Prendergast, C., and R. H. Topel (1996). Favoritism in organizations. *Journal of Political Economy 104*(5), 958–978.

Rabin, M. (1998). Pyschology and economics. *Journal of Economic Literature 36*(1), 11–46.

Rahman, D. (2012). But who will monitor the monitor? *American Economic Review 102*(6), 2767–2797.

Raiffa, H. (1953). Arbitration schemes for generalized two-person games. In H. W. Kuhn and A. W. Tucker (Eds.), *Contributions to the Theory of Games (AM-28)*, vol. 2, 361–388. Princeton University Press.

Rajan, M., and S. Reichelstein (2006). Subjective performance indicators and discretionary bonus pools. *Journal of Accounting Research 44*(3), 585–618.

Ramey, G., and J. Watson (1997). Contractual fragility, job destruction, and business cycles. *Quarterly Journal of Economics 112*(3), 873–912.

Ramey, G., and J. Watson (2002). Contractual intermediaries. *Journal of Law Economics and Organization 18*(2), 362–384.

Rawls, J. (1971). *A Theory of Justice*. Harvard University Press.

Rayo, L. (2007). Relational incentives and moral hazard in teams. *Review of Economic Studies 74*(3), 937–963.

Riley, J. G. (1979). Informational equilibrium. *Econometrica 47*(2), 331–359.

Rochet, J. C., and P. Chone (1998). Ironing, sweeping, and multidimensional screening. *Econometrica 66*(4), 783–826.

Rogerson, R., R. Shimer, and R. Wright (2005). Search-theoretic models of the labor market: A survey. *Journal of Economic Literature 43*(4), 959–988.

Rogerson, W. P. (1984). Efficient reliance and damage measures for breach of contract. *RAND Journal of Economics 15*(1), 39–53.

Rosenbaum, P. R. (2010). *Design of Observational Studies*. Springer.

Rosenbaum, P. R. (2017). *Observation and Experiment*. Harvard University Press.

Roth, A. E. (1995a). Bargaining experiments. In J. H. Kagel and A. E. Roth (Eds.), *The Handbook of Experimental Economics*, 253–347, Princeton University Press.

Roth, A. E. (1995b). Introduction to experimental economics. In J. H. Kagel and A. E. Roth (Eds.), *The Handbook of Experimental Economics*, 3–109. Princeton University Press.

Roth, A. E. (2002). The economist as engineer: Game theory, experimentation, and computation as tools for design economics. *Econometrica 70*(4), 1341–1378.

Roth, A. E. (2018). Marketplaces, markets, and market design. *American Economic Review 108*(7), 1609–1658.

Roth, A. E., and J. K. Murnighan (1978). Equilibrium behavior and repeated play of the prisoner's dilemma. *Journal of Mathematical Psychology 17*(2), 189–198.

Rothschild, M., and J. E. Stiglitz (1976). Equilibrium in competitive insurance markets: An essay on the economics of imperfect information. *Quarterly Journal of Economics 90*(4), 630–649.

Rothstein, M. A., and L. Liebman (2007). *Employment Law*. 6th ed. New York, NY: Thomson West.

Rubinstein, A. (1982). Perfect equilibrium in a bargaining model. *Econometrica 50*(1), 97–109.

Rubinstein, A. (1989). The electronic mail game: Strategic behavior under "almost common knowledge." *American Economic Review 79*(3), 385–391.

Rubinstein, A. (1991). Comments on the interpretation of game theory. *Econometrica 59*(4), 909–924.

Ruff, C. C., and E. Fehr (2014). The neurobiology of rewards and values in social decision making. *Nature Reviews Neuroscience 15*(8), 549–562.

Salanié, B. (2005). *The Economics of Contracts*. 2nd ed. MIT Press.

Salop, S. C. (1979). A model of the natural rate of unemployment. *American Economic Review 69*(1), 117–125.

Samuelson, P. A. (1938). A note on the pure theory of consumer behavior. *Economica 5*(17), 61–71.

Sannikov, Y. (2008). A continuous-time version of the principal-agent problem. *Review of Economic Studies 75*(3), 957–984.

Sapolsky, R. M. (2018). *Behave: The Biology of Humans at Our Best and Worst*. Penguin.

Saunders, R. (1750). *Poor Richard Improved*. B. Franklin and D. Hall.

Savage, L. J. ([1954] 1972). *The Foundations of Statistics*. Dover.

Schelling, T. C. (1980). *The Strategy of Conflict*. Harvard University Press.

Schmidt, K. M., and M. Schnitzer (1995). The interaction of explicit and implicit contracts. *Economic Letters 48*(2), 193–199.

Schmieder, J. F., and T. von Wachter (2010). Does wage persistence matter for employment fluctuations? Evidence from displaced workers. *American Economic Journal: Applied Economics 2*(3), 1–21.

Schultz, T. W. (1961). Investment in human capital. *American Economic Review 51*(1), 1–17.

Schwartz, A. (1979). The case for specific performance. *Yale Law Journal 89*(2), 271–306.

Selten, R. (1965). Spieltheoretische Behandlung eines Oligopolmodells mit Nachfrageträgheit. *Zeitschrift für die gesamte Staatswissenschaft 121*(2), 301–324.

Selten, R. (1975). Reexamination of the perfectness concept for equilibrium points in extensive games. *International Journal of Game Theory 4*(1), 25–55.

Selvin, S. (1975). A problem in probability. *American Statistician 29*(1), 67–71.

Sen, A. (1977). Starvation and exchange entitlements: A general approach and its application to the great Bengal famine. *Cambridge Journal of Economics 1*(1), 33–59.

Shaked, A. (1994). Opting out: Bazaars versus "high tech" markets. *Investigaciones Económicas 18*(3), 421–432.

Shaked, A., and J. Sutton (1984). Involuntary unemployment as a perfect equilibrium in a bargaining model. *Econometrica 52*(6), 1351–1364.

Shapiro, C., and J. E. Stiglitz (1984). Equilibrium unemployment as a worker discipline device. *American Economic Review 74*(3), 433–444.

Shavell, S. (1980). Damage measures for breach of contract. *Bell Journal of Economics 11*(2), 466–490.

Silver, D., A. Huang, C. J. Maddison, A. Guez, L. Sifre, G. van den Driessche, J. Schrittwieser, I. Antonoglou, V. Panneershelvam, M. Lanctot, S. Dieleman, D. Grewe, J. Nham, N. Kalchbrenner, I. Sutskever, T. Lillicrap, M. Leach, K. Kavukcuoglu, T. Graepel, and D. Hassabis (2016). Mastering the game of go with deep neural networks and tree search. *Nature 529*(7587), 484–489.

Silver, D., J. Schrittwieser, K. Simonyan, I. Antonoglou, A. Huang, A. Guez, T. Hubert, L. Baker, M. Lai, A. Bolton, Y. Chen, T. Lillicrap, F. Hui, L. Sifre, G. van den Driessche, T. Graepel, and D. Hassabis (2017). Mastering the game of go without human knowledge. *Nature 550*(7676), 354–359.

Simon, H. A. (1951). A formal theory of the employment relationship. *Econometrica 19*(3), 293–305.

Sjöström, T. (1991). Ståhl's bargaining model. *Economics Letters 36*(2), 153–157.

Skinner, B. F. (1948). "Superstition" in the pigeon. *Journal of Experimental Psychology 38*(2), 168–172.

Sloof, R., and J. Sonnemans (2011). The interaction between explicit and relational incentives: An experiment. *Games and Economic Behavior 73*(2), 573–594.

Smith, A. (1776). *An Inquiry into the Nature and Causes of the Wealth of Nations*. W. Strahan and T. Cadell.

Sobel, J. (1985). A theory of credibility. *Review of Economic Studies 52*(4), 557–573.

Sobel, J. (2006). For better or forever: Formal versus informal enforcement. *Journal of Labor Economics 24*(2), 271–297.

Solow, R. M. (1956). A contribution to the theory of economic growth. *Quarterly Journal of Economics 70*(1), 65–94.

Spence, M. (1973). Job market signaling. *Quarterly Journal of Economics 87*(3), 355–374.

Spier, K. E., and M. D. Whinston (1995). On the efficiency of privately stipulated damages for breach of contract: Entry barriers, reliance, and renegotiation. *RAND Journal of Economics 26*(2), 180–202.

Ståhl, I. (1972). *Bargaining Theory*. Economics Research Institute.

Startz, M. (2016). The value of face-to-face: Search and contracting problems in Nigerian trade. Available at SSRN:https://ssrn.com/abstract=3096685.

Stevenson, B., and J. Wolfers (2006). Bargaining in the shadow of the law: Divorce laws and family distress. *Quarterly Journal of Economics 121*(1), 267–288.

Stole, L. A., and J. Zwiebel (1996). Intra-firm bargaining under non-binding contracts. *Review of Economic Studies 63*(3), 375–410.

Svejnar, J. (1986). Bargaining power, fear of disagreement, and wage settlements: Theory and evidence from United States industry. *Econometrica 54*(5), 1055–1078.

Sweet, J. (2000). *Legal Aspects of Architecture, Engineering, and the Construction Process*. 6th ed. West.

Tadelis, S. (1999). What's in a name? Reputation as a tradeable asset. *American Economic Review 89*(3), 548–563.

Tadelis, S. (2002). The market for reputations as an incentive mechanism. *Journal of Political Economy 110*(4), 854–882.

Taylor, C. R., and H. Yildirim (2011). Subjective performance and the value of blind evaluation. *Review of Economic Studies 78*(2), 762–794.

Telser, L. G. (1980). A theory of self-enforcing agreements. *Journal of Business 53*(1), 27–44.

Tirole, J. (1986). Procurement and renegotiation. *Journal of Political Economy 94*(2), 235–259.

Tirole, J. (1999). Incomplete contracts: Where do we stand? *Econometrica 67*(4), 741–782.

Toikka, J. (2011). Ironing without control. *Journal of Economic Theory 146*(6), 2510–2526.

van Damme, E. (1989). Renegotiation-proof equilibria in repeated prisoners' dilemma. *Journal of Economic Theory 47*(1), 206–217.

van Damme, E. (1991). *Stability and Perfection of Nash Equilibria*. Springer.

Vanek, J. (1970). *The General Theory of Labour-Managed Firms*. Cornell University Press.

Vaughan, E. J. (1997). *Risk Management*. John Wiley.

Vitruvius (1914). *The Ten Books on Architecture*. Edited by M. H. Morgan and H. L. Warren. Harvard University Press.

Von Neumann, J., and O. Morgenstern (1944). *Theory of Games and Economic Behavior*. Princeton University Press.

Waldman, M. (1984). Worker allocation, hierarchies and the wage distribution. *Review of Economic Studies 51*(1), 95–109.

Watson, J. (1999). Starting small and renegotiation. *Journal of Economic Theory 85*(1), 52–90.

Watson, J. (2002). Starting small and commitment. *Games and Economic Behavior 38*(1), 176–199.

Watson, J., D. A. Miller, and T. E. Olsen (2020). Relational contracting, negotiation, and external enforcement. *American Economic Review 110*(7), 2153–2197.

Weiss, A. (1980). Job queues and layoffs in labor markets with flexible wages. *Journal of Political Economy 88*(3), 526–538.

Williams, S. R. (1999). A characterization of efficient, Bayesian incentive compatible mechanisms. *Economic Theory 14*(1), 155–180.

Williamson, O. E. (1975). *Markets and Hierarchies: Analysis and Antitrust Implications*. Free Press.

Williamson, O. E. (1979). Transaction-cost economics: The governance of contractual relations. *Journal of Law and Economics 22*(2), 233–261.

Williamson, O. E., M. L. Wachter, and J. E. Harris (1975). Understanding the employment relation: The analysis of idiosyncratic exchange. *Bell Journal of Economics 6*(1), 250–278.

Wolak, F. A. (1996). Why do firms simultaneously purchase in spot and contract markets? Evidence from the United States steam coal market. In D. Martimort (Ed.), *Agricultural Markets*, 109–168. Vol. 234 of *Contributions to Economic Analysis*. Emerald.

Yildiz, M. (2004). Waiting to persuade. *Quarterly Journal of Economics 119*(1), 223–248.

Zabojnik, J. (2014). Subjective evaluations with performance feedback. *RAND Journal of Economics 45*(2), 341–369.

Zanarone, G. (2013). Contract adaptation under legal constraints. *Journal of Law Economics and Organization 29*(4), 799–834.

Zhu, J. Y. (2018). A foundation for efficiency wage contracts. *American Economic Journal: Microeconomics 10*(4), 248–288.

Index

Note: Endnote information is indicated with n with chapter and note number following the page number.